THE ANTILLES AND THE SPANISH MAIN

1624-1692

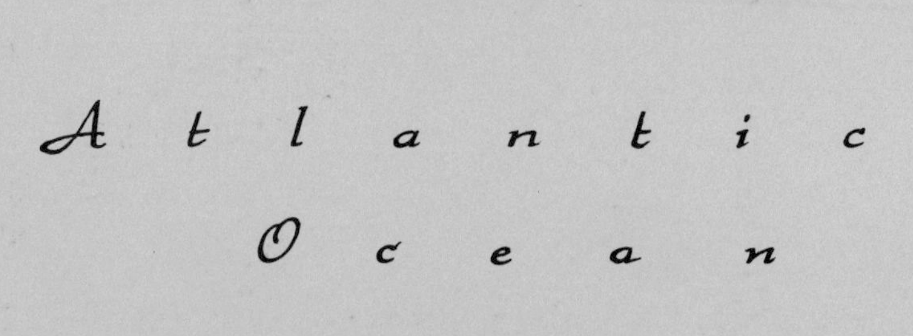

From the founding of St. Christopher in 1624 to the terrible earthquake that destroyed the metropolis of Port Royal in 1692, the English and Irish who emigrated to the West Indies struggled to establish permanent colonies, as did their fellow countrymen in New England and on the Chesapeake. Adaptation to the tropical environment was difficult, the attempt to use indentured white servants ended tragically, and only when new staple crops — cotton and sugar — and a new labor force from Africa were introduced did the Caribbean colonies improve economically. Even with these radical changes, however, well-rounded societies did not form in the Leeward Islands or Barbados during the seventeenth century.

The Spanish, French, and English maintained that peace in Europe did not extend to the Caribbean. Foreign wars, Carib raids, and freebooters disrupted all normal activities, and white men also had to battle the climate and epidemic diseases, which always seemed to ravage the West Indies. Further, human greed, the failure of religion, and the cruelty of the age insured that there would be "no peace beyond the line" for anyone who ventured to the West Indies.

This fascinating narrative is the first to deal with the daily lives of all the people — white and black — who inhabited the British West Indies in the seventeenth century. With sympathetic insight and a firm grasp of the social and economic conditions of the time, the authors describe the hardships faced by

NO PEACE BEYOND THE LINE

BOOKS BY CARL BRIDENBAUGH

The Beginnings of the American People
I VEXED AND TROUBLED ENGLISHMEN 1590–1642

II NO PEACE BEYOND THE LINE:
The English in the Caribbean 1624–1690 (co-author)

MITRE AND SCEPTRE:
Transatlantic Faiths, Ideas, Personalities, and Politics 1689–1775

CITIES IN THE WILDERNESS:
The First Century of Urban Life in America, 1625–1742

CITIES IN REVOLT:
Urban Life in America, 1743–1776

PETER HARRISON, FIRST AMERICAN ARCHITECT

THE COLONIAL CRAFTSMAN

SEAT OF EMPIRE:
The Political Role of Eighteenth-Century Williamsburg

MYTHS AND REALITIES:
Societies of the Colonial South

REBELS AND GENTLEMEN:
Philadelphia in the Age of Franklin (co-author)

GENTLEMAN'S PROGRESS:
Dr. Alexander Hamilton's Itinerarium, 1744
(edited, with an Introduction)

No Peace Beyond the Line

The English in the Caribbean 1624-1690

CARL AND ROBERTA BRIDENBAUGH

New York
OXFORD UNIVERSITY PRESS
1972

Library of Congress Catalogue Card Number: 70-182421

Printed in the United States of America

For
Panchita and Norton Canfield
of
Saint Croix

Preface

THE YEARS BETWEEN 1600 and 1700 constitute one of the most boisterous, brilliant, significant centuries in all recorded history. In a very real sense, this seminal epoch belonged to the English more than to any other nation of Europe, not excepting the industrious Dutch or the Sun King's Frenchmen. One of the most dramatic scenes for their activity was the Caribbean. Of the several authors who have written excellent histories of the Leeward Islands, Barbados, and Jamaica, only Edward Long paid much attention to social and cultural conditions, and to the lives of ordinary West Indians, white or black. This book is about the peoples of the Antilles.

The most serious problem that historians of this fascinating region face is that of sources. Time, war, weather, and man have deprived us of essential materials. There are great gaps in the story that will never be filled. Many descriptions or narratives are one-sided or partisan, and conclusions drawn from them must of necessity be informed guesses. Where populations and the West Indian economy figure so prominently, it is, unfortunately, impossible to provide the quantitative evidence that some readers will reasonably desire. But most regrettable of all is the paucity of human sources—diaries, journals, personal and business correspondence—so essential to this genre of history. With its every limitation, however, this is a story that must be told, because of its interest and its very great importance to The Beginnings of the American People.

To compensate in some measure for these unavoidable deficiencies and to lessen the dangers inherent in extrapolating from contemporary white sources or in working backward from modern opinions, we have sampled extensively the variety of the West Indies and tried to sense the conditions of the past by inspecting by car and from planes the many islands: St. Thomas, St. Martin, St. Christopher, Nevis, Antigua, Trinidad, Curaçao; and also Surinam on the Main. In addition to visual research and library and archive study at St. Croix, Barbados, and Jamaica (on two occasions), we have also made considerable use of neglected contemporary maps, engravings, and sketches, extraordinarily fruitful sources, some of which are reproduced as illustrations and referred to throughout the text.

One glaring weakness of much social history is the disregard of strict chronology. Most West Indian historians stress society as it existed in the second half of the eighteenth century, largely because of the more abundant sources. There is nothing wrong in this. Our account is restricted exclusively to *the seventeenth century* before 1690, with the single exception of the accounts of the earthquake at Port Royal in 1692. A rigorous insistence upon a decent respect for chronology, we fondly hope, will explain to our readers why we may appear at times to "have looked upon truth askance and strangely."

CARL AND ROBERTA BRIDENBAUGH

Providence, Rhode Island
4 March 1971

Acknowledgments

DURING THE very long time that this book has been in the making, we have levied heavily upon friends, colleagues, mere acquaintances, and total strangers for information, advice, and sundry kinds of assistance. Without exception, these have been promptly forthcoming. Our study of West Indian history began in 1956 at Berkeley, where William S. Hanna (now of the University of Oregon), a rare research assistant, initiated us into Caribbean lore and shared his knowledge of Spanish colonial life. The late J. Harry Bennett, a scholar whom, alas, we never met, collected many documents and other materials in England, especially the Helyar Papers, which we were privileged to use in microfilm through the courtesy of Barnes Lathrop and other members of the Department of History of the University of Texas. Edwin B. Kretzmann of Mystic, Connecticut, generously put his time and wide knowledge of the German language at our disposal by translating the *Kurze Reise* of Heinrich von Uchteritz for us. Here in Providence, our patient friend, William P. Buffum, Jr., spent many hours assisting us to understand and visualize something of the vernacular architecture of early Barbados.

At the John Carter Brown Library, Samuel Hough and Mrs. Joseph Hardy brought us every book we asked for and told us of others. A major contributor to this undertaking is Jeannette D. Black, who told us of maps and prints in the collection over which she presides, gave wise advice on many occasions, and always listened willingly and patiently when we were thinking out loud. At the

John D. Rockefeller, Jr., and John Hay libraries of Brown University, David A. Jonah provided every assistance possible, including a roomy study; and Miss Sara Deluca procured many books for us through interlibrary loan.

Mr. David Simpson of the Royal Commonwealth Society, London, kindly told us about the Sparke Papers and gave us unrestricted access to the N. Darnell Davis Collection, which we have used extensively. As always, the officials and staffs of the Public Record Office and the British Museum made our visits to their collections memorable. And to Dr. Helen Wallis we owe special thanks for procuring certain photographs so promptly.

In the Barbados Museum and Historical Society and the West India Reference Library are two collections of books and manuscripts of very great value. At Bridgetown, Neville Connell went out of his way to show us his holdings and share his wide knowledge of Barbadian history. During two visits to Kingston, the most recent in January 1971, Miss Glory Robertson and her staff saw to it that we consulted every manuscript pertaining to Jamaica in our period, supplied a microfilm of the unique Coppie Booke of William Freeman, and in many other ways lightened our labors. The most delightful "field trip" one of the writers ever experienced was dining at the home of Mrs. Peter King of the Institute upon a deliciously cooked West Indian sea turtle (once so common and now so rare a dish in Jamaica).

When Professor Richard Dunn of the University of Pennsylvania learned that we were writing a book that covered much of the timespan of his forthcoming *Sugar and Slaves: The Rise of the Planter Class in the English West Indies, 1640–1713,* he accepted the fact with a friendliness, generosity, and grace that are today rare in unplanned scholarly competition.

Other individuals to whom we are beholden in more ways than one are: Professor David Beers Quinn of the University of Liverpool, Professor C. R. Boxer of Yale, Professor J. H. Bromley of Southampton, Dr. Charles F. Carroll, Professor Elsa Goveia of the University of the West Indies, Professor Jerome Handler of Southern Illinois, Professor Robert McColley of Illinois, Professor J. H. Parry of Harvard, Joyce Olson Ransome of Providence, Professor Walter Schnerr of Brown, the late Raymond P. Stearns, and Bradford Swan of Providence. Mr. John Alden received one of the authors with great enthusiasm and opened the fine West Indies collection of the Boston Public Library to us.

On many occasions in the past three years Mary and Edwin Wolf of the Library Company of Philadelphia have brought out their Caribbean treasures for our use and then welcomed us at their home in Wyncote.

We are most grateful for the generosity of the John Simon Guggenheim Memorial Foundation, which made possible travel for research in the West Indies and Britain.

Dr. and Mrs. Norton Canfield of St. Croix, friends of very long standing, introduced us to the West Indies and made certain that we saw "Whimsy"—a real, old-fashioned sugar plantation. To them we dedicate this book.

Note on Documentation

COMPLETE DOCUMENTATION of a work on life in the West Indies such as this would require more space for footnotes than for text. We have therefore used facts, incidents, statistics, and quotations *to illustrate* rather than *to prove* the conclusions we have reached. We have not sought to tell all. Behind most statements lie many authorities which are not cited. We believe that this kind of documentation will content virtually all of our readers, but for the few who will wish to pursue the subject further we refer to the following excellent guides:

Frank Cundall, *Bibliographia Jamaicensis* (Kingston, 1902); and a *Supplement* (Kingston, 1908).

Frank Cundall, *Bibliography of the West Indies* [excluding Jamaica] (Kingston, 1909).

Jerome Handler, *A Guide to Source Materials for the Study of Barbados History, 1627–1834* (Carbondale: University of Southern Illinois Press, 1972).

Kenneth Ingram, Deputy-Librarian of the University of the West Indies, Jamaica, has in manuscript a massive listing of manuscripts relating to the history of Jamaica.

Manuscripts and printed sources were consulted in the following repositories and libraries in England, the West Indies, and the United States:

Barb. Mus. Barbados Museum and Historical Society, Bridgetown.
Bodleian Bodleian Library, Oxford, England.
BM The British Museum, London.

HCL Harvard College Library (including the Houghton), Cambridge, Mass.

Inst. Jam. West India Reference Library, Institute of Jamaica, Kingston.

JCB John Carter Brown Library, Brown University, Providence, R. I.

LC Library of Congress, Washington.

LCP Library Company of Philadelphia.

JH John Hay Library of Brown University (Special Collections).

NYPL New York Public Library.

PRO Public Record Office, Chancery Lane, London.

RCS Royal Commonwealth Society, Northumberland Road, London.

PUBLICATIONS AND BOOKS FREQUENTLY CITED

APC Col. *Acts of the Privy Council, Colonial Series.*

CSM Pubs. Colonial Society of Massachusetts, *Publications.*

CSPC *Calendar of State Papers, Colonial. America and West Indies.*

CSPD *Calendar of State Papers, Domestic.*

Davis Coll. N. Darnell Davis Collection of Notes and Transcripts of Barbados court and other records, since destroyed by fire, in the Royal Commonwealth Society's Library. Fifteen boxes, each containing many envelopes of documents.

DAB *Dictionary of American Biography.*

DNB *Dictionary of National Biography.*

Ec. Hist. Rev. *Economic History Review.*

Force, *Tracts* *Tracts and Other Papers, Relating to the Origin, Settlement, and Progress of the Colonies in North America,* comp. Peter Force (Washington, 1837).

Harlow, *Colonising Expeditions* Vincent T. Harlow, ed., *Colonising Expeditions to the West Indies and Guiana, 1623–1667* (Hakluyt Society, 2nd ser., No. LVI, London, 1925).

HMC Historical Manuscript Commission, *Reports.*

JBMHS *Journal of the Barbados Museum and Historical Society.*

Ligon, *Barbados* Richard Ligon, *A True and Exact History of the Island of Barbados* [1647–1650] (London, 1657, 1673).

MHS Colls. Massachusetts Historical Society, *Collections.*

MHS Procs. Massachusetts Historical Society, *Proceedings.*

NEHG Reg. *New England Historical and Genealogical Register.*

RHS Trans. Royal Historical Society, *Transactions.*

Stock, *Debates* Leo F. Stock, ed., *Proceedings and Debates of the British Parliament respecting North America.*

WMQ *William and Mary Quarterly,* Third Series.

Winthrop Papers *Winthrop Papers* (Massachusetts Historical Society, Boston, 1929–47, in progress).

Contents

List of Illustrations

NOTE: Most readers think of illustrations and maps as material inserted to embellish a book, as the seventeenth century would have put it. Here, they are used as detailed descriptions of certain matters and as authorities to buttress the text and notes. In the legends given below we have tried to point out the significance and importance of each illustration, and in the text we refer to the appropriate *plate* for further information. Many of these illustrations have never before been reproduced.

Endpapers WEST INDIES AND THE SPANISH MAIN

Plate 1 A WEST INDIAN COTTON GIN, 1688

Dr. Hans Sloane described "A GINN COTTON about Four Foot High," in *A Voyage to the Islands Madera, Barbados, Nieves, S. Christophers and Jamaica . . .* (London, 1725), II, 68, and Plate 100, as follows: "*A.B.* 2 round rollers of about an inch & ½ diameter made smooth, with only 2 or 3 shallow furrowes in them. They are turn'd about 2 several ways by the help of 2 wheels, *C&D,* by the Negroes feet sitting before it and placed at *E* or *F. G&H* are made to make the 2 rollers stand nearer or further from one another, so as to suffer the cotton to pass thro' leaving the seeds. *I* is a board about 2 foot & ½ long & 8 inches broad, where the cotton is laid to be drawn through between the 2 rollers, that so the seeds may be left in this side and the cotton go into a bagg on the further side, purged from its seeds, unless the seeds be chaw'd by ratts, in which case they go through between the rollers and foul the cotton." This kind of gin, for long-staple cotton, can be traced back some centuries to India, and can be claimed for neither Eli Whitney nor the Russians.

Plate 2 THE ISLAND OF BARBADOS, 1650, BY RICHARD LIGON

Artistry and accuracy were but two of the many remarkable qualities displayed by Richard Ligon during his brief Caribbean sojourn. Wild hogs, cattle, asinegoes, camels carrying bags of sugar, and horsemen pursuing runaway servants or slaves, were daily sights on the insular scene that he depicted in *A Topographicall Description and Admeasurement of the Yland of Barbados in the West Indies, with the M[aste]rs Names of the severall plantac̃ons.* The map was first published in his *A True and Exact History of Barbados* (London, 1657). Courtesy of the John Carter Brown Library.

Plate 3 AN INDIGO PLANTATION AND WORKS

The indigo plants are seen growing in a fenced field at the top of the engraving. When they came into blossom they were cut and immersed in a vat of water (A) to steep. Next, the liquor was drawn off into a lower beating vat (B), where three slaves agitated it vigorously (2, 3) with special long-handled tools in order to give it as much air as possible while it fermented. At a certain critical stage, determined by the overseer, the fermenting was stopped by the addition of limewater, and the suspended matter allowed to settle, after which the waste-water was drained off. In the lowest vat, or basin (C), the precipitated indigo "mud" was strained, pressed, and poured into bags (6, 10) for further draining until it attained the consistency of soft cheese. Finally it was put in boxes and dried in the sun (11), then cut into small cubes, dried further in the drying-house, after which it was ready for marketing. On this French indigo plantation the rotting vat (A) was 10 feet long by 9 feet in width and 3 feet deep; the beating vat (B) was 10 by 7 by 5 feet. Élie Monnereau, *Le Parfait Indigotier, ou description de l'indigo . . .* (Nouvelle edition, rev., Amsterdam, 1765), Frontispiece. Courtesy of the John Carter Brown Library.

Plate 4 SUGAR CULTURE IN THE FRENCH WEST INDIES, *ca.* 1665

A French composite view of the sugar industry: at the left slaves are loading bundles of sugar canes on the back of an asinego for transport to the ingenio; while at the right female blacks pile them on a platform (*barbecue*) for feeding the ingenio. Two oxen harnessed to each sweep and driven by slaves turn the great vertical roller, whose cogs (C) rotate the two smaller ones. Two other slaves feed the canes between the rollers which crush them. In the foreground the juice flows into a basin (D, E). At either side are the great kettles for boiling the juice that workers skim frequently (K). "La Figure des Moulins à Sucre," from Charles de Rochefort, *Histoire naturelle et morale des Isles Antilles de l'Amerique* (2nd ed., Rotterdam, 1665), 332. Courtesy of the John Carter Brown Library.

Plate 5 THE UPRIGHT OF THE INGENIO OR MILL THAT GRINDS SUGAR CANES

This, and the succeeding plate, provide further evidence of the skill of Richard Ligon as a technical draftsman. The legend on the plate sufficiently explains the diagram, but it may be pointed out here that the Barbadian mill has six sweeps instead of just two as in the French mill in Plate 4; presumably one horse or ox was harnessed to each sweep. Ligon, *History of Barbados,* 84.

Plate 6 THE PLAN OF AN INGENIO AND BOILING ROOM

(a.) The ground-plat, upon which the pillars stand. (b.) The pillars or posts. (c.) Wall between mill-house and boiling-house. (d.) The circle where the horses and oxen draw the rollers around. (e.) The sweeps that turn the rollers. (f.) The frame of the ingenio. (g.) The brackets that support the frame. (h.) The door and nine steps down to the boiling-house. (i.) The cistern into which the juice flows underground from the ingenio. (k.) The cistern that holds the temper, for use in the three last coppers to cause the syrup to "Corn." It is a sort of lye. (l.) The boiling-house containing five coppers in which the sugar is boiled, the largest being the clarifying copper, the smallest, the tatch. (m.) The cooling cistern, after which the liquor is poured into pots made of boards, tapered from 16 inches at the top to a point, commonly 30 inches long with a capacity of 30 to 35 pounds of sugar. (n.) Door of filling-room. (o.) Filling-room where pots are set for two days and two nights until the sugar is cold and hard. (p.) Tops of pots, 16 inches square, which stand between two timber stanchions about 13 to 14 inches apart; the pots are 4 feet above the ground or floor. (q.) The frame for the coppers is 1½ feet high, made of Dutch bricks and plaster of Paris. There are also small gutters besides the coppers to convey the skimmings of the three smaller ones down to the still-house, where kill-devil is made, and the skimmings of the two great coppers, being worthless, flow out in other gutters. (r.) Door and stairs down to the fire-room, where the boiling furnaces are, indicated as *z.* (s.) Little gutter in wall from first cistern to the clarifying copper, from which the liquor is ladled by Negroes into the other coppers. The slaves attend day and night and blacks and cattle work four-hour shifts. (t.) All windows. (v.) The fire-room. (w.) The still-house. (x.) The cistern to hold the skimmings until they begin to sour. (y.) Two stills. (z.) Boiling furnaces. From Ligon's Index and diagram, *History of Barbados,* 84.

Plate 7 A WEST INDIAN VILLAGE, 1660+, BY FRANS POST

This scene is described in detail on page 133 of the text. The painting hangs in Queen Anne's Dining Room, Kensington Palace (No. 71), and is reproduced by gracious permission of Her Majesty the Queen.

Plate 8 WEST AFRICAN BLACKS AND PALISADED HOUSE

Note that the house has a conical roof of thatch; the whole strongly resembling the kind of shelter the Negroes would have in the Caribbean. The man inside is playing on a *balafo,* or xylophone, having gourds underneath to serve as resonators. John Churchill, comp., *A Collection of Voyages and Travels* . . . (London, 1732), V, Plate III, p. 51.

Plate 9 NEGROES CARRYING BLACK SLAVES TO SHIPS AT MANFROE

In this engraving by the well-known Johannes Kip are shown, from left to right, some leading West African slave-trading posts: Mouree, Manfrou (Manfroe), Cape Castle, St. Iago, and Mina. The great dugout canoes were very much like those used in the Caribbean. From Churchill, ed., *A Collection of Voyages and Travels* . . . , V, Plate IX, facing p. 156.

Plate 10 ENGLISH SETTLEMENTS IN SURINAM, 1667

The title of this manuscript map is self-explanatory: "A Discription of the Colony of Surranam in Guiana Drawne in the Yeare 1667: the planters names as they are settled in their Plantations in the Severall parts of the Cuntry: the Land is Low and very full of woods: Its very Bad Travelling from one Plantation to an other without Boats." Going southward upstream on the Surinam River one came first on the west shore to "The Fort" (now Parimaribo); then to "The Towne" of Torarica; and farther on to Parham Hill, where Mrs. Aphra Behn stayed. Going upriver, on the east bank, one reached the seat of General Byam (the governor), and shortly beyond a number of the plantations of Sephardic Jews and the Synagogue adjacent to them. This map, here redrawn, is both accurate and beautifully executed. It is to be found in the John Carter Brown Library (Ea 667 Di Ms Map).

Plate 11 PROSPECT OF BRIDGE TOWN IN BARBADOS, 1695, BY SAMUEL COPEN

Engraved in London by Johannes Kip, this is the finest and most accurate seventeenth-century view of an English seaport in the New World. Its various features are discussed in the text on page 313. Courtesy of the British Museum.

Plate 12 AMSTERDAM, THE MART OF THE WEST INDIES

A portion of the view engraved by Jan Pieterszoon Saeuredam in 1606, which is reproduced here for comparison with Samuel Copen's prospect of the Bridgetown waterfront shown in Plate 11. The principal difference between the two seaports is largely one of scale. *Amstelodamum,* 1606. Courtesy of the Rijksmuseum, Amsterdam.

Plate 13 PORT ROYAL, JAMAICA, BEFORE AND AFTER THE EARTHQUAKE OF 1692

"A General Plan of Port-Royal in which the Different States of the Town are Accurately laid Down. NB. the Whole is an exact plan of the Town as it stood before the Earthquake, the hatched part & that within the hatched lines being all that was left after the Shock, and the dotted Space, a representation of the land thrown up Gradually by the Sea, or Made by Art since that time." References: (A.) Ft. James. (B, C, D.) Carlisle, Rupert, and Charles Forts. (E.) Mather's Line. (F.) Morgan's Line. (G.) White's Line. (H.) The Church. (I.) The King's House. (K.) The School. (L.) The New Yard. (M.) A Store House. (1.) Thames Street. (2.) Queen Street. (3.) High Street. (4.) Broad Street. (5.) New Street. (6.) Canon Street. (7.) York Street. (8.) Tower Street. (9.) Church Street. (10.) The Parade. (11.) Lime Street. (12.) Fisher Street. The plan is printed as an insert on Patrick Browne, *A New Map of Jamaica* (London, 1755). Courtesy of the John Carter Brown Library.

Plate 14 CARIBBEAN SEA TURTLES

Top: turtles laying eggs; *below:* the manner of turning turtles. From Jean-Baptiste Labat, *Nouveau Voyage aux isles de l'Amerique* (2d ed., Paris, 1742), I, plate facing p. 313.

Plate 15 SPECIFICATIONS FOR A BARBADOS GLEBE HOUSE, 1679

A portion of the most detailed building instructions that survive from the seventeenth century. "The House to be built for the Minister," in Parish Vestry Minutes of St. John's Barbados (Ms., Barbados Museum and Historical Society, Bridgetown), p. 29. The specifications are transcribed in full in Appendix IV of this work. Courtesy of Neville Connell.

Plate 16 PLANTATION JAMAICA, 1684

At this date the valleys of the river Cobre and of the streams that flowed into the present Kingston Harbor were the most densely settled, and only a little less so to the eastward along the southern coast. Cattle and hog ranching was prominent to the westward. In *A New & Exact Map of Jamaica* (London, 1684), Charles Bochart and Humphrey Knollys not only gave the names of the planters or plantations, but indicated which had sugarworks, cacao walks, indigo works, hog crawls, and cattle ranges; churches and towns were indicated as well. The central portion of the map is reproduced here, and its location is shown in the inset. From the copy in the John Carter Brown Library.

Plate 17 A LONDON VERSION OF THE JAMAICAN DISASTER OF 1692

One of several broadsides hawked about London: *A True and Perfect Relation of that most Sad and Terrible Earthquake, at Port-Royal in Jamaica.* Courtesy of the British Museum and the Institute of Jamaica.

NO PEACE BEYOND THE LINE

Introduction

THE TITLE OF THIS SECOND VOLUME of The Beginnings of the American People has ordinarily had a strictly diplomatic connotation. One reads of "les lignes de l'enclos des amitiés" in the Treaty of Vervins (1598) between Henry IV of France and Philip II of Spain. "Beyond the Line" means the boundless area west of the longitude of the outermost of the Azores and south of the Tropic of Cancer. No matter how friendly relations were among the nations of Western Europe, no such amity bound the men who ventured west and south of the Line. "No peace beyond the Line" was *the* maxim that governed both the official action and private conduct of all Englishmen (Frenchmen, Dutchmen, and Spaniards too) in the Antilles throughout the seventeenth century.[1]

Our purpose in the following pages is to convey to readers something of the tough, fibrous character of those people who sought an outlet for their astounding English vitality in the islands of the Lesser Antilles. They all went out expecting to improve their fortunes—the rich to get richer, or recoup fortunes, the poor to get land, and the hopeless to find security—and at the same time to transplant as much of Old England as possible. In pursuit of these goals they reversed the Christian order of things by worshipping

1. Jean Dumont, *Corps universel diplomatique du droit des gens; contenant un recueil des traitez d'alliance, de paix . . . faits en Europe . . .* (Amsterdam, 1726–31), V, 561–6.

Mammon all of the time and God only occasionally. The obstacles in the way of success were many and gigantic. From the very beginning they had to fight natives, or other Europeans, or nature, but whether they contended with Caribs or white men or with the jungle, or were striving to recover after devastating hurricanes or earthquakes, or, as buccaneers, were raiding the Spanish Main, their story is fascinating, sometimes incredible, and often instructive.[2]

The tale also has a sad and somber side, one which will be evident most often. The settlers never achieved more than a partial success in transferring English institutions and civilization to the Caribbean. Nor could they dwell for long in peace, even among themselves. The overwhelming majority who came in search of land and security found neither. In time a small number, whose fortitude and persistence in their drive for success evoke admiration and astonishment, grew rich. Only a small fraction of these men, let alone the small planters, servants, or wage laborers, ever experienced inner satisfactions or spiritual comforts. In an age of faith, these were secular men and women.

Around 1650 when the white men seemed about to attain their objectives, the very foundations of their existence, through their own doing, suffered a profound and permanent change. Two kinds of unfree immigrants converged in force on the Caribbean islands—white and black, European and African, Christian and pagan, temporary servant and chattel slave—but they never combined or amalgamated to form unified West Indian branches of English colonial society. The very presence in each island of a vastly superior number of Africans inspired fear and foreboding in all of the whites, for here was an unprecedented situation with which they were ill-equipped to deal. The blacks too were frightened, albeit for totally different reasons. This is no chronicle of hope and progress.

The question which we pose is the most important one that historians can ask: What did this portentous meeting of whites and blacks (also a few reds) mean in human terms, not "to the bloodless units of generalization" or "depersonalized caricatures of a

2. For the vitality of the English people, see Carl Bridenbaugh, *Vexed and Troubled Englishmen, 1590–1642* (New York and Oxford, 1968), 474, *et passim.*

partisan legend" but to actual men and women? Any effort to assess the seventeenth century must inevitably be limited by such materials as come to hand, but running through the sources we have used for our answer, like a leitmotif, is the theme that socially, economically, politically, mentally, and morally the men of the Caribbean seldom felt free from external or personal conflicts or agitating passions. Beyond the Line from 1624 to 1690 assuredly there was no peace of any kind.

Part I

White Men's Plantations

1624–1650

I

Peopling the English Colonies

THE HISTORY of the settling of human beings of three different races and complexions in the English islands of the West Indies during the seventeenth century divides naturally into two chronological periods, each having a theme peculiarly its own. Taken together both eras exhibit unprecedented growth and profound change over a term of nearly eight decades. First, starting with the founding of the earliest colony on St. Christopher in 1624, there was the attempt to create viable societies of white men in the Leeward Islands and Barbados by thousands of Englishmen and Irishmen in conjunction with hundreds of Scotsmen, Dutchmen, and Frenchmen.[1]

Just as it seemed that this mighty colonizing effort was about to succeed, the most thoroughgoing social revolution in the history of the New World set in, and by 1690 was nearly complete: a diversified agricultural economy was replaced by a predominant sugar culture; the possibility of insular self-sufficiency had vanished forever; and the incipient rural societies of white, English-speaking Europeans were, with unexpected finality, being transformed into communities dominated by the fear of, if not by the management of, tens of thousands of servile blacks, most of whom were newly

1. In the West Indies today *Leeward* is pronounced leé-ward, not *loó-ard,* as the sailors say, and in modern usage one does not use the *the* and there is no *e* in *Barbados;* and *St. Christopher* is preferred to *St. Christopher's* and *St. Kitts.*

come from West Africa and unable to speak any of the white man's languages. Here is a history of human tragedy.

II

Desire, verging on greed, for land, advancement, rank, and power, as well as desire to participate in the recently uncovered opportunities to exploit tropical soils for the production of exotic staple crops, animated the promoters of the first permanent English colonies begun at St. Christopher in 1624 and Barbados in 1627. Upon the urging of Sir William Courteen and James Hay, first Earl of Carlisle, a number of venturesome merchants, among them Ralph Merrifield, Maurice Thompson, Thomas Stone, and the elder John Powell, formed syndicates to furnish the funds, equipment, and settlers needed for these colonizing enterprises. Maurice Thompson—whose later career in the Caribbean, along the coast of North America, in the African slave trade, and traffic with the East Indies would make him possibly the most notorious, certainly the most wide-ranging, English colonial merchant—actually crossed the ocean with sixty Negro slaves in 1626 to plant in St. Christopher. The following year he sent out two ships, one of which he commanded, with supplies for his tobacco plantation, the patent for which he had wrung from a reluctant Earl of Carlisle, together with a ten-years' freedom from customs.[2]

Maurice Thompson and fellow merchants of London and the outports realized their greatest profits from the human cargoes in the ships they dispatched to the West Indies. When once assured of enough to eat, the planters' most urgent demand was for labor, for servants bound for a stipulated period to serve in cultivating tropical crops. This traffic in servants had grown to such proportions by 1629 that the ever alert Hollanders and Zeelanders were vigorously striving to secure a substantial share of it. By 1650

2. Harlow, *Colonising Expeditions,* 26–7; *Travels and Works of Captain John Smith,* ed. Edward Arber (Edinburgh, 1910), II, 900–903; *House of Lords Journals,* IX, 50. Two English scholars have treated the settlement and political history of the islands in detail: James A. Williamson, *The Caribbee Islands under the Proprietary Patents* (Oxford, 1926) [*q. v.*, pp. 17, 31, 64–5, 125–6]; and Vincent T. Harlow, *History of Barbados, 1625–1685* (Oxford, 1926).

English and Dutch merchants had successfully recruited and shipped to the islands thousands of discontented or audacious European men and boys, and occasionally some women.[3]

One of the curious facts about the English occupation of the West Indies is that, in marked contrast to the contemporaneous settling of the Chesapeake and New England regions, there was no literature issued to promote the Caribbean before Daniel Gookin published *Certain Inducements to Well Minded People to Transport Themselves to the West Indies* in 1645. The explanation may lie in the belief of the promoters that the kinds of individuals whom they sought to enlist could not be attracted by pamphlets and sermons, for most of them were either illiterate or rootless or both. Glib promises made by promoters, "spirits," and captains that the exiles would receive small plots of land to plant as their own at the expiration of their times of service proved to be almost the sole attraction for those who shipped to the Caribbean voluntarily. We do know, however, that the merchants did use some reprehensible means of recruitment.[4]

Neither in England nor in the islands did the authorities keep any systematic records of servants' indentures, departures from Britain or Ireland, or arrivals in the colonies as did the notaries of France. Several lists of passengers sailing to the West Indies from Dartmouth and Plymouth in 1632 give the occupations of the emigrants: husbandmen make up about 65 per cent of the men and boys; apprentices, journeymen-craftsmen, and common laborers account for the rest. Although the majority of all indentured servants who embarked for the islands had been bred to field husbandry in the Old World, very few of them ever displayed much skill at it, and those youths trained in the crafts went out with the knowledge that they would be put to planting rather than to trades.[5]

3. In the previous volume of this series are described at length the devices employed by the merchants—fair, devious, questionable, or foul—to fill the requirements of the planters for labor. *Vexed and Troubled Englishmen,* 412–23, 426–33. See also for the servant trade: Captain John Hawley to the Earl of Carlisle, Sept. 6, 1636, Hay of Haystoun MSS (Scottish Record Office, Edinburgh), Nos. 920–55; and *APC Col.,* I, 270–71, 273.

4. For the promotion literature of Virginia, Maryland, and New England, see *Vexed and Troubled Englishmen,* 398, 400–409, 450.

5. A total of 1397 passengers crossed to Barbados and St. Christopher from Lon-

During the first two decades, the white population of the Caribbees was composed chiefly of young people without any family attachments in the islands. Of the colonists who departed from London in 1635 for Barbados and St. Christopher, the preponderance was male; women and young girls amounted to less than 1 per cent. Most of the emigrants were in their twenties; their average age was twenty-four and one-half years. Of the males, 28 per cent ranged from eleven to nineteen years of age, whereas those over thirty totaled only slightly more than 1 per cent. Such fragmentary figures support conclusions drawn from other kinds of sources.[6]

The rapid growth of the white population in the English islands, especially in St. Christopher and Barbados, is astonishing, though its magnitude was grossly overestimated at the time—and has been frequently since then. One must agree with the historian of Jamaica, Edward Long, who exclaimed in 1774 at the large totals mentioned by Richard Ligon and Daniel Searle for Barbados: "nor is it easy to conceive by what means that island, which is not so large as some of the parishes in Jamaica, became so well stocked with white inhabitants in so short a time." The average ship carried about one hundred passengers, and, considering the unusually heavy demand for passages to New England, Virginia, and Maryland in these same years, it is extremely doubtful whether enough English and Dutch vessels of all tonnages were available to transport all of the servants to the West Indies who were said to have been sent there.[7]

Early in 1639, Sir Thomas Warner, governor of the Caribbee Isles, including Barbados, warned the Earl of Carlisle that "about 20,000 planters" in his patent lived in constant danger of attack by the Caribs or foreign enemies. This is as informed and accurate an estimate of population as we have. Bound servants of many nationalities and free Englishmen with their followers crossed the ocean in shoals during the next ten years, raising the white population of the islands to its greatest height between 1645 and 1647.

---

don, 1634–35, in thirteen ships according to data in John C. Hotten, *Original Lists of Persons . . . who went . . . to the American Plantations* (New York, 1874), 147–53.

6. Hotten, *Original Lists,* 38–136.

7. Edward Long, *History of Jamaica* (London, 1774), I, 263; *Vexed and Troubled Englishmen,* 427–8*n.*

With genuine diffidence we may suggest the population of the Caribbee Isles in 1650 to be somewhat as follows.

MASTERS, SERVANTS, AND SLAVES

Barbados	30,000
St. Christopher (English Quarter)	20,000
Nevis	5,000
Montserrat	1,000
Antigua	900
	Total 56,900

About this time, Père Pelleprat, a Jesuit missionary, reported the French population of French St. Christopher, Guadeloupe, Martinique, and the smaller French holdings in the Lesser Antilles to be between 15,000 and 16,000; Irish and other Europeans not enumerated did not enlarge the total very much, but the 12,000 to 13,000 black slaves did.[8]

An explanation of this unprecedented influx of people and the means by which they were seated on the plantations is essential to any understanding of early Caribbean history. The first Englishmen to arrive in the islands found St. Christopher alone to be occupied by any formidable number of Caribs; only a few of these fierce aborigines lived on Nevis, Montserrat, or Antigua. No natives of any kind dwelt on Barbados; it was an uninhabited island. The English, therefore, encountered no large native populations ready for exploitation (and eventual extinction) as had the Spanish in the Greater Antilles in the previous century. Thus, at the outset, a

8. Both the English and the French in the West Indies always distinguished between *population* (white) and *slaves* (black)—a significant indication of racial attitudes. Authorities in England were told in 1643 that Barbados contained 26,900 white people and about 6000 blacks; and the House of Commons was informed that the island had "upwards of 15,000 men." Another report gave 18,600 men and 5680 slaves. *CSPC, 1574–1660,* p. 295; *1661–68,* p. 529; for the year 1645 John Scott calculated from the muster rolls 18,300 men. Description of Barbados, BM: Sloane MSS, 3662, fol. 54b; Stock, *Debates,* I, 146; John Davies, *History of the Caribby-Islands* (London, 1666), 9, 177; see also Harlow, *Colonising Expeditions,* 44; *HMC, Franciscan,* 243; *A Collection of the State Papers of John Thurloe* (London, 1742), III, 754–5; Pierre Pelleprat, *Relation des P. P. de la Compagnie de Jésus dans les isles . . . d l'Amerique meridionale* (Paris, 1655), 5, 15, 16, 54–5.

shortage of labor hampered the English planters, a deficiency that Maurice Thompson and other merchants hastened to lessen by shipping them cargoes of indentured servants as fast as they could be assembled.

The merchants could never procure enough servants from East Anglia and the south and west of England, and consequently turned to other countries for them. Ireland became the principal supplier of white servants to the English planters in the West Indies. At Kinsale, early in the 1630's, a profitable traffic in young Irish servants sprang up. English, Dutch, and even a few Irish shipowners engaged in the trade; agents reported to their principals that all the men there were set upon going to St. Christopher where, they had heard, the planters paid annual wages. Such payments were not the custom, but a master usually paid freedom dues of £10 in money or goods to each servant. Father Andrew White was delighted to find some Roman Catholics, both English and Irish, at Barbados in 1634, and at Montserrat lived an impressive number of Irish Catholics. Thomas Anthony, supercargo of the *Abraham,* wrote from Barbados in 1637 to his employer, the well-known Puritan Matthew Cradock, that he had sold 53 male and female Irish servants to the planters for more than 500 pounds of tobacco each, except for ten he had let Governor Henry Hawley have for 450 pounds apiece. Six years later the Franciscans in Paris were told that the Irish working in the fields of St. Christopher numbered 20,000. Exaggerated though this figure was, it is still significant as an indication that the inhabitants of that English colony were overwhelmingly Irish. The presence of these Hibernian servants among the English settlers (and among the French too) demonstrates that neither religious persecution nor the political and social dislocation caused by Oliver Cromwell in Ireland were primary causes for the migration of the Irish from their homeland; the movement had begun a decade earlier, in the thirties. Like the members of every other nationality who risked their lives in the Caribbean, these Irish peasants hoped in some vague way to escape from famine and unrelieved poverty.[9]

9. Upon arriving at Kinsale, County Cork, in April 1637, Thomas Anthony heard that a "flymishe shippe of Amsterdam" had cleared out recently with 120 to 140

From Irish ports during the decade after 1640, English and Dutch merchants or ship captains sent off thousands of peasants gathered for them at Kinsale or Limerick by native Irish "spirits," who unscrupulously used every means to further this profitable commerce in human beings of their own country. Yet one inevitably concludes that a very large majority of Irish emigrants went off willingly, if not wisely. So numerous had these Roman Catholics become in the islands that Protestants of other nationalities there, mindful of the massacre of their coreligionists in Ireland during the Rebellion of 1641, feared them as potential enemies in the event of war with Spain or France. And, not without some reason, they also looked upon the Irish settlers as a turbulent and disturbing element in the population at the same time that they condemned them *en masse* for shiftlessness and sloth. The Barbadian aversion to Irish servants took official form on August 29, 1644, when the Assembly prohibited the landing of Irish persons. The act did not end the practice, however, and the law eventually became obsolete. Before long John Dryden, lampooning Thomas Shadwell, caused Dullness to exclaim:

> Heavens bless my son, from *Ireland* let him reign
> To far *Barbados* on the westerne maine.[10]

From the very first days of settlement, the Dutch (Hollanders, Zeelanders, Flemings) called at St. Christopher and Barbados to pick up cargoes of tobacco and cotton. When Captain Charles

---

servant passengers for St. Christopher, and that a local vessel with another 100 was destined for the same island within a month. The procuring of Irish peasants for the *Abraham* is described in PRO: High Court of Admiralty, 30/636. The obvious printed sources, together with Jesuit documents, pertaining to the Irish in the West Indies have been assembled by the Reverend Aubrey Gwyn in *Analecta Hibernica* (Dublin, 1932), No. 4, pp. 153–286; also relevant are Father Gwyn's articles in the Irish quarterly *Studies,* XVIII, 377–93, 651–63. *Narratives of Early Maryland, 1633–1684,* ed. Clayton C. Hall (New York, 1910), 37–8; Gabriel Debien, *Les Engagés pour les Antilles* (*1634–1715*) [Paris, 1951], 90–91; Richard Pares, *Merchants and Planters* (*Ec. Hist. Rev.,* suppl. 4, Cambridge, England, 1960), 15.

10. Some Observations on the Island of Barbados, PRO: CO 1/21, No. 170; Davis Coll., IV, Envelope 1; for the Rebellion of 1641, see Samuel R. Gardiner, *History of England from the Accession of James I to the Outbreak of the Civil*

Saltonstall, son of Sir Samuel, reached Barbados on November 26, 1627, with a store of all kinds of commodities to relieve the plantation, he learned that some Hollanders had been there before him and taken all the tobacco away with them. "Hoping to make a voyage," the mariner decided to stay on and plant a crop of tobacco, but when he finally sailed for home, he had to leave all of his trading goods behind him on trust. An English official counted forty Dutch ships in port at the Cape Verde Islands in 1630, all of them bound for the West Indies. In August of the next year, thirteen sail of the Holland Fleet, laden with salt from St. Martin, called to water at St. Christopher, because the water at their island was brackish. Between their two bases, St. Eustatius and St. Martin, and the English Leeward Islands, the Dutch carried on a vital exchange of goods almost weekly. More than a few Dutch sailors and petty traders remained in the English islands, there to congregate with their countrymen wherever one of their vessels came to anchor. By 1640 the Dutch made up a numerically small but very influential fraction of the Barbadian population.[11]

Masters sailing from England sometimes filled their complements of passengers in the Channel Islands, and those seeking many servants called at St.-Malo or La Rochelle to take on *engagés* before proceeding to the Caribbean. In 1627 the island of St. Christopher was divided by a treaty into three areas: the French occupied both ends, and the English controlled the middle. A genuine tragedy occurred in 1639 when all of 200 *engagés*, who had been lured away from St.-Servan by a rascally English captain from Jersey, died shortly after landing in Barbados. In January 1655 a party of French gentlemen with *engagés* came ashore at Barbados and purchased a plantation. Much to his surprise, Abbé Biët discovered many Roman Catholics there; in truth he reported that there were more than two thousand of them, and he privately celebrated the

---

War, 1603–1642 (London, 1884), X, 64–9; *Selected Works of John Dryden,* ed. William Frost (New York, 1959), p. 20, lines 140–41.

11. *Travels and Works of Captain John Smith,* ed. A. G. Bradley (Edinburgh, 1910), II, 902; Arthur P. Newton, *The European Nations in the West Indies, 1493–1688* (London, 1933), 145; Harlow, *Colonising Expeditions,* 94; *CSPC, 1574–1660,* p. 113; *CSPC, 1661–68,* p. 529.

mass without any interference from local officials. At the end of this period, a sizable body of Frenchmen dwelt and planted in the various islands under English rule in addition to those engaged in the expanding brandy and wine traffic with Dieppe and La Rochelle.[12]

In the years 1645–47, ship after ship arrived annually from England, Ireland, and France bringing servants and slaves, both men and women, to Barbados and St. Christopher; and from these islands a number were transported in small craft to Nevis, Antigua, and Montserrat. Civil war in the Mother Country started an emigration of English gentlemen, Roundheads and Cavaliers, who with some wealth and often many followers, contributed measurably to the beginnings of the culture of sugar, as well as to the social and political improvement of the colonies. On the other hand, they also brought over with them their political quarrels and kept the islands in a continual state "of mutiny and internal dissentions." After Drogheda, in 1649, a few hundred Irish common soldiers were exiled to Barbados; their fate was not that of slaves, as is so often charged, but of servants who eventually became free but could not return to the Emerald Isle. They merely added to the grand total of the Irish, which, as we have noted, was composed chiefly of men and women who shipped as cargo and who, incidentally, bequeathed a pronounced brogue to English-speaking West Indians. Despite meager evidence it is difficult not to conclude that in the English West Indies in 1650, the Irish settlers constituted more than half of the entire population and outnumbered even the English. Some Spaniards, French, Portuguese traders and planters, and a few Sephardic Jews from Brazil made up the rest of the white population of these five cosmopolitan colonies under the English rule. And all of them, the white settlers of each Caribbee island, as well as the black, were imported people.[13]

12. Debien, *Les Engagés,* 49, 86–7; Antoine Biët, *Voyage de la France équinoxiale en l'isle de Cayenne entrepris par les français en l'année MDCLII* (Paris, 1664), 276, 294.

13. The anonymous author of *A Short History of Barbados* (London, 1768), pp. 7, 9–10, alleges that the inhabitants increased so fast between 1640 and 1650 it was "computed" there were 20,000 white men, and that at musters of the militia 10,000 foot and 1000 horse attended. Ligon, *Barbados,* 40, 43; Sir Richard Schomburgk, *The History of Barbados* (London, 1872), 144.

The false promises and repugnant methods used to snare young men and women into binding themselves for service in the tropics (where sooner or later at least half of them succumbed) gradually became common knowledge all over England and Ireland. The verbal expression "to Barbados" a person gained wide currency, and English men and women could be recruited only with great effort. Furthermore, the Great Migration to America subsided with the calling of the Long Parliament, and as men began to question the benefits of emigration a subtle change of attitude emerged that deterred many of them from setting sail for the Caribbean.

Emanuel Downing wrote as early as 1645 from London to his nephew in Connecticut that "the people generallie here now begyn to disrealishe the West Indyes . . . and torne theire faces towards New England, which is in better creditt among all sorts and degrees than it hath ben for some yeares past." This was certainly true of men with puritan persuasions, but individuals of different sympathies held much the same opinion.* Any Englishman could more or less have endorsed the conclusion reached by Henry Whistler about Barbados in 1654: "This Iland is inhabited with all sortes: with English, french, Duch, Scotes, Irish, Spaniards they being Jues: with Ingones and miserabell Negors . . . This Illand is the Dunghill wharone England doth cast forth its rubidg." Nevertheless, Barbados, the pearl of the Caribbees, had already conferred on itself the sobriquet "Little England" and stood first among the islands.[14]

The Europeans who sailed away to the West Indies were pursuing a will-o'-the-wisp; very few of them ever achieved the better life they all believed that somehow they would find. Land—land of their own to hold in fee simple; land—the possession of which would bring them well-being, contentment, and a recognized place in society; land was the promise for which one risked the unknown. Voluntarily or Barbadosed, they set forth to these small islands, whose vast importance has always been obscured by their size.

* In this volume, as in *Vexed and Troubled Englishmen,* the term *puritan* will be used to denote *an attitude* toward God, the Church, morals, and behavior; whereas *Puritan* will refer to *a party* or *the radical wing* of the Church of England.

14. *Winthrop Papers* (Boston, 1929), V, 22; *The Narrative of General Venables,* ed. Charles H. Firth (RHS, *Camden,* London, 1899), 146.

The five principal colonies of the Earl of Carlisle's proprietary patent embraced a mere 421 square miles!

Barbados	166
Antiqua	108
St. Christopher (French & English)	65
Nevis	50
Montserrat	32

The smallest state of the American Republic, Rhode Island, with 864 square miles of land, is more than twice as spacious as the entire lot of these islands; the Isle of Wight with 147 square miles has an area only 10 per cent smaller than that of Barbados. When Jamaica, 4396 square miles in extent, was added to the English West Indian colonies in 1655, it was destined by its very size to dominate all of the other islands. We must never forget in the discussion of the peopling of the Caribbees that we are dealing with exceedingly small portions of the earth's surface.[15]

Ten years after the founding of Barbados, nearly all of the land bordering on the shores had been given out. Although a few privileged individuals acquired large tracts, most of the grants were made in parcels of five to thirty acres. In 1638 there were 766 proprietors with small holdings settled along the littoral. A mile or so inland, where there were no paths or roads, the vegetation stood too thick for a small planter or newly freed man to clear with his own hands. A report of 1651 giving the number of "considerable proprietors" as 760 shows clearly that there had been no increase in their number since 1638. Richard Ligon's map reveals the interesting fact that only 18.2 per cent, or less than one-fifth, of the earlier landowners were still in possession of their lands in 1650. The occupied and cultivated parts of the islands, with few exceptions, were still located along the shores, and no sustained effort to clear away the forest had been made.[16]

15. The two largest and most important French islands in 1650 were Guadeloupe and Martinique, with 619 and 380 square miles of territory respectively. For convenient data on the areas of islands, see *The World Almanac 1966* (New York, 1966), 238, 287.

16. The holders of ten or more acres of land in 1638 are listed in *Memoirs of the First Settlement of the Island of Barbados and other Carribee Islands* (London, 1743), 70–84; also in *NEHG Reg.*, XXXIX (1885), 132–44 (763 names); "A Topographical Description and Admeasurement of the Island of Barbados . . . with the Masters names of the Severall Plantations," folding map probably drawn

Into this very limited arable area, English and Dutch skippers had poured great numbers of people. By the end of the period about 30,000 human beings lived on less than half of the acreage: Barbados, with more than 362 persons per square mile, supported one of the densest populations in the known world. Since 1640 the value of ordinary land had risen at least 200 per cent, and far more than that for sugar land; a man could procure a plantation only by buying out one or more of the existing proprietors. The allotting of five acres of land to each person coming out of his service in Barbados, so sincerely promised by Governor Philip Bell, came to naught, as the Earl of Carlisle conceded in his proclamation of 1647.[17]

In 1631 Sir Henry Colt remarked that the plantations in St. Christopher were larger and better cleared than those of Barbados, but there, too, very little ground had been cleared inland away from the shore. Immigrants from Europe crowding into St. Christopher gave it possibly an even denser population than that which Barbados sustained. The settlers in the English quarter numbered about 4000 in 1635; fifteen years later Père Pelleprat thought that there were 20,000, most of them Irishmen, bound and free. Though we lack reliable information, we do know that visitors to St. Christopher marveled at "the multitudes that live upon it." [18]

Beginning in 1628 colonists from St. Christopher crossed the narrow strait to people Nevis; and four years later Montserrat and Antigua received surplus population from St. Christopher. The two smallest islands quickly filled up with Irish. Captain Anthony Brisket, governor of Montserrat, recruited Irish planters and ser-

---

by the author, in Ligon, *Barbados* [Plate 2]; David Watts, *Man's Influence on the Vegetation of Barbados 1627 to 1800* (University of Hull Publications, Occasional Papers in Geography, No. 4, 1966), 38–43; *CSPC, 1661–68,* p. 529.

17. Harlow, *Colonising Expeditions,* xxxviii, 44; Thomas Southey, *Chronological History of the West Indies* (London, 1827), I, 293; *A Declaration by James Earl of Carlisle, Lord of the Caribee Islands . . . Manifesting His care of and affection to the good and welfare of the Inhabitants of the Island of Barbados . . .* (London, 1647), BM: Thomason, 669.11 (115); also *Photostat Americana* (Mass. Hist. Soc.), No. 174; Ligon, *Barbados,* 86.

18. *Winthrop's Journal,* ed. James K. Hosmer (New York, 1908), I, 151; Harlow, *Colonising Expeditions,* 91; Thurloe, *State Papers,* III, 754. In 1634–5, St. Christopher received 1397 servants. Hotten, *Original Lists,* 38, 50, 80, 126, 134, 154; Pares, *Merchants and Planters,* 66, *n*32.

vants in 1636 and succeeding years, and before long all the arable land there had been granted. Held up by threats of Carib raids and the monopolistic land policy of Governor Henry Ashton, settlement of Antigua proceeded far more slowly. After carrying out what was, in essence, his first "diplomatic mission," to investigate each of the Caribbee islands for Governor John Winthrop, Jr., young George Downing sent a report back to Connecticut in 1645 on "the state of the Indyes." He recommended settling at Nevis or St. Croix (as big as Barbados, "as healthy as any Iland," and containing about 300 English and 300 French planters); nevertheless he strongly favored Antigua and would have remained there had he been certain that John Winthrop, Jr., would come there also to plant.[19]

III

Ships crossing the Atlantic with cargoes of servants usually made direct for Barbados or, but less often, St. Christopher; seldom did one call at any of the smaller Leeward Islands. These larger places received accessions of population regularly, and by the mid-forties suffered from overcrowding, but migrations of considerable groups of settlers from St. Christopher and Barbados had started long before the shortage of land and the consequent pressure of population grew acute.

In the beginning, these outpourings were carefully induced rather than spontaneous voluntary departures. Proprietorial promoters of the stripe of Sir Thomas Warner and Robert Rich, Earl of Warwick, seeking to colonize the uninhabited islands of the Lesser Antilles, initiated the first transfers of pioneers from the crowded parent islands. In 1628 Anthony Hilton, who had started a plantation on the windward side of St. Christopher with servants procured from some gentlemen of Ireland, joined with several planters backed by Thomas Littleton of London to open Nevis for the English. There were about 150 settlers, half of them from Hilton's plantation and the remainder from England and Ireland. Despite

19. Davies, *Caribby-Islands,* 169–70, 177; *CSPC, 1574–1660,* p. 240; PRO: CO 1/9, No. 23; *Analecta Hibernica,* No. 4, p. 262; Gwyn, *Studies,* XVIII, 649; Williamson, *Caribbee Islands,* 158–9; *Winthrop Papers,* V, 42–4.

the expulsion of the French and English from St. Christopher by a Spanish force in 1629 and the destruction of all crops on Nevis, the undertakings on both of those islands revived the following year, and by 1632 planters, settlers, and servants from St. Christopher had begun to colonize Montserrat, Antigua, and Barbuda.[20]

When Sir Thomas Warner was making his plans for settling the island of Metalina in 1636, he confidently expected to raise about 500 men in Barbados. At that time there were, as he reported later, about 6000 inhabitants on that island, and it was no secret that the planters were grumbling about the 20 per cent tax on their produce; some of them had even taken up arms. After mounting the expedition in St. Christopher, Warner sailed for Barbados, but he had misgauged the attitude of Governor Hawley, who prevented any malcontents from leaving the island. Two years later, however, the Governor reversed his position and permitted agents of the Earl of Warwick to entice Barbadians into going to Tobago, and in 1639, while Hawley was in England, his brother gave the same kind of encouragement to recruiters of settlers for St. Lucia.[21]

In later years, adventuresome and crafty men, many of whom were leaving because of persistent political struggles, cajoled or inspired servants just freed, runaway bondsmen, unsuccessful freemen, and debtors to embark as soldier-settlers. Some were lured by the prospects of plunder; others by the promises of land—agricultural opportunities on virgin soil (as yet uncleared) where tobacco and cotton of superior quality and higher prices might be grown. Some colonists were sent off as undesirables. Food shortages—at times virtual starvation—and epidemics figured prominently in decisions to leave, and so did a pervading restlessness compounded of absence of opportunity, failure, and, among not a few, despair. In truth, the selfsame emotions and needs that prompted emigra-

20. Harlow, *Colonising Expeditions,* 4–6; Capt. John Smith, *Travels and Works,* II, 910–11; Williamson, *Caribbee Islands,* 94–5; John Barbot, *A Brief and Historical Account of the Caribbee Islands . . .* in John Churchill, *A Collection of Voyages and Travels* (London, 1732), V, 642.

21. It was reported in 1639 in London that Warwick's agents at St. Christopher, Barbados, Nevis, and Montserrat "doe underhand labor to allure such people as can be spared or gotten off . . . to goe with them on their designs." PRO: CO 1/10, Nos. 12, 13; Williamson, *Caribbee Islands,* 152; *CSPC, 1574–1600,* pp. 130, 240; Harlow, *Barbados,* 18; Harlow, *Colonising Expeditions,* xxvi, xxvii*n; APC Col.,* I, 290–91.

tion from Europe operated in the West Indies, except that the element of desperation weighed in the latter; and to all of these we may add a new and governing inducement, the inability of many colonists to adjust themselves to living in an unfamiliar and terrifying environment.

By 1640 it was obvious that Barbados was in a decline. English merchants had ceased to send over servants and supplies, and land was virtually unattainable for all but the rich. An informed planter drew attention to what was to become the chronic complaint of the decade: "Inhabitants . . . daily run from the Island in Boats, being much indebted both to the Merchants, and also to one another." Sometime after 1640, Richard Hackett, listed as the possessor of ten or more acres of land in Barbados two years earlier, led a party of Englishmen raised in his island and at St. Christopher to settle in Hispaniola. When some of Captain William Jackson's privateers landed at Cape Tiburon in 1645, they found human bones and skulls, supposedly of the men of the Hackett expedition who had, in all likelihood, "starved to death for want of Doggs to Hunte, and Armes, Ammunition to kill beasts." Jackson himself had had no difficulty in persuading more than 500 men of Barbados and 250 others from St. Christopher to forgo planting and join in a buccaneering adventure to the Spanish Main. Captain Robert Marsham easily enlisted another several hundred Barbadians for the Earl of Warwick's projected settlement at Trinidad, which ended in disaster: Marsham was killed, and the others abandoned Trinidad to the Caribs and removed to Tobago. Warwick sent out a second party of about 200 men under Captain Marshall of Barbados in 1642 to plant tobacco and indigo on Tobago. When, after a year, this venture also proved to be a failure the discouraged settlers took off for Surinam on the Main where, in 1645, they were murdered by Carib warriors.[22]

Colonists also began to leave St. Christopher in droves by 1640 because of the ban on planting tobacco, which was ordered by Sir

22. Nicholas Foster, *Briefe Relation of the late Horrid Rebellion acted in the Island of Barbados . . .* (London, 1650), A–4; *The Voyages of Captain Jackson (1642–1645)*, ed. Vincent T. Harlow (*Camden Miscellany*, 3d ser., XIII, 1924), xiii–xiv, xvii, 2, 15, 21–2; BM: Sloane MSS, 3662, fols. 46–8; Harlow, *Colonising Expeditions*, 117–18.

Thomas Warner in an attempt to raise the price of that staple. Two years later Governor Ashton of Antigua reported to the Earl of Carlisle that the island was actually running to ruin. More than 800 men had fled to Santa Cruz, a similar number had crossed to nearby Nevis, and at least 500 more, carrying their arms with them, had gone off to other places. The departure of all these men left every third Englishman remaining on St. Christopher unarmed.[23]

Insular discontents and repercussions in the Caribbean of the Civil War in England launched further migrations from Barbados between 1643 and 1647. Once again hundreds of men set forth in vain attempts to colonize Trinidad and Tobago, and a large contingent removed to Virginia, and others, after 1646, to Surinam. But the most important and lasting of all the outgoings in this era was the little-noticed departure of 1200 Barbadians for New England. This migration must be looked upon as an individual, not a mass exodus. Nor did the New Englanders actively solicit the West Indians. Those persons who sailed to the northern colonies did not seek large land grants or plunder, but inasmuch as they were puritans to a degree, they must have welcomed the reign of the "Saints" if they did not purposely seek it out. Possibly, too, they longed to dwell in a healthier climate. Moreover they fervently wanted to locate where political tranquility prevailed and where they would be free from the Royalist coercion so openly practiced in Barbados. In some instances benefits were mixed, as in the case of Francis Brinley who, with some other Royalist Barbadians not relishing the climate, removed to salubrious Newport on Rhode Island. There the new arrivals thrived but were never, right down to the American Revolution, entirely comfortable because of their Royalist sympathies, whether for King Charles or for King George. The seasoned oldsters, always secure in the possession of broad acres, stayed on in Little England and continued to rule over it and to prosper.[24]

Recognizing that all was not going well with the humble settlers in his patent, the Earl of Carlisle, after he had leased it to Lord Willoughby of Parham, distributed a remarkable proclama-

23. Gov. Ashton of Antigua to Earl of Carisle, 1642, Hay MSS.

24. *CSPC, 1574–1660,* p. 529; Henry F. Waters, *Genealogical Gleanings in England* (Boston, Mass., 1901), I, 13.

tion for the purpose of encouraging immigrants from England, as well as for the freed servants of Barbados and St. Christopher, to emigrate to the smaller islands under his command: "Whereas divers People have been transported from the Kingdom of England to my Island of Barbados in America, and have there remained a long time as servants, in great labour for the profits of other persons, upon whose account they were first consigned thither, expecting that their faithful services according to the Covenants agreed upon at their first entrance there to make some advantage to themselves by settling of Plantations for their own use; but by reason of the great number of people who repaired thither, and who by the blessing of God have multiplyed there; the land is now so taken up as there is not any to be had but at great rates, too high for the purchase of poor servants. In consideration hereof, and out of a hearty affection towards the wellfare and happinesse of all such people as have left their native Countrey to settle under my Government in so Remote parts, I have thought fit to declare, that each freeman who is unprovided of land, and shall therefore desire to go off from the Barbados, shall have a proportion of land alotted to him in my Islands of Nevis, Antigua, or any other Island under my command according to the Custome of the Countrey." [25]

Coming ten years after migrations from the island had begun, it is difficult to determine how much stimulus this new policy gave to an exodus already nearing floodtide or how, when, and where the new governor, Lord Willoughby, carried it out. It may have been of greater benefit to the richer or middling sorts among the planters of Barbados who could envisage the possibilities of exploiting new soils, and who commanded sufficient resources or the credit to ship themselves, their servants, and their goods to distant islands. Some of the freed servants took up land in Antigua in 1647, but the growth of this island lagged behind the others. The migrants were composed chiefly of landless freemen and debtors, of whom a large majority appear to have been Irish. Whatever their place of birth,

25. The Earl of Carlisle leased his islands for 21 years to Francis, Lord Willoughby of Parham, on Feb. 17, 1647. His proclamation, issued on Nov. 22, 1647, left the execution of the new land policy to Lord Willoughby. The Earl also promised to encourage settlement of Antigua by guaranteeing a regular supply of ships twice a year. Carlisle, *A Declaration;* Williamson, *Caribbee Islands,* 122–3.

"those desolate English, Scotch, and Irish" in St. Christopher, as well as in Barbados, could travel along very few avenues leading to security and prosperity in the year 1650.[26]

By noteworthy coincidence, the hard times that New Englanders passed through from 1639 to 1642 stimulated many men, as John Winthrop noted with regret, "to inquire after . . . the great advantages supposed to be had in . . . the West Indies." This trend was developing in spite of the fact that those "countries (for all their great wealth) have sent hither . . . for supply of clothes and other necessaries; and some families have forsaken both Providence [Island] and the other Caribee Islands . . . to come live here." And Winthrop went on to say that "though our people saw what meagre, unhealthful countenances they brought hither, and how fat and liking they became soon, yet they were so taken with the ease and plenty of those countries, as many of them sold their estates to transport themselves. . . ." Actually the emigrants from New England were few, and the majority of them moved to Barbados with enough capital to make a comfortable beginning there as either merchants or planters. Outstanding among them was William Vassall, a leading citizen of Roxbury and Scituate. In 1646 his pronounced Presbyterian views caused him to seek redress in England against persecution; two years later he located in St. Michael's Parish, Barbados, both for trading and planting.[27]

IV

Between 1645 and 1647 the white population of the English islands reached its peak: in numbers, wealth, and power it prevailed over red men and black. It still consisted of imported Englishmen, Irishmen, and a few other Europeans. An amorphous lot, these colonists,

26. Tortuga, soon to be the rendezvous of the buccaneers, was first settled from Nevis and Providence Island in 1630–31, and had a population of about 300 in 1640. When the Spanish conquered Providence Island in 1643, most of the English inhabitants fled to Barbados. Arthur P. Newton, *Colonising Activities of the English Puritans* (New Haven, 1914), 104–10, 192, 193; Harlow, *Colonising Expeditions,* 15; BM: Sloane MSS, 3662, fol. 60b.

27. *Winthrop's Journal,* I, 333, 335*n;* William Hubbard, *A General History of New England . . .* (Cambridge, Mass., 1815), 375–6, 378–9; *JBMHS,* XIV, 165–6; XV, 132–4; Thomas Hutchinson, *History of the Colony and Province of Massachusetts-Bay,* ed. Lawrence S. Mayo (Cambridge, Mass., 1936), I, 93.

without any question, continued to live within the confines of their heritage from the late Middle Ages, including the established social ranks of their homelands. The financial and social condition of the majority of them was distinctly below that of the New England Puritans and probably lower than that of the settlers of the Chesapeake country, if only because half or more of them were poverty-stricken peasants from Ireland.

Outstanding among the human characteristics of the members of this great migration were youth, predominance of the male sex, and the fact that they had no family ties; these give us the keys to understanding nearly everything about their lives in the New World. Young men were shipped off or went of their own accord to the West Indies by the thousands, each of them alone for the most part. In modern parlance, this was an atomized movement.

Late in the seventeenth century, Sir Josiah Child told his English readers in pungent terms that the Caribbee Isles were first settled by "a sort of loose vagrant People, vicious and destitute of means to live at home, (being either unfit for labour, or such as could find none to employ themselves about, or had so misbehaved themselves by Whoreing, Thieving, or other Debauchery, that none would set them on work) which Merchants and Masters of Ships by their Agents gathered up about the Streets of London, and other places, cloathed and transported, to be employed upon Plantations . . ." Severe as these strictures are, they contain much truth as far as English emigrants are concerned, including the few English women sent to the plantations as servants. Some lusty, unspoiled, chaste colleens proved "reddear to goe than men" from Kinsale in 1636, but upon the whole the women colonists of the West Indies turned out to be a sorry, reluctant lot. Richard Ligon writes that in 1647 divers of them aboard his ship went ashore at a Portuguese island to wash clothes. There they promptly fraternized with white men and Negroes who "I cannot say Ravish'd them; for the major part of them being taken from Bridewel, Turnball street, and such like places of education, were better natur'd than to suffer such violence." [28]

28. Josiah Child, *A New Discourse of Trade* (London, 1693), 170; Ligon, *Barbados,* 13; and for the London purlieus of these women, see *Vexed and Troubled Englishmen,* 372–4.

With few exceptions the indentured servants arrived in the West Indies without any rational plan or guidance for their lives. Unaccustomed or unwilling to perform the hard tasks demanded of them, the newcomers nevertheless had to toil long hours under a scorching sun, subsist on a poor diet, had little or no recreation, and were unsustained by any religious impulses. Working conditions improved somewhat after the land had been cleared, but servants required constant supervision. Otherwise, as Sir Henry Colt reported to Barbadian masters in 1631, they would idle away the time. He recalled seeing some of them spend entire days hanging about the ships that came in order to avoid working.[29]

Family ties and domesticity were ruled out for most of these poor creatures during the first twenty years of settlement. Excessively high mortality, continual replacements from overseas, and lack of cleared land for the freemen precluded marriage for them. Under such a dispensation they did not reproduce themselves: children were few in contrast with their numbers in Old and New England. Only a handful of rich planters ever experienced the comforts, responsibilities, solace, and joys of family life, the foundation of all civilized societies. Not until after 1640 did the family begin to figure in the life of the English islands, and even then, among the mass of the people, it developed very slowly.

Whatever promise the Caribbean had once held out to these unfortunate mortals had vanished by the time they emerged from three to five years of servitude (if indeed they survived at all). Psychological troubles resulting from homesickness, uncertainty, fear, frustration, and, only too often, despair, battened down the spirits of the pioneers, crushed all ambition and hope, and left them so many beaten men, ever more frightened, quarrelsome, and devoid of much moral sense. Such men must be depicted not as individuals but in the mass, for they failed to leave behind them even the short and simple annals of the English poor, and they found no chronicler. The literate minority, alas, seldom wrote home and kept no diaries or journals. But the inescapable fact is that they too were people—the essential human stuff of West Indian history.

In dealing with these chaps in the mass, however, we cannot

29. Harlow, *Colonising Expeditions,* 66.

overlook a small though potent body of adventurers. Every white man, whatever his rank, who felt any ambition at all and could withstand the heat and the discomforts of the tropics, was very much on the make in the Caribbean. Some of the members of this element were scions of good families in England. Greedy for pelf and power, men of courage with admirable fighting qualities, ordinarily quick tempered and ready with pistol and sword, they sometimes commanded small amounts of capital—in hundreds of pounds not thousands—which in the Caribbean enabled them to acquire land and exercise talents unrecognized or undeveloped at home. Here in the islands they proved to be self-reliant, often remarkably shrewd, and eager to manage or to lead their fellows; and these men and their families appear frequently in the annals of the islands in the company of members of their class temporarily residing there as agents or factors for English mercantile houses. But by the very process of the peopling of the islands, only a few individuals felt any sense of community parallel to their vivid and memorable experiences at home. Nor did many of them entertain much hope of permanence either for themselves or for society in this era.

V

After landing fifty Englishmen and eight or ten slaves, captured during his outward passage to establish the first settlement at Barbados in February 1627, Captain Henry Powell left his nephew John in charge and sailed away to the Dutch colony in Guiana on "the Mayne." There an old friend, Governor Amos van Groenewegen, made him welcome and introduced him to the headmen of the Arawaks. In after years Powell explained that he had gone to the Essequibo region to trade with the Indians "for all things that was to be gotten for the planting of this Iland of the Barbadoes," and within a few months he was successful in getting what he wanted. As he dropped down the river in the *William and John,* the captain noticed that three large canoes, manned by some of the Arawaks he had chaffered with, were following him. When he inquired why they did so, "there answer was that they did perceive by the things that I had bought of them that I was bounde to plant an Iland," one which one of their forefathers had described. "They had a desire to goe with me *as free people* . . . and that I would allow them a peice of Land, which I did, and they would Manure those fruits and bring up their children to Christianitie; and that we might drive a constant trade between that Iland and the Mayne for there was manie more of the Indians . . . that had a desire to come for that Iland the nexte yeare if I would come there again."[30]

The Arawaks, to the number of thirty-two, including some wives and children of men who remained at Essequibo, willingly boarded the *William and John* and sailed with Powell for Barbados in May 1627. Thus it came about that in the first months of that year, white, black, and red men arrived to inhabit this vacant island. The Arawaks lived up to their bargain by cultivating the plants and teaching the English how to do so, but the English broke the contract by enslaving the Indians. Few more outrageous displays of man's ingratitude to man are recorded in the sad annals of English colonization. Internecine political disturbances prevented Henry Powell from going back to Essequibo for more Indians the next year as he had planned. In fact twenty years elapsed before he discovered, to his great distress, that Yow, an Indian woman, and her three children, and a boy at Colonel Ellis's were still held in bondage—the sole survivors of the original thirty-two good Indians. In a bitter and eloquent appeal to Governor Daniel Searle, Powell explained that he had "lefte them heere free people," and that a former governor had made them slaves. His protest eventually brought freedom to the five miserable Indians. Other Arawak and Carib slaves had been brought in in the meantime from nearby islands or the Main. In an inventory of an estate made in 1645, an Indian man and woman were appraised at 5000 pounds of tobacco! Richard Ligon discovered Indians in use when he arrived in 1647. The planters valued the women for their knowledge in making cassava bread, and the men, "with their own bowes and arrows," proved to be experienced fishermen. By 1650 the

30. Harlow, *Colonising Expeditions,* 30, 37–8, 39; Jerome S. Handler, "The Amerindian Slave Population of Barbados in the Seventeenth and Early Eighteenth Centuries," in *Caribbean Studies,* VIII, No. 4, pp. 38–64.

relations between the white man and the red man in Little England had nearly ended.[31]

Throughout the seventeenth century the Caribs, intractable and exceedingly warlike, presented a threat to the Leeward Islands. Soon after Governor Thomas Warner and the first colonists started to build a fort at St. Christopher in 1624, "King Tegreeman" planned a surprise attack to wipe out the English, but fortunately a warning came from an old Indian woman that enabled Warner's men to fall upon the Caribs. They killed the king as he lay in his hammock and slaughtered many of his people who were lying about in a drunken stupor; some of the Indians managed to reach their canoes and paddle off to other islands. Doubtless the fear of a return of the Caribs explains Warner's willingness to permit Sieur d'Esnambuc and the French to settle on the island. The Caribs came close to counterbalancing their losses when, in 1625 or 1626, a large raiding party arrived in canoes to drive the French from Basseterre, but with English assistance they were driven off. So many Europeans arrived in 1628, "about thirtie saile of English, French, and Dutch ships," that they were able to expel these dangerous Indians from St. Christopher. Those whom Sir Henry Colt saw on a visit to the islands in 1631 were a tame lot. He comments on the "many naked Indians, and although ther bellyes be to great for their proportions, yett itt shewes the plenty of the Island in the nourishing of them." Today we know that the distended "bellyes" are apt to be a result of malnutrition or starvation, and conclude that the aborigines may have been "tame" because of lack of

31. Mistress Susannah Winslow of Marshfield in Plymouth Colony sold to John Mainsford, a Barbadian merchant, on Feb. 11, 1648, "one Indian man called Hope, servant to . . . Mr. Winslow," then in England as agent for the Massachusetts-Bay Colony, "to have and to hold to him . . . according to the Orders and Customs of English servants in the said Island, both for maintenance, and other recompense." The term was ten years. One would like to know whether Hope (probably a Pequot) survived to greet his former master when Edward Winslow arrived as a Parliamentary Commissioner in 1655. *Winthrop Papers,* I, 357, 361; V, 197; BM: Sloane MSS, 3662, fols. 62–61 (paged from back of the volume); Harlow, *Colonising Expeditions,* 32, 37–8; *Memoirs of the First Settlements . . . of Barbados,* 20; Davis Coll., VII, Envelope 15; Ligon, *Barbados,* 54; N. N. [Thomas Peake], *America, or An Exact Description of the West Indies* (London, 1655), 169.

energy. We do know that the crops had been destroyed in 1629 and that Spanish assaults had almost wiped out the colony.[32]

The elimination of permanent Carib populations from the Leeward Islands by 1628 saved the English from the difficult times the French and Spanish passed through during native revolts. Nevertheless these islands lay open to raids by the Caribs, who could muster sufficient numbers and transport them rapidly across the open water in their great dugout canoes. Antigua suffered frequent incursions, and the Indians attacked St. Christopher in force in 1640 and again in 1654.[33]

Of the "lesser breeds," the blacks from West Africa were destined in the long run to transpose the composition of the population of the Caribbees. The first Negroes to arrive in Barbados were the eight or ten slaves landed by Captain Henry Powell in 1627; they must have come off a Portuguese prize. Within two years fifty Negroes drudged in the colony. The status of the black, as well as of the red men, remained in doubt until the decision of Governor Hawley and Council in 1636 stipulated "that Negroes and Indians that came here to be sold, should serve for Life, unless a contract was before made to the contrary." This was the earliest law governing slavery in the English dominions. Negro slavery did not develop on any extensive scale until well after 1640, because insular agriculture was conducted on small farms cultivated by a plentiful supply of white indentured servants or freedmen.[34]

In St. Christopher, as in Barbados, black slavery did not immediately take hold, even though Maurice Thompson carried sixty Negroes there in 1626, because of the abundance of white servant labor. The French resorted to slave labor before 1636, because not enough *engagés* came over to work for the planters and also be-

32. Harlow, *Colonising Expeditions,* xix, xx, 2–4, 93; Capt. John Smith, *Travels and Works,* II, 901–2.

33. According to a German gentleman indentured to a Barbarian named Whitaker in 1652, his master owned "100 Christian, 100 Moors and 100 'wild ones' [Caribs?]" as slaves. *Kurze Reise Beschreibung Hr. Heinrich von Uchteritz . . . auf der Insel Barbados . . .* (Schleswig, 1666), 5; Noell Deerr, *The History of Sugar* (London, 1949), I, 155.

34. There is no foundation for the tradition that a slave market existed near The Bridge in the 1630's. *JBMHS,* I, 49–50; BM: Egerton MSS, 2395, fol. 62; *Memoirs of the First Settlements . . . of Barbados,* 20.

cause Dutch slavers, from their base on St. Eustatius, stood ready and eager to supply blacks to any purchasers. In 1636 Governor d'Esnambuc threatened to set the French slaves against the English. The first slave revolt occurred in 1639 when sixty blacks escaped to the hills with their women to form the first settlement of Maroons. Slavery did not become an important institution in the other Leeward Islands for many years.[35]

Conflict in England interrupted the flow of white English and Irish servants to the West Indies just as it did to New England and the Chesapeake region, 1639–41. Again the observant Dutch merchants relieved the shortage by persuading owners of large insular plantations producing tobacco and cotton to purchase Negro slaves on very easy credit terms. Barbados contained only a few hundred blacks in 1640, but five years later George Downing reported: "I beleive they have bought this year no lesse than a thousand Negroes; and the more they buie, the better able they are to buye, for in a yeare and a halfe they will earne (with gods blessing) as much as they cost." It is evident that, despite the assertions of many writers, the shift from indentured white servants to black slave labor in Barbados originated on the tobacco and cotton plantations *before* sugar had become a regular staple, because a supply of slaves was readily at hand and because they were cheaper than white labor. The planters made this important discovery during a period of depression, and by 1645, before sugar production became commercially feasible, they were using 5680 blacks purchased from the Dutch.[36]

The successful cultivation of sugar cane and the mastery of the techniques of manufacturing Muscovado sugar after 1647 gave the Barbadians their first truly profitable staple. As a result their

35. All of the French islands suffered from a shortage of white labor. At Guadeloupe, Governor Daniel Houel complained in 1647 of the problem and of the inadequacy of the *engagés,* suggesting that they be "replaced by slaves who already have so largely contributed to the great rise of Barbados." Debien, *Les Engagés,* 253; Jean-Baptiste Du Tertre, *Histoire générale des Antilles habitées par les français* (Paris, 1667), I, 153; Williamson, *Caribbee Islands,* 149.

36. The statement of 1667 that there were "not even 6000 Negroes" in Barbados in 1643 is patently erroneous. *CSPC, 1661–68,* p. 529; *Winthrop Papers,* V, 43; BM: Sloane MSS, 3662, fol. 54. Père Pelleprat estimated the Negro slaves in all of the French islands in 1650 at 12,000 to 13,000. *Relation,* 3, 15, 54.

entire agricultural economy underwent a far-reaching transformation. They proceeded to purchase ever increasing numbers of black slaves from Dutch skippers—they "buy them out of the ship," Ligon wrote, "where they find them stark naked, and therefore cannot be deceived in any outward infirmity. They choose them as they do Horses in a Market." In the last years of this period, a good sound male slave fetched £30 and a woman £27; "the Children are at easier rates . . . for if they have more Men than Women," Ligon explained, "the men who are unmarried will . . . complain." [37]

To supply slaves to the English West Indian colonies and shut out the Dutch from carrying both sugar to Europe and slaves from Africa, the Guinea Company, in which Maurice Thompson was deeply involved, now began, understandably, to stress the trade in black instead of white ivory. Another interested person, Samuel Saltonstall, strove to break the Guinea Company's monopoly to the advantage of himself and his kinsmen among the Barbadian planters. The new lucrative traffic in slaves, opened by the Dutch in the forties, must certainly have figured in the passage of the Parliamentary acts of 1650 and 1651, as well as the war with the Netherlands in the following year.[38]

Ironically, the very years in which the white population of the Caribbee Isles reached its greatest height and when forced migrations from St. Christopher and Barbados occurred were also marked by the rapid rise of the black population, which would, in the course of time, prevail in the islands. The red men had almost disappeared from the English possessions; the white men were beginning to depart; the black men had come to stay. The peopling of these tiny uninhabited islands early in the seventeenth century was the first significant transformation of the Caribbees; now we must examine how the new West Indians met their strange environment, how they attempted to wrest a living out of it, and how some of them, at least, managed to survive and prosper.

37. Ligon's figure of 50,000 blacks is fantastic! *Barbados,* 43, 46–7.

38. *Documents Illustrative of the History of the Slave Trade into America,* ed. Elizabeth Donnan (Washington, 1930), I, 128, 129*n*.

II

Survival and Adaptation

FOR THE ENGLISH and the peoples of continental Europe, the seventeenth century was not fundamentally a materialistic age; for the inhabitants of England's Caribbean colonies, it was little else. As Abbé Biët said bluntly of the ruling clique in Barbados: "They all came here in order to become rich." Certainly the promoters of each colony thought exclusively of profits, and the statement applies equally to all the white men and women, regardless of their rank or degree, who emigrated from Britain of their own free will—it was also true of the Spanish, Dutch, and French throughout all of the Antilles. In the first years, everyday human needs for food, shelter, and health loomed larger than any other concern in these tropical islands where people often lived perilously near the level of subsistence and in a state of continuous insecurity. In fact it was a long time before the settlers could give attention to anything other than the problems of mere survival and adjustment to their new and unfamiliar surroundings.[1]

II

The first colonists at St. Christopher and Barbados brought supplies and provisions from Britain to sustain them until they could produce crops in the islands. No wealth of any kind existed; men had

1. Charles Wilson, *Profit and Power: A Study of England and the Dutch Wars* (Cambridge, England, 1957), 157; Biët, *Voyage,* 292.

to start from scratch and, by their own labor, create it. Barbados, for example, had to have seeds and plants, for both food and exportable staples, from the outside. It was to obtain these necessities that, after landing his passengers, Captain Henry Powell promptly sailed off to Essequibo on the Main. Meanwhile the first efforts of the settlers he left behind in his nephew's charge were directed toward erecting some kind of shelter on the island, "then vacante without house or inhabitants." They needed immediate protection from the burning sun, from the steadily blowing Northeast Trade Winds, from the tropical rains and torrential storms, and, in late summer and early autumn, from terrifying and destructive hurricanes. Quite as much as seeking shelter from the elements, these people hoped to avoid the extreme discomforts and dangers brought on by myriads of insects, unfamiliar vermin, and vicious rats. For a gentleman of some means or the leader of an expedition, such as Sir Henry Colt or Captain William Jackson, a few tents might be available which could be pitched on the beaches until more permanent abodes could be constructed, but the ordinary sort of men, apprehensive and miserable, had to shift for themselves wherever they could. Years later Captain James Holdip regaled Abbé Biët with a colorful story of how he, Colonel Drax, William Hilliard, and others of the first settlement in Barbados in 1627 shielded themselves from the strong winds in a depression in the rocks.[2]

The firstcomers to Barbados immediately "cutt doune trees and made houses," Henry Powell records, but when he uses the word *house,* he really means hut—or anything suitable for habitation. Furthermore, when he asserts that the men cut down trees to make houses, it must not be inferred that the settlers hewed timbers and sawed boards from tall trees, but rather that they stuck forked sticks into the ground for frames. No sawyers or carpenters crossed in the ships of 1627, and it is doubtful if one of these pioneers had ever felled a tree with an axe. These points must be labored because of the persisting log-cabin myth and the misconception of the meaning of *house* imposed upon later generations by historians who, themselves, knew next to nothing about forest or jungle conditions.

2. Harlow, *Colonising Expeditions,* 39; Biët, *Voyage,* 294.

We are fortunate that a contemporary, Charles de Rochefort, in his *Histoire naturelle et moralle des isles Antilles de l'Amérique* (1658), describes exactly what these early shelters were like: "At the first coming of the foreign Nations into the Islands, they were lodg'd much after the same manner as the natural Inhabitants of the Country, in little cots and hutts made of the wood they fell'd upon the place as they clear'd the ground. There are many still to be seen, in several of the newly-planted Colonies, many of these weak structures, which are sustained only by four or six forks planted in the ground, and instead of walls are encompass'd and palizado'd only with reeds, and cover'd with Palm or Plaintain-leaves, Sugar-canes, or some such material." In 1628 three men from St. Christopher told Captain John Smith that the "Palmeta [tree] serveth to build Forts and houses, the leaves to cover them, and many other uses . . . ."[3]

Adopting the construction methods and designs of the Arawaks and Caribs, the Powells and their company put up at least a hundred "houses," as they called their huts. The next year, 1628, Anthony Hilton and his companions quickly threw up the same kind of shelters when they settled at Nevis which they had previously raised on St. Christopher. Fabricated out of forked sticks, withes, and leaves, and situated under the shade of tall trees, such cabins afforded a measure of protection against sun, rain, and insects. As a rule, when a new lot of indentured servants arrived at a plantation, the owner would order them to construct their own cabins immediately. Ignorant of how to proceed, they had to rely on the advice and instructions of old hands among the servants or else lie on the damp ground. An occasional master might prepare housing for servants in advance of their arrival as did Thomas Verney, who wrote home in 1639: "I am now building a sorry cottage to harbour the men when I have them." Throughout the century, most servants and not a few slaves continued to occupy these flimsy

3. As noted above, the misconception so ably dispelled for the continental colonies in Harold N. Shurtleff's *The Log-Cabin Myth* (Cambridge, Mass., 1939), naturally took a somewhat different form in the West Indies. Rochefort's account was translated into English and published at London in 1666 by John Davies. The quotation is from his *History of the Caribby-Islands,* 177; Harlow, *Colonising Expeditions,* 2, 40; Capt. John Smith, *Travels and Works,* II, 905; and for Shurtleff on Harlow and Barbados, *Log-Cabin Myth,* 5.

structures long after their masters had acquired better dwellings. During the first years of settlement, a servant ordinarily received a small tract of land at the end of his term of service. Having no servants of his own to start out with, he and his successors lived in huts hastily put up on their lands just like the ones they had grown accustomed to in bondage.[4]

The early governors and the few men with means soon employed their servants to erect more substantial quarters for them. At St. Christopher, Thomas Warner was living in a modest timber dwelling by 1628, and what was just as important, he had a "great tobaccoe house that stood to the windward." Sir Henry Colt had endured the discomforts inherent in living in a tent on the beach for only a few days when he set about, rather hastily as it turned out, to have a house built for him on a site he had selected. The cabin was to be fit to house beds, a candlestick, wax lights, a tablecloth, napkins, dishes, glasses, a tankard, and "a chamber pott basin"—in fact all the accessories required by this Admirable Crichton of 1631. As he wrote to his son, "now comes one of the greatest labours and cares that is for the suddaine buyldinge of a house." The location he had picked out was between two rivers, "for water is to be prised above any thinge els, yett was the place wonderfull discommodious." Unfortunately he had failed to recognize the difficulties of conveying all of his belongings and the materials needed to start the building to his property, an abandoned, overgrown Carib plantation without path or access to it. It was half a mile from the sea and all uphill, and everything had to be carried there on men's shoulders. So arduous, almost impossible, was it for inexperienced axemen to clear the ground that the disgruntled knight, after weeks had passed without any appreciable progress being made, gave up the undertaking. Sixteen years after

4. Houses, huts, cabins—all were flimsy shacks that could be put up in a day. It is erroneous to believe that the "ten-acre men" of Barbados were settlers who received ten acres or less as freedom dues; rather ten-acre men were those who, by law, had to maintain one white servant for every ten acres granted to them. Davis Coll., VII, Envelope 14 (Lucas MSS); Harlow, *Colonising Expeditions,* 5, 30; Ligon, *Barbados,* 44; *Voyages of Capt. Jackson,* ed. Harlow, 26; Biët, *Voyage,* 289; *Memoirs of the Verney Family,* ed. Frances P. Verney (London, 1892), I, 151; Pares, *Merchants and Planters,* 9.

the first settlement, the "houses" of the Barbadians were characterized as "mean, with things only for necessity." [5]

The best-informed gentleman, architect, and engineer who ever went out to any of the English plantations in the seventeenth century arrived at Barbados in 1647. Expecting to see houses such as he had known in France and Italy, with thick walls, high ceilings and roofs, and deep cellars, all calculated to counter the tropical heat, Richard Ligon found "timber houses, with low roofs, so low, as for the most part of them, I could hardly stand upright with my hat on, and no cellars at all." Indoors the owners nearly stifled, for in order to exclude the winds, they had no openings on the east sides of their houses; alleging that the rain drove through glassless windows, they never thought to fit shutters to them. Conversely, the western sides of the houses were left open to the unbearable heat of the afternoon sun. Ligon blamed this unintelligent planning on the "poverty and indigence" of the planters, great and small. One must also give weight to the innate conservatism of colonists, who always want to repeat what they have known at home. Indubitably, the Barbadians would all have built with timber and boards if they had been available, but most of them, once ensconced in their forked-stick framed cabins with the reed-and-palm-leaf siding and roofs, which they had copied from the Indians out of sheer necessity in the beginning, were then too unimaginative or slothful to construct solid and comfortable houses designed for their new environment.[6]

One of the items of household furnishings that Sir Henry Colt thought indispensable for his well-being was a good English bed (leather if possible). Few of the poor even in Old England and Ireland had one, and in the islands only the very richest colonists

5. Harlow, *Colonising Expeditions,* 7, 90–91, 100; *CSPC, 1661–68,* p. 529.

6. Almost the only improvement in construction came with the substitution of the native Royal Palm for roofing and siding for the ordinary palm leaves. Ligon points out "the use our Planters made of them at first coming, before they knew how to make shingles, was, to saw the bodies of these trees to such length, as might reach to the ridge pole, to the Eves of the house; for they were hollow, and then sawing them long wise, there were two concaves, which they laid together, setting the hollow sides upward; and where they close, one to cover them, with the hollow side downward, and so the whole house over." Ligon, *Barbados,* 40–41, 78–9, 102; *CSPC, 1681–85,* p. 70.

aspired to them; but to sleep on the ground in the West Indies was unthinkable. Ants, cockroaches, chiggers, and other insects made one's life miserable, and lizards, land crabs, and snakes crawled about everywhere. Long before the English settled on the islands, Indians had evolved the hammock to alleviate these ills; sailors had observed them and made use of them aboard ship; so much so that in the first English book on seamanship (1628), Captain John Smith listed as a regular part of a ship "the hang cabben," where the crew slung their hammocks.[7]

When the firstcomers arrived in the islands, they too recognized the merits of the hammock. Father Andrew White stopped off at Barbados on his way to Maryland in 1634 and found to his surprise that "they use noe bede, but onely hamachoes, which are curious blankets of fine cotton neatly wrought and painted on the outside, and hung up a yard or lesse from the ground by a rope at each end fastened to two posts when they goe to rest, and on the day time taken away and carried about with them when they travaile." The need for them was obvious, for everyone suffered from "such aboundance of smale knatts by the sea shoare towards the sun goinge down that bite so as noe rest cann be had without fyers under your Hamaccas." To ensure additional protection from ants and cockroaches, the islanders tarred the strings of their hammocks. To Père Du Tertre, a hammock also had the advantage of being inexpensive, "because no pillows, sheets, or quilts are necessary: so that a good cotton bed lasts a man for a life." Richard Ligon on the other hand firmly believed that "Irish Ruggs such as are made at Killkennie" were beneficial for servants to wrap around themselves when they came in all overheated and sweating from their labors and lay in their hammocks. Fastidious Sir Henry Colt declared that: "Hammaccas are naught, they are to cold, and you cannott turne yourself in them." He used one only in the daytime. Whatever their opinions concerning the virtues of hammocks, the white men, sleeping in them every night, never gave a thought to

7. Cotton hammocks were widely known in England. "I had promised my Cosen an Hamacca," Colt noted as his ship raised Dominica. "These [Carib] people are thought to have the best." As early as 1555, Richard Eden mentions them in *The Decades of the New Worlde* (London, 1555, p. 200r): "Theyr hangynge beddes whiche they call Hamacas." Harlow, *Colonising Expeditions,* 77; Capt. John Smith, *Travels and Works,* II, 793.

the fact that they were indebted to the red man for this acceptable contribution to their comfort and sanity.[8]

III

Well into the 1650's, the French traveler, Rochefort, said of the Caribbees: "the greatest part of these islands are cover'd with several sorts of excellent Woods, which being green at all times, offered a very delightful prospect." Indeed most Europeans approaching an island admired the entrancing sylvan scene, but once ashore they soon came to realize, as did Sir Henry Colt, that the jungle was in many ways their primary problem. Gazing at the forest on Nevis in 1607, Captain John Smith described its primitive state: "It is all woddy . . . in most places the wod groweth close to the water side, at a high water marke, and in some places so thicke of a soft spungy wood like a wilde figge tree, you cannot get through it, but by making your way with hatchets, or fauchions." [9]

The most formidable obstacle to settling and farming in any of the islands was the presence of these dense and often impenetrable jungles, which stretched right down to the littoral and had to be cleared away to allow for habitations and fields. In our own days of bulldozers and dynamite, it is virtually impossible to imagine how appalling and gigantic the prospect of clearing the ground appeared to the English settlers. They came from a land where timber was scarce, and they understood very little of the techniques of the woodsman. Englishmen, Irishmen, Frenchmen, had little or no experience with the axe and not the slightest knowledge about felling or stripping great trees, let alone of clearing away tough parasitic vines. All of this was American and very strange. Even the most skillful and hard-working English and Irish husbandmen and planters had to undergo a second strenuous and difficult period

8. The colonists valued Indian women for making hammocks from large pieces of cloth "with loop-holes at each end; through which, by putting a cord or some small line, they hang them up in their houses upon beams or Tainters made for that purpose. . . ." N. N., *America,* 170; *Narratives of Early Maryland,* 35; Harlow, *Colonising Expeditions,* 65, 100; Du Tertre, *Histoire générale des Antilles,* II, 451–2; Ligon, *Barbados,* 44–5, 109.

9. Davies, *Caribby-Islands,* 4, 28; Ligon, *Barbados,* 20; Capt. John Smith, *Travels and Works,* II, 909.

of apprenticeship in the West Indies before they were able to contend successfully with nature in these tropical lands.[10]

In each island, the clearing of the jungle back from the water's edge proved to be an incredibly slow process. Once having acquired the know-how, the settlers expended years of back-breaking toil applying it. Sir Henry Colt suggests that in some places the islanders resorted to the easy but very dangerous course of burning the jungle. In 1634, seven years after Barbados had been settled, a visiting Jesuit observed: "The place is a plaine ground, growne over with trees and undershrubs without passage, except where the planters had cleared"; and six years later, Laet described the northern coast as everywhere covered with green trees. In his usual fashion, Richard Ligon summed up the situation in 1647. The first pioneers had cut down only enough trees to make small plots in which to plant provisions and tobacco: "For the Woods were so thick and most of the Trees so large and massie, as they were not to be falne with so few hands; and when they were laid along [the ground], the branches were so thick and boysterous, as required more help, and those, strong and active men, to lop and remove them off the ground . . . We found both Potatoes, Maies, and Bonavists, planted between the boughes, the Trees lying along the ground, so Short was the ground then of being clear'd." And the colony was then twenty years old! [11]

In the Leeward Islands, the colonists encountered similar difficulties. Colt noticed in 1631 that Montserrat was mountainous and heavily wooded, and Nevis was "all full of woods." St. Christopher,

10. Far more difficult to clear away than tall trees were the "withes," parasitic vines of several sorts, that climbed trees 80 to 100 feet high, and were unusually strong plants. Ligon tells of Col. Drax's "Axemen" who were felling a tree and, concluding how it would fall, got clear; but the "withe" that entwined it was also fastened to another tree and pulled down a great branch of it that nearly crushed them, leaving both of them badly injured. Ligon, *Barbados,* 97.

11. David Watts attributes the slow recession of the forest and undergrowth at Barbados chiefly to unsettled political conditions, insecure finances, frequent changes in ownership of property, and repercussions of the English Civil War. These are sound reasons, but the ignorance of woodmen's techniques, the formidable jungle, and especially the large number of hands needed to effect the clearing seem to us to be even more weighty. Watts, *Man's Influence on the Vegetation of Barbados,* 39; Watts, in *JBMHS,* XXXII, 54; Harlow, *Colonising Expeditions,* 66, 67, 69–70; *Narratives of Early Maryland,* 37; Jean de Laet, *Histoire du nouveau monde, ou description des Indes occidentales* (Leyden, 1640), 30; Ligon, *Barbados,* 24.

on the other hand, had large plantations that seemed "somewhatt cleerer than the Barbados" though "the woods are thick, the mountaynes and hills manye." When he and his servants attempted to clear the ground for his house, they discovered that they had no helve for their *only* axe, and spent most of a day fashioning one! Then, he wrote plaintively, unforeseen obstacles arose: "The wood we must cut downe is the pricklye tree hard and tough. This beinge doone we come to the wood that we must deale with. The trees are butt smale, some hard some soft, butt the withes of a nutt that is green and rownd as bigg as a warden [pear] . . . gives us the greatest Impediments; for the withes of these runns upp to the topps of trees and then downe to the bottome, running about like roaps soe entangle the trees, the one with the other as we could not devide them without cuttinge downe 4 or 5 together." As late as 1645 Guillaume Coppier described St. Christopher as "full of forests of tall trees." Ligon commented on the prevalence of woods and jungles, deploring the lack of "smooth Champion to walk or ride on, with variety of Landscapes at several distances; all there being hem'd in with Wood." [12]

By 1650, in spite of the smallness of these islands, only the littoral of each one had been cleared, and the interiors were almost universally covered by a tangled mass of small and large trees, vines, bushes, and every sort of lush vegetation that grows in a hot moist climate. There were just not enough white men to perform this Herculean task. At this date all that the Europeans had accomplished was the learning of the techniques for clearing land. Paths and highways leading inland from the seashore had not yet been opened, and until they should be, The Great Clearing still lay in the future.

IV

One obvious trait perceivable in all colonists is that no matter how advanced or unorthodox in opinion or customs they may be, when

12. The planters of St. Christopher and Nevis cut and exported logwood (*Haematoxylum campechianum*) in the thirties. Gordon C. Merrill, *The Historical Geography of St. Kitts and Nevis, the West Indies* (Mexico City, 1958), 15; Harlow, *Colonising Expeditions,* 74–5, 83–4, 87, 90–91; Guillaume Coppier, *Histoire d'un voyage* (Lyon, 1655), 30; Ligon, *Barbados,* 106.

it comes to diet they want food such as they had in their childhood. Even the most radical or obstreperous men yearn for pie like mother used to make. In food and drink they invariably turn out to be conservative; no human characteristic is more ingrained, and one must take cognizance of this fact in trying to understand the settlers' intransigence in adapting themselves to conditions in their island homes. Only with the greatest reluctance did they make an effort to accommodate themselves to new and more suitable kinds of food. In this matter they moved even more slowly than they did on shelter.

At St. Christopher in 1624, then at Barbados, the firstcomers immediately planted wheat brought from England, and though this cereal matured in three months, it never did well enough in the tropics to meet the demand for bread. At times, as in 1631 in Barbados, the crop was burned and blasted, and that of St. Christopher was eaten up by rats. Father Andrew White spoke of Barbados as "the granarie of all the Charybbies" in 1634, but it was not wheat that made it so; by this time the inhabitants had turned, unwillingly, to planting unfamiliar grains that were better adapted to the soil and climate of the islands.[13]

When Captain Henry Powell and his thirty or so Arawaks came from Essequibo early in May 1627, they had with them seeds and cuttings not only for staple crops but also for many kinds of food, among them cassava, maize or Indian corn, yams, sweet potatoes, and pulses, plantains, bananas, oranges, lemons, limes, pineapples, and melons—"to all which Barbados was naturally a stranger." The object of the Indians in coming was "to assist and instructe the english" in growing them, and accordingly they promptly fell to work on the tract granted to them by Captain Powell called the Indian Plantation. The soil proved to be favorable and every one of the varieties grew quickly and unusually well, and soon the 170 or more white, red, and black inhabitants were producing food enough to sustain themselves.[14]

For the English, one of the assets of Barbados, and to a lesser extent of St. Christopher, was the presence of a superabundance

13. Harlow, *Colonising Expeditions,* 67, 93; *Narratives of Early Maryland,* 34.
14. BM: Sloane MSS, 3662, fols. 62b, 60a; Harlow, *Colonising Expeditions,* 30, 40.

of wild hogs, some of them weighing as much as 400 pounds. The story goes that Pedro à Campos, a Portuguese, stopped off at Barbados in 1523 to take on water during a voyage to Margarita. He left some hogs there, which, disturbed only on rare occasions by hunting parties of Caribs from St. Vincent, increased in numbers over the century. Unaccustomed to any kind of regular diet of "bone meat" at home, the English settlers proceeded to slaughter the swine indiscriminately and to gorge themselves on pork.[15]

A graphic description of the reckless and wholesale killing of the pigs has been left to us by Sir Henry Colt, who recognized that the colonists were creating a conservation problem of the first magnitude, and unnecessarily. "The Barbados have moor wilde hoggs than St. Christophers, butt ther lavish expences have well nigh roated them all out. They usually kill 1500 a week, a waste to great to be continued. Lett them remember that when they want to hunt hoggs ther custome was when they had taken 10 or 12 to binde them togeether, and let them lye, and to proceed further to catch moor; which beinge doone, they would nott take the paynes to returne and fetch the first, beinge to farr out of ther way home, butt left them soe tyed to starve. Alsoe every man must have his hogg with an allowance alsoe for ther doggs to eat. Butt this plentifull world of thers is now past. They needed nott have made such a hasty distruction of them." Thus did Englishmen, with brutal thoroughness, make their first assault on the ecology of the Caribbean islands. Within a few years the luscious iguana, a large and plentiful lizard, was subjected to the same senseless slaughter at St. Christopher and Nevis and soon became extinct in these islands.[16]

The people of Barbados passed through a deadly "starving time" in the years 1630 and 1631. Most of the planters and ser-

15. On the absence of meat in the diet of the average Briton, in the seventeenth century, see *Vexed and Troubled Englishmen,* 94–5; Ligon, *Barbados,* 33–4.

16. After addressing the Barbadians metaphorically about hogs, Sir Henry Colt continued sardonically: "I eat one of them baked in a pye at ther governours and it liked me soe well, as I durst sware ther fathers and predecessors that lived and dyed in England weer never fed dayly with soe good meat. Yett weer they farr better men then you are." Harlow, *Colonising Expeditions,* 92; J. H. Westermann, *Nature Preservation in the Caribbean* (Utrecht, 1953), 23–57; Capt. John Smith, *Travels and Works,* II, 904.

vants had concentrated on growing tobacco, which, with a little cotton, served as the only staples to exchange for Dutch and English provisions and manufactured goods so much needed in the little island. In attempting to increase the production of tobacco and cotton, the planters neglected their provision crops, leaving the raising of food to the Arawaks. The latter could not increase the supplies commensurate with the increase in population, and the whites had irresponsibly depleted the meat supply by their extermination of the hogs. As yet no dependable supply of food outside the islands had been found. Furthermore, many freemen and some servants, succumbing to the enervating climate, slowed down and did not produce as much as they might have, if they did not stop working altogether; while their betters broke up into turbulent, lawless factions struggling for power.[17]

Very gradually, as a result of near starvation, shameful waste of resources, and the system of bondage among the English, some of the settlers had to adjust themselves to eating the exotic West Indian foods. First in Barbados and St. Christopher, and shortly thereafter at Nevis, Montserrat, and Antigua, newcomers added to the plants and trees introduced by Captain Powell in 1627. Figs, various vines, pomegranates, peas, and a species of kidney bean known as bonavist, guavas, pawpaws, excellent red peppers, all were added to the diet of the islanders, as well as such English fowl as chickens, turkeys, ducks, peacocks, and pigeons, and also the cow, "whose milk tasts better then in England." Probably the best husbandman in Barbados was Captain James Futter, noted for the excellence of both his household and his fields. One afternoon in 1631, he served a great feast for Sir Henry Colt: "We had piggs, capons, Turkey, chickins: from the field, Indian wheat, Cassavi, and Cabidges, whose stemme or stalk was 200 foot long and you must cutt them downe with an ax." And the knight believed the captain when he boasted that he could do the same every day.[18]

17. Because a shipload of provisions from England failed to arrive at St. Christopher in 1627, the colonists were on the verge of starvation. Perhaps the Barbadians first discovered that their rats "eat in tast like younge rabbitts" during "the Starving Time"; the rats at St. Christopher were more numerous and, also, considered "good meat." Harlow, *Colonising Expeditions,* xvii, 68; and for political troubles and lawlessness, Harlow, *Barbados,* 11–13.
18. The "Cabbidg Tree" or palm, which often grew to 100 feet in height, had a tender or unexpanded center or terminal bud that was edible, though extract-

During the first days of each island's settlement, the planters, merchants, white servants, and slaves subsisted on essentially the same kinds of foods; their diet was both scanty and monotonous. As months and years went by and some of the colonists prospered, class lines were sharply drawn. The rich could afford the costly foods and beverages the Dutch brought over from Europe in their ships, and though the diet of the ordinary people improved somewhat as provision crops were established in the islands, the demands of the soaring white population soon exceeded the supply of local cereals and fruits. Since no arrangements for regular importation of food from elsewhere existed, the mass of the people were often faced with short rations and sometimes experienced periods of actual starvation. When this situation occurred, men, seeing little hope of change, began to migrate.[19]

The settlers who were unable or unwilling to risk making a new start in another location, depressed in spirit by food shortages and hard labor, fell into "a declining and yielding condition." Newly arrived from Strawberry Bank in New Hampshire, the Reverend James Parker described for Governor John Winthrop the plight of the "common people" of Barbados in 1646. He found them "very meane in respect of provisions, little flesh if any, noe bread but casader, a bread I approve not off, though its true the rich live high." Two years later Sir Edmund Plowden, echoing this report, added that for servants the usual diet was peas, potatoes, and roots.[20]

Richard Ligon was exceptional for his interest in diets, good eating, and wide knowledge of how to prepare and cook foods. Landing at Barbados in 1647, during a time of famine and pestilence, he noticed immediately that in addition to the scarcity of provisions, the ordinary Barbadian lived on "a slight diet." Most

ing it killed the tree. BM: Sloane MSS, 4070, fols. 19–21; Harlow, *Colonising Expeditions,* 67–9, 76; Coppier, *Histoire d'un voyage,* 30–31.

19. Ligon, *Barbados,* 19.

20. For bread, the settlers used a mixture of maize and cassava flours. Ligon explains the preparation of edible cassava flour and the removal of the poisonous juice from the root, as well as the baking of the unsalted cassava dough on an iron "Pone" into something akin to a pancake. The latter task was always left to the Indians, and Ligon persuaded an old Arawak woman to show him "the right way of it." Ligon, *Barbados,* 29–30, 41; *Winthrop Papers,* V, 84; Force, *Tracts,* II, No. 7, p. 5.

of the lesser planters did not eat bone meat more than twice a week in the forties, and white servants never tasted any unless an ox died, "and then they were feasted, as long as that lasted." Otherwise, "we have a way to feed our Christian servants with this Mayes, which is, by pounding it in a large Morter, and boyling it in water, to the thickness of Frumenty; and so put in a Tray with a quantity, as will serve a mess of seven or eight people; give it them cold, and scarce afford them salt with it. This we call *Loblollie.* But the Negroes, when they come to be fed with this, are much discontented, and cry out, *O! O!* no more *Lob-lob.*" Some masters gave their slaves ears of maize to roast, but it was not until the blacks had planted and harvested a good crop of plantains that "they were heard no more to complain." Not surprisingly, the Negroes were as wedded to their former diet as the whites were to theirs.[21]

Although the waters about Barbados teemed with many varieties of edible fish, it is astonishing to learn that they were seldom used for plantation food. They spoiled within six hours of being caught, and fishermen therefore hastened to sell them to the taverners at The Indian Bridge rather than risk peddling them to the plantations that still could not be reached by path or road. With few exceptions, one being Colonel Humphrey Walrond who maintained fishermen with a seine at his seaside estate, planters refused to release their servants or slaves from cultivating staples to go out fishing. All kinds of fish figured in the diet of the inhabitants of the Leeward Islands: white servants even enjoyed the delicate meat of the great green sea turtle on occasion. One result of the famine of 1647 was the forcing of the planters of the Caribbees to expand their hitherto small traffic in provisions and salt fish (or "poor John") with New England and Virginia, as well as with Ireland, Old England, Holland, and Russia.[22]

By the time Richard Ligon went back to England in 1650, the

21. Ligon, *Barbados,* 21, 31, 43.
22. To the West Indies from New England came sturgeon, "so ill cook'd, as 'tis hardly to be eaten," for want of skill in the boiling and seasoning; and from the Leeward Islands to Barbados went pickled turtle, "but so uncleanly ordered" as to be fit "only for servants and sometimes for the Negroes." Ligon, *Barbados,* 35, 37, 113.

entire dietary situation of the West Indies had improved remarkably, a condition that he attributed to the better husbandry of the ordinary planter. "There was greater plenty, both of the victuals they were wont to eat, as [sweet] Potatoes, Bonavist, and Loblolly, as also of the bone meat, viz. Pork, salt Fish, and powder'd Beef, which came hither by sea, from forraign parts, in so much as the Negroes were allowed each man two Macquerels a week, and every woman one; which were given out to them on Saturday in the evening after they had their allowance of Plantines, which was every one a large bunch, or two little ones, to serve them for a weeks provision; and if any cattle dyed by mischance, or by any disease: the servants eat the bodies, and the Negroes the skins, head and intrails which was divided amongst them by the Overseers; or if any horse, then the whole bodies of them were distributed amongst the Negroes, and that they thought a high feast, with which never poor souls were more contented." [23]

If any one individual deserves credit for the noticeable improvement in diet that took place after 1647, it was Richard Ligon himself. *Un gastronome veritable* (and a very early one) and dietitian combined, this exile taught the richest planters and merchants the pleasure of appetizing and well-prepared food. He showed Joan Fuller and Mr. Jobson, his "pupils" in the inns at The Indian Bridge, how to fry fresh fish in oil or poach them in vinegar in the absence of good butter; and he convinced many of the planters of the real benefits arising from feeding their servants and slaves some meat and salt fish to balance their rations of loblolly and plantains. He tried, but in vain, to convince the colonists that their excessive consumption of spirituous liquors was harmful. Of his many contributions to the bettering of West Indian life, Ligon's almost single-handed accomplishment in aiding both the whites

23. In calculating the cost of a sugar plantation in 1650, Ligon stressed the feeding of servants and slaves over and above what was raised locally: for about 30 Christian servants: 4 barrels of beef and 4 barrels of pork per year; 2 barrels of salt fish, 500 poor John (from New England). Negro slaves were to be given 4 barrels of turtle (from the Leeward Islands), 4 barrels of pickled mackerel, 2 barrels of herrings. All of this, with local fruits, amounted to £100 annually. £500 was to be allowed to replace Negroes, horses, and cattle. Ligon, *Barbados,* 35, 37, 113. For a brief sketch of the West Indian diet in 1650 that corroborates Ligon, see Harlow, *Colonising Expeditions,* 46–7.

and blacks to adjust their tastes to New World foods was the greatest and the most lasting, and what he imparted to the Barbadians was quickly picked up by the planters of the other islands.[24]

For centuries, the peoples of Western Europe and the British Isles had recognized threats to health and life itself that came from drinking water; most of it, including that from springs, was badly polluted and consequently unsafe. On the Continent, the common drink of all classes was wine; in Britain beer and ale were the favorite beverages, except in the southwest where Devon cider was consumed in large quantities. On long sea voyages, the brewed drinks often spoiled, and "stinckinge beere" proved not only offensive to the tongue and nostrils but downright unwholesome. The first colonists to land on a tropical isle with thirsts unslaked drank immoderately of the water they found there, pure or impure. It was not long before all the springs and streams became contaminated, and their contents caused all manner of disorders and complaints in both white men and black. Imported beer and ale, if they arrived unspoiled, were too costly for most of the colonists, and the failure to produce such English grains as barley, rye, and wheat, let alone hops, meant that no brewing or distilling of familiar beverages could be conducted in the islands. Some substitute had to be found.[25]

As in so many instances when the Europeans found themselves baffled by tropical limitations, they got the answer to their problems from the aborigines, though they seldom admitted that they owed their survival and ultimate adaptation to the new environment to these despised Indians. From the Caribs and the Arawaks, the first whites of St. Christopher and Barbados learned how to make a drink called *mobbie,* derived from fermented sweet potatoes. Ligon thought it tasted much like new Rhenish wine. The juice of the mashed tubers had the great quality of working within a few hours and being ready for consumption the next day. With the

24. Richard Ligon's contributions to fine eating among the richest planters will be discussed in Chapter IV. Ligon, *Barbados,* 35.

25. The Negro slaves had been heavy drinkers in Africa, especially of palm wine. William Bosman, *A New and Accurate Description of the Coast of Guinea* (London, 1705), in *Voyages and Travels,* ed. John Pinkerton (London, 1814), XVI, 386.

monotonous diet of loblolly, masters gave white servants "Mobbie and sometimes a little Beveridge"—the latter a concoction made of spring water, white sugar, and orange juice; the Negroes were given nothing but "fair water." Uchteritz observes that the rich planters made a liquor from "Batatas," to which they added sugar and lemon juice. Regardless of how much wine and beer the planters imported, they were very expensive, said this former indentured servant in 1652.[26]

The Indians made fermented drinks from other native plants. In their opinion, *perino* was very wholesome despite the fact that it was made from the poisonous cassava root. According to Ligon, old Arawak women who had a few remaining teeth would chew the roots and spit them out into water (like the Mexicans of today making *pulque*). The mixture was boiled, and the juice, no longer poisonous, fermented within a few hours and was considered by some of the islanders to be better than wine. The Indians made other liquors from wild plums and plantains, but mobbie remained the common thirst-quencher throughout this period. It was not until the sugar culture attained full development that rum replaced it.[27]

V

"The most important feature of economic life in a colony or newly settled community is its commercial connection with the outside world," Guy Stevens Callender pointed out over sixty years ago. Although historians have tended recently to ignore this sage observation, nearly three centuries earlier both the promoters and the first planters of the English West Indies learned this truth by bitter experience: they came quickly to understand that the colonies

26. "The West Indie [Sweet] Potatoe (by much more delicate and large than what wee have here [in Virginia] growing), besides that, it is a food excellently delicious and strongly nourishing, fixes himselfe wherever planted, with such an irradicable fertility that being set it eternally grows: of this an extraordinary pleasing and strong drinke may be composed." Edward Williams, *Virginia Richly Valued* (London, 1650), 42. Ligon gives a careful description of the making of mobbie in *Barbados,* 31, 32, 33, 38; Harlow, *Colonising Expeditions,* 46; Uchteritz, *Kurze Reise,* 7–8.

27. Ligon, *Barbados,* 32; Capt. John Smith, *Travels and Works,* II, 904–5.

would never flourish unless the inhabitants succeeded in establishing a profitable commerce to supply them with provisions, tools, clothing, other necessaries, and some luxuries as well, in exchange for staple products.[28]

The English, the French, and the Dutch, farming peoples though they were, had no experience at all with tropical agriculture upon which to draw. For more than twenty years, the English fumbled about in search of a suitable staple to plant and export. The crop had to be one that a freeholder and three or four white servants could cultivate on small plantations of fifty acres or less. In an attempt to match the earlier achievements of the planters of Virginia and Bermuda with tobacco, the men who colonized St. Christopher began to cultivate that plant as soon as they landed in 1624. A hurricane destroyed their first crop, but they persisted and succeeded, at least to the extent of raising crops and shipping them off to London. The Bermuda Company of London recommended to its planters not to grow any more tobacco, because the international market was oversupplied with superior Virginia leaf and because of the "very good" tobacco coming from St. Christopher. Captain Thomas Warner was encouraged, at a considerable charge for materials and labor, to build a "great tobacco house" near the waterside in St. Christopher for the storing and curing of his tobacco crop.[29]

Contemporaries attributed the greater success with tobacco at St. Christopher to the superiority of its soil and husbandry to those of Barbados. Furthermore its white servants appeared to be more industrious. The culture of tobacco spread from St. Christopher

28. "The history of modern colonization does not show a single case where a newly settled country has enjoyed any considerable economic prosperity, or made notable social progress, without a flourishing commerce with other communities. This dominance of foreign commerce in economic affairs may be considered the most characteristic feature of colonial economy." Guy S. Callender, *Selections from the Economic History of the United States, 1765–1860* (Boston, 1909), 6; Ligon, *Barbados,* 24.

29. "At the beginning all the foreign Inhabitants of the Caribees apply'd themselves wholly to the culture of Tobacco, whereby they made a shift to get a competent livelihood, but afterwards the abundance that was made bringing down the price of it." Davies, *Caribby-Islands,* 187; J. H. Lefroy, *Memorials of the Discovery and Early Settlement of the Bermudas* (London, 1877), I, 398; *APC Col.,* I, 122; Harlow, *Colonising Expeditions,* 7; *CSPC, 1574–1660,* p. 295.

after 1628 to Nevis, and to Montserrat and Antigua by 1635, where it promptly became and long remained the staple and standard for exchange. As the population mounted in St. Christopher, production figures rose and shipments increased through 1638 and then fell off sharply.

	lbs.
1637	263,599
1638	470,732
1639	107,312
1640	138,973

Consignments from Virginia in these years ran into millions of pounds, and soon the world supply became so plentiful that the price plummeted. The sharp drop in shipments from St. Christopher may also be explained, in part, by the opposition of the Crown to the West Indian insistence upon growing tobacco to the exclusion of provisions, and also by the fact that many planters began raising cotton. In addition, some decline in the yield of a crop that rapidly depletes even the richest soil must have occurred.[30]

When Captain Henry Powell returned from his voyage to Guiana in 1627 with tobacco, cotton, indigo, and annatto [dye] seeds, the settlers of Barbados, without much thought for the future, proceeded to plant tobacco and to neglect the raising of foods. They thought, as we have seen, that they could live on provisions from home, wild hogs, and the produce raised by the Arawaks who came back with the captain. Powell himself had a tobacco colony in mind from the very beginning; in England he persuaded young Henry Winthrop to give up a career at sea and join him in planting tobacco. Emigrating along with his servants, this son of John Winthrop of Groton in Suffolk shipped the proceeds of his first planting to London in 1628. His father was forced to break the bitter news that the rolls of tobacco he had sent arrived so "very ill conditioned, fowle, full of stalkes and evil coloured" the London

30. PRO: CO 1/9, p. 124; Harlow, *Colonising Expeditions,* 91; BM: Add. MSS, 35,865, fol. 247, printed in *Caribbeana,* III, 197–8; Harlow, *Barbados,* 23; George L. Beer, *Origins of the British Colonial System, 1578–1660* (New York, 1908), 99–100; BM: Egerton MSS, 2395, fols. 54, 58, 70; BM: Sloane MSS, 3662, fol. 61a; Thurloe, *State Papers,* III, 754.

grocers would not give five shillings a pound for them. John Jones of "Redriff," master of the *Marigold*, laded "700 and odd weight" for Peter Pett, also of Barbados, and then called at St. Christopher to take on 600 pounds more before sailing homewards. Messrs. Wheatly & Banister, his principals, had an excellent opportunity to judge the quality of the two lots. As is so often the case in a new country, a few astute or merely lucky men succeed while their fellows fail. James Drax, James Holdip, William Hilliard, and three or four others of the first planters of Barbados were such men: they fared so well with their crops of 1627-28 that Drax took the tobacco to England at a time when the commodity was scarce and sold it for a tidy sum. Investing the proceeds in forty-odd servants, he returned to the island determined to employ them in growing a more acceptable staple.[31]

Although the Barbadians increased their production of tobacco steadily, they were never able to improve its quality; it continued to be "earthy and worthless." Samuel Atkins, a London merchant, frankly told a Barbadian on July 21, 1643, that out of 150 rolls he had sent over, only twenty or thirty were worth the freight: "They were the rotinest, dryest, basest goods as ever I saw in my life." If, as John Scott averred years later, the planters averaged only three farthings a pound for their crop in 1646, tobacco growing was a losing business. Ten years after the first crops were shipped, James Hay tried consigning his tobacco to Amsterdam, for he had heard merchants and mariners say that Barbados leaf "would not yeeld any money in England, and that it was one good commoditie in holland." Declining figures of London imports of Barbados tobacco confirm his decision:

	lbs.
1637	124,593
1638	204,956
1639	28,010
1640	66,895

As seen in retrospect, if the Dutch ships had not taken off quantities of the poor tobacco, the economy of Little England would

31. *Winthrop Papers,* I, 338, 338*n,* 356–7; II, 66; *Genealogical Magazine,* n. s., IV, 73; Biët, *Voyage,* 294.

have collapsed. This unfavorable situation did force a few planters, however, to look about for a staple that might be profitable.[32]

When the Spanish came to the continent of South America, they found cotton growing and widely used by the Indians. Recent investigations demonstrate that four, and only four, species of cotton embrace the whole vast diversity of cultivated cottons: two of them native to the Old World, two to the New. Along the coast of the Spanish Main from Panama eastward beyond Trinidad to the delta of the Amazon flourished the *Gossypium barbadense,* and thence northward to the Lesser Antilles. The perennial *Gossypium hirsutum,* var. *marie-galante,* grew in large shrubs or trees, often as much as twenty feet in height, in the villages of the natives. Writing of the Amazon country in 1626, Robert Harcourt must have been referring to this variety of cotton, "which (truly is) the finest of all other, there may be gotten infinite quantities, with little or no charge, and with easie labour: for it groweth upon trees, and every Indian house hath commonly store of those trees already about it, which yeeld them Cotton more then sufficient for their own uses which (if we require them) they will gather for us, and within the yeare return us a good quantitie of, either ready spunne, or in the wooll, and if we either set the seeds, or cut some of the branches of the Cotton trees into small stickes about halfe a yard in length, and pricke them into the ground, they will speedily growe up, and bear Cotton within the space of two yeares, as hath been proved often by experience." [33]

32. We have not been able to find any contemporary authority for C. R. Boxer's unsupported statement that improved methods of cultivating tobacco were introduced from Pernambuco into the Antilles (*Dutch in Brazil* [Oxford, 1957], 114). As late as 1645, Guillaume Coppier said of Barbados: "Ils y font du Petun," which they sell in England, Scotland, Ireland, and Holland. James Hay shipped his tobacco crop of 1638 to Amsterdam in the Dutch ship *Waterdog*. Coppier, *Histoire d'un voyage,* 28; 1637–38, Hay MSS; Ligon, *Barbados,* 28; Davis Coll., XIII, Envelope 16; BM: Sloane MSS, 3662, fol. 60b.

33. It is altogether possible, even probable, that seeds or plants of the *Gossypium barbadense,* var. *brasiliense* were introducted in the Lesser Antilles by the Dutch or English, either from Guiana or directly from the Pernambuco area of Brazil. It is not clear when the *Gossypium hirsutum,* var. *marie-galante,* the largest of the cottons first appeared in the islands. It is a large shrub or small tree, growing to 20 feet. See plates VI–VIII, figs. 9, 10, and pp. 98–108 of J. B. Hutchinson, R. A. Silow, and S. G. Stephens, *The Evolution of Gossypium and the Differentiation of the Cultivated Cottons* (Oxford and New York, 1947); and the corrections made by J. B. Hutchinson in "History and Relationships of the World's Cottons,"

Captain Thomas Warner had been to Guiana and seen this culture; in 1628 three of his men, back in England, told Captain John Smith that on St. Christopher "There is two sorts of Cotten, the silke Cotten as in the East Indies groweth upon a small stalke, as good for beds as downe; the other upon a shrub, and beareth a cod bigger than a Walnut, full of Cotten wooll [*Gossypium barbadense*]." Cotton had become an important export from the plantations of Brazil, and it is not unlikely that the Dutch, who settled in Guiana under Amos van Groenewegen and others in 1615, imported some techniques there which were unknown to the Arawaks.[34]

Powell's Arawaks had brought cotton seeds and taught the Barbadians their way of planting them in 1627. Subsequently, led by James Drax, many islanders, abandoning tobacco-growing and using the manual labor of white servants, turned to raising the new staple. Sir Henry Colt noted in 1631 that "Now the trade of Cotton fills them all with hope." One of the most optimistic and enterprising of the Barbadian planters was James Holdip, whose plantation was but a year old when Colt saw it. "This man is the beautye, hands, eyes, feet, of all other planters. He hath in one year that which any other hath, and alsoe more than any other hath." The sight of so many cotton trees delighted Father Andrew White in 1634. When the boll bursts, he exclaims, there "appeares a knot of cotton white as snow, with six seede in the middle . . . which with an *invention of wheeles* they take out and soe keep it till the merchants fetch it from them." What must have been one of the larger plantations in the island in 1640 was "Rendezvous," 360 acres owned by Captain Lancelot Pacey. It was valued at more than 58,000 pounds of cotton, and, besides a cotton warehouse at 4000 pounds, the mansion at 6000, there was "a Mill House [gin]" appraised at 9600 pounds of cotton. The eminent

in Smithsonian Institution, *Annual Report,* 1962, pp. 497–515 (also in *Endeavour,* XXI [1962], No. 81); Robert Harcourt, *The Relation of a Voyage to Guiana performed by Robert Harcourt* (rev. ed. enlarged, London, 1626), 43.

34. PRO: CO 1/2, No. 18; Capt. John Smith, *Travels and Works,* II, 905; John H. Parry, *The Age of Reconnaissance* (London, 1963), 287; Engel Sluiter, in *Pacific Historical Review,* XI (1942), 36; Hans Sloane, *A Voyage to the Islands Madera, Barbados, Mevis, St. Christopher and Jamaica* . . . (London, 1725), II, 69–70.

Major Hilliard owned a great cotton "Carding house of 100 foot long, and 40 foot broad." [35]

Here we have the exciting proof that by 1634 (a mere three years after cotton-growing began in earnest), the planters of Barbados had installed in their island, whole and intact, the cotton culture as it was then known. This was an astounding and thorough adaptation of agriculture and industry in a colony where only seven years earlier not a single component of the system had existed—people, seeds, plants, or machinery. It is not impossible, though we can only conjecture, that in 1627 Henry Powell (who had been in Pernambuco) brought a small cotton gin along with the seed from Essequibo, which he had procured through the good offices of his friend Amos van Groenewegen. Perhaps a more likely explanation is that Dutch traders from Brazil introduced the already well-developed Portuguese cotton culture, gin and all, to Drax, Holdip, and their fellows in Barbados with the hope of promoting a more marketable staple crop than tobacco.[36]

Much more complex than the planting, growing, and processing of tobacco was the establishing of the cotton culture in three or four years by totally inexperienced Barbadians, an agricultural accomplishment of the first magnitude which has been obscured by the later overwhelming triumph with sugar. So rapidly did the raising of cotton (or *cotton wool,* as contemporaries knew it)

35. Bodleian Library: Rawlinson MSS, C94, fol. 8, transcript in Davis Coll., VI; Harlow, *Colonising Expeditions,* 69, 75; Biët, *Voyage,* 294; *Narratives of Early Maryland,* 35 (our italics); Davis Coll., II, Envelope 19; Ligon, *Barbados,* 35.

36. The cotton gin (*Churka*) originated centuries earlier in India. Rochefort described the West Indian gins in 1658, but the best contemporary account is Dr. Hans Sloane's, *ca.* 1687/8: "The Instrument by which they separate the Seeds and Filth from the Cotton stands as a turning Loom, and is made of two, long, small, round, Cilinders of Wood, on which are three or four small Furrows; these have more or less Space between them, as the Master desires, but generally are so close, as only to suffer the fine Cotton to go thro', whereas the Seeds are kept back, and the Cotton is drawn by one of these Cilinders, and thrust away by the other, they being turned by the Feet two contrary Ways, the one from the other. . . ." Sloane, *Voyage to the Islands,* II, 68, and pl. 190 [reproduced in this volume, as Plate 1]; Davies, *Caribby-Islands,* 47, 198. Père Labat states that a good worker could clean 55 to 60 pounds of cotton a day with a "moulin-à-coton." He means by using a gin with a foot-treadle; if the slave turned the rollers by a crank, his output was much smaller. Jean-Baptiste Labat, *Nouveau Voyage aux isles de l'Amerique* (2d ed., Paris, 1742), IV, 168–73.

spread that by 1640 it equaled tobacco in value among exports of Barbados and had virtually superseded tobacco as the principal commodity money.[37]

The manufacture of cotton cloth began to make considerable advances in Northern Europe during the latter part of the sixteenth century, especially after the fall of Antwerp and the dispersal of the Flemish workers. By 1600, spinners and weavers at Amersfoort were working up raw cotton imported at Amsterdam a few miles away, and French artisans at Rouen had begun to develop a flourishing industry. Over in England there sprang up by 1600 in Lancashire under Walloon impetus a manufacture of fustians, "made of a kind of Bombast or Downe, being a fruit of the earth growing on little shrubs or bushes . . . commonly called Cotton Wooll." Thereafter the cotton industry spread over the rural northern counties from Norwich to Manchester. When arguing for the diversifying of England's economy in 1641, Lewes Roberts described with evident satisfaction how the merchants of Manchester "buy Cotten wooll, in London, that comes first from Cyprus and Smyrna, and at home worke the same, and perfit it into Fustians, Vermilions, Dymities, and other such Stuffes; and then returne it to London, where the same is vented and sold, and not seldom sent into forrain parts, who have meanes at far easier termes, to provide themselves of the said first materials." To this, the same year, Henry Robinson added that encouragement of cotton growing in the plantations would provide the colonists with a staple, free the English reliance upon Levantine raw materials, and "set our people awork." [38]

As though by a miracle, the Barbadians discovered their new staple at the very time that the demand for raw cotton rose in Lancashire, and English mercantile writers began to teach the

37. When supplies no longer came from England after 1642, Governor Winthrop of Massachusetts-Bay noted that "men began to look about them, and fell to a manufacture of cotton, whereof we had store from Barbados." Though the traffic did not last, the Barbadians took hope for the development of a market in New England. *Winthrop's Journal,* II, 122; Harlow, *Barbados,* 21, 21*n*. The estate of Sergt. Major Hunckes, late governor, was appraised in 1641 at 35,400 pounds of cotton. Davis Coll., VII, Envelope 1.

38. Sneller, in *Annales d'histoire économique et sociale,* I (1929), 201–2; Alfred P. Wadsworth and Julia de L. Mann, *The Cotton Trade and Industrial Lancashire, 1600–1730* (Manchester, England, 1931), 15–23, 35, 45; Lewes Roberts, *The Treasure of Trafficke* (London, 1641), 33, 41; Henry Robinson, *England's Safety in Trade's Increase* (London, 1641), 9.

need to get away from their island's almost total dependence on the woolen industry. Similar demands for a larger supply of raw cotton came at this time from the Low Countries and Northern France. By 1641 at least two colonial factors were shipping Barbados "white cotton" (probably in Dutch bottoms) to Benian Fletcher, an English merchant at Rouen. Cotton may be credited with having averted a collapse of the island's economy. Conversely, as Henry Robinson foresaw, the trade with Turkey would inevitably fall off "because wee must likely forbeare those Country['s] Cotton Woolls which used to furnish us for returnes, being now served with better cheape of our owne plantation in the Westerne Islands." [39]

In the islands, small planters, as well as large, found their salvation in cotton, which they could easily raise on their small holdings. An acre of ground yielded from 200 to 400 pounds. Not infrequently yeomen proprietors divided their parcels into cotton, tobacco, ginger, and more rarely indigo, fields. The fifty-acre estate of Thomas Horne was appraised in December 1640 at 6450 pounds of cotton—eight acres in sweet potatoes at 2400; 33 acres of "Fowle ground and standing ground" at 1650; nine acres "with cotton Trees" at 900; and all the housing "with the Boards" at 1500. With remarkable foresight, James Drax began quietly in 1640 to buy up small parcels of land from freeholders whenever he could and to turn them into cotton plantations. In June of that year he purchased 200 acres and 20,000 feet of sound cedar board from Samuel Andrewes for 8000 pounds of cotton, and in November he acquired another 200 acres from Captain William Hawley. A member of the St. Christopher Assembly, Phance Beecher, commenced buying in small plantations in 1643. Clearly, the consolidating of small into larger holdings was well under way in Barbados five years or more before the cultivating of sugar cane became commercially important. From St. Christopher the culture of cotton spread to the other Leeward Islands, with the exception of Nevis, and throughout the seventeenth century cotton continued to be a widely cultivated crop.[40]

39. Davis Coll., II, Envelope 17; Robinson, *England's Safety*, 9.

40. William Johnson to Carlisle Trustees, April 4, 1642, Hay MSS; Dalby Thomas, *An Historical Account of the Rise and Growth of the West India Colonies* (London, 1690), 21–2; *Winthrop Papers*, V, 172; *Timehri*, n. s., X (1896),

Among the contemporary comments that reveal some side effects of the cotton production is one by Thomas Peake (about 1654). We learn from him that the English came to value particularly the services of Indian women for their skill in carding, spinning, and weaving cotton yarn into superior sail-cloth, tent-covers, and "certain hanging Beds." The latter "are webs of a great strong sort of Cotton Cloaths, woven about eight or nine foot long, and an ell broad. . . ." The looms of the New World were not as technologically advanced as those of Europe. Borrowing from Brazil and Guiana, the Indians of the Caribbees fashioned their looms with "two round sticks about nine foot long, and three or four inches in diameter, the two ends whereof lie a-cross, on two pieces of wood, lying eight or nine foot from the ground, more or less, according to the length they design to make the bed [hammock]. The other round stick hangs directly under this, to which they make fast the warp of the bed. They use a kind of shuttle thrust thro' the thread after the manner of our clothweavers [John Barbot explained]; but with this difference, that they put the shuttle thro' thread by thread, one above and the other below, which renders the work very tedious, and requires the stock of patience they generally have." Evidently the cotton boll figured prominently in perpetuating the enslavement of a small number of Indians in the islands for many years.[41]

The successful production of cotton did not, however, solve the problem of returns for the Caribbee islands, and particularly for Barbados. Great quantities of cotton were soon transported from the islands, and eventually it, like tobacco, was of very little value. It was partly for this reason that some planters sought to diversify by planting small crops of ginger, and others tried their luck with the more complicated production of indigo. But all of these commodities, "one with another were not worth to the Planter above one penny per pound, at the first Cost of their Goods in England." Moreover, farming by inexperienced white men on small plots was not an economical form of agriculture. Draxes and Holdips, for-

---

97–8. See copies of appraisals and inventories in Davis Coll., I, Deeds; VII, especially Envelopes 5, 14.

41. N. N., *America,* 169; Barbot, in Churchill, *Voyages,* V, 554.

tunate enough to have the wherewithal to enlarge their operations, were turning to cheaper slave labor on large units.[42]

At the close of the period, tobacco remained the principal crop of all in the English West Indies in spite of the fact that there was little if any profit in it for the small planter. One acre of ground would produce only 2500 pounds of leaf, and that, John Scott declared, was as much as one man could tend, cure, and make up into rolls, besides raising his own provisions. For such heavy work, he received only about £7 10*s*. 3*d*. a year! Scott was right: "Tobacco thus beaten down . . . was their Staple." To their great dismay, the English colonists were finding out that *"les cultures sont filles, non sœurs de commerce."* [43]

VI

That the settling of all the islands of the West Indies was a maritime enterprise must be constantly borne in mind as we seek to fathom the nature of life in them. Their well-being depended upon safe and regular commerce along the sea lanes much more than did that of the English settlements on the North American continent. Throughout most of the year, the Northeast Trade Winds blew fresh and steadily, bringing ships from Europe in about six weeks but delaying and lengthening the homeward passage from seven to ten weeks. Almost every year, too, the inhabitants and visiting mariners went through the frightening experience of the West Indian hurricane. One of these great windstorms beat down the entire tobacco crop and all of the flimsy huts of the planters at St. Christopher on September 19, 1624; and in twenty-four hours one day in 1642, the second of three hurricanes that year devastated

42. Ligon wrote of the years after 1637 that indigo was planted and "so well ordered, as it sold in London at very good rates; and their Cotton wool, and Fustick [dye-] wood, prov'd very good and staple commodities." By the time of his arrival in 1647, the leading planters were beginning to grow sugar cane. *Barbados,* 24, 40; Foster, *Late Horrid Rebellion,* 1–2; George Gardyner, *A Description of fthe New World, Or, America, Islands and Continent* (London, 1651), 74; Uchteritz, *Kurze Reise,* 6–7; Biët, *Voyage,* 289; BM: Sloane MSS, 3662, fol. 60b.

43. N. N., *America,* 470–71; BM: Sloane MSS, 3662, fol. 60b; Debien, *Les Engagés,* 38.

the same island, wrecking twenty-three laden vessels, blowing down all the houses, and completely destroying the cotton and tobacco crops. Of the islands, Barbados alone possessed a good, safe harbor; the others had only open roadsteads where ships anchored at the mercy of the elements.[44]

The sea led men to the West Indies, and away from them. A unique fact about the Caribbee islands was that all the inhabitants—Caribs, Arawaks, white planters, merchants, and servants, and black slaves—had arrived by sea in very recent times. To these islands, with their motley populations, merchants and factors came and went with some regularity; they brought craftsmen, servants, and slaves to the West Indies. Communication from one island to another by means of small sloops was both facilitated and obstructed by the incessant trade winds; Barbados lay so far eastward of the Leeward Islands that very little exchange took place. All life, everywhere, depended on wooden hulls: on the outward passage they carried food and supplies of all kinds, and wines from Madeira and the Canaries; on the homeward voyage they took back the island staples and a few passengers.

Everyone in the Lesser Antilles found his welfare and destiny linked to the maritime environment. Unlike the people of Northampton and Hadley in New England, the settlers of the Caribbees all lived within a mile of the ocean prior to 1650. Some of them went out daily to fish; the men of Nevis and St. Christopher sailed regularly in their small boats to catch sea turtles off St. Eustatius. Unsuccessful small planters, persons in debt, landless freemen, and newly discharged servants, plus black and white runaways, seeking afloat the living that had eluded them ashore, sailed with the buccaneers; occasionally even a man of substance joined in such adventures. The island of Tortuga, about two miles off the northwest coast of Hispaniola and close upon the northern entrance to the Windward Passage, became a base for these freebooters and sea rovers—English, French, Dutch, Spanish, and Portuguese.

44. Ships returning to Europe had to work their way northward to about 27° before they could pick up the Anti-Trades that would then carry them northeastward from Florida along the Atlantic coast and then along the great-circle course to Europe. Capt. John Smith, *Travels and Works,* II, 900–902; Southey, *Chronological History of the West Indies,* I, 294; *CSPC, 1661–68,* p. 534.

Without naval protection, the islands could be, and were, easily attacked by foreign enemies; and, with the exception of Barbados, they were never secure from depredations by the Caribs, who swooped down in their great *periaguas,* which carried fifty to sixty warriors.[45]

The most enterprising and experienced sea-going people of this age, the Dutch, helped to create and largely sustained for more than three decades the economies of the English and French islands as well as that of their own. The chartering of the West India Company in 1621 enabled the Dutch to launch a carefully planned assault on the Spanish and Portuguese colonies in the Caribbean and on the mainland of South America. From their Brazilian base at Pernambuco, they moved westward to the deltas of the Amazon and Essequibo rivers. The English settlers, who combined various skills in agriculture, industry, and the managing of other men with a sound understanding of commerce, now and then joined with the Dutch in mutually profitable undertakings. The governor of the colony in Guiana was Amos van Groenewegen, who had sailed in the Courteens' ships with Henry Powell, and it appears that the latter's prompt departure from Barbados to Essequibo early in 1627 was part of a plan worked out in London by Sir William Courteen. We know, too, that Thomas Warner had been in communication with the Dutch on the Amazon before he founded the colony on St. Christopher in 1624. Thus in the very first years, the English colonists established themselves in the Caribbean with Dutch aid; and though they eventually yielded reluctantly to British law, they never entirely severed the Dutch connection during the seventeenth century.[46]

45. On the early history of Tortuga (or Association), consult: Newton, *Colonising Activities of the English Puritans,* 103–10, 192–3, 279–80.

46. Charles Wilson has written a charming and authoritative sketch of *The Dutch Republic, and the Civilisation of the Seventeenth Century* (London, 1968); see also Paul Gunther, *Daily Life in Rembrandt's Holland* (New York, 1962). George Edmundson, "The Dutch in Western Guiana," in the *English Historical Review,* XVI (1901), 651, 657, 659–60; Richard Hall, *A General Account of the First Settlement and of the Trade and Constitution of the Island of Barbados, Written in the Year 1755* (Barbados, 1924), 2; Harlow, *Colonising Expeditions,* xv. Probably the greatest gap in our knowledge of colonization in the New World is the lack of a work in English on Dutch settlement and trade in Guiana and the Caribbean islands.

Trade, not colonizing, was the Dutch objective in the Caribbean. The merchants of Holland and Zeeland who composed the West India Company had capital to invest; each year they had more and more ships to freight with cargoes to and from the islands: they had provisions, manufactures, and animals to exchange for tobacco and other tropical produce. They recruited English and Irish servants and carried them to both St. Christopher and Barbados in the twenties, and they procured Negro slaves in Africa to dispose of to the planters. In 1631 Sir Henry Colt told of "St. Martins wher the Hollanders ride at Anchor for salt," and if the Spanish fleet, then cruising, had gone there, they could have "taken 48 sayle of Hollanders, all unrigged, ther sayles ashoar, ther ships nott ballasteed, for they mean to ballast with salt," so much wanted for the North Sea herring fishery, the dairy industry, and preserving food in the Netherlands and the Baltic countries.[47]

"The settlement of this Island," a governor of Barbados insisted in later years, "came first from the Dutch, who made a Trade with them for some yeares for *smale gaines upon future hopes of Commerce,* and they are a people the planter is not jealous of, they joining this Caracter of them: that they are good marchants, but ill planters, and are for quick returns though with easy gaines, for to expect upon future improvements they are not much inclined to it." Finding themselves shut out from trading with the English islands by the Parliamentary Act of 30 October 1650, forty Dutch merchants of Holland and Zeeland implored their High Mightinesses of the States General to take up their cause, alleging that "they have traded for upwards of twenty years past, to all the Caribbean islands. . . ." Also they exported thence

47. One of the Courteen ships stopped at Barbados in 1624 on its voyage home from Pernambuco, and it brought the first reports of the island to Britain. In 1629 the Dutch occupied Tobago; in 1634 they took over Curaçao (which they never relinquished); in 1635 St. Eustatius, and in 1648 St. Martin. From these ports of call they could easily dominate the commerce of the Spanish Main and the Antilles. For the background, see three works by Charles R. Boxer: *The Dutch in Brazil, 1624–1654* (Oxford, 1957); *The Dutch Seaborne Empire, 1600–1800* (London, 1965); and *The Portuguese Seaborne Empire* (London, 1969). Arthur P. Watts, *Une Histoire des colonies anglaises aux Antilles (de 1649 à 1660)* [Paris, 1924], xv; *CSPC, 1574–1660,* p. 113; Harlow, *Colonising Expeditions,* 15, 81.

annually "several million" of guilders and brought back tobacco, cotton, indigo, and sugar to about the same amount.[48]

When the Spanish drove the Dutch salt men away from Punta de Araya in 1622 and erected a fort to keep them off the peninsula, skippers sailed their ships to the Lesser Antilles where smaller, though satisfactory, salt deposits on St. Martin and St. Christopher provided them with cargoes. The reports of the widely traveled merchant-skipper David Pietersen de Vries, in his *Korte Historiael,* verify that by 1632–34 there existed a much-used intercolonial trade route from Pernambuco to Guiana and the islands of St. Martin, St. Eustatius, and Saba, soon to be occupied by the Dutch and lying close to the English Leeward Islands, then via New Netherland to the fatherland. De Vries left St. Martin in 1632 with a cargo of salt and sailed to Nevis "to take in wood and water because they were both better there than at St. Christopher." On shore he visited Governor Littleton, who persuaded him to carry some Portuguese prisoners to St. Christopher and put them aboard a ship bound for England. Two years after that, de Vries traded for tobacco with the French on St. Christopher, as well as with Governor Warner in the English quarter. He was at Nevis on December 13, when five Holland ships put in on their way from Pernambuco to Curaçao for wood and salt.[49]

As soon as the English planters produced merchantable crops of tobacco, Dutch traders appeared to buy them, and from about 1630 onward they were the principal dealers in the leaf. At about the same time they induced the English to diversify their crops. After the world price of tobacco fell so precipitously in 1638, English ships stopped coming to Barbados, but fortunately the Dutch

48. Jonathan Atkins, Answers to Queries, July $\frac{4}{14}$, 1676, PRO: CO 1/37, fol. 23 (italics ours); *Acts and Ordinances of the Interregnum, 1642–1660,* eds. C. H. Firth and R. S. Rait (London, 1911), II, 425–9; *Documents Relative to the Colonial History of the State of New York,* ed. Edward B. O'Callaghan (Albany, 1856), I, 436.

49. For the history of the Dutch salt trade to 1621, see articles by Engel Sluiter in *Pacific Hist. Review,* XI (1942), 30, 38; and in *Hispanic-American Hist. Review,* XXVIII (1948), 179. The West Indian portions of de Vries's *Korte Historiael* are translated in New-York Historical Society, *Collections,* 2 ser., III, Pt. I, pp. 20–21, 68–70, 83–4.

willingly bought its low-grade product, and when the supply of servants simultaneously failed, the Hollanders, having African slaves to sell, persuaded the planters to use Negro labor in their tobacco and cotton fields. So completely did the Netherlanders monopolize commerce in the Caribbees, that when Lord Willoughby of Parham, a Royalist, arrived as governor in 1650, he offended Parliament by ordering "the mannege of trade to be only with Hollanders." In 1652 the Earl of Warwick wrote sternly to the President and Council of Barbados: "I have received advertisement from divers planters &c. That the trade and habitacion of the Dutch in your Island and other parts of his Majesties Territories in the W. I. hath been very prejudiciall to the English Trade, which might be better dispenst with all if ballanced with their admitting of the English to trade in those parts of the W. I. that are under theire Jurisdicion which as I heare they refuse to doe." No rule is prescribed now, the Earl continued, and I await your advice. "In the meantime youl doe well to cherish your oune Countreymen by giving them all just advantage of Trade before strangers according to the Lawes and Customes established amongst you." Such admonitions had small effect on those who had of late been more or less ignored by the English.[50]

The Dutch monopoly of the commerce of the English West Indian colonies produced some interesting adjuncts. Young Samuel Winthrop, who left Harvard College without taking a degree because of his father's financial difficulties, set out to make his fortune in Madeira. In 1647 he sold a shipment of wine in Barbados at a good profit and then proceeded to St. Christopher to set up as a merchant. A year later, while in Rotterdam on business, he met and married a Dutch woman before sailing back to Barbados, "where in all probability I can live better then in other places" as a trader. During the years of the English Revolution, most of the

50. Although the Dutch won the traffic of most of the islands, an occasional English vessel still went there after 1641. The *Star* of London, owned by Sir Nicholas and Samuel Crispe, and John Wood, merchants of London, arrived at Barbados with a cargo of Negro slaves in 1641, which sold for cotton and tobacco. Davis Coll., VII, Envelope 2; Harlow, *Colonising Expeditions,* 45; *HMC, 10th Report,* Pt. 4, pp. 284–6; Sparke Papers (Royal Commonwealth Society, MSS), 7 (RC 1), 1649; BM: Sloane MSS, 3662, p. 2; BM: Stowe MSS, 184, fol. 126b.

correspondence originating in English America, especially from New England and the Caribbean, went to and from the Mother Country by way of Holland. Even Lord Willoughby sent his official communications from Barbados by the Dutch ships that touched there. To his father in London, Giles Sylvester explained in 1651 that "I have writ by most posts of Dutch and English that are gone from hence." A year later Sylvester would be in Amsterdam acting as a factor for Barbadian planters. It was Samuel Brown, English bookseller at the Hague who, in 1651, printed and sold for Barbadian authorities their reply to the Parliament's prohibition of trade with Virginia, Bermuda, Barbados, and Antigua. In *A Declaration Set Forth,* they freely conceded that "all the old Planters well know how much they have ben beholding to the Dutch for their subsistance, and how difficult it would have ben (without their assistance) ever to have settled this place, and even to this day we are sensible what necessary comforts they bring us and how much cheaper they sell their Commodities to us then our owne Nation; but this comfort must be taken from us by them whose will must be our law: But we do Declare that we will never be so ungratefull to the Dutch for former helps as to deny them or any other Nation the freedome of our Ports. . . ."[51]

Edward Winslow remarked in 1655 that "the Barbadians doted on the Dutch commerce," and he could have included the planters of the Leeward Islands, for the Hollanders had done more with their ships and their credit to get the colonies started than had the merchants of England. They supplied provisions and servants; they urged and enabled the colonists to try the cotton culture; they sold them slaves on easy terms. They performed all of the functions of middlemen that the English merchants had failed to do, and at lower rates. Though the Dutch were very friendly and most helpful, they were no philanthropists. With foresight and patience, the Dutch recognized the mutual needs of themselves and the English planters and were willing to wait for the rewards which, when they ultimately came with sugar, turned out to be very substantial.

51. *MHS Colls.,* 5th ser., VIII, 234*n; Winthrop Papers,* V, 242–3, 280; Watts, *Histoire des colonies anglaises aux Antilles,* 40*n;* Harlow *Colonising Expeditions,* 48, 51; *A Declaration Set forth by the Lord Lieutenant Generall, the Gentlemen of the Councill & Assembly* (The Hague, 1651).

Because Hollånders and Zeelanders went to live as factors or traders in the islands, and built warehouses, docks, and town dwellings, and because they frequently intermarried with the English, they naturally became intimately associated with the settlers and realized that what was good for the English was also good for the Dutch. To cap all this, the men from the Low Countries finally succeeded in introducing the settlers to a staple, the production of which so completely transformed their society and economy that the English West Indian colonies became known as the Sugar Islands.[52]

52. That the Dutch commercial success in the West Indies was agitating English mercantile leaders is well known. In a powerful tract, Henry Robinson argued that the Hollanders have "almost worried us out of the East Indian Trade . . . as also in the West Indies . . . Guiney," and that they not only furnish the English and others with commodities, "but even plant Colonies there" and employed English ships and seamen in expanding their commerce. *Brief Considerations Concerning the Advancement of Trade* (London, 1649), 7; Winslow, quoted by Watts, *Histoire des colonies aux Antilles,* 123.

III

A Staple from Brazil

THE LEADING PLANTERS of the English and French islands in the Lesser Antilles succeeded spectacularly during the fourth decade of the seventeenth century in starting a change-over in their economies from cultivating tobacco and cotton to producing sugar. They performed this agricultural and industrial miracle almost exclusively under the auspices of the Dutch, who guided the transfer of this industry *in toto* from Brazil and caused it to flourish in the West Indies. As middlemen in this remarkable undertaking, the Dutch, of both Holland and Brazil, perceived that such a transplanting had to be complete—an entire culture in fact. Few enterprises in the history of agriculture in modern times approach this in ingenuity, completeness, and in ultimate economic consequences.

In some respects this achievement is a twice-told tale, but virtually unrecognized, or ignored, even at the time, was the outstanding contribution of the Portuguese planters of Brazil, which was as essential as the managerial feats of the Dutch. It was the Portuguese-Brazilians who taught the English the lore of planting and raising sugar cane. It was they who demonstrated the ways to boil and skim the juice, and how to process the syrup and make the crystallized Muscovado and clayed sugar, ready to be shipped off to Europe for refining. What the colonists of the three nations accomplished by working in concert was the transplanting, within little more than seven years, of sugar canes, machinery, materials, and methods of labor, manufacture, and marketing from Pernambuco in the spacious land of Brazil, where the culture had developed gradually over more than a century, to the confined areas of the small Caribbean islands, where it had never before been attempted.[1]

The colonial monopoly of Spain in the Caribbean region began to crack perceptibly under persistent Dutch pressure as soon as the Twelve Years' Truce expired in 1621. Portuguese Brazil was situated close by the Antilles, and because Portugal was then under Spanish domination, the skippers of the newly formed Dutch West India Company looked upon Brazil as fair game. In a series of attacks which began with the partial capture of Bahia, the Dutch gradually extended their conquests to all of northern Brazil. Starting in 1630, one-third to one-half of the Brazilian sugar exports were annually carried in Dutch bottoms to Rouen, Hamburg, and especially to Amsterdam. During the struggle, such widespread devastation of sugar plantations occurred that by 1636 only 127 sugarworks remained intact. The Dutch had destroyed some of them, but the Portuguese themselves had burned or dismantled most of them rather than leave them to their captors.[2]

The Dutch West India Company sent out Prince Maurice of Nassau as governor of the Brazilian territory in 1637. Finding the sugar industry in ruins, he instituted an enlightened policy of not only encouraging the Portuguese to resume growing and grinding the canes but also of stimulating the Portuguese Sephardic Jews of Holland to migrate to Brazil and invest in sugar mills and serve as brokers and slave dealers. Under this impetus, the industry revived and flourished. During Prince Maurice's stay, a total of 166 Brazilian sugar factories produced for the European market 154,634 tons of Muscovado, or brown sugar, and 34,574 tons of

1. There is no evidence that the older sugar industry of the Spanish islands had the slightest influence on that of the English or French in the West Indies. During the period of the transplanting from Brazil, the sugar culture of San Domingo actually declined. Ward Barrett, "Caribbean Sugar Production Standards in the Seventeenth and Eighteenth Centuries," in *Merchants and Scholars,* ed. John Parker (Minneapolis, 1965), 169*n*8.

2. The growth of the sugar industry of Brazil rendered that of Madeira, from which it sprang, obsolete by 1600, and the islanders turned to making wine. Deerr, *History of Sugar,* I, 100–105; and for the Dutch conquest, Boxer, *Dutch in Brazil,* 1–66, 97.

clayed white—an average of 23,651 tons a year from 1638 to 1645. Under Dutch rule, Brazil dominated the sugar trade of the Western World.

Although the Portuguese of Brazil rose in revolt soon after their Mother Country acquired her independence from Spain in 1640, it was not until 1645 that the war of liberation began to turn in their favor. There was no sharp decline in their sugar exports before that, and the final evacuation of the Dutch did not take place before the fall of Pernambuco in 1654. The Brazilians treated both the Dutch and the Jews with praiseworthy lenience; it was the Jesuits who forced the expulsion of the latter after 1654. To maintain that the Dutch were in such straits as early as 1640 that they had to get out of Brazil is patently contrary to fact.[3]

During the period from 1636 to 1645 when the Dutch controlled Pernambuco, the sugar plantations continued as before, under the supervision and operation of the Portuguese planters and their Negro slaves. The number of resident Dutch planters and ordinary colonists was very small. One Brazilian remarked in 1640 that "although there are at present many Dutch owners of sugar-mills, yet they cannot dispense with the Portuguese factors and small holders for the management and overseeing of the same." The Hollander, John Nieuhoff, frankly admitted that "the Portuguese did not only surpass all the rest, at least ten to one in number, during my abode in Brasil [1643–49], but were in possession of all the Sugar-Mills and Lands, except what was possess'd by a very few Dutch who applied themselves to Sugar-Planting. . . ."

3. Deerr, *History of Sugar,* I, 106–7. For the often misunderstood role of the Jews and their relatively small numbers in Brazil, see Herbert I. Bloom, *Economic Activities of the Jews in Amsterdam in the Seventeenth and Eighteenth Centuries* (Williamsport, Pa., 1937); and A. Wiznitzer, "The Number of Jews in Dutch Brazil, 1630–1654," in *Jewish Social Studies,* XVI (1954), 107–14; Wiznitzer, "The Exodus from Brazil and Arrival in New Amsterdam of the Jewish Pilgrim Fathers," in American Jewish Historical Society, *Publications,* XLIV (1954), 80–97. Nieuhoff said of the Jews he saw in Brazil: "Among the Free-Inhabitants . . . that were not in the Companies' Service, the Jews were the most considerable in number, who had transplanted themselves thither from Holland. They had a vast Traffick, beyond all the rest, they purchased Sugar-Mills, and built stately Houses in Receif. *They were all Traders* [our italics], but not planters. . . ." John Nieuhoff, *Voyages and Travels into Brasil and the East Indies* [1643–49], in Churchill, *Voyages,* II, 146; Boxer, *Dutch in Brazil,* 114, 243.

In 1645 Gaspar Días Ferreira demanded rhetorically: "Show me the Hollander who up to the present day in Pernambuco was a workman in making sugar, or who wished to learn it or any other position in a sugar-mill . . . There are but few Flemings who devote themselves to the sugar industry or to the maintenance of the mills in Brazil, and only rarely do they own them, and thus both the Negroes and the sugars have to pass through the hands of the Portuguese." In short, everything about the culture of sugar except the shipping and marketing of the product remained in the hands of the Portuguese colonials; the Dutch were neither planters nor technicians, they were middlemen—merchants and traders.[4]

The system of sugar production used in Brazil evolved from that imported from the island of Madeira. The owner of a sugar plantation, known as the *senhor de engenho,* customarily rented most of his land to five or ten small planters called *lavradores* in return for an agreed-upon share of the sugar they produced. The *lavrador* would get one-third to two-fifths of it; the larger share and by-products would go to the *senhor de engenho*. Each leasehold, about 150 acres, was presupposed to yield, on an average, 160 tons of sugar. The *lavrador* would require twenty slaves to plant, weed, cut canes, and transport them to the owner's mill; he was also expected to supply any tools, utensils, and *caixas,* or chests, necessary for shipping his share to market. Small planters who owned their land also took their canes to a nearby mill, and they ordinarily received 50 per cent of the sugar their canes produced.[5]

All the improvements devised for the production of sugar in Brazil, which made that system the most technically advanced of any in the world at that time, were made by the Portuguese under Dutch rule. At the mill-house the ingenio (*engenho*) was composed of three vertical rollers, turned by oxen or water power; a slave fed the canes between the first two to the other side, where an-

4. Boxer, *Dutch in Brazil,* 143; Churchill, *Voyages,* II, 146.

5. See the excellent descriptions of the Brazilian sugar industry in Boxer, *Dutch in Brazil,* 140–41, and Deerr, *History of Sugar,* I, 108. For complete details on every aspect of the industry one must consult the classic treatise of 1711 by André João Antonil, *Cultura e Opulencia do Brasil por Suas Drogas e Minas* (Paris, 1968), 84–167. This edition contains the Portuguese text on one page and on the opposite page a very good French translation with editorial notes by Andrée Mansuy.

other slave turned them around the middle roller and back again. This twice-crushed cane, called *bagaco* (*bagasse* to the French and English) belonged to the millowner, who gave it to his oxen or used it for fuel in the boiling furnaces. The cane juice, therewith released, dropped into troughs that led to the boiling-house. There it was boiled in a copper caldron and skimmed. Then, after workers had ladled the syrup into smaller "coppers," it was allowed to cool and, though it still contained a large amount of molasses, was poured into cone-shaped clay molds by slaves. A cone contained about thirty-two pounds of sugar, which, after crystalizing, went to the purging-house for a week. On the top of each cone, the slaves poured wet clay—hence the term *claying*. As the water drained down through the sugar toward a small hole in the bottom of the cone, it carried most of the molasses with it. For the better grades of sugar, this process was repeated two or three times. The white sugar, which filled the top of the cone, was tipped out and put in the sun to dry; that which remained in the bottom or clung to the sides, because of its molasses content, was brown in color and was called by the Portuguese *Mascavado*.[6]

Two by-products of this method of making sugar are of particular interest. One, called *garapa* by the Portuguese, was a cane juice derived from the skimmings taken from the boiling syrup. Sweet at first, it quickly soured and fermented, and the resultant strong liquor was exceedingly popular among the Negroes. From the "fine syrup" or molasses, the residue from boiling and crystallizing the sugar, the planters distilled *agua ardente* (*eau de vie*). André João Antonil urged them not to give any of this potent concoction to the blacks lest, becoming intoxicated, they perpetrate all manner of disorders—he mentions that some men in Brazil grew rich selling *garapa* and *agua ardente* to the Negroes and Indians, for once they developed a taste for it, they would pay good money for more. Ships crossing from Brazil to São Tomé for slave cargoes always carried large quantities of this liquor for trading along the coast.[7]

6. Boxer, *Dutch in Brazil,* 141–2; Antonil, *Cultura e Opulencia do Brasil,* 168–271, 285–9.
7. Antonil, *Cultura e Opulencia do Brasil,* 132*n,* 252–3, 266*n;* Labat, *Nouveau Voyage,* IV, 168–73.

In appearance a Brazilian sugar plantation resembled a small farming village. Two buildings dominated the scene: the owner's mansion (*casa grande*) and the sugar *engenho*.* The latter, much the largest structure, was located lengthwise on a hillside wherever possible (to make use of gravity for speeding up operations), with the downhill side open to the air. Round and about, one saw the small houses of *lavradores* and the slave shacks. Nearly all of the structures had thatched roofs, even the mill, despite the fire hazard; only an occasional house had a covering of shingles or the sightly red Dutch tiles. From the large trees in the adjacent woods came the huge timbers required for erecting the mill-house and constructing the machinery; from the woods, too, came the sawn boards, or shooks, used to fabricate the chests in which the planters always shipped their sugar, for each plantation produced its own timbers and lumber. Transportation costs were too high for an independent lumber industry to develop.[8]

Accompanying Prince Maurice of Nassau to Brazil in 1637 as a member of one of the most unusual colonial entourages of the age was Frans Post of Haarlem, a painter of much merit and considerable popularity. From notes, sketches, and memory of the years from 1637 to 1645, he produced a large number of charming landscapes and genre paintings of life in Brazil and the Caribbean, which give posterity a unique pictorial record of the Portuguese-Dutch colony and its slave population, far surpassing what the literary remains tell us.[9]

Prince Maurice worked wonders in restoring the Brazilian sugar industry by 1640, but the Dutch, at home in Holland and in

* Strictly speaking, *engenho* (ingenio) meant the cane-crushing rollers, the machinery, but by extension, as in *mill* in English, it came to include the entire building or sugarworks.

8. Erik Larsen, *Frans Post: Interprète du Brésil* (Amsterdam and Rio de Janeiro, 1962), plates 29, 34 (Village avec Casa-Grande), 34, 44, 46, 47, 47a, 48, 49, 50, 51, 53 (Moulin à sucre en lisière de la forêt vierge), 61, 74, 75, 94 (Les bâtiments de la plantation de sucre), 97, 99; Antonil, *Cultura e Opulencia dô Brasil,* 194–5.

9. Nearly 100 of the 132 paintings definitely ascribed to Post are reproduced by Larsen, *Frans Post.* See Catalogue des Oeuvres, 185–204, and plates 25, 40, 42, 49, 60, 92, 94, 96, reproduced in color, go far to recover the Brazilian plantation scene.

Zeeland, found themselves confronting several serious problems having to do not merely with the sugar industry but with trade and navigation in general. In Amsterdam and other cities of the Low Countries, merchants and bankers had in hand much saved capital that they needed to invest, and they were prepared to put it out for long terms at low interest rates in order to expand Dutch commerce overseas. In like fashion, Dutch manufactures and those collected from the Baltic countries, France, and even England, were piling up in their warehouses and on wharves; markets had to be found for them, and sources of raw materials were needed to further manufacturing. Ship-building went on apace, and a burgeoning merchant marine needed more and more cargo each year for both outward and homeward voyages. In 1641, with the capture of Loanda in Angola and the island of São Tomé in the Gulf of Guinea from the Portuguese, and early the next year, the island of Axim in Ghana,"the best and most populous breeding ground for Negro slaves," came under Dutch control. The slave merchants consequently set out to drum up more purchasers for the cargoes of blacks they were sending from Africa.[10]

Sugar—raw sugar—provided the way out of most of these difficulties. In truth, sugar was to become by 1650 the largest single item of exchange for the Dutch. Ten years earlier, the world supply of this exotic came principally from Brazil, then from Madeira, the Canaries, and Sicily; but the growers in those areas and those in the newer plantations of São Tomé could not furnish enough for the Amsterdam refiners who, in turn, had to meet the demands of an ever widening European market. Though sugar production in Brazil expanded steadily and the Netherlanders bent every effort to increase it and provide the Muscovado sugar which the refiners of Amsterdam clamored for, the Dutch-Portuguese colonials could not produce enough to fill up all the cargo-space of the twenty-one new ships built each year for that specific trade.[11]

Attempts to create additional supplies of sugar had actually begun in 1616 with the encouraging of both Dutch and English planters at Essequibo and elsewhere in Guiana. A decade later,

10. Boxer, *Dutch in Brazil*, 106–7.
11. Deerr, *History of Sugar*, I, 146–8; Bloom, *Jews in Amsterdam*, 36.

Robert Harcourt told of the expectations of "great benefit and wealth" to be drawn from cultivating sugar there based upon "the long experience of the Portugals, and Spaniards, in Brasill and the Ilands of the Canaries. . . ." Dutch settlement in the thirties at Curaçao had been designed to support a factory, or station, from which trade with the Spanish on the Main might be promoted; whereas that at St. Eustatius would serve as the entrepôt for the English and French colonies of the Lesser Antilles. In establishing colonies on these two islands, the Dutch had four main objectives: to provide havens for their ships to water, careen, and refit; to sell their goods and services and supply capital to needy planters of other nationalities (thereby augmenting a traffic begun long since); to open markets for the plentiful supply of African slaves; and to purchase such staples as tobacco and cotton, as formerly, but especially sugar. Success with all of these would give them a virtual monopoly of the commerce of the Caribbean and Spanish Main, such as they had already in the tobacco trade of the Chesapeake from their base at New Amsterdam. These shrewd and venturesome traders realized fully that by transplanting the culture of sugar from Brazil to the Caribbee Isles, they could tap one of the most promising sources of Muscovado. Their activities must be viewed then as the outcome of a determination to put all of their financial resources, agencies, and techniques to work to increase the economic power of the Dutch nation.[12]

II

The manner of transplanting the sugar culture and industry resembles very much the earlier transplanting of the cotton culture, but it was far more complicated and costly. None but men of considerable means or liberally supplied with credit could afford to embark on such a formidable project. Halting attempts to introduce sugar cane at Barbados went on for many years before success

12. Charles de Rochefort reported about 1600 men, headed by merchants of Flushing and Middleburg, living at St. Eustatius in houses as neat and well furnished as those of their native Zeeland. "There are also Store-houses so well furnish'd with all things requisite to life, and the accommodation of the Inhabitants, that many times they have wherewith to pleasure their Neighbours." Davies, *Caribby-Islands,* 25, 170; Harcourt, *Relation,* 41.

came, and in view of this, it is important to dispel certain widely held misconceptions about these first efforts. To do this, we shall do well, as far as the sources will permit, to adopt the rigorous attitude of the seventeenth-century European historians who tirelessly addressed themselves to the study of chronology.

Included among the many plants and seeds brought to Barbados from Essequibo by Captain Henry Powell in 1627 were sugar canes. The Arawaks planted them, but for at least ten years, the settlers made no attempt to develop sugar as a staple; they merely grew small amounts of canes to suck and chew for the sweet taste. Tobacco, cotton, and indigo absorbed their attention. According to John Scott, Pieter Brouwer [Brower] of North Holland introduced the first sugar to Barbados from Brazil by accident in 1637. Little more than a year after this, the Earls of Warwick and Carlisle expressed their "intentione to set up a sugger works" in the islands but apparently never carried out the project. Further along in his narrative, Scott credits James Holdip with being the first to plant a field with sugar canes that he had procured from a ship from "Guinea" (doubtless an error in the spelling of Guiana). This event took place some time after the arrival in 1640 of Governor Philip Bell, perhaps as late as 1642. Both John Scott and Nicholas Foster point out that the low price of tobacco, "their Staple," had put some Barbadians "upon making of Sugar." Foster described what, as a planter in Barbados, he had actually witnessed: "The decaying condition of this island (so plainly appearing) some of the ingenious spirits set their wits at worke to consider which way the desolation of this Plantation might be prevented; which could not possibly be effected, without the producing of some richer commodities to invite the Merchant to supply them [with the shipping and the European goods they wanted] . . . And considering Sugar not the least of commodities, (finding the scituation of the place promising that way) [they] resolved to make tryall thereof, and accordingly did; and with *divers yeares [of] paines, care, patience, and industry, with the disbursing of vast summes of money,* brought the same to perfection."[13]

13. On March 31, 1643/4, Captain James Holdip contracted with Thomas Applegate, citizen and clothworker of London, to sell him at least 200 acres of land, also pasturage for 20 cattle on other property of Holdip's and to deliver "so many good Sugar Canes to plant" as Applegate should need. Two other

Concerted efforts to grow sugar cane seem to have been started in 1642 by the selfsame first planters of Barbados who introduced the cotton culture. James Holdip more or less failed in his experiment, but another planter succeeded beyond all dreams. Sugar-growing, said Scott, "came to little untill the great industry and more thriving Genious [*sic*] of . . . James Drax, engaged in that great worke, who brought . . . Holdups essay, to soe great perfection that many were encouraged to undertake the makeing of Sugar." Drax, an enterprising man, a considerable landholder, and well connected in Barbados from the earliest times, embodied all of those virtues commonly associated with his group of conforming English puritans. It took a year or two of experimenting before he, his white servants, and his few black slaves succeeded in making a low-grade merchantable brown sugar. By August 6, 1644, he was ready to lay out a large sum on thirty-four Negroes. For payment Drax engaged with three London correspondents to ship them "soe much Suger or other merchantable commodities as shall amount to £726 sterling." He also contracted to share the risk of shipping the slaves and to absorb charges for their passage at the usual rate. Drax's friend William Hilliard agreed on July 30, 1644, to buy thirty blacks for £660 sterling, payable in "Indigoe, Suger, cotton-woole or Tobacco." Thomas Wall and Edward Pye, gentlemen, Governor Philip Bell, and Thomas Bartlett purchased African slaves at that same time, but they paid for them in cotton or tobacco. Sugar had not yet become an important crop for the planters; Hilliard and Drax alone among them had sugar to trade, but even with them, there was a choice of three commodities for payment. A charge made several years later (and therefore may have been mere political malice) asserted that James

---

points are significant here: Applegate planned to send out 50 white men servants for whose passage Holdip was to pay according to "the Custom of the Country," which meant, at this time, either in tobacco or cotton; and that Holdip was selling land, not consolidating holdings. He was growing sugar canes, but they do not figure prominently in his arrangements. Holdip sold land again in 1648 to Andrews & Wardell of London. Copy of Indenture in Davis Coll., VII, Envelope 22; *JBMHS,* I, 91; Harlow, *Colonising Expeditions,* 30; BM: Sloane MSS, 3662, fols. 60a, 55b; *Memoirs of the First Settlements . . . of Barbados,* Appendix 1 (where Guinea is used, which we assume is a slip); *Jamaica Historical Review,* V (1965), 20; Foster, *Late Horrid Rebellion,* 2 [A-3] (our italics).

Drax had kept the secrets of the art of sugar-making from the islanders at large for several years.[14]

Whatever the cause, it is evident that not until 1645 did sugar begin to be an important crop in Barbados, and when it did, the product was inferior. The average planter who raised tobacco, cotton, or indigo on a small plot began to experiment in planting sugar canes when he found out that he could produce as many pounds of sugar as tobacco on an acre and get "four times the price." James Parker, a Puritan minister who had come from Piscataqua, informed Governor John Winthrop of Massachusetts-Bay in June 1646 that Barbados "is now and like to be very wealthy, full of sugar, cotton, indigo, and ginger; some have made this yeare off one acre off canes about 4000 weight of sugar, ordinarily 3000." When he said that "a man with about 200 off pounds, in an ordinarie way off providence, might quickly gaine an estate by sugar," he had in mind a small planter who had no sugarworks and simply grew canes. In July of 1647 Richard Vines, another settler from Piscataqua, also wrote the elder Winthrop that his prospects in Barbados were very good: he had a practice of physic worth 10,000 pounds of tobacco a year, sixteen acres of cotton and the same of maize (for provisions), besides tobacco, all from his two adjoining plantations which totaled only fifty acres purchased from emigrating freeholders. His land and slaves had stood him 40,000 pounds of tobacco, and he could not at present, therefore, plant sugar as most men seemed to be doing, but he intended to do so the next year. Barbados had indeed become a boom island by 1647.[15]

14. The absence of any mention of sugar in the instructions sent from London to Humphrey Kent, a factor in Barbados, on March 5, 1640/1, indicates that it had not yet become an important item in the economy. Davis Coll., II, Envelope 17; VII, Envelope 15; BM: Sloane MSS, 3662, fol. 60a; Ligon, *Barbados,* 85–6. In reporting on "the state of the Indyes" in August 1645, the always alert George Downing failed to mention sugar. *Winthrop Papers,* V, 43–4; Thos. Robinson to Thos. Chappell, Sept. 24, 1643, Carlisle Trustees to Governor, Council, Assembly, Barbados, April 17, 1644, Hay MSS. For the charge that Drax concealed his sugar secrets, Southey, *Chronological History of the West Indies* (I, 284–5), who does not cite his source.

15. James Carr of Boston bound himself in an indenture of Nov. 16, 1646, to serve John and Anne Bayes of Barbados for two years, and they covenanted to pay him at the end of his term £9 in cotton-wool, indigo, or sugar at the price

At this very time, Richard Ligon arrived at Barbados in the same party with Thomas Modyford (Royalist but also a cousin of General Monck), who purchased half of William Hilliard's large plantation, one of the few lying inland. Ligon's description and analysis of the entire sugar culture is the earliest and fullest that we have and serves as the most reliable summary of the progress made up to 1650.

"At the time we landed on this Iland, which was in the beginning of September, 1647," this eye-witness tells us, "we were informed, partly by those Planters we found there, and partly by our own observations, that the great worke of Sugar-making, was *but newly practised* by the inhabitants there. Some of the more industrious men having gotten Plants from Fernambock [Pernambuco], a place in Brasill, and made tryall of them at Barbados; and finding them to grow, they planted more and more, as they grew and multiplied on the place, till they had such a considerable number, as they were worth while to keep up *a small Ingenio* [Drax's], and so make tryall what Sugar could be made upon that soyl. But, the secrets not being well understood, the Sugars they made were very inconsiderable, and [of] little worth, for two or three years." After they discovered some of their errors around 1645, the planters began to improve the agriculture of Barbados, and *"by new directions from Brasil,* sometimes by strangers, and now and then *by their own people,* (who being covetous of the knowledge of a thing, which so much concerned them in their particulars, and for the generall good of the whole Iland) *were content sometimes to make a voyage thither, to improve their knowledge* in a thing they so much desired." Returning from Brazil with "more Plants, and better Knowledge," these enterprising men went ahead with great hopes, "but still short of what they should be skilfull in," says Ligon, "for, at our arrivall there, we found them ignorant in three main points that much conduced to the work." These deficiencies were: the manner of planting canes, the time of cutting them, and the proper placing of the copper caldrons

---

there current. *Aspinwall Notarial Records* (32d *Report of the Record Commissioners of the City of Boston,* Boston, 1903), 39; BM: Sloane MSS, 3662, fols. 55b, 59a; *Winthrop Papers,* V, 83–4, 172; Davis Coll., VIII, Envelope 2.

for boiling the juice; furthermore they had not yet learned to sheathe the rollers of the mill with plates of iron or brass. Both Ligon and Modyford found many sugar mills operating in 1647, but the sugars the planters made were "bare Muscavadoes," and very little of their product was merchantable, for it was moist and full of molasses.[16]

When Ligon left to return to England in 1650, all operations from planting to shipping had been "much better'd"; and some observers thought them perfected. In 1648 Sir Edmund Plowden noted that some of the men in Barbados were growing rich. Certain it is that in the twenty months prior to 1650, the sugar produced had helped to raise the total value of Barbados crops to the amazing sum of £3,097,800. Prosperity had arrived with sugar.[17]

From scattered sources, we know that the sugar culture reached the Leeward Islands either direct from Brazil or by way of St. Eustatius or St. Martin, independent of the transplanting into Barbados. "The English were the first in condition to make sugar at St. Christopher," said Père Labat, "their histories date it at 1643." One account suggests that the islanders forced the secret of making a clayed white sugar out of a Portuguese who landed at St. Christopher from a Dutch ship. The French on this island moved more slowly; not before 1648 did they begin, under the direction of a Dutch refugee from Brazil, to plant canes. The planters of Nevis seem to have promptly acquired canes from St. Christopher, and before long their sugar had won the reputation of being the best made in any of the English islands. Sometime before 1649, Montserrat planters had turned to growing sugar with sufficient success to attract the canny London merchant, Samuel Atkins,

16. Thomas Peake remarked of the Barbadians: "Their chief Trade is Tobacco, and a kind of course Sugar, which we call Barbados-Sugar, and will not keep long; not that the Countrie is unapt for better, but, as 'tis rather supposed, because the Planters want either skill or stock [capital] to improve things to the best." Though published in 1655, this information probably dates before 1650. N. N., *America,* 471; Ligon, *Barbados,* 22, 85 (our italics).

17. Not until Feb. 4, 1650/1 did the Assembly of Barbados, in an act to relieve persons imprisoned for debts not exceeding 2000 pounds of sugar, specify that commodity as a money equivalent instead of tobacco or cotton. *Acts of Barbados* (Hall) [London, 1764], 16; Ligon, *Barbados,* 85, 96; Force, *Tracts,* II, No. 7, p. 5.

into investing heavily in a sugarworks requiring twenty horses from overseas.[18]

III

The manner in which the English planters transferred the sugar industry from Brazil to Barbados and the Leeward Islands is of more than antiquarian interest. It is a central concern in the economic history of the seventeenth century. In Barbados in 1642, more than 8000 landed proprietors, with the help of thousands of white servants, farmed small tracts of land ranging from five to thirty acres in size. For them to shift from tobacco, cotton, indigo, and ginger to sugar meant that each one must have access to capital or credit to purchase more hands—and those black—and additional acres. Even the more substantial planters commanded very little capital or sufficient land. One of the true bigwigs, James Holdip, held but 500 acres in 1650, but he and James Drax, William Hilliard, and others of the puritan old planters had small amounts of capital saved from sales of tobacco and cotton, and from trading in land to start off with—but not very much. Imagination and considerable daring they did have, however—the gambling instincts of the pioneer.[19]

In any new country, and Barbados and the Leeward Islands were no exception, the creation of capital out of land and natural

18. M. Tresel, a Dutch merchant of Rouen, went to Martinique in 1641 to introduce the culture of sugar, but he did not start planting until about 1644. Biët wrote in 1652 that in 1647 one of the "Principal Dutchmen" from Brazil persuaded the governor of Guadeloupe that sugar would grow well there, and soon had the French planters busy clearing land and planting canes. When Père Pelleprat was in the French islands in 1650 and 1654, he reported excellent sugar being produced, especially at St. Christopher "where there are several sugar works." Du Tertre, *Histoire générale des Antilles,* I, 109; Stuart L. Mims, *Colbert's West India Policy* (New Haven, 1912), 32–6, 250, 260; Biët, *Voyage,* 314–15; Pelleprat, *Relation,* 194. On sugar in the Leeward Islands, see Labat, *Nouveau Voyage,* III, 327, 331, 369, 377; Alice P. Canabrava, "A Influencia do Brasil na Tecnica do fabrico de acuar nas Antillas. . . ." in *Annuario da Facultade de Ciencias, Economicas e Administrativas* (São Paulo, 1946–47) as quoted by Matthew Edel in *Caribbean Studies,* IX (1969), 32; Gardyner, *New World,* 74; *CSPC, 1574–1660,* p. 331; Robinson to Chappell, Sept. 24, 1643, Hay MSS.

19. Deerr, *History of Sugar,* I, 161; *JBMHS,* I (1934), 91; Ligon, *Barbados,* 22.

resources is always a slow process, and aid and support must come from the outside. It was at this point that Dutch assistance proved decisive. "The Hollanders that are great encouragers of Plantacions," John Scott explained in his history, "did at the first attempt of makeing sugar, give great Credit to the most sober Inhabitants, and upon the unhappie Civill warr, that brake out in England, *they mannaged the whole trade in our Westerne Collonies,* and furnished the Island with Negroes, Coppers, Stills, and all other things appertaining to the Ingenious [*sic*] for makeing of Sugar and that were any other way necessary for their comfortable Subsistance." Dalby Thomas confirms this view: The Dutch, "who being eternal Prolers about, and Searchers for moderate Gains by Trade, did give Credit to those Islanders, as well as they did to the Portugalls in Brasile, for Black Slaves, and all other necessaries for planting, taking as their Crops throve, the Sugar they made; thus with light but sure Gains, they nourisht the Industrious and consequently Improving Planters, both before, and during the Civill Wars in those Islands." [20]

Beyond all doubt, in 1650, Amsterdam not London was the metropolis of the Caribbean. (Plate 12) In 1644 Captain Cornelius Hartgers, a merchant at Medemblick on the Zuider Zee, and the Flemings, Simon and Henrique Casseres of the same town, placed Michael Vanderserver as agent at The Indian Bridge to dispense advice and extend ample credit at rates of interest lower than English merchants would grant it. Indicative of the enterprise of the Barbadians is the fact that several merchant-planters, among them Constant Sylvester and Charles Jacobson, went over to Amsterdam to solicit financial aid directly from the Dutch merchants and bankers, as well as to act as factors for handling incoming cargoes of colonial produce. Men such as these were the ones who worked out credit arrangements for the sugar planters.[21]

These arrangements "put Barbados into a flourishing condition, but it was attended with this Inconvenience, in that the more Industrious and Prudent Planters became Storehouse-keepers for

20. BM: Sloane MSS, 3662, fols. 60a, 60b; Thomas, *Historical Account . . . of the West Indies,* 36–7 (our italics).
21. Notes on Barbados merchants, Davis Coll., VII, Envelope 2, 13.

the Dutch, and soe by giving Credit to their profuse and some times Necessitous Neighbours on Severe Termes, insensibly in [a] few yeares wormed out the greatest part of the small proprietors, for the makeing of Sugar requires many Negroes, and Considerable quantitys of land." Christopher Codrington, the Brothers Holdip, and Gerard Hawtayne were among the old planters who bought up small tracts of ten to fifty acres along the coast from migrating freemen after 1645. A comparative newcomer, Captain Waterman, told John Scott in later years that his 800 acres had at one time been held by forty different individuals.[22]

As the London merchants sensed how much the Dutch were profiting from the traffic with the English colonies, they, too, began to pour large sums of additional capital into the islands, albeit in new ways and on stiffer terms. Robert Page and William Eyton went out in 1647 to act as agents for their "Loving Cozen" of London in acquiring a plantation for a sugarworks at Barbados; in part payment they sent home in the *Seaflower* 6000 weight of sugar valued at £120. About this time also, Maurice Thompson & Company and William Pennoyer, both of London, and "divers other planters at Barbados, whoe are erecting sugar workes there," petitioned the House of Lords to permit them to send over "drawing horses and oxen for the mills"—Thompson bought more than a hundred oxen in Virginia. In 1649 one of the London brothers of John Norton of Ipswich planned to send over £500 to £1000 worth of goods annually for their younger brother, William, to dispose of in the Bay Colony, and "to have retornes made to Barbados to supply his sugar workmen." [23]

As one might suspect, this trend to establish sugar plantations created a demand for land that brought about an increase in its price. William Hilliard's 500-acre plantation could have been purchased in 1642 for £400 sterling, but five years later Thomas Modyford had to pay £7000 sterling for one-half of it and half of the stock on it! Clearing the ground for an inland plantation

22. BM: Sloane MSS, 3662, fols. 60a, 60b, 59a; *Timehri,* n. s., VII (1893), 17–26; X (1896), 109, 115.

23. For meager evidence of the beginnings of English investments in sugar lands, see Pares, *Merchants and Planters,* 52–5; Davis Coll., VII, Envelope 2; Stock, *Debates,* I, 196–7; *Winthrop Papers,* V, 301; Foster, *Late Horrid Rebellion,* 3–4.

required a great deal of slave labor and took a long time to effect; small investors did better to buy the tobacco or cotton fields of migrating freeholders. This was the advice given to the leaders of Père Biët's little party in 1652 by their compatriot César du Mesnil, who had married a Holdip heiress. They bought a small parcel of cleared land for 20,000 pounds of sugar, which they paid for by selling six slaves and the services of most of their white *engagés.* Though a Cavalier, Richard Norwood, knowing that he was not one of "the men of the first rate, who wanted not money or credit to balance the expence necessary to the carrying on the sugar works," wisely chose to settle in Virginia.[24]

The size of the investment required rose year by year, not only because of the mounting prices of land, cleared or uncleared, but also because, in addition to more ground, the prospective sugar planter needed utensils, expensive machinery, buildings, animals, provisions, and, above everything else, African slaves. Although the Dutch advanced long-term credit at low interest, planters found themselves buying many essential items "at deere rates," and if they turned to the English merchants, the goods cost more and the interest rate was higher. One had to have a stock, "both quick and dead," of at least £2000 sterling, "which was counted no great beginning." The estate of John Price of St. Peter's Parish, Barbados, appraised at his death in 1650, probably represents an average middle-sized investment during the transition to sugar: 130 acres in tobacco, 38 acres in sugar, an unstated number in provisions; also a dwelling-house and a still-house valued at 5500 pounds of sugar; 13 white servants, a Negro slave couple; 17 horses, one ox, and several little donkeys. Ligon's analysis of that same year, which was intended for his English readers and based upon the Hilliard-Modyford plantation, called for an outlay of £14,000 spread over three years. Perhaps it was the awareness of these sums that impelled Lucy Winthrop Downing to pass on a bit of news she had received from Barbados to her brother in Pequot

24. We may recall here that Ligon found very little ground cleared away from the shore in 1647; it took hard work by slaves to prepare lands for planting and this goes far to explain the very high cost of land along the littoral before 1650. Ligon, *Barbados,* 24, 86, 112–15; Biët, *Voyage,* 274; William Powrey to Archibald Hay, April 8, 1646, Hay MSS; Force, *Tracts,* III, No. 10, pp. 3–4.

(New London): that Thomasine, daughter of William Hilliard, once "our overthwart neighbour in fleet street," had taken as her second husband Mr. Thomas Noell: "They are rich and have great sugar workes." In 1654 they occupied the mansion house at Mt. Clapham.[25]

The bright prospects of fortunes to be reaped from the sugar industry, which attracted investors from overseas, came about through the earnest efforts of the Barbadians who had come to realize that nothing less than the smooth functioning of the entire inter-related system would bring any measure of success; they had failed between 1642 and 1646 when they tried to produce sugar without fully comprehending the complete process. On their several journeys to Pernambuco in the company of their Dutch backers, the Barbadians came to understand that they must take home an intricate combination of related Portuguese and Dutch elements: agricultural, industrial, mechanical, laboring, maritime, and commercial elements that made up what we might call the Sugar Complex. They also, without previous experience themselves, had to learn all the details and put them into practice with totally inexperienced white and black laborers. And so, we are told, they "bent all their endeavours to advance their knowledge in the planting and making sugar: Which knowledge, though they studied hard, was long a learning." Between 1646 and 1650 they began to approach their goal. This was a superb effort that must have astonished themselves and their Dutch partners; and we know that the once indifferent but now envious members of the mercantile community of England experienced astonishment and dismay.[26]

25. The powerful Noell family and connection was well established in the West Indies by 1647; Thomasine Hilliard's first husband was also a very rich planter, Lancelot Pacey. *Winthrop Papers,* V, 291; *Timehri,* n. s., X (1896), 106; BM: Sloane MSS, 3662, fol. 59a; Egerton MSS, 2395, fol. 283; Thomas Tryon, *The Merchant's, Citizen's, and Countryman's Instructor* (London, 1701), 201; Davis Coll., VI, Envelope 25; Ligon, *Barbados,* 112–15.

26. As if to compensate the Portuguese in part for their aid in teaching the Barbadians the art of making sugar, the West Indians swapped crops in 1642 by sending indigo seeds to Brazil by Gillan Venant. By official order some planters experimented, but pissmires "consumed most of the leaves." Finally, with the ants eliminated from cleared ground, the plants grew and several grades of indigo were shipped to the Netherlands. Nieuhoff, in Churchill, *Voyages,* II, 140; Ligon, *Barbados,* 24; BM: Sloane MSS, 3662, fol. 55b. For a very good descrip-

At the outset, difficult problems of organization and management had to be faced. Those planters who, like Drax, possessed from 300 to 500 acres of tobacco or cotton land already cleared could adopt the *senhor de engenho–lavrador* leasing system if they chose, but to extend the culture of sugar to the smaller plantations (small farms, despite the name) they had to persuade some of the thousands of small freeholders to plant and tend sugar canes. Very few of these yeomen-planters went in for sugar exclusively before 1650, and their method of planting was simply to stick the canes endwise into small holes poked in the soil. The three or four sprouts that grew from each one had no resistance to the high winds and entire crops were lost in a single storm, or were washed out by heavy rains. In the manner of farmers everywhere, they were slow to adopt new agricultural methods, and the millowners could not control them the way the *senhor de engenho* did the *lavradores.* The great planters, responding possibly to suggestions from Dutch merchants or to observations made during their visits to Brazil, perceived that large units farmed by slave labor would be cheaper to operate, more efficient, and yield higher profits. Well-to-do planters began to follow the example of Drax and his associates and consolidate, by purchase, small parcels of ten, twenty, and thirty acres, then "in poor mens hands," into plantations of five, six, or seven hundred acres. According to Ligon, this process had only begun in 1650. The great transformation and full flowering of the sugar culture would come in the next decade.

The English now began to practice "the right way of planting" canes, which they had learned from the Portuguese in Brazil. Up and down an entire field, they dug small trenches in parallel lines, six inches deep and six inches wide. Into these they placed two canes, side by side and end to end for the length of the trench, and covered them with soil. By this method, every knot in the canes put forth a sprout and its own root, thereby fixing them firmly in the ground. Growing thickly, they could support each other against the wind and rain, and choke out weeds and withes;

---

tion of the manufacture of indigo, see Davies, *Caribby-Islands,* 197. The culture of tobacco will be described in detail in the volume of this history dealing with the Chesapeake colonies, but there is a good account in Davies, 188–93.

filling in void spots was one of the most important features of cane growing. Carefully cultivated, sugar canes attained a diameter of about an inch and averaged eight feet in height.[27]

In Brazil the Barbadians also learned that they should wait fifteen months before cutting their crops instead of twelve, as they had been doing. They made several plantings at regular intervals during the wet season between May and October so that all of the canes would not ripen at the same time and swamp them and the ingenio with work. With "little hand bills," the white servants and black slaves cut the mature canes about six inches above the ground and stripped off the blades and tops, which they loaded into carts to be carried to the barn, there being no pasturage in the islands. Other hands bound the canes into faggots and loaded them on the backs of *asinegoes* (small donkeys), saddled Devonshire fashion, and thus the canes were carried to the *barbacoa* (Fr.: *barbecue,* or railed platform) that stood in front of the mill. After the faggots were unloaded there, these "understanding" little beasts turned around and plodded back to the field. Obviously such a procedure worked only on the few large plantations; the ordinary grower had to load faggots on his asinego and then either he or a servant had to lead it across several fields to the nearest mill-house, for paths or roads still did not exist.[28]

Most contemporary accounts credit James Drax with introducing "the Dutch Sugar Mill" to Barbados by means of an imported model. If he used a model, almost certainly he brought it back from Pernambuco, for no grinding-mills existed in Holland. He did import from there, as did the Brazilians, many necessary utensils and copper caldrons for boiling juices. Soon after the sugar-works seemed to be operating satisfactorily, carpenters, joiners, millwrights, and masons arrived from England—they had been enlisted by the promise of good wages to help build the sugar mills and grinding machinery. In the islands, which lacked running streams, the Brazilian water-powered mill could not be imitated,

27. This discussion of the steps and processes in sugar-growing and sugar manufacture rests entirely, unless otherwise stated, on Ligon's account. Ligon, *Barbados,* 85, 87, 88, 89.

28. The platform or *barbacoa* (Fr. *barbecue*) may be readily seen in plates 46, 47a, and 51 of Larsen's *Frans Post;* Ligon, *Barbados,* 89.

but the English artisans seem to have made several technical improvements in the works, especially in the boiling-houses. "These Mills are built of very solid and lasting wood," an observer at St. Christopher stated, "and are more convenient in these Islands than those used to the same purpose at Madera and Brasil: Nor is it to be fear'd in the former, as many times in the latter, that the fire should get to the boiling Coppers, and set all into a flame, to the destruction of those who are employ'd about the work, for the Coppers in these Islands are seen to boil, yet the fire that causes it is made and kept in on the outside by furnaces, which are so well cemented, that neither the flame nor the smoak does any way hinder those who are at work. . . ." Out of heavy timbers, expert English and continental artisans fashioned the mill-houses, fabricated the grinding rollers and other machinery, built and arranged the boiling-furnaces and the stills used in making rum. Throughout the West Indies the English referred interchangeably to the mill-house and all of its equipment as the ingenio (*engenho*), or the mill, or the sugarworks. Parenthetically, we may point out here that nearly every technical term pertaining to the growth and manufacture of sugar was a clumsy English rendering of some Portuguese word, and never of Dutch origin: *ingenio, barbycue, bagasse, Muscovado.*[29]

The grinding machine, which, as in Brazil, consisted of three vertical rollers turned from local ironwood, geared together with ironwood cogs, and rotated, usually by five oxen or five horses harnessed to sweeps. (See Plates 4 and 5) The faggots, or canes, having been brought by white servants or slaves from the barbecue, passed twice through the rollers; the crushed canes (*bagasse*) were carried away by young Negro girls and kept for fodder or for fuel in the boiling furnaces; the juice dripped down into a "receiver," from which it ran underground, in a pipe, to the "cistern." Thence, within twenty-four hours, the juice had to be conveyed to the boiling-house lest it sour. Then began a series of operations, cycles in which the juice was boiled, skimmed, and ladled from one "clarifying copper" to another. As the scum rose, "dirtie and drosse," in

29. *Memoirs of the First Settlement . . . of Barbados,* Appendix 1; *NEHG Reg.,* XXXIX (1885), 135; Ligon, *Barbados,* 40, 42, 74; Davies, *Caribby-Islands,* 194; *Aspinwall Notarial Records,* 40.

the first two boilings, it was thrown away, but the skimmings from the subsequent three boilings were conveyed to the still-house and allowed to sour. The sugar-liquid, now sufficiently refined, was permitted to cool somewhat, and then the workmen poured it into pots, or cones, in the "filling-room." After two days the men opened the pointed bottom-ends of the cones and let the molasses drain off down a gutter into cisterns. These operations went on for twenty-four hours a day, with "fresh supplies of Men, Horses, and Cattle" working in regular shifts, Monday through Saturday, when the workers put out the fires in the furnaces.[30]

The pots, now filled with sugar, continued to drain for at least a month before the sugar was considered to be "well cur'd." The cones were next turned upside down and gently tapped, or "knocked," until the core, which amounted to about two-thirds of its contents, dropped out. This bright-colored, brown substance was the product so earnestly sought, Muscovado sugar. That which remained, sticking to the sides of the cone because it contained so much molasses, went back to be boiled again with the molasses in the cisterns and converted into *peneles* (Portuguese: *panela*). "And this is the whole processe of making Muscavado-Sugar, whereof some is better, and some is worse, as the Canes are: for ill Canes can never make good Sugar." Thus wrote Richard Ligon, who never directly states that it was the Portuguese method, borrowed with only minor modifications, from Pernambuco.[31]

Planters did not pack the Muscovado sugar at the mill; rather they sent it down daily in leather bags on the backs of asinegoes or camels (one of them could carry 1200 pounds) to The Indian Bridge. There warehousemen packed it into casks of various sizes and stored it in their buildings until ships came to carry it off to Amsterdam or Hamburg or, less often, to London and Bristol. The

30. Ligon, *Barbados,* 89–91.

31. "Many of the Inhabitants who are not able to get so many Coppers, nor furnish themselves with those great Engines whereby Canes are squeez'd, have little Mills made like Presses, which are wrought by two or three men, or are driven about by one horse; and with one or two Coppers they purifie the juice gotten out of them, reduce it to the consistence of Syrup, and make good Sugar without any further trouble." Charles de Rochefort wrote this before 1658, but since Ligon does not mention these smaller sugar mills, they may have been an innovation after 1650. Davies, *Caribby-Islands,* 196; Ligon, *Barbados,* 91.

sugar was not uniform in grade or quality. Colonel Drax, Colonel Walrond, Mr. Francis Raynes, and a few other major planters performed all of the steps in the knocking process with great care, but the "greater number, when they knock out their Sugars, let all go together, both bottom and top, and so let the better bear the worse." Shrewd merchants gave but £3 10*s*. per hundredweight for the poorer quality but would pay £6 4*s*. and above for the best Muscovado.[32]

Inevitably, during their trips to Pernambuco to learn the mystery of making sugar, the gentlemen-planters of Barbados also found out how to make *agua ardente* from molasses and skimmings. Once back home, they permitted the skimmings to sour before passing them through the still. Off came a spirit so strong that a flame of a candle brought near an open bunghole of a hogshead or butt filled with it would fire the contents. *Agua ardente* was one Portuguese term that the Dutch, French, and English in the West Indies did not adopt, possibly because it suggested French brandy, *eau de vie*. Relishing the taste and potency of the liquor, the English appropriately called it "Kill-devill," because a man who imbibed it promptly became boisterous, reckless, and daring. Also, as Ligon explained, it possessed "the vertue to cure" many Negroes of colds and allied ailments contracted from lying on their boards without any covering through the cool nights; it drove the devil out of them. A dram of this elixir was the accepted dosage issued by plantation apothecaries. Kill-devil, furthermore, refreshed and comforted white servants after they had sweated in the hot sun for ten hours a day.[33]

The new sugar drink rapidly found favor with men of all classes and conditions—and with more than a few women as well—in every American colony. Ligon told of sending quantities of it down from Modyford's plantation to the retailers at The Bridge. "Some they sell to the Ships and is transported into forraign parts, and

32. "And those that use this care, have such credit with the Buyer, as they scarce open the Cask to make a tryall, so well they are assured of the goodnesse of the Sugars they make." White (or clayed) sugar sold in London for 20*d*. a pound, but none was produced in the English islands before 1650. The larger planters, as well as the merchants, had storehouses at The Indian Bridge (Bridgetown). Ligon, *Barbados*, 89, 91–2; Davis Coll., VII, Envelope 13.
33. Ligon, *Barbados*, 27, 93.

drunk by the way. Some they sell to such Planters, as have no Sugar-works of their owne, yet drink excessively of it, for they buy it at easie rates"; the price in 1650 was half a crown a gallon, though it would shortly go higher. He estimated that from the skimmings and molasses of a 500-acre plantation, the kill-devil distillery would pay a profit of £30 a week, and that was allowing for what the labor force and other men of the establishment consumed.[34]

Somewhere, somehow, for its origin is obscure, kill-devil acquired a new name. Ligon never used it, but an anonymous Barbadian of 1650 indicated that it already enjoyed currency: "The cheife fudling they make in the Iland is Rumbullion, alias Kill Divill, and this is made of Suggar cones distilled; a hott hellish and terrible liquor." The name was soon shortened from *Rumbullion* to *rum,* and from this Dutch and English word we get the French *rhum* and Spanish *ron.* Caribbean rum shortly became a prime article of commerce, though not always an approved one, for the General Court of Connecticut ordered in 1654 that "whatsoever Barbados Liquors, commonly called Rum, Kill Devill, or the like," either landed or sold aboard ships in the colony should be confiscated. Pressure from thirsty Yankee farmers finally, five years later, forced the repeal of this measure.[35]

That the work of managing a sugar plantation demanded all of the time, intelligence, and energy of the owner must be immediately recognized. Unless he had a superior overseer, a rare creature at any time, the owner was advised to superintend both planting and weeding in person (Ligon considered the latter task most important for the success of the venture). Next in priorities was the supervision of the ingenio or sugar mill, "the Primum Mobile of the whole work" with its many rooms, coppers, furnaces, and utensils. "If anything in the Rollers, as the Goudges, Sockets, Sweeps,

34. Barbados rum was not only the best produced in the Caribbean area but because so much care was used in the distilling it retained its primacy for more than a century. Georges Butel-Dumont asserted that "Rum or Tasiat" yielded almost nothing to the *eau de vie* of France. *Histoire et commerce des Antilles angloises* (Paris, 1758), 22–3; Ligon, *Barbados,* 93.

35. Harlow, *Colonising Expeditions,* 46; *Oxford English Dictionary,* q. v. *rum; Public Records of the Colony of Connecticut,* ed. J. Hammond Trumbull and Charles J. Hoadly (Hartford, 1850), I, 255.

Cogs or Braytrees, be at fault, the whole work stands still." Trouble in the boiling-house with the coppers or the furnace, and the constant danger of fire, could cause similar interruption of work. Most disastrous of all was the loss of animals: oxen and horses, along with camels and asinegoes, all had to be imported, not bred in the islands, and some of them died from rare or undiagnosed diseases within a day or so of their arrival. The stoppage of work, for any of these reasons, meant that the canes might overripen and be unfit for grinding. In addition to managing his fields, works, and labor force, the plantation owner had to deal with shrewd and demanding merchants and factors, or be one himself, in order to ensure proper packing and shipping of his sugar and other produce; he also had to arrange for the importing of servants, slaves, animals, clothing, tools, provisions, and such luxuries as he wanted for his family. "They are men of great abilities, and parts," the admiring Ligon concluded, "otherwise they could not go through, with such great works as they undertake, being a work of such latitude, as will require a very good head-peece, to put in order, and continue to do so. . . ."[36]

Planters such as Drax, Hilliard, Codrington, Holdip, Hawtayne, and Yeamans had gone out to the West Indies in the twenties and thirties to make their fortunes, and they had to wait a long time before they could see prosperous futures ahead of them—James Drax's entire stock did not exceed £300 in 1627, but twenty years later he declared he would not retire to England until he could purchase an estate of £10,000 yearly; and Thomas Modyford often remarked that he would never set his face toward Britain before sugar-planting earned him £100,000 sterling. Foreseeing that the big money would be in sugar, and also that land in Barbados, St. Christopher, Nevis, and Montserrat would become increasingly scarce and high-priced, these men drastically limited the number of acres planted in food crops, because they knew they could buy provisions from outside and show a better profit on their acres with sugar crops. Their imitators among the lesser planters went even further and one by one gave up raising any food at all.[37]

36. Ligon, *Barbados,* 55–7.
37. Ligon, *Barbados,* 43, 96.

This move toward a monoculture demanded regular and dependable imports of all provisions and necessaries from elsewhere. In the early days, of course, English merchants had supplied St. Christopher with servants and provisions, as did Ireland. The Dutch, too, sold goods, food, cattle, and horses to islanders. With the spreading of the sugar culture, which included bringing in more and more slaves and the abandoning of nearly all food crops except sweet potatoes and plantains, the colonists needed to import increasingly large supplies of heavy timbers, lumber, barrel staves, and hoops; and, for turning their mills, they needed more oxen and horses than the Dutch ships could bring from Europe. It was their good fortune to discover that the merchants of the northern colonies were ready and eager to trade all of these articles in sufficient amounts. Richard Vines sent a letter to Governor Winthrop in July 1647 by John Mainford, a Barbados merchant sailing for Boston "to trade for provisions for the belly, which at present is very scarce, by reason of 5 or 6 months drythe, and not that only, but men are so intent upon planting sugar that they had rather buy foode at very deare rates than produce it by labour, soe infinite is the profitt of sugar workes after once accomplished." [38]

Lying athwart the routes of ships homeward bound from the Caribbean, New England and Virginia each enjoyed intermittent contacts with the West Indies in the early thirties. The pressing need for salt for the fisheries and meat-packing, and cotton wool for the nascent cloth industry, led the New Englanders to seek more regular connections. The sea captains of the outlying colonies of New England seem to have moved a bit faster in finding outlets for their products in the West Indies than did those of Massachusetts-Bay. The inhabitants of the town of Portsmouth on Rhode Island agreed in 1640 to co-operate in making up a cargo of pipe staves, clapboards, bolts, planks, and shooks for making casks and houses for planters. Westward, in Connecticut, the General Court directed Governor Hopkins to send a ship laden with local wheat and pipe staves, "as the country shall afford," to one of the West Indian islands to exchange for cotton wool. The proceeds of this voyage amounted to £440 and, as directed, the adventurers

38. For the provision trade between Ireland and Barbados, see James, *WMQ,* 3d ser., XX (1963), 576; Ligon, *Barbados,* 37; *Winthrop Papers,* V, 172.

laid it out in cotton for Connecticut spinners and weavers. In 1641 the General Court set standard sizes for all exported staves. Captain Thomas Chammock of Black Point in the Province of Maine died in 1643 in the West Indies (almost certainly at St. Christopher), where he had been dealing in "merchantable Codfish, Refuse fish," and oil for illumination.[39]

The foremost figure of the English colonies in the New World before 1660, Governor John Winthrop, had had connections with Barbados in 1627 through his son Henry, two years before he really knew much about his future home in Massachusetts-Bay. Although Joshua Scottow and other Boston and Salem traders had trafficked in the West Indies prior to 1640, Governor Winthrop's first mention of "looking out" to the West Indies for a trade in cotton was not until 1641. The New Englanders were drawn to the islands from two directions: along the old familiar route, directly southward, which they had long known, and in the forties from the eastward, when they began to carry wines to the planters on their homeward voyages from Madeira and the Canaries. Learning about the new developments in the Caribbean, they solicited trade, and many of them started taking cargoes of salted beef and pork, Indian corn, wheat, and cattle, assembled at home or picked up in Virginia and Maryland. Seeing a market in food for the growing slave population, they also took down quintals of "refuse fish."[40]

As the sugar industry gradually overtook the production of cotton and tobacco, the Bostoners began shipping forest products

39. The master of a ship from New Haven sought a cargo of cotton at Barbados in 1648. A few years later, William Couzens of Piscataqua purchased a vessel from Symon Overze, merchant of Rotterdam, on the ship's return from Barbados. *Records of the Colony and Plantation of New Haven . . .*, ed. Charles J. Hoadly (Hartford, 1852), I, 337, 439; *Early Records of the Town of Portsmouth (1639–1697)* [Providence, 1901], 10; *Conn. Col. Recs.*, I, 59–60, 67–8, 79, 116, 200; Will of Capt. Thomas Chammock, Sept. 2, 1640, and a Deed to Chammock from the Council for New England, Nov. 1, 1636, in Chammock Family Papers (Maine Hist. Soc., Portland); James Savage, *Genealogical Dictionary of New England* (Boston, 1847–), II, 570; *Aspinwall Notarial Records*, 359; *Province and Court Records of Maine*, ed. Charles T. Libby (Portland, 1928), I, 158.

40. Chammock Family Papers (Maine Hist. Soc.); *Winthrop's Journal*, II, 24, 89, 126, 154, 157, 176; *Winthrop Papers*, V, 62–4; Hubbard, *History of New England*, 378, 379; Force, *Tracts*, II, No. 7, p. 6; *Aspinwall Notarial Records*, 8, 75, 394, 397, 401.

of every sort to the West Indies: heavy timbers for the frames and machinery of the mills, boards for the siding of the mills and the planters' houses, even some prefabricated "frames of houses." Thousands of red-oak "shaken casks," or shooks, to be coopered into sugar and molasses hogsheads, barrels, and tierces, made up the largest single kind of shipment because of the shortage of timber in the islands. Mrs. Joan Swane of Boston put in twelve dozen "wooden dishes" in a venture cargo of onions, mackerel, and butter for Barbados in 1649, and Ralph Woory of Charlestown in the Bay became one of the more active merchants dealing with Barbados, particularly in "bread," or ship's biscuits. And now sugar and molasses became valuable commodities at the New England market. When John Parris and his fellow merchants of Boston lacked ships for these voyages, they "hyred" Dutch skippers, such as Gerrard Lawler, master of the good ship *Hope* of Rotterdam. Edward Johnson had every right to exult in 1647 that "in a very little space, every thing in the country proved a staple-commodity," as New England fed, housed, and supplied the containers for their insular compatriots, making it possible for them to concentrate on the highly profitable manufacture of sugar.[41]

Ligon considered the proper feeding of servants and slaves a matter of the first importance in the management of a plantation and so advised any prospective planter from England. "You must be sure to have a Factor, both at New England and Virginia," he added, "to provide you of all Commodities those places afford, that are usefull to your plantation; or else your charge will be treble. As from New England, Beefe, Porke, Fish, of all sorts, dried and pickled; from Virginia live-Cattle, Beefe and Tobacco; for theirs at Barbados is the worst I think that growes in the world;

41. From 1647 to 1650, the *Aspinwall Notarial Records* show that fish of many kinds and provisions were being shipped not only to Barbados but to St. Christopher, Nevis, Montserrat, and Antigua. See *pari passu,* 11, 140, 164, 165, 174, 177, 215, 220, 225, 228–9, 255, 259, 411, 423. *Winthrop Papers,* V, 70–71; *Johnson's Wonder-Working Providence, 1620–1651,* ed. John F. Jameson (New York, 1910), 246–7. John Parris, a Boston merchant, first traded to Barbados, then acquired two plantations there and got into the slave trade to Guinea. When he died in 1660, he had three plantations, land at The Bridge, and a stone house at Reade's Bay. *Suffolk Deeds,* ed. William B. Trask (Boston, 1880), I, 119; Waters, *Genealogical Gleanings,* I, 143–4.

And for Cattle, no place lyes neerer to provide themselves, and the Virginians cannot have a better market to sell them; for an Oxe of 5£ price at Virginie, will yield 25£ there." [42]

The animals, vital to the success of the sugar industry, came from several lands. Dutch vessels transported asinegoes, camels, and oxen to the West Indies from Europe, Africa, or Virginia, and Curaçao. They were employed primarily for turning the rollers of the mills, but sometimes for riding. For heavy transport, where there were deep gullies, the planters used the sure-footed little donkey. As soon as the sugar mills required them, the New England farmers sent their surplus horses southward. In June 1648 the *Welcome* of Boston, 300 tons, rode in Charlestown Harbor, ready to sail for Barbados with eighty horses and 120 tons of ballast. Valentine Hill, a Boston merchant, owned a one-third share in a cargo of horses and other goods dispatched to the West Indies in 1649 in a Dutch vessel, with Paul Allestre as factor. From Barbados, Giles Sylvester wrote to his father in London in 1650 that poor horses would bring only 2400 pounds of sugar each, while a good one commanded 3000 pounds: "My brother Nathaniel is not come from [Shelter Island] New England as yet" with Connecticut horses. The sugar mills of the Caribbean thus provided an outlet for a new staple for the New Englanders, and by 1650 the farmers of Rhode Island and Connecticut were raising "naggs" for export to the island market.[43]

IV

Few if any of the economic activities of the first English settlements in the Caribbean had been planned in advance. Vague no-

42. Ligon, *Barbados,* 113.

43. New England ships in the West Indies trade at this time were often of no more than 15 or 20 tons burthen and seldom over 50, too small to carry many horses. Richard Malbone of New Haven bought a nag at Windsor in 1648 intending to ship it to Barbados, "but he was too big to goe into the vessell." Dutch ships of 200 to 300 tons had far better accommodations. *New Haven Records,* I, 419; *Winthrop's Journal,* II, 345–6; *Suffolk Deeds,* I, 106; Deane Phillips, "Horse Raising in Colonial New England," in Cornell University Agricultural Experiment Station, *Memoir,* 54 (1922), 890–97; Force, *Tracts,* II, No. 7, p. 5; Harlow, *Colonising Expeditions,* 52; Ligon, *Barbados,* 58.

tions governed the promoters and leaders of the colonies; at times they appeared incorrigibly romantic. All they did was to send out colonists with a supply of provisions to last until they should be self-sufficient. To the modern mind, habituated to all kinds of research and development, such an absence of foresight seems almost incredible. Alone of the parties that left England for America during the Great Migration, the Puritans who went to New England in 1629–30 made a sustained effort to plan and carry out a carefully reasoned theory of colonization.

Alternately hasty or impatient, sometimes wise and sometimes foolish, occasionally dilatory, the white settlers in the Caribbean Isles managed somehow to keep going from 1624 to 1640. To maintain that the white men made a success of their colonies prior to 1645 is to press the evidence too hard. Their numbers actually increased astonishingly after 1638, despite some heavy emigration. And amid political uncertainties in each island and civil strife at home, as well as insular failures of many kinds, these men, fresh from relatively civilized surroundings in salubrious Britain, did manage in some measure to adjust themselves and to make a living in the tropics. On the human side, they had found out by actual contact how to live with the Dutch, Irish, French, and Portuguese in their midst—though never with the Spanish. In a much different way, they devised rules of behavior by which the red men and the black had to live as inferiors with them.

Very little European agricultural lore and experience could be applied in the islands. The colonists had to begin anew and, as it were, go to school to the Indians, albeit with the greatest reluctance and disdain. Not that they ever admitted the fact, but by trial and error, and by imitation, by wholesale borrowing, the Europeans learned how to build Indians cabins, to sleep in Indian hammocks, to eat and ultimately to relish some Indian foods, and to befuddle themselves with Indian beverages, to hollow-out and travel in Indian canoes, and, beyond everything else, to plant and cultivate Indian tobacco and cotton as staples with which to make returns to Old-World merchants. By 1650, however, the white man had extorted from the Arawak and Carib all that he needed or wanted and had, by extermination, exorcised much of the tawny incubus. At the same time, he was beginning to use the members of another race, the black Africans, to perform the arduous labors he had formerly had to perform himself, but which were repugnant to the white man in tropical climates.

Largely by chance, the settlers hit upon a scheme of agriculture that may be said to represent a progressive technology. Tobacco required little more than careful hoeing and no processing before it was shipped off to market. Cotton represented a more complicated culture. The preparation of the indigo necessitated several intricate operations and a sizable investment in equipment before it was ready for market. But the making of merchantable Muscovado sugar was the crowning agricultural and industrial achievement of these early years in the West Indies.

The Englishmen could envisage a very profitable future ahead in 1650 as the sugar culture spread gradually from Barbados and St. Christopher to Nevis, Montserrat, and Antigua. Planters would grow, harvest, and carry on the manufacture of raw sugar in the islands, using a black labor force regularly replenished with importations of Negroes from West Africa. Both the masters and the slaves would be fed in large part by the auxiliary colonies of New England and the Chesapeake region, and to a much smaller degree, from nearby islands and the Main. Upon the forest civilization of New England, they would draw for the wood products they so signally lacked and which turned out to be superior to the kinds used in Brazil. Ingeniously the Caribbean English improved upon the Brazilian boiling furnaces and made them more resistant to fire. Their demonstrated mastery of the techniques of planting and processing sugar in so brief a time is the true accomplishment of these West Indians. In commenting upon the making of sugar, Richard Ligon perceived this clearly: "the right and best way they practised, when I left the Island . . . will admit of no greater or farther improvement." He was right, right as much about the organization and management of the entire industry as about sugar-growing and sugar manufacture, for the partnership with the Dutch completed the scheme of things.[44]

Although sugar was "the very soul of the place," thus far only a handful of the planters had amassed any wealth. But future ex-

44. Ligon, *Barbados,* 86.

pectations dazzled nearly all the rest. Englanders at home, Puritan and Cavalier alike, were rapidly realizing that westward in the islands new opportunities to invest a little capital and to reap large returns awaited them, and their representatives in Parliament were standing poised to oust the Dutch at the first opportunity. The total accomplishment was spectacular. It had been a remarkable adaptation against great odds, this transforming of uninhabited islands from a wild state into lucrative sugar-producing colonies in little more than twenty years, and without official support. The unsolved question was what kind of a society was possible for the West Indians—red, black, and white—and how successfully men and women could adapt themselves to it.

IV

Servile Islanders

NO FEATURE of English colonizing in vacant or recently emptied lands is more arresting than the rapidity with which the settlers endeavor to transfer and transplant the attitudes, customs, and institutions of the Mother Country to their new-found homes. Did not the Barbadians demonstrate this when they prematurely called their island "Little England"? Their insistence upon ways and things British was due in part to nostalgia for the remembered sociability of their rural villages, loneliness for the homely and the intimate. An inbred yearning and capacity for self-government, as well as habit, and a pressing need for self-reliance, all combined to impel the colonists to try to create a familiar civilization in an unfamiliar land, characteristics not found to the same degree among the Dutch, French, or Spanish. Nor can the significant contributions of a few, and absolutely necessary, leaders be overlooked. Many a younger son of good birth and some able men from the middling sort of Britons, who emigrated imbued with the expectation of rising to power and prestige while winning their way to wealth, attempted to establish law and hierarchy in colonial life such as they had known in England.

A baffling environment, unsettled political conditions, and above all, the absence of the great English institution of the family, to which the puritan colonists showed a more lasting attachment than any other white inhabitants, made for a slower transit of English civilization to the islands than to New England. It was, perhaps, even slower than in Virginia or Maryland because of the long, discouraging search for a profitable staple. In one or two respects, however, the transplantation may have been easier than for the Saints of New England, for life in the Lesser Antilles was fundamentally rural and agricultural, and familiar medieval landed ideals governed every activity. Along the littoral of every island as late as 1650, small tracts of land up to thirty acres in extent, each farmed by a freeholder and several white servants, predominated. Although all freeholders were *planters* in the contemporary sense, only a tiny minority of them lived on large estates, or *plantations,* as they were beginning to be called. Save at The Indian Bridge in Barbados, villages and towns failed to develop, and the state of the population was, at best, a transitory one. But the all-embracing difficulty was that of incomplete adjustment to the New World. A society resembling any in the Old World cannot be said to have been formed.[1]

II

Any discussion of the inhabitants of the Caribbee islands must be based upon very few sources, but in every one of them it is obvious that here were rural populations whose members had grown up in a land where degree and station were the norm and who desired to establish them intact and without alteration as soon as possible. Habituated to the Roman Catholic hierarchical discipline, the Irish, who had come by 1645 to constitute the largest proportion of the whites, unquestioningly acceded to these ideas. But what no colonist grasped was that in the West Indies, from the very inception of every colony, social conditions would inexorably

1. A useful comparison may be made with the French colonial family. Rochefort said of St. Christopher before 1658, that the English had superior houses, better furnished, than those of his countrymen because of "their constant abode" in the island and the significant fact that most of them were married and took "greater pains to supply themselves with all things requisite then those . . . who lead single lives, as most of the French do." Davies, *Caribby-Islands,* 177–8. For the Old-World differences between English and French families, compare *Vexed and Troubled Englishmen,* 27–41, 83–91, 140–41, 312–13; and Joan Thirsk in *Past and Present,* No. 27 (1964), 120–22; with the classic French treatment by Phillippe Ariès, *Centuries of Childhood* (New York, 1962).

force a fundamental alteration or mutation of the ancient scheme of rank and position.

During the thirties, as the reputation of the Caribbees as a refuge or as lands of promise progressively worsened with the better sort of prospective colonists in Britain, authorities agreed that the quality of the English servants steadily degenerated. Competition with the mainland colonies for indentured servants intensified, and more and more peasants were recruited in Ireland. When the price paid by merchants and ships' captains for servants delivered by peddlers and "spirits" rose from 18*s.* to 22*s.* a head, these procurers, eager to capitalize on a rising market, paid less and less attention to the kinds of human beings they tempted into going to the plantations or to the propriety of the means by which they persuaded them to sign labor covenants. From Barbados in April 1642 Thomas Verney wrote his father asking him to round up 100 men "with the great help of bridwell and the prisons." Recognizing officially "a great want of servants" in the plantations, the House of Lords acted in 1647 to encourage the transporting of English emigrants, provided that they were neither forced into going nor apprentices nor "children under age admitted without express consent of the parents." [2]

It is extremely doubtful if any of the young men who were lured into signing up as indentured servants had any realization of the conditions under which they were going to live and work in the islands. Granted that they came from poor backgrounds, were accustomed to plain food, and had, perhaps, heard sailors tell of the hardships of life at sea, they nevertheless thought themselves capable of handling whatever demands would be made of them in the New World. Alas for them, they had not reckoned on how debilitating the cramped quarters and foul air for weeks on end could be, or the seasickness, or the insufficient and bad rations. Many of them suffered strains and bruises from being thrown against

2. Newton, *Colonising Activities of the English Puritans,* 169*n;* BM: Egerton MSS, 2395, fol. 277; *Memoirs of the Verney Family,* I, 154; Stock, *Debates,* I, 185–6. The indenture and the process of covenanting in England are described in *Vexed and Troubled Englishmen,* 172–3, 420–21. For a parallel difficulty in procuring servants in France, see Pelleprat, *Relation,* 21–2; and Debien, *Les Engagés,* 34–46, 98–140.

bulkheads and stanchions during heavy weather. More often than not the men, for most of the servants were males, arrived at their destination weakened, unnerved, and utterly unfit to start in on the hard physical labor for which they had covenanted.

When the ship arrived at Barbados or St. Christopher, the planters were waiting, eager to go aboard and buy the time of such of the miserable passengers as would suit their needs, usually for £6 apiece, which represented a handsome profit for the shippers. Ordinarily the newly arrived servant would be taken off promptly to a farm, where he might be one of several servants or the sole one and where he would work along with his master; or else he might be taken to a large plantation having from twenty to a hundred servants. Planters, great and small, put most of their capital into indentured servants and were commonly determined to get the most out of their investments. With unbelievable shortsightedness, they allowed the poor wretches no time to recover from the effects of the crossing or to adjust to the new environment and enervating climate but put them to work immediately. A bell rang at six o'clock the next morning, and out to the fields went the new hands. There they toiled in the sun under the direction of a master of a small freehold or the supervision of an overseer until eleven when the bell rang again and they returned to their huts for a "dinner" of strange foods—loblolly, bonavist, or sweet potatoes. At one in the afternoon they had to go back to the fields and work until six o'clock. The night meal was the same as the one at midday, far from nourishing or satisfying. They were probably too tired to resent having to sleep in a hammock instead of a bed.[3]

The only possessions a servant had, unless he had practiced a trade or had special skills, was a suit of ill-fitting clothes provided when he signed his indenture. In the fields he wore the standard West Indian garb of a shirt and drawers of linen, and shoes, which seldom lasted more than a month. Although the master and overseers had broad-brimmed hats to protect them from the sun, the flat, round, knitted Monmouth cap, which was tight-fitting and totally unsuited for wear in the tropics, was allotted to the servants.

3. Ligon, *Barbados,* 44; Hall, *First Settlements . . . of Barbados,* 8. For similar conditions in French arrivals at Guadeloupe in 1647, see Debien, *Les Engagés,* 253.

When the laborers came back from the fields at the end of their day's work, dripping with perspiration or soaked from working in the rain, they had no change of clothes. If they removed their garments, insects bit them unmercifully and the cool night struck into them with the result that those having weak constitutions easily fell sick, and not a few of them succumbed.[4]

Work in the tobacco, cotton, and sugar fields was both monotonous and exhausting. Answering people who thought cultivating tobacco was easy, one observer remarked: "if they had themselves seen the poor Servants who are . . . expos'd the greatest part of the day to the scorching heat of the Sun, and spending one half of the night reducing it to that posture wherein it is transported to Europe," they would harbor different ideas about "the sweat and labours of so many miserable creatures." Hoeing, weeding, grubbing, worming, picking cotton and tobacco, bagging and barreling, performing the many operations in growing and processing sugar, and, above everything else, the hand-blistering, back-breaking work of clearing the wild jungle were some of the many tasks that soft and inexperienced young men and boys were put to; weeding seems to have been the principal field work for women servants.[5]

The terms of service stipulated in the indentures varied with the nature and skills of the servants, their ages and sex, and with the supply of labor available. Lads under eighteen ordinarily served for seven years or until they reached twenty-one, like apprentices in England, and less time if they were older. At Bristol, Joseph Whettal of Shropshire bound himself to Thomas Heathcote to serve in any of the Caribbees for seven years after his arrival there. In consideration for this, the merchant allowed him meat, drink, apparel, and lodging "according to the Custom of the Country" during his servitude; and at the completion of his time, Heathcote promised Whettal vendible commodities worth £10 sterling. This servant was carried in the *Jonathan* to Barbados where the captain

4. For Monmouth caps, "the headgear of colonization," see *Vexed and Troubled Englishmen,* 215–16; Uchteritz, *Kurze Reise,* 8; Ligon, *Barbados,* 8, 44, 114–15; Harlow, *Colonising Expeditions,* 51; *APC Col.,* I, 270, 273; Davis Coll., VII, Envelope 2.
5. Davies, *Caribby-Islands,* 192; Ligon, *Barbados,* 44.

sold him, probably for the usual £6. Two French boys, Peter and Nicolas Pulveset, with seven years to serve, were sold with a tract of fifteen acres in Barbados by Alexander Lindsay in 1640. These terms and conditions were standard for the West Indies.[6]

Sometimes a planter needed laborers so badly that he did as Robert Lea did when he contracted with John Burroughs to bring over by May 1, 1645, six able men to serve him six, five, or four years, as it could be arranged, "but all were to be not under eighteen or above thirty years of age." Lea promised to pay £46 10*s.* and each servant was to be furnished with one suit of clothes besides the one he brought with him.[7]

In 1647 Richard Ligon stated that "according to the Law of the Iland," the term of each servant was five years, but the author of the "Briefe Description" of 1650 gave four years as "the Custome for a Christian servant," and apparently these terms applied to both males and females, whatever their nationality. But to the newly inducted servant, the very prospect of the smallest term must have been depressing, even under a reasonable overseer or a benign master. Throughout this whole period many a forlorn soul, standing on the shore at eventide and gazing sadly out across the blue water, must have longed for the friendly little village somewhere in England or Ireland, which he or she would never see again.[8]

Men who knew West Indian life at first hand agreed that during their years of servitude, the white servants, in contrast to the Negro slaves, "have the worser lives, for they are put to very hard labour, ill lodging, and their dyet [is] very sleight." In most instances, those who worked on small estates under freeholders, who employed but five or ten servants and labored along with them, stood a better chance for decent treatment. On the other hand, nobody could have been a more vicious taskmaster than a recently

6. Unscrupulous masters resorted to every kind of pretext to keep servants in bondage, sometimes doubling their period of service. An act of October 1652 stated that all servants brought from England who were under 18 years of age should serve 7 years, and those over 18 should serve 5 years. *Acts and Statutes of Barbados* (Jennings), 15–16; Davis Coll., I, Deed of Dec. 14, 1640; VII, Envelopes 5, 22.

7. Davis Coll., VII, Envelope 22.

8. Ligon, *Barbados,* 43; Harlow, *Colonising Expeditions,* 44.

freed small planter trying desperately to get established by endeavoring to get every penny out of his investment in labor. Surely few overseers surpassed the ferocity of Francis Leaven and his brother-in-law Ensign Samuel Hodgkins who "did inhumanly and unchristianlike torture John Thomas, a Servant, by hanging him up by the hands and putting fired matches between his fingers, whereby he hath lost the use of several joints, and is in great danger to lose the use of his right hand." After hearing this case, the Council of Barbados ordered the two freemen to pay Thomas 10,000 pounds of cotton "apiece," free him immediately, and Leaven was to "take a speedy course for his cure." Hodgkins was sent to jail. Still we doubt whether such prompt and severe justice did much to assuage the poor man's agony.[9]

"As for the usage of the Servants, it is much as the Master is mercifull or cruell," but on the larger plantations the master's mercy did not always extend as far as the fields. Twenty or more servants laboring under the supervision of an overseer led the most wearisome and miserable lives. One had no choice but to do as he was told and hope that somehow he would get through ten working hours each day. If a servant complained, the overseer would beat him; if he resisted, the master might double his time in bondage. "I have seen one Overseer beat a Servant with a cane about the head, till the blood has followed, for a fault that is not worth the speaking of; and yet he must have patience, or worse will follow. Truly [Ligon continued] I have seen such cruelty there done to Servants, as I did not think one Christian could have done to another." In this harsh judgment Père Biët fully concurred: "All are very badly treated. When they work the overseers, who act like those in charge of galley slaves, are always close by with a stick with which they often prod them when they do not work as fast as is desired." The cost in lives of such inhuman treatment is incalculable, but it was very, very high.[10]

Certain human beings will not yield to authority no matter how brutally it is administered; they do not lose their spirit, they rebel. Among the white servants of the English colonies were men with the capacity to lead and sufficiently imbued with resentment to

9. Ligon, *Barbados,* 44; Davis Coll., VII, Envelopes 14, 22.
10. Ligon, *Barbados,* 44; Biët, *Voyage,* 290; *Acts of Barbados* (Hall), 3.

unite their fellows against the masters. During the Spanish attack on St. Christopher in 1629, the servants "proved treacherous" by deserting their masters and swimming to the Spanish ships to give Don Fadrique de Toledo information concerning "in what case our Islands stood." Sir Henry Colt believed in 1631 that the island could be well defended "if the men servants who are the greatest number could be brought to fight." When Father Andrew White reached Barbados in January 1634 he discovered 800 men of the militia in arms: "The servants of the Iland had conspired to kill their masters and make themselves free, and soe goe to sea." One of them turned informer, and the Brothers Weston were seized; one of them was executed as an example. Thus rigorously was the first rebellion suppressed.[11]

There took place at Barbados in 1649 "such a combination" of servants "as the like was never seen there before." So acutely had their sufferings increased and so widely had "the intollerable burdens they labour'd under" been bruited about, that some of them "whose spirits were not able to endure such slavery, resolved to break through it, or die in the act. . . ." They proceeded to conspire with those of their acquaintance whose sufferings equaled their own and drew "many of the discontented party into this plot." A day was set for the rebels to fall upon their masters, cut their throats, and become "not only freemen, but Masters of the Iland." The plot, carefully kept a secret until the day before the outbreak, was revealed by a servant to Justice Hethersoll, his master. The planters were aroused and eighteen of the "contrivers" were summarily executed as a warning against future uprisings.[12]

Even though open and organized rebellion seldom occurred, unrest among white servants was more or less chronic. As the abortive law of 1644 against bringing in Irish servants implied, the

11. Harlow, *Colonising Expeditions,* xxiii, 10, 87; *Narratives of Early Maryland,* 34.

12. A more skulking way to even accounts with the hated masters was to set fire to their cane fields. James Holdip and Constant Sylvester had cane-fires costing them £10,000 sterling in 1650. Whether or not mistreatment of servants caused these two incidents is not known, but Ligon testified that several masters had so mistreated their servants as to provoke retaliation. Ligon, *Barbados,* 45–6; Schomburgk erroneously ascribed the servile revolt of 1649 to African slaves. *History of Barbados,* 267.

sons and daughters of Erin were looked upon as undependables and malingerers, or even more dangerous types, but the same charges could have been leveled against many of the English and other nationalities. Planters and overseers had to keep a weather eye on all of their small craft lest runaway servants steal them and flee the island.[13]

Towards 1650, as "discreeter and better natur'd men" came to rule, some commentators thought that the miseries of white servants eased somewhat. Possibly a stronger reason for less heartless treatment was the marked decline of the servile white population brought about by heavy mortality and migration which left the ranks of the insular militias much depleted. In any case, on some of the great plantations servants now slept in hammocks slung in warm, dry rooms, and those who came in wet had a shift of shirts and drawers. Colonel Humphrey Walrond, seeing his servants all wet through with sweat or rain, sent over to England for "rug Gownes, such as poor people wear in Hospitalls." The Cavalier planter and others were learning too that by feeding their servants fruit, vegetables, salted beef, and a little Irish butter several times a week they got more work out of them. Such concern on the part of Walrond won him the devotion and respect of his grateful laborers, but enlightened treatment of this sort had not become the general rule by the end of the period, because the small planter, who actually lived little better than his servants, could not afford it.[14]

Brutal, rigorous, and discouraging as the term of bondage was, now and then there emerged from a faceless mass of servile laborers a sturdy individual who, by mere chance or good management, made a career, sometimes a name, for himself. In their wills, kind and grateful masters occasionally left legacies to faithful servants. William Beresford, surgeon, directed in 1650 that "my Servant Andrew Bayley have his freedom with my Phisicke

13. *Acts of Barbados* (Hall), 35.
14. Richard Ligon's scheme for a plantation of 500 acres with 30 white servants and 30 black slaves called for stockings for both men and women, as well as several "shifts" of other clothing, rug gowns, and 12 pairs of shoes for each servant every year. For food they were to have salted beef and pork, salt fish, and "500 poor Johns from New England." Ligon, *Barbados,* 44, 113, 114.

bookes, linen and woollen cloathes." Thus equipped and presumably trained, Bayley could set up in practice for himself. Big, bad, bold Henry Morgan began his flamboyant career as a youthful servant of fifteen in Barbados in 1650.

> I'm going to be a pirate with a bright brass pivot gun,
> And an island in the Spanish main beyond the setting sun,
> And a silver flagon full of red wine to drink when work is done,
> Like a fine old salt-sea scavinger, like a tarry Buccaneer.

He ended up a rich man, lieutenant governor, then senior member of the council, and commander-in-chief of the forces of Jamaica—and also a knight.[15]

In no instance did the element of chance figure so prominently as with Heinrich von Uchteritz of Meissen, who was one of the prisoners taken at Worcester in 1651. Later, in London, Oliver Cromwell announced that "he was of a mind to give us sugar to eat . . . and that is what happened." After three months in prison, 1300 Royalists were shipped off to Barbados. There the young German and nineteen of his comrades were purchased for 800 pounds of sugar each by "Graf" Jabez Whitaker, one of the richest planters, who was not a count as Uchteritz thought but "a Christian" and a gentleman. On his first day at the plantation near The Hole, Uchteritz writes, "I, for my part, had to sweep the courtyard . . . feed the swine the next, and thereafter carry out all sorts of tasks which befit the slaves." But at least he was not sent out to work in the cane fields. After eighteen long weeks of "miserable life in such servitude," Uchteritz learned of the arrival of several ships from Hamburg. He implored his master to let him go so that he might see his parents and fatherland again. A Cavalier officer confirmed his assertion that he came from a good family, and Whitaker agreed to let him go when the merchants of one of the ships purchased his time for 800 pounds of sugar (which was later recovered in Hamburg from his family). Uchteritz came close to the truth when he wrote of his experience in the *Kurze Reise* that of the 1300 prisoners Oliver Cromwell exiled to the Carib-

15. Davis Coll., XV, Index to Wills, Sept. 19, 1650; J. H. Parry and P. M. Sherlock, *A Short History of the West Indies* (2d ed., New York, 1968), 85; *Dictionary of National Biography*, XXXIX, 17, q.v. Henry Morgan.

bean, "no one but myself, as far as I know came out again." [16]

What little we can learn about women servants indicates that their fate was usually somewhat better than that of the men. Not all of them had to work in the fields; some of them were "house women," who were favored in many ways. Women servants seem to have been issued ample clothing: they had smocks, waistcoats, coiffes or caps, and shoes provided for them in Ligon's plan. All but the very worst or ill-favored of the women must have had opportunities to marry in these overwhelmingly male settlements. George Haddock, a freeman of Barbados, covenanted with a gentleman-planter, William Light, in June 1640, "to serve for Anne Mitchell who is now my wife," for the remainder of her time "for which she came over" on December 8, 1637. All in all, the single woman could look ahead to her freedom, a prospect denied the unmarried man.[17]

Of all the white servants, the most fortunate were those artisans trained in one of the crafts needed in the islands: carpenters, joiners, coopers, smiths, masons, bricklayers, tailors. A journeyman in any one of them could indenture himself voluntarily in order to get to the West Indies and, when his term was up, succeed in finding employment as a master craftsman. M. Bigot, one of Père Biët's party, had two trades which brought him a great many customers and won for him the friendship of important people. He began in Barbados working for "a very fashionable French tailor," and in a brief time had earned 500 pounds of sugar, which helped to pay his passage back to France. He was also skilled in repairing watches, at which he made even more money. The number of timepieces brought to him to be put back in running order is a telling index of the affluent state of the sugar planters. The priest remarks that several of his party's *engagés* who knew different trades "made good money." Some of them earned as much as twenty-five or thirty pounds of sugar a day, and most of them used it to buy their freedom.[18]

16. Uchteritz, *Kurze Reise,* 3–10.

17. Ligon, *Barbados,* 115; Davis Coll., VII, Envelope 22.

18. When Witham Hall, Barbados, was sold in 1646, fifteen white servants went with it: Jeremy Axam, James Neale, Teague McShane, Dermond Butler, Hugh Clarke, Damish Bryant (carpenter), Henry Spong (bricklayer), James Browne,

Every year a class of servants graduated, as it were, from the servile state. Years of labor in bondage had paid for the passage of each one from Europe and enabled him to learn a little something about growing tobacco, cotton, indigo, or sugar. To each one, after the custom of the country, masters gave £10 in local commodities and, in some cases, a suit of clothes, and turned them loose to shift for themselves.

In the first decade at Barbados, and presumably at St. Christopher, freedmen received small grants of three to five acres of land. In some instances the indenture specified some land as part of the freedom dues. In *Certain Inducements to Well Minded People* (Puritans, that is), Daniel Gookin advertised as late as 1645 for people in straitened circumstances because of the decay of trade or injured by the "Cavaliers" to go to the West Indies. One of the inducements was the promise that when their term of servitude was up, each one would be allotted six acres within four miles of a town, or sixty acres somewhere farther off. Like Governor Bell's earlier intention, this proposal was apparently never put into practice, and in 1648 Sir Edmund Plowden said of Barbados: "Here was no store of land for our 100 men and their families. . . ." The same situation existed in St. Christopher. The Earl of Carlisle had hoped to ease the shortage of land for freemen by handing out tracts in Nevis and Antigua, but migration there required considerable expenditures for passage, provisions, and tools, which men without credit could not afford. Servants in bondage received from their masters at least a minimum of patriarchal protection, but when freedom came, more than one must have looked ahead and asked himself rhetorically: "Freedom for what?" [19]

III

Most of the English who had earned freedom by service found that it brought great hazards as well as opportunities, and it was

---

Edmund Spillane, Henry Parker (tailor), Christopher Lumers (shoemaker), Eleanor Tompkins (maid servant), Thomas Berry, Ambrose Parker, and John Goodson. For the fifteen, there are "13 Narrow Hamocks." Davis Coll., VII, Envelope 14; Biët, *Voyage,* 276–7.

19. [Daniel Gookin] *Certain Inducements to Well Minded People to Transport themselves to the West Indies* (London, 1645), 17–18, 22; Force, *Tracts,* II, No. 7, p. 5; Carlisle, *A Declaration.*

very difficult to balance the two. For the Irish, shackled by their faith, a telltale brogue, and their general reputation, whether deserved or not, it must have been doubly hard. In all ages, including the present, only a small percentage of human beings willingly accept responsibility, let alone seek it out. It was not a mere simple matter of joining or of being absorbed into a community for those newly freed men. The large majority of ex-servants were young people who had never really been on their own before and whose knowledge of planting was very limited. Furthermore, at no time after 1640 in either Barbados or St. Christopher, and probably Nevis, was there any land cheap enough for a man to purchase with his freedom dues of £10. The dreams and hopes that had encouraged these men to emigrate failed to materialize, and the vast majority never became landholders in the Caribbean.

In view of all the circumstances, it should not surprise us that throughout the forties in both St. Christopher and Barbados there existed large numbers of "loose, idle, vagrant persons," whose condition stemmed not so much from sloth or sluggishness as from "a decay of their spirits by long and tedious labour" capped by the inability of many of them to gain a livelihood. Thieving was a natural concomitant of such an economic predicament: hungry men took to stealing "Fowls, Hogs, Sheep, Cattel, Cotton, Tobacco, Sugar, Indico, Ginger, Money, Cloathes," and provisions of all sorts from plantations. If convicted, hired-men or servants had to serve the despoiled masters an additional three years without salary. Migration to undeveloped islands provided a way out for the venturesome and energetic freemen, but their departure in considerable numbers from 1640 onward from the parent islands must not be permitted to obscure the far more significant fact that economic and social conditions in the oldest islands created the greatest concentration of poverty-stricken freemen in any of England's dominions before 1776.[20]

Opportunities did arise for some of the servants fortunate enough

20. Rather than hire freemen, planters preferred to import more servants: they were cheaper, healthier, and more willing to work. See permits for two Bristol merchants and one Londoner to carry 500 peasants from any Irish port to the Caribbees in 1652. *CSPC, 1574–1660,* p. 387. For a New England servant bound to serve for two years in Barbados in 1646, *Aspinwall Notarial Records,* 39; Ligon, *Barbados,* 41; *Acts and Statutes of Barbados* (Jennings), 18, 39–40, 46.

to have served as "sub-overseers" to become salaried overseers of white servants or black slaves upon release from bondage. Also, those who had learned and practiced skills on plantations could earn livings when freed; some of the artisans in Barbados moved to The Indian Bridge to set up as independent craftsmen. Without any of these qualifications, however, and faced with what seemed to be insurmountable barriers, almost the only way the landless freedman could maintain himself was to hire out to his former master or some other planter as an overseer, asinego-driver, faller of trees, "or other whatsoever," which meant being a field worker and no better off than a servant. Where and how such hired-men lived on the low wages paid to them is not recorded, but the chances are that in many instances life was, at best, precarious.[21]

Until 1645 there were always some freeholders added each year to the old-timers who had received small grants in the thirties. Many of the new proprietors managed to get credit, first from the Dutch merchants and factors, and then from resident planters of rich estate who made a good thing out of financing their needy neighbors. Having borrowed to acquire land, tools, buildings, and especially servants, they set up as small planters and proceeded to raise staple crops suited to small-scale agriculture on their five to thirty acres. They deemed that "it was only proper to rayse so much Tobacco, Cotton, ginger, and such like as would just afforde the Inhabitants a Livelyhood." According to a muster-roll seen by John Scott, Barbados contained 11,200 proprietors in 1645 but thereafter the yeomanry began to shrink rapidly. Famine and disease struck down thousands in 1647 and 1648, and the total mortality in white men and women in only five years was the greatest of the entire seventeenth century in the West Indies. How many freeholders remained in the two larger islands in 1650 cannot now be gauged with any accuracy.[22]

Many of the new freeholders faced financial ruin as the forties advanced, for they had incurred debts larger than they could repay during a time of falling prices of the staples they raised. Thousands of them disposed of their land to more prosperous planters. George Adams was one of these; he sold his twelve acres in 1643. They were moving to New England, Virginia, and other islands in the

21. *Acts and Statutes of Barbados* (Jennings), 18.
22. BM: Sloane MSS, 3662, fols. 60a, 54b.

hope of re-establishing themselves. Some of the debtors ran away to avoid paying what they owed to merchants and to each other.[23]

There were very few avenues open to the freemen who failed to earn the livelihood they had gambled on. Many of those who lacked skills sold themselves back into servitude to satisfy their creditors. In consideration of a release from a bill for 1000 pounds of cotton due, Peter Crosland agreed to serve John Barton in Barbados from April 20, 1640, to April 21, 1641. Ricketts Meloe bound himself as a servant to Mills Morant, surgeon, for sixteen months in default of paying 600 pounds of cotton for credit or medical services in 1640 or to give the surgeon some other satisfaction. About this time John Nile, "Planter," contracted to serve Alexander Glover for one complete year; he was to pay for all his clothes, necessaries, and charges himself. Whether Nile owed money to Glover or merely sought some way to live is not clear. John Keyes covenanted to work two years "in such lawfull imployment and service" as Paul White thought fit to satisfy an unpaid debt of 4000 pounds of tobacco. To men such as these, voluntary servitude seemed preferable to imprisonment for debt. The Assembly of Barbados, recognizing "the extreme poverty of several poor persons . . . and their inability to satisfy their several Creditors, and [that] by reason thereof [they] suffer long and tedious imprisonment, without any hope of relief," passed an act in February 1651 directing that such debtors be bound out to serve any creditor who would give the greatest wages per month until payment was made for debts not exceeding 2000 pounds of sugar.[24]

Economic and social conditions denied most of the comforts and all of the amenities to those hard-pressed freeholders who managed to hang on during the forties. Ligon characterized their dwellings as "rather like stoves then houses," in which neither the owners nor anyone else would remain for long without sweltering. "So loath are poor people to part with that, which is their next immediate help" that they, and some rich planters too, would not spare their servants' labor to erect better abodes. After storms demolished many of the old huts—particularly the hurricanes of

23. Davis Coll., VII, Envelope 14; BM: Sloane MSS, 3662, fol. 62; Foster, *Late Horrid Rebellion*, A-4.

24. Davis Coll., VII, Envelope 22; *Acts of Barbados* (Hall), 16.

1642, which razed thousands of flimsy shacks on St. Christopher and Nevis—better houses did replace them. And those planters who had accumulated wealth in the thirties had already replaced the temporary cabins of their early days in the settlements with permanent frame houses sheathed with cedar plank, and some of them had roofs of ironwood shingles instead of the old familiar thatch.[25]

Household furnishings were still meager, consisting of necessities only. The inventory of John Higginbotham, made in 1643, mentions only sieves, lamps, pewter platters, tubs, trays, two runlets, and some "smythes tooles." When Captain Philip Bell bought a fifty-acre estate, "Cannoe Hill," the only things in the house were tables, frames, forms, and benches, and "one room with appurtenances, 2 pairs of cards, and 3 cedar Tubbs." No tools, and no hammocks remained if they had once been there. Some of the planters lighted their houses with new wax candles they made from materials brought in from Africa; there was no beeswax in the islands. The small freeholder had to be satisfied with imported tallow candles that lumped together in the heat.[26]

For the ordinary planter and the island's yeomanry, life was very primitive; it took hard labor merely to survive. Family life was lacking for the vast majority, because women were few, and children are not mentioned in the surviving records. As late as 1647 most planters did not have meat twice a week, and freemen ate the same monotonous, unsavory, and poorly balanced meals

25. *CSPC, 1574–1660,* p. 529; Ligon, *Barbados,* 41, 102.

26. Samuel Vassall and two associates took over in 1634 a plantation whose inventory reveals the sparseness of a male establishment: firearms, sword, pots, kettles, 1 hand-mill to grind cassava or maize, a scales, 24 wooden trenchers, 2 pewter salts, 4 hoops, 2 spits, 4 iron wedges, 2 baking pans, a hammer, a fire shovel, 1 iron lamp, 1 pair of tongs, 3 hammocks, 1 bill, and 2 old table cloths. With the plantation also went Bernard Jemmott, a bound overseer, Thomas Williams, a servant, "An Old Woman Servant," and the indentures of five other bound whites. The owner must have been a devout, literate Anglican, for he possessed "a Booke of Common Prayer," "The Practice of Piety," and a "Book of Homilies." Listed in a deed of sale of a 40-acre plantation in August 1643 are 1 iron kettle, 1 brass kettle, 2 pewter dishes, 12 pewter spoons, 9 trenchers, 1 wooden tray, 1 milk pail, 2 tables, 1 form, 1 old cask, 1 jar, 1 wash tub, 2 bills, 2 hatchets, 4 muskets and 1 old gun, 1 old sword, 3 bandoliers, 2 hammocks, and 1 trough. Davis Coll., II, Envelope 26; VII, Envelope 5; Ligon, *Barbados,* 30; *CSPC, 1661–68,* p. 529.

they handed out to their servants. There being no leisure, recreation and play were out of the question, unless heavy drinking of mobbie or rum in the evenings be so counted.

IV

The number of white men released from bondage each year did not reduce the servile population of the Caribbees, for, with the importing of slaves from Africa, it actually increased. Only the composition of the population changed. Dutch merchants had very early persuaded those planters with money and credit that a black slave, who would serve for his lifetime, would be cheaper in the long run than a white servant bound for only five years. Consequently the blacks, first used about 1643 to raise tobacco, cotton, and indigo, were purchased in ever larger numbers as sugar became the prime staple in the islands. According to John Scott, Barbados contained 5680 slaves in 1645; unquestionably the white man still predominated in the West Indies at that time.[27]

One hundred ships a year, or thereabouts, came to Barbados with servants and slaves in the late forties. From the Dutch slavers the planters bought men or women from £27 to £30, and children for smaller sums. In terms of sugar, a prime male slave cost about 1000 to 1100 pounds of that staple. Père Biët estimated that the annual maintenance of each slave amounted to only one-twenty-fifth of the profit he or she earned for the master. This may be somewhat low, but there can be no doubt that slaves cost far less and were a better investment than servants.[28]

Slaves fresh from West Africa knew next to nothing about

27. Next to nothing is known about slavery in the Leeward Islands. Reporting to John Winthrop, Jr., on the West Indies as a whole in August 1645, George Downing concluded that "a man that will settle ther must looke to procure servants which if you could gett out of England for 6 or 8 or 9 yeares time onely paying their passage . . . it would do very well, for so therby you shall be able to doe somthing upon a plantation, and in short tim be able with good husbandry to procure Negroes (the life of the place) out of the encrease of your owne plantation." *Winthrop Papers,* V, 43–4; BM: Sloane MSS, 3662, fol. 54; Ligon, *Barbados,* 46–7.

28. The African background of the slave trade, the notorious Middle Passage, and the English slave traffic will be considered in Chapter VIII; Ligon, *Barbados,* 40, 44, 46–7; Harlow, *Colonising Expeditions,* 44; Biët, *Voyage,* 290.

West Indian staples or how to cultivate them. They had to be taught their tasks by sign language principally, for they could not speak the tongue of their masters or even of their fellow slaves, so many dialects there were among them. In handling their slaves, the Barbadians appear to have followed practices they had noted in Brazil and which were used by the Portuguese planters there. As for the slaves, they had to submit to the strange new discipline of responding to the bell, working ten hours a day, and performing every kind of task in the fields. Many of them also proved to be adept at the work of the ingenio. Their women, even when pregnant, labored, for the most part at weeding—"a stooping and painful work." A woman had a fortnight to recover her strength after childbirth and then, carrying her child on her back, she returned to the field and resumed weeding.[29]

At all of their labors, in these years, the slave and white servant worked together without any distinction being made of race or task, but commentators in the West Indies seem to agree that, because they had paid a bigger price for a slave, the planters treated the black better than they did their "Christian" white servant. Even the Negroes recognized this and did not hesitate to show their contempt for those white men who, they could see, were worse off than themselves—Barbados and St. Christopher, and Nevis had their "Po' Buckras" long before they appeared in the Carolina Low Country.[30]

The greatest single advantage the black had was his family. If it had been broken up in Africa by war or by native black slave traders, the planters wisely and actively sought spouses for men who had lost their wives or who were unmarried, for experience showed that the married men were more contented and better workers. The result was that every plantation with adult slaves also had black women and children. "The small Negroes and Negresses go about completely naked until they are fourteen or fifteen years of age." The men went around entirely naked except for a loincloth, save on Sunday when they put on "some

29. Ligon, *Barbados,* 47–8.

30. Buckra: white man, possibly from *bockorau,* an African word, later meaning buccaneer. *South Carolina Gazette,* April 23, 1727.

worthless breeches and a shirt. . . ." In Ligon's plan, drawn up in 1650, each year three pairs of canvas drawers were provided for every man and two petticoats for every woman.[31]

On some of the best plantations there were framed houses with plank sidings for the field hands, but ordinarily, not far from the mansion house, were small cabins, "none above six foot square," where the slaves lived. "Built of inferior wood, almost like dog huts, and covered with leaves from trees which they call plantain, which is very broad and almost shelf-like and serves very well against rain," each one was occupied by a Negro family. Aside from the fact that the blacks did not sleep in hammocks but on boards laid on the dirt floor, these quarters, which Uchteritz describes, were the same as the ones in which the white servants slept. Slaves also had small gardens, which they cultivated on Sunday, their free day, and grew yams, maize, and other edibles; they were also permitted to raise their own poultry so that they might have eggs for their children. In the absence of meat, careful masters gave out portions of salted West Indian turtle and New England mackerel or "poor John" with the weekly ration of plantain. Père Biët was probably right in maintaining that no nation fed its slaves as badly as the English, but except in a very few cases the blacks ate as well as, and sometimes better than, the mass of white servants—and many freemen.[32]

Now and then the records afford us brief glances at some of the human aspects of Negro slavery that we are denied of white servitude. Nearly all of the slaves lived together on large plantations, whereas most of the white servants belonged to little groups working on small farms. The blacks were, in general, clean about their persons. Even though they lacked soap, they would repair to ponds, often in companies, and wash themselves during the hottest weather.

31. Uchteritz, *Kurze Reise,* 8; Biët, *Voyage,* 274–5, 290.

32. M. Debien has pointed out that the food and diet problem of the blacks is central to the story of colonial slavery. The French planters did not feed turtle meat to their slaves before 1660. Gabriel Debien, "La Nourriture des esclaves sur les plantations des Antilles françaises aux XVIIe et XVIIIe siècles," in *Caribbean Studies,* IV (1964), 3–5; Uchteritz, *Kurze Reise,* 5; Biët, *Voyage,* 5, 290–91; Ligon, *Barbados,* 113; and for illustrations of Brazilian slave cabins, Larsen, *Frans Post,* plates 27, 34, 35.

Ligon shuddered at this practice, for the water from the same ponds was used for drinking and cooking. Those who lived near the shore, bathed in the ocean. Better swimmers than the white servants, they loved to disport themselves in the sea. Inveterately fond of dancing and their African rhythms, they frolicked together whenever possible. Some of the Barbadian slaves who had lived among the Portuguese were adept at singing and fencing with the rapier or playing "very skilfully" with the dagger.[33]

Like the white servants, the black slaves suffered abuse, mistreatment, and worse from unscrupulous and cruel overseers. Père Biët noted that they could be beaten with cudgels if they went beyond a plantation's limits: "these often bruise them severely." He appears to be unaware of the act passed by the Assembly of Barbados in 1652 restraining *either* white servants or black slaves from "wandering about" without written permission from their masters, and authorizing anyone who detected a vagrant to correct or whip him before returning him to the master. For the same offense, a white man had to serve an extra month for every two hours of absence. Many Negroes were punished for stealing, a habit that was not uncommon among the natives in Africa. This was an age of cruelty among all races and nationalities, and at its best, chattel slavery was still very cruel. Before 1650, however, the greater victims of man's inhumanity were the mass of white Christian servants who suffered at the hands of callous, white Christian masters. For the time being, with all of their troubles, the blacks had it better.[34]

It is quite evident, moreover, that slaves were not thought to be dangerous. To explain this, Ligon pointed out that "they are fetch'd from severall parts of Africa, who speake severall languages, and by that means, one of them understands not another." They could not, therefore, easily cabal. No slave code had been framed as yet, and in 1639 Peter Hancock could arrange that if his Negro woman Asha would serve for twelve months after his

33. Ligon describes with admiration the Negroes' swimming strokes. *Barbados,* 28, 47, 48, 52.

34. Père Biët tells of a Negro woman of thirty-five whose body was covered by scars made by firebrands applied to it—an act that parallels in barbarity the treatment of the white servant John Thomas mentioned earlier. Biët, *Voyage,* 291; *Acts and Statutes of Barbados* (Jennings), 81–3.

death, she was to be "manumitted and from thenceforth be a free woman to all intents and purposes whatsoever." [35]

At the end of this period, perhaps 20 per cent of the population of the island was black; the transition from white to slave labor had barely begun. Major William Hilliard, one of the leading sugar planters, had 96 Christians, 96 slaves, and 3 Indian women and their children to work his 500 acres in 1647. In a survey of Anthony Ashley Cooper's plantation made in 1652 by Captain Gerard Hawtayne, his Barbados agent, there were 21 white servants having five to eight years to serve, and 15 slaves, 3 men, 6 women, 2 boys, 2 girls, and 2 suckling boys. The inhabitants of the English islands were still predominantly white despite the rising number of blacks in Barbados and St. Christopher. A revolutionary change in the composition of the population had begun, but the fact that a formidable proportion of the people continued unfree, whether they were white or black, was the salient social feature of these colonies.[36]

V

Whatever an individual's rank or station in the Caribbean might be, weather and climate profoundly conditioned his or her adjustment to the new life. Climatically, these volcanic islands are described by geographers as moderate tropics because of the steady-blowing, cooling Northeast Trades. "The sunne never freckles nor tannes the skinn except of such as works in the heatt therof all day," was the revealing comment of Sir Henry Colt. "I never ware gloves, and yett my hands were never whiter." James Parker moved to Barbados to settle and reported back to New England in June 1646: "The country to my sense is not very hott, but that which I like well off." [37]

35. Ligon, *Barbados,* 29, 46; Bodleian Library: Rawlinson MSS, A289, transcript in Davis Coll., VIII, Envelope 11.
36. Ligon, *Barbados,* 22; Davis Coll., VIII, Envelope 9.
37. The average annual temperature in the Leeward Islands is 79° F; the mean monthly temperature in January is 74.4° F, and in July, 80.9° F. "Air of moderate warmth, combined with a relative humidity of approximately 75 per cent throughout the year and a steady cooling breeze off the ocean, all make for human comfort," according to Gordon Merrill (*Historical Geography of St. Kitts and*

In contrast to these favorable comments is Richard Ligon's account of the climate: "Eight months of the year, the weather is very hot, yet not so scalding, but that servants, both Christians and slaves, labour and travel [travail] ten hours in a day." Not only does a high average annual humidity of 75 per cent keep a man damp or wet with perspiration most of the time, depleting his energies, but "the moisture of the air causes all our Knives, Etweese, Keys, Needles, Swords, and Ammunition to rust . . . Our locks, too, that are not often made use of, will rust in the wards . . . and Clocks, and Watches will seldome or never go true. . . ." Another writer deplored this same situation saying: "The Air there is so moist, that if any Instrument of Steel is never so clean, let it lie one Night exposed to the Air, it will be rusty by next Morning, which . . . occasions the Necessity of frequent Supplies" of tools and goods from abroad. To the Europeans, accustomed to frequent changes of weather within reasonable ranges of temperature, the West Indian climate must have seemed unusually and injuriously monotonous as well as enervating.[38]

Other tropical conditions besides the hot sun and excessive moisture forestalled prompt, even eventual adaptation to the Caribbean environment. Insects of all kinds tormented the unprotected settlers so persistently day and night that many of them must have been affected nervously as well as physically by their biting. Although white servants and freemen had mobbie to drink after the first few years, water was all the blacks ever had, and it brought on many kinds of complaints, including the bloody flux or dysentery. Sanitation did not exist in any modern sense. Malnutrition lowered the resistance of the mass of the people to disease, and overeating on the part of the rich planters rendered them peculiarly susceptible to ailments. All of the whites, hoping to cool themselves, tended to overindulge in liquids, and ordinarily

---

Nevis, 25); but to one who has, like the writers, been in these and other West Indian islands, such "scientific facts" completely omit the debilitating effect of the heat, and especially the humidity, from May through December on individuals acclimated to cooler and dryer regions. Harlow, *Colonising Expeditions,* 73; *Winthrop Papers,* V, 84.

38. Ligon, *Barbados,* 27; John Oldmixon, *The British Empire in America* (London, 1708), II, 157.

they drank alcoholic beverages. Nothing in European experience had prepared the colonists to look after their health properly in the tropics. In this respect they were tragically ignorant. Nor did they have either the inclination or the wisdom to follow the Arawak and Carib regimen. It is essential, therefore, that we temper the conclusion of those historians who have argued that the extensive white population of the Caribbees was "vigorous" before it was "ruined by war, capitalism, overcrowding, soil exhaustion, and the introduction of the negro with his diseases." [39]

For the West Indians of all complexions, health was not merely a matter of well-being; it was a matter of life or death. To adapt oneself physically to living in the tropics proved to be the most difficult of all adjustments for the white man, because in almost every ailment or disease the syndrome included unrecognized psychosomatic symptoms. Life expectancy in England was from thirty to thirty-five years, but servants in the islands soon came to the belief that they would not outlive the five to seven years of their bondage. Though unfortunately no vital statistics have survived, a very large fraction—more than a third, possibly a half—of those between sixteen and twenty years of age did not live to attain their freedom. With them death was an everyday occurrence. Richard Ligon was shocked to learn upon his arrival that in a decade or fifteen years each island had undergone an almost total turnover in population: most of the Barbadians were "new men, for few or none of them that first set foot there, were now living." [40]

39. In his vigorously argued book, A. Grenfell Price does not analyze the effect of climate and the health of the white colonists in the English West Indies before Negro slavery won out; yet they were the determining factors in the capacity of the whites to survive. *White Settlers in the Tropics* (New York, 1939), 29, 32, 99, 232, 234–5, 237.

40. Like true Englishmen, valetudinarian planters were seeking relief before 1631 at "the hott bathe, whose excellencyes and propertyes in the Cure of all maladyes the Barbadians themselves will confess it." In 1639 Governor D'Olive of Guadeloupe was in such poor health that he went to the English colony of Nevis to try the waters. It was a long distance to go for the cure, but by 1650 James Blomfield was but one of the many sick West Indians who, "in my greate distresse and weakness," traveled all the way north to Boston at great expense for "dyet, physick, and apparel . . . to recover my health." Harlow, *Colonising Expeditions,* 92–3; Southey, *Chronological History of the West Indies,* I, 283; *Aspinwall Notarial Records,* 283–4. On English spas, see Charles F. Mullett,

The blacks from torrid West Africa could accommodate themselves to the West Indian climate and environment in nearly all ways better than the whites, but in a few they could not. They appear to have been more susceptible to a variety of pulmonary diseases, and sleeping on boards on damp, earthen floors in their cabins obviously did them no good. "The soil itself seems to be poisoned," Uchteritz remarks, "for if someone lays himself down upon the naked earth even if only for an hour, he rapidly begins to swell up and develop running sores." From Africa the blacks brought strange maladies for which the whites did not know how to prescribe. And to all this was always to be added the trauma of being forced into slavery.[41]

The human price paid in bad health, chronic ailments, and death for the settling and maintaining of the English West Indies was appalling, and so nearly incredible that most historians have avoided mentioning it. One inevitably concludes that from 1624 to 1646 more of the colonists of Barbados and St. Christopher died than emigrated to other parts.

There were never enough physicians, "chirurgions," and apothecaries in any of the islands to meet the daily demand for their services. In 1640 the authorities in Barbados gave orders to Messrs Thomas Perkins and John Ourey, surgeons, and eight women (presumably midwives) to "search and veiwe the severall chests of all the Chirurgeons, which are to be lycensed too practise in this Island," and to report truly to the governor "how they are furnished with medicaments and instruments. Soe Helpe you God!" No earlier effort to regulate the medical profession is known in any of the English colonies.[42]

Many barber-surgeons came out from England to the islands, where their services were sorely needed, especially when the slave population began to grow. "Anthony Ker, Chirurgion and free

---

"Public Baths and Health in England, 16th–18th Century," in *Bulletin of the History of Medicine,* Supplement No. 5 (Baltimore, 1946), 1–10; and for life expectancy in England, *Vexed and Troubled Englishmen,* 25; Ligon, *Barbados,* 23, 117; *Winthrop's Journal,* I, 333.

41. Uchteritz, *Kurze Reise,* 8.

42. The earliest attempt to regulate medical men on the North American continent was in Massachusetts in 1645. Carl Bridenbaugh, *Cities in the Wilderness* (New York, 1938), 88; Davis Coll., VII, Envelope 3.

man of London," indentured himself in March 1644 to William Powrey for four years. He was to take care of all the sick in Powrey's family and receive "what is owing for physicke and what he shall hereafter earn," besides £20 sterling in freedom dues. William Gay, surgeon, who bought fifty acres of land in St. James's Parish in 1645, was only one of several medical men who were able to pay high prices for tracts of twenty to fifty acres after they had completed their contracts with such planters as Powrey. Coming to Barbados in 1647, Richard Vines estimated his yearly earnings at 10,000 pounds of tobacco. Vines himself fell ill in 1651 and, in his will, gave his servant William Maxwell two years of his time and allowed him "to practice the Remainder of his Time" provided he stayed with Mrs. Vines to get in debts and make up accounts. "A certain very capable French surgeon named César du Mesnil," who, though evidently a Huguenot, had served in the army of Charles I, went out to Barbados after the Battle of Worcester. His reputation became such that he could marry a rich minister's widow who was a kinswoman of Colonel Holdip.[43]

In Barbados, Richard Ligon suffered the griping agonies of the stone. Although believing that health in the islands would improve as soon as suitable drugs and medicines became available there, he had nothing but contempt for "the several drenches our Ignorant Quacksalvers there gave me." After having nearly died three times at the Modyford plantation, he risked returning to England only to be thrown into the Upper Bench Prison as a political offender.[44]

At the very moment that the English planters were discovering the key to prosperity in sugar, they experienced a disaster that permanently altered the demography of the Caribbees. Upon landing at Barbados early in September 1647, Richard Ligon, Thomas Modyford, and their party were startled by the appearance of trade and shipping; what they called "the plague" was in progress. Before the month was out, the mortality was frightening, and its incidence was equally great at St. Christopher.

Whether this grievous contagion came in by sea or "by the distempers of the people of the Iland, who by the ill dyet they

43. Davis Coll., VII, Envelopes 3, 6; *Winthrop Papers,* V, 172; *NEHG Reg.,* LIV (1900), 148; Biët, *Voyage,* 274.
44. Ligon, *Barbados,* 118.

keep, and drinking strong waters, bring diseases upon themselves, was not certainly known." Ligon attributed it to the latter, because for one woman who died, there were ten men, and they "were the greater deboysters [debauchees]." He does not indicate whether he recognized the ratio of men to women in the population to be ten to one. On the other hand, influenza was raging in epidemic proportions from French Canada to New Netherland at this same time, and it may well have reached the islands. Englishmen were familiar with the symptoms of the plague, if such it was; and in the islands, everlastingly infested with rats, were all the conditions for fostering an epidemic. It would have taken but one disease-bearing rodent from an incoming ship from England or the Low Countries to infect the hordes of rats that fed on the sugar and other crops in each island and this could account for the ravages of the plague.[45]

"In this sad time," the Barbadians could not determine which divine visitation hurt them most sorely, the plague or a concurrent famine. The latter was relieved by the arrival of quantities of provisions from New England, but the sickness continued to take a toll of lives for months; The Indian Bridge became both a pest center and a charnel house. "The living were hardly able to bury the dead" (a familiar cliché of the age), and they resorted to throwing "the dead carcasses into the bog," which infected the water supply. After it was observed that those who drank of it

45. "America certainly became a melting pot of diseases as well as of people, as Indians, Europeans, and Negroes engaged in a free exchange of their respective infections," Richard Shryock remarks in *Medicine in America* (Baltimore, 1966), 1–2. Dr. Ernest Caulfield, historian and pediatrician, discusses this early influenza epidemic in "The Pursuit of a Pestilence," in American Antiquarian Society, *Proceedings,* LX (1950), 26–7. He tells us that the high incidence of the Caribbean visitation suggests something like the bubonic plague. Hubbard, *History of New England,* 531–2; *Winthrop's Journal,* II, 326; Hutchinson, *History of Massachusetts-Bay,* I, 128–9*n,* links the West Indian pestilence with New England. From 1640 to 1648 "London was a plague-ridden city," says Charles Mullett. The disease also spread to Nottingham. English or Dutch rats could easily have carried the disease to the islands, where rodents flourished beyond most other living things and lived luxuriously off sugar cane. Founded in 1612, the Bermuda colony was so infested by rats off the ships that the leaders feared they "wilbee the subversion of this plantacon." Mullett, *The Bubonic Plague and England* (Lexington, Ky., 1956), 176–8, 184–5; New York Public Library, *Bulletin,* III (1899), 161; Ligon, *Barbados,* 21.

"dyed in [a] few hours," others took warning and "forbare to taste any more of it." Dr. Richard Vines notified Governor Winthrop in April 1648 that "the sicknes was an absolute plague, very infectious and destroying, insomuch that in our parish there were buried 20 in a weeke, and many weekes together 15 or 16. It first seased on the ablest men both for account and ability of body. Men who had begun and almost finished greate sugar workes, who dandled themselves in their hopes, but were suddenly laid in the dust, and their estates left to strangers. Our New England men had their share, and so had all nations, especially Dutchmen, of whome died a great company, even the wisest of them all." Samuel Winthrop, the old Governor's son, nearly died during the epidemic at St. Christopher. Vines believed the contagion was well over but proved wrong, for it flared up again, and as late as January 1649 Lucy Downing's two seafaring sons hesitated to ship out "in respect of the sad sicknes still at barbados." By April, however, the disease had apparently run its course, but in the following year, 1650, a drought of nine months' duration again threatened the health of the islanders.[46]

From September 1647 to April 1649 this epidemic scourged the Caribbee Isles. Toward the close of 1648, William Powrey estimated that 6000 "Christians" died in Barbados alone; Sir Edmund Plowden put the figure at "10,000 brave men," and to this should be added those white men who died before the end of April 1650. Contemporaries maintained that St. Christopher lost very heavily too. The number of white victims of this pestilence almost certainly ran from 10,000 to 12,000 for all of the islands; we cannot estimate the incidence of it among the blacks, but if it was bubonic plague or some disease previously alien to Africans, it must have been

46. Learning in March 1648 of the ravages of the infectious disease at Barbados and St. Christopher and the other Leeward Islands, "to the great depopulation of those" colonies, the General Court of Massachusetts-Bay ordered that all vessels entering from those places stop at the Castle in Boston Harbor and that, upon a penalty of £100, no persons were to go ashore or land goods without inspection. Nor could any local person go aboard any ship from the Caribbean, upon pain of a fine of £100. *Records of the Governor and Company of the Massachusetts-Bay in New England,* ed. Nathaniel B. Shurtleff (Boston, 1853–54), II, 237; III, 168. Ligon, *Barbados,* 21, 25; Hubbard, *History of New England,* 532; Harlow, *Colonising Expeditions,* 52; Lawrence S. Mayo, *The Winthrop Family in America* (Boston, 1938), 76; *Winthrop Papers,* V, 219–20, 290, 297.

very high. Allowing a conservative figure of 15,000 as the total losses (including blacks and whites in Nevis, Montserrat, and Antigua), the mortality resembled that of a prolonged and bloody war. A human catastrophe had occurred. How many persons starved to death during these three terrible years can never be known, but in the West Indies, the "immanence of death" was no mere cant phrase.[47]

Had not such acts of God—drought, famine, pestilence—occurred all at the same time, the leaders at Barbados and St. Christopher would have had to confront a problem of crowded populations such as had not been experienced hitherto in the Western World. The loss of life through disease and famine must be coupled with loss of population through emigration, for the specters of hunger and disease impelled many men to depart for less-populated and less sickly islands. This decrease in numbers makes it possible to understand why the population of Barbados, estimated at about 45,000 in 1645, was put at only 30,000 in 1650.[48]

The mortality in Barbados alone stimulated the importing of more blacks from Africa to relieve the labor shortage on the plantations. It also speeded the changeover to the culture of sugar after 1650. Hundreds, nay thousands, of the victims of the epidemic were freeholders whose small tracts went on the market to be bought up by the great planters. And the famine, deepened by the acute labor shortage but lessened by the timely arrival of provisions from New England, led as much as any one factor to the permanent reliance upon the mainland colonies for food and other goods. Accompanied by the black steed and its rider, Death on a pale horse rode down on the unsuspecting inhabitants of these islands and, in three years' time, created the greatest tragedy ever suffered in the colonies of the First British Empire; the consequences linger on into the present age.[49]

47. In his study of the whites in the Caribbean, Mr. Price overlooked completely this three-year period of death. See two letters of William Powrey to Archibald Hay, 1648. Hay MSS, p. 835; Force, *Tracts,* II, No. 7, p. 5. Schomburgk says that in 18 months (1647–48) the French islands lost nearly a third of their population by the epidemic. *History of Barbados,* 80.
48. *CSPC, 1661–68,* p. 217.
49. Revelation, 6:5–8.

V

Incomplete Societies

HERE AND THERE among the undistinguished, ignorant, and indigent people who composed the white populations of the English islands before 1650 were some younger sons of country gentlemen or prominent merchants, each with useful connections at home and a few hundred pounds to venture in the New World. Those who had strong constitutions survived and grew accustomed, or "seasoned," to tropical life took first to planting tobacco, then cotton, indigo, ginger, and ultimately sugar. Some of the first colonists added one or more small parcels purchased from less fortunate neighbors to their grants of land from the Earl of Carlisle or his local governors to build up estates of 300 to 500 acres of cleared ground on which, by the close of this period, gangs of white servants and black slaves produced highly profitable Muscovado sugar. These planters formed the only nearly complete social group in the Lesser Antilles. Successful, newly rich, politically influential, they constituted a tiny ruling oligarchy in each island, one that ordered all human affairs in its own interest. They held that what was good for them was good for the colony.[1]

1. Prominent among the old planters of Barbados were: Benjamin Berringer, Christopher Codrington, James Drax, Gerard Hawtayne, William Hilliard, James Holdip, Lancelot Pacey, and John Yeamans. At St. Christopher, John Jeaffreson and William Freeman were equally influential in a small group of planters that included Phance Beecher, William Sommers, John Jessen, and Roger Butler. At Montserrat, Samuel Waad ("one of the eminentest men") enjoyed a similar position. For the activities of these men, see the Index to this volume; and for St. Christopher in particular, Hay MSS, Nos. 920–55. Child, *A New Discourse of Trade,* 170.

The failure of the settlers to develop profitable staples before 1640 and the uncertainties of insular politics combined to keep most freeholders on the same level, but the rapid rise of the white populations, a pressing need for resourceful economic leadership, and the repercussions in the West Indies of civil war in England thrust able colonists to the fore. Most Barbadian planters were undoubtedly new men, as Richard Ligon claimed, but his *History of Barbados* clearly indicates that economic and political power rested with the old planters. That nearly all of these men were conforming puritans, supporters of Parliament, and later of the Commonwealth, is of first importance in any estimate of their efforts to build a Little England.

By virtue of a title of nobility and long possession of the proprietary patent that gave them control of all ungranted lands and rights to rents from those under cultivation, the first two Earls of Carlisle exercised the greatest power in these incipient societies. Officials and agents appointed by them shared conspicuously in the proprietorial prerogatives and enjoyed the greatest social eminence in the islands. Sir Thomas Warner, from Framlingham in Suffolk and a friend of the Winthrops, served as governor of St. Christopher for life (1629–49) and contributed as much as any Englishman to the colonizing of the West Indies. His lieutenant, John Jeaffreson, and Captain Anthony Brisket, for twenty years governor of Montserrat, as well as two governors of Barbados, the detested Henry Hawley and the highly regarded Philip Bell, were the principal appointees around whom men clustered in the search for favors and political power.[2]

Associated with the old planters from the beginning were certain English merchants who had financed them and maintained connections between metropolis and colony. Maurice Thompson, William Pennoyer, and Thomas Povey were such merchants, and all of them, too, were involved in the slave trade through the Guinea Company. Not infrequently they acquired tracts of land and sent out agents to manage them, particularly after the sugar culture proved so profitable. During the late thirties and forties, a number of Dutch merchants also participated actively and

2. Aucher Warner, *Sir Thomas Warner* (London, 1933), 18–58; *Narratives of Early Maryland,* 39; Williamson, *Caribbee Islands,* 10, 21; Harlow, *Colonising Expeditions,* 18–20, 29*n*; *Analecta Hibernica,* No. 4, p. 219.

decisively in the affairs of the colonies. As shipping from New England to the Caribbean expanded in volume, several Bostonians located in Barbados and St. Christopher as factors and agents, and more than one shifted from commerce to planting. One of those who won distinction in the islands was Samuel Winthrop, who set up as a merchant at St. Christopher and then at Barbados, ending up as a sugar planter in Antigua. The mercantile interest, both Dutch and English, not only made the islands the pivot of world commerce but also linked the rising oligarchies socially to similar groups in Amsterdam, London, and Boston.[3]

In the two decades before they began to prosper, the principal planters and their merchant associates worked very hard and lived very simply, almost frugally. Sugar and new men changed all this. Nicholas Foster explained in 1650 that a "generation of young *Cavees* lately come over . . . and being heires to great inheritances in England . . . pretend all is sequestered by Parliament, and they having lost that they never had right to there, intend to make that theirs here, which was never intended them." Making every allowance for the strong bias of a harassed puritan planter, we must concede that basically he was right. The Cavaliers came over with the expectation of becoming rich and powerful. Of late years they had had all they could take of "the chaos, when degree is suffocate." Now they were determined above all other things to create and preside over a new English gentry in the Caribbees and to go on living in the luxurious manner they believed to be their birthright. Two imperious brothers from a gentle family of Somersetshire, Humphrey and Edward Walrond, who landed late in 1645, immediately made a strong bid for leadership of the planters of Barbados. Closely associated with them were William Byam, a soldier of fortune with a remarkably beautiful wife, Thomas Modyford, Richard Ligon, and César du Mesnil, the French surgeon, and certain other Cavaliers. In the last years of this period, many Royalists crossed with their families and sufficient capital to purchase cleared plantations, which already had

3. A life of Maurice Thompson would light up nearly every dark corner of English expansion, 1624–66. Waters, *Genealogical Gleanings,* I, 85; II, 1349–50; Donnan, *Documents . . . of the Slave Trade,* I, 74*n,* 82, 84*n;* Stock, *Debates,* I, 188–9; J.E. Farnell, in *Ec. Hist. Rev.,* 2d ser., XVI (1964), 443–6; Mayo, *Winthrop Family in America,* 75–6; *Winthrop Papers,* V, 220.

buildings on them, and were producing sugar. These additions lent strength to the Walronds' faction.[4]

The family as a civilizing insular institution became firmly rooted with the coming of the Cavaliers. Families of the old planters had been joined by marriages in earlier years, as when Thomasine Hilliard married first Lancelot Pacey and then Thomas Noell. In the later decades, despite bitter and deep-seated political differences, sons and daughters of violently opposed families were forming unions: an active puritan, Constant Sylvester, fined and imprisoned by the Walronds, later took Grace Walrond as his wife. Intermarriages such as these went far to consolidate the great planters economically and socially. Samuel Winthrop's union with a woman of Amsterdam is but one of many marriages that illustrates the gradual joining of mercantile and planting families of the West Indies with New England and the Low Countries, as well as with Britain, and which would in time fuse them into a sort of Atlantic society. The offspring of such unions enabled the ruling groups to perpetuate themselves, in striking contrast to the inability of the great mass of less-favored whites to do so.[5]

II

It was on the rural estates of the great planters of each island that permanent units of society first began to form. From 1640 onward, those planters who had risen from the great body of colonists possessed sufficient wealth to support families, which they hastened to do. Richard Ligon met most of the more than 260 leading planters during the three years he passed on the Hilliard-Modyford plantation and located them meticulously on the map in his history. By visiting these plantation villages in fancy we can better understand what the emerging Caribbean gentry was like.[6] (Plate 2)

4. Foster, *Late Horrid Rebellion,* A-5; *Troilus and Cressida,* I, iii, 101–3, 125; Harlow, *Barbados,* 45–6; Biët, *Voyage,* 274–5, 279; Ligon, *Barbados,* 22; Nikolaus Pevsner, *South and West Somersetshire* (Harmondsworth, 1958), 208–9.

5. *Winthrop Papers,* V, 291; Biët, *Voyage,* 294; Waters, *Genealogical Gleanings,* I, 17, 19.

6. Throughout his work, Ligon mentions several major planters whose estates are not included in the 260 on his map; perhaps ten more should be added. The

A painting in oils by the Dutch *genre* artist Frans Post helps us to envisage a plantation village. (Plate 7) Although Post probably depicted a scene at Curaçao seen during his travels around the Caribbean before 1644, there is good reason to believe that in broad outlines and in many details it represents the general arrangement and appearance of the several structures on a plantation village of Barbados, St. Christopher, Nevis, or Montserrat. Post's "West Indian Village" bears a strong resemblance to the estates of the middling planters of Brazil and, considering the wholesale borrowing of the sugar culture and works by the English visitors, it would have been strange indeed had not James Drax and his friends also taken note of the arrangement of buildings and the opulent style of Brazilian life and followed them when they created their own island estates.[7]

Necessity and utility, however, had to come first with the English planters, which meant that, as a Barbados act of 1652 stated, ". . . the whole Wealth of the Inhabitants of this Island, consisteth chiefly in the labour of their servants." Additional wealth went into the purchase of African slaves and an ingenio with all of its accoutrements. Shortly after the period ended, what Père Biët said of rural Barbados also applied to the other islands: ". . . most of the plantations in the country are like as many villages whose size varies according to the number of [servants and] slaves each plantation has . . . The sugar works take up a lot of space. There are also the cabins of the indentured servants . . . and the dwellings of the Negro slaves. Each household has its own dwelling; they are all close to one another. This whole collection resembles a village . . . where there are two or three hundred persons. . . ."[8]

There was no dwelling worthy of the name of "great house" in Barbados when Ligon arrived in 1647. He writes that carpenters and masons had recently come there to help build the sugar mills,

---

Indian Bridge was the only aggregation of inhabitants in these years worthy of the name of a town.

7. The Indians shown in the background at the left are more characteristic of the Leeward Islands than of Barbados. Frans Post's "West Indian Village" hangs in Queen Anne's dining room at Kensington Palace. Larsen, *Frans Post,* 122.

8. *Acts and Statutes of Barbados* (Jennings), 18–19; Biët, *Voyage,* 289.

some of them "very great Masters in their Art: and such as could draw a plot, and pursue the design they framed with great diligence, and beautifie the tops of their Doors, Windows, and Chimney-peeces, very prettily; but not many of those, nor is it needful that there should be many, for though the Planters talk of building houses, and with them up, yet they weigh the want of those hands in their sugar work . . . they fall back, and put on their considering caps." During his first year there, gentleman-architect that he was, Ligon prepared twenty sets of plans. Applying what he had learned about building in France and Italy to the tropical scene, he produced designs that are still in use today. Although the planters liked them well enough, only two, Captains Thomas Middleton and George Standfast, actually used them; Ligon adjudged their houses to be the two best in the island when he left for England. Two years later Uchteritz observed that the finest houses were built of cedar boards and roofed with cedar shingles. The upper part of the house was open on all sides so that the air circulated throughout, and removable shutters fitted the windows to prevent rains from damaging the houses during storms. There was a large chamber on the first floor with an adjoining sleeping room. Evidently some of Ligon's architectural ideas were beginning to influence the Barbadians, but even the best plantation house had not yet become a *casa grande*.[9]

9. Here are Ligon's ingenious specifications for a livable house cooled by the trade winds: "I would have a third part of my building to be of an East and West line, and the other two thirds to cross that, at the West end: in a North and South line, so that at four a clock in the afternoon, the higher buildings will begin to shade the other, and so afford more and more shade to my East and West building till night; and not only to the house, but to all the walks that I make on either side of that building, and then I would raise my foundation of that part of my house wherein my best rooms were three feet above ground; leaving it hollow underneath for Ventiducts, which I would have come into every room in the house, and by that means you shall feel the cool breeze[s] all the day, and in the evening when they slacken a cool shade from my North and South building, both which are great refreshings, in hot Countreys: and according to this Model, I drew many plots [plans] of several sizes and contrivances, but they did not or would not understand them: at last I grew weary of casting stones against the wind, and so gave over." New Englanders had only begun to introduce ready-hewn and fitted house frames to the islanders in 1652. They had first to create a market for the materials at the price of £40 17*s.* they

As more women appeared in the colonies, household furnishings began to accumulate, and the old pioneer, masculine atmosphere dissipated in the better plantation houses. In addition to a cotton "Engine" mentioned in George Bulkley's inventory of 1640 are pewter plates, kettles, a clock, and "Hangings for 2 Rooms and [table] Carpitts, with 5 Cushings." The excessive moisture, however, played havoc by mildewing or rusting almost all furnishings, which explains why Ligon avowed some years later that "Hangings we dare not use, for being spoyl'd by Ants, and eaten by the Cockroaches, and Rats, yet some Planters that meant to handsom their houses, were minded to send for gilt leather, and hang their rooms with that, which they were more than perswaded those vermine would not eat." Cedar wainscoating had to satisfy most of the newly rich and the Cavaliers. They protected their beds and cedar tables from pests by standing the legs in bowls of water—meat was suspended from ceilings of cupboards by tarred ropes. Most of the mansions were sparsely furnished: few of them contained chairs; benches and "joyned stooles" had to serve, and there is no record of pictures before 1652.[10]

The impressionable Barbadians who accompanied James Drax to Brazil in the 1640's could scarcely have failed to be dazzled by the high social position that sugar wealth assured the master of a great plantation. He was served, obeyed, and respected by everyone, not merely by his retainers. As Antonil observed later in the century, the *senhor de engenho* properly looked upon himself, as he lived in his *casa grande* on a scale of magnificence and luxury, as being on a par with the gentleman of Portugal. Aspirants to repeat this splendid existence increased with the arrival in the Caribbees in 1646 of the *Cavees* bringing ample money and credit with them and the habit of keeping gentle and showy establishments for the rest of the populace to see and admire. Dignity, taste, good manners, *noblesse oblige,* a certain imperiousness, culture—the contributions of the Walrond brothers, Thomas Modyford, and,

asked. *Barbados,* 24, 42–3, 103–4; Uchteritz, *Kurze Reise,* 5; *Suffolk Deeds,* II, 156, 163.

10. Davis Coll., II, Envelope 5; VIII, Envelope 9; Ligon, *Barbados,* 41, 42, 64; Connell, in *JBMHS,* XXIV (1957), 102–5.

above all others, Richard Ligon—turned out, with the passage of time, to be more lasting and more important in the civilizing of the Caribbean colonies of England than their economic and political activities.[11]

If sufficient wealth and labor were not yet available for the erection of mansions, most of the rising gentry were ready and able to lay out considerable sums of money on fine clothes and sumptuous wining and dining. Imports of the best linens, "Holland and Dovelace," for the planters and their wives and children, Devonshire kerseys and other woolens, no matter how unsuited for a hot country, fashionable hats and thin leather gloves, these and many other articles gradually found as ready a market at the merchants' warehouses as tools, cheap clothing, and utilitarian goods. We have seen that nearly every substantial planter displayed a gold watch, an outward and visible evidence of rank. More and more luxury goods for aspiring ladies and gentlemen appear in the mounting traffic with Holland and England—silks and satins, gold and silver lace, with colored ribbons—at prices ordinarily double or more than those asked in London. Pins were in such demand that a man could get almost anything he asked for them. "The ladies and young women are as well dressed as in Europe, and they economize on nothing to dress well." When one of them would pay eight or ten pounds of sugar for a bit of lace, a Frenchman thought one could easily estimate how much an entire outfit would cost. Small wonder that in her will of 1650, Mary Browne bequeathed to Joan Obring her "Read Fancy Wascoate and . . . Colloured Petticoat" as well as 1000 pounds of sugar.[12]

After viewing some of the plantations and observing how the

11. Antonil, *Cultura e Opulencia do Brasil,* 84–5.

12. Better attendance at the shop than formerly given was now required: "The Goods being stowed in a Ware-house . . . your Correspondent must reserve a handsome room for a Shop, where his servants must attend; for then his Customers will come about him. . . ." Ligon advised the merchant to "be careful whom he trusts; for, as there are some good, so there are many bad pay-masters." The merchant must ride about the country to make half a dozen good acquaintances, who can "enform him how the pulse beats of all the rest. . . ." Ligon, *Barbados,* 109–11; Davis Coll., II, Envelope 5; Bodleian: Tanner MSS, 54: fols. 153–4, quoted in Harlow, *Barbados,* 38–9*n*; Biët, *Voyage,* 277, 292.

owners were served by a dozen or more house slaves and white servants, "whom they command as they please," an English visitor concluded that they lived far better than their counterparts in England. A French priest declared that sugar had made them all so rich that they lived like princes, and we may recall that Uchteritz called Jabez Whitaker a count, as he certainly would have been addressed in Saxony. Many of the great planters displayed gentle personal qualities: they were helpful to strangers, sharing their knowledge and aiding in buying land, as both Ligon and Biët testify. "Loving, friendly, and hospitable to one another," though of several political and religious persuasions, they were upon the whole discreet and got along reasonably well together—until 1647 at least.[13]

III

The First Gentleman of Barbados, indeed of the whole Carlisle Patent, was not a Cavalier as one would expect but one of the earliest to arrive of the old planters, one who was branded by the Royalists as "that devout Zealot (of the deeds of the Devill, and the cause of that seven headed Dragon at Westminster)." His "ayme is wholly to Cashere the Gentry and Loyall, to change for our Peace Warre, and for our Unity Division." Calumny apart, not one of the jealous Royalists who fined and imprisoned him in 1650 had family connections to match those of James Drax.[14]

Where in England James Drax came from and who his family was are facts unknown today, even to his descendants. It can be readily assumed in the light of his career that he was a younger son of a good family in England, whose members inclined toward puritanism. He exhibited nearly every quality of the English country gentleman of the seventeenth century, the pioneer, and the founder of an empire: high intelligence, ambition, initiative, driving energy, courage, persuasiveness, and leadership. And to these must be added two rare assets, a strong constitution and sound health.

13. Venables, in RHS, *Camden,* LX, 146; Biët, *Voyage,* 278, 294; Ligon, *Barbados,* 57.

14. Foster, *Late Horrid Rebellion,* 24–5.

Both moderate and wise, he nevertheless thought in large terms, and throughout his life acted accordingly. John Scott's accolade of "genious" was well conferred.[15]

Well connected, apparently personable, and successful, Drax married a daughter of James Hay, first Earl of Carlisle, by his second wife, the beautiful and witty Lucy Percy of the celebrated Northumberland family. This union not only ensured power and influence but also drew the young Barbadian close to the Parliament men during the forties, doubtless through the good offices of the bold, intriguing Countess of Carlisle, closest friend of Queen Henrietta Maria and at the same time an intimate of "King Pym." Among the earliest to arrive in Barbados, Drax and his kinsman William Hilliard were among the first to reap fortunes in tobacco, then cotton, and in the late forties, in sugar. The first Christopher Codrington, a good friend of Drax, though a Royalist, espoused the planter's daughter Frances, thereby uniting two of the most distinguished West Indian families. Both Drax and Codrington served as colonels in the militia regiments and sat on the Council in Barbados.[16]

Through the eminence of his family, his own personality, and abilities, Drax, like Sir Thomas Warner at St. Christopher, emerged as the head of the planting gentry of Barbados. He excelled as planter, official, and host. The Cavalier Ligon tells us that the puritan colonel "was not so strict an observer of Sundaies, as to deny himself lawfull recreations," such as having his slaves swim after ducks to amuse his guests. Drawing upon his English background, what his wife knew of life at the Court, and what he had seen of plantation elegance in Brazil, James Drax became famous in the forties for the open and bounteous hospitality he dispensed. Always a good judge of men and quick to pick up new ideas, Colonel Drax was one of the very first planters whom Ligon induced to practice the "Art of Cookery"—to serve "Fricases," "Quelquechoses," "Excellent Stews," and other French dishes,

15. Ligon, *Barbados,* 96.

16. Lucy Percy had married James Hay in 1617 against the wishes of her father, the ninth Earl of Northumberland, who wanted no more "Scottish jiggs." *DNB,* XXV, 267, 272; *Caribbeana,* IV, 315–16; Vincent T. Harlow, *Christopher Codrington, 1668–1710* (Oxford, 1928), 6, 7; Wm. Hilliard to Archibald Hay, June 22, 1640, Hay MSS.

by importing gourmet items from Holland and England, and by introducing luscious West Indian fruits and other viands at his board. Almost alone of all the planters before 1650, Drax would now and then kill one of his beefs, which had been fattened on twelve acres of bonavist, for one of his Lucullan spreads. Feasting and wining, virtually the only mode of recreation and amusement available for the planters, spread over several hours, and the remainder of the afternoon was spent in consuming French brandy or punch made from brandy or rum.[17]

Père Biët was on hand to report the pageantry at The Indian Bridge when Drax sailed for England in 1654: "We saw the esteem in which he was held, for the day of his departure he came to visit the Governor [Daniel Searle] who entertained him and many others. Then, after dinner, he was accompanied to the place where the ship was to embark by more than two hundred of the island's most important people, all well mounted and marching two by two in a column headed by the Governor and Colonel Drax. When he arrived at the embarkation place, the ship fired a volley of all its guns; and after he had set foot in the long boat to go out to the ship, all the persons accompanying him fired their pistols. Then having seen him go up into the ship, they turned back so as to escort the Governor, marching in the same order in which they had come." The unparalleled services rendered to Barbados by James Drax in promoting its staple crops and his faithful support of the Good Old Cause were rewarded at home when he and Martin Noell were granted an interview by the Protector on January 1, 1657/8, after which Oliver Cromwell knighted him as an honor to his island.[18]

IV

The moral behavior of the islanders in the early years differed little from that common to any pioneer society composed almost wholly of lusty young males. Authority being lax, and normal

17. So important was feasting as the first instance of conspicuous display that one of Drax's spreads is described in Appendix III. Ligon, *Barbados,* 33, 34, 35, 36–7, 52, 56–7, 64, 80, 99; Biët, *Voyage,* 278.
18. Biët, *Voyage,* 295; BM: Add. MSS, 11411, fol. 55b.

family and religious restraints mostly absent, it would have been a miracle if the settlers had not sought release or solace in drunkenness, and not a few of them in such unnatural practices as sodomy and bestiality. Everywhere men were boisterous and extremely quarrelsome, given to making false charges, and calling all sorts of names. Sir Henry Colt blamed the climate for their idleness and waywardness.[19]

In the Caribbean, men's passions were seldom far from the surface. With the slow extension of authority after 1638, profanity and dueling, always frowned upon, were severely dealt with by the rulers of a puritan cast. Furthermore, any man who criticized the officials, regardless of his position, found the courts dealing out prompt and ruthless punishment. In 1641 the justices ordered John Wiborne to be nailed by the ears to the pillory with tenpenny nails for writing a libelous book against Master Hilliard, after which he was whipped and branded. In the same year, Captain James Futter, who had feasted Sir Henry Colt ten years previously, asked Judge Read "in open Court, If all whore-masters were taken off the Bench, what would the Governor [Henry Huncks] do for a Council," and added that "my Lord of Carlisle himself was too much given to drink." One hour in the pillory at noon on a hot day was the sentence imposed on this planter for speaking what was not too far from the truth, for Sergeant Major Huncks was reputed to have seduced the wives of at least three of his friends in Antigua. Mr. Huncks declared that he did not care threepence what people said about him. Of his behavior while he was governor of Barbados we are not told, but Captain Futter's outburst suggests that he had not reformed.[20]

The greatest of all the vices of the English colonies in Père Biët's opinion was lewdness. "It is a horrible thing to think about: adulterers, incest and all the rest." According to one report there was, in 1650 in Barbados, a standing commission for punishing adultery and fornication, though it rarely exercised its powers. Among the female servants at most large plantations, and some small ones,

19. Harlow, *Colonising Expeditions*, 65, 67.
20. Biët, *Voyage*, 293; N. Darnell Davis, *The Cavaliers and Roundheads of Barbados* (Georgetown, British Guiana, 1887), 61; Richard Pares, *A West-India Fortune* (London, 1950), 25; Wm. Jeaffreson to the Earl of Carlisle, Aug. 9, 1641, Hay MSS.

were many "suspected whores," who never lacked custom on the Sabbath, the authorities maintained. Rogues and whores and similar people were the kind generally sent to the Caribbees. Henry Whistler declared that a "rodge in England will hardly make a cheater heare; a Baud brought over puts one a demuor comportment, a whore if hansume makes a wife for sume rich planter." In the moral sphere, as in all else in the West Indies, there was no peace, and many of the colonists bore witness to "the debaucht lives of the people." [21]

More than one man who left a wife in England when he sailed for the Caribbees married again in the islands. Such a one was Captain Nicholas Foster—stalwart Roundhead and author, in 1650, of *A Briefe Relation of the Late Horrid Rebellion*—who had gone out to Barbados in 1639 and married a woman there. His English wife waited for eight years for his return before espousing William Welborne of the East India trade. When Foster returned from Barbados to escape persecution by the Royalists, he learned that Welborne had been long in the Indies. On the advice of some of his Puritan friends, who said it was sinful to live apart, Foster again co-habited with his first wife. Other Londoners petitioned against him as a bigamist. At this juncture, Elizabeth Lake of Dover came to the city to buy wedding clothes in expectation of marrying Foster who, she claimed, had proposed to her upon landing from the West Indies. She returned home when she learned about his first wife. His island spouse could most certainly have acquired another husband had she so wished.[22]

21. Among servants and freemen, brawling was a sport that often followed drinking bouts, so that it seems that it was the Englishmen in the West Indies as much as or more than those on the Virginia frontier who regularly engaged in the knock-down-and-drag-out fight. "They settle their differences by fist fighting. They give each other black eyes, scratch each other, tear each other's hair, and do similar things. The onlookers let them do this and surround them so as to see who will be victorious. If they fall down they are picked up, and they fight until they can no longer do so and are forced to give up." Colt held in 1631 that "St. Christopher shewes moor valour in the quarrels then the Barbadians." Biët, *Voyage,* 293; Ligon, *Barbados,* 101; Harlow, *Colonising Expeditions,* 43, 74, 93; Thomas Ashe (1806), in *American Social History as Recorded by British Travelers,* ed. Allan Nevins (New York, 1923), 58–60; Thurloe, *State Papers,* III, 507; Venables, in RHS, *Camden,* LX, 146; *Acts and Statutes of Barbados* (Jennings), 79–80.
22. Davis Coll., I, Envelope 9.

Drunkenness was widespread, especially among the lower classes. White indentured servants and freemen, and also blacks when they had the opportunity, all imbibed deeply and desperately. At Barbados, Sir Henry Colt discovered that he had gone from drinking two up to thirty drams of spirits at a meal, and feared that within a few days he would be consuming sixty drams! He believed that there were numerous "good drinkers" in St. Christopher but not as many as at Barbados: evidence is not lacking that both islands supported confirmed drunkards. Tom Verney wrote home about seeing first one and then another besotted man lying along the highway when he was going to church on a Sunday. There were instances of men having their fingers and toes bitten off, and even being killed, by landcrabs without their rousing from their drunken stupor. Verney considered these inebriates to be beyond redemption, mere "beasts," and felt no inclination to assist them. At The Indian Bridge all buildings not warehouses were inns or grog-houses. "For the merry planter, or freeman to give him a Caracter," one visitor bantered in 1650, "I can call him noe otherwise then a German for his drinking, and a Welshman for his welcome, hee is never idle; if it raines he toapes securely under his roofe, if faire hee plants and workes in the feild; he takes it ill if you pass by his doore, and not tast of Liquor." [23]

The great planters worked out a ritual for their drinking; and they too quaffed deep and long. The abstemious Père Biët describes graphically the drinking during and after dinner at the Drax plantation: "When they dine, no one is forced to drink, one drinks willingly. They present whatever drink one wants: wine from Spain, Madeira, the Canaries; French wines, and sweetened mobby for those who do not want wine. But after one has dined, and the table has been cleared, a trencher full of pipes and another full of tobacco is put on the table along with a bowl full of brandy, into which is put plenty of sugar . . . Egg yolks are also thrown in, then this is set alight, and they let it burn down to two-thirds of its former volume. The host takes a little silver cup, fills it with this punch and drinks to the health of whoever is in front of him. After he has drunk, he refills the cup and gives it to the person whose health he has just drunk; this person does the same thing to

23. Harlow, *Colonising Expeditions,* 44, 66, 91; *Memoirs of the Verney Family,* I, 150; Biët, *Voyage,* 288, 293; *Winthrop Papers,* V, 83–4.

another, and this procedure is continued until there is nothing left in the bowl. During this festivity, well-built young slaves refill the pipes, which they present on their knees. The afternoon passes thus, in drinking and smoking, but quite often one is so drunk that he cannot return home. Our gentlemen found this life extremely pleasant." [24]

V

Almost every man or woman who went out from England to settle in the Caribbee Isles shared in some degree the massive concern of their compatriots about their relation to God, and they agreed with John Selden that religion was the "cement of society." A further indubitable fact was that a majority of the promoters and early colonists were puritans of some complexion, usually conforming puritans; and another was that, until the Restoration, those English settlers favoring Parliament and the Commonwealth were more numerous than the supporters of the Stuarts. Bible-reading was not confined to Old England and New; in the islands more than one reader must have found comfort in such apposite texts from Isaiah:

> He shall not faile nor be discouraged
> till hee have set judgement in the
> earth; and the isles shall wait for his Law

and,

> The innocent shall deliver the yland,
> and it shalbe preserved by the pureness
> of thine hands.

The course of Puritanism as a whole requires an understanding of what happened in the West Indies as well as in Britain, the Chesapeake colonies, and New England.[25]

24. Biët, *Voyage,* 278–9; Ligon, *Barbados,* 33.
25. For the intense religiosity of the English after 1641, see Thomas Edwards, *Gangræna* (London, 1646); and for earlier years, *Vexed and Troubled Englishmen*, 239–73. Isaiah, 42:4; Job, 22:30 (Geneva version, 1608). The only available study for the West Indies is Babette M. Levy, "Early Puritanism in the Southern and Island Colonies," in American Antiquarian Society, *Proceedings,* LXX (1960), 69–348.

Organized religion made a very slow and shaky start in the Caribbees. Himself a courtier, though no bigot, the first Earl of Carlisle left all matters of piety and morals in his patent to his governors. They too appear to have been more concerned with the thousands of servants dumped in the islands as a labor force than with congregations. Among peoples of many creeds, a broad measure of toleration developed in practice from sheer necessity—the presence of a very large number of Roman Catholic Irish without their priests further restricted any attempt to establish and maintain religious uniformity. More than any other condition, however, the absence of families to provide the essential base for organized religion by means of daily prayers, regular readings of Scripture, and other household observances acted to weaken and attenuate the originally strong religious impulse.

Services from the Book of Common Prayer began at St. Christopher in 1626 when Master John Featley of All Souls arrived, but in the next decade puritan influences grew strong enough to call for repression by the officials in the interest of the Established Church. For talking against the Bishops, Parson French was cruelly whipped, pilloried, forced to wear a paper in his hat proclaiming his offense, then imprisoned, and eventually sent to England in irons in 1643. There the Puritans arranged for his release. A merchant with puritan views who lived in St. Christopher from 1630 to 1645 complained that the inhabitants were very wicked despite the existence of three Anglican churches. Master William Collins, "a young scholar, full of zeal," who had preached privately at Gloucester, and Master Hales, also bred a scholar, won many settlers by their Familist preaching. After being persecuted and having their liberty restricted, the two sold their possessions and, together with some of their followers, sailed northward to New Haven in 1640. There they dispersed; some of them returned to Ireland; Collins and Hales ended up at Aquidneck, where they became disciples of Mistress Anne Hutchinson, the notorious Antinomian. Collins married his leader's daughter, Anne, and both of them were massacred by the Indians near Pelham (New York) in the present Westchester County in 1643. Pestered by religious controversies, especially with Roman Catholics, Governor Thomas Warner resorted to root and branch methods in

1643 by banishing a party of Irish to Montserrat, and other malcontents to Antigua.[26]

First settled by Roman Catholic Irishmen, whom the Virginians had rejected, Montserrat had become, by 1634, a sizable plantation. Two years later the governor, Captain Anthony Brisket, apparently an Anglican, informed King Charles of his intention to carry out more settlers and that he was "erecting a church of stone and brick." An order promulgated by Governor Brisket and his Council in 1638 provided for proper observation of the Lord's Day and a fine of 1000 pounds of tobacco for each violator. By 1643 the Catholic Irish, who had become very numerous in the Leeward Islands, dispatched a petition to the Jesuits in Paris asking for spiritual assistance for "souls that are in danger" in St. Christopher and neighboring localities. It was the Capuchins, however, who sent out the first priest. We know next to nothing of these activities save that the English expelled several priests from Montserrat prior to 1650.[27]

Talking to Père Biët, James Holdip, one of the oldest residents in Barbados at the time, remarked: "It is enough to believe that there is a God, and that Jesus Christ died for us." This attitude of sweet reasonableness prevailed among most Barbadians, though to the disapproving Frenchman it signified that they were close to being without any religion. No records of the beginnings of religious observances in the island before 1629 exist. In that year Governor Sir William Tufton divided the island into six parishes, but whether six rectors presided over them or the measure was intended merely for local administration is not known. After about 1631 the islanders built five or six church edifices, which were, with perhaps a few slight improvements, similar to their cabins.

26. During the "Second Revolt" at St. Christopher in 1642 against Sir Thomas Warner's harsh rule, one of the grievances was that "the division of Keyon doth desire to have their minister put out, and to have Mr. Palmer againe, the new incumbant being a contentious man, and one that hath sowed much discord among his parisioners by his scandalous tongue." William Johnson to Carlisle Trustees, Feb. 8, 1641/2, Hay MSS; Davis Coll., VI, Envelope 27; *Winthrop's Journal,* I, 151; II, 7–8, 39–40, 138; *Mass. Col. Recs.,* I, 336, 344; Hubbard, *History of New England,* 340–43; Harlow, *Colonising Expeditions,* xxvii–xxviii.

27. *Narratives of Early Maryland,* 38; PRO: CO 1/9, fol. 23; *Acts of Assembly passed in the Island of Montserrat (1668–1740)* [London, 1740], 26; Pelleprat, *Relation,* 37–41; Gwynn, in *Studies,* XVIII, 653–63.

In 1637 Master Thomas Lane, writing to Archbishop Laud about the state of the Church, complained that Governor Hawley chose the clergy and agreed with them or not as he pleased. Each parish had a vestry possessing the power to engage and remove ministers and set a levy for their salaries. As for the ministers, the parson said they were "made and esteemed no better than mercenaries." Furthermore, he added, they had to pay poll taxes on their wives and children above the age of seven. We "live in a declining age of the world," the clergyman lamented, "wherein there is not found that youthful zeal of God's house which was wont to eat up men." [28]

Since there was no representative assembly in Barbados until 1639, the establishment of the Church of England in the early thirties must have been ordered under the authority of the governor and council. Reporting on the "particulars of what good doctrine" he found in Barbados, Thomas Verney deplored the fact that "our teaching it is not soe good as I wish it were." He hoped that if the Earl of Warwick bought the island (as was rumored), the Barbadians would have better order. Here we get a glimpse of a conforming puritan's point of view.[29]

As the religious scene in the Mother Country clouded over in 1641, Philip Bell, an Anglican with puritan tendencies, became governor of Barbados. Almost at once he reorganized the island and made eleven parishes: two of them, St. George's and St. Thomas's, were inland. He also rebuilt the church of St. Michael's at The Indian Bridge with strong timbers. The following November, Bell and the Council removed James Anderson from the cure of the chapel of St. Thomas's, because "his violent and turbulent Carriage procured the ill Opinion and distrust of the Parish." Master Anderson may have been a Familist like William Collins, who had preached for a time in Barbados before being driven out and going to St. Christopher. At any rate, Bell, writing to

28. Biët, *Voyage,* 293–4; Schomburgk, *History of Barbados,* 92; PRO: CO 1/15, p. 70.

29. Arthur L. Cross effectively disproved the old claims for the Bishop of London's jurisdiction over the colonies in *The Anglican Episcopate and the American Colonies* (Cambridge, Mass., 1902), 15–22. Thomas Verney's brother, Sir Ralph, opposed Laud and sat in both the Short and Long Parliaments before refusing the Covenant and going abroad in 1643. *Memoirs of the Verney Family,* I, 148–9.

Governor Winthrop in 1641, complained of the distracted state of his island brought about by "divers sects of familists . . . and their turbulent practices, which had forced him to proceed against some of them by banishment, and others . . . by whipping." He beseeched the Governor to send down some godly ministers and men of good principles, but none of the northern colonists ventured to come.[30]

In religion, as in politics, the practical puritans who governed Barbados steered a middle course, which they hoped would enable Anglicans, Puritans, and Roman Catholics to arrive at an acceptable *modus vivendi.* To accommodate a handful of Sephardim from Brazil, they permitted the erection of a synagogue at The Indian Bridge sometime before 1644. Until the coming of the Walronds, Byam, and other bigoted and violent Cavees in 1647 and later, Philip Bell succeeded so well with his reasonable ecclesiastical policy that the planters, exhibiting both tolerance and discretion, enjoyed peaceful relations one with another. Some of the better sort even managed to introduced a bit of good humor in a self-imposed rule among themselves by ordering that whosoever "nam'd the word Roundhead or Cavalier, should give all those that heard him a Sho[a]t and a Turkey, to be eaten at his house. . . ."[31]

When in 1646 the Committee for Foreign Plantations sent out a commission to guarantee the Barbadians liberty of conscience, the puritan governor, the moderate Anglican Christopher Codrington, and four others of the Council remarked, with some asperity, that they were being assured of nothing they did not already have. In this very year James Parker, a Puritan minister from New England, arrived and was asked to preach "for the present" by Governor Bell, whom he deemed a good man who honored religion according to his lights, even if it were not the New England Way—he exposed only heresies, which abounded on the island. Richard Vines testified that Parker met with approval and was opposed by

30. Harlow, *Barbados,* 25; Hubbard, *History of New England,* 346; Barbados Council Minutes, I (1641–53/4), in Davis Coll., IV, Envelopes 28, 30.

31. The synagogue is mentioned in a conveyance of land. Eustace M. Shilstone, *Monumental Inscriptions in the Burial Ground of the Jewish Synagogue at Bridgetown, Barbados* (New York, 1952), xvi; Ligon, *Barbados,* 57.

none, unless by the Antinomians and "such like." Living on a twenty-acre plantation, receiving numerous gifts as well as a good stipend, Parker had good reason to report to Governor Winthrop that he had been received with great respect by both government and people. Here was grass-roots toleration indeed: "a godly man and a scholar," a New England Puritan, inducted by the Governor into an established Anglican cure and welcomed by the parishioners! [32]

The following year, the religious policy of Barbados was spelled out by a public act: "Whereas divers opinionated and self-conceited persons, have declared an absolute dislike to the Government of the Church of England, as well by their aversion and utter neglect or refusal of the Prayers, Sermons, and Administration of the Sacrament and other Rites and Ordinances thereof, used in their several Parish-churches; as by holding Conventicles in private houses and other places; scandalizing Ministers, and endeavouring to seduce others to their erroneous opinions, upon pretence of an alteration of Church-government in England . . ." all persons were ordered to give due obedience to the church established in the island; and justices of the peace, ministers, and churchwardens were to enforce the law. The statute also required families to conduct morning and evening prayers, and all masters to have daily prayers read to their servants. Inhabitants were expected to attend divine services every Lord's Day or, if they lived more than two miles from the church, at least once a month. Led by the Walrond brothers, the recently arrived Cavaliers won control of the Assembly and, on May 30, 1650, forced the Governor to issue a proclamation in the name of King Charles II that required exclusive use of the Book of Common Prayer every Lord's Day as "the only Pattern of true worship." Until then the Barbadians had skillfully achieved what at the end of the century would be called comprehension, a notable example of forbearance so rarely exhibited by Christians of that time.[33]

32. Stock, *Debates,* I, 191; *Winthrop Papers,* V, 83, 172; *Winthrop's Journal,* II, 89–90.

33. Ministers received no tithes, as they had in England, but a yearly allowance of one pound of tobacco for every acre a man held. Ligon's map of 1650 shows only four church edifices in the parishes—Christ Church, St. Michael, Speight's

In England the rudiments of education, both religious and secular, were generally taught to children in the home by their parents. After that they proceeded to more formal schooling. The inability of the great majority of the Englishmen in the Lesser Antilles to establish the family as a fundamental institution during the early decades seriously limited any significant development of education. In the first place, most children of ten years or more had been brought over to work in the fields, and very few babies were born or survived in the islands so that before 1650 schooling was not a pressing matter. When the widespread illiteracy of the numerous Irish servants is taken into account, along with a similar deficiency among many of the English, it is evident that the proportion of the islanders who could read and write must have been well below the high level attained at home.[34]

There is indisputable evidence that some young people did receive at least elementary education. Robert Sandford, who became a justice of the peace, a lieutenant colonel, and a councillor in Surinam tells us that about 1642 ". . . I was transported in my child-hood into the West Indies; where I spent my whole puerility and adolescence, all the time proper for Erudition, and the polishings of my now-ended virility." This sentence alone indicates a capacity to write Latinate English, which must have been the result of instruction in the colonies. In a will made in June 1647 Matthew Halsey of Barbados, gentleman and an old planter, left ninety acres in cotton and tobacco to his wife, gave his two bound nephews their freedom, and desired that "John (son of Mary Chapman) have maintenance and be put to school . . . and shall never be a servant." [35]

Bay, and St. Lucy. These may have been built with Barbados stone and brick; other less pretentious wooden structures may have been omitted because they were being destroyed by termites. (Plate 2) *Acts of Barbados* (Hall), 4–5; *Acts and Statutes of Barbados* (Jennings), 11–12; Foster, *Late Horrid Rebellion,* 109.

34. For schooling in Britain, see *Vexed and Troubled Englishmen,* 141–2, 276, 311–39. This was a time of great educational ferment in England. See, for example, Henry Robinson, *Certain Proposals in Order to the Peoples Freedom* (London, 1652), for "free Publick Schooles" for teaching reading, writing, grammar, and even swimming, because the parents of the poor do not instruct them sufficiently.

35. Robert Sandford, *Surinam Justice* (London, 1662), To the Reader; *JBMHS,* XI, 184; *NEHG Reg.,* XXXIX, 136.

Peter Hancock, who died in 1645, left his plantation and all appurtenances to found and erect "a free school for the Teaching and instructing of Youth, the Sons of poor Parents, in Grammar, and the Knowledge of the Latin Tongue, &c., and for the maintenance of the said poor Schollars and their Master." The trustees were to give preference to children of poor servants from London, and all scholars were to wear gray coats of a uniform pattern. There is no record that this school ever started, but the bequest reflects perfectly the eleemosynary spirit of contemporary Englishmen and also the determination of Barbadians of substance to create a real Little England in their island. The earliest known reference to actual educational institutions in the Caribbees comes from Uchteritz. Commenting on the Anglicans in 1652, the Lutheran asserts that "they even have their schools here too." This probably meant that the ministers taught school in addition to their weekly duty of catechizing children prescribed by the act of 1647, for formal education would naturally be conducted under the aegis of the Church. Whether or not a planter paid fees to send his sons and daughters to such a school was a private decision. In time the islanders would achieve a measure of success in providing for education, but at the close of the century they still would not have reached the point already arrived at in 1650 by the Puritans in New England.[36]

VI

In not one of the Caribbee islands did the English inhabitants succeed before 1650 in establishing a sound white society. Constantly changing and shifting populations and the single-minded pursuit of material gain did not allow sufficient leisure for healthy recreation, let alone for any kind of culture. The West Indians

36. Several Latin grammar schools already flourished in Massachusetts-Bay and Connecticut, and were sending boys to Harvard College, which, by 1650, had graduated 45 students. John Jones of the class of 1643 was "imployed in the Western parts in Mevis" as a preacher in 1651. John L. Sibley, *Biographical Sketches of Graduates of Harvard University* (Cambridge, Mass., 1873), I, 77, 20–256; Samuel E. Morison, *Intellectual Life of Colonial New England* (Ithaca, 1961), 17–18; Davis Coll., VIII, Envelope 11; Uchteritz, *Kurze Reise,* 9; *Acts and Statutes of Barbados* (Jennings), 13.

had no Prince Maurice of Nassau to act as Maecenas, no half-dozen good painters headed by Frans Post and Albert Eckhout, no assemblage of forty-four other learned and skilled men to create botanical and zoological gardens, an aviary, and an astronomical observatory to keep records of winds and rainfall. Nor were these settlements served by any 130 or so graduates of English universities, such as began as early as 1633 in New England to seek support for the erection of a school of learning, "a colledg among us." Culture in the Caribbean was, as the modern phrase goes, a one-man show, but, as with so many other promising young men in the islands, a distinguished career ended within three years because of a breakdown of health.[37]

Richard Ligon—so heavily leaned upon in these pages—arrived at Barbados in the *Achilles* in 1647. Very little is known about his previous life. Obviously of gentle birth and a kinsman of the famous Berkeleys of Gloucestershire, he had had as good an education as the age permitted, even though he did not attend a university. During his travels in France and Italy he absorbed by observation and much reading as much as any one intelligent Englishman could. A riotous mob in the Lincolnshire fens kept this calm and well-tempered Royalist out of a large estate. Subsequently he sought to recoup his fortunes on a plantation in Antigua, but illness forced him to stay with Thomas Modyford in Barbados.[38]

Richard Ligon demonstrated beyond all doubt that he was the true Renaissance man in capacity, in knowledge, in spirit and action. In fact it would be difficult to discover among the colonists of any other nation in the New World throughout the seventeenth century a more cultured individual. This talented and resourceful amateur strove successfully to improve the diet of the average man and to introduce the rich planters to the delights of French and Italian cooking at a time when very few of his countrymen knew anything about it. In like fashion, as we have noted earlier, he

37. Boxer, *Dutch in Brazil,* 112–16; John Eliot to Sir Simon D'Ewes, Sept. 1633, *Harvard Library Bulletin,* VIII (1954), 273–4.

38. Astonishing, too, is Ligon's knowledge of ship-handling and navigation, and of animal husbandry. William D. Ligon, *The Ligon Family and Connections* (New York, 1947); Ligon, *Barbados,* 1–2, 22.

drew up plans for houses suited to the climate and attempted to persuade the planting gentry to seek beauty as well as utility in their dwellings. Indeed, he was full of ideas of all sorts, ever ready with his skills, and in a very real sense the premier pioneer of culture in the West Indies. Unfortunately, his fellow colonists often failed to listen. His was a voice crying in the wilderness.

Ligon had great hopes when he arrived in Barbados that the Cavalier planters would transplant and perpetuate the great English traditional music. He found some congenial spirits with "musicall minds," but the majority of them were "so fixt upon, and so rivetted to the earth, and the profits that arise out of it, as their souls were lifted no higher; and those men think . . . that three whip Sawes, going all at once in a Frame or Pit, is the best and sweetest musick that can enter their ears; and to hear a cow of their own low, or an Assinigo bray, no sound can please them better." Their souls, he went on, echoing Sir Thomas Browne, were never lifted so high "as to hear the musick of the Sphears." He and other music lovers formulated a plan of sending for the musicians who played at Black Friars. They were prepared to allow them salaries sufficient to permit them to live as well as they did in England. The plan failed because Ligon, who knew them personally, fell ill and could not negotiate with them about coming to the Caribbees.[39]

The rhythms of the blacks fascinated Ligon, who recognized their musical import. Certainly he was one of the first Europeans to sense this, and had he not been ill so much of the time he would have tried to give the slaves some "hints of tunes . . . for time without tune is not an eighth part of the Science of Musick." When he discovered that Macow, the keeper of the plantain grove on the Hilliard-Modyford plantation, had a gift for music and displayed curiosity about the theorbo, he taught him to play the instrument. The slave also fashioned a primitive xylophone of six notes with six wooden billets, each one above the other. Ligon successfully explained to him about sharps and flats, and nominated him "our Chiefe Musician." (Plate 8) [40]

Early in the century, the Earl of Arundel asserted that "one

39. Ligon, *Barbados,* 107.
40. Ligon, *Barbados,* 47–9, 107.

who could not design a little would never make an honest man." Richard Ligon easily met this test with his architectural drafting, but he can also be designated a cartographer and watercolor artist. The map, *A Topographical Description and Admeasurement of the Yland of Barbados in the West Indies with the Mrs. Names of the severall plantacons,* in his *History* is both accurate and curiously embellished with vignettes of ships and dolphins, of wild boars, camels, Negro slaves, long-horned cattle, and planters on horseback. (Plate 2) Six plates in this book of 1657 are very early representations of New-World flora: palms, pineapples, bananas, plantains, pomegranates, and prickly pears. Three diagrams of an ingenio, or sugar mill, are remarkable for the clarity with which technical matters are presented. Originally Ligon had planned to include several plates showing Negroes in various postures to illustrate their sports and work. He had sketched them on Barbados and intended to have them reproduced in color but had to settle with his bookseller for black and white.[41]

Vivid accounts of all his efforts, achievements, and failures are set down in *A True and Exact History of the Island of Barbados,* written in the King's Bench Prison where he was thrown upon his return to England in 1650 to regain his health. In time his friends procured his release. First published in 1657, and again in 1673, and in a French translation at Paris in 1699, it is the most detailed and informing account of any English colony in the seventeenth century. A notable book of travel, its clear and fascinating prose makes it good reading as well. It is, moreover, a very early and excellent example of the *essai sur les mœurs,* for in addition to the many topics already alluded to, its author dealt fully with the flora and fauna of the island in the text as well as in the illustrations. John Evelyn read about pineapples in "Captain Ligon's History," and it is pleasant to imagine these two votaries of horticulture conversing about exotic plants and fruits. Ligon also contributed to the beginnings of Caribbean anthropology with shrewd observations about the black man and the red. To the gradually emerging conception of the Indian as a noble savage, Ligon supplied a

41. Ligon used Albrecht Dürer's proportions in describing the Arawaks. Horace Walpole, *Anecdotes of Painting in England,* in *Works* (London, 1798), III, 207; Ligon, *Barbados,* Epistle Dedicatory, 51.

firsthand account of an Indian woman servant at the Hilliard-Modyford plantation. Modest to a fault, she went about naked, "was of an excellent shape and colour, for it was a pure bright bay; small breasts, with nipples of a porphyric colour." One of her daily duties was to remove "Chegoes" [chiggers] from Ligon's feet. In England the story of her tragic love affair with a white man, when told in Addison's *Spectator* (No. 11), attained great popularity and inspired George Colman's play of 1787 "Inkle and Yarico." [42]

VII

The history of the English people in the West Indies is much more than a chronicle of past politics, but the establishing of English governmental institutions and the struggle to control them did, however, greatly complicate and often hinder economic and social development. From 1629 to 1650, proprietary rule rested heavily on the inhabitants of each island, and was exercised for the private profit of the two Earls and their lessee, Lord Willoughby of Parham. It was to the proprietors and their agents that the leading colonists looked for grants of land and other favors.[43]

The puritan colonizer, Sir Thomas Warner, went out as governor of St. Christopher for life in 1629; in 1636 he received a commission as lieutenant general of all the islands in the Carlisle patent, Barbados included. With the aid of a council appointed by himself, he ruled St. Christopher arbitrarily, at times ruthlessly, in the proprietorial interest. He made a treaty in May 1639 with the Chevalier de Poincy to stop the planting of tobacco in the British and French islands for eighteen months in order to raise its price; later Warner extended the period for the English colonies until October 6, 1641. Governor Henry Ashton of Antigua told

42. Henri Justel first published the French translation of the work in *Recueil de divers voyages faits en Afrique et en l'Amérique . . .* (Paris, 1674, reissued 1684); Ligon, *Barbados,* 54–5, 65; *Diary of John Evelyn,* ed. H. B. Wheatley (London, 1906), II, 231.

43. From the few available sources, J. A. Williamson and V. T. Harlow worked out in detail what was known in the 1920's of the political and constitutional history of the Caribbee islands. The late J. Harry Bennett of the University of Texas, using the Hay of Haystoun MSS, wrote the most authoritative account of the period 1642–46 (*WMQ,* 3d ser., XXIV [1967], 359–72).

of the desperation and impatience with which the colonists had to bear with the impositions of the government: "The long Cessation hath reduced them to this pointe of undoeinge, having spent their whole Tyme in pedling and chaffering to the multiplying of debt, the infecting them with the love of long accustomed Idlenes, and the Disableinge them to renewe their stockes of servants whose tymes in this vacancy have been unproffitably worne out. . . ." Three years of debt, bad weather, and the probability of having to pay back rents to the proprietor brought about the "First Rebellion" against arbitrary government and for the redressing of grievances at St. Christopher in December 1641. Sir Thomas peremptorily rejected all demands of the committees chosen by the planters and imprisoned the three leading spokesmen.[44]

A second rebellion, and a successful one, erupted as 1500 aroused men forced Warner to issue a general pardon by February 1642, but their great achievement was ending one-man government by Sir Thomas Warner and the calling of an elected assembly of twenty-four burgesses. The first representative body met in February or March. According to the receiver general, William Johnson, it was completely controlled by Ensign Phance Beecher and three other militia officers. Although he had been in the island only three years, Beecher, a "most arrogant and nowe sawcye proude fellowe," acted as if he were the only governor of the island and in that capacity forced Warner to accede to all of the islanders' demands by March 1642. The fact that Beecher, a merchant, was a kinsman of Sir William Beecher, Clerk of the Privy Council, gave him a high standing with the planters, who rejoiced when he declared in the presence of the Council and Sir Thomas Warner that he was as well descended and as good as any man there. More than one of the other rebels was a man of repute among the planters, and though the Governor managed to recover some of his old authority by December of that year, the representative assembly continued as a permanent branch of the government in a "free Colony." [45]

44. Henry Ashton to James Hay, Feb. 8, 1641/2; Anthony Brisket to Proprietary Trustees, Nov. 7, 1642, Hay MSS; Bennett, *WMQ,* 3d ser., XXIV, 360–61.

45. Phance Beecher, merchant and planter, was an early Nathaniel Bacon. An enemy accused him of "Cutthroate dealinges in buyinge and sellinge of planta-

Fear that the success of the second insurrection at St. Christopher would precipitate similar uprisings in the other Leeward Islands agitated Sir Thomas Warner. He was reassured by Anthony Brisket of Montserrat, who reported in February 1642: "God be praysed our people here are all quiet." Nine months later, however, there was trouble, which Brisket attributed to the example set by St. Christopher. He alleged that there were very few landholders who refused to pay the lord's levies, but many, many poor planters did not have the means to pay, and he was unwilling to use any "extremety" with them. On Nevis the Governor managed, "by a wile," to capture four rebel leaders, who were sent to prison at St. Christopher; and he forestalled possible disorders by announcing that no rents due the lord would be collected on that island during the prohibition of planting. From 1642 until his death in 1649, Governor Warner managed to contain political unrest in the Leeward Islands. Although Henry Ashton of Antigua revealed that the French and Irish in English St. Christopher were "starke weary of his Government," the English settlers, outnumbered and overawed, remained silent. It is not unlikely that the colonists, on the whole, were sympathetic to the Royal cause, but they wisely maintained a benevolent neutrality.[46]

Political uncertainties, if not always actual turmoil, plagued Barbados through this entire period. The struggle between Sir William Courteen and James Hay, first Earl of Carlisle, ended in victory for the Scot in 1629. Then ensued ten difficult years, during

---

tions, as alsoe by putting of Comodityes . . . at unconscionable rates, as playinge Cards which cost not above 3*d.* at 20 [pounds] . . . of tobacco p[er] paire (some say at 30 . . .), pinns, needles, lynnen, Canvas, and other Comodityes at like rates . . . ." He bragged of being worth 300,000 pounds of tobacco, "all men paid" up! Beecher's supporters in the new Assembly were the nucleas of a local Anglo-Irish planting gentry, along with Jeaffreson and the Warner officials: Rice Nowell, William Crowe, Thomas Branshie, John Powell, John Gill, Hugh Ford, Henry Lawther. William Johnson to Proprietary Trustees, Jan. 17, April 2, 4, 1642; Aggrievances of the Inhabitants, Feb. 8, 1642; Warner to Earl of Carlisle, April 1, 1642, Hay MSS; Bennett, in *WMQ,* 3d ser., XXIV, 363–6.

46. As Sir Thomas recovered some of his former authority toward the end of 1642, George Butler, a burgess, enticed many settlers to leave St. Christopher for St. Croix, where they "dyed miserably in the woods." Johnson to Trustees, Dec. 24, 1642; Warner to Carlisle, April 1, 1642; Brisket to Carlisle, Feb. 13, Nov. 7, 1642; Johnson to Carlisle, April 2 or 4, 1642, Hay MSS; Bennett, in *WMQ,* 3d ser., XXIV, 366.

most of which the unscrupulous Henry Hawley governed, exacting high rents for himself as well as for the Proprietor. When the spendthrift Earl died in 1636, three trustees assumed control of the revenues to pay off the creditors; his son James Hay, as second Earl of Carlisle, succeeded to what assets remained in the patent. In 1639 the young Earl, with a view of recovering proprietary authority, dismissed the unpopular Hawley, who, in a bid to retain his office, sought local support by summoning an elected assembly to advise with him. In 1640, however, the settlers obediently received the new governor, Henry Huncks. He, in turn, making a great effort, succeeded in wresting control of the revenues from the Trustees by persuading the Assembly to consent to a new annual rent of three pounds of tobacco or cotton per acre in place of the forty pounds of tobacco exacted by Hawley for each adult laboring on the land. By this act, the Barbados Assembly ceased to be a mere advisory body. The next year brought a new acting governor, Philip Bell; he induced the Assembly to return to the old rent based on polls but consistently recognized this body as a regularly constituted legislature.[47]

Philip Bell was an old Caribbean hand when he assumed office at Barbados in 1641. He had been governor of Bermuda, 1625–29, of Providence Island, 1631–36, and in 1640, following an unsuccessful attempt to settle 120 Englishmen at St. Lucia, he and some followers moved over to Barbados. "A very honest just man" with "a very plentifull fortune of his own," Bell concentrated upon promoting the general welfare and advancing trade in conjunction with men of great estates in the island who sat on the Council by

47. Unless speedy changes in government are made in Barbados, William Powrey notified Archibald Hay in 1640, some kind of upheaval will occur: "The ablest and best sort of people are seling and disposing of their estates here and prepareing for to remove hence. The whole Island in generall great and small doeth murmure and say in their hearts although they do not speake it with their tounges, lett us be gon. I know no other caus of this their discontent but the soe Rigid and too too severe Governor [Hawley]. Hee sayes all is for the profitt of my earl of Carlisle." Evidence from the Hay MSS strongly indicates that it was under Huncks in 1640 rather than Bell after 1641 that the Assembly was recognized as a legislative body. William Powrey to Archibald Hay, Oct. 5, Nov. 17, 1640; Archibald Hay to Peter Hay, Aug. 3, 1641; James Brown to Proprietary Trustees, Aug. 15, 1643, Hay MSS; Bennett, *WMQ*, 3d ser., XXIV, 367–8. Cf. Harlow, *Barbados*, 13–20; and Williamson, *Caribbee Islands*, 145–6.

fostering good laws, encouraging trade with all comers, especially the Dutch, and setting up local parish government modeled as nearly as possible on that in Britain.[48]

From 1641 to 1650 the leading Barbadians applied themselves and their resources to the developing of a profitable staple. When the political upheaval came in England, the most striking fact about the island was the "quiet Enclination of the People." Governor Bell and most of the old planters favored the Parliament, but outwardly they were "bound up with the Principles of Neutrality," which they shrewdly adhered to until 1647 while, for the first time in their brief history, they prospered. "If we should pertake or declare ourselves on eyther side, we wer undone," Philip Bell warned Archibald Hay in 1645, "for against the kinge we are resolved never to be, and without the freindshipe of the perliment and free trade of London ships we are not able to subsist . . . what unreasonable tearmes on both sides!" After 1646 hundreds of the Royal party taken prisoners were sent to Barbados as servants, and many officers came to the island with the hope of recouping their fortunes. They came in such numbers that "by the Civility of the first Settlers, they got into the Principal Offices of that Government and by degrees drew the People if not absolutely to decline their former Peaceable Resolutions, yet in a great measure, to incline to the lost Cavalier Party, by making the Current of all Preferments and Authority to stream to those that way affected." The Walronds and Colonel Byam first forced one of their own faction, Guy Molesworth, into exile, then turned on James Drax, whom they branded the "factor to the Rebells in England" and the promoter in Barbados of "disloyalty, Rebellion, and ruin." "My ayme is at Drax, [Thomas] Middleton, and the rest," read one of their inflammatory posters. "Vivat Rex!"[49]

48. The earliest surviving local records of Barbados are the Parish Vestry Minutes of St. John's in the Barbados Museum and Historical Society. In 1649 the parish officers consisted of 2 churchwardens, 2 sidesmen, 6 constables, and 7 "surveyors." Among the 24 vestrymen were Thomas Modyford, Edward Walrond, and "Mr. Ferdinande Paleologus" (a descendant of a Byzantine Emperor), see p. 1. Each parish elected 2 burgesses to the Assembly. Stock, *Debates,* I, 145; BM: Egerton MSS, 2395, fol. 629, pp. 1412–13.

49. Governor Bell to Archibald Hay, July 21, 1645, Hay MSS; A. B., *A Brief*

By playing upon the fears of aged Governor Bell, the extremists got the upper hand in the Assembly, where they rammed through several acts designed to crush the "Independents." The tacit compromise between Roundhead and Royalist broke down completely; violence and bloodshed threatened to erupt everywhere after the proclamation of May 3, 1650, that Charles Stuart was the rightful king of England! By this time the Walronds and their supporters were in the saddle and spurring every inhabitant of Barbados against the "Parliament men." Their secret plans to ruin Drax and others were revealed by Christopher Codrington, a Royalist but also a moderate, an old planter, and a son-in-law of Drax; he was also a Barbadian patriot and was aghast at the extremes to which the Walronds proposed to go. The aim of "these new model'd Magistrates" seemed to be to eliminate all men of opinions contrary to theirs. Twenty Parliament men, including James Drax, Thomas Middleton, Constant Sylvester, Lewis Morris, and Nicholas Foster, were brought to trial for planning to subvert Church and State, condemned upon spurious evidence, and fined from 5000 to 80,000 pounds of sugar, the highest amount being levied against Drax.[50]

The Barbadians' enjoyment of virtual independence and free trade with all nations was soon to end. The strong men of Westminster could not be expected to endure for long a Royalist island trading with the greatest rivals of the merchants of England. On October 1, 1650, they declared through Parliament that the people of Barbados, Antigua, St. Christopher, Nevis, Montserrat, Bermuda, and Virginia, for refusing to subject themselves to the Parliament of England, were "notorious Robbers and Traitors, and such as by the Law of Nations are not to be permitted any maner of Commerce or Traffique with any people whatsoever." In a puni-

---

Relation of the Beginning and Ending of the Troubles of the Barbados With the True Causes Thereof (London, 1653), 1–6; also Foster, *Late Horrid Rebellion,* 24, 26, *et passim.*

50. Foster lists the principal Royalists and Parliament men, and prints several letters directed against Drax and his party, as well as the oath demanded by the Walronds. This ordinance and A. B.'s narrative demonstrate how completely this was a struggle within the nascent gentry of rich planters, who had so much in common socially and economically. Foster, *Late Horrid Rebellion,* especially pp. 5, 8–12, 24–6, 43, 47, 54, 59, 67–70, 86–7.

tive clause, all intercourse with these colonies was prohibited, and the Council of State was authorized to send an expedition to reduce the recalcitrant provinces and settle their governments.[51]

VIII

CONCLUSION TO PART I

English promoters and colonists, with thousands of servants from the British Isles, a majority of whom were Irish, established five permanent colonies in the Lesser Antilles during the two and a half decades before 1650. In that year in St. Christopher and Barbados, thousands of white men, some women, and fewer children formed the two most densely populated communities of the known world. The smaller islands of Nevis and Montserrat were also crowded with settlers; alone of the Leeward Islands, Antigua remained relatively undeveloped. Everywhere, save at Barbados, Irish indentured servants or freemen predominated. The native redmen had been almost eliminated from these islands.

Emerging from a long, hard, and tragic struggle for survival and adjustment to the strange and formidable environment, these Europeans had at last succeeded in producing the staple crops so fundamental to colonial economies. With the priceless assistance of the Dutch merchants, shipping, and credit, the leading planters, given a little good fortune and domestic and civil quiet, could look ahead to a promising future. This was a signal accomplishment.

The mood of the common folk in the English islands could not, however, be considered optimistic. At least half of all the white people who had been brought from the British Isles had died in loneliness, misery, and despair. They could not adapt themselves to the New World. Overpopulation and lack of land forced many freemen to seek relief by migrating, while into Barbados and St. Christopher, Dutch slavers were beginning to pour thousands of black Africans to supplant the white servants. Displaced Europeans were now becoming displaced West Indians.

Within each island, life was conducted almost exclusively in the interests of the large planters, who represented what little

51. Firth and Rait, *Acts and Ordinances of the Interregnum,* II, 426–7, 559–62.

stability there was. For everyone else, existence continued in doubt; at best they looked upon life somberly, desperately, often hopelessly. Nostalgia for the home they would never see again, bitterness and exhaustion from toil in the present, and fear about the near future possessed thousands of men and women. Life in the Caribbean was temporary, fleeting; death appeared almost the sole certainty for persons of all ranks. In no aspect of their experience had there been the kind of peace for which simple folk yearn. The Europeans had failed to create a Little England; in truth they had not formed a viable white society. By 1650, though they did not grasp the fact, the opportunity to build a white man's civilization in these islands had passed by forever.

Part II

Black Men's Plantations

1651–1690

VI

Acts of God and Man

THE MEN AND WOMEN of the European nations in the West Indies, whether they were white, black, or red, lived in a continual state of transition throughout the seventeenth century. We have seen that because of unsettled human, physical, economic, and political conditions, radical transformations were under way but far from complete in any of the English settlements. Permanent well-rounded societies had not yet formed in the Leeward Islands or Barbados.

From 1650 to 1690 several outside influences combined with economic uncertainties to retard the civilizing of the peoples or, in some instances, to disrupt all normal activity. Some of them were man-made; others were natural occurrences or, as men of that day thought, acts of divine retribution beyond all human capacity to fathom, let alone combat. Foreign wars, organized violence by freebooters, Carib raids, devastation by storms and hurricanes, and a steady erosion of life caused by endemic or epidemic diseases seemed always to ravage the Caribbees. For forty years in the Antilles, Englishmen enjoyed little peace of mind. Attacks on or by the Spanish, Dutch, French, or aborigines occurred so frequently that they were deemed to be normal happenings; and when respites did come, Nature seemed to conspire against the people. Often, too, the islanders quarreled bitterly among themselves. Disrupting change and insecurity were the lot of every Englishman. All of life, it seemed, was violent.

II

"The wars here are more destructive then in any other partes of the world; for twenty yeares' peace will hardly resettle the devastation of one yeare's warre," remarked Christopher Jeaffreson as he reviewed the terrible decade 1665–75 from his plantation in depopulated and ruined St. Christopher. In not one of the forty years after 1650 did the West Indians experience a surcease from strife. During twenty-six of them, England was formally at war, both in Europe and the Caribbean, with Spain, the Netherlands, or France. Alone of the Caribbees, Barbados escaped invasion. Based upon the doctrine of no peace beyond the line, the English and the Dutch waged undeclared war at sea; the English-led privateers or buccaneers attacked or captured Dutch islands or Spanish cities on the Main; and on St. Christopher the English and the French always lived uneasily in enmity and fear of each other. Among the English, French, and Dutch, the entire period was one of intense competition for trade that upon occasion involved the use of force, legal or illegal. There is no necessity here to chronicle the course of conflict; what needs to be emphasized is the several ways in which it determined the lives of the English colonists in the West Indies.[1]

Threats of declared wars and informal struggles kept the Caribbean peoples in a constant fever of apprehension. As dwellers in the islands they lived a decidedly maritime existence. Everything and everybody came and went in ships, small craft, or great dugout canoes: food, wood for fuel, draft animals, European goods, servants, slaves, merchants, and Caribs. In times of war, obviously, each colony's trade was vulnerable, and each lay open to attack from the sea. The sudden foray of Admiral de Ruyter from the Mediterranean against the English islands in April 1665 is but the most dramatic example. With his ships severely battered by shore batteries when he attempted to bombard The Indian Bridge, the

1. A chronology of strife in the Caribbean may be found in Appendix II. Professor Charles Wilson has pointed out that in the years between 1600 and 1667 only in 1610 did all of the great European states enjoy peace. *Profit and Power*, 1; *A Young Squire of the Seventeenth Century from the Papers of Christopher Jeaffreson*, ed. John C. Jeaffreson (London, 1878), I, 215.

greatest naval commander of the age stood away from Barbados for Nevis, where he captured sixteen English ships from that island and Montserrat. In one of these merchantmen from London, Governor John Winthrop, Jr., of Connecticut lost goods worth £2000. De Ruyter also raided shore stations at each place. On the other hand, buccaneers organized by Governor Thomas Modyford of Jamaica and led by Colonel Edward Morgan captured St. Eustatius, Saba, and later Tobago; and from St. Christopher, Governor William Watts sent off an expedition that plundered the Dutch half of St. Martin; and Captain Morris with a force from Barbados attacked and sacked Pomeroon and Essequibo, Dutch settlements in Guiana. By the close of 1665 the Dutch had been virtually driven out of the Caribbean, having only Curaçao left in their possession. A sound strategic conclusion enunciated later by Governor Sir William Stapleton of the Leeward Islands was: "Whoever is master of the sea, and has good soldiers, from October to June, can carry or destroy the strongest islands." [2]

The people of all nations in the Antilles greatly dreaded the consequences of any extension of European quarrels to their regions and, with the exception of the Spanish, their public officials strove constantly and earnestly to preserve peace beyond the line. The treaty between Sir Thomas Warner and Sieur d'Esnambuc, concluded first in 1627 and renewed many times down to 1666, rested upon the assumption that the French and English had come out to the Caribbean as allies against the Spanish and the Caribs rather than as members of enemy nations. Both parties ardently desired to remain clear of European struggles, and one might say that the isolation of the New World proclaimed so pungently by Tom Paine in 1776 had its origins in practice more than a century earlier in the Lesser Antilles.

In 1659 the French governors of Guadeloupe and St. Christopher agreed with the English officials of Nevis, Montserrat, and Antigua on an offensive-defensive alliance against the Caribs; and in 1660 the two nations appeared to be getting along peaceably in the West Indies. Within three years, however, Lord Willoughby's plans to expand on St. Lucia and St. Vincent aroused the French

2. *MHS Colls.*, 5th ser., VIII, 134; *CSPC, 1661–68,* pp. 292–3, 297–8, 319–20, 329, 331–2, 355; *1675–76,* p. 499; *London Gazette,* May 14, 1666.

to protest what they properly considered breaches of the treaty. In January 1666, the very same month that Louis XIV honored his Dutch alliance and declared war on England, the French and English on St. Christopher renewed their treaty of neutrality; but neutrality and peace ended abruptly and finally with the King's declaration, notwithstanding desperate efforts by French insular authorities to extend the treaty and fend off conflict. After the Peace of Breda (1667), Sir William Stapleton energetically attempted to arrange a general treaty of neutrality between the two nations in the West Indies. In 1668 an accord was actually reached with Governor de Blénac for "peace, union, concord, good correspondence, amity, and neutrallyty" in the islands under the control of the negotiators. The French mistakenly assumed that the agreement would include Barbados and Jamaica; their government, understandably, insisted upon the inclusion of the two largest and strongest islands, but the English Lords of Trade dissembled and delayed, with the result that the treaty was never ratified in either France or England. From that time forward the colonists and planters of the two countries were in for nearly a century of unceasing hostilities, open or undeclared.[3]

The exclusively maritime nature of war in the West Indies meant that Dutch trade inevitably and inescapably suffered from it. In 1662 Pieter de la Court warned in *Het Interest van Holland* that "above all things War, and chiefly by Sea, is most prejudiciall, and Peace very beneficial for Holland." This was doubly true in the Dutch islands and other settlements on the Main, for their inhabitants had to defend themselves against "Sea-Robbers or Enemyes" in peacetime, and when war came, besides ships, they lost goods and debts due. The merchants of St. Eustatius and Curaçao had not waited for buyers to come to them; they carried their goods to

3. The French and English signed a general treaty guaranteeing a peaceful settlement of all disputes in their plantations in America from Dec. 1, 1687, until Jan. 1, 1688/9. Immediately after this brief interlude, the two nations were at war again, however. For the Anglo-French neutrality treaties, see Frances G. Davenport, *European Treaties bearing on the History of the United States and Its Dependencies* (Washington, 1927), II, 81–5, 256–60, 309–29, 329; *CSPC, 1685–88,* p. 475; C. S. S. Higham, *The Development of the Leeward Islands Under the Restoration, 1660–1688* (Cambridge, England, 1921), 32–6, 40–41, 113–17; and for the French view, Du Tertre, *Histoire générale des Antilles,* III, 277–9, 280–81.

the English and French islands for the chapmen to take up and ordinarily allowed a year's time for payments. More and more, now that sugar was becoming the prime staple, supplies of food came in from New England, and war threatened shipments from there as it did those from Ireland, the other main source of provisions. In 1666 one Evans, master of a small ketch from New England, thinking he was to the leeward of Surinam, beat to windward for five days and then fell a prize to Admiral Abraham de Cryñsen's fleet. Lord Willoughby wrote home of the "friendship and bounty of New England" in providing £1200 sterling worth of provisions for the fleet before Nevis. "Thank God," exclaimed Governor Edwin Stede, when reporting the shortage of shipping at Barbados in 1690, "we have been kept fairly well supplied by ships from New England." When war with Holland was being debated in 1664, George Monck, Duke of Albemarle, in soldierly fashion, blurted out the truth: "What matters this or that reason? What we want is more of the trade the Dutch now have." In the West Indies during the Second Dutch War (1665–67), which was the first of the great colonial conflicts, the Hollanders and Zeelanders appear to have been the heaviest losers, because they were the greatest shippers and traders. To them this struggle was truly "an incredible great Blow." [4]

Although Spain was a once-great power, now in decay, and her colonial monopoly on the Main had been breached early in the seventeenth century, her rulers blindly and stubbornly refused to recognize the realities of the new age of war as an extension of commerce. In the Treaty of Tordesillas (1494) the Portuguese and the Spaniards had accepted the pope's division that gave the latter nation exclusive right to and possession of all lands west and south of the "line of Demarcation." Never acknowledging the Spanish monopoly, the Dutch, French, and English in the seventeenth century, seized small, unoccupied islands in the Lesser Antilles, colonized them, and opened a forbidden traffic with the Spanish col-

4. Ascribed to John De Witt, but written by Pieter de la Court, this influential tract was published in English as *The True Interest and political Maxims of the Republic of Holland and West Friesland* (London, 1702), 230–31; William Byam, Journal of Guiana, in BM: Sloane MSS, 3662, fol. 30; *CSPC, 1661–68,* p. 526; *1689–92,* p. 249; George Monck, quoted by Alfred T. Mahan, *The Influence of Sea Power on History, 1660–1783* (Boston, 1923), 107.

onies. Justifying the English designs in a memorandum of 1660, a writer disdainfully asserted the attitude of all other European nations: "The Popes Donacion is of little vallidity, for he hath given to the Kings of Spayne the Crownes of England, which he might more Legally doe, then give him the Indyes, the English having been subject to his power, the Americans never." Still, as late as 1666, in defending the issuing of privateering commissions to buccaneers to sail against them, Governor Modyford of Jamaica insisted that "the Spaniards look on us as intruders and trespassers wheresoever they find us in the Indies and use us accordingly; and were it in their power . . . would soon turn us out of all our Plantations . . . It must be force alone that can cut in sunder that unneighbourly maxim of their Government to deny all access of strangers." The English conquest and colonizing of Jamaica in 1655 were not explicitly admitted as accomplished facts by Spain until 1670 in the Treaty of Madrid.[5]

Enemy depredations on English shipping reached the point in the Second Dutch War that for the first time, to protect merchant vessels, the Admiralty resorted to convoying them. On February 16, 1665, such ships were ordered to return from the West Indies in fleets with naval escorts; ships from Surinam were to join those of Barbados; on November 11 a system for both outgoing and incoming merchantmen in the Caribbean and Virginia traffic was instituted. The *London Gazette* reported the arrival at Lyme in Dorset on August 1, 1668, of the *Concord,* one of twenty ships accompanied by two frigates that crossed the Atlantic in six weeks from Barbados; two days later another convoy of thirteen vessels came into Deal from the same island. Even though the Peace of Breda, July 21/31, 1667, officially ended the war with France and Holland, protection of English shipping apparently was still thought necessary both beyond the line and in home waters.[6]

5. Spanish exclusiveness, though less and less complete, did serve to prevent any kind of Spanish social and cultural influence from affecting the Dutch, English, and French, thereby insulating the English colonies not only against Spanish Roman Catholicism but against nearly everything else. BM: Egerton MSS, 2395, fol. 613; *CSPC, 1661–68,* p. 407; Davenport, *European Treaties,* I, 221*n,* 231*n*8; II, 94, 97, 99, 107, 189, 194, 195.

6. *CSPC, 1661–68,* pp. 328–9, 453; *CSPD, 1665–66,* pp. 51, 514, 546; *APC Col.,* I, 401–2; Frank Cundall, "Migration from Surinam to Jamaica," reprint from

From the first days of settlement, defense had been a major consideration with the colonists at each island, and some kind of military force was provided. As regular government was established, one or more militia regiments were formed, with the leading planters serving as officers. A law of 1652 at Barbados placed the responsibility for internal policing of servants and slaves upon the masters. Abbé Biët remarked there two years later that all the plantation masters carried the title of captain or colonel; not a few of these officers had gained experience in England under King Charles or Oliver Cromwell. The rank and file in the regiments were made up of thousands of white freemen. Upon occasion the colonial militia could put up a stout defense against invaders. This was demonstrated when Admiral George Ayscue was prevented by Lord Willoughby's men from forcing Barbados under Parliamentary rule in 1651–52 until Colonel Thomas Modyford's Windward Regiment reinforced the admiral's side; and also when shore batteries held off de Ruyter in 1665. The proximity of the French on St. Christopher necessitated an alerted militia most of the time.[7]

The large migrations of freemen and runaway servants from Barbados and St. Christopher cut down noticeably the numbers of white men available for militia duty at the same time that the black population was soaring; such a loss of manpower grew critical after 1660. During the Second Dutch War all of the Leeward Islands lost white population, St. Christopher drastically. After observing that only 2000 out of 7000 men able to bear arms could be depended upon in emergencies, Governor William Willoughby notified King Charles in 1666 that His Majesty's forces were badly needed: "Neither will the country be better for the future against an enemy, unless some way be found to give a comfortable livelihood to the meaner sort." From the days of Cromwell, military patrols ranged about nightly in Jamaica; in 1681 the Assembly passed a strict militia law emphasizing regular training and good discipline. The same year the Barbadians endeavored to elevate the status and authority of their militia regiments by ordering

---

Timehri, VI (1919), 146; *London Gazette,* Aug. 6, 1668; Arthur P. Middleton, in *WMQ,* 3d ser., III, 183–4.

7. *Acts and Statutes of Barbados* (Jennings), 116–25; Ligon, *Barbados,* 29; Biët, *Voyage,* 294; Thurloe, *State Papers,* III, 39.

red coats and black hats for the foot without the least regard to the suitability of the traditional English woolen uniform for tropical service. In times of peace, the militia could maintain public order, but it required help against an invading enemy when war broke out. Forts with heavy ordnance, regular English troops, and protection at sea from enemy war vessels were continually needed but not always forthcoming. So militarily weak did a Jamaican named Nevill consider his island in 1677 that he proposed to the Earl of Carlisle that all newcomers be required to plant inland away from the defenseless coast.[8]

At all times, the Leeward Islands lay open to raids by the Caribs, whose fierceness aroused extreme apprehension among the inhabitants. For this, the English policy of exterminating the natives was chiefly to blame, with the result that, as Charles de Rochefort wrote of the Caribs before 1658: ". . . there hardly passes a year but they make one or two irruptions, in the night time, into some one of the Islands . . . and then, if it be not timely discover'd, and valiantly oppos'd, they kill all the men they meet, ransack the Houses and burn them," and carry off all of the women and children with their booty. While seeking volunteers for the Penn-Venables Expedition in 1655, Captain Gregory Butler carefully refrained from recruiting on Antigua, because the Caribs of Guadeloupe, Dominica, and St. Vincent constantly harried the island, which had only 1000 militiamen to protect it. In the Anglo-French War of 1666–67, the Caribs paddled in their *periaguas* to the windward of Montserrat and Antigua, "the winds and currents making access easy," surprised the people, and burned their houses. When William, Lord Willoughby retaliated by attacking the Caribs on St. Vincent, Governor Modyford complained to Lord Albemarle that Willoughby did it only to colonize "an agueish island called Antigua, which those Indians might infest." The Caribs, he said, cannot be easily conquered, because his Lordship's action has

8. Governor Dutton wrote home concerning the Barbados militia: "They are now clothed like the King's army in red coats, black hats." He planned also to "model" the horse and reduce half of them to dragoons. *CSPC, 1681–85,* pp. 141, 281; *1661–68,* pp. 383, 432; *1675–76,* p. 420; *1685–88,* p. 535; Long, *History of Jamaica,* I, 123; II, 31; *Interesting Tracts Relating to the Island of Jamaica . . .* (St. Iago de la Vega, 1800), 106.

driven them right into the arms of the French; he would have done better to make peace with them.[9]

The Peace of Breda, 1667, held no meaning for the Caribs, who went right ahead with their hit-and-run raids and carrying off slaves, who quickly learned to serve them. In 1672 Governor Stapleton estimated the number of Indian bowmen in Dominica, St. Vincent, and St. Lucia to be 1500, and the runaway slaves taking refuge with them at 600. "The French have them always at command," he added, "and made . . . bloodhounds of them in the late war; and they are more terrible to some of our people than their neighbours." This former soldier suggested a joint Anglo-French campaign to wipe them out, but nothing came of it. In April 1683, after further raids by the "hellish villains" on Montserrat and Antigua, he took a small fleet to Dominica where he succeeded only in checking the offensive capacity of the Caribs by destroying eleven of their canoes. Later on, thirty-five more were destroyed at St. Vincent. The limited success of the venture may be attributed, in part, to the unwillingness of the Barbadians to join in the enterprise. Their governor, Sir Richard Dutton, made it clear that his people were "so little interested in the well-being of the Leeward Islands, which can never be useful to them, as they think, growing too fast upon them already, that they would be well content to see them lessened rather than advanced." Until the forced removal of 5000 Caribs from St. Vincent to the island of Ruatan in 1796, the embittered natives continued to menace the islanders.[10]

The enemy within their own ranks posed a threat almost as great as did the foreigners. Everywhere multitudes of Irish servants and freedmen, some of whom had borne arms against the English, aroused suspicion and fear. In resentment of the callous treatment by English settlers, the Hibernians had grown disaffected. So many of them wandered about Barbados, refusing to labor, threatening

9. Davies, *Caribby-Islands,* 19, 159; Thurloe, *State Papers,* III, 754–5; *CSPC, 1661–68,* pp. 553–4; *1677–80,* p. 642.

10. If Jamaica were not so far to leeward, we would help you, Sir Thomas Lynch wrote Governor Stapleton. "I am therefore amazed that at Barbados they should tell the captain that they would not spend 20£ to save the Leeward Islands and Jamaica. God be thanked our people here are not of that humour." *CSPC, 1681–85,* pp. 127, 140, 181, 197, 358–9, 431; *1669–74,* pp. 392, 399; PRO: CO 1/36, fols. 90–91; Higham, *Leeward Islands,* 122–42.

the inhabitants, and attempting to secure arms, that the governor, Daniel Searle, issued a proclamation in 1657 requiring all Irish servants to carry tickets from their masters when they went abroad in the island, and all Irish freedmen with no constant place of abode were to be whipped. They were feared, too, because of their Romish religion and the possibility that they might defect to the Catholic enemy should war break out. As a precaution in 1660, church-wardens were ordered to make a census of the Irish in each parish of Barbados. Throughout the Caribbees, the authorities hesitated to enroll the Celts in their militias. That such fears were not unreasonable was proved in 1666 when the Irish in St. Christopher rose against their masters and went over to the French cause for two years until the Peace of Breda. At Montserrat the overwhelmingly Celtic population revolted in January 1666 and remained in control of the colony until June. The English attitude was voiced by William, Lord Willoughby, at Barbados a year later: "We have more than a good many Irish amongst us, therefore I am for the downe right Scott, who I am certaine will fight without a Crucifix about his neck." [11]

Resentment against the Irish Catholics in the West Indies subsided somewhat in the decade 1667–77 as the need for white servants took precedence over other matters. Christopher Jeaffreson alleged in 1676 that most of the white inhabitants of restored St. Christopher were Hibernians, but the better sort were English. All of the old suspicions, animosities, and fears quickly surfaced again in 1689 when the English and French began to fight. Joseph Crispe wrote in alarm from Nevis that they had a still worse enemy than the French in the Irish Catholics; at Montserrat, Christopher Codrington preferred to entrust defense to the few Englishmen and their black slaves rather than depend upon the Irish whose loyalty was suspect and who predominated three to one. After 130 Celtics and others said openly that they would desert the English

11. After the French had plundered Antigua in 1666, Lord Willoughby reported that some Irish colonists, who adhered to the Gallic cause, destroyed what was left on the island. He personally saw to the hanging of some Irish rebels at Montserrat. *CSPC, 1661–68,* p. 547; *1574–1660,* p. 483; Thurloe, *State Papers,* III, 39–40; *Analecta Hibernica,* No. 4, pp. 236–9, 243; BM: Stowe MSS, 755, fol. 19b.

on Montserrat, the authorities on adjacent Nevis disarmed all of the Irish there and sent them off to Jamaica. In advising the governor of Montserrat about the probable defections of the Hibernians to the enemy if the island should be attacked, and what should be done about it, Lieutenant General Codrington frankly reminded him that "the Irish have never had any great kindness from the English, and as affairs are now, less than ever, witness Ireland itself and St. Christopher. Again, the Irish being Papists may be expected to welcome Papists . . . They also have a grievance against you, and doubtless hope for revenge." The only way out, Codrington continued, is to appeal to their self-interest and advantage by allowing them to enjoy estates in the island as freely as do the English. Here was an acute human problem dangerously exacerbated by war.[12]

Up to 1667, in the three islands of Barbados, St. Christopher, and Nevis, the annual freeing of hundreds of white servants for whom there was no land available and who did not wish to labor in the fields for low wages or who could not get work, created a large landless male population. Required to serve in the local militias, these freedmen had acquired some small preparation for service on expeditions against England's foes in the West Indies, and several times recruiting officers appealed to them successfully. For the projected conquest of Hispaniola that resulted in the conquering and colonizing of Jamaica in 1655, the agents of General Venables managed to enlist nearly 4000 Barbadians. The majority of them were rootless freedmen, but faced with raising so numerous a force, the recruiters also accepted debtors and runaway servants without much discrimination, even though they had been strictly enjoined not to enlist bondsmen. As Colonel Modyford saw it, however, "ther indentures not being written in their foreheads, they were by some ignorantly, and by others willfully received, and when once they were gott into the huddle there was no findinge them." Similar volunteers from St. Christopher and Nevis, numbering 1300, went aboard the fleet at the former place. Thus there went off more than 5000 colonials, "besides Women and

12. Jeaffreson, *Young Squire,* I, 180; *CSPC, 1689–92,* pp. 65, 73, 112–13, 123, 235.

Children that went with a Design to plant." Almost none of this large contingent ever returned to their islands: some were killed in battle and an unknown but large number succumbed to disease on shipboard or in Jamaica when they attempted to settle there. In 1666 Lord Willoughby, the crews of his ships, and his more than one thousand soldiers on their voyage from Barbados to "suppress the Insolencyes of the French and Dutch" and to retake English St. Christopher were virtually all drowned off Guadeloupe during a violent hurricane. Similar losses of colonists being used as soldiers demonstrated over and again that the wars suddenly and radically reduced and altered the composition of the white populations of the Caribbees.[13]

Buccaneering syphoned off the most adventurous, pugnacious, and greedy of the landless males of the crowded English islands. The prospects of booty and plunder from the cities of the Spanish Main, let alone the promise of three meals a day with plenty of meat, sufficed to attract them to the seventeenth-century Foreign Legion based on Tortuga. In the forties Maurice Thompson and some Cornish merchants backed "the valiant and victorious General Captain William Jackson" in privateering ventures against the Spanish; most of his men signed on from Barbados and St. Christopher. After 1655 the buccaneers commonly sailed under commissions issued by the governors of either Tortuga or Jamaica, and in this decade the excitement and the plunder increased their numbers noticeably. The primary source of their manpower was servants or *engagés* who had run away from their exacting and relentless masters. Sir Thomas Lynch estimated that between 1668 and 1671 Jamaica alone lost about 2600 men on buccaneering raids against Tobago, Curaçao, Porto Bello, Granada, and Panama; in the last expedition four-fifths of the men from Jamaica died, and

13. Lt. Col. Francis Barrington frankly admitted the mistake of enlisting Barbados servants with time to serve: "the doing of this hath much injured poor people, even to their undoing, and prejudiced many of the rich, some losing ten servants, some fifteen, some more, some less, none escaping us." But he believed the freemen were a greater loss to the island, especially the artificers. *HMC, 7th Report,* 572; Thurloe, *State Papers,* III, 620; *A Briefe and Perfect Journal of the Late Proceedings . . . in the West Indies.* By I. S., "an Eye Witness" (London, 1655), 11; BM: Egerton MSS, 2395, fol. 60; PRO: CO 1/37, fol. 60a; Harlow, *Colonising Expeditions,* 196–8.

planting was greatly retarded by the labor shortage thus created. On the favorable side, however, was the victory of the buccaneer force raised in Jamaica by Governor Modyford that captured St. Eustatius and Saba for the English in the Second Dutch War in 1665.[14]

Every economic activity in the West Indies—agricultural, industrial, commercial—by the English, French, and Spanish was delicately arranged. From the early days of settlement, Holland and Zeeland skippers and merchants shrewdly maintained a monopoly of trade and navigation, and English and French colonists had adjusted their economic activities in the light of this fact. Changing conditions in Europe, however, brought significant modifications shortly after 1650, and following the Treaty of Breda in 1667 Dutch predominance in the Caribbean disappeared forever.[15]

Parliament began the English effort to prevent its colonies from trading with the Dutch in the Act of 1650 and strengthened the restrictions in the Navigation Act of 1651. Sir George Ayscue's fleet seized twelve Dutch merchantmen lying unladen in Carlisle Bay in 1651; in 1654 Admiral William Penn surprised twenty more, took much contraband in the same harbor, and again "spoilt the sport" a few months later by taking Peter Stuyvesant and three ships that had come to Barbados to open "a fair trade" with New Netherland. In 1658 Captain Christopher Myngs captured six alleged Dutch vessels at Barbados in violation of the Act of Navigation. During the three Anglo-Dutch wars, 1652–74, commerce between the two nations in the West Indies broke up completely. But in the intervals between periods of open warfare, the Dutchmen and colonials energetically endeavored to restore peace-time exchanges, both legitimate and illegal. Although direct trade of Am-

14. Clarence H. Haring, *The Buccaneers in the Caribbean in the Seventeenth Century* (London, 1910), especially 59–66, 73–9, 238–9; "Mercurius Americanus," Captain William Jackson's Journal, 1642, in BM: Sloane MSS, 793 or 894; Alexander Olivier Exquemeling, *The History of the Buccaneers of America* (3d ed., London, 1704), is the fullest account of this Dutch *engagé's* classic experience as a buccaneer. *CSPC, 1669–74,* pp. 74, 75, 298; PRO: CO 1/18, fol. 95; CO 1/27, fol. 7; *London Gazette,* May 14, 1666.

15. Wilson, *Profit and Power,* 7, 41, 44–5, 115, 128, 142; W. J. van Hoboken, in *Britain and the Netherlands,* ed. J. S. Bromley and E. H. Kossmann (London, 1960), 41–2.

sterdam and Flushing with the English islands more or less ended after the Peace of Westminster in 1674, much clandestine traffic went on from depots of goods at St. Eustatius, Curaçao, and Surinam.[16]

The prevalence of war-time conditions throughout most of these forty years prevented the English planters from achieving any kind of stable economy in their islands, for with any disruption of trade came a breakdown in agriculture. Furthermore, in human and material terms, the costs of conflict to the English West Indies were incalculable, but conspicuously enormous. The loss of lives from disease, accidents, starvation, death in raids, from drowning, in addition to those of the men who went on military expeditions, was staggering. Some people died near their home settlements; others as refugees in far-away places.

One aspect of these years of conflict was the steady growth of strained relations among the several English colonies. The Barbadians grew envious as St. Christopher and Nevis began to produce sugar, and they also feared the potential competition from the great island of Jamaica and the large plantations at Surinam, not only for the growing of sugar cane, cotton, indigo, and ginger on them but for the capacity of these places to attract much-needed white men. They directed their resentment particularly against settlements undertaken on other islands by the Lords Willoughby as part of a policy of expansion. Prior to the Dutch conquest of Surinam in 1667, former Barbadians developed a flourishing sugar culture there and made superior Muscovado. One of the planters, Renatus Enys, wrote to Sir Henry Bennet in 1663 that "The sworn enemies of the colony are the Dons of Barbadoes, whose chief interest is to keep the planters in that island to balance the power of their negroes." At this time there were about 4000 planters along the Surinam River. In explaining why he surrendered the colony to the Dutch, Lieutenant General Byam charged that neither the King nor the Proprietor gave any assistance in arms or medicines, "nor can we have any thoughts of any Kindness or Succour

16. Bodleian: Tanner MSS, 55, fol. 85, cited by Harlow, *Barbados,* 70; BM: Egerton MSS, 2395, fol. 60; Thurloe, *State Papers,* III, 251; Beer, *Origins of the British Colonial System,* 391; Charles M. Andrews, *The Colonial Period of American History* (New Haven, 1938), IV, 117.

from Barbadoes, who soe late by word [were] very unwilling to spare a little Limestone." [17]

The Leeward Islanders had their grievances, too, and complained bitterly of the Barbados Council and Assembly; they asserted that Barbadians were known to have "wished these Islands sunck." The quarreling and discontent reached the point in 1667 that the planters of St. Christopher, Montserrat, Nevis, and Antigua petitioned for a separation of the Carlisle Patent into two governments. They charged the Barbadians with desiring to forestall any further settlement in the Leeward group, because if they were lost to the French or the Dutch, one pound of Barbadian sugar would be worth as much as two pounds if it did not have to compete with the product of the petitioners. The rejoinder of an agent of Lord Willoughby in Barbados that with the Patent divided debtors would escape to the Leeward Islands, jumping from island to island, may have been true, but the statement as a whole appears to be mere sophistry. That these rivalries continued is evidenced by the unwillingness of the Barbadians in 1681 to join Governor Stapleton's foray against the Caribs.[18]

For many years, in the train of the wars, the displaced person became a familiar figure of island societies. The French historian Du Tertre placed the English exodus from St. Christopher in 1666, the year the French captured the English sector, at 8000, though Sir Charles Wheler later fixed the number at 5000. In any event, Christopher Jeaffreson held that in 1677 the English part of the island contained only a quarter of the people it had had eleven years earlier. The bulk of the small landowners had dispersed to other islands or to the continent of North America. To the thousands who fled from St. Christopher must be added hundreds from Antigua and Montserrat; many of them sought safety on tiny Nevis, where they created a serious refugee problem until they could be transported to Jamaica or resettled in their own colonies. Major William Freeman told how hundreds of poor, homeless people, suffered by the French to settle among them on St. Christopher, found themselves to be no better off than slaves. They re-

17. *CSPC, 1661–68,* pp. 166, 593–4, 602; BM: Sloane MSS, 3662, fol. 33a.

18. *CSPC, 1669–74,* p. 157; *1685–88,* pp. 512, 553; BM: Egerton MSS, 2395, fols. 455, 459–60.

ceived only a third to a half of the wages the English had paid them.[19]

The unfortunate victims of the wars were not necessarily servants or poor freedmen. Samuel Winthrop, brother of the governor of Connecticut, reported the loss of a large estate at St. Christopher, as well as his sugarworks, goods, and slaves at Antigua, where he had settled after removing in 1654 from the former island. One of the richest and most influential of the first planters of that same island, William Freeman, who had lost a limb in the course of forty-two years spent in the service of his country, was stripped of his entire estate, which he had been long accumulating: plantation house, Negroes, cattle, and his sugar and cotton mills, which had brought in £800 a year. Sending his family of twenty-two offspring to Jamaica, he remained at Nevis in an attempt to salvage something, but in August of 1668 a hurricane destroyed all that was left.[20]

In the early decades of colonization the English and French had managed to live side by side in the Lesser Antilles in a reasonably friendly fashion. Forgotten, however, were the days of amity during the years of war, 1666–67. The French conquerors carried away the timbers of the English churches, demolished the forts, and commandeered all of the lumber in houses and plantation buildings abandoned by the owners or belonging to men slain in combat. They also sold for a pittance all the sugar coppers taken from the works they destroyed. Any horses, slaves, and servants they caught were similarly sold. Worst of all, in a sense, they cut down the trees in the woods and on the mountains to prevent the English from rebuilding. The physical damage cannot be exaggerated. Although St. Christopher was restored in time, it never regained its former prestige. Actually it became the least prosperous of the Leeward Islands, and the seat of government passed to Nevis, and then, in 1688, on to Antigua.[21]

19. Du Tertre, *Histoire générale des Antilles,* IV, 62–3; *CSPC, 1661–68,* p. 388; *1669–74,* p. 441; Jeaffreson, *Young Squire,* I, 215.
20. *MHS Colls.,* 5th ser., VIII, 135, 241–2; *CSPC, 1669–74,* pp. 46, 80; PRO: CO 1/29, fol. 18 (Case of William Freeman under Article 8, Treaty of Breda).
21. A volume in the British Museum contains correspondence concerning the Anglo-French differences over property at St. Christopher after 1667. BM: Add. MSS, 11,409, fols. 37, 205 (also Institute of Jamaica Transcripts); *CSPC, 1669–74,* p. 47; *1689–92,* p. 235; Harlow, *Colonising Expeditions,* 22.

The aftermath of the war brought ineradicable bitterness. A list of reasons drawn up by the French at St. Christopher proved the impossibility of the two nations living in peace. The Jesuit, Du Tertre, wrote in his *Histoire générale:* "The hatred between these two nations is such, and they are so aroused against each other, particularly the English people who are so haughty and proud by nature, and who, having always been beaten by the French in St. Christopher, will never be content that they be not avenged, in one way or another." Carib raids, inspired by the French, added to this enmity. Such an attitude is understandable when it is known that, between 1665 and 1667, tiny Montserrat and thinly populated Antigua lost 1300 slaves to either the Indians or the French. After retaking St. Christopher, the English had their revenge at Guadeloupe in 1691 when they burned towns and destroyed the best plantations. Christopher Codrington estimated the extent of devastation on Guadeloupe at half a million pounds sterling.[22]

The period closed with a great war already in progress, and the specter of insecurity, as so often since 1651, loomed over the peoples of the Caribbean. This time Jamaica experienced more than its share of disasters. Three years of guerilla war with the Maroons after 1685 both exhausted and stirred up the planters. The merchants of Port Royal and other towns suffered from the attacks of pirates and Biscayners upon their shipping; these same raiders destroyed many coastal plantations. The Glorious Revolution of 1688 brought no political advantage to Jamaica as it did to New England, and the outbreak in the West Indies in 1689 of a struggle with France that would drag on for eight years set the Jamaicans back measurably. Finally, in 1692, they lost completely, in less than an hour, the town of Port Royal, the leading urban center of the English West Indies.[23]

The war of the English with the Dutch and French, 1665–67, ended an era in the history of the European nations in the West Indies. With the passage of the Acts of Trade and Navigation, the agriculture and commerce of the Antilles passed under the control of London. Never again, without serious restrictions, would Dutch

22. Du Tertre, *Histoire générale des Antilles,* IV, 355; *CSPC, 1669–74,* p. 391; *1689–92,* pp. 458–9; 489.

23. Agnes M. Whitson, *The Constitutional Development of Jamaica, 1660–1729* (Manchester, 1929), 128.

traders be permitted to serve the English and French colonists as they had done in the past. Patient and statesmanlike negotiations of nearly four decades to ensure friendship and neutrality between the English and French were brushed aside within two years, never again to be renewed. Petty resentments and genuine jealousies arose among the English themselves, almost paralleling in intensity their hatred of the Gallics. Untouched by the conflict, Jamaica began to forge ahead to eventual economic supremacy among the king's West Indian possessions, while St. Christopher, Nevis, and Montserrat lagged far behind Barbados and growing Antigua. The disruptions caused by the wars retarded social and cultural improvement, depleted the white populations, and prolonged their male character. At the same time the slowly growing Caucasian societies turned more and more into substantially black ones, merely sheathed with a white veneer.

III

Although fire not drawn from the heavens was an act of man, most of the people of the seventeenth century looked upon a major conflagration such as the Great Fire of London as a sign of divine displeasure and retribution. During these four decades, fires caused a number of violent ruptures in the economic and social life of the Lesser Antilles. Plantation fires, breaking out usually in the boiling rooms of the sugar mills, often consumed the entire works, the slave quarters, and the master's house. The most devastating conflagrations occurred in the principal insular towns, such as that which destroyed more than sixty warehouses at Basseterre, French St. Christopher, in 1663. Resident Dutch merchants lost more than two million livres' worth of goods, and for five months—until new shipments of salted meats, oils, brandy, flour, cloth, and of necessary supplies came from Holland—both the French and the English (who traded clandestinely at Basseterre) suffered severely.[24]

Disasters by fire took place almost periodically in Barbados at

24. Ironically, after the fire, such quantities of meats, wine, and brandy arrived from Holland and Zeeland, which could not be preserved for long, that the Dutch merchants had to sell them at two-thirds of their value and thereby incurred a second financial loss. Du Tertre, *Histoire générale des Antilles,* I, 586.

The Indian Bridge, or as it was coming to be called, Bridgetown or St. Michael's. During the six years of Daniel Searle's administration, two very destructive fires broke out. In that of February 2, 1658/9, about 200 dwellings and storehouses burned down—and the colony's records along with them. John Hull of Boston mentioned in his diary that a number of New Englanders shared in the loss. In May the vestry of St. Michael's Parish voted that two men be chosen by the town's merchants to join them in setting a levy to procure leather buckets and other fire-fighting equipment; and they ordered the constables to nominate 100 townsmen to be ready to assist in case of fire. In October 1666, immediately following the Great Fire of London, the vestrymen, suddenly realizing how vulnerable their town was, ordered a "cuple of Water Enjins" for parish use from London, and in the next month, sent for broad axes, ladders, iron hooks, chains, ropes, and additional leather buckets. The inhabitants learned that even with all their new apparatus they could not cope with a spectacular fire such as occurred at 5:00 p.m. on April 18, 1668. Whether it was caused by the carelessness of a boy with a candle or by a spark from the chimney that ignited the countinghouse of John Bushell and Francis Bond is not known, but the flames spread quickly to the public magazine next door. One hundred and seventy barrels of powder exploded causing a general conflagration which consumed 800, some said 1000, buildings—a loss of property estimated at £400,000 sterling. The few remaining structures at Bridgetown, weakened or shattered by the explosion, were unfit for habitation or use.[25]

Governor Lord Willoughby acted promptly to provide for orderly rebuilding according to "a form" drawn up by appointed commissioners, notwithstanding the aversion of many people to planned urban development similar to that used in London at the same time. By August 6, London newspapers reported that re-

25. The two fire engines ordered in 1666 were the first in American colonies of England; Boston did not acquire its first engine until 1679. Bridenbaugh, *Cities in the Wilderness,* 59; BM: Sloane MSS, 3662, fol. 58a; "The Diaries of John Hull," in *Archaelogia Americana* (Worcester, Mass., 1851), III, 187; *JBMHS,* XIV, 173; XV, 121–2; John Bushell, *A True and Perfect Narrative of the Late Dreadful Fire . . .* (London, 1668); *CSPC, 1661–68,* pp. 556, 561, 563, 578; *London Gazette,* June 11, 18, 1668.

building had commenced; the Barbadians had hired many ships to bring timber down from New England. By December 10 it was reported in Plymouth that more than a half of the town had been again rebuilt. Although such speed suggests sleazy construction, still John Ogilby tells in his book *America* (1670) of St. Michael's "many fair and large Buildings, whereof some are of Stone and Lime." What gave promise of a remarkable civic improvement at Bridgetown was rudely halted on January 24, 1672/3, when a night fire on "New-England Street" consumed thirty to forty warehouses, including most of the available provisions brought in from Boston, Virginia, and Bermuda, together with "their great magazine of pipe staves and hoops" for sugar casks. Further rebuilding of Bridgetown received a crippling setback from the devastating hurricane of August 1675 which did great damage along the leeward coast where the town was situated, but eventually recovery did come. Four destructive fires and a terrible hurricane had cleared out every vestige of the early days, and when, sometime after 1692, the Dutch artist Samuel Copen drew his beautiful view, more fireproof structures of stone and brick of several stories set off the skyline of the metropolis of the Lesser Antilles. (Plate 14) [26]

IV

Whatever uncertainty existed in men's minds about great fires being the punishment of sinners by an angry God, there were other events, today recognized as natural, that a helpless generation attributed directly to the Divine Being.

Most of the acts of God in the Caribbean had some connection

26. To guard against fire at Charles Town and Morton's Bay on Nevis, the Assembly passed an act in 1682 against keeping fires in the streets to dress victuals. The same year the Jamaica Assembly made fire and building regulations for Port Royal. At Antigua in 1686 the Assembly passed a measure concerning building in towns to prevent the erection of thatched-roofed houses adjacent to well-framed brick and shingled structures. *An Abridgement of the Acts of Assembly passed in the Island of Nevis (1664–1732)* [London, 1740], 6; *An Abridgement of the Laws in Force and Use in Her Majesty's Plantations* . . . (London, 1704), 95–6; *London Gazette,* Aug. 6, Dec. 10, 1668; John Ogilby, *America* (London, 1671), 379; Hull, "Diaries," 235; *CSPC, 1669–74,* p. 465; *1675–76,* pp. 294, 421; *1685–88,* p. 159; *A Prospect of Bridge Town in Barbados, 1695, By Samuel Copen* (Johannes Kip, fecit, London, 1695).

with the climate and the weather. After spending several years in Jamaica, Edward Hickeringill—graduate of Caius College, chaplain, and soldier—published *Jamaica view'd* in 1661. ". . . I never came in more temperate Climes than those of Jamaica, Hispaniola, St. Kitts, Barbadoes, &c. so slanderously calumniated, the heat in the day time being alwaies alloy'd with the Sea Breezes, and the nights naturally cool. . . ." This enthusiastic pamphleteer told some of the truth, but not all of it. Governor Edwin Stede's experience led him to complain in September 1685 that Barbados had been troubled by "ill weather," and again, the next year, of "the cold and unknown weather." The temperature was either too high or too low to suit the Europeans and Africans inhabiting the islands, and always too humid. From time to time long droughts resulted in crop failures, and the populace faced the possibility of famine. On rarer occasions the rains came too heavily. On November 1, 1668, began four days of rain that drove down on Barbados like a monsoon. Along the south shore it washed away many houses and caused stone structures to collapse. The rector of Christ Church Parish told Nicholas Blake that the rushing waters cut a gully about 50 feet wide and 150 feet long in the churchyard, and that coffins and the bodies of about 1500 people, the corpses of all the parishioners who had been buried within the past thirty years, were washed out into the ocean! "It was a dismal [yea, macabre] sight to see the [floating] coffins striking on each side of the banks of the beach," not waiting for the Resurrection to rise out of the ground. In truth, nature under divine management was serving the West Indians scurvily.[27]

Occasionally the islands became infested with more than the usual swarms of insects, and crops and people alike suffered from them. The year 1661 was a particularly bad year in this respect for Barbados. Tiny poisonous "chiggers" and large poisonous worms caused severe infections. Most of the men went barefooted and were bitten unmercifully by little mosquitoes that attacked their legs and toes. Men were even known to die as a result of the bites. The entire West Indies were visited in 1662 by hosts of caterpil-

27. Edward Hickeringill, *Jamaica view'd . . .* (London, 1661), 10; *CSPC, 1685–88,* pp. 96, 343; J. E. Reece & C. G. Clark-Hunt, *Barbados Diocesan History* (London, 1925), 79, 85; Barbados Council Minutes, Jan. 18, 1669/70, p. 105.

lars that ate every kind of green thing, and if it had not been for the timely arrival of provisions from New England, the common folk would have starved. At Port Royal in Jamaica, Colonel William Beeston recorded in his journal for December 4, 1664: "About this day appeared first the comet which was the forerunner of the blasting of the cacao trees, and after which time they generally failed in Jamaica, Cuba, and Hispaniola." So much for the theory of portents! [28]

The most terrifying of all acts of God were West Indian hurricanes and earthquakes. Anybody who has been through either of these is well aware how agonizing and frustrating it is to feel so utterly helpless. The one certain fact about hurricanes was that they were likely to arise in the Caribbean at any time from July to September. As the Antillean proverb had it:

> June too soon, July stand by; August you must;
> September remember; October all over.

Every year one or more tropical storms blew up in the Caribbean and whether or not men called them hurricanes depended upon their force. About 1670 an anonymous sea captain, familiar with the West Indies, wrote a piece "Concerning Hurricanes and their Prognosticks and Observations of my owne Experience thereupon," which is now among the Egerton Papers in the British Museum. He claims that the English and French used to send about June to the Caribs of Dominica and St. Vincent to learn if one or more hurricanes could be expected in a given year. About ten or twelve days before one was due, the Caribs sent the word, and a big blow very rarely failed to follow. Some people branded such predictions witchcraft, but this author defends them. Our mariner learned how to forecast hurricanes himself after careful observation of the storms of 1657, 1658, 1660, 1665, and 1667. He believed that they came either on the day of the "full Range or Quarters of the moon," and that August was the most dangerous month, though

28. The Swiss physician, Dr. Felix Christian Spörri, made a great deal of the poisonous insects whose bites caused the death of many Caribbeans. *Americanische Reise—Beschreibung Nach den Caribe Insslen und Neu Engelland* (Zurich, 1677), [JCB copy], 14–16, and trans. in *JBMHS,* XXXIII (1969), 6; *CSPC, 1661–68,* p. 167; *Interesting Tracts Relating to Jamaica,* 284.

he warned about July. At the first sign of a big blow, all ships must immediately run out to sea, for no vessel at anchor or tied up could ever ride out a hurricane.[29]

When a great hurricane struck one or more of the islands, it "reduced most of those miserable people to their first principles," as Lord Willoughby said of the colonists on war-torn Antigua and St. Christopher in 1667. The most destructive hurricane of the seventeenth century crippled the Barbadian economy for several years. On August 31, 1675, black clouds appeared in the sky, the winds rose rapidly, veering to all points of the compass, then settling in the north, all the while accompanied by lightning and heavy rain. That night the tempest grew furious and did not abate until the next morning. When the terrified inhabitants surveyed the scene, they found scarcely a single house without one person dead in it. In one dwelling in Scotland District seventeen had been killed, and there were instances where entire families had been buried in the ruins of their houses. In all, 200 Barbadians lost their lives. Governor Jonathan Atkins told of the storm flattening fifteen stone and timber sugar mills valued at £500 sterling each in just one parish; and throughout the island, the canes were all ruined. Many of the churches were blown down along with scores of dwellings in the leeward part of the island, and any standing timber had been leveled. Most of the sugar pots were broken and other equipment destroyed. At two plantations belonging to John Bawden and John Sparke of London the losses amounted to £6000. Atkins advised Whitehall that £200,000 would not repair the damage, and he requested temporary permission to have free trade or an abatement of the 4½ per cent duty on exports to help in the rehabilitation of the colony. In addition to the devastation on land, every ship in Carlisle Bay had either been driven ashore or broken up. One planter summed up the situation with the remark that "Such another blow will bring Barbados near the Horizon." [30]

29. PRO: CO 1/37, fol. 58a; Merrill, *Historical Geography of St. Kitts and Nevis,* 27; BM: Egerton MSS, 2395, fols. 619–24; Spörri, *Americanische Reise,* 12.

30. *CSPC, 1661–68,* p. 547; *1675–76,* p. 425; *1677–80,* p. 501; PRO: CO 1/31, fols. 72–3; Griffith Hughes, *The Natural History of Barbados* (London, 1750),

In many respects the aftermath of the disaster turned out to be even more trying than the storm itself. With nearly every structure in the island in ruins, most of the sugar mills out of commission, and many fallen trees to be cut away, the process of cleaning up and rebuilding had to begin at once. Masters, freedmen, servants, and slaves had to shelter themselves in huts for a year or more. Fear of the unrestrained blacks whose masters had died or who were otherwise on the loose mounted daily. With all of the shipping destroyed along with all food crops, famine stalked the colony; and because of King Philip's War, the obtaining of provisions and lumber from New England was uncertain if not impossible. Many a trader turned scoundrel by monopolizing foods and holding them to gain outrageous prices. Credit failed, and formerly opulent families faced ruin. Governor Atkins and the Assembly acted quickly to protect debtors and save them from having to flee the island, which would have left those remaining whites open to great danger from the Negroes. No relief came from a parsimonious king, and the desperate planters had to pull themselves up by their own bootstraps.[31]

Hurricanes menaced all of the islands every summer, and sooner or later the inhabitants of each one suffered. In September 1680 the Leeward Islands fortunately escaped the worst blow ever known at Martinique. Governor Stapleton learned that it had blown down all houses, forts, churches, and left scarcely a tree or plant standing. A little less than a year later, however, Christopher Jeaffreson was but one of many planters on St. Christopher who lost heavily in a hurricane on August 27, and on October 4 in a second great blow. The latter hit Antigua hardest, driving several ships on shore. Jamaicans congratulated themselves on being free of hurricanes, but when John Austin arrived at Bybrook Plantation on August 7, 1690, he discovered that because a great hurricane had blown down "all our planton walke we was like to starve the negroes,"

25–6; Oldmixon, *British Empire in America,* II, 36–8; *A Continuation of the State of New England Together with an Account of the Intended Rebellion of the Negroes in Barbados* (London, 1676), 19–20; Daniel B. Updike, *Richard Smith* (Boston, 1937), 114.

31. John Poyer, *History of Barbados* (London, 1808), 104–5; Oldmixon, *British Empire in America,* II, 36–8; Schomburgk, *History of Barbados,* 295.

provisions proving so dear. They managed to subsist on "a sort of Corne that grows here." All of the growing canes on every plantation in the vicinity had been flattened by the storm.[32]

In these volcanic islands earthquakes were bound to happen, and when they did, the loss of life was often greater than from hurricanes. A subterranean shift in 1690 caused severe tremors on Nevis and St. Christopher late in the afternoon of April 25. All of the stone or brick houses in Charles Town on Nevis dropped "of a sudden from the Top to the Bottom in perfect Ruines," whereas many wooden ones stood. At nearby Antigua the quake resulted in the death of some people and the leveling of many buildings; Governor Codrington, who was the loser by £2000, reported that in the Lesser Antilles, French as well as English, scarcely any stonework was undamaged and that tremors were felt almost daily for a month after. Of this quake the *London Gazette* stated that the greater loss on Antigua resulted from most of the houses, buildings, sugarworks, and windmills being of stone, whereas timber construction prevailed in the other islands.[33]

Captain John Boylston arrived at Charlestown in Massachussets-Bay on August 3, 1692, with the news of "the Amazing severity of God towards Jamaica." A year later Londoners read of the full extent of the tragedy in *The Truest and Largest Account of the late Earthquake in Jamaica. June the 7th, 1692.* "The Lord has spoke terrible things in righteousness," declared the author, "a Reverend Divine" of Vere Parish. Beginning about 11:45 in the morning, a series of tremors shook the entire island with great violence for six or seven minutes. In the countryside, nearly every brick or stone building collapsed, and in many places the earth opened and spewed out water from holes twelve to twenty feet deep. The whole of St. Iago de la Vega, church and all, was left in ruins. Port

32. PRO: CO 1/46, fol. 5; Jeaffreson, *Young Squire,* I, 274–9; Somerset Record Office, Taunton: John Austin to William Helyar, Aug. 7, 1690, Helyar MSS (1669–1712).

33. A letter written in Nevis to a London merchant pointed out that "the Rivetings of woodden Structures are far stronger, and not so easily disjoynted as the co-agmentations of Cement and Mortar." Experience thus gained led to marked modifications in the types of buildings erected thereafter. *An Account of the Late Dreadful Earthquake in the Island of Nevis and St. Christopher . . .* (London, 1690); *CSPC, 1689–92,* p. 278; *London Gazette,* June 30, 1690.

Royal presented a scene of horror and devastation: "three parts swallowed into the Sea," as the neck of land on which it was built sank quickly, and within a few days ships and shallops were riding at anchor where once there had been the dwellings of merchants and warehouses. The loss of life was estimated at somewhere between 1500 and 2000 "besides Blacks" (mark the words!), who were probably some 600 or 700 more—"a multitude . . . whose Corps floated a great many days after from one side of the Harbour to the other," creating such "an intolerable stench, that the Dead were like to destroy the Living." Eventually some bodies sank, some blew away, some washed ashore and lined the beaches of the south coast for many miles. People at far-off Boston heard on December 15 that about 4000 Jamaicans had succumbed to disease and starvation after the earthquake. Thus the total loss of life in the greatest recorded single catastrophe affecting Europeans in the New World amounted to about 6000 people.[34]

This divinely ordained event happened when the English were at war, and their French enemy promptly seized the occasion to land a force on the north shore of Jamaica. Meanwhile at Port Royal, every vile and base element of human nature instantly asserted itself. Depredations, robberies, and violence took place almost immediately; "no man could call any thing his own." Gold, silver, plate, slaves, were carried off by vandals who came in canoes and wherries to perform their ghoulish work of stripping the dead and their houses. The mart town had disappeared into the bowels of the earth, never again to rise on that spot, which only in our own day is being dug by archaeologists. To make matters even worse, in town and country many masterless blacks, "those Irreconcilable and yet Intestine Enemies of ours, who are no otherwise our Subjects than as the Whip makes them," looted and often ran away in the name of liberty. The possibility of famine or of extreme scarcity of provisions at high prices, if a six weeks' drought did not

34. In the English period the Jamaicans had experienced at least one other severe earthquake, which occurred on Sunday, Feb. 19, 1687. The one-story Spanish houses stood up well, but the English dwellings, most of which were of brick, did not withstand the shock. Oldmixon, *British Empire in America,* II, 285–6, 386; Sloane, *A Voyage to the Islands,* I, xlvii–lix; *MHS Procs.,* 2d ser., VII, 163, 164; *The Late Dreadful Earthquake in Jamaica,* A2-s, 1–12.

break, added to the woe of the survivors. President John White and the Council re-established the government on board a merchantman anchored in the harbor, from which they attempted to handle the salvage and looting problems, and to apprehend "Thieves, Fellows and Robbers," as well as to distribute food to the poor. Then they set about restoring the island, sounding a new ship channel, and coping with the French invasion on the north side. Years would pass before the stricken Jamaicans finally recovered from their shattering experience.[35] (Plate 13)

V

Samuel Winthrop wrote from Antigua on November 8, 1663, to his brother John at New London concerning God's controversy with the men of the Caribbean. "It has been his pleasure to visit this island with much sicknesse this winter;—a violent fever and fluxe with most; and others no fluxe but great costivenesse [constipation]. A great many lusty young men are dead of it. My family hath escaped as yet; only my selfe, I have had it very sorely, but am by God's goodness recovered." Rats and mice, brought by the ships to the islands where none had existed in 1627, multiplied so rapidly by feeding on sugar canes, maize, and other crops that they became dangerous pests, as in the years of the plague, 1646–48. Desperate settlers imported cats, who gave the rodents no quarter; but they continued to multiply, and when vessels discharged freshly infected vermin, they quickly spread disease throughout the Antilles. Pestilences variously described as violent fevers, plague, malignant fevers, and disease proved to be longer lasting and more often fatal because of the favorable warmth of the tropics and lack of frost. In 1665 the vestry of St. Michael's Parish, Barbados, hired Richard Morris, the bricklayer, to build a pest house (60′ x 20′ x 9′) with walls of stone two feet thick and plastered and painted

35. Many of the people who survived at Port Royal moved over to "the Rack," which became Kingston. A fire finished off what remained of Port Royal on Jan. 9, 1702/3, after which the authorities ordered that all residents should move to Kingston, where streets were laid out and which soon became a populous place. Oldmixon, *British Empire in America,* II, 288–95, 310–11, 316; *The Late Dreadful Earthquake in Jamaica,* 5–12; Jamaica Council Minutes (Institute of Jamaica Transcripts), V, 338, 340, 344, 399.

throughout. Two years later they purchased a hearse and horse to convey the dead of Bridgetown to the cemetery.[36]

Seldom did many years go by in any one of the islands without some kind of epidemic disease attacking the inhabitants. In 1667 one carried away more than 200 white men, besides women and children, at Torarica in Surinam, which had but recently been highly praised for its health and "kind women." The fact that both the Caribs and the Europeans were at this time "strangely troubled with the Indian Pox" raises doubts as to the soundness of that judgment. It seems scarcely to be a coincidence that Barbados, where the most ships touched, also had the largest number of epidemics. Wait Winthrop learned in Boston in the winter of 1670/1 from his father that the mortality in Barbados was causing people to abandon it for Nevis. Again, in 1673 John Winthrop, Jr., wrote to his son of the epidemics: many important persons and hosts of others had died within three months. From August 1689 through February 1690 the inhabitants of Nevis suffered from multiple epidemics: smallpox, bloody flux (dysentery), fever, and ague, causing Christopher Codrington to lament that during the war with France the strongest of the Leeward Islands had become the weakest. Fifteen hundred white men in all, with women and children in proportion, and many Negro slaves succumbed. The inhabitants of all the Leeward Islands were infected with various communicable diseases brought by the crews and soldiers in the fleet sent from England in 1691 to defend them against the French attack. Barbados was a veritable pest center, and the next year a virulent fever destroyed most of the seamen of both merchant and naval vessels in Carlisle Bay and carried away more than a third of all the inhabitants.[37]

36. *MHS Colls.,* 5th ser., VIII, 250; Davies, *Caribby-Islands,* 154; *JBMHS,* XV, 99–100, 126.

37. In 1683–84, in comparatively healthy Jamaica, and also at Montserrat, the smallpox raged "like the plague." Samuel Sewall of Boston postponed the sailing of his ketch from March to June because of the presence of smallpox in Barbados, lest his partner Nathaniel Dummer "help to make up the tale of those that die of that mortal disease." *MHS Colls.,* 6th ser., I, 26, 29; 5th ser., VIII, 161, 384; BM: Sloane MSS, 3662, fols. 29, 38–9, 55; George Warren, *An Impartial Description of Surinam* (London, 1667), Preface; *CSPC, 1681–85,* pp. 592, 609; *1689–92,* pp. 175, 219, 225, 228, 229, 389; Oldmixon, *British Empire in America,* II, 56, 58, 102.

From Barbados in August 1660, Richard Leader notified John Winthrop, Jr., that he intended to return to New England in the spring. "My cheifest end being to see to recover my lost health, which this clyme hath in great measure deprived me of. Being a weaknes and feebleness in all my lymbes, being the dreggs of a desperate disease which we call the Belly-ake, which is only restored by remove into the coulde clyme as experience teacheth." This is the earliest description of the dry belly-ache or dry gripes the authors have found. It first appeared in Barbados and St. Christopher, and at Nevis within a short time. In explaining to the Lords of Trade and Plantations in 1695 about the serious threat to the health of the Barbadians from an epidemic that swept away hundreds of people, Governor Russell referred to another distemper that was "catching." This was the dry belly-ache. "It deprives those whom it seizes of the use of their limbs, and the only cure for it is to go immediately to a cold climate. If it be not taken at once, but allowed to hang upon any one for but a little time, it is absolutely incurable, and the party remains a cripple for life." [38]

Physicians and laymen alike devoted much thought and time to observing, diagnosing, explaining the cause, and treating the dry belly-ache. It was not merely a gentleman's affliction, for persons of all ranks, rich and poor, white and black contracted it. Down to about 1700 the standard treatment, according to Griffith Hughes, F.R.S., was to purge with both cathartics and clysters or enemas, but with little success. The first insight into the cause of the malady came from Dr. Thomas Trapham, who went out to Jamaica in 1676 as physician to Governor Lord Vaughan. Two years later he published a book on the state of health in the island, which contained a conception about the "dry Belliach." Its "most urgent symptome, which is exquisite pain in the belly," he believed could be cured with care, especially the liberal use of baths in a tub. He did not prescribe a colder climate. Dr Trapham blamed the disease on mineral gases issuing from caverns and descending from the mountains to cause the same effects as "the lead works in Derby, where the fumes of the separating Oars" produce great pain, convulsions, and death. Here was the identification of lead poisoning, although

38. *MHS Procs.*, 2d ser., III, 196–7; *CSPC, 1693–96,* p. 445.

the physician failed to grasp the fact that it was the evil that came from rum distilled in leaden pipes. This was first pointed out at Philadelphia in 1745 by Dr. Thomas Cadwalader in his important *Essay on the West India Dry-Gripes; with the Method of Preventing and Curing that Cruel Distemper.* Neither Thomas Tryon (1684) nor Dr. Hans Sloane, F.R.S. (1680), also physician to a governor of Jamaica, perceived that rum caused the dry gripes, even though rum-distillers, sugar-boilers, and overseers, and many of the poorer sort were known to contract the belly-ache "from drinking new hot Rum" or "strong Punch" made of rum that their betters quaffed in prodigious quantities.[39]

Thus it was that contemporaries who brooded on the "general frailty of Humane life" in the Caribbean, usually ended up by attributing the shorter span of existence there to the will of God. With Thomas Tryon, many West Indians tended to blame their fellows more than the climate for arousing divine anger. What they failed to comprehend was their own inability to adjust themselves properly in their eating and drinking to tropical conditions—even after sixty-five years of experience under "Sea Brezes partaking of the universal vivifying saline nature." [40]

39. Hughes, *Natural History of Barbados,* 34; Dr. Thomas Trapham, *A Discourse of the State of Health in the Island of Jamaica* (London, 1679), 129–30; Philotheos Physiologus [Thomas Tryon], *Friendly Advice to the Gentlemen-Planters of the East and West Indies* (London, 1684); Sloane, *Voyage to the Islands,* I, cxx.
40. Tryon, *Friendly Advice,* 48; Trapham, *State of Health in Jamaica,* 1–4.

VII

The Dispersal of the White Men

THE WILL OF JOSEPH HORBIN, merchant and planter of St. Michael's Parish in Barbados, was proved early in 1692. Some personal effects went to a kinsman, Andrew Russ, who lived on Horbin's plantation in Carolina. To his sea-going son John, if he still lived, for he had long been a captive at Sallee, the father devised half of a plantation in Jamaica and all of the Carolina estate. Sarah Horbin, Joseph's widow, was a sister of Ralph Lane, a Barbados gentleman; she was also connected with the Oistins and Empereurs of Christ Church Parish, as well as with the members of the latter family living in Lower Norfolk County, Virginia. Besides John Seabury of Barbados, she had had, since at least 1662, six Seabury cousins residing at Duxbury in Plymouth, now Massachusetts-Bay. The far-flung membership of this clan, with roots firmly set in Old England, surprises us at first, but upon further inquiry we discover that in this age it was far from unusual. For the past seven decades colonial expansion had scattered scions of many English families in much the same fashion along the vast periphery of the Atlantic Basin. Mercantile, planting, religious, and political concerns had brought about this dispersal, and intermarriage among these largely voluntary exiles extended and perpetuated it in the colonies.[1]

1. Members of the Corbin family of Staffordshire, Dorsetshire, and Wales could be found in New England by 1633, in Barbados by 1638 or earlier, and in Virginia in 1654. Harvey M. Lawson, *History and Genealogy of the Descendants*

This circulating of Englishmen throughout the West Indies and along the Spanish Main is a remarkable social phenomenon, which explains more about the history of the area from 1650 to 1692 than almost any other element except the coming of the blacks. Although historians have often described Barbados as the "nursery for planting . . . other places," there is abundant evidence that each of the four other Caribbean colonies also contributed liberally of its inhabitants to the forming of new settlements. Migrations had actually begun with the founding from St. Christopher of a colony on Nevis in 1628, and within a few years two more were established on Montserrat and Antigua. There is no doubt that the parent island had lost a larger proportion of its people before 1650 than had more renowned Barbados. Resettling had been in train in the Lesser Antilles long before the maturing of the sugar culture.[2]

If sugar and slavery did not start the movement of white inhabitants away from the Caribbees during the boom decade, 1650–60, they exacerbated profoundly the existing conditions, which generated additional incitements for seeking new homes. Barbados, St. Christopher, Nevis, and even Montserrat (but chiefly Barbados), were "pestered with a super-numerary glut of Inhabitants," and each island had become "too small a Hive for such a swarme of people," as Edward Hickeringill perceived in 1661. Surplus populations accumulated, some by natural increase for the first time since the islands had been colonies but, for the most part, by intermittent though often large importations of Irish, English, and Scottish prisoners or voluntary indentured servants. Between 1649 and 1655, according to a planters' petition, the Barbadians alone received and employed 12,000 prisoners of war and "many thousands of other persons." Scots, sold to Martin Noell and fellow merchants of London for transportation after the battles of Dunbar and Worcester, turned out to be the most reliable and the hardest workers, and they established the high regard in which their nation was held thereafter. Though frowned upon as formerly, contingents of Irish prisoners and servants continued to arrive in great numbers, whereas

of Clement Corbin (Hartford, 1905), 7–14; Barbados Council Minutes, 1654–58 (PRO: Typescript), I, 167; *NEHG Reg.*, LXVII, 363; Charles H. Pope, *Pioneers of Massachusetts* (Boston, 1903), 405; *Suffolk Deeds,* III, 525.

2. *CSPC, 1661–68,* p. 47.

the English were fewest of all. A new policy of issuing pardons under the Great Seal to offenders on condition of their going overseas started the great transportation of felons in 1655. As a result, some hundreds of convicts crossed to the Lesser Antilles and were sold into service before 1660. When such accretions of people, not only in Barbados but at St. Christopher and Nevis, were added to those already there who had served their time, the pressure of population upon the island resources increased alarmingly. In the pungent, inelegant phrase of a Puritan pamphleteer, "Barbados (with the rest of those small Islands) . . . are now so filled, that they vomit forth of their superfluities into other places." [3]

Contemporaries found in the absence of land for freed servants a simple explanation for a very complex situation, the departure of hundreds, even thousands, of the island peoples. There were other factors, however, which were just as important and which, by affecting the lives of humble white folk of the West Indies, served to drive out the indigent, the drifters, and the adventurers, as well as the landless men. By 1654 the consolidating of holdings by the great planters had "wormed out" some of the small ones who raised tobacco, cotton, indigo, and ginger. Many of the latter were finding that the soil was depleted from growing those crops year after year, especially at St. Christopher, and numbers of them had fallen heavily into debt. The mass of the freemen were Hibernians, believed by the English to be reluctant to work for wages. All of the whites, moreover, disliked the exhausting job of clearing land, which had become so necessary inland after 1650, whereas the Africans showed themselves adept at it. To add to the worries of the poor white men, owners of ingenios had begun to have the sugar-boiling and artisans' work performed by blacks. As a group, the white men suffered from the hot moist climate—most visitors remarked their universally sallow complexions—and the great bulk of the islanders continued to subsist on a bad and sometimes insufficient diet. Such unfavorable conditions, taken together, bred a

3. Hickeringill, *Jamaica view'd*, 21–2; Debien, *Les Engagés*, 77; BM: Add. MSS, 11,411, fol. 9; *CSPC, 1574–1660*, pp. 363, 421, 433; *Acts and Statutes of Barbados* (Jennings), 115–16; Abbot E. Smith, *Colonists in Bondage* (Chapel Hill, 1947), 95–6; Barbados Council Minutes, 1654–58, I, 53, 55, 144; I. S., *Briefe and Perfect Journal*, 6.

discontented or defeated set of men, but their listlessness and hopelessness required strong inducements or severe prodding from their superiors to persuade them to begin over again elsewhere. On the other hand, the overwhelming majority of the insular peoples consisted of young males, and few family ties or obligations existed to restrain their departure.[4]

When Francis, Lord Willoughby of Parham, became governor of the Caribbees in 1650, he pursued an energetic policy of Barbadian expansion by which, with romantic optimism, he hoped to reduce the island's population. He proposed to follow the Greek example of founding a colony from a colony, as the men of St. Christopher had done earlier. Immediately he fitted out a ship with ample supplies for the former privateersman and extreme Royalist, Anthony Rous, who was to explore the coast of Guiana between the Maroni and Surinam rivers. A year later, in August, the Governor wrote enthusiastically to his wife that he was sending a hundred men to take possession under Major Rous, and he fully expected "in a few years to have many thousands there." He had been particularly encouraged by the report that Surinam was a healthful place. The first expedition had been out there for five months, and not one of forty persons engaged in it had had so much as a headache.[5]

In 1652 Lord Willoughby went to Surinam himself with 300 Barbadians (mostly Royalists) to begin planting along the great river. This undertaking, which cost him £20,000, had the reassuring support of Thomas Modyford, who overconfidently predicted that in seven years' time Surinam would surpass Brazil in the production of sugar, cotton, tobacco, indigo, and ginger. If the Commonwealth government would but supply three or four ships of forty to fifty tons' burthen to transport passengers, Barbados could send at least 1000 men to the new colony every year—"(I speak within Compass), soe many yearely removing out of their lands, and knowing not how to be employed, must of necessity goe to other Ilands, or rashly attempt to settle new, (which many have done) [and] be miserably distroyed." At St. Christopher, Nevis,

4. *CSPC, 1661–68,* pp. 529–30.
5. BM: Egerton MSS, 2395, fol. 249; BM: Sloane MSS, 3662, fols. 40b–41; Schomburgk, *History of Barbados,* 274–5.

and Montserrat too, there are supernumeraries "that doe but look for encouragement" from England. By guaranteeing 100 acres of land as freedom dues to each servant who completed his time in this vast country, Thomas Modyford believed that the place might be settled very quickly, and a great nation arise. In 1654 he even thought of trying to lure settlers farther westward to the Orinoco.[6]

In the first years, in spite of Modyford's optimism, Willoughby Land, as Surinam was often called by the colonists from Barbados, grew slowly. Some of the Cavees on Barbados were exceedingly bitter about Thomas Modyford's regiment's supporting Sir George Ayscue when he arrived to compel the Barbadians and Antiguans to submit to the authority of the Commonwealth, and also about Lord Willoughby's capitulation. Actually such extreme Royalists as Anthony Rous, William Byam, the Walronds, and their followers could not stomach being governed by the Puritan Daniel Searle, whom Ayscue left behind when he sailed for the Leeward Islands, and considerable numbers of them prepared to leave Barbados and move to Surinam.[7]

After the fall of Pernambuco in 1654, some Jews came to Surinam. The attractions for them were freedom of conscience, the right to erect a synagogue, eligibility for election as burgesses, passage to Holland in Dutch vessels, and from seven to twelve years' exemption from taxation. In a charter of 1662, Charles II confirmed all of these privileges except that of tax-relief. Many more Hebrews came from Cayenne after the French captured the island from the Dutch.[8]

As the culture of sugar flourished, Surinam's population rose. From St. John's Hill in August 1662 John Treffry wrote: "I hope that we shall see this colony wonderfully prosper by reason of the

6. In a paper on Guiana, December 1654, Colonel Modyford reported: "We already have a colony at Surinam . . . of about 600 men, besides women and children, who will readily quit the place to come [to the Orinoco] where the beavers are" [i.e., Indians who can be enslaved and put to work]. Thurloe, *State Papers,* III, 63; BM: Egerton MSS, 2395, fols. 249, 280; PRO: CO 1/11, fol. 41, I.

7. *CSPC, 1574–1660,* p. 374; James A. Williamson, *The English in Guiana and on the Amazon, 1604–1668* (Oxford, 1923), 153, 158; *HMC, Portland,* III, 280, 284; BM: Egerton MSS, 2543, fol. 123 (Inst. Jamaica Trans.), III.

8. Privileges granted to the People of the Hebrew Nation which are to goe to the Wilde Coaste, *ca.* 1654, BM: Egerton MSS, 2395, fol. 46; Merrill, in *Caribbean Studies,* IV, 39.

decline of Barbados, whence we daily expect sixty passengers and planters by the *Guiana*." Though Roundheads and Cavees who came to Surinam carried on their old insular feud, the colony continued to grow. Renatus Enys told of the bustling activity of the new settlements: supplies arrived weekly—nine ships had brought in provisions in the past two months—and its sugar brought a better price than the Muscovado of the parent island. Inhabitants in 1663 numbered close to 4000, and great hopes were entertained for a succeeding generation, for the women "are very prolifical and have lusty children." Following short terms by Anthony Rous and Richard Holdip, the settlers chose Colonel William Byam as governor, and it was this ardent Royalist who remained in office until the Dutch conquest in 1667.[9]

Surinam attained its greatest prosperity in the years from 1660 to 1666. From Parimaribo, fifteen miles from the mouth of the river, for thirty miles up-stream to the capital at Torarica, which could be reached by vessels of 300 tons, and for thirty-five miles beyond, plantations lined the banks. In all there were about 500 estates and between forty and fifty sugarworks, which were profitable ventures for the settlers. (Plate 10) According to Mrs. Aphra Behn, who had lived in Surinam, the finest plantation was St. John's Hill, which was managed by John Treffry for its absent owner, Sir Robert Harley. Suddenly, beginning with a heavy mortality in 1666 from a pestilence that drove some people to leave the valley, the great and real promise of this tropical Eden came to an end. The *coup de grâce* came the following February with the surrender of the colony to the Dutch by Governor Byam. Despite its recapture in October 1667, Surinam went back to the Dutch by the Treaty of Breda in exchange for New Netherland. Once more the ex-Barbadians and other Englishmen, with their slaves and movable goods, emigrated to resume an insular existence in Antigua and Jamaica. In 1675 all but a handful had sailed away from the Main.[10]

9. *HMC, 10th Report,* VI (Bouverie MSS), 96; *Caribbeana,* II, 14, 15; *CSPC, 1661–68,* pp. 166, 167; BM: Sloane MSS, 3662, fols. 27–37.

10. The extent of plantation settlement may be gauged from the map of Surinam of 1667 reproduced as Plate 10. The most complete account of the colony is in Warren's *An Impartial Description of Surinam,* see especially pp. 1, 2, 8, 16–17,

The Cromwellian Western Design, aimed at the Spanish colonies, substantially reduced the surplus population of the Caribbees. Though the assaults did not occur in a time of declared war, Barbados supplied about 4000 recruits and the Leeward Islands about 1200 more for the abortive attack on Hispaniola, which ended fortuitously in the conquest of Jamaica by the English in 1655. General Venables employed sixteen Dutch vessels seized at Barbados for trading with contraband goods to transport the more than 5000 troops and supplies to Jamaica. An eyewitness wrote disdainfully of the rawness of the soldiers brought over from England, but, he exclaimed, "certainly these Islanders must be the very scum of scums, and meer dregs of corruption, and such upon whose endeavours, it was impossible to expect a blessing." Daniel How, another participant, thought the colonials "prov'd good for little . . . for they have been for the most part such old beaten runaways as that they know how to do little else than plunder. . . ." Old-timers among the freemen, who had been in the islands before 1645 and who owned small tracts, remained behind and continued to raise cotton and tobacco.[11]

Nearly all of the contingent from the Caribbees were landless men, and few of them had any intention of going back to their islands after the expedition was concluded. Planting, not soldiering, was their design. The large number of women and children, "whom out of ill grounded confidence, and high presumption" some of the freemen took along, made them seem "rather as a people that went to inhabit some Country already conquered, then to conquer: but for this perhaps they had too good a President." These men had completed their time of service. The vast majority, however, were unmarried bondsmen, recently arrived servants with time still to serve, who had little or no experience in the tropics. Some of the

---

19, 28; *Oroonoko: Or the Royal Slave,* in *The Novels of Mrs. Aphra Behn,* ed. by Ernest A. Baker (London, 1913), 1, 39, 51; *HMC, Portland,* III, 284, 285, 308–9, 310; Williamson, *English in Guiana,* 151–65; Oldmixon, *British Empire in America,* II, 281; BM: Sloane MSS, 3662, fols. 27–37; Surtees Society, *Publications,* L (1866), 45.

11. Venables, in RHS, *Camden,* LX, 8, 40, 145; BM: Egerton MSS, 2395, fols. 60, 134; William Blathwayt, comp., History and State of Jamaica under Lord Vaughan . . . (MS: Inst. Jamaica), 10; I. S., *Briefe and Perfect Journal,* 10–11; *Interesting Tracts Relating to Jamaica,* 37; *CSPC, 1661–68,* p. 529.

rich planters lost ten servants, some fifteen, and others still more. Inasmuch as the value of a servant's time for nine months was estimated at £20 or more, the departure of servants represented a crippling loss to masters. Even so one contemporary deemed the loss of freemen, artisans especially, even more costly in the long run.[12]

Martin Noell, Stephen Winthrop, and other London merchants, together with the officials in Jamaica, used every device to people the new colony. At Barbados they received aid from Colonel Thomas Modyford, one of the architects of the Cromwellian policy. Writing to Secretary Thurloe on June 20, 1655, he expressed his regret over the failure of the forces at Hispaniola, but admitted that he was not sorry they had gone to Jamaica. With its good harbor, land aplenty, and a suitable climate, "it will be sooner filled." The Colonel avowed that he had nearly a hundred families ready to leave Barbados, but he warned that the leading planters would try to prevent further emigration out of resentment of Jamaica, "all grounded upon the malicious apprehension they have against this settlement in the Indies (forsooth) it will make sugar cheap, and then this island of people, which when the wood is gone (and that cannot be long first) must fall of itself." Other than a trickle of craftsmen, lured by good terms, not many people left Barbados for Jamaica before 1662.[13]

Knowledge of the terrible mortality in Jamaica during the first years of English rule discouraged additional large bodies of West Indians from settling there—most of the members of the invading forces and their families had perished by 1657. The one notable exception to this colonial avoidance of the island came from overcrowded Nevis. Governor Luke Stokes informed Major Robert Sedgwick on May 12, 1656, that ". . . I find in this Island the greatest part of the inhabitants, with their wives, children, and servants, are willing and ready to accept" the Protector's liberal terms for settlement. The Governor had reference to the poor, who were the "greatest part," for the richer inhabitants were not willing to make the move. Other islands, according to Stokes, were "forward" and only waiting for transportation. Bermuda, also over-

12. I. S., *Briefe and Perfect Journal,* 11; *HMC, 7th Report,* 572.
13. BM: Egerton MSS, 2395, fol. 123; Thurloe, *State Papers,* III, 565, 566.

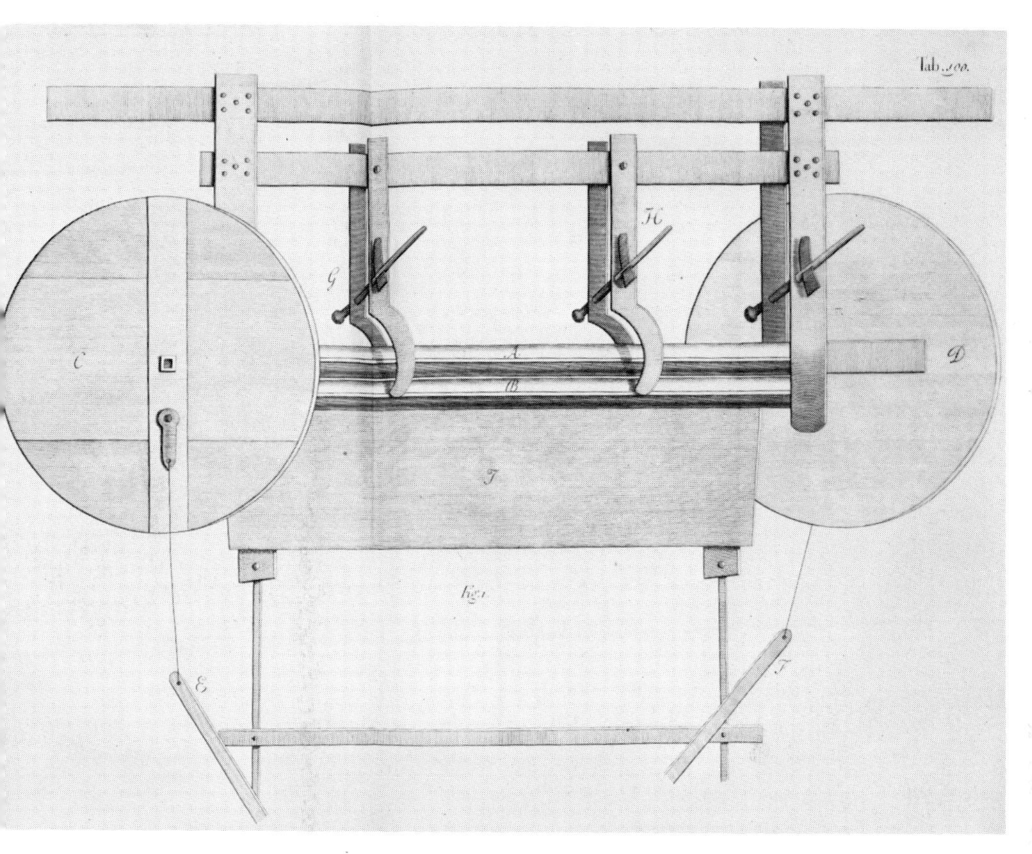

A West Indian Cotton Gin, 1688

The Island of Barbados, 1650, by Richard Ligon

A topographicall Description and Admeasurement of the YLAND of BARBADOS in the West INDYAES With the Mrs. Names of the Seuerall plantacons

An Indigo Plantation and Works

Sugar Culture in the French West Indies, *ca*. 1665

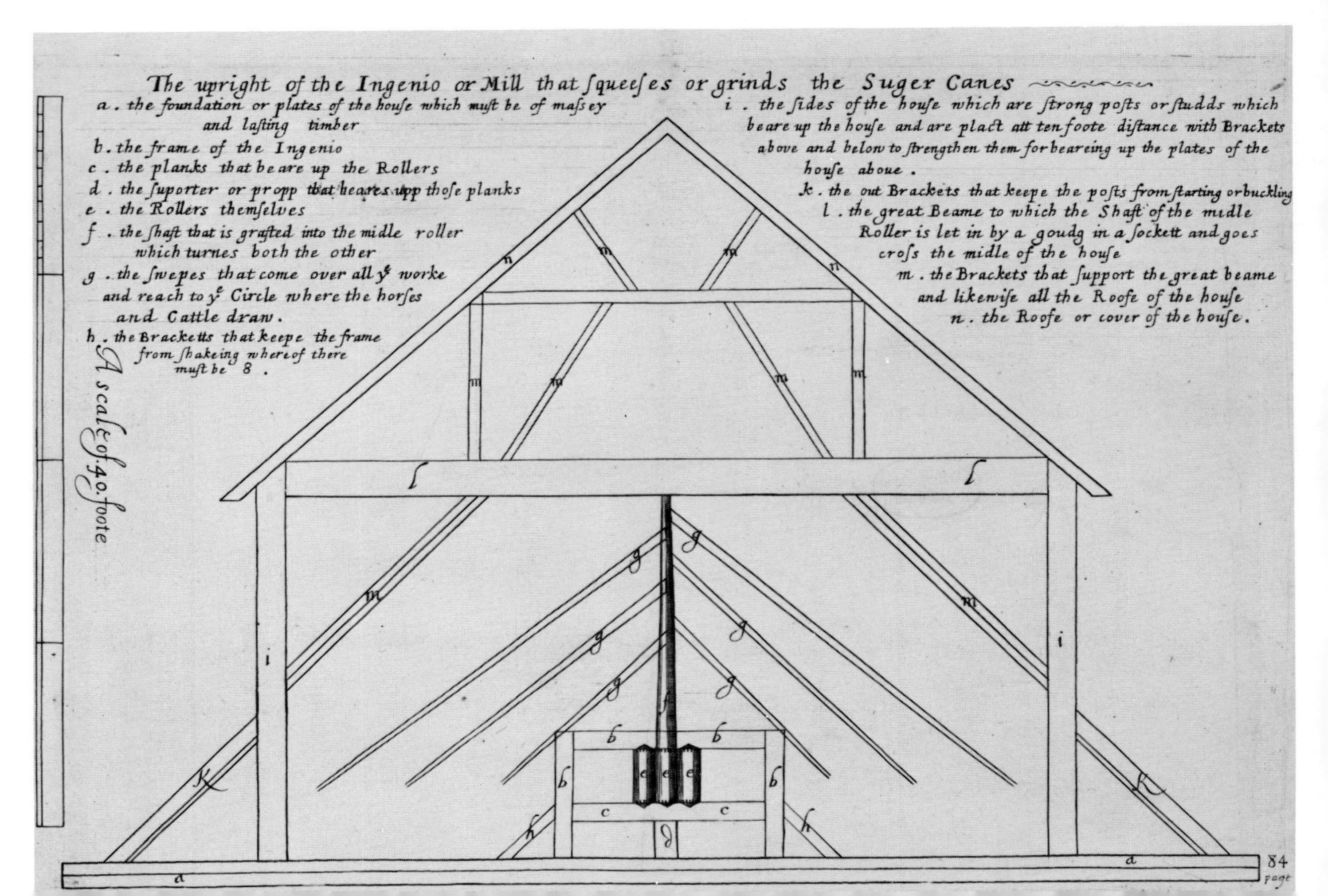

The Upright of the Ingenio or Mill That Grinds Sugar Canes

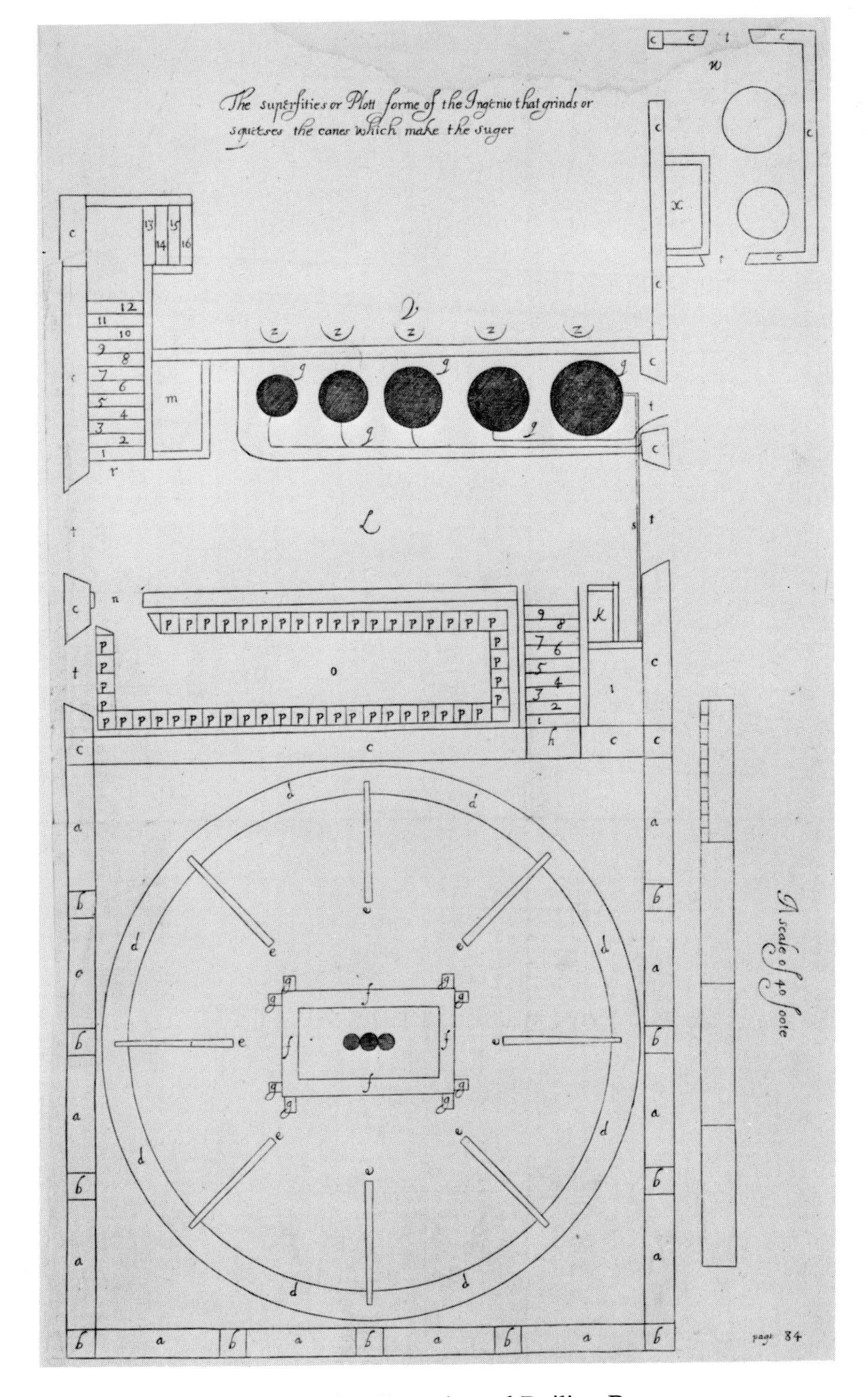

The Plan of an Ingenio and Boiling Room

A West Indian Village, 1660+, by Frans Post

West African Blacks and Palisaded House

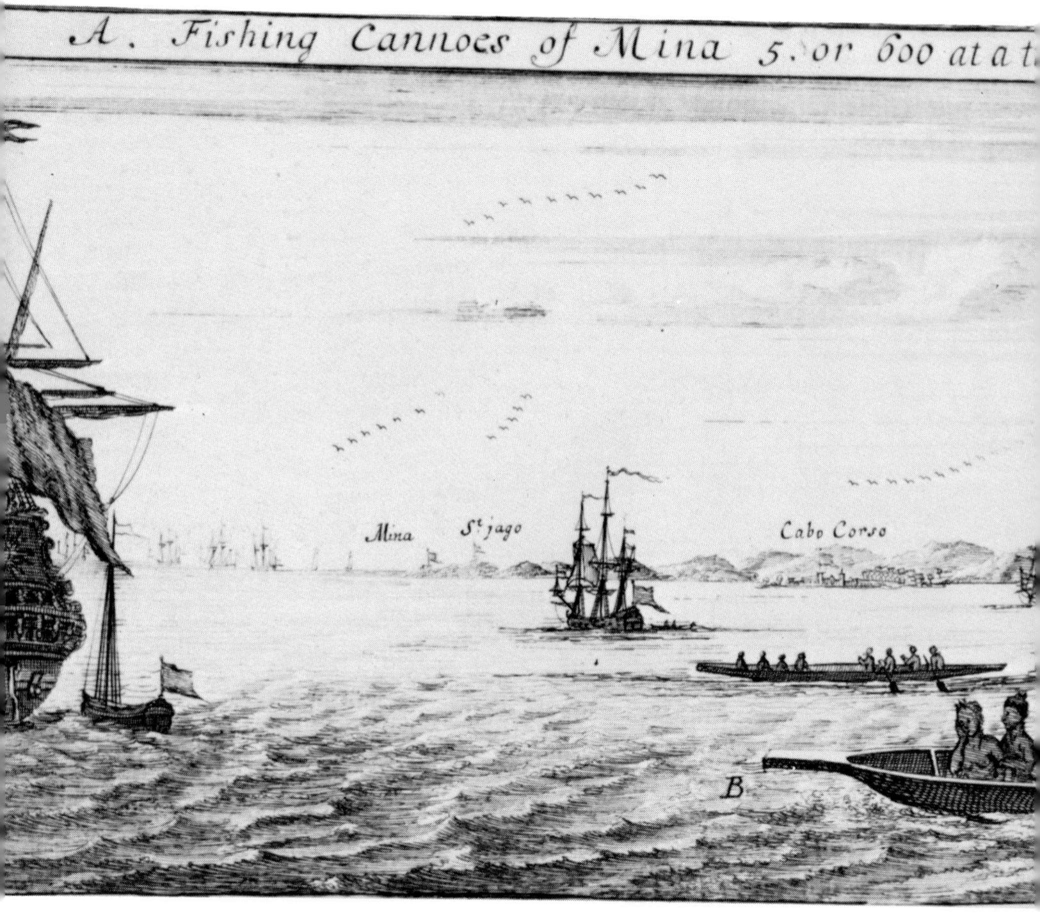

A. Fishing Cannoes of Mina 5. or 600 at a t

Mina

S^t jago

Cabo Corso

B

Negroes Carrying Black Slaves to Ships at Manfroe

Armadill
Hill
Sanford
St. John's Hill
Mapauny or Willughby River
Com ma wena
Speckle-wood Country
Tomountibo
cash ip pory
Jews
Mor ganam
Kings
Gen. Byam
Surrin am R
cash iwini ca
Erackirak
Seri no
Occomico
Ri ver
Serin
Powells
Commetawena
wiampebo
Cot ti co
Commawena Ri.
Mud Creeke
The Sea Coast to windward of Surrinam River
Byam's
A T L A N T I C

A Discription of the Colony of Surranam in Guiana
·:·Drawne in the ÿeare 1667 :·
(Redrawn by Vaughn Gray, 1971)

The Plantations as they are Settled in the Severall parts of the Country.
The land is low and very full of woods; it is very Bad travelling from one Plantation to an other without Boats.

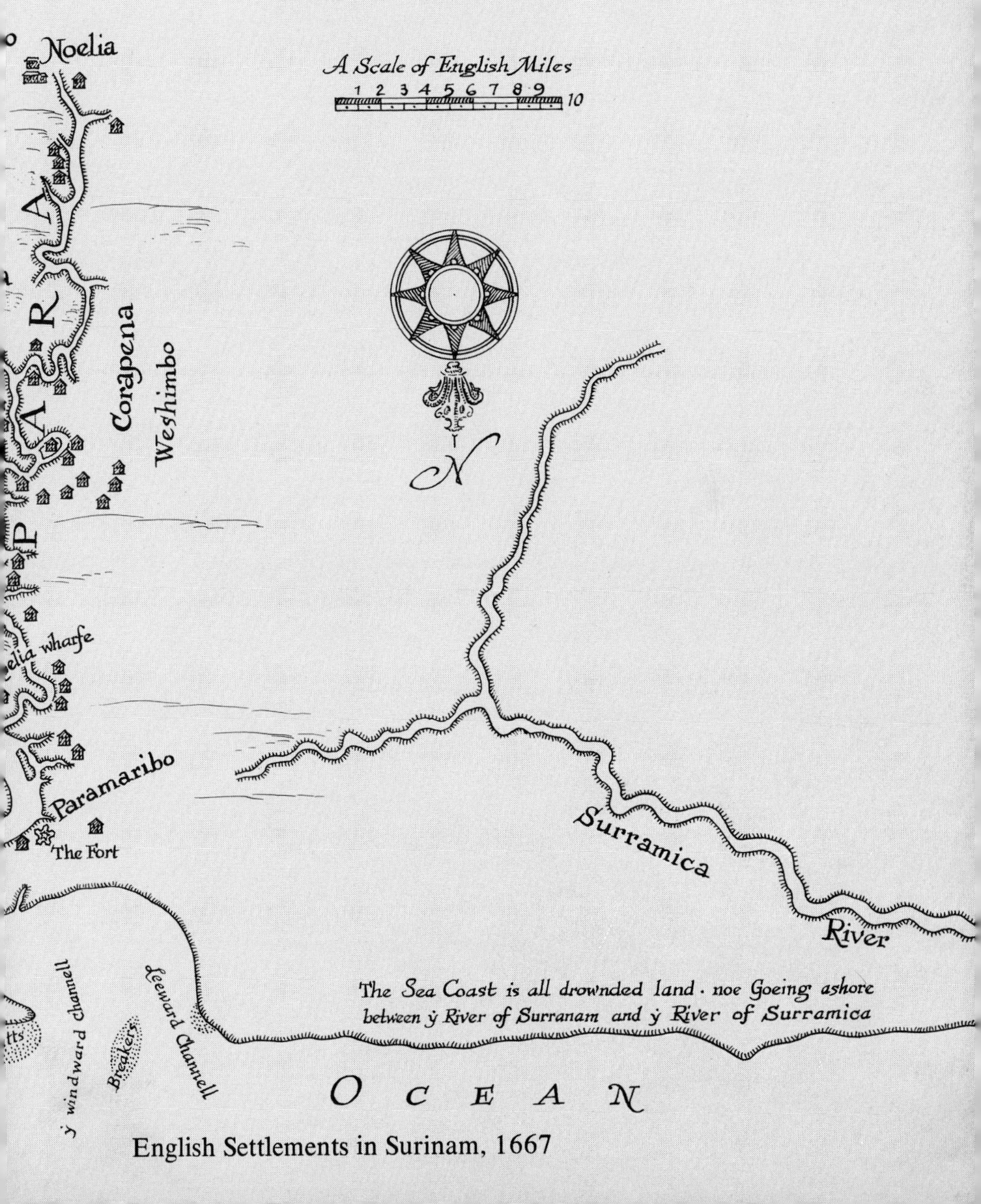

English Settlements in Surinam, 1667

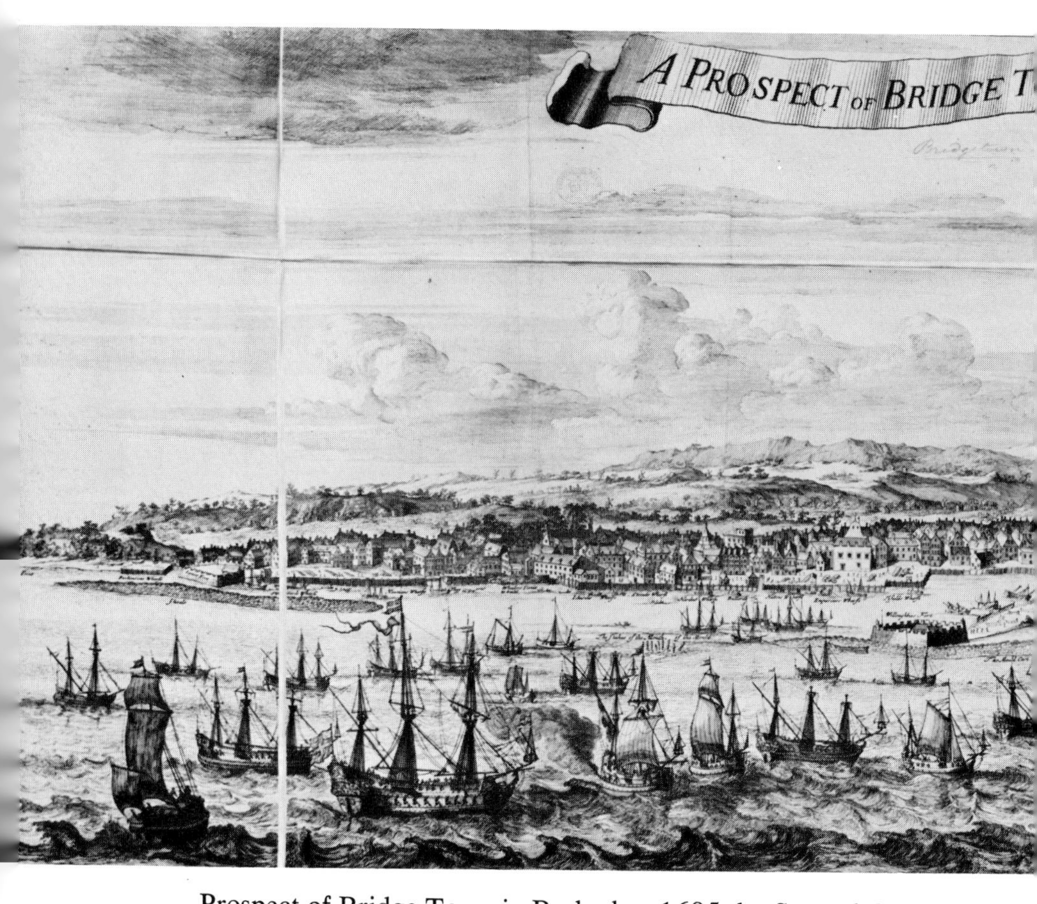

Prospect of Bridge Town in Barbados, 1695, by Samuel Copen

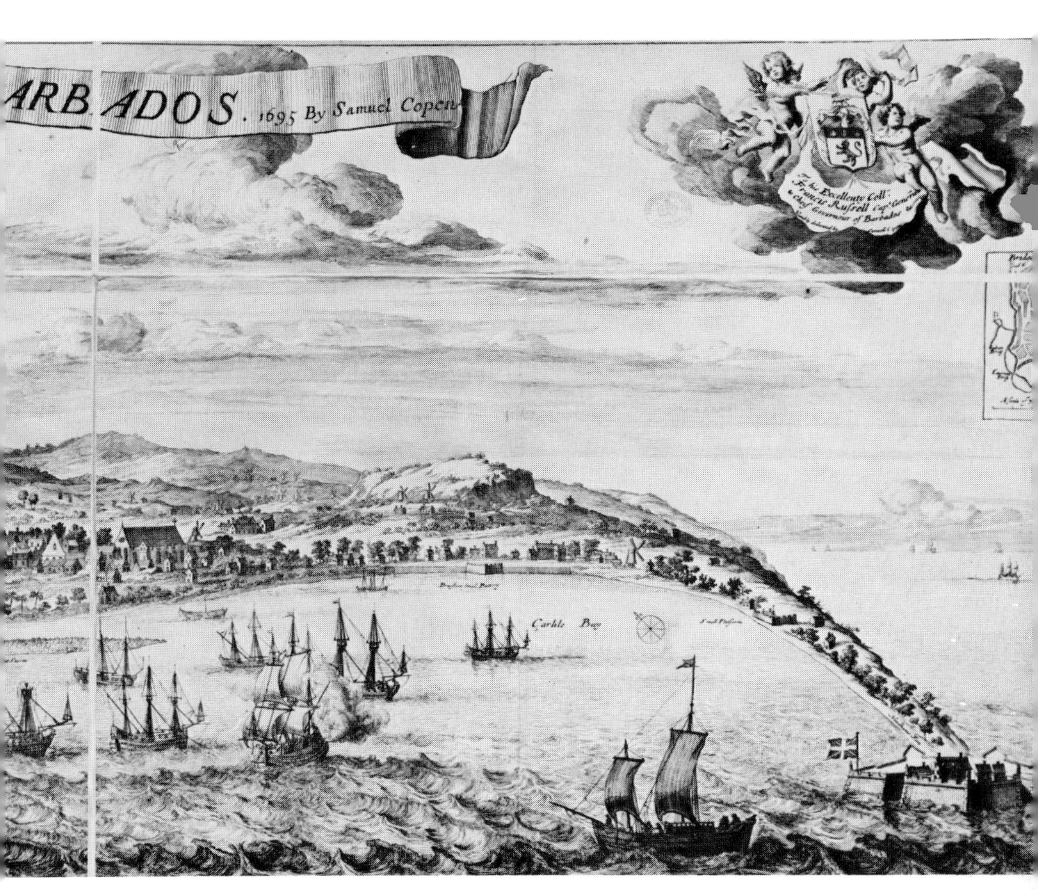
ARB ADOS. 1695 By Samuel Copen
To his Excellency Coll.
Francis Russell Cap.t General
& chief Governour of Barbados
Carlile Bay

Amsterdam, the Mart of the West Indies

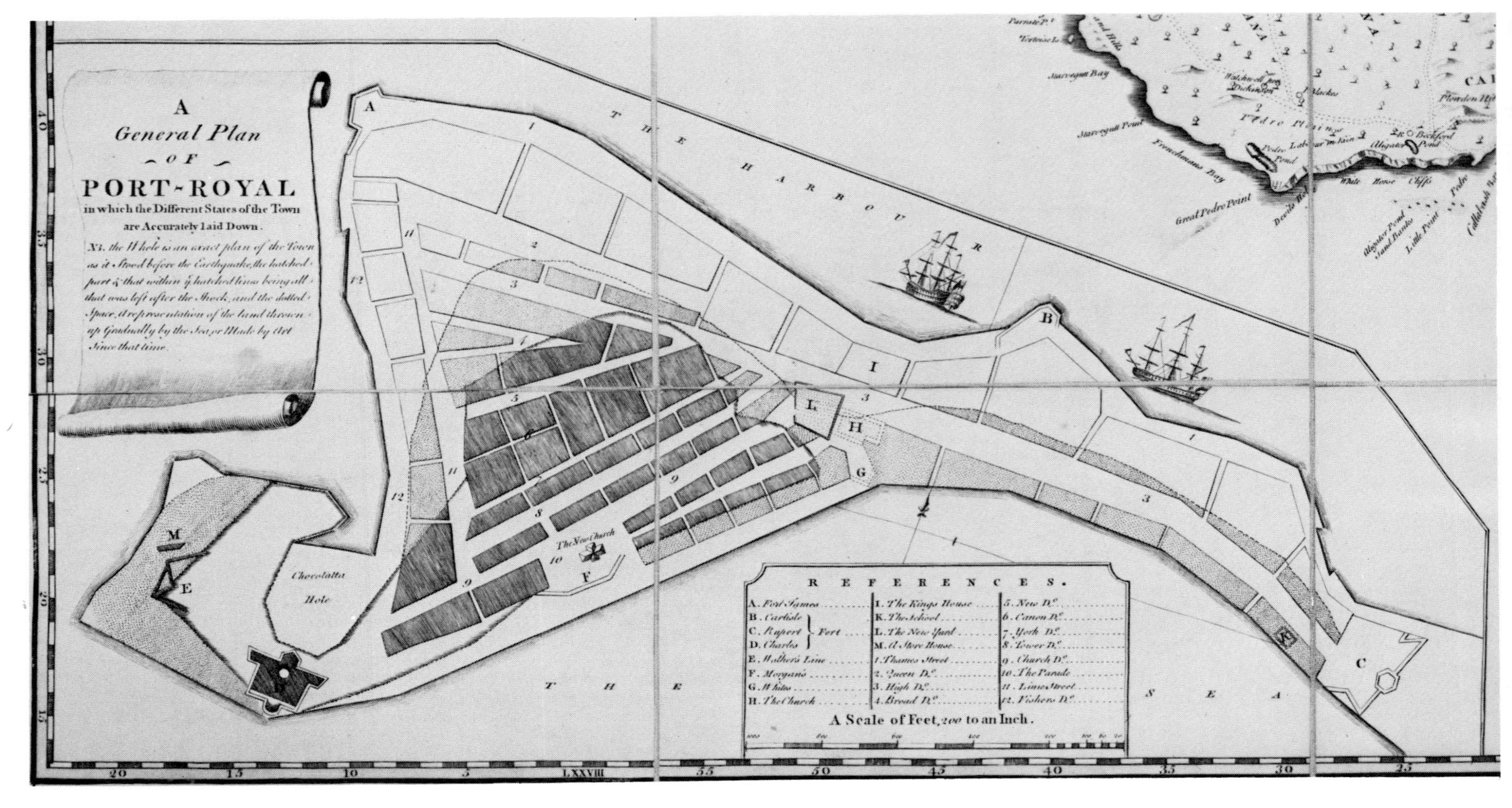

Port Royal, Jamaica, Before and After the Earthquake of 1692

Caribbean Sea Turtles

The House to be built for the Minister is to be Forty ffoote long and Twenty one ffoote wide from Out to Out and to have a porch building Twelve and ffourteen foote square, A staire Building Sixteen and ffourteen foote square Two Shades each of them ~~Twelve~~ and ffourteen and Twelve foot square, all these dimensions are from out to out./

The body of the House porch & staire must be of Stone walls Two foote thick and Eighteen foot high and the Shades of the same thicknesse — Tenn ffoote high with shadeing and Gable ends./

The Roomes contained in ye Dwelling house will be as followeth. Vizt/

In ye 1st Story
- A porch tenn foote sq:
- A Hall Twenty and seventeen foote sqr:
- A parlor sixteen & seventeen foote sqr:
- A staire Case Twelve foote sqr.
- A Shade Twelve & Tenn foot sq:
- A Shade Tenn and Twelve foote sqr:

In ye 2d story
- A porch Chamber Tenn foote square
- A Hall Chamber Twenty and seventeen foot square
- A parlor Chamber sixteen and seventeen foote square
- A staire Case Twelve foote square
- A shade Chamber ten and Twelve foot square
- A Shade Chamber Tenn & Twelve foote square

In the 3d Story
- A Garrit 10 foot square
- Hall and parlor Garritt Thirty six and Seventeen foote square
- A staire case in ye Garrit Twelve foote square

All ye Ground ffloores to be paved belonging to the House with paving bricks laid in Mortar, all ye roofs to be covered with plaine tyles pinned and laid in Mortar./

The Walls to be all plaistered within, pointed without and ye Corners ffreestone./

The partitions to be on both sides lathed and plaistered./

The second ffloore to be laid with boards plained and Joynted./

The Third or Garrett story to be laid with boards plained and Joynted./

In one of ye Shades is to be a Chimney and Oven./

Doore Cases this house will need in the 1st story 8 & 7 of wch: are to be in Stone Walls. / In the 2d Story 5 & 4 of which are to be in Stone Walls./

Windowes in the ffirst story will be needed 9 } These 17 all in Stone walls./
In ye Second ———— 8 }

The preceeding Doore Cases and windowes being Twenty Eight in Stone Walls must have Lintells of Timber. The Windowes must be all Glassed, the doore cases fitted with Doores, and the three outmost with Locks and Keyes;/ Timber for the body of the house &c./ All of Masticks as followeth/

Six beames ~~x~~ 3 19½ foote long./ 3 21 foote long all tenn Inches square./

One Hundred Twenty & five foote of Wall plate ten Inches broad ffive thick./

Ninty Six Joyce 9 foote 9 Inches long, or ffourty Eight Joyce Nine and a half foote long, Forty Eight Joyce Tenn foote long all five and three Inches square./

ffive paire of principalls Two pair Eighteen foote long, three pair fifteen foote long all seven and ffive at bottome, ffive square at Topp./

ffive Coller beames each Twelve ffoote long six and ffive Inches square Tenn purlins six of them Tenn ffoote long ffour ffive foote long all six and ffive Inches square, Twenty ffive pair of small rafters seaventeen & a half foote long, or ffifty pair half 10½ foote long half 7 foote long all three Inches square./

Timber for the porch building as followeth

Seven Joyce Twelve foote long Six Inches and three square / One beame fourteen foote long Tenn Inches and Eight square / Fourteen Joyce Six foote long five Inches and Two and a half square, Forty ffoote of Wallplate Eight Inches and ffoure square / Two pair of principalls, 1 pair Tenn and a half foote long, 1 pair thirteen long Six Inches and ffive square. Twelve pair of Rafters thirteen foot long or Twenty four pair half five foote long, half Eight foote long all three Inches square / Seaventy ffoure foote of purlin Coller beame and brace Six inches and three and a half /

Timber for the staire Case followeth vizt:

The Standards, Railes braces and Joyce for the staires will require some Twenty five foote Timber /

ffourty Six foote of Wallplate Eight Inches and ffoure /

Eighty Eight ffoote of Coller beame purlin and brace Six Inches and three and a half square: Two paire of principalls one paire Twelve foote long, One pair fifteen foote all Six Inches and five square, ffourteen paire of small rafters fourteen and a half long and Twenty Eight paire Ditto half six foote long, half Eight foote and a half long all three Inches square /

Timber for the Shades followeth

Two Wallplates Tenn Inches and five thirteen foote long: ffourteen Joyce four of which sixteen foote long Six Inches and Seaven square. Teen Joyce fifteen foote long Seaven Inches and foure and Two paire of principalls Twenty foot long Nine Inches and Six square at bottome Six square at topp, Two pair of purlins Tenn foote long each seaven and ffive Inches square / Twelve pair of small rafters Twenty Two ffoote and a half long or Twenty four half tenn foote long and half Twelve and a half foote long all three Inches square / ffour braces Six foote long, Six and foure Inches square, A Mantle Tree for the Chimney and Timbers to lay in y^e house Wall to fasten y^e four great shade Joyce there-bute may take some fifteen foote of Timber /

Specifications for a Barbados Glebe House, 1679

Montego Bay
JAMAICA
1684
Savanna la Mar
Port Royal
Caribbean Sea
AREA SHOWN IN DETAIL
0
50
100 Miles
CLARENDON
Clarenden Parke
PARRISH
St. DOROTH
VERE
PARRISH
St. Anns Gut
Mino R.
Vere R.
Vere Park
Round Hill
Milke Savana
Kettle Spring
The Cross
Old Harbour
Towne
Brid Port
Pig bay
Dorrels bogg
Salt Savana
Portland
Long Bay
Swift River
Flint Bay
Milk R.
Maccary Bay
Maccary Pt.
Mino R.
Michaels hole
Rocky Pt.
Taylors bay
Long Bay
The Pitch of Portland
Portland Cays
Sandy Banck
Pidgeon Is
Langleys Land
Parsons
Beckford
Tomson
Manour
Modyfords
Littleton & Dawkins
Masters
Fuller
Halstead
Long
Watson
Watson
Watson
Booth
Iry
Sutten
Sutton
Sutton
Tennent
Rimes
Harding
Scta Maria
Rimes
Savana
Spirry
Lewy
James
North
Sutton
Rimes
Pickeing
Marshall
Gent
Watson
Cotes
Dawkins
Hazard
Halee
Dawkins
Browne
Halce
Young
Savana
Buller's Sarana
Rimes B.
Cooper
Ashurst
Long & Story
Barnes
Peeke
Hunt
Hales
Halce
Maning
Smart Castle
Pye
King
Swarton
Morant
Keen
Sheen
Wright
Peeke
Barclau
Edmonds
Iry
Goodwin
Corner
Rippon
Phelps
Durant
Colier
Fawcet
Fisher
Wolascot
Varney
Carlisle
Banister
Banister
Colebeck
Winter
Bodle
Knight
Moleswerth & Barnard
Topiboa
Wright
Vrpeth & Bouchar
Best
Long
Palmeto
Davis
Reeve
Watson
Bennet
Sykes
Groves
Read

Plantation Jamaica, 1684

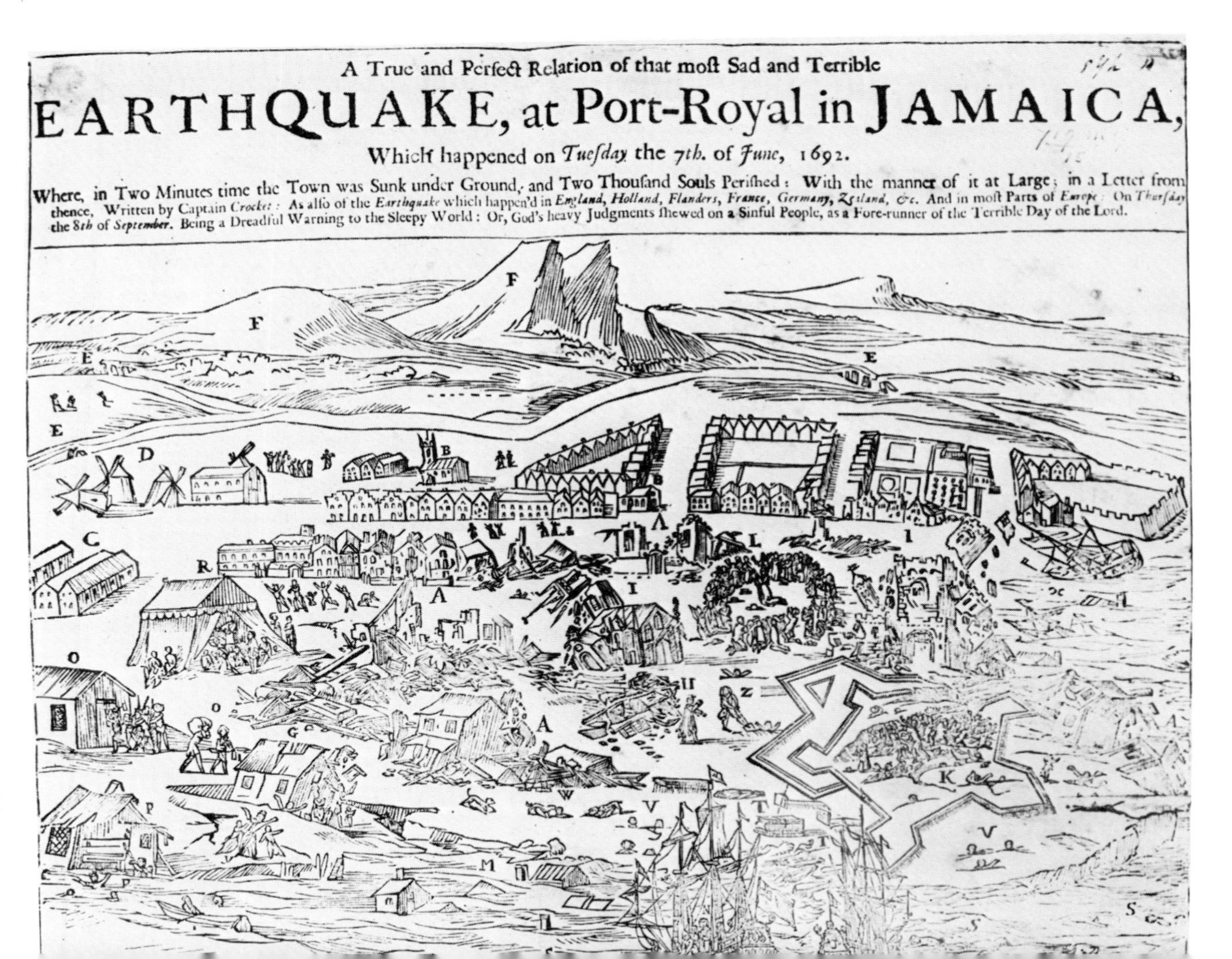
A True and Perfect Relation of that most Sad and Terrible

EARTHQUAKE, at Port-Royal in JAMAICA,

Which happened on *Tuesday* the *7th.* of *June*, 1692.

Where, in Two Minutes time the Town was Sunk under Ground, and Two Thousand Souls Perished: With the manner of it at Large; in a Letter from thence, Written by Captain *Crocket*: As also of the *Earthquake* which happen'd in *England*, *Holland*, *Flanders*, *France*, *Germany*, *Zealand*, &c. And in most Parts of *Europe*: On *Thursday* the 8th of *September*. Being a Dreadful Warning to the Sleepy World: Or, God's heavy Judgments shewed on a Sinful People, as a Fore-runner of the Terrible Day of the Lord.

A London Version of the Jamaican Disaster of 1692

populated, contributed some settlers to Jamaica at this time. In all, between 1600 and 1800 white people and Negro slaves from Nevis, St. Christopher, and Montserrat embarked for Jamaica with Governor Stokes and his family. Making such a long voyage in heavy Flemish ships unfit for tropical service caused many of the passengers to contract scurvy at sea, and when, in January 1657, they all settled at Morant Point where they were sheltered only in tents, heavy rains contributed to fevers, and a fifth of the party died. Stokes and his wife died within a year, and sickness or starvation carried off most of those who survived the first days. According to Governor D'Oyley of Jamaica, not eighty of the miserable immigrants remained alive in 1660.[14]

Oliver Cromwell's eagerness to settle experienced colonists from New England in Jamaica was blocked by the objections of the Puritan leaders to the scheme and the unwillingness of contented New Englanders to move. With Puritan foresight they had dispatched two agents to investigate the prospects for their people, and the men had given "an evell report upon the island in respect of the unhealthfulness thereof" and warned of the threat of a return of the Spanish. The Protector's emigration agent, Daniel Gookin, wrote home that letters received in Massachusetts-Bay and Connecticut from Jamaica reported that only half of the 8000 souls landed there initially had survived. If, however, a more suitable place were to be chosen, "whole Churches would remove." Closest of all to the truth was John Leverett who, with Puritan directness, explained that, although great riches like those amassed by a few men in the West Indies were not attainable in New England, "yet, take the body of the people and all things considered, they lived more comfortably like Englishmen than any of the rest of the Plantations." Consequently, Cromwell's plan to resettle some New

14. The preamble to an act of the Nevis Assembly of 1680 to confirm existing land titles stated that so many inhabitants did "leave and desert their Estates, transporting themselves, with all their Chattels moveable, to Jamaica, or elsewhere, leaving the said Lands and Plantations void of Inhabitants." *Acts of Nevis,* 3–6; Thurloe, *State Papers,* IV, 51–2, 603; V, 66, 374, 500, 652, 668, 769, 771; Frank Cundall, *The Governors of Jamaica in the Seventeenth Century* (London, 1936), 3–4; *CSPC, 1574–1664, Addenda,* p. 114; *CSPC, 1661–68,* p. 177; BM: Egerton MSS, 2395, fol. 83 (names of emigrants from Nevis); Long, *History of Jamaica,* I, 261, 264, 266; BM: Add. MSS, 11, 410, fols. 10b–11.

Englanders failed. Only 300 people, more or less, a large proportion of them women, subscribed to migrate to Jamaica if shipping were provided.[15]

For more than five years after the conquest, the population of Jamaica increased at a very slow rate in spite of the fact that in the first year the Council of State ordered the Commissioners of the Admiralty to send out from Ireland 1000 girls and 1000 boys aged fourteen or under. Among several tracts written to promote settlement was one by Edward Hickeringill, published in 1660, to combat the reputation of the island as a death-trap. His claim of "Every ship that comes from the Wind-ward Islands of Barbados, Nevis, St. Christopher, etc., being crowded above convenience with all sorts of people" was doubtless correct, for the number of vessels was few, and they carried all immigrants crossing from Europe at the time. An estimate of 1658, which seems too high, gave Jamaica 4500 white and 1400 black inhabitants. The whites consisted of disbanded English and colonial troops, some of them with families, youthful Irish servants, and immigrants from the Caribbees and Bermuda. In human lives, a very high price had been paid for the settlements: 6000 persons had died, almost two for every one that survived.[16]

15. The Protector had instructed Daniel Gookin, a prominent and devout Puritan, to promote the settling of New Englanders in Jamaica. Despite his disapproval of the scheme, Gookin issued a broadside printed at London: *To All Persons whome these may Concern . . .* (Broadside, 1656. Bodleian), stating that he was authorized to agree with "any convenient number" in New England who desire to go to Jamaica. *CSPC, 1574–1660,* p. 429; Thurloe, *State Papers,* III, 6–7, 148; IV, 130–31, 440, 449, 634; V, 6, 7, 147–8, 509–10; Hutchinson, *History of Massachusetts-Bay,* I, 163*n*. For a detailed account, see Frank Strong, in Amer. Hist. Assoc., *Annual Report* (1898), 77–94.

16. About the year 1660, in Considerations about the peopling and Settling of Jamaica, the probable author, Thomas Povey, argued hard against restricting the trade of that island to "our avaritious and diffident English Merchants . . . Itts well knowne that all our Collonyes in the West Indies had perished in their infancye, and non of them had come to anie kind of maturitye, if they had not beene releived, and supplyed, by the curtesie, and trade of the Dutch . . . Whereas noe English Merchant yet ever brought to Jamaica, eyther Slaves, Servants, Coppers, or such things as tended directly to the Settling of the Island, But onely Wynes, and such Trifles for which they have carryed away all the Mony that was ever brought to the Island." BM: Egerton MSS, 2395, fol. 283; Long, *History of Jamaica,* I, 375; *CSPC, 1574–1660,* p. 431; Hickeringill, *Jamaica*

In the meantime, runaways, freemen, and a few freeholders continued to leave Barbados, St. Christopher, Nevis, and Montserrat for other less populated islands of the Lesser Antilles. In the twelve years after 1650, the French islands of Guadeloupe, Martinique, Marie Galante, and also Dutch Curaçao and Tobago, attracted some 1600 English settlers. Not a few of these migrants had been prisoners exiled by the Protector, and they were now labeled "notorious delinquents and offenders" by Governor Searle of Barbados. Some West Indians with property and family or business connections to the northward sailed to plant tobacco in Virginia and Maryland; others embarked for New England to locate themselves in a mercantile way in a more salubrious and politically and religiously congenial atmosphere. How many people fled from their islands to sit down elsewhere or went off to fight and never returned can never be stated exactly; but in this decade it must have exceeded 12,000.[17]

By 1660 the 421 square miles of available land of the five Caribbee islands had been expanded ten-and-a-half times by the acquisition of Jamaica's 4396 square miles and the boundless acreage in Surinam (which in 1954 encompassed 55,400 square miles). Land in abundance had come under the control of the English, who were now confronted by the same problem the Spanish had in the sixteenth century: could they assemble or induce enough men and women from the British Isles and their four overpopulated islands in the West Indies to colonize and develop the new territories?[18]

II

As the decade of the sixties began, population, which had reached the saturation point, appeared to be the chief problem. An author

---

view'd, 15; *A True Description of Jamaica* (London, 1650), in *Interesting Tracts Relating to Jamaica.*

17. In 1660 the area of the islands held by the Dutch—Curaçao, Aruba, Bonaire, St. Eustatius, Saba, and one-third of St. Martin—totaled 383 square miles. *World Almanac 1966,* pp. 287, 625; *CSPC, 1661–68,* p. 529; *1669–74,* p. 442; Thurloe, *State Papers,* III, 743; IV, 6–7, 625; Chandler, in *JBMHS,* XIII, 114.

18. *World Almanac 1966,* pp. 287, 648.

of a contemporary tract stated it very clearly: "Every Person knowes how full all the Caribbee Islands are of Inhabitants, and how incapable they are of giving them subsistances, and that there is an absolute necessity that very many of them doe immediately transplant. . . . "[19]

Fully aware of the critical situation, Lord Willoughby strove to relieve the pressure of population by renewing the policy of expansion begun with Surinam in 1650. His views fitted in with current London opinion, which stressed warm tropical settlements over colder northern colonies. Indeed, his Lordship may have inspired a promoter of 1660 to point out to Englishmen with some capital the vast benefits of planting among "the innocent Charibdens." Calling attention to a Dutch venture in Guiana in 1659 commanded by Sir Balthasar Gerbier for the States General, the author recommended Tobago and Guiana as regions where immediate success with slave labor seemed certain. Not only would smaller amounts of clothing and equipment be required, but the colonist might count on a larger yield of the exotic products so valued in Europe.[20]

The restoration of King Charles II in 1660 brought about a series of changes in the Caribbean, which stimulated substantial migrations from the overcrowded islands, particularly from Barbados. Lord Willoughby minced no words in 1662 when he warned the King that "Barbados decays fast." His Lordship and the chief planters attributed the "decay" directly to the enumeration of sugar and other restrictive features of the Navigation Act of 1660, which barred their former lucrative traffic with the Dutch and caused an irreparable fall in the price of sugar. To the duties on sugar imported into England was added a 4½ per cent export duty granted to the king, which further reduced the profits of the island planters. The departure of many rich Cavalier planters with their servants and slaves for Surinam, in addition to "some thousands" of small

19. BM: Egerton MSS, 2395, fol. 283.

20. The list of articles needed for establishing a new tropical plantation as given in the promotion tract is the most complete one that the present writers have seen. Sir Balthasar Gerbier, *A Sommary Description Manifesting that Greater Profits are to bee done in the hott then in the colder parte of the Coast of America . . .* (Rotterdam [or London], 1660), A1–3.

landholders and freemen from Barbados to neighboring French and Dutch colonies, where complete freedom of trade still existed, pointed up the severity of the economic depression the islands suffered in the early sixties.[21]

In spite of the pressing need to relieve Barbados of its superabundance of men, it was difficult to induce hard-pressed islanders to go to Jamaica. The reputed unhealthful conditions and the popular belief that the soil was unsuited for planting deterred the poor from emigrating, and the principal planters were "very averse from acting anything to the good of Jamaica." The position of the landholders was anomalous: they had to rid themselves of freedmen whom they could not or would not employ, but they feared that the expelled whites might contribute to the prosperity of a formidable, rising competitor; they clamored for the importation of more and more blacks, but still they hesitated to reduce the number of freemen eligible to serve as privates in the militia. A few Barbadians were persuaded to emigrate in November 1661 by agents, who then sailed for the Leeward Islands to transport to Jamaica as many settlers there as were free to go. A year later, Lord Windsor, newly appointed governor of Jamaica, experienced the same obstructionist tactics: relying on a Royal Proclamation, he began taking servants aboard his ships, but the Council of Barbados insisted that he must post the names of every servant seven days in advance. One planter, writing to friends at Boston, complained that many passengers went with Lord Windsor, "and what of our Debtors are gon I know not. . . ."[22]

Some venturesome Barbadians made their way to the nearest island where they could cut much needed wood for fuel for the sugar furnaces and raise cattle and provisions for their own island. When Lord Willoughby was questioned about this incursion into St. Lucia by M. de Laubière, governor of Martinique, which maintained a small colony there, he insisted that a treaty had been made to purchase the island from the Caribs, who were willing to allow

21. *CSPC, 1661–68,* p. 167; Broadside describing Barbados, undated but after 1665, Bodleian: Rawlinson MSS (reprinted in *West Indian Commercial Circular,* No. 395, Nov. 18, 1913, BM: 1879, C7).

22. PRO: CO 1/15, No. 90; *CSPC, 1661–68,* pp. 96, 97, 99–100, 102, 103; *CSM Pubs.,* XXIX, I, 51.

further settlement. In 1664 Willoughby actually sent more than 1000 Barbadians, led by Colonel Carew, together with 600 Caribs from Dominica under "Indian [Thomas] Warner." The French gave way, but disease, financial difficulties, and the Caribs ruined the undertaking. Many of the men died; others abandoned the island and went elsewhere, and by 1667 a mere eighty-nine of the original party remained. An expected 3000 planters from Virginia and New England never arrived, and St. Lucia reverted to the French, who soon reoccupied it.[23]

At the Restoration, Thomas Modyford, who was one of the leading public servants of Barbados and a shrewd politician, again changed his allegiance by resigning as governor of Barbados to become speaker of the Assembly. He was thoroughly aware of the population problem of the island and had, as early as 1655, stated positively that Barbados could not sustain large numbers of inhabitants much longer. In 1663 the Proprietors of Carolina chose him and Peter, son of Sir John Colleton, to promote a settlement from Barbados. A group of some 200 "gentlemen of good quality," who appeared ready to emigrate to Carolina, formed the Barbados Adventurers. When their demands for home rule and other privileges were rejected by the Proprietors, however, most of the planters declined to risk the costs of migrating in such hard times without the concessions. Only one or two of the ninety prominent Barbadians who had backed the enterprise went to Cape Fear, where the colonists proposed to cut timber and plant provisions for use in Little England. Within a year the colony had more than 800 settlers drawn from the continent as well as the islands. In 1667, however, "the rude Rable" decided almost unanimously to abandon Cape Fear. Some of them went to the Albemarle settlements, others to Virginia and New England, while others returned to Barbados. Internal dissensions had disrupted the group, and the onset of the Second Dutch War prevented more Barbadians from going to the

23. In a neutrality treaty of 1687, France conceded England's possession of St. Lucia, and two years later Dr. Hans Sloane reported a small number of Barbadians living there and cutting wood for the larger island's sugar furnaces and the galleys of many of the ships that called at Bridgetown. Sloane, *Voyage to the Islands,* I, 41; PRO: CO 1/17, No. 79; Du Tertre, *Histoire générale des Antilles,* III, 81–2, 86–90, 243–4; *HMC, Portland,* XIV, Appendix, Pt. 2:2; *CSPC, 1661–68,* pp. 230, 297–8, 329, 413; *1685–88,* pp. 296–7; *1700,* pp. 617–19.

mainland to reinforce their fellows against the more numerous pioneers from New England.[24]

When the Cape Fear colony proved to be disappointing, Thomas Modyford again turned his attention to promoting the settlement of Jamaica and, for a time at least, with more success. Shortly after he was created a baronet by Charles II in March 1664 he became governor of that great island. Within two months he had dispatched a party of several hundred Barbadians to make a permanent settlement there; within a month or so of their departure, he himself, accompanied by 400 would-be colonists, set out and were followed shortly by another vessel with about 300 more persons. In all, Modyford claimed to have taken 987 persons from Barbados by June 1664, nearly all of them free from debt and members of "composed families." Writing to Lord Arlington, he asserted that if the King would provide shipping and victualing for those who were too poor to pay their passage, settlers could be had at a rate of 1000 a year. Somehow, Barbadians continued to flock to Jamaica in the next two years, but all did not go well with them. In February 1665 Modyford notified Lord Arlington that already numbers of those who had come with him were dead, though the island itself was healthful. Not one immigrant, aside from himself, had yet made any plantation: "They came down very poor, and went into the woods without provisions, and there fall sick before they have houses or victuals." [25]

From 1660 to 1665, Irish and English colonists, predominantly male, emigrated in amazing numbers from all the English West Indies, and the populations of Barbados and the Leeward group continued to shrink in the next few years. The apparent causes varied from island to island. The low return for staple crops was blamed by some—Sir Peter Colleton figured that the fall in the price of sugar was proportional to the decline in the population of

24. Robert Sandford, whom we met earlier in Surinam, became registrar and treasurer at Cape Fear, and conducted an exploring voyage to the Port Royal region. *North Carolina Colonial Records,* ed. William L. Saunders (Raleigh, 1886), I, 39–41, 57–9, 95, 118–39, 145–6, 159, 161; Thurloe, *State Papers,* III, 566; *CSPC, 1661–68,* p. 153; South Carolina Historical Society, *Collections,* V (1897). 10–12. A later volume will treat the Carolinas, 1680–90.

25. BM: Add. MSS, 12,408, fol. 8; PRO: CO 1/18, fols. 38, 67, 80; *CSPC, 1661–68,* pp. 180, 189, 207, 219, 277–8.

the Sugar Colonies; Barbados fell from 14,000 fighting men to less than 8000, and men were still leaving the island. Another explanation was soil exhaustion, and there were efforts made to encourage the use of dung. The predicament of many of the meaner sort of planters on Nevis, who had formerly lived in some comfort, explains the problem facing all the small planters everywhere in the Caribbees. Employed solely in growing tobacco, they could no longer sell their crops, because the Dutch purchasers were excluded from the traffic and English ships did not call at that island. Being too poor to buy sugar machinery or slaves, they had no choice, as Governor James Russell put it, but to leave. Consequently, to the more than 7000 Barbadians must be added a number unknown, but certainly in the thousands, from St. Christopher, Nevis, and Montserrat who left their islands in search of land and prosperity elsewhere: in Surinam; on Jamaica, or the smaller islands; in New England, Virginia, or Carolina on the continent of North America.[26]

The nature and quality of these migrating colonists have often been misconceived, as they were at the time. Edward Hickeringill, who was attempting to show Jamaica in the best light, wrote in 1661: "The Major part of the Inhabitants being old West Indians, who now Naturalized [seasoned] to the Countrey grow the better by their transplantation, and flourish in health equivalently comparable to that of their Mother-soil. For which I need not beg credit, since there is no Countrey Disease (as at Virginia and Surinam) endemically raging throughout the Isle. . . ." He was partly right, but the sad truth is that more transplanted islanders succumbed than survived. If the climate was unexceptionable, then the health and resistance of the newcomers must have been poor. Thompson, Povey, Noell, and the London sponsors of Jamaica could not have been properly informed about such conditions in 1660 when they praised the fitness of the migrants: "1000 of them being capable probably of doeinge more in a new Plantacion, than 5000 out of England." One suspects that they discreetly overlooked certain facts in the interest of promotion and trade.[27]

26. BM: Egerton MSS, 2395, fols. 640b–41a; Chandler, in *JBMHS,* XIII, 115; *CSPC, 1661–68,* pp. 204–5.

27. Hickeringill, *Jamaica view'd,* 100; BM: Egerton MSS, 2395, fol. 283.

The long-held belief that runaway or newly freed servants, most of whom were Irish peasants who had served a mere four or five years performing a few simple tasks under strict supervision on a sugar, cotton, or tobacco plantation, were the human stuff of which *pioneers* were made is just not correct. Every statistic and every estimate that we possess indicate the opposite. Settlers from the British Isles or the European continent enjoyed sounder constitutions, better health, and were less debauched by rum than the men of the Caribbean. Above all, they were psychologically sounder and fitter. Lord Willoughby of Parham, who had an unsurpassed knowledge of the colonists in the West Indies, wrote on June 27, 1664, that experience had taught him that "in all new settlements whither people are removed from old ones, 10 die for one that comes fresh and raw out of Europe." He referred his correspondent to the physicians for an explanation, but all of the evidence we now have supports his conclusion.[28]

The Second Dutch War, 1665–67, had profound effects upon the populations of the Caribbees. Because it was a maritime struggle, normal migrations from island to island and to the Main, which had served to cut down the ranks of those unable to make a living for themselves, ceased almost entirely. However, more than a few thwarted colonizers attained their goals by shipping out as soldiers, sailing away on expeditions that drained certain islands of any surplus fighting men they had and left others virtually defenseless. A substantial proportion of these men lost their lives by disease or in combat, and the great preponderance of those who survived never returned to man the weakened militias of the parent islands. After the war, the usual stream of emigrants began again, finding in migration the easiest way out of their dilemmas.

Though all of the colonists of the English West Indies suffered in some measure during the Second Dutch War, the greatest losers appeared to be those living on St. Christopher. Before the conflict began, a few rich planters cultivated sugar with the labor of some hundreds of black slaves, but the great majority of the inhabitants, those possessing tracts of ten or twelve acres, grew tobacco with the

28. *CSPC, 1661–68,* pp. 217–18.

help of one or more white Irish servants. As long as "the weed was a good Comodity," servants stayed on when their time was up and began to plant indigo and ginger as well as tobacco on their newly acquired land.[29]

When the English surrendered their part of St. Christopher to the French on April 11, 1666, the Gallics were just beginning to produce sugar. Rapaciously they carried off as plunder to their own plantations all of the slaves and equipment for sugarworks, later valued at £400,000. Altogether, the English lost 438 plantations, small and large. Their lands overrun, stripped of their means of livelihood, between 5000 and 8000 white settlers fled from their homes. Some of them managed to get to Jamaica, others to Virginia and New England, but the largest body of refugees crossed in haste to nearby Nevis, and some 300 went to Montserrat—communities whose resources could ill support them. Antigua received others, and when passage was available, several hundred located on Anguilla, where Captain Abraham Howell became their governor. Not long after the conquest of St. Christopher, Antigua surrendered to the enemy, and in 1667 Montserrat fell into French hands. In all probability the refugee populations of the Leeward Islands outnumbered the inhabitants who remained on their land.[30]

Apprehension and terror of the growing power of the French in the Caribbean, according to Sir Peter Colleton, drove some prudent planters to seek greater security in the northern colonies. From recently acquired New York in June 1667, Samuel Maverick reported that several men had arrived from Barbados who had been commissioned by "persons of quality" to buy farms or estates and houses; "some are already bought, more in chase." By all odds the most important of these émigrés was Lewis Morris, formerly a sea captain, a colonel under Cromwell, a rich planter, now a Quaker, and a member of the Barbados Council. Together with his brother Richard, a prosperous merchant of Bridgetown, Morris purchased a tract of 500 acres on the Harlem River, known then

29. BM: Add. MSS, 11,409, fol. 77; *CSPC, 1669–74,* p. 441.

30. Early in 1672, Sir Charles Wheler found only five English families living on St. Christopher (before the French returned it). BM: Add. MSS, 11,409, fol. 71; PRO: CO 1/26, No. 57; Du Tertre, *Histoire générale . . . des Antilles,* IV, 62; *CSPC, 1661–68,* p. 587; *1669–74,* pp. 286, 441; BM: Egerton, 2395, p. 1029.

as Bronck's land and today as The Bronx. Colonel Morris sailed northward to locate permanently in 1672.[31]

When the former English colony on St. Christopher was restored to the English by the Treaty of Breda in 1667, the returning planters met with all manner of obstacles when they tried to regain their property. The figure of 6352 slaves claimed seems exorbitant, but Governor Stapleton said that 243 landholders had not retrieved their lands in 1672. In all, the colony contained 3182 English, 3371 French, and 270 Dutch, or 6823 whites. Four years later, according to Colonel Philip Warner, there were still less than 4000 English in the "mother island" of the Caribbees. The land was barren—"There is no wood"—and so "Extreame poore" were the people that St. Christopher never recovered its former population or its economic prosperity and political importance. In June 1689 the Irish in the English section openly declared themselves for King James and the destruction of "all that belongs to the Protestant interest." Immediately the English planters set about sending their women and children to Nevis for safety. War began on July 18, and in August the English capitulated but were permitted to join their families on Nevis. Codrington wrote home at this time that should St. Christopher remain in French hands, there most certainly would be a mass emigration from all the Leeward Islands "to some secure country." [32]

Barbados was never invaded, but it did lose 1300 "Stout English men" in the abortive colonization of St. Lucia, and another 1500 perished with Francis, Lord Willoughby in a hurricane as they were on their way in 1666 to retake St. Christopher. Perhaps 500 more died in the unfortunate failure at St. Christopher when his successor, William, Lord Willoughby, sought to recover it from the French.[33]

31. BM: Egerton MSS, 2395, fol. 638b; *MHS Colls.,* 4th ser., VII, 319; *Suffolk Deeds,* VII, 226; Davis Coll., I, Envelope 30; *DAB,* XIII, 213.

32. BM: Add. MSS, 11,409 (Inst. Jamaica Trans.), fols. 13–16, 37, 56, 77; BM: Egerton MSS, 2395, pp. 1029–30, fol. 530; *CSPC, 1675–76,* p. 367; *1689–92,* p. 305.

33. Early in 1670, Nicholas Blake of Bilbao plantation informed King Charles II that Barbados had lost 1500 men to St. Lucia "about four years past." This same year, Scott put the number at 1300. *CSPC, 1699, Addenda,* p. 591; BM: Egerton MSS, 2395, fol. 633b; BM: Sloane MSS, 3662, fol. 55b.

The number of King Charles's white West Indian subjects who became displaced persons in the war years or who were made so by the Peace of Breda approximates 12,000—8000 from St. Christopher and 4000 from Surinam. The victims of conflict on Antigua and Montserrat were not estimated, nor do we have any figure for the blacks lost on the three captured islands. Men, women, and children, their servants and slaves became refugees on other islands, dependent upon the charity of strangers for their very survival. For the white inhabitants of the English West Indies, this struggle had been a major catastrophe, and by 1669 it was evident that more than 15,000 of them, how many more we shall never know, and an uncounted body of blacks had been forced to move from their homes and huts or had died in military service. Never again would there be complaints about the excess of white men in the English colonies of the West Indies.[34]

III

The loss of so many white settlers from Barbados and the Leeward Islands by migration and the heavy mortality of the wars in the sixties actually created a shortage of fighting men that colonial leaders realized with genuine dismay. When Thomas Modyford departed for Jamaica in the spring of 1664, Lord Willoughby, writing to Lord Clarendon, described it as a great "blowe" because "the loss of our planters (by the incouraigement they will take from him) in thire adventuring thither whereby wee shall be soe thinned of Christian people, a great many haveing alreddy ingaiged uppon settlin of Carolina . . . I feare our negrose will growe to[o] hard for us." William, Lord Willoughby, upon his arrival in Barbados in 1666, reported back to the King that a mere 2000 out of 7000 men could be depended upon to fight if the enemy attacked; "the remainder made up of small planters . . . freemen, and servants, who, impoverished and disheartened, and without interest or hope

34. A petition to the King from Barbados in 1671 stated that "upwards of 4000 inhabitants" have deserted the island, many of them for foreign plantations. *CSPC, 1669–74,* p. 284, ii; PRO: CO 1/21, No. 170.

of benefit here," have no inclination to expose themselves to danger.[35]

An absentee planter, Sir John Colleton, made a vivid social analysis of the island's inhabitants as he had known them, which supports Lord Willoughby's view. The population, by 1666, had shrunk to a figure reminiscent of the estimates of the forties—760 "considerable proprietors" and no more than 8000 effective men. Two-thirds of them were "of noe interest or reputation, and of little innate Courage, being poor men that are just permitted to live, and a very great part Irish, derided by the Negroes, and branded with the Epithite of white slaves. And, indeed, except the Proprietors, Merchants, some Tradesmen and those few officers, with the dependents of the same, the rest are onely such, that have not reason enough to discern their abuses, or not Courage to embarque and leave the Island, or that are in debt, and cannot goe, while others, more strict Computists of their Injuries, have at severall tymes gone off [since 1643] at least 12,000 good men, formerly proprietors and tradesmen, wormed out of theire small settlements, by theire more settled and greedy Neighbours." [36]

Notwithstanding the loss of men in the wars and the loss of the vast land areas of Surinam to the Dutch by the Treaty of Breda, and the return of St. Eustatius and Saba, which they had occupied in trust from 1672 to 1682, the English expanded the area of the territories they controlled in the Caribbean more than twelvefold between 1650 and 1690. During these years the English turned out to be by far the most aggressive of the Europeans, and either by conquest or by settling unoccupied lands, they pursued fitfully a policy of colonial expansion and displayed in the process, as a Frenchman wrote, "la présomption ordinaire à cette nation." The urgent need for land upon which the thousands of freemen in the four densely populated islands might seat themselves and raise profitable staples and meet the military requirements for soldiers going on expeditions of conquest were the primary causes for the migrations to new territories; then with the passage of time, the

35. Willoughby to Clarendon, March 5, 1663/4 (Bodleian: Clarendon MSS, 81, fol. 129), Davis Coll., V; *CSPC, 1661–68,* p. 431.

36. PRO: CO 1/21, No. 170.

planters on such islands developed an insatiable demand for white labor to exploit virgin soils. A large proportion of the white settlers of the newer colonies came from the older overcrowded islands.[37]

ENGLISH EXPANSION IN THE CARIBBEAN
1650–1690

1650	*Anguilla,* from the Leeward Islands
1650	*Surinam,* from Barbados and the Leeward Islands
1655	*Jamaica,* from the Caribbees and Surinam
1660	*Antigua,* from the Caribbees and Surinam
1661	*Barbuda,* from Antigua
1662	*Campeachy,* by buccaneers and Jamaicans
1663	*Carolina,* by Barbadians at Cape Fear
1663	*St. Lucia,* by Barbadians
1666	*Bahamas,* from Bermuda
1672	*Tortola,* from the Leeward Islands
1672	*St. Eustatius* and *Saba,* by Leeward Islanders (to 1682)
1672	*Tobago,* from Barbados (abandoned, 1683)
1678	*Turks Island,* from the Leeward Islands
1680	*Virgin Islands,* from Anguilla

Following the Peace of Breda, William, Lord Willoughby made plans to revive his brother's scheme for extending the English settlements to the Windward Islands. At the same time, Nicholas Blake importuned King Charles to allow him to people St. Lucia, which he believed could soon attract 5000 colonists because it lay only twenty-five leagues from Barbados. The King, however, favored Lord Willoughby, who professed that he could not "endure to suffer the Dutch to Burrow soe neare to Barbados" as Tobago. When Sir Tobias Bridge expelled the Dutch from Tobago in December 1672, Lord Willoughby pressed the Assembly of Barbados to help in settling the island but was told "they desired noe people might be sent off this Island to Tobago, this place much wanting funds." According to Jonathan Atkins, Francis, Lord Willoughby

37. See list of English and French possessions included in a proposed neutrality treaty of 1679, *CSPC, 1677–80,* pp. 385–86; J. Clodoré, *Relation de ce qui s'est passé dans les isles et terre-ferme de l'Amérique* (Paris, 1671), I, 129.

had spent more than £50,000, ruining his fortune, to expand English influence on what was "too much for any man's undertaking though hee had beene a Prince considerable." Five hundred men were all that could be enlisted to send over to settle Tobago. By 1683 all of the English at St. Lucia had died or abandoned the settlement, and in another five years the Caribs had driven away to New England the Courlanders who had been living on Tobago and cutting wood. When M. Marrin, deputy governor of Tobago, went to Bridgetown to open a timber trade for money with which to restore the settlement under French auspices, Governor Edwin Stede declined to enter into any agreement.[38]

At the conclusion of the Second Dutch War, most of the English and Irish who went out to the West Indies with servants of their own nations went to Jamaica, where they took up large tracts of land on easy terms. Every governor of Jamaica from 1660 to 1690 earnestly endeavored to encourage white immigration. To erase from the public mind the reputation of the island as an unhealthful place, descriptions of the salubrious climate and fruitful soil of the island, nearly as unrealistic and deceptive as modern Caribbean travel "literature," were issued to allure the prospective colonists. An act for naturalization, passed in 1675, was intended by the Council to attract qualified planters to Jamaica: "no one's poverty ought to be alledged [against him], and the interest and stock they bring with them is the best Security Foreigners can give for their Allegiance." A report of passengers and servants landing there between June 25, 1671, and March 25, 1679, listed 3522 from Europe and 1874 from Barbados.[39]

38. In 1682 M. Hesselberg, agent for the Duke of Courland, who claimed to own Tobago, stopped at Bridgetown, took on 135 passengers, and then sailed to Tobago to load firewood for Barbados and return for more passengers. A storm drove him to Jamaica where Governor Lynch learned from him that the Dutch could supply Tobago goods 35 per cent under the price the English colonists paid for American produce. Lynch feared the sloops from Tobago would supply Barbados and ruin English trade there. *CSPC, 1669–74,* pp. 114–15; *1681–85,* pp. 285, 320; BM: Egerton MSS, 2395, fol. 483; Barbados Council Minutes, II, Jan. 4, 8, Feb. 18, 1672/3; PRO: CO 1/37, fol. 22; BM: Sloane MSS, 2441, fol. 16; *JBMHS,* XII, 122. In general, see John Poyntz, *The Present Prospect of . . . Tobago* (2d ed., London, 1695).

39. Persistent attempts to attract New Englanders to Jamaica largely failed. Capt. John Blackleach explained this to John Winthrop, Jr., in 1671: "All matters

During this period, English gentlemen of substance, former Royalists who had been exiled to Barbados by Cromwell and then moved to Surinam to avoid a sticky insular political situation, found themselves harried by their Dutch rulers after 1667. Those who could arrange to emigrate with their slaves came chiefly to Jamaica. In two ships "so filled that they had scarce room to lodge in," 105 families numbering 517 persons came from there with Major James Bannister in 1670. Hundreds of additional Surinam planters, "being weary of a strange government," were eager to follow them, but the Dutch court at Parimaribo deliberately slowed down the process of arranging the sale of their estates and goods. In September 1675, however, Edward Cranfield succeeded in evacuating more than 250 white people with 981 slaves to Jamaica.[40]

Because these newcomers to Jamaica, who had arrived with their families, slaves, and considerable property, were all in good health after a long voyage, let alone well seasoned after living on the Main for more than twenty years, many leading Jamaicans welcomed them as experienced planters and looked upon them as

---

considered, I judge our husbandmen in Connecticut doe live better then a great part of the inhabitants here" in Jamaica. The heat is offensive, "and the diet of the common sort of people is not so houlsome nor soe good, in my apprehension." *MHS Colls.,* 4th ser., VII, 152; BM: Sloane MSS, 3662, fol. 59a; PRO: CO 1/15, fol. 94; Jamaica Council Minutes, III, 77; PRO: CO 1/43, p. 59; *CSPC, 1677–80,* p. 344.

40. Some idea of the distress and losses of the Surinam planters may be gained by studying the sad case of Jeronimy Clifford, who was an English subject living at Corcabo plantation on the Commewijne River in 1667 when the Dutch acquired the colony permanently. The Dutch governor blocked any sale of the estate: houses, 68 slaves, sugar machinery, live stock, and 1500 acres on both sides of the river. In 1685 Clifford tried to sell it to a Negro man, Henry Macintosh, for 6000 pounds of sugar, but soon the transaction fell through. He removed to Jamaica, where he owned 480 acres in St. Elizabeth's Parish, in that same year. He was still trying to recover damages in 1717. Even though the Board of Trade had reduced the amount of the claim from £31,892.11*s.* to £13,514.11*s.8d.,* there is no record of whether he ever received anything. *The Case of Mr. Jeronimy Clifford, Merchant and Planter of Surinam* (London, *ca.* 1705); *The Case and Proceedings For and Against Mr. Jeronimy Clifford Merchant and Planter of Surinam* (London, 1717), 6–8; PRO: CO 1/43, p. 59; Barbados Council Minutes, II, 172–3; *CSPC, 1675–76,* pp. 284, 285–7, 289–92; *1669–74,* p. 319; BM: Add. MSS, 12,408; fol. 15; Beeston's Journal, in *Interesting Tracts Relating to Jamaica,* 291; Frank Cundall gives a careful account in *Timehri,* VI, 145–60; PRO: CO 1/36, No. 75, (I–IV), fols. 175–90; CO 1/37, fols. 4–11.

"worth four times the number of people from Europe." As old comrades-in-arms and now protégés of King Charles II, they were assisted by a proclamation of Lord Vaughan, the governor, who enjoined all inhabitants to treat them well and see that they were received with all manner of "Friendship and Kindliness." The proclamation also set penalties for overcharging or defrauding them. In Jamaica, they proceeded to St. Elizabeth's Parish and located in the midst of earlier colonists from Surinam and at once prospered as sugar planters. A capable, selected lot, they stand out vividly as the exception to the general rule about the inferior quality of the Caribbean pioneers.[41]

Every year between 400 and 600 people departed from Barbados as individuals, not as a part of any group migration or military expedition. This continuing exodus of Barbadians was a matter of comment among officials. Sir Peter Colleton put the number of people departing in 1669 at 2000, "thereof the Sobriest and the Richest to the parts about New England, some to the French plantations, and the looser sort out of hopes of plunder to Jamaica." A few years later, in 1675, Jonathan Atkins reported to his superiors in England that "People frequently go to the other plantations in America, some for change, others with persuasion of mending their fortunes." Because of the Indian troubles in New England and Virginia, he thought many would gladly return if they could. Of the few white servants who still came to the colony, he asserted that, when their time was served, they preferred Virginia, New York, and Jamaica, "where they can hope for land, to Barbados, where there is none." To prevent servants from running away and debtors from fleeing their creditors, an official regulation required anybody who desired to leave the island to register with the Secretary's Office three weeks before sailing, to procure a ticket marked "time out," and to post security for debts and dependents. The list for 1679 has survived and is given here.[42]

41. Jamaica Council Minutes, III, 77, 99, 100–102.

42. This revealing list of persons leaving Barbados in 1679 is in PRO: CO 1/44, fol. 47, XXVI, and the University of Pennsylvania Library has a microfilm (1038:6–7); it is printed in *JBMHS,* I, 155–80, and in Hotten, *Original Lists,* 347–418. Because of some ambiguities, counts of heads are bound to vary slightly; our count differs very little from that given in Richard B. Dunn's excellent article in *WMQ,* 3d ser., XXVI (1969), 27, which we follow with adjustments

DESTINATIONS OF PERSONS LEAVING BARBADOS
1679

NORTH AMERICA		CARIBBEAN		ENGLAND	
Boston	68	Antigua	65	London	151
Rhode Island	6	Nevis	14	Bristol	39
New England	22	Montserrat	1	Liverpool	8
New York	34	Leeward Islands		Beaumaris	3
Virginia	62	[St. Christopher]	15	Topsham	3
Carolina	38	Jamaica	35	Poole	1
Newfoundland	3	Tortuga	3		
		Surinam	5		
		Bahamas	12		
		Bermuda	4		
	233		154		205
Total: 593				Holland	1

If 1679 was in any way a typical year, some data are pertinent. Of the 593 persons who left Barbados, 552 were free, and only 41 were servants. The sex ratio was 8.8 to 1; 11 married couples went out and 59 single women. These émigrés were definitely not runaway servants, for 73 per cent of the tickets bore the statement "time out," which was marked on the tickets of all free persons; and security for wives and children left behind had been posted by 20 per cent, men who were either freemen or freeholders. That many of the individuals were intending to resettle was also obvious, because 233 went to the North American continent, more than half of them locating north of as yet unsettled Pennsylvania. Other Caribbean colonies, notably Jamaica and the Leeward Islands, lured 154 of them. Interest in Carolina had apparently been rekindled, for 38 Barbadians went there (2 married couples, 25 single men, and 9 single women); but half of this group later returned to the Caribbean. Fifteen of those who remained took out land warrants. Arthur Middleton and Robert Quintyne, the latter accompanied by a servant, came from great planting families in Barbados, and they promptly occupied places of power and profit

for Rhode Island and New England. Oldmixon, *British Empire in America,* II, 41; *CSPC, 1675–76,* p. 348; BM: Egerton MSS, 2395, fol. 641a; *CSPC, 1669–74,* pp. 141, 458.

in the northern settlement, and in the course of time Barbadians dominated the colony and imparted to it a characteristic Caribbean flavor.[43]

Together with migrants from Nevis, St. Christopher, and Montserrat, Barbadians had helped to people Antigua, which in 1655 had an estimated population of only 1000 inhabitants. The island was nearly as large as Barbados, could boast of good harbors, fertile soil, plenty of standing timber, and a healthful climate, but great unsettled tracts of land granted to absentee proprietors discouraged possible colonists. At the end of the French occupation in April 1668 the Assembly sought to develop the island by promising ten acres of land, free of feudal obligations, to any individual who would bring in a laboring person "to abide." Antigua now began to fill up as rich Barbadians, led by Christopher Codrington, sought large grants of land to extend the sugar culture. Small planters from St. Christopher and other nearby islands also poured in, all of them seeking virgin lands on which to grow cotton, tobacco, and sugar.[44]

Forty thousand acres of arable land and a total of 4480 inhabitants (1052 white men and 570 slaves) in 1672 are proof enough of the influx of people after the war. Subsequently the number of immigrants slackened somewhat; 65 arrived in 1679 from Barbados, however, and 102 whites and blacks from Surinam landed at Antigua toward the end of that year. More would come, as soon as the Dutch governor would permit them to leave. Governor Stapleton of the Leeward Islands believed that such substantial planters would ensure a real "advancement to the Setlement of the Island." Governor Sir Nathaniel Johnson moved the government there from Nevis in 1688, because it paid more customs to the king, even though he believed it to be subject to more bad weather and only one-third of the land was settled. From that day forward, Antigua proved to be the most important and productive island of the group and was thought to contain 2000 white inhabitants besides slaves.[45]

43. Dunn, in *WMQ,* 3d ser., XXVI, 28–30; Hotten, *Original Lists,* 390–91; *CSPC, 1669–74,* pp. 100 ff., 141, 184–5, 620.

44. BM: Add. MSS, 11,411, fol. 1; BM: Egerton MSS, 2395, fol. 288; *Acts of the Assembly Passed in the Charibbee Leeward Islands, From 1690 to 1730* (London, 1734), 30; PRO: CO 1/27, No. 52.

45. Another count for 1672 gives the number of blacks on Antigua as 1739. BM:

Barbuda and Anguilla, two very tiny islands colonized from the larger ones, served principally as auxiliary food-producing areas. Sir Thomas Warner had attempted to settle Barbuda in the thirties, but Carib raids had forced the English to abandon it. Men from Antigua finally made a settlement there in 1661, and within a decade 500 men were said to be supplying cattle, maize, and other provisions to the rest of the Leeward Islands. Christopher Codrington, who seems to have had a share in so many ventures, owned the entire island in 1689 and kept several small sloops for the interisland trade in provisions. Plantations on Anguilla were also cultivated by Antiguans beginning in 1650. They were joined by refugees from St. Christopher in 1667, and many of the latter stayed on when the war was over. Governor Stapleton's census of 1676 gave Anguilla 100 white men, 150 white women, 300 children, and no slaves. Small holdings predominated on this fertile island. Well stocked with cattle and sheep, Anguilla, like Barbuda, was subject to frequent Indian attacks, and population growth was very slow.[46]

IV

The departure of so many people from Barbados, St. Christopher, and Nevis caused a genuine depopulation of the whites in these colonies. Although Francis, Lord Willoughby, had warned of the drain of freemen and small landowners in 1664, the Barbadian planters had not realized the gravity of their situation for some years, for, as one of them explained, the white people imported from Ireland and England between 1652 and 1668 more or less counterbalanced the mortalities and those who departed. This was also true of the year 1683 when the free whites who left Barbados numbered 446 (285 for other plantations and 161 for Eu-

Egerton MSS, 2395, fols. 530, 533; PRO: CO 1/42, fols. 220–41; CO 1/29, fol. 14: IV; fol. 61, p. 163; *CSPC, 1685–88,* pp. 512, 553; *1677–80,* pp. 476, 479; PRO: CO 1/44, fol. 21.

46. Oldmixon, *British Empire in America,* II, 263–5; Frederick H. Watkins, *Handbook of the Leeward Islands* (London, 1924), 2; *CSPC, 1677–80,* p. 266; Nathaniel Crouch, *The English Empire in America* (3d ed., London, 1698), 152; Sloane, *Voyage to the Islands,* I, 46.

rope) while 325 freemen and 385 servants arrived; the latter probably came in response to an act of the previous year "to encourage the bringing in of Christian Servants." [47]

Jamaica, which had been the Mecca of so many émigrés, was losing population in the seventies, as Sir Thomas Lynch discovered when he became governor in 1671. In a communication, The State of the Case for the Sugar Plantations in America, which he wrote for the Lords of Trade and Plantations, he pointed out that the low price of sugar would force small planters to "wander into other parts as 1600 have (within a year past) done from Barbados alone, and perhaps may be wonne to go over to the French or Dutch Plantations . . . where many English Planters have gone. . . ." The following year, Sir Thomas mentioned to Lord Arlington that 2600 of "the bravest sort of people had been lost or had left off planting to participate in forays against the Windward Islands, Curaçao, Porto Bello, Granada, and Panama, besides those carried aboard particular privateersmen, "so that warr will infinitely retard the settlement of this island." [48]

Officials of the four oldest colonies, thoroughly aroused by the wholesale departures of white settlers, took measures at the eleventh hour to stop them and lure white servants into coming over from the British Isles; and because they never received sufficient migrants to fill their labor requirements the authorities of the newly settled islands also made overtures to immigrants from Europe. A law of 1670 was directed at preventing the "spiriting" of servants and freemen from Barbados, especially artificers for the new settlements. And to forestall the consolidating of small holdings into large sugar estates, the Assembly passed an act the next year against depopulation which prohibited the pulling down or allowing to fall into decay of any "mansion house." [49]

After they had rid Nevis of the refugees who crowded in during the Second Dutch War, the planters of that island suddenly realized that they too were losing many of their own white people to Jamaica

47. BM: Sloane MSS, 3662, fol. 55b; Sloane MSS, 2441, fols. 17–22; PRO: CO 30/5, fol. 44.

48. *CSPC, 1669–74,* pp. 215, 298; BM: Egerton MSS, fol. 639.

49. *Acts of Barbados* (1721), 80; PRO: CO 30/2, fols. 89–93.

and Antigua. The Assembly acted in 1672 to stimulate the bringing in of white servants by offering any importer a bounty of 400 pounds of Muscovado sugar, which was more than enough to make up for the £10 given to each servant as his freedom dues. Three years later the Assembly raised the bounty to 800 pounds of sugar, but reduced it in 1682 to the original figure, for the planters were making a handsome profit from the awards. Though no legislation was enacted in St. Christopher, a bounty of 400 pounds of sugar was paid out to those who bought white servants. No bounty was paid at Montserrat, for all of the servants there came from Ireland.[50]

The increasing number of families wanting to remove to Jamaica induced the Assembly to intervene in Montserrat sometime before 1678. In January Captain Carryl, a planter of "considerable condition" at Montserrat, landed in Jamaica with his family of twenty-five persons. He described to Lord Carlisle the difficulty he had had in getting his family away because of the removal law. The Governor at once wrote to Secretary Coventry to point out that inasmuch as the King wanted families at St. Christopher to remove to Jamaica, he must certainly want to have them from other islands to ensure security against the French. English officials concurred in his view. Not long before this incident, the Council of St. Christopher had tried hard to attract Englishmen residing in the French islands but with very little success.[51]

An elaborate act passed by the Assembly of Jamaica in 1682 stipulated that every master of five black slaves must keep one white servant, overseer, or hired man for three months of the year at least upon penalty of £5 for each white man lacking. To encourage the masters of ships to bring over white men, any vessel carrying more than fifty was to be released from port charges. A supply of white servants became available in 1684 when James II ordered "the Western Rebels" to Jamaica. Eventually, 164, "both sick and well," arrived. The miserable wretches were not allowed to redeem themselves with money and had to serve a minimum of

50. After the surrender of St. Christopher to the French in 1689, Nevis once again received droves of refugees, who soon became victims of a severe epidemic of smallpox. *CSPC, 1689–92,* p. 175; *1669–74,* pp. 48, 458–9; *1675–76,* p. 237; *Acts of Nevis,* 10–11; PRO: CO 154/2, p. 340; Higham, *Leeward Islands,* 166–8.
51. *CSPC, 1669–74,* p. 442; *1677–80,* p. 333; PRO: CO 1/43, fol. 61.

ten years. In spite of strenuous efforts, however, the white population of Jamaica approximated only 15,000 of all ages and sexes. In truth, the efforts of the insular assemblies to stop the outpouring of the white populations of the islands and to bring in more whites from Europe largely failed.[52]

A modern authority estimates that almost 30,000 Barbadians, most of them males, had gone off never to return; and to this number must be added about 10,000 who died in the years of the plague, 1647–49, together with some thousands more during several epidemics after 1660. Because of the Second Dutch War, St. Christopher suffered the loss of an even larger proportion of its inhabitants, and Nevis also experienced a marked decline in its freemen and small proprietors. Montserrat, on the other hand, appeared to be more than holding its own in 1671. As a group, the Leeward Islands had lost about 5000 souls in the plague years. From the several migrations, the French and Dutch islands gained considerable populations, but the principal beneficiary was Jamaica.[53]

The population statistics given below are most inadequate, mere estimates or guesses in many instances, and therefore not susceptible to any kind of refined analysis. They do disclose, however, several remarkable facts. Perhaps the most significant one is that Barbados contained more than half of the population of the English islands as late as 1690. In 1650 the island had an estimated 24,000 whites; an enumeration of 1683 gave it 19,568; and another estimate of 1690 indicated about 20,000. Throughout four decades, therefore, despite a high rate of mortality and continuous migration, the white population of Barbados remained comparatively stable: from 1668 to 1692 it scarcely varied at all. Contrariwise, the number of blacks in the island mounted from 6000 in 1650 to 46,602 in the census of 1683 or, if we allow for the concealing of one-third

52. PRO: CO 138/5, fol. 84d; CO 1/58, No. 90; *Abridgement of Laws of Plantations,* 136, 140.

53. Governor Sir Nathaniel Johnson told the Lords of Trade and Plantations in 1688 of receiving several petitions from "poorer inhabitants" of Nevis and from all settlers on Anguilla and Tortola for permission to settle on Crab Island (Vieques). People here at Nevis "are daily leaving us for want of subsistence." *CSPC, 1685–88,* p. 506; Chandler, in *JBMHS,* XIII, 134; *CSPC, 1661–68,* p. 587; *1669–74,* p. 227.

ENGLISH CARIBBEAN POPULATIONS
1650–1690

Year	White	Black	Total	Source
			BARBADOS	
1650	24,000	6,000	30,000	Harlow, *Colonising Expeditions,* 44
1653	26,000	20,000	46,000	BM: Egerton MSS, 2395, fol. 625
*1673	21,309	33,184 [44,245]	54,493 [65,554]†	*CSPC, 1669–74,* p. 495
*1676	21,725	32,473 [43,279]	54,198 [65,022]†	*CSPC, 1675–76,* p. 349
*1684	19,568	46,602 [62,136]	66,170 [81,704]†	BM: Sloane MSS, 2441, fols. 17–18
1690	20,000	60,000	80,000	*CSPC, 1689–92,* p. 311
1768	22,000	72,000	94,000	*Short History of Barbados,*116
			ST. CHRISTOPHER	
1650			20,000	This work, p. 13
1665	10,000 "at least"			*CSPC, 1669–74,* p. 112
*1678	1,897	1,436 [1,914]	3,333 [3,811]†	PRO: 1/42, fol. 98
			NEVIS	
1650			5,000	This work, p. 13
*1676	3,595	3,849 [5,132]	7,444 [8,727]†	PRO: CO 1/42, fol. 201
			MONSERRAT	
1650			900	This work, p. 13
1677	2,682	922 [1,229]	3,604 [3,911]†	PRO: CO 1/42, fol. 213
			ANTIGUA	
1650			900	This work, p. 13
*1678	2,308	2,172 [2,896]	4,480 [5,204]†	PRO: CO 1/42, fol. 98
			JAMAICA	
1655				
*1661	3,360	514 [685]	3,784 [4,045]†	PRO: CO 1/15, fol. 98

*1665			17,298	Long, *Jamaica,* I, 316
*1670	12,698	2,500 [3,333]	15,198 [16,031]†	PRO: CO 138/1, fols. 61–80
*1673	7,764	9,504 [12,672]	17,268 [20,436]†	Includes 800 seamen, Long, *Jamaica,* I, 316
1677	15,000	15,000	30,000	*CSPC, 1675–76,* p. 339
1680	15,000	20,000	35,000	Blathwayt

* Actual contemporary count
† In 1673 Sir Peter Colleton, President of the Barbados Council, stated that there were 33,184 slaves listed for the island and suggested that one-third be allowed for concealments not reported by the planters because the tax levy was on polls. Governor Stapleton reported the same from the Leeward Islands in 1676. Similar information came from Jamaica. The figures given above in brackets are adjusted for this hidden third of the slaves. *CSPC, 1669–74, p. 495; 1675–76,* p. 501.

in official counts, 66,136; and the latter figure is fairly close to Governor Kendall's estimate for 1690. The count of 22,000 whites and 70,000 blacks eighty-five years later, in 1768, seems to indicate that by 1682–83 Barbados had attained the proportion of three Negro slaves to one white that existed in the island throughout the eighteenth century.

The populations of the several Leeward Islands were strikingly different, one from another and from that of Barbados. St. Christopher, which had about 20,000 inhabitants (predominantly white)

POPULATION OF ENGLISH COLONIES
1673–1678

Year	*Colony*	*Whites*	*Blacks*	*Total Population*
1676	Barbados	21,725	43,297	65,022
1678	St. Kitts	1,897	1,914	3,811
1676	Nevis	3,595	5,132	8,727
1677	Montserrat	2,682	1,229	3,911
1678	Antigua	2,308	2,896	5,204
1673	Jamaica	7,764	12,672	20,436
Totals		40,851	67,140	107,111

in 1650, had lost heavily even before the capture by the French in 1666; and an enumeration in 1678 lists only 1897 white proprietors, servants, and freemen. However, the blacks at this time amounted only to 1436 or, adding one-third for those concealed, 1914—an even balance between the races. At Nevis in 1676, the whites and blacks were also nearly equal in number, while on Montserrat the Irish colonists outnumbered the slaves by 2783 to 992 (or adding a third, 1323). In contrast, by 1678 the black population of Antigua already exceeded the white, and this island was well on its way to achieving in the eighteenth century the ratio of three blacks to one white, such as Barbados experienced.

In the great and distant Jamaica, the population differed radically from that of the Caribbees. The total number of inhabitants rose between 1661 and 1670 from 3874 to around 15,199, of whom only 2500 were black. But by 1680, when there were about 15,000 white people, the black slaves had increased to about 20,000. The total of 35,000 inhabitants marked the beginning of a period of very rapid growth for Jamaica, but in 1690 it still contained only a little more than half as many people as Barbados.

V

Like the Spaniards on the continents of North and South America in the previous Century of Conquest, the English had spread themselves pretty thin over the Antilles. In doing so, they had drawn principally upon the four original and overpopulated islands after 1650. Within twenty years insular officials began to realize that the process of depopulation had so reduced the older colonies that they no longer had enough white men to fill the ranks of their militia regiments now so sorely needed to counter the Gallic menace. Of course, they exaggerated their losses to some degree, but the situation was critical nevertheless. White labor, moreover, was alarmingly scarce in the older plantations. Equally discouraging was the fact that, because of the great loss of life in the newer colonies and the even greater need for white labor in these settlements, as well as for defense against the Caribs and the French, agriculture developed far more slowly than the founders had expected. It was evident to observers by 1690 that the planters of all the English colonies (and also of the French and Dutch islands) recognized that the only way to solve their many problems was to purchase black slaves from Africa in ever greater numbers. At the very time that the migrations depleted the English islands of their white men, the slave traders were bringing in thousands of Africans to the islands—a traffic which next claims our attention.

VIII
Black Floodtide

THE DEPARTURE of countless numbers of white people over a span of more than four decades would have created, under normal conditions, a labor shortage fatal to the economies of the four original English Caribbean islands had not another—and better—kind of labor become available concurrently. Disaster, possibly the abandonment of the settlements, never ensued, nor was there ever any labor vacuum, because the English planters substituted black slaves from Africa for the white servants. It is very difficult to distinguish cause from effect in this fundamental exchange of persons; perhaps the introduction of the blacks forced the white migration. Whatever the relationship, a radical *bouleversement* of the populations of the English possessions had taken place by 1690 as the Negro replaced the white Irishman and Englishman in the labor force and outnumbered them everywhere except in the tiny islands of Montserrat, Barbuda, and Anguilla. Whence, and how, did he come to the Caribbean, and what manner of man was this Negro? *

II

Nearly all of the blacks who toiled in the West Indies during the seventeenth century had been brought over in Dutch and English

* Contemporaries always used the noun *Negro* to label the black African. We follow their practice and, to avoid monotonous repetition, use *black, African, slave,* and *native* interchangeably with *Negro*.

slavers from West Africa. This vast region had a coastline of about 3500 miles extending from the Cape Verde Islands and the mouth of the river Senegal southward to Sierra Leone, then eastward along the Windward (Grain), Ivory, and Gold Coasts to the Bight of Benin and Old Calabar, then turning southward again past the mouth of the Congo and the island of São Tomé to the Dutch fort at Loanda in Portuguese Angola. Inland from the shore, West Africa embraced an immense, vaguely defined area reaching northward to the desert of Sahara, eastward beyond Lake Chad, and southward to the great valley of the Congo. The entire inland region was part of Western Sudan.[1]

The West African littoral was the homeland of a very large number of Negro tribes—peoples of varying shades of color, who spoke a confusion of tongues and lived with a surprising measure of privacy and neatness in well-arranged villages. Theirs were ancient societies, which were much farther advanced, complex, and highly organized than those of the Arawaks or Caribs in the New World. The people of West Africa displayed all of the variety and individuality of the members of the other two branches of the human race, but it is their many common characteristics that they took with them to the Caribbean which concern us here. There are no records written down by the black men; we know them only from the reports of a few ships' captains and merchants who engaged in the slave trade. The European commentators were describing human beings strikingly different from themselves and, as might be expected, they applied Christian standards of morality and customs to pagan and Muslim tribesmen who were unrestrained by any of the moral or legal codes that Christians recognized as valid and binding. Naturally, therefore, the conclusions they drew were more often than not unfavorable. One-sided though such descriptions be, if they are studied with an awareness of their inherent bias, they reveal much about those Africans who, by 1690, had become the determining element of the Caribbean population.

Almost the first feature of West African life noticed by the

1. Small numbers of black slaves were brought to the Caribbees from Portuguese Angola, and fewer still from far-away Madagascar. The six regions of the "Coast" are clearly described in Kenneth G. Davies, *The Royal African Company* (London, 1957), 213–22; Donnan, *Documents . . . of the Slave Trade,* I, 94.

newcomer from Europe was "the great Number of Villages, composed of Houses which are round at the top and encompass'd with Mud Walls or Hedges [thatch]." (Plate 8) Next, he observed the denizens themselves, who could be accurately described in all their strangeness, for they habitually went about scantily clad or altogether naked. The Negro men appeared "well limb'd and lusty" and, for the most part, boasted fine physiques. Strong and capable of hard work, they labored only when they had to and were actually indolent and slothful.[2]

Traders often admitted reluctantly, and usually indirectly, that in intelligence many of the principal blacks matched the whites with whom they dealt. "The negroes are all, without exception," said Dutch William Bosman, "crafty, villainous and fraudulent, and very seldom if ever to be trusted; being sure to slip no Opportunity of cheating an European, nor indeed one another." This is, perhaps, too harsh a judgment, but John Barbot, a moderate Huguenot, warned: "They are of a pilfering temper, and will steal anything they can well come at from strangers," and are also "great mumpers" (or beggars) of presents. Quarrelsome and warlike, both by nature and training, and living in communities lacking the rule of law, the Negro men were considered by the Europeans to be "generally of a turbulent temper," and known to be often very cruel toward each other. Some tribes practiced cannibalism. Near Calabar in 1672, a youthful English seaman, John Watts, saw his boatswain from the *Peach-Tree* beheaded and two com-

2. Each house in Gambia was round, having a wall "of Reede, platted and made up together, some six foot in height." Some natives built their walls "of loame, which after it is tempered and layde up together," becomes hard and reddish like durable brick. The Africans made their houses round to lessen the force of the winds on them. Richard Jobson, *The Golden Trade, or A Discovery of the River Gambia* . . . (London [1623], 1968, 47–8, 53–4. The many excellent engravings by Johannes Kip illustrating life in West Africa in John Barbot's *A Description of the Coasts of North and South Guinea* . . . [1682], first published in Churchill's *Voyages* [1732], V, greatly facilitate visualizing the exotic scene. William Bosman, *A New and Accurate Description of the Coast of Guinea* . . . (London [1679], 1705, LCP copy), 304, 315; also printed by John Pinkerton, in *Voyages and Travels* (London, 1814), XVI; Capt. Thomas Phillips, *A Journal of a Voyage made . . . in 1693 to Africa . . . and Barbados* . . . in Churchill, *Voyages*, VI, 214. A useful modern introduction is Robin Hallett, *The Penetration of Africa: European Exploration in North and West Africa to 1815* (London, 1965), 19–36.

panions killed by the blacks, who broiled them in strips in revenge for one of their fellows who had been carried off by white men the year before.[3]

From the European point of view, all the West Africans, except the worshippers of Mohammed, seemed to be very intemperate, and there were numerous comments upon their excessive appetites. Though they ate "poorly" as a rule, "they drink the more, being great Lovers of strong Liquor; and let the World go how it will, they must have Brandy in the Morning, and Palm-Wine in the afternoon." Later in the century it would be rum. They were equally addicted to tobacco and would pay almost any price for Brazilian or Portuguese leaf. Native potters spent almost as much of their time making clay pipes for smokers as they did jugs and bowls for households.[4]

Negro sexual behavior scandalized Roman Catholics and Protestants alike. Polygamy prevailed everywhere. The Koran limited black Muslims to four wives and kings to seven, but they could have any number of concubines. Every other male could marry as many women as he pleased, or could support, which on the Gold Coast could mean as many as twenty. The kindly Frenchman Barbot censured the men for being "luxurious to excess, always talking of their sport with women." Whoredom was widespread, and black masters freely enjoyed the bodies of their female slaves.[5]

The sexual appetites of the black women, as depicted by Barbot, exceeded those of the men in some respects. Females of North Guinea impressed him as being "very well shaped, tall, lusty, strait, active, and of a very bright black colour, extreme wanton, and of pleasing countenance; their temper hot, and lascivious, making no scruple to prostitute themselves to the Europeans for a very slender profit, so great is their inclination to white men; which often occasions mighty quarrels with their husbands." Many women, be-

3. Bosman, *Coast of Guinea,* 100, 325; Barbot, in Churchill, *Voyages,* V, 110, 138, 155; [John Watts] *A True Relation of the Inhumane and Unparallel'd Actions and Barbarous Murders . . . Committed on Three Englishmen in Old Calabar . . .* (London, 1672), 4–5.

4. Barbot, in Churchill, *Voyages,* V, 138; Bosman, *Coast of Guinea,* 107, 268–70, 286; Jobson, *The Golden Trade,* 155.

5. Jobson, *The Golden Trade,* 65–7, 77; Barbot, in Churchill, *Voyages,* V, 35, 138; Bosman, *Coast of Guinea,* 169, 172.

cause they considerably outnumbered the men, remained unmarried for a long time, but they did not hesitate to indulge their desires: "It is no manner of scandal," an astonished mariner reported, "nor are they rudely accounted whores." Once married, however, the members of some tribes proved remarkably faithful to each other.[6]

Foreign observers agreed that the Negro women, toiling daily in the fields and laboring industriously at household chores in their huts and yards, worked harder than the men. In addition, the women wove the cloth, and mothers taught their daughters at an early age how to spin cotton yarn and weave cloth out of it, or else to fashion mats from straw and rushes. They bore their babies with remarkable ease and then returned promptly to work. A thrifty Dutch Calvinist remarked: "Child-bearing is here as little troublesome as the Men can wish; here is no long Lying-in, nor expensive gossipping or Groaning-feasts." [7]

The most attractive positive trait of the blacks of both sexes, which stemmed in part from their great sexual desire, was their devotion to family life. An unmarried state was frowned upon, and in the household good humor, laughter, and kindliness predominated. Indeed, the Africans valued the conjugal tie, given its difference from the European, quite as much as did the white men. They loved their children and indulged them excessively, thereby earning the stern disapproval of the Europeans, whose offspring were seen but not heard. From the family, black youth learned its habitual courtesy and respect for a carefully distinguished hierarchy of social ranks.

Around the family and the household revolved all economic activities. Most of the men along the Coast served as husbandmen or worked as canoemen, fishermen, thatchers, palm-wine-makers, potters, or salt-boilers. Elsewhere weavers abounded and won acclaim for the excellence of their cloth, and the work of saddlers and leather-dressers was always in demand. Using small anvils, numerous blacksmiths fashioned out of iron the cutlasses, knives, shackles for slaves, and all sorts of arms, while the more skilled smiths hammered out bracelets and other articles from the gold and silver mined inland. Woodworkers and carvers kept busy meeting

6. Barbot, in Churchill, *Voyages,* V, 34; Bosman, *Coast of Guinea,* 180.
7. Bosman, *Coast of Guinea,* 104–5, 169; Barbot, in Churchill, *Voyages,* V, 36, 38.

the requirements of hundreds of villagers for wooden bowls, cups, troughs, chairs, and other articles needed in everyday living. There were also artisans who specialized in making musical instruments such as "snappers" (like castanets or bones), drums, reeds, and flutes; and in Gambia, they turned out a *balafo,* or xylophone, with gourds or hard shells of fruits attached underneath as resonators, which could be heard an English mile away. Richard Ligon had marveled at a balafo made by Macow and thought that the clever slave had invented it there in Barbados, whereas it was an instrument that had a history in Africa. (Plate 8) Contemporary Europeans may have disagreed over the degree of skill attained by black artisans—Bosman thought that there were very few good craftsmen and that the work of most of them was crude—but all would have agreed to their presence in force and to the variety of occupations.[8]

Throughout the seventeenth century, a lively trade went on among the coastal villages, and between them and the communities of the interior. Barbot encountered Negroes who served as brokers for the inland blacks with others along the coast. The natives of the Antese country grew rich and powerful from the possession of several gold mines, and because they controlled the pass through which dealers from the interior had to come and go. "The Negroes are very subtle Artists in the sophisticating of Gold," Bosman warned; "they can so neatly falsifie and counterfeit the Gold Dust and Mountain Gold" that white traders are frequently cheated. Europeans arriving in West Africa for the first time usually admitted to being surprised at finding "the Negro inhabitants . . . generally very rich," and their merchants and despotic kings facilely and shrewdly driving a lucrative trade for gold, ivory, and black slaves.[9]

We of the twentieth century cannot remind ourselves too often not to exaggerate both the variety and the quality of civilization in

8. "The Weavers . . . would make very good cloth had they large looms," Barbot decided, "but they wholly apply themselves to weaving of a narrow, thick, strip'd cotton-cloth, seven or eight fingers broad, and about ten ells and a half long, in small portable Looms, made for that purpose." Churchill, *Voyages,* V, 40, 172, 268, 275, 365, plate 3 (O, M, N); Bosman, *Coast of Guinea,* 109; Jobson, *The Golden Trade,* 133–6, 153–9; A. N. Jones, *Africa and Indonesia: The Evidence of the Xylophone and Other Musical and Cultural Factors* (Leiden, 1964), 9–120. For Ligon and Macow, see present work, p. 152.

9. Bosman, *Coast of Guinea,* 5, 22, 70, 73, 304.

West Africa in the seventeenth century. The painstaking Dutch, French, and English reporters of that age gave remarkably perceptive and unvarnished accounts of what they saw, but they were observing human beings who, because their color, customs, religious beliefs, and morals differed so greatly from their own, seemed primitive though in some matters they were considerably advanced. The blacks worshipped pagan gods, often mere idols; then, here and there, one ran into Negroes who were circumcised, and to the Christian, a Muslim was as strange and unacceptable as a pagan.[10]

The multiplicity of tongues in West Africa (seven or eight were spoken along the sixty miles of the Gold Coast in 1690) prevented any diffusion of culture, and no widely accepted code of morals could be maintained. Illiteracy was almost universal, and no system of education under religious auspices prevailed as in Europe, with the exception of that among the recent converts to Islam. Manuscript copies of the Koran, brought by caravan from Barbary, commanded higher prices than anything else sold at Nettico, and male children were taught to read and write at an early age. Shortly after 1693, the Royal African Company gave support to a school at Cape Coast Castle on the Gold Coast to teach the small black children to read and write in preparation for becoming Christians, but their pagan parents refused to allow them to be baptised, and the idea was soon abandoned. Even though to Europeans the Africans were barbarians, the blacks of all kinds possessed a developed sense of beauty, which they expressed in various forms. The dance occupied an important place in their lives. Regularly, at the markets, the multitude danced to "a loud, strange harmony" produced by musicians on drums, fiddles, a xylophone, and a small harp called a gittern. The dance also figured in religious rites, which ordinarily offended the sensibilities of white onlookers by what they deemed its lewdness.[11]

10. A recent judicious treatment of this theme is by David Brion Davis, *The Problem of Slavery in Western Culture* (Ithaca, 1966), especially pp. 181–2, 464–72. Phillips, in Churchill, *Voyages,* VI, 214. On circumcision, see Jobson, *The Golden Trade,* 139–45.

11. Barbot supplied a short vocabulary of the principal languages of West Africa so much needed by the white traders. Churchill, *Voyages,* V, 248–9, 275, 413–20 (vocabulary); Jobson, *The Golden Trade,* 85–6, 94; Phillips, in Churchill, *Voyages,* VI, 207; Davies, *Royal African Company,* 280, 280*n.*

The proneness of the West Africans to certain diseases, particularly those brought from Europe, startled foreigners. There was an extensive loss of life in Sierra Leone from the measles after 1660, and, though Western Europe remained free of the deadly plague after 1666, it continued to rage in West Africa. Smallpox, however, made "the greatest havock among them." In view of the promiscuity of the sexes, it should not surprise us to learn that venereal disease flourished everywhere. It usually took the form among the Africans of chancres and a swelling of the arms, legs, nose, and lips, known as the yaws (frambesia) in the Caribbean, which the Negroes attributed to their overindulgence with common harlots. Another easily observed venereal affliction, thought to be caused by excessive imbibing of palm-wine by the males, was a swelling of the scrotum so great as to prohibit cohabitation. The rainy season in August was the most sickly time of the year; thousands of people suffered from the common ailments of the bloody flux (dysentery), worms, migraine headaches, colic, stomach ache, and various undifferentiated fevers. Nor were white men exempt from these killing diseases. Between 25 and 75 per cent of any group of white men recently arrived died in the first year. According to one modern author, "West Africa surpassed every other region of the tropics in its tales of mortality." The "flaming sword of deadly fevers" slew black and white indiscriminately. An old English sea-chanty ran: [12]

Beware and take care
Of the Bight of Benin,
For one that comes out
There are forty goes in.

When the Portuguese and their rivals first came to the Coast, the enslavement of blacks by blacks was already an ancient institution, universally practiced by Muslims and pagans alike. The ownership of from five to fifteen black slaves was acknowledged in West Africa as proof of riches, and upper-class Negroes along the Coast eagerly bought them. Their kings naturally kept many more. A minority of the slaves had been condemned to perpetual servitude for crimes committed or for debts. "Abundance of little Blacks of

12. Barbot, in Churchill, *Voyages,* V, 118, 195, 277–80; Phillips, in Churchill, *Voyages,* VI, 215; Hallett, *Penetration of Africa,* 9–10, 127.

both sexes," John Barbot exclaimed in horror, "are also stolen away by their neighbours," and many elders too; and some rascals actually sold off their kindred. In times of dearth or famine, some Negroes went to the extreme length of selling themselves into slavery. African tribal armies lacked the European kind of discipline, but all black warriors fought to the utmost out of dread of being taken prisoner and made slaves. Not even kings, other leaders, and the ablest men escaped being enslaved once they were captured, with the consequence that not a few of them ended their days on Caribbean plantations, where once again they sometimes led their black companions. Oroonoko, the royal slave, was no mere creature of the romantic imagination of Mrs. Aphra Behn.[13]

European merchants and factors of the seventeenth century acquired nearly all of their knowledge from and conducted their trade almost exclusively with the native tribes living along the littoral. Coastal kings and merchants jealously kept the trade with the interior in their own hands and acted as brokers for inland traders in the exchange of gold, ivory, and slaves for cattle, cloth, and provisions. William Bosman somehow managed to deal directly with a representative from the interior at St. George d'Elmina, the principal Dutch post on the Gold Coast. He found that "those who come from the inward part of the country to traffic with us are chiefly Slaves: one of which, on whom the Master reposes the greatest trust, is appointed the chief of this Caravan: but when he comes to us, he is not treated as a Slave, but as a very great Merchant, whom we take all possible care to oblige. . . ."[14]

A firsthand account of native practices is furnished by John Watts, a young man from Kent who made a voyage to Africa when he was eighteen, in the year 1668. Captured and enslaved by the

13. "The Blacks of the Gold Coast have traded with the Europeans ever since the beginning of the fourteenth century," Barbot wrote in 1682, and they "are very well skilled in the nature and proper qualities of all the European wares and merchandize vended there." Because they had been imposed upon in former times by "the white men, as they call the Europeans," they now are perpetually on their guard and measure everything carefully. Barbot, in Churchill, *Voyages,* V, 39, 47, 110, 273, 352; Cornelius Hodges's report in Royal African Company, Letter Book, XI, 65, reprinted in *EHR,* XXXIX, 92.

14. Barbot, in Churchill, *Voyages,* V, 44–7, 172; Bosman, *Coast of Guinea,* 22, 70, 80.

blacks while he was ashore at Calabar and sold to an "Aurania," a black master, he experienced the bad diet, hard service, and callous treatment that was a slave's portion. In time, however, he had the good fortune to be sold to the captain of an English ship for forty-five copper and iron bars. "The Slaves they sell to the English are prisoners taken in war: the Kings war much against one another. They have no Holds, Castles, nor Prisons: but keeping those they have taken, until the next Ship comes in, with with[e]s they fasten them to a pole, that they cannot untye themselves and get home. They are also perswaded that they go to help that King to fight against his enemy, and that they shall live idlely, and eat good victuals, drink good liquor, and have cloaths, and that the King will give them great rewards. But if half were performed that is promised, they would be more ready to go, than we to fetch them."[15]

Whether slaves were kept for native use or to be sold to the foreigners, all were badly treated by their own people, "who subsist them poorly, and beat them inhumanely, as may be seen by the scabs and wounds on the bodies of many of them when sold to us. They scarcely allow them the least rag to cover their nakedness, which they also take off from them when sold to Europeans . . . The wives and children of slaves, are also slaves to the master under whom they are married; and when dead, they never bury them, but cast the bodies into some by place to be devoured by birds or beasts of prey." John Watts esteemed the diet and conditions of life accorded a West African slave to be worse than the treatment handed out to the galley slaves of the Moors and Turks.[16]

The traffic in human beings was peculiarly "the business of kings, rich men, and prime merchants." These traders did not have to send more than 200 or 300 miles inland to procure seemingly unlimited numbers of blacks taken, ordinarily, in tribal wars when traffic in slaves thrived. In times of peace, however, prisoners being scarce, all trade except that for gold languished, and conditions at Accra and similar places on the Slave Coast, where the English and Dutch ships called, became "utterly uncertain." This was par-

15. Watts, *True Relation,* 3, 4–5, 6, 9, 10, 16.
16. Barbot, in Churchill, *Voyages,* V, 270; Watts, *True Relation,* 9.

ticularly true at Whydah on that coast, which was almost "constantly at war . . . and all plunder is in men and women to sell for slaves," as Captain Phillips testified. "I have seen nine or ten bags full of men, women, and childrens heads at a time brought to the king's town." In 1681 the merchants of Fida procured a thousand a month, but the next year when peace prevailed, the English slave traders could purchase only eight blacks. A sharp distinction ought to be made between the coastal prisoners of war and the far more numerous "upland Negroes" sought exclusively for the slave trade. The slaves brought down the Senegal and the Gambia "from the very remote inland countries, by way of trade, and sold for things of very inconsiderable value" were generally poor and weak, "by reason of the barbarous usage they have had in travelling so far, being continually beaten, and almost famish'd: so inhuman are the Blacks to one another." [17]

The eagerness of the African kings and merchants to sell off batches of their fellow men more than overmatched the desire of Dutch, English, and French traders to assemble black cargoes. At Bandy, James Barbot, supercargo of the *Albion,* noted: "As soon as the Blacks could see our ship off at sea, they immediately went up the [Calabar] river to buy slaves." The local ruler, King William, guaranteed to furnish at once five hundred for loading, "all lusty and young." On March 15, 1678, Captain Robert Dogood of the *Arthur* at Calabar recorded in his journal: "This day wee haveinge many Cannews on bord and very Likely negroes, wee Bought 11 men, 4 women, 2 Boyes and 1 Girle. Wee had not purchase[d] soe many Butt findinge them very Likely negroes and haveinge then many sick." The ships usually lay at anchor in the road while the natives paddled the captives out in their great canoes. (Plate 9) Kidnapping by unscrupulous white sea captains, though much talked about, now seems actually to have been rare.[18]

Up until the end of the period at least, the Dutch and English

17. Davies, *Royal African Company,* 278; Phillips, in Churchill, *Voyages,* VI, 220; Barbot, in Churchill, *Voyages,* V, 48, 155–6, 184, 270, 271; Bosman, *Coast of Guinea,* 304.

18. With rare exceptions, European slave traders did not enslave free blacks; they accepted and honored the African definition of slavery. J. Holland Rose, ed., *Cambridge History of the British Empire* (Cambridge, Eng., 1929), I, 443–4;

procured the bulk of their slaves at the mouth of the Gambia or on the Gold Coast. To circumvent the Portuguese controlling the business, the agent of the Royal African Company had urged in 1672 that an expedition be sent upriver once a year to buy directly from the inland merchants who brought their slaves, elephants' teeth, and gold to markets hundreds of miles from the littoral. The detailed report of Cornelius Hodges of his expedition in 1689, when he led a party of sixty-eight men from the falls of the Gambia at Barracunda overland to Bambuck, supplied the Royal African Company with most valuable information. Three hundred miles up the Gambia, the tribes had little or no government. Though possibly he exaggerated, Hodges claimed that he discovered notoriously despotic, petty kings presiding over every town of seven or eight houses. The Bissareans, or Muslim proselyters, lived in great fear of the arbitrary actions of these rulers, for they were "very apt for any Roguery" and great thieves. In spite of protests and threats by the Mandingoes, Hodges reached the gold mines at Nettico but found that a severe local famine had shut them down. He did find out, however, that most of the gold of Bambuck went northward by caravan to Tarra, the present Atar of Mauretania, and that the slaves brought down the Senegal and the Gambia came "from very remote inland countries." [19]

Slaves arriving on the coast were terrified by their first sight of the ocean and the loud roar of the surf. Lest they attempt to mutiny or escape, the hungry, exhausted wretches were herded into "trunks" or pens, until the white traders arrived with surgeons, who examined "every part of every one of them," the men and women being brought forth stark naked. The young, best, and soundest Negroes

---

Daniel P. Mannix, *Black Cargoes: A History of the Atlantic Slave Trade* (New York, 1962), 30–32; Barbot, in Churchill, *Voyages*, V, 458, 560; Donnan, *Documents . . . of the Slave Trade*, I, 229.

19. The English first learned about the interior of West Africa in the valley of the river Gambia. In 1621 Richard Jobson went upriver and dealt for gold with a black Muslim merchant. A factor of the Guinea Company named Bowles made a trip up to Barracunda on a barge in 1651. John Barbot listed the European wares for which the Moors would trade gold and slaves in 1682 and reported the presence of the French far up the Senegal River. Jobson, *The Golden Trade*, lx, 17; *HMC, Portland*, II, 31; Barbot, in Churchill, *Voyages*, V, 44–7, 272–5; Davies, *Royal African Company*, 214; Hodges, in *EHR*, XXXIX, 89, 92–3.

were carefully separated from the "refuse slaves"—the small, weak, sickly, deformed, or old people, and those with defective eyes or teeth, and those with yaws or some other venereal or obviously virulent disease. The usual price paid in goods for a black African during the seventies and eighties was £3; in general slaves cost more in North Guinea than along the Gold Coast, and in the Bight of Benin and the Whydah, Negroes were the cheapest of all. If males were plentiful along the Coast, women brought only about one-quarter or one-fifth as much as the men; boys and girls somewhat less. After purchase, the white traders branded all of the merchantable slaves on the chest to prevent theft, and then had them, together with enough refuse slaves to complete a cargo, carried out to the ships in canoes manned by free Negroes.[20]

The long, arduous, and painful journey to the shore, and detention in crowded and loathsome trunks until the slavers arrived, caused a high mortality among the inland captives. The incidence will never be known, but undeniably it was great. "Thus we are sometimes driven many Miles by Land over parching Deserts, and through howling Wildernesses, down to the Sea-Coasts and Factories, being all the way miserably abus'd by our unmerciful Drivers, and wearied and spent with Over-Travel, Hunger, Drought, and excessive Heat, which puts a period to many of our sweet Lives."

20. Among the blacks of Africa, rank had its privileges even in the ugly and sordid business of selling their fellow men to white men. Captain Thomas Phillips was examining some Negroes on shore in 1693: "When we were at the trunk, the king's slaves, if he had any, were the first to be offered for sale, often forced to buy, and [we] observed they were generally the worst slaves in the trunk, and we paid more for them . . . then the cappasheirs [headmen] each brought out his slaves according to his degree and quality, the greatest first, and our surgeon examin'd them well in all kinds, to see that they were sound, wind and limb, making them jump, stretch out their arms swiftly, looking in their mouths to judge of their age; for the cappasheirs are so cunning, that they shave them all close before we see them, so that let them be never so old we can see no grey hairs on their heads or beards; and then having liquor'd them well and sleeked with palm oil, 'tis no easy matter to know an old one from a middle-age one, but by the teeths decay. But our greatest care of all is to buy none that are pox'd, lest they should infect the rest aboard . . . and that distemper which they call the yaws, is very common here. . . ." Phillips, in Churchill, *Voyages,* VI, 218; Mannix, *Black Cargoes,* 47; Du Tertre, *Histoire générale des Antilles,* II, 492; Davies, *Royal African Company,* 236–7; Bosman, *Coast of Guinea,* 340.

There is no doubt, moreover, that such of the miserable blacks who endured and survived the long walk from the interior reached the coast with resistance lowered by fatigue, undernourishment, and frequent beatings—a debilitated state that contributed greatly to the death of so many of them on the Middle Passage.[21]

For this high mortality, their black captors, rulers, and merchants must share the responsibility with the whites. The traumatic experience of the Negro with bondage began not on the high seas, but at the very moment he was taken prisoner in tribal war, or otherwise enslaved, in Africa by his own people. Centuries of human slavery for friend and foe in his native land had taught the awful nature of bondage, and this knowledge aroused great fear in him. Although unnoticed, the psychosomatic effects of this terror produced on the way to the coast and exacerbated on shipboard contributed effectively to the deaths of thousands of blacks. We will do well to bear in mind that, as late as 1690, it was the Africans, not the Europeans, who possessed and exercised power along the entire coast of West Africa.

This was a callous, brutal age, one in which no branch of the human race distinguished itself for sympathy with the downtrodden or practiced what we now call humanitarianism. The avid participation of kings and greedy men—all of the most intelligent and potent blacks in fact—in the traffic in human beings gave it an aspect of legality and respectability that has long veiled the terrible, vicious nature of slavery in Africa as Africans themselves had conducted it for centuries. As far as morality was concerned, there was scarcely a pin to choose between the black kings and the white traders (save that the latter were not regarded in their own countries as leaders or men of the ruling class). Sin, evil, greed, cruelty were certainly no monopoly of the white man; they represented *human,* not just white, depravity. Without condoning in any way the horrors of the Middle Passage and the treatment of the blacks in the West Indies (which happen to be more highly publicized because better documented than slavery in Africa), we must concede a large element of truth in John Barbot's measured

21. Philotheos Physiologus [Thomas Tryon], *Friendly Advice to the Gentlemen Planters of the East and West Indies* (London, 1684), Pt. II, 82.

conclusion that "the fate of such [black slaves] as are brought and transported from the Coast to America by Europeans is less deplorable than of those who end their days in their native country." [22]

III

Under any circumstances a voyage to the West Indies in a slaver was a horrifying experience. As in almost everything else pertaining to seafaring in this age, the Dutch surpassed the English, the French, and the Portuguese in accommodations on their ships, the cleanliness maintained, and the health of the slaves they landed in the Caribbees. For one reason, their ships were the best, ones which had been built for the grim business with more space between decks than those of other nations, and with small ports and lights. Some large vessels carried as many as six or seven hundred Africans, "yet by the careful management of our masters of ships," William Bosman noted with pride, "they are so regulated that it seems incredible" that they "are for the most part clean and neat." The Dutch lost fewer blacks on the Middle Passage, because they took greater care to preserve their lives. They always fed the slaves "indifferent victuals" in ample quantities three times a day. Stripped of their clothes as soon as they stepped on deck, women as well as men remained "stark naked" throughout the voyage. Below the decks the men and women lodged separately, though "they [all] lie so close together as is possible for them to be crowded." [23]

22. Watts, *True Relation,* 4–5, 9–11; Hallett, *Penetration of Africa,* 26; Barbot, in Churchill, *Voyages,* V, 270. Recently Walter Rodney has returned to the abolitionists' position of blaming the Atlantic slave trade for slavery in Upper Guinea and denying the antiquity of slavery in West Africa by implication. For the seventeenth century, at least, his argument is not convincing. *Journal of African History,* VII (1966), 431–43.

23. In perhaps the first English effort to grasp the meaning of this terrible experience to the black African, Thomas Tryon wrote in 1684: We slaves "are sold like Beasts to the Merchant, who glad of the booty puts us aboard the Ships, claps us under Deck, and binds us in Chains and Fetters, and thrusts us into the dark noisom Hold, so many and so close together, that we can hardly breathe, there are we in the hottest of Summer, and under that scorching Climate without any of the sweet Influences of the Air, or briezing Gale[s] to refresh us, suffocated, stewed, and parboyled altogether in a Crowd, till we almost rot each other and ourselves." Tryon, *Friendly Advice,* Pt. II, 82–3; Bosman, *Coast of Guinea,* 341–2.

The English slave ships, Bosman charged, were nearly "always foul and stinking." While the *Hannibal* lay at anchor off Cape Coast Castle in 1693, Captain Thomas Phillips shackled all the black men "two and two" to forestall any attempt to escape or mutiny; likewise he posted guards at every hatchway. On the quarterdeck he had a chest of small arms ready-loaded placed for emergency use. Once the ship put out to sea he ordered the fetters removed, because the blacks seldom rebelled after they lost sight of their homeland. Like many an English master, Phillips fed his slaves twice daily, at 10:00 a.m. and 4:00 p.m., times when he thought them most likely to be restive. The diet consisted of "dabbadabb" (the familiar loblolly that the slaves protested against in Barbados) made up of one peck of cornmeal boiled into mush for twelve men. Three days a week the blacks got horse beans, which they savored and thrived on. The men ate on the main deck and forecastle; the boys and women on the poopdeck. Afterward they cleaned up and went below. To ease themselves they had to go up on deck to a designated place. English captains liked to buy thirty or forty Gold Coast Negroes to guard the Whydahs and others to prevent any quarreling and to oversee them in scraping the decks clean every morning to prevent "nastiness and distemper." Each of the guards received a small cat-o'-nine-tails, which he wielded proudly and frequently. Early in the evening the slaves again came on deck to sun themselves and exercise by jumping and dancing to the sound of bagpipes, harps, and fiddles. Barbot allowed the smoking of pipes on deck, and from time to time distributed coconuts.[24]

Such evidence as survives seems to indicate that before 1667, when the Dutch supplied most of the slaves, conditions were better and the Middle Passage less frightful with the result that a higher proportion of the blacks arrived in good condition than during the last quarter of the century when the Royal African Company transported them. Scarcely a ship landed more than 95 per cent of its original black cargo, but very few met with the excessive mortality of the first voyage of a French West India Company ship to Buenos Aires when most of the slaves, as reported by the anonymous supercargo, wanted to die, and did. Between 1680 and 1688 the Royal

24. Phillips, in Churchill, *Voyages,* VI, 229–30; Barbot, in Churchill, *Voyages,* V, 546–7.

African Company dispatched on the Middle Passage in 249 ships a total of 60,783 Negroes and delivered 46,396 of them in the West Indian islands, or only 76.5 per cent of the cargoes; in other words, the loss of life on the Middle Passage was 23.5 per cent. Sometimes the percentage ranged far higher, as in the case of a voyage of the *Hannibal,* which Captain Phillips commanded in 1693. He sailed for Barbados in August of that year with a cargo of 480 male and 220 female slaves; the crossing took two months and eleven days. There was much sickness on board his ship "among my poor men and negroes," and he buried at sea fourteen members of the crew who succumbed to the white flux, ascribed by the master to an excess of drinking raw rum punch with bad sugar. Smallpox, the greatest scourge of the Africans, broke out, and a hundred blacks had it at a time; but miraculously Phillips lost less than a dozen of them. Other disorders struck, however, and when the voyage ended he succeeded in landing only 372 of the 700 he started with from Africa, a loss that cost the Royal African Company £6500 sterling. "No gold finders can endure so much noisome slavery as they do who carry negroes." They get some respite, we never, Captain Phillips confided to his journal.[25]

Every vessel carried a doctor, but the rudimentary sanitation and hygiene of the age, the overcrowded conditions below decks, and the English habit of keeping the black men in irons, often for the entire voyage, brought about these dire happenings. The absence of any humanitarian concern apart, the self-interest of the Royal African Company, the English interlopers, and the Dutch was to keep down mortality; they paid high prices for slaves in Africa, disbursed large sums for transportation, and the loss of a Negro at sea or on land before sale was more expensive for the captain of the ship than the death of a white indentured servant.

25. Captain Phillip Carteret arrived at Barbados in the *Speedwell* in March 1663 with a cargo of 155 Negro men, 102 women, and 22 boys and girls. "The small-pox hitt unfortunately among them, distroyed many, rendered others unsaleable that had it in the harbor" and left others "very sickly." The agents of the Royal Adventurers in Barbados reported a malignancy at this time among the African slaves of St. Christopher and Nevis, and they were experiencing a great mortality. PRO: CO 1/18, fol. 39; *Journal d'un voyage sur les costes d'Afrique et aux Indes d'Espagne . . . commencé en 1702 & fini en 1706* (Amsterdam, 1723); George L. Beer, *The Old Colonial System* (New York, 1912), I, 343–4*n,* 346; Davies, *Royal African Company,* 292; Phillips, in Churchill, *Voyages,* VI, 230, 234–7.

The passage out to the Caribbean in this period was every bit as much of a living hell for English and Irish servants, however, as it was for the African slaves. John Coad, one of ninety-nine Monmouth rebels condemned in 1685 by Judge Jeffreys to be transported to Jamaica, wrote an account of the six weeks and three days' journey to Port Royal in *A Memorandum of the Wonderful Providence of God* (London, 1849). They were taken aboard ship and immediately confined below deck "in a very small room where we could not lay ourselves down without lying upon one another." The crew gave them no water, provided no heat, and placed only one receptacle in the middle of the room for the use of all. Captain Edward Brookes, a fellow-Englishman, made a miserable gain by keeping the servants on short rations during the entire trip. No sooner did the ship put out to sea than disease broke out: smallpox, calentures, plagues, and ailments accompanied by "Frightful Blotches." In all, twenty-two, or 22.2 per cent, of these miserable wretches succumbed, as did also several free passengers and the mate. Coad tells of "others devoured with lice till they were almost at death's door." Being very weak when he sailed, the writer believed that he too would have died had he and his fellows not been allowed on deck well after the voyage was half over. Inhuman treatment of his own kind was not unique with Captain Brookes; it was, alas, common English practice.

In brooding over the evil of three hundred years ago, we of the present, despite the outrageous crime of the slave trade, might pause and reflect before passing harsh judgments against the blacks and the whites responsible for it that, in our own enlightened day, blacks still enslave blacks in Africa, and white men assist in the traffic; and that the crimes of Biafra, Dachau, Hiroshima, and Mylai are but different, more refined, and far worse misdeeds committed by men upon human beings of all colors and races. Evil is timeless as well as universal.

IV

Since 1563, at least, the English had shown a great interest in trade with Africa, but not until the formation of "The Adventurers of London Trading to Gynny and Bynny" (the Guinea Company) in 1617 did they seriously begin to challenge the Portuguese and Dutch traders along the coast of West Africa. Even then they chiefly sought gold and ivory. At Nettico, far up the river Gambia in 1621, a Negro Muslim merchant, Bucker Sano, was chaffering with Richard Jobson of the Guinea Company: "Hee shewed unto mee certaine young black women, who were standing by themselves . . . which hee told me were slaves, brought for me to buy. I made answer, We were a people who did not deale in any such commodities, neither did wee buy or sell one another, or any that had our own shapes: hee seemed to marvell much at it." This diffidence or reluctance to engage in the slave traffic lasted until shortly after 1640, when Maurice Thompson and Samuel Saltonstall, both owners of cotton plantations in the Caribbees, drew the attention of their fellow merchants in the Guinea Company to the opportunity for opening a profitable trade in slaves with the islands.[26]

Uncertain conditions in England held these traders back for nearly a decade, but in 1650, their Company claimed, with evident exaggeration, to have had sixteen factories on the Coast and still to be maintaining twelve. Parliament renewed the monopoly of the Guinea Company the next year; in December, James Pope was instructed to sail the pink *Supply* to the Coast to pick up "as many good lusty negroes or cattle" as possible and deliver them to Mr. Francis Soane, a merchant in Barbados, for sale to the planters there. Once again Maurice Thompson figured prominently in Caribbean affairs, this time in gearing the African slave trade into the West Indian sugar culture. Thereafter the Guinea Company kept one or two resident agents at Barbados and the other English islands to dispose of its slaves and also to arrange for freighting cargoes of sugar, cotton, and indigo for England. This was a beginning, but the Guinea Company did not succeed in supplying many blacks to the planters between 1650 and 1660, because the Dutch, who conducted the traffic to the planters' satisfaction, virtually monopolized it.[27]

26. Donnan, *Documents . . . of the Slave Trade,* 86; Jobson, *The Golden Trade,* 112.
27. J. W. Blake, "The Farm of the Guinea Trade," *Essays in British and Irish History,* ed. H. H. Cronne, T. W. Moody, and D. B. Quinn (London, 1939),

The dismaying spectacle of their Dutch rivals driving the trade from Africa to the English colonies so successfully and profitably aroused both jealousy and cupidity in Maurice Thompson and the Londoners of the Guinea Company. Mention has been made earlier of how, along with the cultivation of cotton and sugar, the Hollanders and Zeelanders shrewdly introduced to the English colonies the complete plantation system as it had been evolved by the Portuguese in Brazil. The central feature of this system was black slave labor. From entrepôts situated conveniently at St. Eustatius (Statia to the English) and Curaçao, the enterprising servants of the Dutch West India Company first created, then exploited, markets for slaves in the Leeward Islands, Barbados, and Surinam. Looking backward on the years before the Restoration, Edward Lyttleton of Barbados recalled that "we could send to Guinney for negroes when we wanted them, and they stood us in about seven pounds a head." He dared not say openly in London, though he meant it, that the trade was conducted by Dutch merchants, not English. Cheap slave labor purchased on long-term credit at low rates of interest seemed to the planters essential to maintain the boom in sugar and to guarantee insular prosperity.[28]

Parliament responded to the urgings of the London merchants in September 1660 by passing a navigation law directed at rendering illegal most of the Dutch trade with England's colonies (it did not stifle it at once because the Netherlanders opened up forbidden routes of commerce). Within three months, King Charles II had issued a patent of monopoly to a new Company of Royal Adventurers Trading in Africa, in which James, Duke of York, was greatly interested. At the outset, the traders still concentrated on gold and ivory, but they quickly sniffed the profits to be gained by transporting slaves from Africa to the West Indies and to the Spanish Main, as well as the English plantations. Colonel Modyford and Sir Peter Colleton served in Barbados as agents for the Royal Adventurers and, in 1662, the Duke of York notified Gov-

---

87–8, 106; *HMC, Portland,* II, 28–9; Donnan, *Documents . . . of the Slave Trade,* I, 129–31; George F. Zook, "The Company of Royal Adventurers Trading to Africa," in *Journal of Negro History,* IV (1919), 207.

28. Davies, *Royal African Company,* 28–40; [Edward Lyttleton] *The Groans of the Plantations* (London, 1689), 5.

ernor Lord Willoughby that they would be able to ship 3000 slaves a year to the island, and at Jamaica, Lord Windsor was advised to expect 300 blacks annually. The price set by the Royal Adventurers for both islands was £17 a head. In 1667 the Company claimed to have shipped more than 6000 Negroes annually to the West Indies. This figure must have been for the years 1665 and 1666 and is unacceptable, even if some of the slaves went to the Spanish settlements. Thomas Modyford admitted frankly in later years that the slave trade fell off in Africa after Admiral de Ruyter's raid on the Coast in 1665 and again in the Caribbean during the Second Dutch War. Shipments of blacks by the Royal Adventurers ceased almost entirely after the Peace of Breda (July 21, 1667), and such slaves as arrived in the Caribbean in English ships were sold by English traders sailing under licenses issued by the company.[29]

The island planters, hard hit by a sharp decline in the world price of sugar after 1660 and apparently facing harder blows from the Navigation Acts of 1660 and 1663, looked upon the monopoly of the African trade by the Royal Adventurers as intolerable. Drawing upon many years of experience in Barbados and Jamaica, Thomas Modyford affirmed in 1676 "that Barbados had never risen to that perfection wee have lately seene in it, had it not beene lawfull [before 1660] for the Dutch, Hamburghers, our own whole Nation and others to bring and sell them Blacks or any other servants in their Infancy." Competition had kept the price of prime slaves down around £7 sterling a head, and the Dutch had always allowed the planters ample credit on easy terms. With the granting of the monopoly in 1660, many an islander concluded that he would have to mortgage his next crop and go into debt to the

29. Only two months after the Peace of Breda, letters from Barbados were reported in the *London Gazette:* "There were also in Safety arrived at the Barbadoes four ships from Guiney richly laden: two of them upon the account of the Company [of Royal Adventurers] and the other private Adventurers, but their Voyage had proved fatal to the Negroes and the rest of the Company in those Ships by reason of a great sickness that was amongst them." *London Gazette,* Aug. 22, 1667. For the Royal Adventurers, see Zook, in *Journal of Negro History,* IV, 209, 210, 213, 217; and Davies, *Royal African Company,* 41–4; *CSPC, 1669–74,* p. 107; *Diary of Samuel Pepys,* ed. H. B. Wheatley (London, 1924), IV, 292.

English merchants, who demanded £17 a head for the Royal Adventurers' Negroes. In 1662 the Council and Assembly of Barbados petitioned without success for free trade along the African Coast. Regularly thereafter, Barbadians and Leeward Islanders complained about the high price, poor quality, and insufficient supply of slaves.[30]

Replying to the strictures of the planters in 1667, the Royal Adventurers insisted that they had supplied the West Indians with slaves more plentifully and as cheaply as both the Guinea Company and the independent English traders, but they conspicuously omitted any mention of the Dutch, with whom England was then at war. The financial plight of the Company was due in large part to the losses resulting from de Ruyter's raids on the Coast, as well as in the Caribbean, but it might have recouped its losses if the planters and merchants had paid their debts, £90,000 sterling, of which Barbados owed £60,000. This may have been true, and, further, the islanders may have overestimated the number of blacks they could take off annually. What the English planters really wanted was not more slaves from the Royal Adventurers but an end to the monopoly and a lawful return to the old, familiar, less expensive free trade with the Dutch under which they had prospered so much in the forties and fifties. Who among them would not have been elated to see the price of prime Negroes fall from £17 to around £7? [31]

The bad management of the Royal Adventurers, their failure to require careful accounts for each voyage, the Second Dutch War, and above all, the inability of English and American historians of the slave trade to use the archives of Holland and Zeeland have largely concealed what must have been the principal facts governing the supply of black Africans to the West Indians from 1660 to 1672.

Out of fragmentary records we may venture to reconstruct the

30. PRO: CO 1/38, fol. 256b; CO 138/1, pp. 102–3; *CSPC, 1661–68,* pp. 23, 30, 45, 46, 47; Zook, in *Journal of Negro History,* IV, 208; BM: Egerton MSS, 2395, fol. 277; Donnan, *Documents . . . of the Slave Trade,* I, 166, 166*n*.

31. *An Answer of the Company of Royal Adventurers of England Trading into Africa, To the Petition and Paper of Certain Heads and Particulars . . . Exhibited to . . . the House of Commons . . .* ([London], 1667), 1–3, 9–12, 14–15, 18; Stock, *Debates,* I, 347.

actual slave situation in the Lesser Antilles during the twelve years of the existence of the Royal Adventurers. Although they enjoyed exclusively the trade from Africa to the Caribbees in 1660, not until the issuing of their second charter in 1661 did the Royal Adventurers begin to ship large cargoes of slaves to the colonies. From August 1663 to March 1664 they delivered to their factors at Barbados 3075 blacks (1051 men, 1018 women, 136 boys, and 56 girls), for whom the planters paid an average price of more than £16 per head. Later in 1664 the price rose to £20, and during the war with the Dutch and French to £30. An unknown number of slaves went to Surinam and Jamaica, but scarcely any to the Leeward Islands. There is a record of one vessel carrying 294 Negroes to Nevis and St. Christopher in 1663–64 but none for any other island in the Leeward group. Governor William Byam, agent for the Royal Adventurers at Torarica, attributed the short supply of slaves in Guiana to the machinations of some principal Barbadians. On the other hand the Company charged that the planters of Surinam and St. Christopher had received all of the slaves required "on Credit." With all of his islands in mind, William, Lord Willoughby wrote to the King in September 1666, stressing the fact that "these settlements have been upheld by negroes and cannot subsist without supplies of them," and he pleaded that the islands be granted the same freedom of trade that was permitted in England.[32]

The Royal Adventurers experienced great difficulty from 1660 to 1665 in breaking the Dutch monopoly of the slave trade in West Africa, while in the Caribbean they had no naval support for their own monopoly against the incursions of the Dutch and English interlopers. When the war broke out in 1665, shipping was totally disrupted and no slaves reached the islands. After 1667, the Royal Adventurers no longer sent Negroes from Africa, though they did license some independent traders to transport them; Cary Helyar of Jamaica was one of their agents. Making

32. A surviving "Barbados Ledger" of the Royal Adventurers contains accounts with Lewis Morris, Thomas Noell, and a Jew, David da Costa for 30, 43, and 11 slaves each. PRO: Treasury 70/646, fols. 7, 10, 11, 44; Donnan, *Documents . . . of the Slave Trade,* I, 88, 92; Zook, in *Journal of Negro History,* IV, 218, 220; *CSPC, 1661–68,* p. 413.

some allowance for the extreme claims of the Londoners, we may concede that they may have delivered something under 20,000 slaves to the Caribbee islands and Surinam. Barbados and Jamaica together had at least 25,000 more in 1668 than in 1660, and it is known that Jamaica imported none after 1665. Almost certainly in both islands the death rate among the Negroes exceeded the birth rate, as it did with the whites. St. Christopher lost several thousand slaves during the war to the French, who also carried off 1300 from Antigua and Montserrat. Precise calculation is impossible, but we cannot question that at this time in the English colonies there were thousands of blacks whom the Royal Adventurers did not carry there. From where did they come? [33]

Independent English traders, either licensed or interlopers, and possibly a few of the latter from New England, supplied a small number of these Africans, but the bulk of them must have been smuggled into the Leeward Islands and Barbados by the Dutch. Until the records of the West India Company are analyzed for shipment of slaves, no figures can be adduced. The little now available to go on, however, all points to the Dutch as the source. When the *Diamond,* a Dutch vessel with 180 slaves aboard, came into Port Royal to trade in 1662, Governor Edward D'Oyley favored it, but, fearing to violate the Navigation Law, the Council opposed him. He thereupon bought the cargo himself, sold forty blacks to Major John Coape, a Quaker, and the remainder to a Spanish sea captain. Three years later, Governor Lynch was speaking of Curaçao as that "cursed little barren island." More weighty is a comment on the Jamaican planters in the manuscript Reflections on the Royal African Companys Interest in the Plantations (1668)

33. The misadventures of a leaky slaver licensed by the Royal Adventurers in 1688 to carry slaves from Guinea to Barbados but which had to land at Surinam, where Captain Robert Bartlett had to sell his 160 Negroes for "Bully-Tree heading" for sugar casks are told in Barbados Council Minutes, II, 52–3; Zook, in *Journal of Negro History,* IV, 218; Bennett, in *WMQ,* 3d ser., XXI, 55–6; *An Answer of the Royal Adventurers,* 11; Davies, *Royal African Company,* 43–4. The author of the State of the Case of the Sugar Plantations in America (1666) claimed that the French took 15,000 Negroes from 150 sugarworks at St. Christopher, Antigua, and Montserrat. This figure seems very high, but it does point to the magnitude of the loss. PRO: CO 1/26, fol. 57; also *HMC, 9th Report,* Pt. II, Appendix 11; *CSPC, 1669–74,* pp. 214–16, 286, 391–4; BM: Egerton MSS, 2395, fol. 530.

that "though by the Interloping Trade both from Africa and the Dutch Island of Cuiraco they may in Time of Peace be supply'd and perhapps at 10 per Cent lower rates," during a conflict the source will be cut off.[34]

As a geographical, if not a political, part of the Leeward Islands, St. Eustatius was ideally situated for smuggling slaves to the French on St. Christopher and to the English, both there and in the nearby colonies. An admiralty judge of London reported to the Privy Council in 1662 that a witness has testified in his court to seeing "about 12 Dutch Shipps at a time at St. Christophers, and that he believes about 30 Dutch Shipps in a year are there Laden." Then years later Governor Sir Charles Wheler mentioned casually "the Dutch Sloopes necessary for our Trade in the Leeward Islands" with St. Eustatius. Within a few months, Governor Sir William Stapleton stated that the Royal Adventurers had sent no slaves to Nevis, Montserrat, or Antigua "these seven years [since 1665]," and that each island had got 300 blacks from licensed English ships. But altogether these colonies now contained at least 3600 African slaves. Who can question that they were procured from nearby Statia in Dutch sloops? How else can this phenomenon be explained? [35]

Everything we now know points to certain conditions that must have prevailed in the Caribbean between 1660 and 1672. Foremost was that the enforcement of the Navigation Laws was as lax in peace as it was in war. It was one thing to pass the laws, but another to enforce them. And so it was, also, with the Royal Adventurers' charters of monopoly. The crafty Dutch continued long after 1660 to drive a lucrative trade in both slaves and goods from St. Eustatius and Curaçao to the English islands. We may con-

34. Constant Sylvester must have been referring to New England interlopers in a letter to John Winthrop, Jr., of June 24, 1664: "The Ginny, or Royall Company, labor to ingross the whole Trade of Barbados to themselves; if so, as here was news, they allready have effected, then what will become of poor New England, and their trade." The answer was that they were shut out of it for a long time. *MHS Procs.,* 2d ser., IV, 280; *CSPC, 1661–68,* p. 36; *1669–74,* p. 622; Donnan, *Documents . . . of the Slave Trade,* I, 14–15, 154, 169; *APC Col.,* I, 616; PRO: CO 1/18, fols. 152–3; BM: Egerton MSS, 2395, fol. 466.

35. *APC Col.,* I, 339; BM: Egerton MSS, 2395, fol. 522; *CSPC, 1669–74,* pp. 392–4; *1681–85,* p. 285.

jecture further that, given the much increased demand for black labor in the Caribbees, the Netherlanders may have managed to dispose of nearly as many slaves as they had before 1660.[36]

In defending themselves in 1667 against the allegations of the planters, the Royal Adventurers voiced their belief that a secret correspondence had taken place between the islanders and the Dutch West India Company before the former had sent their petition to London. The petitioners, they said, "had taken care to make the Dutch rejoyce at the Ruine of the Royal Company, which is expressed in the *Harlem Gazett* of the 30th of October, So that we have too much cause to suspect that they are under-hand set on by the Dutch West-India Company, who doubtless would purchase the dissolution of this Company with a greater Summe of money than ever was subscribed to support it." This belief was probably based on sound facts. By the end of the Second Dutch War, the Company was a failure, and not until the King chartered the Royal African Company on September 20, 1672, was the English slave trade put on a firm basis.[37]

Disregarding the hazards accompanying the outbreak of the third war with the Dutch, the new company proceeded to deal in African slaves for the steadily growing market in the West Indies. Most of the slaves—purchased in Gambia and on the Gold Coast for about £3 a head—they sold through resident agents in Barbados, Jamaica, and Nevis (for all of the Leeward Islands) at fixed prices of £17, £16, and £15 a head respectively, prices that represented the average charged by the Royal Adventurers. The Company gave the planters of Barbados the best service, sending them about 2000 a year, and in one year, 5000. Over an eleven years' period (May 6, 1673, to May 30, 1684) the Company's

36. In addition to the famous shipping and enumeration clauses, the Navigation Act of 1660 provided that after 1 February 1660/1, "no alien person not born within the allegiance of our sovereign . . . or naturalized, or made a free denizen, Shall . . . exercise the Trade or Occupation of a merchant or factor in any of the said places." This ruled out Dutchmen, at least newcomers, and was definitely aimed at the traffic in the West Indies, but for a time it was unsuccessful. *The Statutes at Large from Magna Carta to 1806*, ed. Danby Pickering (London, 1762–1807), VII, 452–4; Governor Bell to Earl of Carlisle, Feb. 18, 1650/1, Hay MSS.

37. *An Answer of the Royal Adventurers*, 18. The standard authority is Davies, *Royal African Company*, see especially 57–63, 87–100, 318.

agents at Bridgetown sold 15,885 slaves for 7,696,742 pounds of sugar and £48,104 in sterling bills of exchange on London. Nevis, too, was well supplied; it was the only colony from which no complaint was ever received. Altogether 5537 sold in this tiny island for 17,899,051 pounds of sugar (@ 12/6 per cwt.).[38]

The table below shows that the Royal African Company markedly improved the record of its predecessor.[39]

ROYAL AFRICAN COMPANY DELIVERIES
OF SLAVES IN THE WEST INDIES

Year	*Barbados*	*Jamaica*	*Nevis*	*Antigua*	*St. Chr.*	*Monts.*	*Total*
1673	220	—	—	—	—	—	220
1674	1066	410	469	—	—	—	1945
1675	1512	1269	502	—	—	—	3283
1676	1836	1188	571	—	—	—	3595
1677	940	1156	495	—	—	—	2591
1678	2392	990	627	—	—	—	4009
1679	676	464	495	210	201	152	2198
1680	1673	1623	819	—	214	—	4329
1681	2404	1150	738	—	91	—	4383
1682–83	3676	3483	626	—	118	21	7924
1684–85	3630	3841	151	104	—	—	7726
1686–87	3585	6223	678	170	—	159	10,815
1688	1516	447	363	80	—	93	2499
1689	1119	682	368	282	—	244	2695
1690	520	359	—	—	—	—	879
1691	1175	579	—	—	—	—	1754

38. The planters of the other Leeward Islands resented the advantage that Nevis enjoyed as "the Mart or Place for delivering of Negroes for the . . . Charibbee Islands." The Assembly of Antigua complained that all the slaves at Nevis sold before "the Windermost" islands learned of their delivery, and that it was also costly to travel to Nevis to buy Negroes. *Acts of Assembly, Passed in the Charibbee Leeward Islands,* 49–50; Davies, *Royal African Company,* 294–5, 311; PRO: Treasury, 70/646; 70/936–42 (invoices of payments dispatched to the Company in England).

39. The Royal African Company reported delivery of 18,802 Negroes to Jamaica, 1680–88. Davies, *Royal African Company,* 363 (table); PRO: CO 388/10, H 108 (table); also printed in *Report of the Privy Council Committee on Trade to Africa* (London, 1789), Pt. IV, No. 5. Mention should be made of the important study by Philip D. Curtin, *The Atlantic Slave Trade: A Census* (Madison, Wisc., 1969), 51–9. Our figures differ from Mr. Curtin's because of adjustments made for slaves concealed, as mentioned in the previous chapter.

These figures, compiled by K. G. Davies, are the most dependable now available.

Somewhat different figures, collected for the Privy Council in 1689 from the Company's records, shed light on the Middle Passage:

LOSS OF SLAVES SHIPPED BY THE ROYAL AFRICAN COMPANY

Year	*No. of Ships*	*Blacks Shipped*	*Blacks Delivered*	*Per Cent of Loss*
1680	24	5190	3751	27⅔
1681	22	6327	4989	21⅐
1682	31	6330	4494	29
1683	35	9081	6488	28½
1684	22	5384	3845	28½
1685	35	8658	6304	27¼
1686	31	8355	6812	18⅔
1687	24	5606	4777	14⅘
1688	25	5852	4936	15⅔
	249	60,783	46,396	Av. 23½

To the 46,396 blacks carried safely over the ocean by the Royal African Company must be added about 10,000 sold as bulk cargo to contractors, and an unknown number brought in by interlopers. As a result of better enforcement of the Acts of Trade, the traffic in Dutch sloops from St. Eustatius and Curaçao began to fall off after 1674, though the Netherlanders could never be kept away from the Leeward Islands. Free trade, such as they had enjoyed during the Interregnum, which meant trade with the Dutch, always remained the goal of the planters, for at no time did the Royal African Company send them as many slaves as they needed.[40]

40. Mrs. Aphra Behn described contract slaves vividly as she had seen them in Surinam: "Those who wanted slaves, make a Bargain with a Master or a Captain of a ship, and contract to pay him so much apiece, a Matter of twenty Pound a Head, for as many as he agrees for, and to pay for 'em when they shall be delivered on such a Plantation. So that when there arrives a Ship laden with Slaves, they who have so contracted go aboard, and receive their Number by Lot; and perhaps in one Lot that may be for ten, there may happen to be three or four Men, the rest Women and Children. Or be there more or less of either

The chief objection of the Barbadians was the irregularity of the supply of black laborers. In 1676 Governor Jonathan Atkins stated that since he arrived in 1672 not 2000 Negroes had been delivered, yet three times that number could have been sold. Later he insisted that 3000 would sell immediately and at good prices, and that island could take off 2000 to 3000 annually. Such statements were rebutted by Governor Dutton in 1681 when he asserted that the Royal African Company had sent about 2000 slaves every year since 1674. Furthermore five Company ships came into Carlisle Bay between March and June of 1676 from which 1372 Negroes were sold. There were times, according to Edwin Stede, who was chief agent at Bridgetown for almost twenty years, when the Company's agents could not dispose of the cargoes landed. On May 30, 1676, a vessel with 224 slaves arrived, and, unable to dispose of any of the Negroes, the ship proceeded to Nevis; another with 200 blacks went on to Jamaica. The fact that by 1675 the black population in Barbados had reached about 40,000 and remained at that level for many decades suggests that on the whole the island was well supplied and that thereafter it needed slaves only for replacement rather than for expansion of the sugar culture.[41]

The needs of the Leeward Islands and Jamaica for a regular and increasing supply of slaves were relatively greater than those of Barbados, because these communities were still expanding the sugar culture throughout the years 1660–90. St. Christopher's slave population had to be entirely replaced after 1667, as did those of Antigua and Montserrat. The complaint of the planters in these islands was that ordinarily they had to buy Negroes rejected by the planters of Barbados, or, if a slaver stopped at Nevis, the planters there got all the blacks or at least the pick of the cargo. The three agents at Nevis protested to the Company on January 30, 1678/9: "The Negroes that came in the *Golden Lyon* are more than the ordinary complained against, being little better than Refuse," and though they sold them to needy planters for £20 a head, "the

---

sex, you are obliged to be contented with your Lot." *Oroonoko,* p. 5; Donnan, *Documents . . . of the Slave Trade,* I, 216*n*.

41. *CSPC, 1669–74,* pp. 316, 392, 415; *1675–76,* p. 422; *1677–80,* p. 7; *1681–85,* pp. 70–71; BM: Harleian MSS, 7310, No. 17; PRO: CO 1/38, fol. 57a; CO 1/44, fol. 47, XXV.

Country complaines much of them." What they wanted were one or two ships with "Mina Negroes" from Angola or Cape Coast. Antigua, at the end of the line, always got the worst of the lot. In 1680 Robert Helmes estimated that the four principal Leeward Islands could take off 3200 Negroes annually. The Council of Montserrat described the situation to the Lords of Trade and Plantations thus: "As your Lordships require of us how this island may be improved, we shall not only deliver it as our opinion, but are also ready to prove that not one of these His Majesty's colonies ever was or ever can be brought to any considerable improvement without a supply of white servants and negroes." [42]

An insufficient supply of slave labor signally retarded the growth of the economy of Jamaica. Sir Thomas Lynch informed Sir Joseph Williamson that the island had fewer white people in 1671 than in 1664. The 9000 Negroes helped to make up the deficiency, but so great was the demand for slaves in the early seventies that privateers high-jacked Dutch slavers off Curaçao and then carried the cargoes of 500 to 600 slaves to a profitable market at Port Royal. Despite the fact that in the next seven years and nine months 11,716 slaves and 5996 white servants were brought in, there was still a crying need for more laborers. With some reason the Jamaicans charged that the Royal African Company preferred to sell to Spaniards than to their own English brethren. Peter Beckford, founder of the greatest sugar fortune, summed it up in 1676: "The People of this Island are much dissatisfied about the Royall Company for that they are not furnished with Negroes as others of his Majesty's plantacions, and those they have att unreasonable Rates, soe that itts now become a good Trade to buy Negroes of the Royal Company's Factors in Barbados and shipp them for our Island, they buying them there for seaventeen pounds sterling per head . . . and sell[ing] them here at £24 sterling by lott. . . ." Furthermore, the Barbadians allow considerable time to pay, the agents at Port Royal but six months. "If the Company objects that the Island has always had more [slaves] than it could pay for," a petition by the planters to the Lords of Trade and Plantations stated in 1680, the true answer is that it ruins its own chapmen by selling at such rates,

42. PRO: Treasury, 70/15, pp. 5–6, 11, 28, 48; 70/107, p. 11; *CSPC, 1677–80*, p. 574; PRO: CO 1/45, p. 58; CO 1/46, p. 20; CO 157/1, pp. 117A, 121A.

and "it is hard for the poor planter to pay." Many Jamaicans considered the Royal Company overbearing and extortionate.[43]

It was for these reasons that the West Indians resented both the companies possessing a monopoly and the Acts of Trade and Navigation, and, whenever and wherever possible, they opposed them. Contrariwise, the planters regarded the interlopers as the Robin Hoods of the Caribbean whether they were from Old England or New. Picking up cargoes in Africa clandestinely, or openly at Madagascar, they played a considerable part in supplying the islands with slaves, often at lower prices than those asked by the Company. Some of the most prominent planters did not scruple to deal with them. Colonel Christopher Codrington "is a great Favourer of Interlopers," the agents in Barbados reported to the Company in 1678, for he and Colonel Drax and Colonel Sharpe "bought all the cheife negroes out of the Interloper . . . at very low rates." Then of course, there were the Dutch merchants, whom many a planter preferred above all others. The Company's agent at Nevis disclosed in 1686 that ". . . Some of the chiefs of this Island and St. Christopher's often discourse of the greater convenience of buying Negroes from the Dutch on St. Eustatius than from the Company." Inasmuch as no law or charter could prevent the Dutch from going to Guinea and buying slaves and selling them, there was little the Royal African Company could do to prevent it.[44]

The ability of the planters to purchase slaves depended, as it always had, on the amount of credit they could command. Robert Helmes, the agent at Nevis, gave this description of the credit terms he allowed, which the planters considered onerous: "The factors att Nevis take bonds or penale bills of all persons who buy

43. "LAUS DEO PORT ROYALL IN JAMAICA," reads the page-heading in a ledger of the Royal African Company for June 5, 1675, which recorded the sale of 351 slaves off the *Diligence:* to William Drax (5 males), Judith Freeman (1 boy), Lord John Vaughan (6 males), Sir Henry Morgan (8 males, 4 females), Sir Thomas Modyford (16 males, 5 females), and William Beeston (6 males). PRO: Treasury, 70/936, pp. 138, 141; CO 1/38, fol. 171a; CO 1/27, fol. 22; CO 1/43, fol. 37; CO 1/37, fol. 25b; BM: Egerton MSS, 2395, fol. 501; Jamaica Council Minutes, III, 279, 280, 284–5; V, 78; Blathwayt, History and State of Jamaica, 20–21; *Interesting Tracts Relating to Jamaica,* 289; Donnan, *Documents . . . of the Slave Trade,* I, 265.

44. Donnan, *Documents . . . of the Slave Trade,* I, 241; *CSPC, 1685–88,* p. 216; PRO: CO 1/29, fol. 36; Jamaica Council Minutes, V, 155.

the Companies negroes of them, to pay att six or nine monthes or att some shorter time according as they Cann agree with the planters. That att the expiration of the said respective time, according as the bill or bond is taken, if not then paid, the bonds or bills are putt in suite and runn up to a Judgement, by which their Land may be extended and their goods and Chattels sold, butt no interest is allowed by the Law of that Island. That they doe endeavour to take the planters bonds or bills without time, by which meanes they can gett the debt sooner paid." [45]

The Royal African Company presented a picture of its financial losses in defense of its charges: one-third to one-half of the Negroes shipped across the Atlantic from Africa were lost on the Middle Passage, and then there were the credits extended to the planters. The Company had inherited all the debts owed its predecessor. In February 1672/3 both King Charles and the Council for Trade and Plantations wrote to the Governor of Barbados urging "the effectual getting in what is due to that Company." The Assembly, suggesting that the Royal African Company could take the normal recourse of the law, assumed that it had done its duty by merely ordering the letter entered on its books and then deposited it with the Secretary. Two months later the Governor and Council ordered that the letter be published in each parish of Barbados. Still the West Indian planters owed the Company £130,000 sterling in 1683, and by 1690 the sum had reached a peak of £170,000.[46]

By the passage of a number of acts in each island, the assemblies sought to protect local debtors from what they looked upon as harassment on the part of English merchants and companies. On the other hand, the vexations awaiting the creditor in all of these colonies were sometimes beyond credence. A law of 1669 in Antigua permitted a creditor who obtained a court judgment to distrain only upon goods and chattels; action against land could take place only under the most onerous conditions and as a last resort. Colonial legal ingenuity was highly developed, and the sole means of countering it was for the Company to use economic pressure to procure the election of members of the colonial governments who

45. Davies, *Royal African Company,* 318–19; PRO: Treasury, 70/107, pp. 15, 24.
46. *CSPC, 1681–85,* pp. 525, 526; Davies, *Royal African Company,* 318; Barbados Council Minutes, II, 253–4, 256, 269; BM: Harleian MSS, 7310, No. 17.

would act in its favor. Apropos of this, Governor Russell of Barbados remarked in 1695 that the Royal African Company's agents have "such a sway here as almost to stop any proceeding, for if a man does not vote as they would wish for a vestryman or assemblyman they proceed against him for what he owes them for negroes (most of the planters being in their debt), thus ruining him and his family." [47]

By the mid-eighties, the governor of Jamaica, Sir Thomas Lynch, could write: "The Royal Company now begin to supply us well, there being two Shipps with 700 Negros in port," which, if the Spanish buyers do not return, will cause interloping to cease entirely. The interlopers had truly cut in on the slave trade, for Jamaica was a large island where they could land them without detection, and the demand was as great, Lynch wryly said, as money to a courtier. Yet, no significant improvement occurred. Reporting to the King and Queen about the sale of Negroes to the Spanish, the Assembly in 1689 concluded: "Thus the foreigners get the best of the negroes and we only the refuse at £22 a head." In Barbados in 1694, according to Edwin Stede, "many considerable Gentlemen, Planters, Merchants and others . . . who have dealt with the Company's Agents and with privat traders for Negros, say that they were furnished by the Company with better Negros, on more moderate tearmes, and greater conveniences in point of time for payment then from the Interlopers, and for that reason would and did for the future deale only with the Company." [48]

V

The white man's plantations in the English islands had been transformed between 1650 and 1690 into a Negro's domain. At this point, though no satisfactory, simple answer can be offered, one

47. Davies, *Royal African Company,* 319–33; Higham, *Leeward Islands,* 155; PRO: Treasury, 70/16, p. 3; *CSPC, 1693–96,* p. 526.

48. The top planters of Jamaica were not above the kind of slave trading they blamed on the Royal African Company. In 1686 Sir Charles Modyford, Colonel Needham, and some others "cut" young John Helyar in on a private deal to sell some slaves to the Spaniards. Sept. 22, 1686, Helyar MSS; *CSPC, 1681–85,* pp. 286, 486, 525, 532; PRO: CO 138/4, p. 267; Donnan, *Documents . . . of the Slave Trade,* I, 370; BM: Harleian MSS, 7310, No. 17.

may properly ask why did the planters, especially in such thickly populated islands as Barbados, St. Christopher, and Nevis, turn from white labor to black? The situation, containing as many social as economic elements, was exceedingly complex. By temperament, heritage, and experience, as well as physically, the Negro was suited to living in the tropics; the white man was not. Few historical contrasts of the seventeenth century have been more striking.

The overwhelming proportion of the white servants from the British Islands and the Continent failed to make the required adjustment to the environment. They never truly succeeded in adapting themselves to the heat, humidity, and the strange diet of the islands. To maintain with some very able writers that a few white men here and there survived and made good in the Torrid Zone is to beg the question of what happened to the great mass of English and French settlers who went to the West Indies before 1690.[49]

The white servants who emigrated to the Caribbees formed, primarily, a male society; very few were married and consequently lacked the steadying influence of the family and never could recapture the sense of community they had once known in the British Isles. When they came out of their indentures, they wanted, above everything else, to have small plantations of their own; they did not want to work for wages. Because land in Barbados, St. Christopher, and Nevis became scarce if not unavailable to them, many migrated to other islands. After 1660 the reputation of the West Indians for mistreating white servants was so widespread that even the dregs of English and Irish societies refused to go there. Of those who went, with the exception of the Scots, few were good workers, and their knowledge of farming was negligible. The inescapable conclusion is that, on the whole, these white men were a low-grade set of people at best, ones whom servitude degraded and debilitated further, leaving them in a depressed state when they became freemen. Perhaps the explanation lies in an observation

49. A. Grenfell Price makes the best case for the white man in the hot countries, but even he admits that in the Caribbean during the seventeenth century, the insecurity of life in the islands, wars, and disease made existence discouraging. "One can, perhaps, go further and say that under such a policy and treatment it was almost impossible for white workers to succeed." *White Settlers in the Tropics*, 21, 23, 27–8, 249; Pares, "Merchants and Planters," 19.

made long ago by Herman Merivale: where Negro slavery prevails extensively, no white man is industrious.[50]

Despite the limitations inherent in bondage, many features of the African heritage made it possible for the black man to adjust to the new environment. When the Negroes were brought to the West Indies, they came to a better environment because the Northeast Trade Winds kept the Caribbee Isles cooler than the steaming equatorial homelands in Africa. Moreover they were given food similar to the diet they were used to: yams, bananas, plantains, and fruits, and in time, refuse, though edible, salted fish from New England. The more affluent planters also fed their slaves turtle meat and salt beef, and allowed them to raise their own chickens. The huts, or houses, in which the blacks lived on the West Indian plantations closely resembled their African dwellings (Plate 8), and in many instances after 1660, intelligent masters provided well-built houses for "their people," which visitors from Europe thought superior to the shelters of the white indentured servants.

Far better than the white servants or the newly freed men, the Negroes were able to live as families and to develop a genuine sense of community life which they expressed so fascinatingly in music and the dance. Herein lay an inestimable human advantage, which was denied the bulk of the whites. Such enumerations as survive show that the sex ratio was about three to two, which made this possible. Masters had grasped the fact that the Negro men worked better and were more tractable when they had wives and children, and, as in Ligon's time, they usually tried to procure wives for their men or to bring separated couples together on one plantation. The vast majority of the blacks proved willing, or at least remained amenable, to chattel slavery when they were treated well, and under careful supervision worked as effectively as most white servants. Some strong-minded Negroes rebelled or ran away as did some whites of the same stripe, but the capacity of Africans fresh from the Coast to adapt themselves to the New World of the Caribbean and to many of the white man's ways under slavery was nothing short of miraculous.

That the Africans were a selected people is a truth that cannot

50. Herman Merivale, *Lectures on Colonisation and Colonies* (London, 1841), I, 59–60.

be passed by, and if one accepts present-day assertions about a fundamental equality among races, they represented a choice of human beings that was superior to the selection of white Europeans who were sent to the West Indies. From a social point of view, it may be said that in the English West Indian colonies, a body of inferior whites was supplanted by a much more numerous and superior body of blacks from West Africa.

Behind this social revolution lay Dutch persuasiveness backed by prompt and relatively inexpensive services for every need of the planters, for in spite of the fact that all these social conditions contributed substantially to the substitution of black labor for white in the Lesser Antilles, the primary determinant was economic. Edward Gibbon Wakefield (one of the great authorities of all time) made this clear in 1851: "Hitherto in this world, labour has never been employed on any considerable scale, with constancy and in combination, except by one or two means; either by hiring, or by slavery of some kind. . . . Slavery is evidently a make-shift for hiring; a proceeding to which recourse is had, only when hiring is impossible or difficult. . . . The method of hiring would be preferred if there was a choice: it is adopted because at the time and under the circumstances there is no other way of getting labourers to work with constancy and in combination." [51]

The English colonies of the Caribbean and Spanish Main provide perfect illustrations of this profound generalization. As Gibbon Wakefield said, there was no choice. Freemen would not work for

51. Gibbon Wakefield first advanced this view in *England and America: A Comparison of the Social and Political State of Both Nations* (London, 1834), II, 1–46; and elucidated it in final form in *A View of the Art of Colonization, in Letters Between a Statesman and a Colonist* (London, 1851), 322–30, from which the quotation is taken. This important book was reprinted at Oxford in 1934, with an introduction by James Collier. The pertinent passages of Wakefield are printed in Guy S. Callender's *Selections from the Economic History of the United States,* 738, 742–8. A lengthy and thorough sociological treatment of the subject is by Herman J. Nieboer, *Slavery as an Industrial System* (2d ed., The Hague, 1910); and for a recent formulation, with a model, by an economist, Evsey D. Domar, *The Causes of Slavery: An Hypothesis* (The Rand Corp., n.d., P-3482), and *Journal of Economic History,* XXX (1970), 18–32. Wakefield also held that "Slave labour is on the whole much more costly than the labour of hired freemen. . . ." Today it is impossible to determine whether this was true in the Caribbean plantations. In any event, hired labor in sufficient numbers could never be secured. Wakefield, *A View of the Art of Colonization*, 3.

wages, and they found what they thought was a way out in migration. Lord Willoughby was right that Barbados would have to provide some kind of "a comfortable livelihood for the meaner sort" to keep them on the island. The shift from white to black labor had begun shortly after 1640 on the cotton plantations, but the voracious requirements of the expanding sugar culture speeded the transformation after 1645 in Barbados, then St. Christopher and Nevis. After 1660 the influx of servants ceased, even the Irish peasants avoided the Caribbees, and very few were willing to try Jamaica.

Karl Ritter pointed out 130 years ago that the plantation system originated from the close relationship between sugar-growing and the manufacture of sugar, and that it prospered in the tropics. In the planters' view, Negro slaves were both cheaper and more plentiful; they were also as capable in performing plantation tasks. An African slave could be purchased in 1650 for as low as £7, and at the end of the period for from £17 to £22, and the planter had his labor as long as he lived. A white servant cost about £10, and one got only three or four years' work out of him if he lived that long. Food, shelter, and clothing costs ran about the same for both kinds of laborers. There was truly no choice, not even between two kinds of bondage.[52]

When the balance is struck, it is abundantly evident that in the English (and French) West Indian plantations, all of the credits went into the black column and most of the debits into the white. Physically, psychologically, socially, culturally, the African black was better suited for the work in the tropical Sugar Colonies than the ordinary white European. If the planters were to expand their acreage and increase their production of sugar to meet the constantly widening European demand, resort to black labor was inevitable. With this vital economic problem solved, however, there still remained the great question of what form the societies on these islands would take.

52. Leo Waibel, "The Climatic Theory of the Plantation: A Critique," in *Geographical Review,* XXXI (1942), 307–10.

IX

Plantation People and Staple Crops

THE MOST WIDELY ACCEPTED BELIEF about the English colonies in the Caribbean during the seventeenth century is that the planters confined their activities almost exclusively after 1660 to the growing and processing of sugar. This has very little foundation in fact. The extent and rate of advance out of the original jungle were very uneven: Barbados, Surinam, Antigua, and Jamaica had each reached a different stage by 1690, and not even Barbados had achieved anything like a monoculture by the close of the period. In fact, the word "monoculture," like most jargon terms, is not only misleading but undescriptive. A better understanding of the state of agriculture in the islands and in Surinam may be had if we distinguish carefully between crops raised by small landholders and those grown by the large planters. In common, the colonists did carry specialization in staples for export to such a degree that, for the first time in recorded history, they thought it more profitable to import most of their food than to grow it themselves.

To satisfy rapidly rising demands in Western Europe for all sorts of tropical commodities, English, Dutch, and French merchants called for more and more produce from the planters of the West Indies. The primacy of sugar among them must not be permitted to conceal the importance of other colonial staples in contributing to the unprecedented expansion of agriculture in the English dominions.

II

In nearly every colony, the fifteen years before 1665 may properly be called the era of The Great Clearing. The first requirement for expanding Caribbean agriculture was to reduce the forests and jungle areas to arable fields free of all stumps. Little ground had been cleared beyond the littoral of each island before 1650. The cutting away of the jungle underbrush, felling of trees, and grubbing-up of roots and stumps was a time-consuming undertaking that called for the labor of many men with strong backs; it was by far the hardest kind of labor. Only a few acres could be cleared at a time, and it was only land hunger among recently freed servants and the insatiable appetite for profits from sugar that forced men inland after 1650.[1]

To make way for sugar and cotton fields, the Barbadians systematically denuded their island of its primordial vegetation in about fifteen years as they moved away from the seacoast. Lord Willoughby requested his English agents in 1651 to send out promptly: "24 sawse . . . The Timber of this cuntry is very hard and therefore the tooles would be made accordingly, as . . . six iron crose . . . 500 pounds of steele for pickaxes. . . ." Some selective lumbering of cedars, bully-trees, and locusts went on to provide beams and boards for mills and houses, barrel heads, crude furniture, utensils, and to fencing fields. In the arduous tasks of clearing, the white servants, chiefly Irish, proved reluctant and unsatisfactory axe and pick men, sawyers, and grubbers, and the free whites shrank from the strenuous tasks of clearing. Black slaves could be ordered to the work and, besides, turned out to be far more willing and capable at the job; many of them preferred work in the woods to hoeing sugar canes or rows of cotton in the open sun-drenched fields. Good timber was disappearing so rapidly

1. A survey of the plantation in Barbados owned jointly by Sir Anthony Ashley Cooper and Gerard Hawtayne in 1652 gives 95 acres of "Standing woode," and 105 acres planted in several crops out of a total of 205 acres. Davis Coll., VIII, Envelope 9. For the extent of the land cleared in 1650, based on Ligon's map, see Watts, *Man's Influence on the Vegetation of Barbados,* fig. 8, pp. 39–45; Merrill, *Historical Geography of St. Kitts and Nevis,* Map 1, pp. 32, 37; J. S. Beard, *The Natural Vegetation of the Windward and Leeward Islands* (London, 1949).

from the interior of the island by 1655 that Thomas Modyford predicted the end of the supply; and the Assembly soon passed an act to prevent greedy planters from encroaching on their neighbors' lands by cutting down "marked and timber trees of a good value" by setting a fine of 500 pounds of sugar for anyone felling a boundary tree and 100 pounds for cutting down any other tree.[2]

Such legislation notwithstanding, the remaining timber and underbrush vanished from all but the deepest gullies and a few inaccessible spots in the hilly and unproductive northeastern part of Barbados. When John Reid arrived in August 1665 he made a remark, which both Governor Atkins and Governor Dutton repeated in later years, that the whole island "appeared to be one Garden." From Tobago in 1667 came word that "at the Barbadoes all the trees are destroyed, soe that wanting wood to boyle their sugar, they are forced to send for coales to England." The Barbadians, finding the Newcastle product too costly, bought quantities of timber from Antigua up to 1669, when the authorities of that island forbade further exports in order to preserve wood for their own inhabitants. St. Lucia and Tobago were "very wealthy in large Timber Trees fit for all uses," and Barbadians sailed there to cut wood for house timbers and, especially, for cedar rollers for their sugar mills. In answering queries from London in 1676, Governor Jonathan Atkins said "that there is not a foot of land in Barbadoes that is not employed even to the very seaside." At the end of this period the need for wood of all kinds was very great, and the only sort of fuel available for boiling sugar was the stalks of Indian and Guinea (sorghum) corn.[3]

2. In 1650 Richard Ligon spoke of fencing made of "faln trees, with the ends laid cross upon one another," but which "were apt to rot" and decay fast; they were slowly replaced by plantings of the "physic-nut" tree, which the cattle avoided. *Barbados,* 66, 73; Watts, *Man's Influence on the Vegetation of Barbados,* 39–40; Willoughby to Edward Lincolne, Welbeck MSS, VIII, 49 (Davis Coll., I, Envelope 29); Thurloe, *State Papers,* III, 565; *Acts of Barbados* (Hall), 25; and for the restriction upon a clergyman using or "disposing of any would" on the glebe tract in St. Michael's Parish, *JBMHS,* XIV, 136, 173; XV, 17.

3. Sir Richard Dutton wrote home in 1681: "as for the Countrey, it is one great Citty adorned with gardens." Dutton to Blathwayt, March 15, 1680/1, Blathwayt Papers (Colonial Williamsburg), XXX; PRO: CO 1/19, fol. 91; CO 1/21, fol. 171; CO 29/2, fol. 49; *CSPC, 1675–76,* pp. 419, 422; William Dampier, "Two Voyages to the Bay of Campeachy," [1674–75], in *Collection*

Being of volcanic origin, the islands of St. Christopher, Nevis, and Montserrat consisted of high mountains surrounded by a certain amount of littoral and arable lowlands on which nearly every vestige of the original natural vegetation had given way to fields of sugar canes, cotton, and tobacco. Only on the mountain tops on St. Christopher could one still see thick woods in 1672. In fact, Governor Stapleton wrote home this same year, "most of the Islands are destitute of timber, Antigua only excepted." Every bit of timber had been cut down in the lowlands for sugar fires and the construction of buildings. Complaint was made against the governor of St. Thomas in 1682 for allowing the Danes to settle there because the Leeward Island merchants "have no place to get timber but from the Virgin Islands." At Nevis, Dr. Hans Sloane reported in 1687, the cleared ground extended almost to the top of the central mountain, where a small stand of timber still sheltered runaway slaves.[4]

No shortage of wood hampered the planters in Surinam or Jamaica, because of the great expanses of unsettled land in each place. When the English returned the province on the Main to the Dutch in 1667, the banks of the Surinam and Commewijne rivers and their tributaries were lined with plantations, close by one another, but settlement had not yet moved into the back country.[5]

Of the islands under English rule, Jamaica was nearly always a special case during these years. From the maps of 1671, 1677, and 1684 may be traced the slow spreading of settlement along the south shore and inland up the valleys of the streams flowing southward into the Caribbean, Old Harbour, and the roadstead of Port Royal. Along the extensive north coast of the island only a few scattered plantations could be found; and natural savannas for grazing already existed. The interior of Jamaica, especially the northeastern portion, was very hilly and mountainous, and

---

of Voyages (London, 1729), II, Pt. II, 4–5; John Poyntz, *The Present Prospect of the Famous and Fertile Island of Tobago* (London, 1683), 4; Sloane, *Voyage to the Islands,* I, 34.

4. Richard Blome, *Description of the Island of Jamaica . . .* (London, 1672), 3, 11, 77, 98; Sloane, *Voyage to the Islands,* I, 42; Merrill, *Historical Geography of St. Kitts and Nevis,* 32, 37; *CSPC, 1669–74,* p. 392; *1681–85,* p. 323.

5. See Plate 10; also Surinam and Commewijne rivers, *Blathwayt Atlas.* Vol. I. *The Maps,* ed. Jeannette D. Black (Providence, 1970), Map 38.

covered throughout with tall forests in 1667. This was still true in 1689, though Dr. Hans Sloane mentioned that on the plantations where firewood was scarce, *bagasse,* or marc, and Guinea corn-stalks were coming into use as a fuel "where a less degree of Fire is sufficient." The shortage of fuel was largely the consequence of transportation costs, for Jamaica still had a superabundance of forest land.[6]

Everywhere the clearing of land proceeded with frustrating slowness. "According to the custome of the country," Cary Helyar wrote to his brother William, squire of East Coker in Somerset in 1671/2, a plantation is best made in Jamaica by beginning with an overseer and two or three Negroes, who can clear about three acres of ground during the first year on which they can plant provisions and some merchantable crop. Gradually, "in seven years' time it will produce a hopefull business . . . This Sir is what my eyes see every day, so it is no new thing. . . ." John Taylor was more specific: slaves working with axes and hoes cut the wood down to knee-high and burned it when it had dried. Following the next rains, they hoed the ground and planted peas. Then they prepared more ground, none of it being fit for canes the first year, because the roots had first to rot and the stumps be pulled up. Therefore they planted maize, tobacco, and cassava. The crops for the second year were ordinarily potatoes and yams, and with the third year the ground was totally cleared of roots and stumps and ready for sugar canes, indigo plants, or cotton. Settlers on all of the islands followed this same routine in clearing their land, which, to them, represented freshly created wealth.[7]

Inevitably the deforestation disturbed the ecology of the English islands. Nearly all of the plants of Barbados today, like the first food and staple plants brought by Captain Powell from Guiana in

6. BM: Egerton MSS, 2395, fol. 609; Sloane, *Voyage to the Islands,* I, xv; II, 19; *Novissima et Accuratissima Jamaicae Descriptis per Johanem Ogiluium Cosmographun Regium* (London, 1671); James Moxon, *New Mapp of Jamaica according to the last Survey* [2d state of Map of Nov. 1672] (London, 1677); Charles Bochart and Humphrey Knollys, *New & Exact Map of Jamaica* (London, 1684), all in JCB; also *Blathwayt Atlas.*

7. Cary to William Helyar, Jan. 22, 1671/2, Helyar MSS (Somerset Record Office); [John Taylor] Multum in Parvo, or Taylor's Historie of his Life and Travells in America and other parts [1688] (MS, Institute of Jamaica), II, 532–5.

1627, are introduced species; virtually none of the original vegetation survives. Ever since the late fifties, about 80 per cent of the land had been covered with sugar canes, as a comparison of the maps of Ligon, 1650 (Plate 2) and Richard Ford (about 1674) demonstrates. Likewise the original fauna was killed off. Inasmuch as the human beings of all three races residing there had all come in recent times, the ecological transformation of Barbados was almost total. The unfortunate consequences were soil erosion and loss of moisture. A dense tropical forest with its two canopy layers, which were so admirably suited for the island's deficiency of moisture, had been replaced by an open landscape; all had been destroyed by man in less than four decades. Large sugar plantations dominated the Barbadian scene after 1665. The alteration of the island since 1627 "and the speed with which this was effected," a geographer tells us, "must be without parallel in an agricultural area." Further, the deforestation of Nevis, St. Christopher, and Montserrat brought about ecological changes made only slightly less radical by the presence of high mountains.[8]

The clearing of land in the interiors of the islands became possible only by the opening of roads where there had been no access, save by an occasional path, before 1650. Thus the hauling or dragging out of timber and, eventually, of produce was facilitated. At Barbados, imported bulk commodities, such as wine, olive oil, and corn, could not be transported to plantations more than two miles from The Indian Bridge, and then on the backs of asses or camels, or increasingly on the backs or heads of black slaves. The growing number of sugarworks forced the Assembly into passing two acts for clearing public roads before 1649. Upon complaint in 1652 that the highways were "very bad, and impassable to the great hindrance of trade," another law provided for the appointment of commissioners of the highways for each parish. The importance attached to such service is evidenced by the prominent planters chosen: Lieutenants Colonel Robert Hooper and Richard Rous, Mr. Francis Raynes, William Vassall, and Captain James

8. [Richard Ford] *New Map of the Island of Barbados* (London, *ca.* 1674), Blathwayt Atlas (JCB); also in *Blathwayt Atlas,* No. 32. Watts, *Man's Influence on the Vegetation of Barbados,* 34–5, 36, 38, 45; Montserrat Island, 1673 (JCB); also *Blathwayt Atlas,* No. 30.

Holdip, Colonel Lewis Morris, and Lieutenant Colonel Benjamin Beringer—some of the most influential and richest men of the island. They received power to appoint surveyors of the highways and to order the building of roads. In St. Michael's Parish a stone bridge was ordered rebuilt across the Gully, and a gravel way to The Bridge Town. The next year another act passed for mending existing roads, and among the new commissioners designated were Colonel James Drax, Thomas Modyford, John Burch, and Christopher Codrington.[9]

A law of 1654 authorized the laying of a tax to support highway repairs and an additional one to pay for the high costs of the new foot-and-horse bridge and causeway. This last measure levied a fine of 2000 pounds of sugar on any freeman and three years of extra service for any servant who should cut down the posts erected to keep carts off the new structure. The highway act of 1654 stipulated further that common roads "in the woods" were to be not less than 40 feet wide, and 20 feet in the open. Two years later, the "Trustees" were directed to set a rate requiring that the labor of one servant (including blacks) for one day be furnished by every owner of five acres of land, and each landless freeman had to work one day himself, as did all the owners of less than five acres. Thus did the Barbadians apply the well-known English parish highway policy to their island. By 1657 all of the parishes elected annually a surveyor of the highways. A new law of 1662 provided for widening the thoroughfares: 24 feet in the open, 40 feet with the woods on one side, and 60 feet through "standing wood." Opening the forests and jungle for roads in itself was a phase of The Great Clearing; often it meant little more, for "in many places the Highwayes are very deep or scarcely passable." Though in 1670 an old planter, Robert Rich, deplored that the wet season "makes the Roads not Cartable," with the passage of time Barbados came to have roads fit for carriages as well as for horsemen and carts, and they drew favorable comment from more than one English visitor.[10]

9. Schomburgk, *History of Barbados,* 184; Ligon, *Barbados,* 39; *Acts and Statutes of Barbados* (Jennings), 103–6, 154–9.

10. The path from Rio Cobre to Sixteen-mile Walk had gone around the mountain until 1670 when "a very ingenious Gentleman," Cary Helyar, cut a short one via Hollow Rock. Dampier, *Voyages,* II, Pt. II, 7; *JBMHS,* XIV, 128–9,

Road building began later in the other islands, as did The Great Clearing, though as early as 1625, the English and French joined in cutting "a path round the Island" at St. Christopher for common defense. Eventually this way was widened, and from it paths or lanes led inland. Some narrow roads had been opened into the woods of Antigua before 1669, for in that year the Assembly ordered that all of them be enlarged and kept clean. The hilly terrain of Montserrat made boats the only means of access; a map of 1673 shows not a single road, and at Jamaica, too, the many streams suitable for light craft and canoes served as the most used highways. Not until 1676 did the Jamaican Assembly order the vestrymen of each parish to choose annually four surveyors of the highways, and emphasize the duty of inland parishes to contribute to the building of the first roads. In 1682 Jamaica followed the Barbadian law of 1654 in standardizing the width of highways. The presence of so many large streams made bridges an important concern. John Helyar of Bybrook Plantation said in 1686 that "as long as our Roads are but for horses and mules," the cheapest transport is along the waterways in canoes. Nearly a century later, Edward Long attributed the slow development of Jamaica to the lack of good roads. All that the colonists had done was to cut down trees as close to the ground as possible, and the stumps were left to be flattened out by the wheels of carts and carriages. Once a year they filled the ruts and hollows with loose mould; the rains always rendered the roads impassable.[11]

At the close of the period, the ecology of Barbados and the four most important of the Leeward Islands had been irrevocably transformed from their former balanced state. It had taken much toil and many decades for white men and black to carry out The Great Clearing of the jungle and the slaughter of its animal denizens. They had considered this necessary in order that men might arrange the landscape and erect plantation houses and buildings. Charles de Rochefort's description of St. Christopher about 1658

132, 137; *Acts of Barbados* (Hall), 45–51; *Acts and Statutes of Barbados* (Jennings), 171–2; Ogilby, *America,* 380.

11. Harlow, *Colonising Expeditions,* 4; *CSPC, 1669–74,* p. 48; PRO: CO 1/36, fols. 150–51; *Abridgement of Laws of Plantations,* 108–10, 213–17; Long, *History of Jamaica,* I, 466–7; John to William Helyar, Nov. 30, 1686, Helyar MSS.

would have applied to all islands thirty years later: "The delightful bright-green of the Tobacco, planted exactly by the line, the pale-yellow of the Sugar Canes [with their tassels], when come to maturity, and the dark-green of Ginger and Potatoes, make so delyghtful a Landskip, as must cause an extraordinary reaction to the unwearied eye." Once accomplished, what had formerly been free or comparatively cheap land was transmuted into pounds sterling for those who possessed it. Governor Jonathan Atkins gave it as his opinion in 1669 that "whoever will have land in Barbadoes must pay dearer for it than for land in England." [12]

III

From the times of their founding to about 1650, the English Caribbean colonies stood out as places of refuge and opportunity where ordinary white freemen might acquire small plots of land in fee simple. By 1666, however, it had become clear to all concerned that a very few large proprietors had succeeded in taking over much of the land on Nevis, and that at Barbados consolidation of small tobacco and cotton tracts into estates of 200 acres or more devoted largely to sugar cane was well under way. On St. Christopher the small planters were almost wiped out by the French conquest of 1666, while at Antigua and Montserrat rich proprietors were rapidly gaining the upper hand. A special situation existed in Jamaica. Nevertheless, at the opening of the great Anglo-French conflict in 1689, the small landholders still figured very prominently in the Caribbean economy, as an examination of their agricultural activities reveals.

An unforeseen consequence of the removal of the original vegetation from the Caribbee Isles was the immediate introduction of not only such promising staple plants as tobacco, cotton, sugar cane, indigo, and ginger, but of hundreds of other species from the Spanish Main, Europe, Africa, and Asia. For the king's use in 1690, James Reed, "gardener," collected the seeds and listed the names of 129 species that grew in Barbados, every one of which had been imported since 1627. A second list sent from the island

12. Rochefort, in Davies, *Caribby-Islands,* 22; *CSPC, 1675–76,* p. 419.

two years later contained the names of 144 different imported plants. Here is convincing proof of the ecological revolution, which, though it took place first and most completely at Barbados, soon transformed St. Christopher and the other Leeward Islands. Among the new plants were delicious fruits previously alien to the taste of the ordinary Englishman: figs, oranges, lemons, limes, mangoes, shaddocks, and pawpaws. There were also many varieties of melons, spices, and cereals, of which Indian and Guinea (sorghum) corn stood out, besides a profusion of brilliantly colored flowering shrubs and trees. Of special significance for the diet of the African slaves were plantains, yams, and bananas, as well as coconut and palm trees. Similarly, such European domestic animals as sheep, goats, hogs, and cattle had been brought across the Atlantic along with all sorts of barnyard fowl.[13]

Many of the alien plants could be raised easily on tiny patches of ground or in small groves by the owners of small freeholds of ten acres or less, on cleared land not rich enough for sugar canes, or on difficult terrain not suited for that culture. Some small farmers grew their own provisions, Indian or Guinea corn, yams, some fruits, such as the pineapple which they came to relish above all others. Now and then one of these planters produced a small surplus to sell in the markets at the seaports. In general, however, the marketable harvest of fruits and roots came off the larger plantations, and the majority of the small proprietors did not grow sufficient food even for themselves.[14]

Tobacco was the poor man's crop. Production of it as an export commodity declined in every island with the shrinking of the white populations, and its value to the economy was almost negligible by 1690; the Europeans wanted only the far superior Chesapeake leaf. The Barbadians gave up tobacco after 1660 because of its poor quality and the greater returns from cotton or sugar cane; what little they grew was for home consumption. At St. Christopher,

13. BM: Sloane MSS, 4070, fols. 17–18, 19–21; 3332, fol. 28 (two lists of plants collected in Barbados for the king's use by James Reed, 1690, 1692, and a list of 140 plants from the island, 1693). For a geographer's view, Watts, *Man's Influence on the Vegetation of Barbados,* 46–55.

14. "Orchards and Gardens are rare in this island," Oldmixon wrote in 1708 in a useful assessment of Barbadian agriculture. *British Empire in America,* II, 101–2.

the French occupation in 1666 drove out the small tobacco planters, and very few of them returned after 1670 to try it again. In 1673 Governor Stapleton failed even to mention tobacco in a survey of the island's crops, and in 1682 Barbot reported that the weed had been abandoned. Jamaica was reputed to make the best tobacco in the West Indies in 1663, but its quality, being unregulated, was uneven; and the Council, hoping to recover the island's credit, ordered the justices of the peace to nominate sworn persons in each parish to serve as "fit Rollers and Makers of Tobacco." The leaf rated among the "excellent commodities" in 1674, but nevertheless it was never again important enough to be grown on large plantations.[15]

Only on the smaller islands did tobacco continue as the staple of marginal planters. Up through the last quarter of the seventeenth century, the Irish colonists of Montserrat went on growing tobacco; their leaf, superior and better graded than that of the other islands, passed as money by a law of 1667. The Antiguans, and the settlers they sent over to Barbuda and Anguilla, raised tobacco because, being "generally very poor," they lacked the capital to shift over to other staples. Fortunately, the Dutch from St. Eustatius were still willing to buy their leaf, and also that of Nevis and Montserrat. Governor Sir Thomas Lynch learned at Port Royal in 1672 that Dutch sloops and colonial shallops had carried only 400,000 pounds of Leeward Island leaf to Statia. This was 70,732 pounds less than St. Christopher alone had shipped to London back in 1638. Montserrat sold 48,000 pounds of its chief crop in England, along with 200,000 pounds of sugar, in a year ending July 1684; the remainder of the crop went to Statia, a market where tobacco was also on its way out as a profitable commodity. By 1690 tobacco had ceased to be a staple for the Caribbean colonies.[16]

15. Richard Ford mentions the raising of some "Tobacco, but not near so much as formerly." *Map of Barbados,* about 1674. Earlier, Ogilby said that uncertain rainfall prejudiced the tobacco crop. *America,* 380; *CSPC, 1574–1660,* p. 295; *1669–74,* p. 548; Barbot, in Churchill, *Voyages,* V, 657; Jamaica Council Minutes, I, 70–71; Blathwayt, History and State of Jamaica, 56–9.

16. *CSPC, 1661–68,* pp. 204, 587; *1669–74,* pp. 226–7; *1677–80,* p. 575; Barbot, in Churchill, *Voyages,* V, 662; Blome, *Description of Jamaica,* 105; *Acts of Assembly . . . of Montserrat,* 16–17; Oldmixon, *British Empire in America,* II, 180; Higham, *Leeward Islands,* 184–7.

The presence of fertile land in Jamaica, the granting of thirty-acre tracts to freemen on easy terms, and the acute shortage of white population (bound as well as free) combined to encourage the raising of minor staples on that island, as they did nowhere else. From a native tree they got the highly valued pimento, or Jamaica pepper (allspice), and, because the pods grew on the ends of the branches, they usually cut off whole limbs, thereby gradually destroying the species. A number of dyewoods grew on the island, such as brasiletto, guaiacum, redwood, and fustic, as well as good cedar trees for shingles and boards, and the all-around coconut tree from which might be had masts, planks, treenails, oakum, and oil. These trees freed the planters, for a time, from reliance upon lumber from New England. An item eagerly sought by the Europeans was tortoise shell, and large amounts of it were shipped away.[17]

Before 1655, the Spanish had made use of the grasslands of the 350,000 acres of savannas of Jamaica for grazing, and the poorer English followed their example with the pasturing of cattle and horses, and the foraging of hogs. About 1675, Governor Lynch imported cattle from Cuba, which brought the price of £12 to £14 a head down to £4 to £5, but the settlers carelessly allowed the breeds of these and other domestic animals to degenerate, and meats were being imported in 1690. On the savannas, the cattle and horses were driven at night into palisaded pens and the swine into sties called "crawls." Grazing required fewer "cowboys" than farming did field hands, and afforded marketable commodities for many a poor freeman from land that he did not have to purchase. The Jamaicans tanned some leather and rendered quantities of tallow from slaughtered beasts. Third in the island's exports for 1673 were the thousands of "large and good hides." A map of 1684 shows large savannas, with cattle pens and hog crawls clearly marked. One of them, called Cowhides, belonged to Peter Beckford, e'er long to be Jamaica's richest planter.[18]

17. Oldmixon, *British Empire in America,* II, 330–31; Thurloe, *State Papers,* II, 547; Sloane, *Voyage to the Islands,* II, 8.

18. Old Cromwellian soldiers were still slaughtering wild hogs outside of parish limits as late as 1664, though the supply was dwindling rapidly. They sold the meat, smoked or jerked, at 15*s.* to 25*s.* a hundredweight (112 lbs.) to planters and merchants. BM: Add. MSS, 11,410, fols. 19b, 20; Thurloe, *State Papers,* III, 546; Bryan Edwards, *History, Civil and Commercial, of the British Colonies*

Ginger, pimento, and dyewoods, minor crops all, were raised by the small planters. Using sugar, they often preserved ginger, orange peel, and various fruits for the English market. Antigua also supplied quantities of lignum vitae from which Jamaican turners made wooden platters and bowls. Taken altogether in the English islands, these secondary products, including cotton, indigo, and cocoa, never approached sugar in bulk or sterling value; nevertheless, they cannot be dismissed as of no economic importance. Legally imported into England, they yielded substantial customs duties, and reached a ready market, while in the islands they enabled the lesser planters to make a meager living.[19]

The small holding, ranging from three to ten or twelve acres in Barbados and probably more in the Leeward Islands—even to thirty acres and upward in Jamaica—was farmed by the owner and his "family," consisting of children (if any), a few indentured servants, and, for the middling planter, one or more black slaves. Many of the small and middling masters fell hopelessly into debt and were forced to mortgage their lands, or not infrequently to migrate, but it was these secondary commodities that enabled more of them to survive than is usually realized. A census of Barbados made in 1683 lists 4056 householders, 17,187 free inhabitants, and 2381 bound white servants. If we assume that the 365 great planters of three years earlier either remained constant, or increased slightly, there still remained thousands of freemen who were neither wage earners nor artisans. They were freeholders and freemen who cultivated the minor staples on small acreages.[20]

---

in the West Indies (London, 1793), I, 301; Taylor, Multum in Parvo, II, 335–7; *CSPC, 1681–85,* p. 500; Blathwayt, History and State of Jamaica, 21; *Present State of Jamaica* (London, 1683), 44; Sloane, *Voyage to the Islands,* I, xvii; *Laws of Jamaica . . . 1683, To which is added* [Francis Hanson's] *A Short Account of the Island . . . about the year 1682* (Wood); Oldmixon, *British Empire in America,* II, 336–7; Blome, *Description of Jamaica,* 10; *New & Exact Map of Jamaica,* 1684.

19. *MHS Colls.,* 5th ser., VIII, 401; Oldmixon, *British Empire in America,* II, 33, 180, 330; Spörri, *Americanische Reise,* 22.

20. The Census of 1680 is in PRO: CO 1/44, fols. 142–379; that of 1684 in BM: Sloane MSS, 2441, fols. 5–22. See especially Richard Dunn's analysis of the enumeration of 1680, *WMQ,* 3d ser., XXVI, 12 (Table III), 17 (Table IV); Higham, *Leeward Islands,* 190.

IV

Year by year, the small farms (or plantations as they were grandiosely called) of the islands under English rule were being gradually consolidated into large estates, which more properly fitted the term *plantation,* or, in such colonies as Surinam, Antigua, and Jamaica above all, great tracts were being opened on freshly cleared land. A plantation was a form of landed estate upon which tropical products such as tobacco, cotton, indigo, cacao, or sugar were raised by gangs of white or black or red laborers in partial or complete bondage. The owners and overseers of the plantation were white men born in Europe or in the islands. As mentioned earlier, this institution originated with the Portuguese in Brazil and, at the instance of Dutch merchants and traders, borrowed by the English and French in the Caribbean. It served as an effective device for organizing large-scale production of staple crops. Moreover, and in some ways more important, the plantation was a way of life as well as an economic institution; it had no clear-cut historical precedent, and it was a development peculiar to the New World.[21]

It would be historically unsound to assume that any one of the islands developed a monoculture of sugar in the seventeenth century, for nearly every planter with a large estate went in for *mixed agriculture.* Richard Ligon described in 1650 the use of land on the Hilliard-Modyford plantation in Barbados:

Acreage	
Sugar	200
Woodland	120
Pasture	80
Provisions	70
Tobacco	30
Ginger	5
Cotton	5
Total	510

21. *Encyclopedia of the Social Sciences* (New York, 1934), XII, 148–9, 152; Waibel, in *Geographical Review,* XXXII, 308–10.

William Waters owned a much smaller plantation consisting of 30 acres in 1657, of which 17 were uncleared and 13 were planted in sugar cane and provisions. Even after 1670, when the Barbados sugar culture was attaining its ultimate development, new plantations designed to produce sugar exclusively were expected to have only 80 acres out of 100 planted in canes, and the other 20 used for foods or for pasture.[22]

Although sugar was a most profitable crop, it never replaced cotton in Barbados and the Leeward Islands as it did tobacco. Actually the cotton culture expanded rapidly, and it could flourish on land where sugar would not grow satisfactorily. Henry Whistler listed sugar and cotton as the leading crops of Barbados in 1655, and six years later Dr. Spörri rated it next to sugar: "whole fields are planted. Every year cotton is raised from seed" and the plants grow six feet tall or higher. Governor Jonathan Atkins placed cotton second in the list of sixteen commodities he reported to the Lords of Trade and Plantations as late as 1676.[23]

Much cotton was planted in Jamaica. "I pray send mee worde whatt price good Cotton Bares Reddy ginned," Charles Sparke inquired in 1660 of his brother Arthur, citizen and fishmonger of London. Observant Edward Cranfield reported to Londoners in 1675 that Jamaica's cotton was "not inferiour to any in the Indies . . . The great Product and returns from New England made it very profittable, especially to the middle sort of Planters, that cannot compasse a Sugar work." Not until about 1680 did sugar emerge as the leading staple of Jamaica, and in that year the planters of that island exported 581 bags of cotton (110,390 pounds), and in the years 1688 and 1689, increased the amount to 903 bags (or 171,570 pounds).[24]

22. Ligon, *Barbados,* 22–3, 112; *Timehri,* VII, 16–43; Davis Coll., II, Envelope 5; PRO: CO 31/3, fols. 120–24; *CSPC, 1685–88,* pp. 93–4; Thomas, *Historical Account of . . . the West Indies,* II, 363–4.

23. *JBMHS,* V, 184; Spörri, *Americanische Reise,* 20–21; Thomas, *Historical Account of . . . the West Indies,* II, 369–70; PRO: CO 1/37, fol. 23. In shipments of 2000 to 3000 pounds, cotton-wool brought to Newbury in Massachusetts-Bay by Captain Abraham Toppan seems to have been profitable. Joshua Coffin, *Sketch of the History of Newbury . . .* (Boston, 1815), 112.

24. Sparke Papers, Feb. 20, 1659/60 (Royal Commonwealth Society); PRO: CO 138/2, fol. 116; CO 390/6, fols. 16, 18.

In his comments on the four Leeward Islands in 1672, Governor Stapleton placed cotton third after sugar and tobacco in exports. In a single year, 1678, Barbados, Jamaica, Nevis, and St. Christopher shipped the remarkable total of 57,409 pounds of cotton to other English colonies; Barbados was responsible for 52,989 pounds of that total, of which New England imported 54,403 pounds. New England ships appear to have taken much of the crop in 1686. Among those entered at Boston that year were: the *Nevis Merchant,* Captain Timothy Clark, with 15 bags; the *Adventure*, John Welch, with 100 pounds; the *Lydia,* from Anguilla, with 31 bags; and from Antigua, the *Hannah,* with 16 bags, and the *Adventure,* with 15 bags. Cotton was also being grown in the new settlements in the Bahamas, and John Graves, the collector of customs there in 1688, insisted that it was "the best of Cotton in all the Indies." [25]

Everywhere in the English Antilles in 1690 cotton stood second to sugar among the exportable staples. Admittedly it was far behind in acreage and value, but production of the plant had increased enormously since 1650. This increment was due in part to the requirements of a rising Caribbean population. Black slaves ginned the wool in the islands, and cloth for clothing, ships' sails, and hammocks, all consumed locally, were woven by females, red or black. (Plate 1) Dr. Griffith Hughes of Jamaica wrote that quantities of cottonseed oil were used by the inhabitants, who thought it would prevent and remove freckles. In 1668 the Barbados Assembly ordered the giving out of premiums for domestic processing of cotton-wool; in 1671 Mrs. Mary Parrott won "a flagon of plate of forty ounces weight," or its value in sugar, for producing 50 pounds of the best balls of "Cotton spun yarn"; and Rebecca, wife of John Devonish, received a gold chain worth £12 sterling for "the best bed, curtaine, valence, and furniture for a

25. At Bybrook Plantation in Jamaica, planted principally in sugar canes in 1685, the Helyars grew three bags of cotton worth £21 4*s*.8*d*. Helyar MSS, 1685. A bag contained 190 pounds. Papers of Robert Shrimpton and other Families, *ca.* 1675–1760 (MHS, MSS), Nov. 15, 1676; A. P. Thornton, "Some Statistics of West Indian Produce Shipping and Revenue, 1660–1685," in *Caribbean Historical Review,* II (1954), 256, 257, 259; PRO: Intercolonial exports, 1677–1678, CO 1/43, fol. 180; CO 5/848 (Mass. shipping), Pt. I, pp. 8–14; John Graves, *A Memorial: Or a Short Account of the Bahama Islands* (London, 1708), 5.

Chamber &c." Mary Parrott won the prize for cotton yarn again the next year. Deliverance Bourne was awarded one dozen silver spoons of 20 ounces weight for weaving "the finest piece of white Dimity" of 24 yards' length, and her husband John received the silver sugar box weighing 26 ounces for the best colored dimity. These encouragements to home industry seem to have lapsed after Mary Duke won a gold chain in May 1673 for "the best suit of curtains and valance." [26]

The principal stimulus to the expansion of the cotton culture in the British West Indies, however, came from the mounting demands of the cloth manufacturers of Lancashire for ever more amounts of "white wool." In 1654, the Manchester clothiers procured all the wool they needed from the Levant, and looked upon the supply from Barbados as "not worth naming of late years." The situation had altered noticeably in another six years as encouragement to raise cotton within the king's dominions became a cardinal feature of colonial policy; the Navigation Act of 1660 included cotton among the enumerated articles, which could only be carried to the possessions of the Crown. Englishmen began to import more and more of the West Indian cotton-wool at Liverpool as they came to realize that it was finer than the Levantine product. The duty on cotton in England was but a halfpenny a pound, and in the years 1680–84 Jamaica alone supplied 620,550 pounds (4137 bags) of cotton-wool, while the planters of Barbados sent home 2860 bags containing 543,400 pounds between 1680 and 1683. The Lancashire clothiers were apparently getting about 70 per cent of their ginned raw cotton from the West Indies in 1690, and Barbados still led all islands in the amount produced—a vital element in that island's economy. In less than a year, from May 11 to November 12, 1690, the merchants at Bridgetown shipped out 57,095 pounds of cotton to other plantations and 62,343 pounds to England; in the short period from November 13, 1690, to February 12, 1691, they dispatched an additional 13,677 pounds to the plantations, much of which doubtless was re-exported

26. For cotton-growing, ginning, and baling, see Labat, *Nouveau Voyage,* III, Chapter II, 30–46; *Recueil de planches* (Paris, 1672), I, plates I–V; William Hughes, *The American Physician . . .* (London, 1672), 68–71; Barbados Council Minutes, II, 153, 200–201, 285–6, 287–8; *CSPC, 1669–74,* p. 141.

to the Mother Country. A Barbados merchant, James Bates, wrote to Weston & Norris of Liverpool in July 1692 recalling that "about 20 yeares past we had a Constant trade from and to Liverpool . . . carried . . . on, to a good avail." [27]

Ginger was a profitable "enumerated" West Indian product, which has been overlooked. Although the small landowners grew some, most of it was raised on the larger estates where it was possible to "confect and preserve" the root with local sugar in "whole barrels full" for export. Jamaica was the main source for ginger, and in 1677–78 its planters shipped 16,240 pounds of it to England; in this year consignments of 12,396 and 2628 went out from St. Christopher and Barbados respectively. Some ginger was also grown in Nevis. The Leeward Islands and Barbados together exported in the years 1681–83 a remarkable total of 1,250,640 pounds of raw and preserved ginger in 13,894 bags weighing 90 pounds each.[28]

Another valuable enumerated tropical product was indigo, a blue dye much in demand on the Continent and in England, where the duty was 2*d*. a pound. Because it required a considerable outlay for vats and labor, it was grown chiefly on the middle-sized plantations. A glance at Plate 3 will confirm this. The making of it also demanded an exercise of good judgment during the period of fermentation before it was made into the hard cakes of dye. The planters of St. Christopher and Nevis manufactured large amounts of indigo; forty-seven works were reported in 1673. Christopher Jeaffreson sent 484 pounds of dye to England in 1676 along with a letter explaining that it passed as commodity money in the island, one ounce being worth a pound of sugar or three halfpence. A year later, however, he advised that "it is esteemed here a great folly for a man to expose his tyme or goods to the hazard

27. Wadsworth and Mann, *Cotton Trade and Industrial Lancashire,* 35*n*, 72*n*, 186; James Bates to Weston & Norris, July 11, 1692, Norris Papers (Liverpool City Library); Tryon, *Merchant's . . . Instructor,* 195–7; Charles Wilson, *England's Apprenticeship, 1603–1733* (London, 1965), 193, 200; Thornton, in *Caribbean Historical Review,* II, 257, 259, 260, 261, 263, 270; *Encyclopedia Britannica* (11th ed.), VII, 265; PRO: CO 396, fols. 26–7.

28. The English duty on ginger was a halfpenny a hundred pounds. Thornton, in *Caribbean Historical Review,* II, 257, 261; Spörri, *Americanische Reise,* 22; Barbot, in Churchill, *Voyages,* V, 654; Taylor, Multum in Parvo, II, 473.

of indigo or tobacco, sugar being now the only thriving and valuable commodity." But the price of sugar fell sharply, and in 1682 he thought indigo a better staple because its price was going up. He could grow two or three crops a year and make four or five cuttings, the whole being produced without great charge. "Were I upon the plantation" (Jeaffreson was now an absentee), "I would plant indigo, the profits of which the planters understand but halfe; having it in low esteeme, only because they made but small quantities, which was all that could be expected from so few hands, as everyone then had." [29]

Forty-nine indigo works on Jamaica turned out 49,000 weight of dye in 1670, and in two years' time sixty of them were operating; and in 1672, sixty-five. It was thought that Jamaica produced the best quality because of its light, sandy soil; at any rate more vats were being erected each year on the island, and during 1677–78 the Jamaicans exported 1355 pounds of indigo, which more than equaled the 1335 pounds from St. Christopher and Nevis in the same period. By 1684 the number of indigo plantations, which flourished on the savannas of Jamaica, numbered seventy-three.[30]

"A West Indian drink called *chocolate,*" first introduced into England about 1652, sold along with coffee and tea; its virtues "are hyperboliz'd upon every post in London," Hickeringill declared, and it became one of the popular drinks of Restoration England. When the English captured Jamaica in 1655, they found cacao or "Cocoa Walks," which had been planted by the Spaniards. Some of these "Walks" covered from ten to twelve acres on which the trees were set, six or seven feet apart as in an orchard. "The famed Chocoletta" was contained in pods, which young trees bore seven years after being planted. John Oldmixon said in 1708 that cacao

29. Between 1680 and 1684, Jamaica planters sent to England 33 hhds., 455 bbls., and 203 tierces of indigo. Thornton, in *Caribbean Historical Review,* V, 258, 260; Père Labat described all aspects of growing and preparing indigo in detail in *Nouveau Voyage,* I, 268–310, and plate facing p. 265. See also Elie Monnereau, *Le Parfait Indigotier* (Nouvelle édition, Amsterdam, 1765. JCB); Spörri, *Americanische Reise,* 21–2; *CSPC, 1669–74,* p. 548; Jeaffreson, *Young Squire,* I, 188, 205, 210, 222.

30. PRO: CO 138/1, fol. 81; Long, *History of Jamaica,* III, 681; map in Sloane, *Voyage to the Islands,* I, facing p. cliv; *New & Exact Map of Jamaica* (1684); Thomas, *Historical Account of . . . the West Indies,* II, 370.

was "at first the principal Invitation to peopling Jamaica," because it earned "so prodigious Profit with little Trouble." When Sir Thomas Modyford arrived as governor in 1664, he promptly planted cacao trees as an example to his neighbors. One of them, his protégé as well, was Cary Helyar, who desired to give over his trade as a merchant in Port Royal and become a planter. Writing to his brother in England in September 1670, Helyar described the six acres on which he had planted young cacao trees "out of a nursery"—probably the adjoining estate of Sir Thomas. He failed to mention the "great dryeth" of the previous summer when the cacao trees were blasted and sugar and indigo crops dried up. Governor Lynch went to the extreme of crossing over to Cuba to inquire of the Spaniards the cause of the failure. One reason may have been the inability of the planters to cultivate them, because they lacked the labor necessary to keep the walks—47 in all—in proper condition. Recovery came gradually; from 1680 to 1684, the planters exported to England 78½ tons, 361½ hogsheads, and 120 barrels of cocoa; but never again did it recover its former importance as a staple.[31]

To the Lords of Trade and Plantations in 1673, Governor Sir Thomas Lynch expressed his conviction that within six years' time, if Jamaica were well governed and defended, "it may produce as much sugars as Barbados." He was also certain that eventually cocoa, indigo, cotton, achiote (a dye), hides, and dyewoods would, together, exceed in value all the sugars produced. To weigh his judgments, we now turn to the famous sugar culture of the English islands in the Antilles.[32]

"The island is a gallant island," said Sir Francis Barrington of

31. Sir Thomas Modyford prepared "Directions about a Cocoa Walke," which would cost £257 10*s*. for 500 acres, 4 white servants, 7 Negro slaves, and overseer, tools, and maintenance for 6 months until provisions could be grown. It is printed in Blome, *Description of Jamaica,* 15–21; and Oldmixon, *British Empire in America,* 325, 328. On the popularity of chocolate in England: *Publick Advertiser,* June 22, 1657; Thomas Rugge, Mercurius Politicus Redevivus (MS: BM) s. v., 1659; Pepys, *Diary,* ed. Wheatley, II, 24; III, 5; IV, 52, 275; Hickeringill, *Jamaica view'd,* 24–6; and for its culture in the islands, Helyar MSS, Sept. 24, 1670; Jamaica Council Minutes, I, 164–5; BM: Egerton MSS, 2395, fols. 643–8; PRO: CO 138/1, fol. 81; BM: Sloane MSS, 1394, fols. 52 a–b; Thornton, in *Caribbean Historical Review, 260.*
32. *CSPC, 1669–74,* p. 477.

Jamaica in 1655, the year of its capture. He found the island very "promising," and predicted that "great estates may be raised by such as have good stocks to begin with." This observation might have been made of every one of the English Caribbean holdings. Men with capital or credit supplied from England had succeeded in acquiring estates ever since the founding of the colony on St. Christopher in 1624. During the fifties many Londoners of both political persuasions either went out themselves to Barbados and the Leeward Islands or to Surinam, or staked kinsmen or agents, to set up as sugar planters. This decade was the era of the great fortunes in sugar at Barbados, and only in a slightly less degree at St. Christopher and Nevis. Boom times for Antigua and Jamaica lay ahead. A sugar plantation required a vast outlay of capital, but a few middling planters, hoping for larger profits, ventured into planting canes, which they sent in ox-carts to the nearest mill on a large estate to be crushed and boiled into Muscovado sugar. In the main, however, a venture in sugar was so expensive and hazardous that only the owners of large plantations who had ample financial backing could avoid failure. As many of the less affluent freeholders went to the wall, the rich bought in their lands.[33]

With the passage of time, one needed more and more capital to start a new plantation. Mills, coppers, stills, horses, cattle, containers, and above all African slaves, in addition to real estate, absorbed the capital of the most affluent planters. Francis Blackmore of Rhimesbury in Jamaica had one plantation for sugar and one for indigo on which he had 250 slaves working, while his neighbor Thomas Sutton had two sugar plantations and one for indigo. Large sugar plantations varied in size from 50 acres at Montserrat and Nevis to 100 or 200 in Barbados, 300 to 400 in Jamaica, and up to 800 at Surinam. The average plantation was like that of Samuel Maynard, gentleman and son of Captain Thomas Maynard of Barbados, who had inherited 70 acres of land, a sugarworks, and about 30 Negro slaves. While on the older islands adventurers tended to purchase going estates, at Jamaica and Antigua, as at Surinam, they had land cleared for the de-

33. *HMC, 7th Report,* 575; *Life of Edward, Earl of Clarendon . . .* (Oxford, 1759), 490; Frank W. Pitman, *The Development of the British West Indies, 1700–1763* (New Haven, 1917), 91.

velopment of new plantations. Thomas Tryon estimated in 1700 that before a man could make one hundredweight of sugar worth not over twelve to fourteen shillings, he would have to disburse between £3000 and £10,000. The halcyon days were over, even for many of the great planters, at the outbreak of the Second Dutch War in 1665 with the accompanying loss of most of the credit formerly extended from Holland and Zeeland.[34]

Only one major change was made in this period in the manner in which sugar cane was grown, as previously described, in the 1640's. This was the extension of the growing time from fifteen months in 1650 to eighteen months, at least in Barbados, in 1685. After the canes were cut, new shoots known as ratoons developed. They did not contain much juice, but two crops of these would be harvested before new canes were planted. Cultivation of the growing canes by blacks with hoes continued to be preferred to plowing, though the former method was one of the hardest tasks to be performed on a plantation.[35]

Staple crops planted year after year inevitably depleted the soil. The land of Barbados had been praised in the fifties for its fertility—"It is a most rich soile all wayes Grene and baring frut; and the Chefest Commoditie is sugar," was Henry Whistler's ap-

34. Dalby Thomas estimated that in 1690 a plantation of 100 acres with 50 black slaves, 7 white servants, 6 horses, 8 oxen "for two teams" to turn the rollers, an overseer at £20 a year, a doctor, a farrier, a carter, and all necessary buildings, utensils, and machinery would cost £5625. Imported clothing and provisions for all of the people would amount to £120 a year. Thomas, *Historical Account of . . . the West Indies,* II, 365–7; Taylor, Multum in Parvo, I, 191–2; Tryon, *Merchant's . . . Instructor,* 201; BM: Egerton MSS, 2395, fol. 528; Barbados Council Minutes, II, 400.

35. Edward Lyttleton wrote up for the Royal Society of London from notes supplied by "Mr. Drake" of Barbados (probably Drax), "The History of the Culture of the Sugar-Cane and Making of Sugar" (*ca.* 1667), which the late Raymond P. Stearns published in *Annals of Science,* I (1936), 178–81. This piece, taken with Antonil's *Cultura e Opulencia do Brasil,* the succinct account by Thomas Tryon in *Merchant's . . . Instructor,* pp. 201–2; and Père Labat's long description in *Nouveau Voyage* constitute an excellent set of treatises on sugar in the Caribbean, 1660–90, which amplify and correct Deerr, *History of Sugar,* I, 158–243. John Taylor's account of sugar-growing in Jamaica (1688) adds little to Ligon's description but does say that new canes were not ready for cutting for 3 years, and that fields were planted 6 months apart. Multum in Parvo, II, 520–24; *CSPC, 1685–88,* pp. 93–4; Pares, *West-India Fortune,* 16.

praisal in 1654. Toward the end of the next decade, however, sugar planters began to complain of the declining yield per acre of their crops. Reports of the soil exhaustion in Barbados in 1672 were a matter of satisfaction to the Jamaicans, who saw in the news a means of attracting settlers to their island. Lord Willoughby exaggerated somewhat when he notified the Committee for Trade and Plantations in 1668 that the island's 100,000 acres "renders not by two thirds its former production by the acre; the land is almost worn out. . . ." This allegation was borne out to a degree by a declaration of the Assembly in 1689 announcing that planters could no longer obtain credit on the security of their land, because their fields were not as well cultivated by the slaves as they formerly were by white servants.[36]

Restoration of the soil's fertility was imperative if the planters were to keep to the level of production attained in earlier years, but the charges and labor needed for gathering and spreading "vast quantities of dung" now called forth one of "the groans of the plantations." One acre needed thirty loads. "We . . . doe rake and scrape Dung out of every Corner. Some save the Urine of their People (both Whites and Blacks) to increase and enrich their Dung." Edward Lyttleton also mentions the great cost of carrying back in carts or on the heads of slaves the soil eroded from the fields by high winds and heavy rains. "Our Negroes work at it like Ants or Bees." Such hysterical remarks, though uttered in support of a political cause, must have had some truth in them. Nevertheless, it is well to note that in 1686, when favorable winds brought temperate weather, Governor Edwin Stede, long an inhabitant of Barbados, wrote: "the crop of sugar, I believe, the largest ever produced in this Island." As in farming anywhere, crops also depended upon the weather. Moreover, as Georges Butel-Dumont shrewdly perceived, the soil in Barbados that Du Tertre represented as wearing out in 1667 and almost exhausted in 1689 was producing as abundantly in 1758 as when the island was first cleared. Land that Tryon described as being "weakened and almost worn out by often Planting" could be brought back by

36. BM: Sloane MSS, 3926, pp. 8–9; *CSPC, 1661–68,* p. 586; *1689–92,* p. 154; BM: Add. MSS, 11,410, fol. 317; Sloane, *Voyage to the Islands,* I, 33.

regular and careful manuring and the use of new sugar plantings each year.[37]

An Englishman spoke of the plantations of French St. Christopher in 1655 as "soe industriously manured [cultivated] that I thought I was in the French gardens, every acre according a family subsistence, noe corne wasted. . . ." Before long, Père Du Tertre pronounced the soil exhausted, but in 1670 several Leeward Islanders insisted that the land and water of St. Christopher "produceth better indico and sugar" than those of Barbados.[38]

Jamaica generally was not as fertile as Barbados, but there was land aplenty for the settlers in the seventeenth century. For a long time people thought that "Barbados was the only nursery for good planters," but the diversity of ground and seasons in Jamaica foiled those men who were accustomed to used and drier land and not to virgin soils. Yet, by 1688, Dr. Hans Sloane could observe: "Their new clear'd Grounds are too rich, those which have been manur'd [cultivated] for a long time need Dung, which now they begin to look after, not burning their Trash as formerly but keeping it in great heaps to rot, in time to make better Dung." On every island a dunging of the land contributed heavily to the rising costs of producing sugar.[39]

The importance of Surinam to the English plantation economy has been almost totally ignored. It was a flourishing sugar colony: along the Surinam River were seventeen sugarworks, and there were three on the Commewijne. In 1675 the Dutch had not yet completed the take-over, which was done under Swedish auspices. On the departure of the English planters, who took much of their sugar-making equipment with them, the Dutch merchants had to replace it. Furthermore, they knew next to nothing about planting

37. Barbot reported the soil of Antigua to be both fertile and productive in 1682. The same was true at Montserrat, but the land in Nevis was less satisfactory. Barbot, in Churchill, *Voyages,* V, 656; Lyttleton, *Groans of the Plantations,* 18–19; *CSPC, 1685–88,* pp. 180, 444; Butel-Dumont, *Histoire et commerce des Antilles angloises,* 16–17; [Thomas Tryon] *England's Grandeur, and a Way to Wealth . . .* (London, 1699. Goldsmith's Library), 11–12.

38. Thurloe, *State Papers,* III, 505; *CSPC, 1669–74,* pp. 97–8; BM: Add. MSS, 11,410, fol. 317.

39. Long, *History of Jamaica,* I, 435–6; Sloane, *Voyage to the Islands,* I, xv, xlv, xlvi.

canes and had "no skill in sugar-making." A report to Whitehall alleged that they were operating with the help of between 1100 and 1200 slaves (Plate 10) and the assistance of "the raggadest Englishmen," whom they offered £200 a year, men who could have earned only £10 15*s.* in Barbados. "All artificers are English." The flight of the English planters from Surinam contributed much to the developing sugar industry on Jamaica and Antigua at the same time that it retarded the growth of the Dutch plantations. Had Surinam remained under the proprietorship of Lord Willoughby of Parham after 1667, its prosperity probably would have increased and the culture of sugar on the great plantations spread so extensively that it would have become the leading English producer of Muscovado and clayed sugars.[40]

V

As Richard Ligon had foreseen in 1650, there was very little room for further advances in the general technology of making sugar, but before 1690 the English planters did effect some minor improvements, most of which pertained to the power for turning the mill rollers. Discovering that oxen did not live very long, they resorted more and more to horses when Rhode Island and Connecticut, the Dutch Islands, North Holland, Ireland, and England could ship them in sufficient numbers. Though human power could never have been used extensively, Dr. Spörri, who arrived at Barbados in 1661 in a vessel bringing horses, said that the mills were turned "either by slaves or by cattle"; and the cartouche of a map of 1670 shows blacks at the sweeps. Even though nags fell in price from £50 in 1650 to £15 in the sixties and seventies, horse-powered mills proved very costly, but horses or oxen had to be used where no other kind of power was available, as in the lowlands of Jamaica and areas on Barbados not open to the trade winds. Wherever streams existed, the familiar Portuguese watermills observed in Brazil were erected. Of the 844 plantations in Barbados in 1684,

40. "How do they [the Dutch] cherish Surinam, though it be one of the basest Countries in the World?" Lyttleton, *Groans of the Plantations*, 31; BM: Egerton MSS, 2395, fol. 526a; *CSPC, 1675–76*, p. 154; *Case of Mr. Jeronimy Clifford*, i-iv, 6–7; *Case and Proceedings for and against Mr. Jeronimy Clifford.*

only a few had watermills, but there were a good many of them in Jamaica.[41]

The idea of harnessing the reliable Northeast Trade Winds must have occurred to both the Hollanders and the East Anglians in Barbados; it may have been a model windmill that James Drax is reputed to have brought or bought from the Low Countries. Henry Whistler claimed in 1655 that the island could be vastly improved if the inhabitants "can bring their desire of wine [wind] mills to perfecktion to grind theyer Shugur, for the mills they now use destroy so many horses that it begors the planters." They succeeded sometime before 1663, when a large property was sold that included two windmills and two sets of "Windmill sails." Richard Ford's map of 1674 shows more than 260 of them; in 1691 a bill levying a tax on windmills passed the Assembly; and Samuel Copen's accurate view of 1695 shows thirty of them in the environs of Bridgetown. In 1673 tiny Montserrat had eight sugarworks, three with windmills, two with watermills, and three turned by horses.[42]

All of the machinery used in the manufacture of sugar was of English design in 1690, whether it was made in England or in the islands. When John Oldmixon said of the Barbadians: "Their Cattle Mills and Wind Mills are made after the same Manner of ours in England," he could also have included the Jamaicans and the Leeward Islanders. During the 1650's, the planters learned

41. About 1672, a Jamaican boasted that "every man may furnish himself with Horses or Assinegoes [as] he pleaseth for travel, for carriage or for grinding att the mill, and that att as cheap rates as in England," and at one-eighth of the cost at Barbados. But Dr. Hans Sloane said in 1688 that horses costing £5 in New England sold for £15 in Jamaica: "they are rougher than the Horses in the Island, usually Pace, and lose their Hair at first coming," because of the hot climate. BM: Add. MSS, 11,410, fol. 316; Sloane, *Voyage to the Islands,* I, lxxxiv; Spörri, *Americanishe Reise,* 10, 20, 45, 47; *Great Newes from Barbados* (London, 1676), 6; Oldmixon, *British Empire in America,* II, 139; Barbot, in Churchill, *Voyages,* V, 641 (water- and horse-mills in the French colonies); Ogilby, *America,* map facing p. 377 (slaves turning a mill); Ford, *Map of Barbados; New & Exact Map of Jamaica,* 1684; *JBMHS,* XXXIII, 7.

42. *JBMHS,* XXIII, 121; XXXI, 47; Venables, in *RHS, Camden,* LX, 146–7; Ford, *Map of Barbados; CSPC, 1689–92,* p. 485; Samuel Copen, *Prospect of Bridge Town in Barbados, 1695* (London, 1695. BM). [Plate 11] But *cf.* Otis P. Starkey, *The Economic Geography of Barbados* (New York, 1939), 36; Map of Montserrat, 1673.

how to sheathe the wooden rollers with iron or copper tubes, or shells, which were manufactured at the foundry of George Sitwell of Renishaw near Derby—one of the first ironmasters to export machinery. From Bybrook Plantation in Jamaica, Cary Helyar wrote to London in 1671 requesting Mr. Charles Modyford to send out copper stills and millwork by the next ship and suggesting that he get in touch with Andrew Orgill, "who is the best contriver for these things as ever came to the Indies." The standard sugar mill had three rollers for crushing the canes, but in 1675 the Assembly of Jamaica passed a private act to encourage Mr. James Lascelles by covering his newly invented mill. It required all persons who constructed mills after his "Modell with four or more Rollers" to pay him £5 provided he gave them the directions for building the machine. The three-roller mill was never outmoded by this new model, which is now of significance only because its inventor received one of the very first colonial patents.[43]

A certain amount of rebuilding and improving of plantation buildings and machinery went on at Barbados and Jamaica. A report from Bybrook in the latter island told how in 1690 Henry Gibbons had "wrighted up the old mill again," after heavy rains had caused serious damage, "and is to have for Compleating it Thirty pounds; he have [*sic*] made a new mill frame, a bridge tree, a water wheele, a sett of Coggs for the three rowlers, and likewise a sett for the maine Shaft, and put two peeces a Crost the beame to raise the Coppoors of the maine rowler. . . ." Gibbons also inserted pieces of timber across the sluices in order to raise the end of the main shaft; and a mason laid fifty perches of stonework. Carts drawn by horses or oxen seem to have replaced asinegoes on the larger plantations for hauling canes from the fields or taking the hogsheads and barrels to the waterside or the warehouse. The Helyars used mules for a time at Bybrook in 1687, for which they had to pay £10 a head. Increasingly, first at Barbados and then

43. Sitwell, in *Journal of the Derbyshire Archaeological and Natural History Society,* X, 38; Oldmixon, *British Empire in America,* II, 139–40; Letter of Cary Helyar, April 15, 1671, Helyar MSS; PRO: CO 1/36, fols. 153a-b. See Plates 4–5, and for engravings of water-, wind-, and horse-mills, see designs for vertical and horizontal rollers in overshot and undershot watermills, in Labat, *Nouveau Voyage,* III, facing pp. 378, 382, 437; Taylor, Multum in Parvo, II, 521.

in all of the islands, the scarcity of wood led to the burning of bagasse and cornstalks in the furnaces at the boiling-houses and distilleries, unsatisfactory though they were.[44]

By such means capable planters, agents, and overseers improved the efficiency of their establishments. Their skill and energy at organizing the entire plantation industry caused one dazed black to exclaim in mixed admiration and awe: "The Devel was in the English-man, that he makes every thing work; he makes the Negro work, the Horse work, the Ass work, the Wood work, the Water work, and the Wind work." [45]

Four kinds of sugar were made on the larger plantations, but the lesser producers continued to confine their efforts to the ordinary Muscovado sugar previously described. A second kind was made by allowing Muscovado to stand in the sun for six or eight hours to harden the grain; this "Sundryed Sugar" did not dissolve in transport or lose as much weight as Muscovado. "These planters that have Houses and Potts enough doe as most profitable, clay all their Sugars that are fitt for it, and these are halfe of the Sugar makers," Governor Lynch explained. A fourth kind was manufactured by melting down plain Muscovado, boiling it again, and then claying it to make a refined white sugar. Richard Leader, who had formerly managed the Ironworks at Saugus, a sawmill in Maine, and a saltworks in Barbados, undertook the refining of sugar on the island in 1659. It is "a trade both ingenuous [*sic*] and profittable, and will give a good subsistance whilst I remain here," he informed John Winthrop, Jr. Only small quantities of the sugar of Barbados and Jamaica were refined, but a petition to Parliament, condemning the "Disorderly Trade of the Plantations," branded the refining of sugar at Barbados an error, which had injured the owners of the thirty sugar houses of London and called for an act to require all of the Sugar Colonies to send only Muscovado sugar to England.[46]

44. Report on Bybrook Plantation by Richard Smith, March 18, 1689/90; Helyar Accounts, 1687; John to William Helyar, June 30, 1687, Helyar MSS; Lyttleton, *Groans of the Plantations,* 17–18. On the fuel shortage, see Sloane, *Voyage to the Islands,* I, 34; and Deerr, *History of Sugar,* I, 165.

45. *Great Newes from Barbados,* 6–7.

46. Most of the sugar refined in Jamaica was for the consumption of the people of that island. W. J. Gardner, *History of Jamaica* (New York, 1909), 86. Bryan

Actually, after experimenting with all four kinds of sugar, most of the planters of Barbados and Jamaica reached the conclusion that their best course was to make Muscovado and distill or sell the molasses by-product. Sir Robert Carr rightly proclaimed in the House of Commons that "Brown sugars are the money of the plantations, and the great concern of the generality of the planters. . . ." The complaint of the London merchants made in 1661 about the "Unmarchandable Sugars" of Barbados was no longer heard in 1690, for the grains of the Muscovado were made much shinier than formerly by the use of limewater. Claying of sugar was more widely practiced in the smaller Leeward Islands. Nevis sugar had been praised as the best in 1650, but at the end of this era both the Jamaican and Antiguan products led all the rest in quality.[47]

The Barbadians still produced more sugar in 1690 than the planters of any other Caribbean island. The cost of production ran higher there than elsewhere and aroused the concern so pungently expressed in Edward Lyttleton's *The Groans of the Plantations* in 1689. Between 1680 and 1683 there were 13,940,000 pounds of sugar shipped to England from the Caribbee islands; just what share of it went from the Leeward Islands is not known, but it was not a large one. Planters at Montserrat sent home 2,001,700 pounds in 1680–84, and those of Nevis dispatched 4,380,000. Sugar-growing had not been resumed in St. Christopher and Antigua after they were captured by the French until 1672 and had not as yet developed extensively, but on Jamaica the sugar culture had increased astonishingly:

Years	*lbs.*
1671–1679 (nine years)	22,911,000
1680–1684 (four years)	35,444,000
1684 alone	8,032,640

Edwards believed that the planters profited more by shipping Muscovado to England and distilling the molasses into rum than by claying or refining their sugar. *History . . . of the British Colonies in the West Indies,* II, 275; BM: Egerton MSS, 2395, fol. 640; William Vassall and John Parris to Samuel Maverick from Barbados, Nov. 1, 1649, MHS Photostats, 1651 box; *MHS Procs.,* 2d ser., III, 195; Amer. Hist. Assn., *Annual Report,* 1892, pp. 38, 40, 41.

47. R. R. Sheridan, The Sugar Trade of the British West Indies, 1660–1756, with

The number of sugarworks in Jamaica rose from 18 in 1663 to 70 in 1670, and to 242 in 1684; and it was said with reason that they turned out a sugar of a finer and lighter grain than the common Muscovado of Barbados and it commanded a much higher price in England.[48]

Small quantities of molasses and rum had been shipped from the West Indies to New England by 1650, but not for another twenty years did these products become commercially valuable by-products of the sugar manufacture. Only when the owners of large estates settled down to making Muscovado sugar did they start either selling or distilling their molasses, for they had found good markets, especially in the northern colonies. The inhabitants of the Bay-Colony took off 150,000 gallons of molasses from the English islands in 1688, and they also procured unknown quantities from the Dutch at Surinam and the French on Guadeloupe and Martinique. A half or better of that which the New Englanders imported was used as a sweetening, for sugar was too costly for their regular diet, and a lot of molasses went into the brewing of small beer. It took some decades before the lower and middle classes of Englishmen acquired a liking for rum greater than their taste for French brandy or acqua vite. Mutiny almost broke out on the Penn-Venables Expedition of 1654 when Commissioner Thomas Povey failed to put 100 tons of brandy on board for the "Land-men," but seldom thereafter does one read about that liquor; all is about rum.[49]

Special Reference to . . . Antigua (Ph.D. Thesis, London School of Economics, 1951); Stock, *Debates,* I, 383, 389; *APC Col.,* I, 314; Tryon, *Merchant's . . . Instructor,* 205–7; Richard Blome, *Present State of His Majesty's Isles, and Territories in America* (London, 1687), 13.

48. BM: Sloane MSS, 2441, fols. 1–22; Add. MSS, 11,410, fol. 153b; Egerton MSS, 2395, fol. 609; *JBMHS,* III, 52; Thornton, in *Caribbean Historical Review,* II, 261; Oldmixon, *British Empire in America,* II, 325; PRO: CO 300/6, fols. 31–4.

49. The New Englanders did not have the distilling capacity to convert more than half of the molasses they imported into rum. For domestic uses of molasses for the brewing and sweetening, see Carl Bridenbaugh, "The High Cost of Living in Boston, 1728," in *New England Quarterly,* V (1932), 800–811; and Gilman Ostrander, "The Colonial Molasses Trade," in *Agricultural History,* XXX (1956), 77–8, 82; PRO: CO 5/848, Pt. I, fols. 14–31. Molasses and rum were not listed in a report on Intercolonial trade, 1677–1688, PRO: CO 1/43, fol. 180; Venables, in *RHS, Camden,* LX, 13, 49.

The demand for rum came annually from the fishermen of Newfoundland and the Gulf of Maine, from the slave traders on the Guinea Coast, and above all from the expanding population of the English colonies in North America. The demand was almost universal by 1670. Because a distillery cost a planter as much as a boiling-house or curing-works, the manufacture of rum became exclusively a large-estate enterprise. The commercial importance of Barbados rum was such that the Assembly passed an act to prevent fraud and deception, which stipulated that any rum that would not take fire from a flame without being heated had to be thrown away or the maker would be fined £100. Since that time the rum of Barbados has always retained its high quality. That of Bybrook and the Modyford plantations in Jamaica also stood high in the international market, for even in England, where the poorer sort of people drank gross acqua vite, Thomas Tryon was delighted to say that rum, "a very noble, lofty, clean Brandy," was beginning to take its place.[50]

The disappearance of wood from the islands forced the planters to look elsewhere for the materials to make the casks needed for packing their staples. The Brazilian *caixas,* or sugar chests, were made of boards from the *jequetiba* and *camassari,* which did not grow in the Antilles. For a time the Barbadians used bully-tree heads and got other woods from Tobago and St. Lucia for staves, and, though they still went to St. Vincent and Dominica in 1676 for most of their headings despite the Carib threat, they ultimately turned to the New England shippers for barrel staves, heads, hoops, and shooks. The West Indians gave up using chests—the last

50. To protect brandy, no colonial molasses or rum could be imported into France, thereby leaving the planters of Guadeloupe and Martinique with £60,000 of these by-products, two-thirds of which were worthless because there was no market for them. About half a million gallons of molasses were thrown away each year. Because the English planters could not satisfy the demands of New England and the other colonies, French sugar-makers asked Colbert for the right to trade rum and molasses to the English colonies for provisions. "The English who dwell near Boston will not worry themselves about the prohibitions which the King of England may issue, because they hardly recognize his authority," they argued shrewdly but in vain. Letter of March 8, 1681, quoted by Mims, *Colbert's West India Policy,* 221–2, 263. PRO: CO 1/36, fol. 152a; Bybrook Plantation Accounts, June 22, 1687, Helyar MSS; Barrett, in *Merchants and Scholars,* 163; Taylor, Multum in Parvo, II, 524–5.

mention of a chest appeared in a letter of Constant Sylvester's in 1659—even though oak shooks could be had from the Piscataqua region. The English *cases* (*caixas*) varied in sizes; those for sugar in 1708 contained from ten to fifteen hundredweight (112 pounds) and were far more difficult to handle than the several sizes of casks, or barrels, which could be rolled easily on shore, along the wharf, or on board ship. Probably as important, if not more so, New England coopers made up casks cheaper than they could be made on many a plantation from local or imported staves and heads, or shooks. Jamaicans, who had ample timber at hand, decided after 1680 that it was less expensive for them to purchase New England casks.[51]

VI

Throughout the seventeenth century the most persistent and acute problem that planters of all degrees had to face was the acquiring, making provision for, and superintending of their labor forces. Regardless of the solution they arrived at, labor represented the investment of the major share of their capital, and, more often than not, they had to procure this capital in the form of credit from merchants.

The first of the four means by which a planter could get labor to farm his acres was the old familiar English system of wage labor. Every freeman, however, wanted land of his own, but as Governor Jonathan Atkins of Barbados, warning against further immigration, explained: "there is neither English, Scotch, nor Irish can come to plant here, there being noe Ground for them to plant upon." Coming out of service, former white indentured Englishmen did not wish to work in the cotton or cane fields alongside blacks; far more numerous Irish freedmen took such jobs because they had no alter-

51. Cask and barrel are general names for cylindrical, wooden containers bulging in the middle; the largest, 1) a *hogshead* (in 1749 the molasses hogshead was standardized at 140 gallons); 2) a *tierce* was one-third of a pipe of wine or liquid, or 42 gallons of molasses, but was also used for sugar, tobacco, tallow, and salt pork; 3) a *kilderkin* was a cask for liquids or fish equal to half a hogshead; 4) a *quintal* held one hundredweight (112 lbs.); and a *keg* was a small cask holding under 10 gallons. *Oxford English Dictionary*. Antonil, *Cultura e Opulencia do Brasil,* 192–4; PRO: CO 1/37, fol. 23; *MHS Procs.,* 2d ser., IV, 277.

native, and they did not prove to be good or willing workers. This type of labor seldom existed on any large scale, and had the West Indian planters been restricted to free wage labor, their enterprises must inevitably have failed, as Gibbon Wakefield pointed out very clearly.[52]

The planters also had the example of the large estate in the Mother Country and the great Brazilian sugar plantation, both of which rested on tenancy. Many small freeholders, who were hopelessly in debt, sold out to richer neighbors but stayed on their land to farm as tenants. If sugar planters, they took their canes to the landlord's mill and, as in Brazil, received in return half of the sugar made from them while the landlord was entitled to the other half and the molasses. The tenant was thus a factor in the process of consolidating plantations. The shortage of white servants became so critical in Barbados after 1670 that some planters resorted to tenancy as a means of getting help. A decade later John Ford, who owned 250 acres of land in St. Andrew's Parish, worked them with four freemen on wages, two white servants, and two tenants who leased plots of ground from him. Captain Abel Alleyne had six tenants for his 316 acres, while Jacob Lucy had four freemen, seven white servants, and four tenants on his great estate. When a hurricane struck Christopher Jeaffreson's plantation on St. Christopher in 1681, it destroyed all of the outhouses and the two sugarworks he operated "to make my tenants sugar," and flattened all of their canes. From the point of view of the freemen just arriving in the islands or those coming out of service, the only choices open to them were tenancy or wage labor, and neither could be called inviting.[53]

The only really satisfactory method of procuring white workers was by indentured bondage. In the first decades after settlement there had been no dearth of white servants, but wars, disease, and migration had produced a serious shortage. Regardless of the hostility of the English planters of the West Indies toward the Hibernians, these much-abused people were almost the only indentured servants available in large numbers. They arrived by the thousands from 1650 to 1660, but thereafter the supply fell off

52. Pares, *West-India Fortune,* 341–2; PRO: CO 1/37, fol. 60a.
53. PRO: CO 1/44, 47, XXXII D; Jeaffreson, *Young Squire,* I, 276–7.

sharply. Furthermore, to quote Jonathan Atkins, the Barbadians grew "weary of them, for they prove commonly *very Idle,* and they do find by Experience they can keep three Blacks, who *work better and cheaper* than one White man." Nevertheless, white servants were wanted to fill jobs as overseers and for the expanding sugar plantations, and the planters were willing to encourage Hibernians in the eighties; eventually their lot improved noticeably.[54]

So pressing was the need for white servants in the newly settled and smaller islands that their assemblies made laws to require the planters to keep and encourage them. The Assembly of Jamaica ruled that each planter maintain one white man for every ten blacks after 1676; Antigua adopted the one-to-ten proportion in 1677, and in 1679 St. Christopher followed suit and, in addition, insisted that owners of large tracts keep one white servant for each twenty-five acres in 1683. By such means, the colonists hoped to fill the ranks of their militias. That they accomplished very little is evident from a census of Barbados for 1684, which showed an increase of only 64 since the count of 1680, but 7820 slaves added in the four years brought the total to 46,602. "We cannot be at the Charges to procure and keep White Servants, or to entertain Freemen as we used to do," Edward Lyttleton protested in 1689, "nor will they now go upon any terms to a Land of Misery and Beggery. So that our Militia must fall: and we shall be in no Capacity to defend ourselves, either against a Forrain Enemy or against our own Negroes." [55]

Nearly every condition of plantation labor proved unfavorable to white servants after 1660. At times heartless overseers pushed them to the physical limit, beyond what they did to slaves. In 1656 Colonel William Brayne wanted the Protector to send Negroes from Africa to Jamaica "because as the planters would have to pay for them, they would have an interest in preserving their lives which was wanting in the case of bond servants." More white laborers succumbed from malnutrition or some disease than Negroes. Often overlooked, too, was a matter emphasized in 1672 by Sir Thomas

54. PRO: CO 1/21, fol. 170; CO 1/37, fol. 171a (our italics).
55. PRO: CO 1/36, fol. 146; CO 154/2, fol. 23; *CSPC, 1677–80,* p. 200; *1681–85,* p. 561; BM: Sloane MSS, 2441, fols. 17–18; Lyttleton, *Groans of the Plantations,* 14; Smith, *Colonists in Bondage,* 31–2, 344.

Lynch: "Plantations are subject to aboundance of ill accidents, especially Sugar workes, because they have so many Machines." Lyttleton told his readers: "If a Stiller slip into a Rum-Cistern, it is a sudden death: for it stifles in a moment. If a Mill-feeder be catch'd by the finger, his whole body is drawn in, and is squees'd to pieces. If a Boyler gets any part into the scalding Sugar, it sticks like Glew, or Birdlime, and 'tis hard to save either Limb or Life." Compensation for the victim of such accidents depended solely upon the whim of the master. When, as Christopher Jeaffreson said, all they got after four years of toil was 300 pounds of sugar, the wonder is that more did not run away. So many fled from Antigua to the Virgin Islands that a law directed the owners of small boats to keep their masts and oars, or paddles, locked up when they were not in use.[56]

White labor had predominated in the islands up to 1650; but in 1668 the preamble to a law of Barbados making slaves legally real estate (chattels) stated: "a very considerable part of the Wealth of this Island consists in our Negro Slaves." This shift had come about primarily because, as John Wilmore, who had long been in the servant trade from London to the Antilles, concluded that the blacks were the real producers. "I dare boldly say no white servant in Jamaica works near so hard as many of our Husbandmen in the Country, or doth much more than half the work of a Black and yet is more chargeable in keeping than five Blacks. . . ." It was acknowledged that the proper operation of a sugar plantation in Barbados required two slaves for each acre because of the necessity of dunging the ground; on the virgin soils of Jamaica and the Leeward Islands, the accepted ratio was one-to-one. For large estates, this meant a heavy investment in the labor force, but their owners recognized the necessity of it and were willing to go into debt to secure the Negroes; they were convinced that the fewer white servants a planter had, the bigger his profit. And not only were the

56. Thurloe, *State Papers,* V, 473; Taylor, Multum in Parvo, II, 536–7; Ligon, *Barbados,* 114; BM: Add. MSS, 11,410, fol. 258; [Henry Pitman] *A Relation of the Great Sufferings and Strange Adventures* . . . (London, 1684), 11–12; Lyttleton, *Groans of the Plantations,* 19–20. For runaway servants, see *CSPC, 1681–85,* p. 323; *1685–88,* pp. 584–5; Jeaffreson, *Young Squire,* I, 207; *Acts of the Leeward Islands,* 42–3.

blacks cheaper in the long run, but they contributed to making the plantation a more stable and permanent institution.[57]

The overseers of the sugar plantations, especially those owned by absentees, worked their slaves pitilessly. In Jamaica they went out to the fields at daylight, "sometimes two hours before," where they were governed at their work by white servants—one for every twenty blacks. When they returned for dinner at 11:00 a.m., they carried wood on their backs "lest they should come idle out of the Field"; back they went at one to work until nightfall. Old, sturdy, and hard Negroes often had to be driven to their tasks, but newcomers, for the most part, went willingly. Only on Sundays were they allowed any time for their own concerns. Christopher Jeaffreson was aghast when a white servant wrote him in England from his plantation on St. Christopher that his overseer, Edward Thorne, had been working the slaves at night: "I am sure that was never practised in my tyme, not by any considerate man that intended not to destroy his people." But many an overseer, agent, or resident planter did destroy the blacks under his control. As with white servants, the kind of treatment accorded Negroes depended upon the intelligence, solicitude, and decency of the individual master.[58]

In the sixties many Barbadians had come to prefer blacks from Africa to whites from the British Isles not just for work in the fields but for all kinds of labor. A surprising number of Negroes, freshly arrived from Africa, had skills that enabled them to serve on plantations as carpenters, masons, bricklayers, smiths, thatchers, and, occasionally, as millwrights. Others appear to have learned very quickly to become acceptable coopers, and their wives were good weavers. "The planters design to have all their tradesmen, sugar boilers, &c. of the blacks, and to put blacks with all their tradesmen [to learn their crafts]. I have seene sometimes 40 Christians, English, Scotch, and Irish at worke in the parching sun without shoe

57. Sir Thomas Lynch estimated the cost of a Jamaica sugar plantation in 1672 at £4488, which included £288 for 24 white servants and £2200 for 100 Negroes. BM: Add. MSS, 11,410, fol. 260b; *Acts of Barbados* (Hall), 63–4; *The Case of John Wilmore . . . or a Looking-Glass for all Merchants and Planters that are concerned on the American Plantations* (London, 1682), 3–4; Barrett, *Merchants and Scholars,* 165.

58. Taylor, Multum in Parvo, II, 539; Jeaffreson, *Young Squire,* II, 62, 69, 77; Spörri, *Americanische Reise,* 17.

or stockin, while their negroes have bin at worke at theire respective Trades in good condition," declared one who knew Barbados well. In 1682 the white coopers of Nevis successfully petitioned the Assembly for a law prohibiting slaves from being taught their trade. "There's a great deal of difference between the Negroes," Oldmixon declared, "those that are born in Barbados are much more useful Men . . . the Creolian Negroes are very preferable to the New Comers (which they call Salt-Water Negroes)"—but in any event, substantial numbers of each kind gradually took over the white men's crafts.[59]

Negroes who were purchased by owners of sugar plantations were soon replacing the white servants in the sugarworks. In explaining the effect of tension and toil on masters in 1700, Thomas Tryon inadvertently revealed how much harder it was for the slaves: "In short, 'tis to live in a perpetual Noise and Hurry, and the only way to render a Person Angry, and Tyrannical too; since the Climate is so hot, and the labor so constant, that the [black] Servants night and day stand in great Boyling Houses, where there are Six or Seven large Coppers or Furnaces kept perpetually Boyling; and from which with heavy Ladles and Scummers, they Skim off the excrementatious parts of the Canes, till it comes to its perfection and cleanness, while others as Stoakers, Broil, as it were alive, in managing the Fires; and one part is constantly at the Mill, to supply it with Canes, night and day, during the whole Season of making Sugar, which is about six Months of the year; so that what with these things, the number of the Family, and many other Losses and Disappointments of bad Crops, which often happens, a Master Planter has no such easy Life as some may imagine, nor Riches flow upon him with that insensibility, as it does upon many in England. . . ."[60]

A report to Parliament in 1650 adjudged that much of the disorder in the Caribbees was traceable to the leading proprietors

59. The promoters of the settlement at Albemarle in Carolina believed in 1664 that they could secure tradesmen and mechanics from Barbados, for those men could not subsist in their island because the "greatest men" were bringing up their Negroes to handicrafts. BM: Egerton MSS, 2395, fol. 664; *CSPC, 1681–85,* p. 248; PRO: CO 1/21, fol. 170; CO 30/5, fol. 44; Oldmixon, *British Empire in America,* II, 121–2.

60. Tryon, *Merchant's . . . Instructor,* 201–2.

and owners of lands residing in England and leaving the management of their plantations to agents or overseers. Absenteeism was a natural concomitant of the West Indian plantation system, and it created problems that became more serious as the century advanced. Maurice Thompson, John Bawden, and William Pennoyer were such men referred to in the report, prominent merchants who lived in London or the outports and seldom if ever saw their land. They must be distinguished from those planters who had grown rich in the islands and returned to England or went to live in the northern colonies on the incomes from their estates. The complaints against all of these absentees are revealed in the preamble to an act of Barbados in 1667: "severall of the most eminent Plantations in most Parishes of this Island do little or no Parochial Duties, by reason the respective Owners of such Plantations have removed themselves to England, or else where, and in their place have left their particular Attorneys, Agents and Overseers, to manage their Estates for them in their Absence. . . ." As Richard Blome remarked of Barbados and Jamaica some years after this, that although plantations ought always to be in the masters' care, "yet few of them (except those of the meanest degree) are without their Overseers." [61]

Promoters in Antigua had difficulty for years with the possessors of large estates who remained in England and neither cleared their lands nor parceled them out to freed servants or immigrants. Samuel Wyllys, who had an interest in several plantations, was a trader and magistrate of Connecticut. He visited his properties frequently but finally sold out and returned to New England. By a strict resettlement law of January 1688/9, the Assembly broke up the large holdings, and the rapid development of Antigua dates from that time.[62]

Few absentee proprietors escaped being fleeced to some degree, if not entirely done in, by their agents or overseers. From London in 1686, Christopher Jeaffreson wrote to one of his reliable servants who had reported on the mismanagement and losses sustained on

61. PRO: State Papers, Colonial, 1, 11, No. 12, Sept. 19, 1650; *Laws of Barbados* (1721), 77; Blome, *Description of Jamaica,* 92; Higham, *Leeward Islands,* 191.
62. Higham, *Leeward Islands,* 24, 165, 182; Sibley, *Harvard Graduates,* I, 323–4; BM: Egerton MSS, 2395, fol. 455; *Acts of the Leeward Islands,* 30.

his St. Christopher plantation: "I perceive my affairs there call loud for me, before my businesse here will admit of my retourne, which nevertheless may be sooner than some men wish for; for I cannot indure to see myself abused . . . I thank you for the account you gave me of my affairs. It was done like a friend. . . ." When Cary Helyar died in Jamaica in 1672, his brother William attempted to operate Bybrook Plantation from Somersetshire through an agent. Sir Thomas Modyford, a onetime companion of Squire Helyar in the Tower of London, wrote the latter in 1677 reporting that "Your chief man Atcherly is a very drunken idle fellow, for which reason my son turned him out of his employ, and by this time you have reason to thinke him a lyeing one alsoe." He has hired as chief overseer one Coffin, the old planter continued, whom I turned away for his drunkenness, and pays him 5 per cent more than I did. He thought Bybrook could be made into the best sugarworks on the island provided a proper course, which he sketched out in considerable detail, be followed.[63]

The proprietor who remained on the islands had business activities and hazards of his own, for he had to be at one and the same time administrator and producer of his own plantation, a man of affairs familiar with all aspects of trading and shipping in a turbulent world alternating between peace and war. In the conduct of it all, the English West Indian planter found little that was truly normal; for him and for those who worked for him, there was no peace.

63. Modyford to William Helyar, July 10, 1677, Helyar MSS; Dampier, *Voyages,* II, Pt. 2, pp. 4, 7–8; Jeaffreson, *Young Squire,* II, 69, 71.

X

Merchants, Mariners, and Shipping

SAMUEL LAMBE OF LONDON offered the Protector in 1658 a "seasonable observation": "That what Nation soever can attaine to and continue the greatest Trade, and number of shipping, will win and keepe the Soveraignty of the Seas, and consequently the greatest Dominion of the World." To achieve this kind of national power, Parliament had passed in 1651 a measure designed to eliminate, or at least to restrain, commercial competition from the Dutch who, as Dr. Benjamin Worsley put it, had been underselling the English by one-third "in all places, and upon all Trades; yea, sometimes in our own Commodities . . . in our Plantations they had three if not four Sail of Ship for our one." This policy of cutting off their credit, chief suppliers, and best customers dismayed all of the English planters in the West Indies and fired them up to protesting periodically and to encouraging willful evasions of the law. "My Lords . . . we may admit as a maxim that Whensoever you intend to plant a new Colloney you must make their port a free port for all people to trade with them that will come," Jonathan Atkins emphatically told royal officials some decades later. The striking difference in outlook between the Mother Country and the colonies also appeared in actual traffic and explains much about the perennially disturbed state of trade and navigation in the Caribbean from 1651 to 1690.[1]

1. Samuel Lambe, *Seasonable Observations Humbly Offered to His Highness the Lord Protector* (London, 1658), 1, 2–13; [Benjamin Worsley] *The Advocate; or*

The mercantile policy of England was never effectively or evenly carried out in the Caribbean during the Protectorate despite the punitive Act of 1650 forbidding all trade with the rebellious colonies, the Ayscue Expedition which forced their submission, the Navigation Act of 1651 aimed at Dutch shipping, and the seizure of Jamaica from the Spaniards in 1655. During the fifties the planters quietly persisted in their old traffic with the Hollanders, who alone provided enough ships, brought over sorely needed manufactures, and took home sugar, tobacco, and cotton. Every maritime current of these years ran in favor of the planters, who preferred the cheaper and better services of the Dutch to the scarcer and far more costly trade with their own countrymen, which was based upon a concept of monopoly and conducted with high prices, high freights, high interest rates, and lower profits for the islanders. Acting in defiance of, or beyond, English law, with a large degree of independence, even of impunity, the insular planters eagerly expanded the culture of sugar and, during the fifties, made great profits. These were the big-money years for the fortunate men who got into the sugar industry early enough.

If the restoration of the Stuarts marked a fateful turning for the English people, it proved even more fateful for their fellow countrymen of the West Indies. During the sixties, a series of events, some of them planned, others accidental, changed the mood of the planters from one of intense optimism to one of unrelieved foreboding. Within a few months of his return, as mentioned earlier, King Charles II granted to the Royal Adventurers a charter of monopoly of the slave trade, which he followed up in 1672 with a more complete monopoly for the Royal African Company. As a result, the cost of slave labor in the islands began to climb.

Promptly, too, with the Restoration, Parliament responded to the urgings of merchants, such as Martin Noell and Thomas Povey, and the diplomat George Downing, for increased statutory control of economic life, especially in the settlements of the New World.

A Narrative of the State and Condition of Things between the English and Dutch Nation in Relation to Trade (London, 1652), 4, 6. The Navigation Act of 1651 is in Firth and Rait, *Acts and Ordinances of the Interregnum,* II, 559–62; and recently discussed by Farnell, *Ec. Hist. Rev.,* 2d ser., XVI, 439–54; and Wilson, *England's Apprenticeship,* 52–6; PRO: CO 1/37, fol. 71b.

The Act passed in 1660 stipulated that only English ships might trade to the colonies. Although colonial produce might be exported freely, the Act *enumerated* seven articles that had to be carried directly from their source to the Mother Country or to one of the other dominions. A Staple Act of 1663 made England the entrepôt for colonial trade by requiring that all European goods destined for the colonies pass through one of its ports. And, in 1673, the Third Navigation Law set a "plantation duty" to be paid at the source if any "enumerated article" was shipped to another colony without bond being given at the time that it would eventually be carried to England, thereby virtually eliminating the possibility of re-exporting it to some port outside of the realm and avoiding the payment of duties in England.[2]

To the men of the Caribbean, the Navigation Laws seemed unduly severe and discriminatory. To begin with, all of the articles enumerated in 1660 came wholly or in part from the islands: brown and white sugar, cotton, tobacco, indigo, ginger, and dyewoods (including fustic and logwood). The principal purchasers of these products had been the Dutch, who actually appear to have increased their traffic in spite of the Act of 1651. Petitioners of 1659 charged that the Dutch had been allowed "to engross the trade" of St. Christopher "to the discouragement of the English." Sir George Downing was one of the very few high officials who had ever been in the colonies, and he, in 1676, reacted angrily to a Barbadian protest: "before the Acts of Trade and navigation above three fourths of all the Ships trading to Barbados were Dutch, and that there were 39 Ships of 40, wheras now there are 38 English Ships of 40 trading in England." There is no gainsaying the truth of his assertion, for during the First Dutch War the Mynheers sailed in small craft from "Stasia" to trade openly at Montserrat warehouses, and as

2. All works on England and her colonies in the 17th century treat the Acts of Trade and Navigation and, because of this and the vast special literature on the subject, these laws will be referred to only when they affect the West Indian settlements directly before 1690. For the purposes of this work the most important treatises are Lawrence A. Harper's classic *The English Navigation Laws* (New York, 1939); and Charles M. Andrews, *The Colonial Period of American History,* IV.

soon as the conflict ended, ships from Holland again crowded Carlisle Bay.[3]

From the vantage point of London, the case for excluding the Dutch and bringing the Caribbean colonies into line seemed clear and unassailable; to the planters, the Navigation Acts spelled disaster. Looking back some years later, an Englishman observed: "But let us do the Colony and our selves Justice, to confess, we consulted our own interests more than theirs, when we tied them to one Market, and obliged them to send all their Commodities to us. Choice of Markets is the greatest Advantage of any Trade." [4]

Parliament had fixed a preferential scale of duties on sugar in favor of the plantations in 1649: 2*d.* a pound for Muscovado, 3*d.* for clayed white sugars, and an additional halfpenny on all foreign sugars. By 1665 the planters were petitioning against high duties on the ginger, sugar, and other articles they exported; and at the same time arguing that their produce gave employment to 20,000 Negroes a year, and that their exports exceeded those of all the Spanish colonies. No relief was granted however; in fact an effort of 1671 to increase the duties on sugar narrowly failed. Sir Peter Colleton held in 1676 that the Acts of Trade had very much altered conditions by their binding the plantations to one market: "Wee must in time, necessarily be eaten out by the French"; and also that the Portuguese of Brazil paid only 7*s.* 6*d.* on £3, while the Barbadians paid 5*s.* out of £2, plus landing charges. But Sir George Downing's arguments prevailed, and the Lords of Trade and Plantations advised against any further alterations either of the Navigation Acts or the customs duties in England. Additions made in 1685 brought the levies on Muscovado up to 18*d.* a hundred pounds and on white sugars to 5*s.* a hundred, which, together with the Act of 1660 making the planters "foreigners" and the 4½ per cent export duty in the islands, placed an intolerable

3. Proof of trade with the enemy may be found in the sequestration of more than a dozen storehouses owned by Dutch merchants on St. Christopher in 1654. BM: Egerton MSS, 2395, fols. 105, 152–65; PRO: CO 391/1, fol. 241; *The Advocate,* 6–7; Deposition of Samuel Waad, 1654, in *Analecta Hibernica,* No. 4, 226; Thurloe, *State Papers,* III, 249–51; *CSPC, 1574–1660,* p. 473.

4. Oldmixon, *British Empire in America,* 11, 24.

burden on the produce of every planter. What is more, it elicited from the agonized West Indians, Edward Lyttleton's famous protest: *The Groans of the Plantations: or A True Account of Their Grievous and Extreme Suffering By the Heavy Impositions upon Sugar, and other Hardships. Relating more particularly to the Island of Barbados.*[5]

Closely linked to the English import duties in the minds of the colonists was the export duty levied "for ever" on all commodities grown in Barbados and the four Leeward Islands. It amounted to "Four and a half in Specie for every Five Score." Always known as the 4½ Per Cent Duty, it had been granted to the king by Barbados in 1663 in lieu of an earlier and more onerous poll tax and export duty, and also for royal confirmation of the titles to the planters' estates. At the time, the colonials understood that the Crown would bear all public charges thereafter. In nearly every respect, this arrangement favored the planters, but the king, ever in need of money, never expended any of the revenue for the purposes stated in the grant. As a consequence, the export duty became the prime Caribbean grievance, one that the planters perennially sought, in vain, to alter or abolish because they felt themselves bound down between two burdens like the Ass of the Tribe of Issachar. And to add to their financial woes, the farmers of the 4½ per cent duty never satisfied them with their methods of collection.[6]

The incidence of the impositions just mentioned must be considered in the light of steadily falling prices for sugar from 1660 to 1680, which meant a diminished prosperity for planter and merchant alike. From 1681 to 1685 a real depression existed. The Barbadians had also become, by 1680, the marginal sugar producers of the region, while the Leeward Islanders and Jamaicans, being less advanced, suffered less. Declining prices were the result of the remarkable increase in sugar production in the islands. En-

5. *Journal of the House of Commons,* VI, 349; BM: Add. MSS, 11,411, fols. 9–10; PRO: CO 391/1, fols. 240–42; Lyttleton, *Groans of the Plantations,* 1–2.
6. Each of the Leeward Islands granted the king a 4½ per cent duty in 1664. *CSPC, 1661–68,* pp. 293, 586; *Acts of Nevis,* 1–3; *Acts of Barbados* (1721), 121–3; PRO: CO 29/1, pp. 47–50; CO 391/1, fol. 242; Edwards, *History . . . of British Colonies in the West Indies,* I, 335–9; BM: Sloane MSS, 3662, fol. 57a; *HMC, Portland,* XIV, Pt. II, 277.

glish imports rose from 6,352,000 pounds to 28,770,520 pounds in 1690, of which two-thirds were ordinarily re-exported, but toward the end of the period, merchants had to compete against rising Dutch and French sugar production, which further depressed prices.[7]

West Indian planters like Edward Lyttleton, still living in 1690, could look back and dream about the great fortunes they had made during the fifties before the slow, inexorable drop in profits which began after 1660 and reached the low point in 1685. They could remember, too, the statutory regulations made by Parliament and the unrequited grants their Assemblies made to the Crown. Corporate monopolies forced up the cost of slaves to more than £20 a head, and few English or Scottish servants were available. These planters could not have forgotten, either, the Caribbean conflicts with the Dutch and the French, or such acts of God as devastating fires, hurricanes, earthquakes, and pestilence. No economic policy ever benefits all the people of a nation, but England's successful quest for national power and industrial diversification worked genuine hardships on every soul in the West Indian islands and justified the *cri de cœur* of the planter at the very moment that John Dryden was singing exultantly of the *Annus Mirabilis,* when:

> Instructed ships shall sail to quick Commerce
> By which remotest Regions are allied;
> Which makes one City of the Universe;
> *Where some may gain,* and all be supplied.[8]

II

The plantation economy of each island centered in its seaport or at the waterside of its roadstead, and we must again stress the singularly maritime nature of all life in the Antilles. One or more small villages or towns quickly appeared after the founding of a colony,

7. Sheridan, Sugar Trade, 308–11; Davies, *Royal African Company,* 15; figures on sugar prices in Higham, *Leeward Islands,* 191–3.

8. Pitman, *Development of the British West Indies,* 156, 175; *CSPC, 1675–76,* p. 304; "Annus Mirabilis," in *The Poems of John Dryden,* ed. John Steward (London, 1925), Stanza 163, p. 36 (our italics).

but most of them failed to develop into genuine communities, even with the passage of time. On the smaller islands, transfer points sufficed at which tobacco and sugar might be exchanged for incoming cargoes of goods and provisions. Such were the several storehouses and retail shops at Sandy Point and Old Road on St. Christopher, which Governer Stapleton listed in 1672 as "places of Trade." Antigua had six spots so designated; only St. John and Falmouth could be rated as towns. Similar places of trade on Montserrat were Kinsale, Plymouth, and "The Roads," and though Nevis had five, according to the act granting the 4½ per cent duty, only Charles Town and Morton's Bay were veritable towns. During the English period at Surinam, Torarica, well up the river, served as the shipping point, but Parimaribo nearer the mouth became the Dutch mart.[9] (Plate 10)

On Barbados, The Hole, or Holetown, Speightstown, and Oistin's Town never fulfilled their promise, but The Indian Bridge, known after 1660 as Bridgetown or St. Michael's, grew into the acknowledged metropolis of the Caribbean, though it was little more than a collection of "storehouses and shops" where merchants and factors transacted their affairs. Père Biët judged that it contained 300 or 400 structures in 1652, most of them storehouses full of merchandise, or inns. Thomas Noell sold to Hewin Hawley in September 1659 the land and building "commonly called the Roe Buck Inn," which obviously had survived the fire of the previous February, which consumed 200 stores and houses. Three times Bridgetown was almost totally destroyed: by a great explosion (1668), a bad fire (1673), and a terrific hurricane in 1675, but because of the essential commercial services performed in the town, on each occasion it was rebuilt.[10]

Under the aegis of the Assembly, Bridgetown was enlarged and restored, principally with structures of brick and stone. Sometime before 1689, Jonathan Hutchinson, merchant and son of Richard Hutchinson of London, operated "the Coffee House," which he bequeathed to his Boston brother Eliakim. Several visitors pro-

9. French Basseterre was the principal town on St. Christopher. Davies, *Caribby-Islands,* 8; BM: Egerton MSS, 2395, fol. 527; *CSPC, 1675–76,* pp. 499–500; Philip H. Hiss, *Netherlands America* (New York, 1943), 27.
10. Carlisle, *A Declaration;* Biët, *Voyage,* 288; Davis Coll., VIII, Envelope 221.

nounced its thoroughfares handsome, and the population in 1680 consisted of slightly more than 2500 (including 1325 Negro slaves). When Samuel Copen sketched this flourishing emporium from the deck of a ship in the road in 1694, Bridgetown made an impressive scene, one worthy of the beautiful large engraving that Johannes Kip published in London the next year.[11]

The most surprising feature of Samuel Copen's *Prospect* is the marked Dutch appearance of the waterfront of the little seaport. The accuracy of his rendition is confirmed by the leading modern Barbadian authority and is the best available evidence that the influence of the Hollanders on the business and culture of the community was sufficiently potent to control the rebuilding of the Bridgetown waterfront as late as 1694. It provides us with outward, visible proofs of great commercial significance. (Plate 11)

As one's eye sweeps across the view from Willoughby Fort to Bagnall's Point, the Dutch character of the waterfront is striking: eleven named wharves and two spacious quays crowded with men rolling and handling great hogsheads of sugar, and in the distance more than twenty windmills, which lend more authenticity to the scene. But it is the storehouses whose architecture and arrangement most resemble the old ports of Holland. Fronting on the harbor are eleven great storehouses of stone and brick, having telltale stepped gables, and twenty-one equally large structures with ogive gable ends—all roofed with the familiar red tiles, and, to our surprise, every one has that West Indian rarity, a brick chimney. The two or three half-timbered structures with jetties or overhangs on the gable end and some small nondescript timber buildings are obviously English but seem strangely out of place in this engraving. The new Bridgetown of 1675–95 resembled much more the Dutch New Amsterdam of 1664 than it did the English Boston of 1690. Ninety-five years before Kip brought out his engraving of Bridgetown, the stalls of Holland had carried an impressive, detailed engraving of the city of Amsterdam, whereon were portrayed the prototypes of the Dutch structures at St. Michael's. The difference

11. A long mole running out from James Fort into the sea, a public undertaking to protect the careenage, was ruined by the tempest of 1694. Oldmixon, *British Empire in America,* II, 80; *CSPC, 1677–80,* p. 507; *1685–88,* p. 357; *NEHG Reg.,* LXVII, 364.

between the two views is merely one of scale rather than of period or style. (Plates 11–12)[12]

A second large English town in the Antilles was the one begun in 1657 by General William Brayne, governor of Jamaica, on the tip of a waterless, barren, sandy strip extending twelve miles from the mainland and enclosing the commodious Port Royal harbor. Known for years as Point Cagua (Englished as Cagway), it contained in 1663 about 400 buildings of all sorts, most of them built of timber and a constant source of worry for the new Dutch fire-master, Nicholas Keine. In this year Governor Lyttleton gave the name of Port Royal to the rising port, then so full of troops from the harbor defenses, old discharged Cromwellian soldiers—turned cattle-hunters—and swaggering buccaneers, all free-spenders providing patronage for the many public houses, victualing places, and brothels. A rich planter of St. James's, John Style, protested in 1670 that "the number of tippling houses is now doubly increased" with more than 100 licenced establishments, besides sugarworks and rum distilleries that sell without licence. Though there were about 800 buildings when Sir Thomas Lynch arrived in 1671, he had to pay dearly for a house and give fifteen shillings an acre for poor land seven miles distant on which to raise provisions. In his opinion, the town was unhealthy, lacking in streets, landing places, house lots, and conveniences for royal officials.[13]

With encouragement from Governor Lynch, Port Royal soon became the center of Jamaica's general prosperity. Its real growth took place after the suppression of the buccaneers commenced in 1672; the little port owed its riches not so much to pirates' plunder as to the far-from-glamorous island staples and the heavy traffic in slaves. Francis Hanson boasted immoderately in 1682: "The town of Port Royal, being as it were the store-house or treasury of the

12. Some writers have been misled by Père Labat's remark of 1700 that the houses of Bridgetown were "well-built in the English taste." At best this could have applied only to private dwellings. *Nouveau Voyage,* VI, 188. For New Amsterdam and Boston, see Bridenbaugh, *Cities in the Wilderness,* Plates 2, 5. Samuel Copen, *A Prospect of Bridgetown in Barbados* (London, 1695), herein reproduced as Plate 11, should be compared with *Amstelodamum* (engraved by Jan Pieterszoon Saueredam, Amsterdam, 1606). (Plate 12) *CSPC, 1681–85,* p. 70.

13. Long, *History of Jamaica,* I, 282; II, 139; PRO: CO 324/1, fols. 253–8; *CSPC, 1661–68,* p. 124; *1669–74,* p. 50; Cundall, *Governors of Jamaica,* 34.

West Indies, is always like a continual mart or fair, where all sorts of choice merchandises are daily imported, not only to furnish the islands, but vast quantities are thence Transported to supply the Spanish, Indians and other nations, who in return exchange us bars and cakes of gold, wedges, and pigs of silver, pistol[e]s, pieces of eight . . . with store of wrought plate, jewels, rich pearl necklaces and . . . of pearls unsorted and undrilled several bushels." Sir Thomas spoke more modestly: "The town is big, and being the chief port is always full of merchants and sailors." [14]

Port Royal was a lively seaport in 1690, pulsating with activities of all sorts, with between 7500 and 10,000 inhabitants (white, black, and red) living and working in the 2000 structures on the sand spit. According to John Taylor's colorful description, 600 of these buildings were of brick construction, four stories high, collared, and "covered with Tile and glazed with Sash Windows," but signally lacking in chimneys unless they were small cookrooms, set apart from the others. "These houses," he continues, "yield as good rents as those in Cheapside in London, seldom less than 80£ to 100£ yearly rent, and lodgings are here very deare, so that you must give six [Spanish] Dollars a Month for one Chamber reasonably furnished." Besides spacious quays, a well-protected landing place for small craft, and three markets each day, Port Royal contained nearly every facility required for extensive commerce and ships' repairs known to the age: many "commodious store houses" belonging to the merchants and a great public warehouse, "large Shops" for dispensing an array of European goods and luxury articles, goldsmiths, and a large cooperage. Along the north side of St. Paul's Church ran a covered, paved walk where the merchants met daily on 'change. As the traveler gazed at the town from the deck of an incoming ship he would have observed its brick buildings with gambrel roofs and been reminded of Great Yarmouth or some other East Anglian port, where he would have also been able to make out an occasional brick structure with

14. On St. Iago de la Vega (Spanish Town), Port Morant, and Passage Fort, as well as Port Royal, see *Present State of Jamaica,* 10–15; Hanson in *Laws of Jamaica* (Wood), 456; and Taylor, Multum in Parvo, II, 509–12; also Buisseret, "Port Royal," in *Jamaica Historical Review,* VI, 21–7; John Cary, *An Essay on the State of England in Relation to Trade* . . . (Bristol, 1695), 77.

stepped gables or curvilinear Flemish pediment roofs to remind him that men from the Low Countries had often sailed into this harbor.[15]

In the main, like the tobacco planters of the Chesapeake, the Englishmen of the Antilles remained rural in their lives and activities; they did not expend time, money, and energy in erecting towns and cities. In this respect they differed markedly from the Spanish colonials with whom they had very little contact. Only Bridgetown, with about the same population as little Newport on Rhode Island, and Port Royal in any way rivaled Boston, Philadelphia, and New York in size or urban attributes. The Jamaican community was a signal exception to the generalization, however, for whether its population totaled 8000 or 10,000 in 1690, it was certainly larger than Boston with its 7000 inhabitants. Taken as a whole, Port Royal was undoubtedly the leading urban center of English America at eleven o'clock on the morning of June 7, 1692, just before the first tremor of a catastrophic earthquake. Nearly 2000 people lost their lives, and more than half of the 53 acres of ground, with the buildings thereon, sank beneath the waters of the Caribbean Sea; the remainder of the town was left "a perfect island of about 25 acres." (Plate 13) Town development had reached its apogee in the English islands; never again before American independence did any Caribbean community rival the five cities on the continent of North America.[16]

III

What most impressed the visitor to Bridgetown, Port Royal, or to one of the tiny settlements at a transfer point was not the usual

15. John Taylor's vivid, though sometimes inaccurate, description of Port Royal in 1688 (Multum in Parvo, II, 491–509) is essential for the state of the seaport just before the earthquake. The devastated area is clearly indicated on "A General Plan of Port Royal in which the Different States of the Town are Accurately Laid Down," insert on Patrick Browne, *A New Map of Jamaica* (London, 1755). [Plate 13] See also Port Royal at 17 minutes before noon, June 2, 1692, an ingenious colored fold-out reconstruction in *National Geographic Magazine,* CXVII (1960), facing p. 152; *Laws of Jamaica* (1683), To the Reader, n. p.; *CSPC, 1693–96,* p. 60; "The Port Royal Project," in *Jamaica Journal,* IV, No. 2, pp. 2–12.

16. The growth of Philadelphia from uninhabited woodland to 4000 people, 1682–90, was unprecedented. Table of Population of Colonial Towns, 1690, in Bridenbaugh, *Cities in the Wilderness,* 6.

structures with party walls, churches with spires, public buildings, and the town houses of the rich but rather the great storehouses. Erected by local merchants, these brick, stone, or timber storehouses, or warehouses, which served as places for dry and safe storage, were ordinarily three or four stories high with windows large enough for hogsheads, large chests, and great bags to be swung through when hoisted from the street to the upper floors by means of a rope passed through an eye-bolt fixed near the top of the gable —one can see these in any Dutch city today. Most merchants and factors set apart a small room in their storehouses as a shop from which they sold goods at retail, for wholesaling and retailing had not yet been completely differentiated. In many of the cavernous structures, there was also a countinghouse where the merchant, his clerks, and apprentices conducted business and made their reckonings. In not a few instances, however, resident merchants had counting rooms and retail shops in their town houses. Weekly, from early on Mondays, the countinghouse was a very busy place until five o'clock on Saturday, when it was "washed" by the prentices, papers and books were laid aside for the Sabbath, and the cash locked in a chest.[17]

A curious observer lingering in front of one of the storehouses and noting the kinds of goods passed in and out could have a very good understanding of the insular economy. Almost daily there came in from the countryside quantities of staple produce in barrels, bags, chests, or paniers on the backs of asses, horses, and occasionally a camel, and even in small bundles carried by black slaves on their heads. After 1660, ox-carts and horse-drawn drays were put into service. Hogsheads of sugar, molasses, rum, and tobacco, smaller casks of indigo and cocoa, bags of cotton and ginger, sticks of logwood, bundles of hides and tuns of fustic, all went into the storehouses. There they were measured or weighed, checked for quality, and stored to await the coming of the English, Dutch, or

17. John Tinker, steward for John Winthrop, Jr., at New London, reported in in Feb. 1660 that he had £150 in sawn and rived timber on hand, and that he wanted a local merchant named Palmer "to accept of soe much slit work for frames for ware houses, to send to Barbados in the frigot. . . ." *MHS Colls.*, 4th ser., VII, 232. *NEHG Reg.*, LXVII, 366; and for trading in a "Convenient Storehouse att the hole," Barbados, see *CSPC, 1661–68,* p. 561; *Suffolk Deeds,* II, 27.

New England ships, which would carry them across the Atlantic to London, Liverpool, Bristol, Amsterdam, Hamburg, or Rouen, or northward to Boston, Newport, and Portsmouth.[18]

From every warehouse—for each of them served as a kind of general store offering to sell any article that the planter or his family required—the motley procession took home a variety of goods. The items sought came from the northern colonies and from across the Atlantic: cheap clothing, hats and shoes for the slaves and servants; wines from Madeira; French brandy; New England fish, pork, pease, and onions; timber products; barrels of salted beef and firkins of butter from Ireland; and Chesapeake, New York, and Pennsylvania flour. In the eighties, all of the islands imported an "infinite Quantity of Iron Wares ready wrought, Thousands of Dozens of Howes, and great numbers of Bills to cut our Canes. Many barrels of Nails, many Sets of Smiths, Carpenters, and Coopers Tools; all our Locks and Hinges," plus weapons of all kinds. These were sold in job lots from the storehouse or by the piece at the shops, along with tinware, earthenware, woodenware, rope, lead, English cloth, especially "Stuffs," hats of beaver and straw, and "thousands of Dozens yearly" of shoes, woolen yarns, and Negroes' caps, also by the thousands, and stockings of wool, worsted, thread, or silk. One planter at Nevis objected bitterly in 1681 to "all things being very dear," and his price list, which he sent to England, substantiates his complaint: 35 pounds of sugar for a pair of shoes for a servant, 250 pounds for a yard of broadcloth, and 12 pounds for a hoe, axe, or bill. Customers repeated his lament at every warehouse throughout the Antilles.[19]

18. The quantities of exports of Muscovado and clayed sugars, molasses, rum, cotton, ginger, and lime juice exported from Barbados warehouses to England and the other plantations from May 13, 1690, to Feb. 12, 1691, are listed in PRO: CO 390/6, fols. 26–7; Taylor, Multum in Parvo, II, 492.

19. Regular market days were appointed for the ports of Barbados in 1661 and 1665; and, to protect both the market people and retail shopkeepers in the latter year, a law prohibited peddlers from carrying packs from house to house and, as in England, provided for the forfeiture of such wares. Peddlers were often accused of dealing with white servants and Negro slaves for stolen goods, which they sold below the prices asked by local merchants. *Acts of Barbados* (1721), 64–5, 71–2; Lyttleton, *Groans of the Plantations,* 28–9; Nevis prices: BM: Egerton MSS, 2395, fol. 597. For markets at Port Royal, see Taylor, Multum in Parvo, II, 494.

IV

All of this importing of provisions, lumber, horses, and many kinds of European goods was managed by the merchants, great and small. When the Lords of Trade and Plantations inquired in 1676 how many such men there were in each colony, Governor Jonathan Atkins replied from Barbados that if they meant by merchants such as the Dutch call them, "which is every man that sells and buy[s] who they call a Copeman, there are many here," but of those who barter and trade commodities by factors, Bridgetown no longer had many. Indeed, in each island, the merchants' community fluctuated in membership and presented a broad spectrum of activities, which are best illustrated by the careers of certain individuals.[20]

One means for a new arrival to become a planter, if he had some stock, however large or small, was to start off in a mercantile way. Cary Helyar, a younger brother of a landed gentleman of Somersetshire, sailed out to Jamaica in 1664 and set up as a merchant at Port Royal, where he enjoyed considerable success. Early in his career, by means of family influence in England, he formed an important and profitable connection with Sir Thomas Modyford, who, in addition to being governor, was an agent for the Royal Adventurers. Sometime before 1669 Cary Helyar became a dealer in slaves, and within two years he had sold 259 blacks, or 10 per cent of the total allowed traders licensed by the Royal Adventurers. He also dealt in wines. Surviving papers indicate that not only had the knight assisted the young merchant in the slave business, but he also guided him in investing the profits in Bybrook Plantation. Many a merchant followed this route from counting-house to plantation, for as Helyar said later, "planting is a happy and convenient way of thriving." One of the more important and interesting of these individuals after the Restoration was Samuel Winthrop, who became deputy-governor of Antigua in 1668—and a Quaker too. Another was Azariah Pinney, a pardoned West Country rebel, who sailed for Nevis in 1685 with only a Bible, six gallons of sack, four of brandy, and £15 in cash. At Charles

20. PRO: CO 1/37, fols. 66, 67.

Town he began as a factor and sold such goods as hoes, axes, and lace supplied by his father, and remitted to him sugar and cotton. Pinney was also sought after as an attorney. Hard work and strict attention to business enabled him to prosper, and in 1697 he purchased the property of Henri Charlot and transformed himself into the founder of one of the largest West Indian sugar fortunes of the eighteenth century.[21]

Christopher Jeaffreson was the head of the second generation of his family to live on St. Christopher. His father John Jeaffreson had been the designated successor to Sir Thomas Warner in 1625 and, not unexpectedly, accumulated a large estate on the island. Supplied with European goods by his cousin, William Poyntz of London, young Jeaffreson crossed to St. Christopher in 1676 to see the estate which he had inherited. He soon learned that "the poverty of this island makes the markett bad, and requires time to vend commodities." Nothing sells so well as Madeira wines: "They are soe generally and soe plentifully drunk." Before long, Jeaffreson was supplying Lady Stapleton with "vallances," cotton hangings, and Smyrna carpets. He acquired an able assistant in William Calhoun, "a bonny Scot," who had been at St. Christopher for many years "to noe small advantage," and was a member of the Assembly. Gradually, over the next six years, the plantation absorbed more and more of the young squire's time and energies. Then in 1682, he returned to England and thenceforth played the role of the absentee, conducting his affairs through overseers and agents, who gave him more worries than satisfaction.[22]

Numerous factors did business in the Caribbean, buying and selling for merchants in London or the outports, customarily for a commission of 5 per cent. They worked for Sir John Bawden, John Gardiner, Sir John Bendish, Sir Peter Leir, and other London merchants prominent in the West India traffic, who often had their

21. Cary Helyar & Co., Accounts, 1669–70, and Helyar MSS, 1664–71, *passim;* also Bennett, *WMQ,* 3d ser., XXI, 54–9; Mayo, *The Winthrop Family in America,* 76–8; Pares, *West-India Fortune,* 9–11, 32–6.

22. The Jeaffreson MSS, containing the valuable letter-book from which the *Young Squire* often supplies only a précis, was used by Higham in 1921 but unfortunately has been lost. Jeaffreson, *Young Squire,* I, 183, 185, 188, 190, 195, 236, 243–7; II, 84–5, 251–2, 263.

own plantations in Barbados and imported sugar in large amounts. As in all ages, some of these factors took advantage of their English employers. Governor Stapleton told of some of these men converting their employers' goods into plantations and slaves, and consequently the ships sailed home empty. John Oldmixon wrote of a number of "dishonest factors" who, when the French took St. Christopher again in 1689, balanced their accounts by transferring a "great Part of their Merchandize, their Negroes especially, to the Planters of St. Christophers." By this devious maneuver, they shifted their own debts to the ruined planters of that captured island, whose debts were patently uncollectable. One man on Nevis payed off his obligation of £10,000 with debts owing from St. Christopher.[23]

All of the men familiar with the West India trade agreed upon one thing: that planters, unless they themselves were also merchants, were in debt to them. As a Barbadian petition expressed it in 1661: "The people of this Country are so generally indebted to the Merchants that were their Estates truly calculated they have a small portion in them for themselves." And what was true that year still held in 1690, and for every other island as well. As for the merchants, Jonathan Atkins believed that none would ever reveal what he was worth in order to guard his credit. Though they were generally esteemed rich men while they were living, when they died, either their factors or their wives ran away with their estates and left little for their creditors.[24]

The letter-book of William Freeman, merchant in London, 1678–84, is possibly the most revealing personal document of the seventeenth century; its pages contain a marvelous tale about every phase of the economic life of the men of the Leeward Islands and their relations with Britain. Freeman was one of the very first settlers at St. Christopher, where he accumulated a large plantation, which he claimed later on was worth £800 a year to him. Along with hundreds of others who were dispossessed by the French when the latter took over the English plantations in 1666, he moved to

23. Edward Hatton, *The Merchant's Magazine, or a Tradesman's Treasury* (2d ed., London, 1697), 208–11, 223–7; *CSPC, 1677–80,* p. 110; *1681–85,* p. 276; PRO: CO 1/37, fol. 67a; Oldmixon, *British Empire in America,* II, 35, 47–8, 249.
24. BM: Egerton MSS, 2395, fols. 305–6.

Nevis. Known there as Captain Freeman, he sought, unsuccessfully, to recover his lost estate from a Frenchman named De Chambre—all the works and the buildings were destroyed by the hurricane in 1668. At this time he went into partnership in a sugar plantation on Montserrat with John Bramley (the ingenio was run by a water-mill). When the newly formed Royal African Company made Nevis its base for the Leeward Islands, Freeman, Robert Helmes, and Henry Carpenter became its agents to record and supervise the arrival and sale of blacks, keep the Company's books, and forward cargoes to England in its ships. They were also expected to see to it that the captains of the slavers did not sneak in slaves of their own and sell them ashore, and to prosecute interlopers. Thus did a long-time planter enter business through employment in the slave trade. Within five years, William Freeman was in England and dispatching Irish servants to the Caribbees, some of them to Christopher Jeaffreson, who also dealt with Freeman's fellow merchant Helmes at Nevis.[25]

William Freeman knew nearly every official, rich planter, and merchant who counted in the life of the Leeward Islands and Jamaica: Governors Stapleton and Lynch, Colonel Philip Warner of Antigua, Samuel Winthrop, and many more. In fact he knew them very well, and furthermore, behind his commercial enterprises lay a very thorough knowledge and understanding of planting, the slave trade, and traffic with England and the European continent. Crossing to London in 1678, he took the final step of joining with his brother-in-law William Baxter in a partnership with Robert Helmes of Nevis, a councillor of the Leeward Islands and still agent for the Royal African Company. This was a family undertaking, for Helmes married Freeman's sister Sarah in 1680, after an engagement dating at least from 1676. They had what seems

25. C. S. S. Higham believed that there were two William Freemans, father and son; a careful reading of the Coppie Booke leads us to conclude that we are dealing with only one; he was sometimes called Captain and at others, Major. In 1678 he was a member of the Council of Montserrat, but "now in England." William Freeman, Coppie Booke of Letres, Anno 1678 to 1684 (MS, Institute of Jamaica), 1, *et passim*. Map of Montserrat (JCB), and *Blathwayt Atlas*, Map 31; BM: Add. MSS, 11,409, fols. 37a-b, 205; PRO: CO 1/29, fol. 18; *CSPC, 1677–80*, pp. 222, 264, 281; Jeaffreson, *Young Squire*, I, 181, 209, 240; II, 202, 304; Higham, *Leeward Islands*, 153, 237.

to be a perfect arrangement for trading from London to the West Indies: an experienced London merchant in Baxter, in Helmes a strategically placed islander, and in William Freeman what today we would call a first-class and bold idea-man. The partners owned several ketches and brigs and were actively concerned in the usual legitimate business of supplying Irish servants and salted beef, candles, butter, salt, and also Madeira wines for Leeward Island correspondents in return for sugar and indigo. With their combined broad experience, the partners were bound to succeed by the proper and prompt use of intelligence, industry, and intrigue.[26]

Had Edward Randolph, the notorious customs snooper who levied charge after charge at the New Englanders for transgressing the Acts of Trade, been permitted a glimpse into the Freeman Coppie Booke he would have discovered what small fry the emerging Yankees really were. William Freeman showed himself a past master at both evasion and smuggling; he knew and used with remarkable skill every trick of trade. In 1678 he ordered from William Helmes in Nevis eighty "Large caske such as are very stronge, and very well hooped and hogsheads" to be sent over to London in the *Olive Branch* for their own use. The partners had purchased, at a good price, the ketch *Batchellor*. Now refitted and laded with the empty casks and a small amount of brandy, the captain, William Clayton, sailed her to St. Martin on the Ile de Ré at the mouth of the Loire, where he was to take on twenty tuns of French brandy, again in the West Indian casks, cover them with salt, and then proceed to Waterford. There he unladed the salt and took on as much salted beef as would make a cargo. The captain's orders were to head for Nevis, stop "an hour or two" at Montserrat, where Robert Helmes would be waiting to give him his instructions, and to see that "all things may be caryed out with Seafety and Silence." There was even a warning not to let the seamen go ashore lest, frequenting punch houses, they talk too much "amongst

26. One way of getting business was by doing favors; in 1678 Freeman wrote to Captain Abel Mathews: "Yor Leadys Trunke of Goods lies in the Custom hous whare I cannot yet get it out unless I will Sware that the Linins there in Contained ware Exported which you know I cannot Doe." He promises, however, to get a warrant from the Lord Treasurer through confidential channels. Freeman, Coppie Booke, 4, 27, 45, 150, 275, 437, 499. On Helmes, see PRO: CO 1/45, fol. 45.

their comrades." William Freeman advised Helmes that *Batchellor*'s cocket would show the entire cargo of French brandy as shipped out of London: "Wee must use a Little art in making a small alteration" of the amounts, so that there can be no evidence against us. At Montserrat, Helmes was to see the beef unladed and sent off to Nevis in a sloop, then to enter the brandy in the Customs. For the return voyage, the ketch was to take on thirty or forty tons of sugar and be cleared either for London or Liverpool in the name of William Fox of Nevis so that the partners' names would not show on the shipping papers. Craft paid off. The voyage of *Batchellor* went exactly as planned save that though Freeman had ordered the best, the French brandy was "not according to Expectations." [27]

For the second venture, the partners acquired a larger vessel, the *Adventure,* and Freeman drew plans to send 20 to 30 tuns of brandy in English beer barrels. This time Captain Clayton made for Nantes where he took on French linens in 20 English-made "truncks" that were listed in the cockets as "Canvis and Dowlies," and 80 hogsheads labeled as "Aquavitae, under which Denomination Brandy is now generally Shipt out." Freeman directed Helmes to try to get "the favor of the Customer of liquors at Mt. Serrat to put it on shore, and Carry it down in what part you think Convenient to Nevis." Helmes, however, was ill and unable to keep a weather eye on the undertaking, and in Antigua his agent Edward Dandy drew the corks on the brandy and watered it, but one of the crew caught him in the act. Nevertheless, this second voyage also succeeded, and, while a return cargo was being assembled, Captain Clayton sailed *Adventure* to Boston with linen and osnaburgs entered as "Rum and Molasses" for Peter Sargent, who sent back to Nevis hogshead and butt staves, deal boards, and 150 barrels of "mackrill" to the value of £300. The shipment was sold in the Leeward Islands and *Adventure* sailed for England with a cargo of sugar. The frugal William Freeman had not insured any of his ships because of the hurricane menace in the Antilles. With what he saved on insurance, the gain from evading the Navigation Acts, the profit from the side trip to Boston, and, with the connivance of Governor Philip Warner, the smuggling of the linens and brandy into Antigua,

27. Freeman, Coppie Booke, 15, 27–8.

this venture also turned in a substantial profit. Thus encouraged, there were further sailings, both regular and illegal, which owed much of their success to William Freeman's meticulous planning and tight secrecy. As a consequence, sometime after October 1679, he was able to contemplate retirement from business.[28]

Here then is the success story of an Englishman with a small stock, but good connections, who went out to the Caribbees, planted, fought and lost an arm in the service of King Charles I, lost his property, but somehow recovered and became a merchant, assemblyman, and later an absentee planter and London merchant. Eventually, in his old age, he retired to the English countryside.

Divers Barbadian planters who made large fortunes in sugar during the forties and fifties returned to England after the Restoration to enjoy their wealth in comfort and luxury. Such able men as Sir James Drax, Sir Peter Colleton, Sir Edwin Stede, Christopher Jeaffreson, and William Freeman often met with the West India merchants of London at the Jamaica Coffee House in St. Michael's Alley near "the West India Walk upon the Exchange." Jointly, as "the Gentlemen-Planters of Barbados in London," they sought to influence policy affecting trade and their island's financial interests. In conjunction with agents sent over by Royal governors and assemblies, these absentees, by looking out for special interests, constituted one of the earliest effective lobbies at Westminster. Although in England they served the West Indies well, their departure deprived the islands of sorely needed talent, as well as considerable working capital, so that their going home was a serious financial and managerial loss.[29]

During the lush times of the forties and early fifties, when the planters were accumulating the wherewithal to retire to their Mother Country, a counter-movement took place of English mer-

28. Samuel Winthrop of Antigua shipped some sugar to Freeman in September 1679 and ordered a new copper made for his boiling-house. Soon he was dealing with William Baxter alone, but Freeman looked after Winthrop's daughter when she arrived in London. Freeman, Coppie Booke, 91, 95, 117, 129, 133, 150, 155, 163, 220, 224, 298.

29. *London Gazette,* March 5, 1673/4; Lillian M. Penson, *The Colonial Agents of the British West Indies* (London, 1924), 10–11; Kenneth G. Davies, "The Origins of the Commission System in the West Indies Trade," in *RHS, Trans.,* 5th ser., II, 89–91.

chants, encouraged by the Navigation Acts, thronging to the island to sell the settlers not only necessities but "all sorts of Delicate things to please their pallates as well as their fancies." As profits began to decline, some of the improvident islanders saw their plantations "swallowed up" by the merchants and themselves turned off their land. Jonathan Atkins related that the more prudent planters "began to trade for themselves of all necessarys and many of them their Neighbors at indifferent Rates." Thus Barbados and the Leeward Islands came to have proportionately fewer men who were exclusively merchants. The planters consigned their produce on their own accounts to such London houses as Bawden & Gardiner, John Eyles & Company, or to individual merchants, such as Thomas Tryon, who charged a commission of 2.5 per cent and .005 per cent for brokerage, and either made purchases requested by the planters or deposited the proceeds in an account on which bills of exchange could be drawn. It was this service that Freeman, Baxter, and Helmes performed for Leeward Islanders.[30]

The Jews had been numerous enough in Barbados in 1644 to justify the building of a synagogue and had lived in apparent harmony with the older residents. After 1654, however, their numbers increased to a point that protests were made to officials that the merchants and traders were suffering as a result of the Jews living and trading in Barbados. An order of 1657 restrained them and other aliens from bringing in goods to sell at retail, but that did not prevent their conducting small shops to sell the English goods they purchased from merchants on the island. The Jews had never been distinguished as planters, but even if they had been so inclined, they could not have succeeded in Barbados, for they were permitted only one slave to a household and could not own white servants. Fifty-four Sephardic families lived on Jew Street (now Swan) in Bridgetown in 1689, and nearly all of them were poor and earned a meager living as moneylenders on personal rather

30. At Barbados in 1669, interest stood at 15 per cent, according to Sir Josiah Child, and his arguments influenced the Assembly to reduce it to 10 per cent in a law of 1690. *A New Discourse of Trade* (1698 ed.), 79. When droughts occurred and fewer ships crossed to England with sugar, the West India merchants of London suffered as well as the planters. William Freeman spoke in 1682 of the scarcity of bills of exchange. Freeman, Coppie Booke, 374–6; BM: Egerton MSS, 2395, fol. 305; Atkins, Answers to Queries, 1676, PRO: CO 1/37, fol. 23; and in general, Davies, in *RHS, Trans.*, 5th ser., II, 33–4.

than real property, usually taking 10 per cent. Like many Jews in other lands, they were pawnbrokers, whom the Grand Jury presented in 1684, along with wandering peddlers, as a nuisance.[31]

By 1680 Jamaica had received Jews who were planters from Surinam, and was attracting others from Barbados by a more lenient policy towards aliens. The English merchants at Port Royal had petitioned the governor and council in 1671 against allowing "the Trading of the Jews," requested an exact census of them, and insisted that the thirteen naturalized Hebrews in their town produce their letters of denization. Again in 1672 a petition was presented to the governor charging that because they practiced a "penurious way of living," they undersold the Christians. In his defense of the Jews, Sir Thomas Lynch argued shrewdly to the Lords of Trade and Plantations: "It is my humble opinion that his Majesty cannot have more profitable Subjects here then they, and the Hollanders, for they have great stocks and correspondence, are not numerous enough to supplant us, and will never find it their interest to betray us." He conceded that no Jamaica merchant was willing to "adventure" the Jews' goods. Captain William Beeston seized Rabba Contÿ's ship *Trial,* which was sailing with a pass from Governor Lovelace of New York, in November 1672 on the grounds that the "Marchant" was not a "Denizen," was evading the Acts of Trade, and was "not an Englishman but a Jew." The case finally reached England, and the Lords of the Privy Council reversed the judgment and ordered the restoration of the ship and cargo of this "Free Burgher" of Manhattan. Such scanty evidence as survives indicates that the Hebrews were never numerous, wealthy, or landholders and, though they were good citizens, they did not figure prominently in insular agriculture or commerce before 1690.[32]

In the countryside of any of the islands only an occasional crafts-

31. Barbados Council Minutes, I, 48, 60; II, 212; *JBMHS,* IX, 130–32; Wilfred S. Samuels, *A Review of the Jewish Colonists in Barbados in the Year 1680* (London, 1936), 8–9, 12; *CSPC, 1677–80,* p. 446; *1681–85,* p. 750.

32. Aboard the frigate *Falcon* on Sunday, December 31, 1687/8, John Taylor recorded in his Journal: "This Morning we pulled up the Jewes [floating] bridges with our Tackles, which hee had there built to hinder our Careening [the *Falcon*] against the Wharff and other timber." Multum in Parvo, III, 676; Jamaica Council Minutes, I, 200; BM: Add. MSS, 11,410, fol. 214; Cundall, *Governors of Jamaica,* 39; PRO: CO 1/29, fol. 50, Nos. II–IV; Samuels, *Jewish Colonists in Barbados,* 32.

man ever succeeded in setting up shop, because, on each plantation, either white servants or black slaves performed nearly all of the required mechanical tasks; an independent smith or mason could find only temporary work among the small landowners. A newly freed man had to have a small stock to purchase tools, rent a shop, and find materials. Furthermore, the urge to get rich on sugar or some other staple worked as inexorably on men with trades as with any others: George Russell, "Blacksmith," who bought three acres of land in St. James's Parish, Barbados, in 1661 was but one of many artisans who abandoned his trade to become a planter. In Barbados in 1685, Dr. Henry Pitman met John Nuthall, "a carver whose condition was somewhat mean and therefore one that wanted Money to carry him off the Island." The physician not only staked him by discharging his debt of £12 for tools, but he bought from a Guineaman in the harbor a small boat in which he joined Nuthall and seven others in fleeing to Curaçao. Ultimately they joined the buccaneers. Lord Carlisle beseeched the king in 1679 to relieve the shortage of craftsmen in Jamaica by encouraging men who were being discharged from the army to migrate there, claiming that "all tradesmen coming hither much advance themselves and improve the Island." But the truth was that such a narrowly agricultural society could never nourish any large number of independent handicraftsmen.[33]

In the great seaports of Bridgetown and Port Royal, skilled craftsmen often made a good living, especially in the luxury trades. The large amounts of bullion and gold and silver coins brought by the freebooters to Jamaica provided work for goldsmiths, one of whom was already working at Port Royal by 1660. In August 1684 Christopher Jeaffreson arranged to send a watch and some silver articles belonging to his neighbor, Captain James Phipps, all the way from St. Christopher to Bridgetown to be repaired by

33. To employ poor white men and keep them from migrating from Barbados, Sir Peter Colleton and other absentee planters in London urged Governor Codrington and the Assembly in 1670 to enact a law requiring all servants and slaves to be clothed in dimity manufactured in the island, and prohibiting Negroes from any craft work other than sugar-making. *CSPC, 1669–74,* p. 141; Pitman, *A Relation,* 12–15; Description of Barbados (MS Map), in BM: Sloane MSS, 2441; *Timehri,* n. s., X, 104; Barbados Council Minutes, II, 198; *Acts of Nevis,* 8–9; PRO: CO 1/43, fol. 61; *CSPC, 1677–80,* p. 330.

a watchmaker and a goldsmith. Some of these craftsmen must have been highly skilled, for the Earl of Inchiquin, who died in 1691, mentions in his will that all of his good plate had been "made up in Jamaica." Before the earthquake of 1692, Port Royal surpassed Bridgetown in the number and variety of its craftsmen. "There are now setled here in this port," Taylor announced, "a sort of Mechanicks and Tradesmen, as Smiths, Carpenters, Bricklayers, Joyners, Turners, Cabanittmakers, Tanners, Curriors, Shoemakers, Taylors, Hatters, Upholsters, Ropemakers, Glasiers, Painters, Carvers, Armourers, and [tortoise-shell] Combmakers . . . all which live here very well, earning thrice the wages given in England, by which means they are enabled to maintain their famalies much better than in England." Taylor thought the tradesmen as a group were much advanced in wealth and strength; but in general throughout the islands, the independent artisan like John Nuthall found it hard to survive.[34]

Colonial societies are always plagued by money troubles, and the shaky financial state of so many West Indians cannot be placed on the shoulders of the merchants or the Jews. In part the difficulties derived from the insufficient supply of money to provide a circulating medium of exchange, which is the bane of all new settlements. Before 1660, the planters seldom dealt in cash or handled coin, and they felt the deficiency keenly. The Barbados Assembly demanded a "Mint House," which would make them "financially equal with New England and Jamaica." Two years later, in November 1661, the English authorities received a "Design for a Bank in Barbados," whose commissioners would give credit on land and goods and not charge over 6 per cent interest. The projectors claimed that it would increase trade and be welcomed by the people because it would use credit instead of specie or commodities, and it would prevent the "Extortion . . . practiced by Jues and others who now sell theire goods for at least 60 per cent annum interest. . . ." Even worse off for a means of exchange were the Lee-

34. One of the Helyars paid £7 10*s*. for a watch in London. Helyar MSS, 1695. During recent excavations at Port Royal a leather-covered watch was found. Biët, *Voyage,* 276–7; *NEHG Reg.,* X, 178; Jeaffreson, *Young Squire,* II, 120; Cundall, *Governors of Jamaica,* 130; Taylor, Multum in Parvo, II, 508.

ward Islanders. The Assembly of Montserrat attempted to ameliorate the shortage by fixing rates of exchange for all foreign coins, and for "all New England monies at its full value, as it passes in New England," whereas in Britain the pine-tree shilling passed at only ninepence.[35]

As early as 1662, in compliance with a request from Jamaicans for a mint to coin the gold, silver, and base metals brought to Port Royal by the privateers, Henry Slingsby, secretary for the Council for Plantations, had agreed to supervise it from London if there were a revenue of £1000 a year to cover the costs of operation. For this reason, probably, the scheme fell through. Ten years later Sir Thomas Lynch expressed the hope that the trade of Jamaica with New Englanders could be lessened, for the northern colonists were taking money out and sending no people. Less and less gold and silver were coming in after the suppression of the buccaneers, and interest rates were rising; by 1675 usury had grown so oppressive that the Assembly limited interest to 15 per cent and fixed a penalty of treble damage for anyone who charged more. At a meeting of the Privy Council in February 1678/9 the Earl of Carlisle raised the idea of a mint again; he pointed out that the traders of the island suffered greatly because the "least coyne" passing in Jamaica was sevenpence halfpenny. Apparently he was directed to issue coins for Jamaica at the same weights as those in England, but the Jamaicans, recalling their past experience, were opposed to the idea, for they were convinced that New Englanders would again carry off the coins.[36]

In an account officially appended to *The Laws of Jamaica,* published at London in 1683, Francis Hanson emphasized the vastly improved economic state and attractions of the island to English investors. Anyone having money available could remit it in bills of exchange at 20 per cent advance or more, and have it lent out at Port Royal for 10 per cent interest; or, with the advice of London merchants, invest his capital in commodities, running only "the

35. BM: Egerton MSS, 2395, fol. 182; PRO: CO 1/15, fol. 89; *Acts of Assembly . . . of Montserrat,* 19, 23; BM: Add. MSS, 11,410, fol. 301b.

36. PRO: CO 1/43, fols. 15, 20, 76; CO 1/36, fol. 151b; *CSPC, 1677–80,* p. 319; *1689–92,* p. 504; and generally, Curtis P. Nettels, *The Money Supply of the American Colonies Before 1720* (Madison, Wisc., 1934).

risque of the Sea, which is so inconsiderable, that it may be ensured for 2 per cent." When the investors recall their money, Hanson added, they can expect a loss of 15 to 20 per cent because of the difference in the value of coins, which they might get back somehow. Moreover, the land in Jamaica increases in value steadily, while it decreases in England, and the entire undertaking should represent a tidy profit. Port Royal was full of gold and silver coins in 1682, most of them gained by the trade in slaves and European goods with the Spanish colonies. Some of this money went out to New England or went home to redress unfavorable balances, but other coins "our Goldsmiths there work up, who but few grow very wealthy, for almost every House hath a rich Cupboard of Plate . . . And whereas most other Plantations ever did and now do keep their accounts in Sugar or the proper Commodities of the Place for want of Money, it is otherwise in Jamaica, for in Port Royal there is more plenty of running Cash (proportionately to the number of its Inhabitants) than is in London." [37]

V

To and from these little maritime communities hundreds of ships came and went regularly along three important sea lanes. The master of a ship of the Royal African Company or of a licensed or interloping merchant of London, Liverpool, Bristol, or Chester would sail down the coast of West Africa to trade for slaves, then cross the Atlantic, usually to Barbados or Jamaica, only occasionally to the Leeward Islands, dispose of his black cargo, and lade tropical commodities for the return trip to England. Such long voyages attracted merchant shipping because they involved the two largest and most lucrative of the plantation trades: sugar and slaves. Merchants such as Freeman, Baxter, and Helmes preferred a direct traffic out to the Caribbean with Irish, English, and French necessaries and luxuries, and a more prompt return of their ships with cargoes of sugar, indigo, ginger, and passengers, more of the last than one would expect. Many vessels sailed out via Madeira to take on wines. A parallel commerce was conducted by the Myn-

37. Hanson's Account in *Laws of Jamaica* (Wood), 451.

heers, either out and back from the West Indies, or via the coast of Guinea.[38]

Contemporary charts and maps gave the distance from Land's End to Barbados as 3430 English miles (2580 to Cape Cod). Even with the advantage of the Northeast Trades, unless the course were altered for a call at Madeira, which frequently happened, it still took about six weeks to sail out. Ships in the West India trade usually made 1.1 voyages a year. The distance to Jamaica was much greater and the passage more difficult because of the winds and ocean currents. It was alleged that one could sail to Jamaica from Barbados in eight days but that it took six to seven weeks to beat back to windward; Governor Atkins estimated ten weeks. Ships sailing from Port Royal to England took the Windward Passage in preference to the treacherous Bahama Channel, but even then they had to sail against the wind until they rounded Cape Morant. Most vessels went out to Jamaica by way of New England and the Windward Passage, "the constant eastern winds obstructing all commerce with Barbados," and Jamaican trade with Barbados normally went on by the roundabout way of Boston and back through the Mona Passage, taking twenty-six days. Joan Vokins, a Quakeress, made a quick and safe trip in 1681 from New York to Antigua. After a week, she set out to visit Friends on Nevis; stiff winds and rough seas made the short passage unpleasant, but the discomfort was nothing to what she experienced when she started for Barbados. The small vessel "laboured three Weeks" and got no farther than Montserrat, usually a trip of one or two days, and during that time all she had to drink was "stinking water." Miserable and sick, she was set ashore, and after being revived, tried again, and again failed to get to Barbados and went back to Antigua. Eventually she did make it to Barbados.[39]

38. Cary, *Essay on the State of England,* 65; Beer, *Old Colonial System,* I, 259*n;* Taylor, Multum in Parvo, II, 505–6.

39. *CPSC, 1661–68,* pp. 319, 534, 551; Morden, *New Map of the English Plantations in America* (London, 1690); *Hydrographia Universalis, or a Book of Maritime Charts* (London, 1690. LCP); PRO: CO 1/37, fol. 23; CO 1/22, fol. 475; Butel-Dumont, *Histoire et commerce des Antilles angloises,* 94–9; Joan Vokins, *God's Mighty Power Magnified* (London, 1680), 38.

The burthen of the craft trading directly from England to Barbados varied from 100 to 200 tons; the "great Dutch ships" from Guinea often ran as high as 300 tons and more. Before 1671 the cargoes from Jamaica were so uncertain that Governor Lynch reported that the "great Shipps durst not venture hither." Lack of good harbors dictated that big ships avoid anchoring in open roadsteads in the Leeward Islands, and consequently those calling at Jamaica and the smaller Caribbees usually ranged from 80 to 100 tons. In the fifties 400 vessels a year from the British Isles traded with the West Indies, and this figure was repeated in 1670; thereafter the number fell off somewhat, possibly because of greater cargo capacity. In 1686–87, London sent out 225 ships of the 391 that sailed from all the English ports; all of them together totaled 44,000 tons.[40]

Samuel Copen's splendid print of Bridgetown shows forty-four ships of various tonnages lying in the harbor in 1694, and from it one gains an accurate idea of nearly every kind of rigging then in use—lateen, square, fore-and-aft—on shallops, sloops, brigs, ketches, barques, brigantines—full-rigged ships, and various small craft.[41]

Travel and communication among the English possessions was infrequent and difficult; in the hurricane months of July, August, September, and October, transport ceased entirely. Because the Caribbee Isles lay so close together, small sloops and shallops served for most of the interisland traffic. On the other hand, Bar-

40. To protect wooden hulls against the destructive *Teredo navalis,* or ship-worm of the tropics, Thomas Rastell at the Customs Office and Francis Dracott at "the West-Indies Walk upon the Exchange" had for sale in 1674 "The new Invention for Sheathing Ships against the Worm &c, with Lead and Lacker." *London Gazette,* March 5, 1673/4; BM: Add. MSS, 11,410, fol. 209; Egerton MSS, 2395, fols. 528–9, 638; Blome, *Description of Jamaica,* 69; PRO: CO 1/37, fol. 23; Ralph Davis, The Organisation and Finance of the English Shipping Industry in the Later Seventeenth Century (Ph.D. Thesis, London, 1955), Tables I, II (entries and clearances from and to the West Indies, 1686), 382–4; Ralph Davis, *The Rise of the English Shipping Industry in the Seventeenth and Eighteenth Centuries* (London, 1962), Table p. 398.

41. See Plate 14, and Montserrat Island, 1673, in *Blathwayt Atlas,* I, Map 30, for 13 craft therein depicted. On rigging, see Henry Bond's widely used *The Boat Swain's Art . . .* (London, 1642, 1670).

bados lay so far to the eastward that about 20 sloops of 15 to 20 tons were sufficient for local transport. The Jamaicans used a sizeable fleet of 60 to 70 small craft for freighting goods along the coast and for fishing off Pedro Cays and the Cayman Islands; and in the eighties, two or three vessels plied constantly between Jamaica and distant Barbados.[42]

Up until 1663 when King Charles II established "a public office or offices for receipt of all letters and postage," the rates according to those set by Parliament, there was no "sure way of intelligence" in the colonies. Heretofore letters and packages had been entrusted to private individuals, but the loss or endless delays in delivering them, which occurred ordinarily after the mail reached the islands, made trade and the conduct of business transactions extremely difficult. The praiseworthy postal service must have died out, for in 1681 the Council of Barbados appointed John Dallison postmaster, and all masters of ships were required to deliver all mail, together with a true signed list to him. At Jamaica in 1671, the marshal was directed to board all incoming ships and get the letters; a list of them was then to be posted at both Spanish Town and Port Royal. Twelve years later, the Council opened a letter-office to receive and deliver all foreign mail and carry "Inland Letters to and from the several Parts of the Island." Most interesting was the injunction to the postmaster to deliver all of the foreign letters within forty-eight hours of their arrival. The merchants of Port Royal protested in 1687 that James Wales, appointed by the Earl of Rochester to be deputy of the "General Post Office" for Jamaica, held up their letters "on Pretence of Postage." After much discussion, the Council decided unanimously: "there is no Post Office" erected in Jamaica, and that Mr. Wales has no power to erect one unless the new governor qualifies him for the office. In 1690, though serious attempts to deal with the problem of the post had been made, nothing satisfactory had been achieved in any of the islands. "We esteem it a quick dispatch of our letters," Governor Atkins of Barbados charged, "if our returns are within six months, often eight

42. Welbeck MSS, VIII, 49, in Davis Coll., I, Envelope 29; BM: Egerton MSS, 2395, fol. 477; *CSPC, 1681–85,* pp. 70–71; Blathwayt, History and State of Jamaica, 66; PRO: CO 138/4, fols. 141–2; CO 1/37, fols. 20, 23.

months; at the time of hurricanes we have no ships here for five months."[43]

VI

"Jesus Christ is good, but Trade is better," ran a Dutch proverb, which Sir Thomas Lynch was fond of quoting. The Acts of Trade and Navigation could not be claimed to be designed for the greater glory of God, but rather to keep the Hollanders and Zeelanders out of the English colonies. But, in commerce, as in other aspects of Caribbean life, there was no amity beyond the line. Several Amsterdam merchants had maintained storehouses on Montserrat and Antigua in 1654 for tobacco men named Barry, Collins, Dougherty, Driscoll, Harnett, and Sullivan. Among others, Claus Jacobs dealt with Sergeant Robert Redwood in sugar as well as tobacco at Antigua. On St. Christopher before 1660, the Dutch warehouses were in the French portion, "soe that the produce of the English plantations was carried either into French grounds, or shipped for Holland, while theire commodities were vended here. 'Tis true the planters found the sweet of this, for they [the Dutch] soulde cheape, and [allowed] a year or two for payment." Christopher Jeaffreson was here describing his father's day, but he ended by saying that in his time all went to England. A modern authority concurs, adding that there were scarcely any complaints after the Treaty of Breda. The evidence at hand, however, proves otherwise.[44]

Shabby treatment by English merchants in both the number of ships and slaves supplied combined with mounting resentment of the Navigation Laws and the 4½ per cent duty to cause the planters of the Leeward Islands, when they attempted to recover from the wars, to continue relations with their oldest and best friends at St. Eustatius. Sir Thomas Lynch told Lord Arlington in 1671 that

43. *London Gazette,* July 14, Nov. 21, 1687; *CSPC, 1661–68,* p. 135; *1675–76,* p. 419; *1685–88,* p. 575; Barbados Council Minutes, II, 312–13; Cundall, *Governors of Jamaica,* 34; *APC Col.,* II, 114–15; Jamaica Council Minutes, IV, 70, 399–400; V, 53–5, 58.

44. Quotation in A. P. Thornton, *West-India Policy under the Restoration* (Oxford, 1956), 23; BM: Egerton MSS, 2395, fols. 54–9; Jeaffreson, *Young Squire,* I, 215; Higham, *Leeward Islands,* 198, 203. Du Tertre presents the classic statement of the advantages of trade with the Dutch in *Histoire générale,* II, 462–6.

most of the produce of Nevis and Antigua was carried off to Statia in Dutch sloops, and Sir Charles Wheler reported that the English merchants took twice as much profit for the goods as the Dutch and gave no credit when the Dutch were generous. Nor would the English take a poor man's tobacco and the lowest grade Muscovado, but the Dutch not only took both but paid well for them.[45]

No person was better informed about what went "out of the back-door for Holland under the name of St. Eustace sugar," which totaled above 1500 hogsheads a year, than Captain George St. Loe, the naval officer detailed to enforce the Navigation Acts in the Caribbees in 1687: "There are generally several ships lying at Statia, any two of them large enough to carry a year's produce of that island. All the rest take in their load [from] the British Colonies. On their way from Holland they generally touch at all our islands on pretext of watering. They generally stay a week, when all the planters go aboard and not only agree for what is on board, but watch their opportunity to get it ashore, to the loss of the revenue and of the [English] merchants who, having paid the duty, cannot sell so cheaply. Having disposed of their cargoes, the ships go to Statia, where they wait for the [English] planters to send their sugar, which they punctually do, though the English merchants, their creditors, for some thousands, cannot get a pound of sugar from them. Most of the islands have so many bays and inlets that it is impossible for the Customs-house officers to check the shipping off of the sugar, and the Dutch ships generally send their long boats to St. Christopher's once or twice a week on pretense of getting water, though one boat load of water would last them a month, but in reality to load sugar. Being loaded, the Dutch ships sail direct to Holland, without paying the King a penny of duty. Brandy and wine are also smuggled into the island from French St. Christophers." [46]

How much illicit trade with the Dutch went on at the two largest

45. Governor Du Lion of Guadeloupe observed to Colbert in 1670: "The quantity of merchandise is so great at St. Eustatius that the Dutch do not know what to do with it and are forced to sell it at very low prices to the English at Nevis, Montserrat, and Antigua. . . ." quoted by Mims, *Colbert's West-India Policy,* 207; *CSPC, 1669–74,* pp. 226, 290.

46. Thomas, *Historical Account of . . . the West Indies,* 382; St. Loe, in *CSPC, 1685–88,* pp. 378–9.

islands is not now ascertainable. Sir Thomas Modyford thought it extensive and, at least up to 1670, essential to Barbados, especially the traffic in white servants and black slaves. Sir Thomas Lynch was convinced in 1672 that the trading sloops of Jamaica would have done well in the islands "if wee were not undersold by great Dutch Ships that haunt the Coast of the Main and Islands." The sugar refiners of Holland, those at Amsterdam in particular, and of Hamburg, could process sugar cheaper than the English and, needing more and more Muscovado, could afford to pay the Caribbean planters a good price and still get it for less than sugar that had passed through customs in England and had been re-exported. Evidence of any clandestine trade is always hard to find, but we believe that there can be no doubt that the Dutch commercial role in the English West Indies was still a vital one in 1690.[47]

The great English maritime tradition notwithstanding, the leading inhabitants of most of the islands made little effort to promote fishing. They deemed it less expensive to import salt fish from New England, which lasted longer in the cask than the fresh, easily spoiled varieties. Richard Ligon had indicated the kinds of fish in the waters off Barbados, but no fleet was ever formed to catch them. On the windward side of the island, the vestry of St. John's Parish expressed concern in 1676 over the "greedy and avaricious desire" of some persons to exclude from the best fishing places "the poorer Inhabitants who draw their principle [*sic*] livelyhood and subsistence by ther Trade and occupation of Fishing." To prevent those who would be deprived of food for their families from going on the poor rates, the vestry petitioned the governor not to grant any fishing monopoly in the parish.[48]

Jamaica, as so often, was the exception, for the need for further economic advance led to the development of fishing. A report of 1675 stated that "Harbours and Baies are infinitely well stor'd with diverse Sorts [of fish] extra-ordinary good, also plenty of Turtle daily caught in Netts in all parts of the Island." The principal fishery after 1670 was conducted on the reefs about ninety-five miles

47. *CSPC, 1669–74,* p. 96; PRO: CO 138/4, fol. 84; Thomas, *Historical Account of . . . the West Indies,* 19–20, 382; Child, *New Discourse of Trade,* 23.
48. Ligon, *Barbados,* 35; Parish Vestry Minutes of St. John's, Barbados (MS, Barbados Historical Society), 21.

south of Port Royal where the sea turtles came from Honduras to lay their eggs, and also where many edible fish could be taken. (Plate 14) "This place has great numbers of People, Vessels, and Seamen, that are maintained by Trade . . . and Fishing in the South Cays," Governor Lynch informed William Blathwayt in 1683. A year later, the "Turtlers" were being systematically beaten off the keys and robbed by Spanish *periaguas* and a French privateersman. When ten vessels returned empty to Port Royal, Governor Molesworth and his Council sent out a galley and several armed sloops to protect the fishing fleet because it employed many "Industrious Inhabitants," and afforded "cheap wholesome Food" for the people of Jamaica. Again, in 1688, Attorney General Musgrave stressed the importance of the turtle fishery, because should its ships be laid up and the crews drift away, "the poorer sort of people" would starve and perish, "Turtle being the Cheife Subsistence. . . ." The scale of the industry is indicated by the maintenance on the southern strand at Port Royal of a large fish market and four crawls for keeping turtles, which were sold live. Fishing off Jamaica, as everywhere else, was a hard and dangerous life, made the more so by enemy harassment. On the Pedro Cays there was no peace.[49]

More remunerative to the Jamaicans than the Apostle's calling was the logwood trade. "This Logwood," wrote Sir Thomas Lynch, "grows all along the Coast of Yucatan for near 150 Leagues, and the beste Sorte is in Morasses and Swampish Grounds, where it is impossible to Plant." The logwood used in trade was cut into "sticks," about a yard long and two or three inches in diameter, from a gnarled hardwood tree having a trunk about two feet thick. The roots were also used. When ground to powder in mills in the British Isles or Europe, dyers used it to give cloth a good base or

49. Exquemeling tells of the buccaneers sailing more than 600 miles from Tortuga to the Cayman Islands to harpoon turtles at night by the light of candlewood torches. Barbuda was the center of turtle-fishing for the Leeward Islands. Exquemeling, *History of the Buccaneers,* 6, 41–2; *CSPC, 1661–68,* p. 534; *1681–85,* p. 393; PRO: CO 138/2, fol. 121; CO 138/4, fols. 141–2; Jamaica Council Minutes, IV, 127–33; V, 50; Diagram of Port Royal, *National Geographic Magazine,* CXVII, 152; Oldmixon, *British Empire in America,* II, 335; Taylor, Multum in Parvo, II, 494. Labat recommended eating turtles as a "remede aisé" for "le mal de Naples" which affected so many Europeans in the tropics. *Nouveau Voyage,* I, 311–12.

foundation for other colors, especially reddish purple and black, all of which could be made brighter by the use of alkali mixtures. When logwood was first introduced to England in Elizabethan days, its importation was banned, but it was illicitly used. The Navigation Law of 1660 made it an enumerated article, and the explanatory act of 1661, repealing the old prohibitory statutes, allowed free importation of logwood upon payment of a duty of £5 a ton with a drawback of £4 if it were re-exported.[50]

The lush growth of logwood along the Spanish Main had been known by the English long before 1662 when Jamaican axemen began to cut it on the coast of Yucatan. In the next decade they had spread their operations from the Isla de Couzemel northward around Cape Catoche (about 710 miles from Port Royal), then southwestward on the shore of the Bay of "Campeachy" (Bahia de Campeche) as far as Laguna de Terminos (about 1136 miles from Port Royal) by 1664. In or before 1665, a ship made the 568-mile voyage from "Blewfields" (the present Nicaragua) with twelve tons of logwood, and Spanish documents place the English at Belize in the present British Honduras as early as 1670. Before the two treaties of Madrid (1667, 1670), the Spaniards merely applied the doctrine of no peace beyond the line toward the intruders. With the cessation of open hostilities in the Caribbean, the privateers and buccaneers, now unemployed, commenced flocking to the logwood camps, especially at Laguna de Terminos. Soon there were twelve ships carrying logwood to Jamaica, where it sold for £25 to £30 a ton. Sir Thomas Modyford believed that two-thirds of the freebooters would enter this profitable business, either at Campeachy, Cape Gracia á Dios, Darien, the Mosquito Coast, Hispaniola, or Cuba—"these new sucking colonies must have some help" from the English authorities against Spain. Once more, there was to be no peace![51]

50. On the logwood trade before 1690, see two fine studies: Arthur M. Wilson, "The Logwood Trade in the Seventeenth and Eighteenth Centuries," in *Essays in the History of Modern Europe,* ed. Donald McKay (New York, 1936), 1–5; and Florence M. Cook, A Study of the British Logwood Trade, 1660–1783 (M. A. Thesis, Yale, 1927), 1–66, especially pp. 1, 11, 12–13; PRO: CO 1/29, fol. 43; Dampier, *Voyages,* II, Pt. II, 57–9; Sloane, *Voyage to the Islands,* II, 183–4.
51. BM: Add. MSS, 12,408, fol. 1b (Edward Long's notes); Jamaica Council

For fourteen days a small Jamaica barque and a New England ketch sailed before the wind from Port Royal until they raised Trist Island in August 1675. On the crew of the barque was William Dampier, an English youth who, preferring uncertain adventure to unremitting management of a plantation in Jamaica, has left us the best account of life at Campeachy that exists. Honduras and Campeachy were the most profitable fields for cutting logwood, for the stick had to be carried but 300 paces to the water's edge; furthermore, Dampier notes that Cape Catoche and Loggerhead Cay had been denuded. The loggers' camp was a genuine frontier settlement, where each man lived in a little hut erected on high ground. Everyone in the camp ate voraciously of beef, pork, pease, and "Soughboys" (sour dough?), and drank deeply of rum in punch or neat. When ships anchored, the cutters boarded, expecting and getting a long, free drunk. The sticks cost £5 a ton where they were cut; the ships' captains paid for them in rum and sugar. The cutters took them out to the ship in rented *periaguas* and each of them was paid off with 250 pounds of sugar. Dampier's return voyage of 1136 miles took thirteen weeks as contrasted with the usual six, for the vessel could not ply to windward. Shortly after his arrival in Port Royal and being paid off, Dampier signed on for another trip, this time as a passenger with Captain Johnson of the New England ketch. Resolved to spend some time in the logwood trade, he took a stock of hardware: hatchets, axes, "Macheats," saws, and wedges, and also "a Pavilion to sleep in." He found the cutters, who were discharged privateers, a rough lot; some of them would spend as much as £40 on a drinking bout when a ship came in, and they defiled the Indian women and sold their husbands into slavery. Not even when soberer men arrived did civil government develop, for all too soon they adopted the debauched ways of the cutters.[52]

Minutes, I, 100, 106–11; Rolf A. Humphreys, *The Diplomatic History of British Honduras, 1638–1901* (Oxford, 1961), 1–2; Davenport, *European Treaties,* II, 106, 194; PRO: CO 1/25, fol. 59; CO 1/29, fol. 33; BM: Egerton MSS, 2395, fol. 481.

52. Dampier had probably learned that New Englanders sold Dutch hardware to the cutters at Campeachy, and then sold the logwood to Holland at prices below the English re-export price. *CSPC, 1675–76,* p. 221; Dampier, *Voyages,* II, Pt. II, 9–131, and folding map.

Captain Johnson was only one of many New England skippers who had entered upon the logwood trade with their tiny ships. In March 1671 a ketch of 30 tons manned by 10 men and commanded by Benjamin Shapleigh of Piscataqua was one of 32 vessels trafficking regularly to Campeachy from Port Royal. One of the Cutt family from the same port was taken by the Spanish a year later. Of the 2000 tons of logwood cut in 1671, at least 600 went to Boston where, according to Sir Thomas Lynch, "its' Reported they send that, and other American Goods to Forreigne Marketts." This was indeed true, for logwood brought good prices at Boston, where merchants re-exported it to Holland and France, thereby evading the king's customs. Lord Vaughan declared in 1675: "At present the New England men reap the whole profit" of the trade; in the following year seventeen Yankee vessels called at Port Royal on their way to Campeachy. Edward Randolph notified Secretary Coventry three years later that the New Englanders took away from the Main 1000 tons of logwood annually. Samuel Shrimpton was one of the Bay-Town's merchants who dealt extensively in logwood, "Brazaletta," "Cuttchaneale," and other dyewoods from Campeachy and New Providence in the Bahamas, which he usually dispatched to London to balance his accounts for imported English goods.[53]

As part of an effort to suppress privateering out of Port Royal, Governor Lynch had given encouragement to the logwood cutters even though England and Spain had been at peace. This policy displeased officials at Whitehall, and he was given no choice in 1682 but to forbid any further logging in Campeachy and at Honduras. The Governor ordered that no more vessels were to go there, and so reported to the Lords of Trade and Plantations, submitting at the same time that the wood was "almost all carried to Hamburgh, New England, Holland, &c., which injures us and the customs and trade of the nation. . . ." His injunction was not very effective, however, for between 1680 and 1684, there were 157

53. PRO: CO 138/1, fol. 112; *MHS Colls.*, 5th ser., VIII, 389; Cook, Logwood Trade, 65; PRO: CO 1/29, fols. 33, 43; CO 1/36, fol. 76; CO 1/43, fol. 37; *CSPC, 1675–76*, p. 282; *1681–85*, pp. 143–4; *Edward Randolph*, ed. R. N. Tappan (Prince Society: Boston, 1898–1909), II, 209; Shrimpton MSS, 1676–83, *passim*.

vessels that took away through Jamaica 1514 tons and 196 sticks of logwood, and in the five years, 1686–91, a total of 4281½ tons and 1217 sticks left Port Royal. One can merely conjecture how much more logwood went to New England and the continent of Europe. Here was an important traffic that did not flow along the routes laid down in the Acts of Trade and Navigation.[54]

VII

Logwood was but one of the articles exchanged in a far larger and more vital commerce between the Caribbean colonies and New England. A lively trade had been in progress for more than a decade before 1650 when Parliament forbade all commerce with Barbados, Antigua, and the other rebellious colonies. Edward Winslow promptly procured a license permitting New England's ships to trade in the islands until July 31, 1651. This action relieved those planters of sugar and cotton who owed so much of their prosperity to the supplies of provisions, horses, and lumber shipped from the northern colonies. The Navigation Act of 1651 restricted the comings and goings of the great Dutch vessels to some degree, but merchants in England failed to replace the Dutch ships with a sufficient number of their own to transport the increasing output of insular produce.[55]

To fill the shipping void, mariners from Piscataqua, Boston, and Newport sailed to the Caribbean. Most of their vessels were tiny craft of 12 to 60 tons' burthen and could put in anywhere in the West Indies. There they bartered away cargoes of salt fish, beef, pork, pease, corn, flour, "bisket," lumber, and horses for sugars, molasses, rum, indigo, logwood or other local produce. Larger New England ships of 100 to 200 tons moved into the trade from the islands to England. The Caribbean merchants could purchase quantities of produce assembled in New England or picked up in the Chesapeake region, New York, or Pennsylvania as the demand enlarged even though they continued to arrive in tiny cargoes from more than 2000 miles away. The *Luke,* Captain Ambrose Lane,

54. *CSPC, 1681–85,* p. 284; Jamaica Council Minutes, IV, 379.
55. Watts, *Histoire des colonies anglaises aux Antilles,* 26–7; Hutchinson, *History of Massachusetts-Bay,* I, xxix; *Suffolk Deeds,* I, 240.

put into Carlisle Bay in December 1652 laden with mackerel, beef, pease, onions, biscuits, and flour, packed in hogsheads, and 92 quintals of fish, all "Shipped by the Grace of God in good order and well conditioned" from Boston by Hezekiah Usher to John Mortimer, merchant in Barbados. The freight was £3 2*s*. per ton, payable in sugar at 4*d*. a pound. About this same time, Hercules Hunking of the Isle of Shoals sent off refuse fish valued at £3 10*s*. a ton to be exchanged at Bridgetown for "merchantable Muscovado sugar" at 3*d*. a pound. Many an emerging Yankee was learning to venture something in this trade. Simon Bradstreet of Andover (well inland from Boston) arranged in 1657 to ship beef and pork worth £100 in several vessels at the price current to Charles Richards of Barbados, who would pay for the meats in good Muscovado sugar at 3*d*. a pound, "free of all charges," and also give Bradstreet an advance of threepence a pound on the provisions. Such, in the simplest terms, was the nature of the commerce with New England.[56]

The volume of imports rose with the expansion of the sugar industry and the constant addition of slaves to the population of the islands. After discharging their cargoes in the islands, if they were paid in pieces of eight or bills of exchange on London, the captains would often return in ballast or else head southward to "Saltertoodas" (near Margarita) for the large-grained salt so much needed for preserving fish and meat—their crews put it in bags at the ponds and trundled them to the ships in wheelbarrows brought along for that purpose. It was some of these ships, which standing in close to the Main on the return, first got into the logwood trade.[57]

Captain Thomas Breedon deposed in 1660 that the mariners of New England and their little ships were "the key to the Indies, with-

56. *Suffolk Deeds,* I, 259; III, 169; "Court Papers, 1652–1668," *New Hampshire State Papers,* XXX, 116.

57. A Connecticut mariner wrote from Bridgetown to John Winthrop, Jr., in 1675: "I brought all my horses saife to an indifferent good markett, viz: 3000 lb sugar per head. Provitions are low espetially flower, pease, and bread, alsoe beef and candles. I have disposed of above one halfe of what I brought for lesse money then it would have sold for in Boston, and see little hopes of goeing for England this 6 weekes or two moneths, heere being little sugar ready, nor any frayte to bee gott home till the London shipps come in, which are dayly looked for. . . ." *MHS Procs.,* 2d ser., VII, 17; Sloane, *Voyage to the Islands,* I, lvi, lxxxiii; Taylor, Multum in Parvo, II, 506; PRO: CO 5/848, Pt. I, 78–9, 98.

out which Jamaica, Barbadoes and the Charibby Islands are not able to subsist." The northerners "chiefly trade here for Sugar, Rum, and Diewood," said John Taylor, and "by this quick and free Trade, the Island begins to gather wealth and strength. . . ." Sometimes the West Indians tacitly admitted their indebtedness, as when in 1664 the Jamaica Assembly consented, after some pressure, that "the part of the act prohibiting New England boards be repealed"; or when the inhabitants of Bridgetown employed many New England ships to bring the timbers and lumber needed to rebuild after the fire of 1668 had destroyed three-quarters of their houses. At the Plantations Council in 1671, Lord Sandwich disclosed the great dependence of the West Indies upon New England for supplies and his fear that it, rather than Old England, would "reap the whole benefit of these colonies." John Evelyn noted that his Lordship called for stricter regulation of such traffic. Much exercised by the rumors of such proposals, the Assembly of Barbados instructed its agent to make it clear to Parliament that the island was so bound to New England's shipping and produce that any legislation against the commerce would be most injurious. The "plantation duty" levied in the Act of 1673, Governor Atkins maintained two years later, "lies so heavy on all these plantations that they will lose all commerce from New England and Ireland, from whence they have all their provisions." [58]

The full extent of the reliance of the islands of the Antilles upon constant exchanges with their northern brethren became particularly apparent during each of the three wars with the Dutch when almost no ships arrived from England and Ireland, and the New England traffic slowed down. In Nevis the merchants spelled out for the Assembly in 1668 that fining New England traders who refused to sell their goods at set prices only impelled them to withdraw from the trade and to say "that this island should suck their paws as bears did in their country in the winter until those usages were foreborne, by which the islanders were ready to famish." The petitioners are still prohibited from free trade (which all West

58. *Documents . . . Colonial History of the State of New York,* III, 40; Taylor, Multum in Parvo, II, 505; *Journal of the Assembly of Jamaica* (Jamaica, 1811), I, 1, 3; *London Gazette,* Aug. 6, 1668; *Diary of John Evelyn,* ed. E. S. Beer (Oxford, 1955), III, 577–80, 844–5; *CSPC, 1669–74,* p. 475; *1675–76,* p. 210.

Indians always ardently desired) and are "now under Censure of devils, who while they never called in their debts were styled Saints." In April 1673 during the Third Dutch War, the Council of Barbados even ordered the frigate *Little David* to convoy ten New England ships as far as Deseado, so highly did they value the northern products. When Governor Codrington heard in 1690 that Sir William Phips planned to winter his fleet in Quebec, he expressed concern for the Leeward Islands: "We can hope for scanty supplies of fish, flesh, or flour" from New England.[59]

Imperceptibly the Puritan and Yankee influence spread over the English Antilles. More New England merchants went to live in the islands to carry on as merchants or to grow sugar or cotton. Joseph, Quaker son of Richard Borden of Portsmouth on Rhode Island, moved to Barbados in 1673, and seven years later he was living near Bridgetown as both a merchant and a planter, with his wife Anne, one apprentice, and fourteen slaves. He dealt in provisions, but chiefly in horses, with Walter Newbury and other Friends in Rhode Island and Barbados. Many English inhabitants envied the "prosperousse estate of New England" and resented the taking away of so much coin from the Caribbean. One Connecticut mariner, badgered by the Governor and Council in 1674 because his people had not retaken New York from the Dutch, explained their military weakness and mollified his critics, but then the sturdy Puritan read the planters a lecture on colonial economics. He told them candidly how dissatisfied he and his fellow New Englanders were with the Barbados duty of 18*d.* per 100 pounds, and that they had resolved to sell the greatest part of their effects to England.[60]

After announcing his intentions to the islanders, this robust Yankee wrote to John Winthrop, Jr.: "Theire rum and molasses heere will becom of no use or vallew to them, with which they have hitherto supplyed theire plantations with provition and horses, being very considerable benefitt to them, and a profitt they will soone

59. PRO: CO 1/21, fol. 162; *MHS Procs.*, 2d ser., VII, 17; *CSPC, 1661–68,* p. 548; *1689–92,* p. 327; Barbados Council Minutes, II, 269, 270–71.
60. *Suffolk Deeds,* II, 44; "The Walter Newbury Shipping Book," in *Rhode Island Historical Society Collections,* XXIV, 76; *NEHG Reg.*, LXVIII, 181; *CSPC, 1675–76,* pp. 343–4; *MHS Procs.*, 2d ser., VII, 16.

misse; and to confirme what I have informed them, all our New England vessells goeinge for sault [at Saltertudas], take none of the Island groath with them, but shipp sugars to England or lay out theire money heere on goods, which still proves the Islands disadvantage and will put them on the consideration of haveing that [customs] tax eased at their next sitting. . . ." The islands would lose out measurably should their rum and molasses not go to New England, for they were vendible in few other parts of the world; in which case New England would prosper by brewing its own beer, distilling its apple cider, and turning the inhabitants to manufacturing wool, flax, and hemp and refraining from growing any surplus provisions. Some accommodation was made, evidently, for the Yankees, followed by the Quakers of Pennsylvania, continued to increase their shipments of provisions and supplies.[61]

VIII

Although no island of the Antilles had achieved a monoculture of sugar in 1690, the trades in Muscovado and slaves already governed the economic and social life of the West Indies. The enormous profits of the fifties, benefiting Barbados most of all, had declined drastically and leveled off as a result of expanded cultivation by the French and Dutch, as well as by the English themselves. Nevertheless the English had wrested the market for Muscovado sugar from their Portuguese mentors in Brazil by 1670. On the other hand, the refiners on the Continent still took most of the raw sugar, and those of London and Bristol figured but little in the making of white sugars as yet. The supply of molasses had already become insufficient for the brewing and sweetening needs of the New Englanders and for the distilling of rum. In the French islands and Surinam, the Yankees were already tapping new sources of supply.[62]

61. *MHS Procs.,* 2d ser., VII, 17.

62. ". . . By reason of this Industry of our Plantations wee have already beate out the Portuguese at Brazil from sending home any Muscovadoes, And have reduced their fine Sugars from 7 and 8 pounds the hundred, unto 50 and odd Shillings, and are by this means the Sole Merchants almost of all that Sugar that is Manufactured into loafe or hard Suger either in Holland, France, or Hamborough as being all made out of our Muscovados." With further encouragement, the writer of The State of the Manufacture of Sugar (MS) was convinced that

Many of the English writers on trade looked upon the Caribbean colonies as the pivot around which the burgeoning commerce of Britain revolved. "The West India Settlements, for these Thirty or Fourty Years past, have been the brightest Gem in our Crown of Trade," Thomas Tryon declared. And yet, this man, and others who knew the Antilles at first hand, must have sensed that the economy of every island was unbalanced and unsound, and that the Mother Country was taking too much from them and giving very little. To a man the planters were greedy, but only a very few of them ever accumulated riches enough to permit them to go home and play the absentee. Governor Christopher Codrington described the Leeward Islands of 1690 as still very much in the barter stage, from which the New Englanders drained the coin and bills of exchange; and Barbados was little better off. That alone of the English Caribbean holdings, Jamaica showed a healthy diversification and some glimmerings of financial maturity for that age was indicated by the action of the Governor and Council in 1688 in granting to John Short of Port Royal a one-year monopoly to operate a "General Intelligence Office . . . for the more speedy disposal of Goods belonging to People living Remote, keeping of Freemen that are non Residents in an Employment, Sale of Lands, Houses, Vessells, or Negroes, that may be the means to keep the proprietors from a Goal, Hire of Land, Houses, Vessells, or Negroes, Loan of Money either Bills of Exchange or otherwise. . . ." [63]

---

the English could beat the Brazilians out of the trade in white sugars and supply Spain and "the Streights." BM: Egerton MSS, 2395, fol. 636; Egerton MSS, 2543, fol. 123; Add. MSS, 11,411, Povey letter of *ca.* 1655; Cary, *Essay on the State of England,* 65.

63. One must keep in mind that the founding of the Bank of England was still six years away, and that Samuel Lambe had argued hard for improved ways of financing the plantation trade thirty years earlier in 1657. *Seasonable Observations,* 11–18; Tryon, *England's Grandeur,* 12; *CSPC, 1689–92,* p. 504; Jamaica Council Minutes, V, 110–11.

XI

Black Men and White

OF FAR GREATER IMPORT than the "sugar revolution" in the long perspective of history, as well as in the years 1650 to 1690, was the radical change in the personnel and in the nature of the inhabitants of the English West Indies: a permanent shift in the plantation labor force from temporary white servants to permanent black slaves. The presence of the African Negroes was the overwhelming human fact in the Caribbean at the close of this period: by mere weight of numbers they had begun to dictate, or force, the direction of insular existence. In every island, black societies were forming, haltingly though inexorably, at the very time that white communities were failing to advance. That neither the blacks nor their white masters realized the fact does not alter its essential truth for the seventeenth century, whatever may have happened in later years.

II

On every plantation of fifty acres or more could be found a Negro village, situated to the leeward of the mansion so that the trade winds would blow away the "nauseous smell" and lessen the noise for the benefit of the master and his family. Villages varied in size with the number of slaves a planter owned—50 to 300 and upward

—but large or small they were veritable communities out of which a recognizable Caribbean society was emerging by 1690.[1]

Immediately after being purchased, newly landed Negroes were taken to one of the villages where, as John Barbot observed, they seldom missed meeting one or more blacks "who are of their own country and language." The very arrangement of the huts and houses, their construction and thatch roofs were the most familiar sight they had experienced since leaving the Coast; and soon some were erecting huts for themselves. For families with children the houses contained several tiny rooms, and on the best-run plantations after about 1670 many of them were sheathed with shingles imported from New England. Most writers agreed that the blacks enjoyed better shelter than the white servants who worked beside them in the fields. Some of the larger estates in Barbados had stone houses for the slaves. But the masters did not issue hammocks or coverlets to protect their "people" against the cool night air, especially of Jamaica.[2] (Plates 7, 8)

Also familiar and very comforting after the monotonous and inadequate diet of "loblob" on shipboard were the small plots of ground surrounding the village, which the master allotted to each Negro family, for raising country provisions such as they had been used to in Guinea. In Jamaica each black man received half an acre of land to clear and cultivate on Saturday afternoons, Sundays, and holy days when plantation work stopped. The master also gave each family a sow and some chickens and issued salted meat or fish once a week. "Wee cannot give the Negros lese then one Case of

1. Tiny black communities even formed on the smaller plantations with 20 slaves more or less, whereas on the great estates of Jamaica and Barbados, with occasionally 200 to 700 Negroes, embryo towns existed. At Montserrat and Nevis such villages were smaller: only 6 planters of Nevis owned more than 60 slaves each in 1678—17 per cent of the entire black population. William Smith, *A Natural History of Nevis and the Rest of the Charibee Islands* (Cambridge, Eng., 1745), 225; Venables, in RHS, *Camden,* 146; Dunn, in *WMQ,* 3d ser., XXVI, 12 (Barbados landholders, 1680); Oldmixon, *British Empire in America,* II, 115; *Caribbeana,* II, 347; III, 81; BM: Egerton MSS, 2395, fol. 598.

2. Connell, in *JBMHS,* XXIV, 114; Biët, *Voyage,* 289; Barbot, in Churchill, *Voyages,* V, 649; N. Darnell Davis, in *Barbados Agriculturalist,* Sept. 28, 1909, p. 3; Oldmixon, *British Empire in America,* II, 87; Blome, *Description of Jamaica,* 89. Labat considered the slaves in the French colonies to be better housed than those of Barbados. *Nouveau Voyage,* VI, 197.

Herring Every Month," one overseer said. Sound shelter and the kinds of food fondly remembered from former days—both of them frequently better in quality—served to ease the adjustment of the majority of the Africans to their new environment.[3]

The opportunity for nearly all of the slaves to enjoy family life is the clue to the eventual emergence of a genuine black society in the English colonies. That it developed in the African rather than the Christian fashion is beside the point. In describing slavery in Jamaica in 1688, John Taylor emphasized that after a planter had acquired 20 or 30 slaves, "he first gives to each man a wife, without which they will not be content, or work." At Bybrook Plantation, the Helyars maintained carefully a balance of the sexes year after year: 38 men and 39 women in 1678; 34 men, 39 women, 10 boys, 21 girls, and 3 small children in 1697. A similar policy prevailed in the Leeward Islands: Nevis had 1422 male slaves, 1321 women, and 1106 children in 1678. For the English colonies in general, the sex ratio of black males to females was three to two, and in Jamaica nearer to a parity. Dr. Hans Sloane confirmed this: "The care of the masters and Overseers about their [slaves'] Wives, is what keeps their Plantations chiefly in good order, when they buy their Wives in proportion to their Men, lest the Men should wander to neighbouring Plantations, and neglect to serve them." Touching testimony to the love some Negro men bore toward their women is found in a letter of 1667 addressed to William Bushey of Barbados. His agent John Batten reports that he has found one of his slaves on a plantation in Maryland, where he had been illegally taken. The new master, Thomas Motley, was willing to give the man up, "but the negro is married and will not part from his wife. If he had not been prevented, he would have hanged himself." Accordingly, Batten sold him to the kind master for 1000 pounds of tobacco, "more by halfe" the price any Negro had ever brought in Maryland.[4]

Mounting numbers of children were constantly being landed by

3. BM: Sloane MSS, 3662, fol. 59; Taylor, Multum in Parvo, II, 538–9; Sloane, *Voyage to the Islands,* I, xv, xlvi, lii; Cary to William Helyar, Nov. 17, 1671; Thomas Hall: list of Necessarys, *ca.* 1670, Helyar MSS.

4. Taylor, Multum in Parvo, II, 538, 542; Sloane, *Voyage to the Islands,* I, xlviii; BM: Egerton MSS, fol. 625; Accounts, June 5, 1678, 1709, Helyar MSS; *Caribbeana,* II, 347; III, 81; Davis Coll., III, Envelope 24.

slavers in spite of the fact that the "naturally fruitful" Negro women added "many lusty young striplings of Natives of the place, whom the Spaniards call Criolias." As Thomas Tryon discovered in Barbados, "our Off-Spring will not maintain the Number" of Negroes, and an annual importation of several thousands was necessary to keep up the slave population. An appalling infant mortality sufficiently accounts for the failure. Dr. Spörri described how "when slave mothers go to work they tie the young children upon their backs. While they work they frequently give the children the breast across the armpits, and let them suckle." Inasmuch as mothers went back to the fields very shortly after giving birth, the babies must have suffered in the hot sun. Those who survived infancy were usually put to work at light tasks at the age of three, much as farm children in England or Europe.[5]

Negro children ran about "quite naked" until they reached the age of puberty, and during the fifties and sixties few planters concerned themselves about clothing the adults, either Negro or Indian. Knowing nothing of African customs, Uchteritz, Dr. Spörri, Père Biët, and John Taylor all expressed distaste at the sight of male and female blacks clad only in a "linnen Arseabout" or "Arseclout" to hide the shame which, of course, they seldom felt. After 1670, when the planters were attempting to match new wealth with elementary refinement, and possibly out of hygienic wisdom too, they began to clothe their "people." Necessaries shipped out for Sir Thomas Lynch's plantation at Port Morant included fifty sets of jackets and drawers for the men and fifty "Frocks" for the women. While Dr. Sloane approved of the canvas jackets and breeches given to Jamaican slaves at Christmas, he criticized his English friends for continuing to wear the heavy garments such as they wore in England that were not conducive to their best health. In dispatching an English woman who would serve for five years on his estate in St. Christopher, Christopher Jeaffreson mentioned that she is a "good needle-woman, can make and mend negroes' or servants' cloathes." An act to govern slaves, passed in Barbados in 1688, stated that thereafter all Negroes should be issued clothing once a year; drawers and caps for the men, petticoats and caps for the

5. Taylor, Multum in Parvo, II, 542–3; Tryon, *Friendly Advice,* 142; Spörri, *Americanische Reise,* 17–18.

women; it also provided for a fine of five shillings per slave for non-compliance. Adult black house-servants wore more clothes, of course, and on a few of the great estates some even donned livery. Clothing added one more element of respectability to the black folk of the Caribbean.[6]

The first slaves in the English colonies were limited both in their work and in social intercourse by the many tongues they spoke, and it was in the plantation village that slowly and painfully they acquired an English vocabulary sufficient to permit them to learn their daily tasks, to serve in the great houses, and obey the master and overseer. As the years passed and slaves from many tribes mingled, the African languages and dialects gradually died out. The "Salt-Water" Negro picked up what he could of his master's English, but learned most of his speech from white bond servants—the first field hands—hence the Irish brogue so prevalent in the West Indies today. Eventually the black Creoles helped out with speech in the villages, for many of them spoke both broken English and some African dialect. An ejected minister, Francis Crow, observed in 1686 that the Jamaica blacks knew no European language and seldom learned English well, "no, not even those that are born here in our houses." And yet they did succeed in evolving a marvelous, colorful, though unrecorded, syntax of their own out of English, Irish, Scottish, Dutch, and Portuguese elements—a Caribbean *lingua franca.* This achievement is preserved in Barbadian proverbs:

> A spoonful o' Molasses ketch mo flies dan a gallon o' vinegar.
> De key hole mek for de key, not fo yu eye.
> Whan de debil cahn go he does sen rum.
> Belly fus and hed aftah.
> All rum good but some bettah dan de ress.

Tribal memories naturally faded along with the languages of these illiterate people; what was essential for survival remained—Creolian, American.[7]

6. Uchteritz, *Kurze Reise,* 8; Biët, *Voyage,* 290; Spörri, *Americanische Reise,* 17; Taylor, Multum in Parvo, II, 539; BM: Egerton MSS, 2395, fol. 599; Jeaffreson, *Young Squire,* II, 278; *Acts of Barbados* (1721), 139; Sloane, *Voyage to the Islands,* I, xlvii.

7. Taylor, Multum in Parvo, II, 546–7; C. J. Cruikshank, "Negro English," in *Timehri,* I, No. 11, pp. 2–3; Crow, in *Jamaica Historical Review,* III, 55; S. E. Brewster, "Rugged Vernacular of Yore," in Davis Coll., I, Envelope 10.

Every evening at dusk upon returning from their labors at the sugarworks or in the fields, men and women slaves first ate a meal in their houses and then assembled with the rest of the villagers around a great fire to sing, dance, or play on a one-string gourd or calabash called a "Kitt," or beat on drums. Because of the sudden drop in temperature at night in Jamaica, they often slept on the ground around the fire. Work stopped at noon on Saturdays, unless it was sugar-boiling time, and then each family received one quart of rum and another of molasses "To make Merry with all." At Passage Fort in Jamaica the blacks enjoyed the sociability of their own market on Saturday evenings until it was prohibited as the penalty for a disturbance in May 1686. Ordinarily the slaves worked in their own garden plots on Saturday afternoons, but on Sundays they frequently gathered to visit their countrymen on other plantations, where they drank rum, feasted, sang, and danced nimbly to a Kitt and drum, "seeming all Mirth, women and men together," in what John Taylor described as "an Antique manner, as if they were all madd." On other occasions the men diverted themselves with swimming and gambling. Activities such as these not only uncovered traits that had originated in West Africa but perpetuated them in the New World. In these ways the blacks merged their family life imperceptibly with almost daily village activities, which built up a sense of community that was wholly missing from the overwhelmingly male existence of the lower-class whites, both bond and free.[8]

Negro moral attitudes and sexual behavior deeply disturbed the few who gave any thought to such matters and drew universal condemnation from most white men, who applied Christian standards to a people who lived habitually by an inherited pagan code that seemed quite proper to them. Clerics and laymen often protested against a black having more than one wife; John Taylor took a more rational view of the practice: each Negro male gets a wife who "proves very honest and kind to her Husband," but he, on the least affront, will leave her and get another from his master or a neighboring plantation. When a surplus of black women occurred,

8. There was little outlet for the creative impulses of the blacks, save in crafts. Unfortunately almost nothing of the rich African artistic tradition was perpetuated in the British West Indies—but neither was the European tradition in art. Taylor, Multum in Parvo, II, 539–40; Sloane, *Voyage to the Islands,* I, xlviii, lii; Jamaica Council Minutes, IV, 15–16.

the African habit of taking more than one wife reappeared in the place of Christian monogamy; and more than one owner encouraged the breeding of slaves. In like fashion, widespread petty thievery by many Negroes aroused resentment in masters and public officials. Yet it also was an imported African habit. By way of reply the slaves slyly encased their attitude in a proverb:

> Wen blak man tief he tief ha'f a bit,
> Wen bukreh massa tief he tief whole plantashun.

The blind and stubborn exclusiveness of the Hebrew-Christian moralists has ofttimes impeded any human understanding of the different ways of black pagans.[9]

The blacks also brought many serious diseases from Africa, and a susceptibility to pulmonary disorders; they had to endure a "seasoning" in the winter—and many of them died in the process—just as the whites had to adjust to the summers. The commonest distemper among them was "the Country Disease, or Yaws." The master of all large estates regularly kept a physician or surgeon to look after his people and paid him good wages. Most of them had been ships' surgeons who were lured ashore, or indentured servants such as Dr. Henry Pitman, who was competent in his art. Christopher Jeaffreson sent "medical drugs" to St. Christopher in 1683 "that my people may have medicine much oftener than the chirurgeon would be willing to furnish." There is good reason to believe that the blacks generally received better and more frequent medical care than the poor white freemen, who could ill afford the high fees charged by licensed practitioners.[10]

The Negro death rate mounted noticeably between 1650 and 1690. One reason was high infant mortality, another was the yaws, and a third was the spreading of the idea that economically the black slave was expendable. Many overseers began to overwork their field hands. Such a policy succeeded, however, only when the

9. Sloane, *Voyage to the Islands,* I, xlviii; Tryon, *Friendly Advice,* 142; Labat, *Nouveau Voyage,* VI, 198; Taylor, Multum in Parvo, II, 542.

10. John Taylor said that Jamaican Negroes were usually healthy, but "naturally afflicted with the french poxe," or the yaws, more so than Europeans. Dropsy was another common black ailment. Multum in Parvo, II, 529. *Acts of Assembly . . . of Montserrat,* 32; BM: Add. MSS, 11,410, fol. 12; Pitman, *A Relation,* 3, 11; Jeaffreson, *Young Squire,* II, 27; *Acts of the Leeward Islands,* 61–2.

supply of Salt-Water blacks was ample. It was Thomas Tryon's belief in 1684 that between one-fifth and one-quarter of the blacks died annually; five years later Edward Lyttleton propounded that a planter needed to replace 6 per cent of his force every year. If he was right, and few planters had more experience, the mortality of the Negroes was probably lower than that of the white servants. Nor do we have any data about the death rate among the lower-class freemen, but we may seriously question whether there was very much difference between the two races in this respect.[11]

With the exception of a minority of Muslims, the religious beliefs of the average African Negro were quite simple. As they were deduced succinctly by Uchteritz, the blacks "worship the devil and explain this as follows to the People: God, who lives in heaven, is a good and pious man, who would do nothing to harm any one, but the devil was very vicious and bad, and he did great harm. Therefore they must pray to him, so that he would not harm them. Whenever anyone among them dies, they say he has gone to his home [in Africa], and to his friends and that he is getting along fine." Not a few of the blacks upon arriving in the Antilles either cut their throats or starved themselves to death in order to hasten the journey back home. The possibility always existed, particularly among the black Creoles, that they could be converted to Christianity. John Taylor became convinced of this after discoursing with several old Negroes of "Witt and Sence." [12]

Somehow the belief arose early among slave owners that a baptized black could claim freedom under the common law. No justification for such insular legal misinformation existed, but landholders persisted in harboring this view and propounding good and real reasons against conversion. A comprehensive act of 1675 concerning slaves in Jamaica contained a provision that each Negro's master must "instruct him in the Christian religion," but for the

11. Tryon, *Friendly Advice to the Planters,* 144; Lyttleton, *Groans of the Plantations,* 18.

12. When Negroes die, their families and friends make a great "adoe" at the burials. They carry the body to the grave singing and shouting in their own tongues, and at the grave put in foods with the corpse, also tobacco and pipes, for the journey to the pleasant hills of the old country. Then they go home and have a feast. Taylor, Multum in Parvo, II, 544; Uchteritz, *Kurze Reise,* 9; Sloane, *Voyage to the Islands,* I, xlviii.

most part, planters everywhere ignored such instructions. "The Planters' Committee" of Barbados announced incisively to the Lords of Trade and Plantations in 1680 that "the conversion of their slaves to Christianity would not only destroy their property but endanger the island, inasmuch as converted negroes grow more perverse and intractable than others, and hence of less value for labour and sale. The disproportion of the blacks to whites being great, the whites have no greater security than the diversity of the negroes' languages, which would be destroyed by conversion in that it would be necessary to teach them all English." The following year the Barbados Assembly told Governor Dutton, when he requested the passage of a law on the subject, that "Their savage brutishness renders them wholly incapable" of it. It was also argued that conversion would ruin the Royal African Company. Finally, in 1685, as John Evelyn recorded, King Charles II resolved "that the Negroes in the Plantations should all be baptized, exceedingly declaiming against the impiety of their masters prohibiting it, out of mistaken opinion that they would be *ipso facto* free." Upon the urging of the Duke of Albemarle, the planters' parliament of Jamaica yielded in 1688 and passed "an Act to encourage and Facilitate the Conversion of Slaves to the Christian Religion. . . ." The planters of Barbados were still resisting the instructions on the conversion of Negroes in 1695, for Governor Russell presented the argument to the Lords of Trade and Plantations that "the keeping of Christian holy days will be the great obstacle, most of the planters thinking Sundays too much to be spared from work." [13]

The claim of the Jesuit travelers that in the French islands converting the slaves was the first order of business for both state and church, and their strictures against the English and Dutch Protestants for avoiding or ignoring their Christian duty were certainly well founded. The Huguenot Barbot scouted all English excuses and praised both the Jesuits and French masters. Conversion, he maintained, imparted self respect to the slaves, and seldom did any

13. Thurloe, *State Papers,* III, 157; Evelyn, *Diary,* ed. Beer, II, 479; *CSPC, 1675–76,* p. 902; *1677–80,* p. 611; *1681–85,* p. 25; *1693–96,* p. 448; Taylor, Multum in Parvo, II, 543; Robert Morden, *Geography Rectified, or a Description of the World* (London, 1693), 609; PRO: CO 1/36, fol. 148a; Jamaica Council Minutes, V, 143; *Journal of the Assembly of Jamaica,* I, 102, 120, 125.

one of them desert from the French, "as we have often heard among the English, especially at Barbados." The Church of England signally failed the Negroes in the Antilles when its resident clergymen weakly and callously decided at the beginning of settlement not to antagonize the planters by preaching the gospel to the blacks. This was indeed "a great blot upon the Church." [14]

It remained for the despised and persecuted members of the Society of Friends to take the first steps to aid the Negroes spiritually. When George Fox visited Barbados in 1671, he set about at once to implement his plans to better the welfare of all the people who served the Friends: the black people ought no longer to be buried in gardens but in their own cemetery; they should be given religious instruction; and overseers must be persuaded to deal mildly and understandably with them. "The Truth is freely preached, both to white people and black people," John Stubbs wrote in December, and "Solomon Eccles and I have had several meetings among the negroes in several plantations. . . ." But George Fox held the most meetings and asked the Barbados Monthly Meeting to keep a separate record book for the blacks. Fox boldly warned Governor Codrington and his Council that God would require an accounting for the treatment of all Negroes and tawnies in Barbados and strongly denied that the Quakers ever taught the slaves to rebel, as had been charged. We teach them the light, he said, and admonish them to be sober and fear God, to be diligent and faithful to their masters, and not to beat their wives, or steal, or drink, or fornicate. The next year he addressed himself with rich irony to the "Ministers, Teachers, and Priests (so called and so stiling your selves) in Barbadoes"; "And if you be Ministers of Christ, are you not Teachers of Blacks and Tawnies (to wit, Indians) as well as of Whites? For is not the Gospel to be preached to all Creatures? And *are they not Men?* And are they not part of your families?" These were searching and disturbing questions.[15]

The Friends of Barbados got their reply from the Anglicans and

14. Dr. Spörri said that at Barbados in 1661 some Negro children were instructed and brought up as Christians. *Americanische Reise,* 17. Barbot, in Churchill, *Voyages,* V, 270–71, 649–50; *Barbados Diocesan History,* 10.

15. *The Journal of George Fox,* ed. John L. Nickalls (Cambridge, Eng., 1952), 598–9, 601–2; George Fox, *To the Ministers, Teachers, and Priests . . . in Barbados* (London, 1672), 5.

Nothingarians in 1673 when the Grand Jury presented them for having Negroes at their meetings. Fear arose and men, growing tense, persecuted the Quakers viciously. After having heard Quaker preaching, it was charged that the blacks threatened the safety of the island, and in 1676 a law passed restraining the Friends from bringing slaves to meetings. Any slave found at a meeting was to be forfeited, with half of the price which he brought going to the informer; and for any "strange Negro" attending on his own, his master would have to pay £10. When the Lords of Trade and Plantations wrote that this act was too severe, Governor Atkins replied that it was intentionally so, for the Quakers' designs for the slaves might have brought about the very ruin of Barbados, for they drew hundreds of blacks to their meetings, who, when they had no mind to work, "claimed the privilege of going." Discreetly he omitted any mention of William Edmundson's letter of February 1676 warning him before it was too late to "use your Power to stop the Current of Wickedness and Uncleanness (which is run over this Island and cries for Vengeance) committed without limit by Negroes and others defiling themselves with one another, as bad or worse than the Beasts of the Field, and go unpunished: For every Man, whether White or Black, ought to have but one Wife; and every Woman . . . but one Husband. . . ." The implication of miscegenation in this statement—the first of its kind in print—could not have been lost on the Barbadians. Friendly concern about morality had evoked the harsh law, which was henceforth directed at the Quakers themselves.[16]

Public Friends persisted in their course despite the law whenever they visited Barbados, for Joan Vokins tells us that during her stay at Bridgetown in 1681: "most Days I had two or three Meetings of a Day, both among the Blacks and also among the Whites." (Perhaps she was the reason for reviving and continuing the Act of

16. Mr. Ramsey, a "priest," made a charge to Governor Atkins, saying of Edmundson: "That I was a Jesuit come out of Ireland, pretending to be a Quaker, and to make the Negroes Christians; but would rise and cut their Throats." After some reasoning, the Governor "grew moderate." William Edmundson, *Journal* (London, 1715), 70, 74–6. *CSPC, 1669–74,* p. 506; *1675–76,* p. 331; *1677–80,* p. 214; *Acts of Barbados* (1721), 106–7; PRO: CO 1/37, fols. 76a, 79b–80a; Joseph Besse, *A Collection of the Sufferings of the People Called Quakers . . .* (London, 1753), II, 306–9.

1676 forbidding the practice.) The writings and admonitions of George Fox and his followers did finally stir the compassion of one Anglican clergyman for the spiritual needs of the slaves. In *The Negro's & Indian's Advocate* and two other tracts published between 1680 and 1685, Morgan Godwyn of Christ Church, Oxford, who had lived in Barbados, accused the planters of "spite against Christianity and Cruelty to the souls of Men, even of their own Slaves," in the fear that baptism might bring freedom. He took the position categorically, moreover, "That Negroes are Men," citing George Fox. But humane preachments fell on deaf ears in Barbados, and such a prominent judge as Alexander Ruddock declared openly that "He was for putting Negroes to death for Example, saying, What was it for Barbados to put twenty or thirty Negroes to Death yearly for Examples-sake?" Concern for property, fear for physical safety, ignorance, and blind prejudice on the part of the planters and their Church denied to the black slave the solace of Christianity.[17]

The mind of the Negro slave was and remains inscrutable. It will never be possible for the historian or psychologist to peer into the souls of the black folk. The Negroes transferred to the Caribbean the deep-seated animosities of tribe against tribe, which had prevailed for centuries in West Africa and were continually exacerbated by warfare. Such hatreds and bitter suspicions died slowly in the Antilles among the first generations of blacks because of the language barriers and diminished quickly with each new generation as the numbers of Creoles rose. But the pugnacity and contentiousness bred in the bones of the blacks did not die out. The blacks, like all peoples, had their vexations. Now and then slaves turned against their masters, but the vast majority proved willing and amenable as long as they were reasonably well treated and satisfactorily fed. These same facts and attitudes applied to the white bondsmen. The bulk of the slaves proved loyal when a test came. Christopher Jeaffreson and other planters were so convinced of the trustworthiness

17. Vokins, *God's Mighty Power,* 43; Barbados Council Minutes, II, 301; Morgan Godwyn's three tracts are: *Negro's & Indian's Advocate* (London, 1681); and *Trade Profess'd before Religion, and Christ made to give Place to Mammon . . .* (London, 1695), especially p. 5; *A Short Account of the Manifest Hand of God . . . in . . . Barbados* (London, 1691), 21, in "Quaker Tracts, 1682–1705," BM: 4152 f 23.

of their people that they armed 1000 of the ablest with spears to help meet the threat of invasions by the French in 1678. Numerous blacks held their masters in high regard, some with real affection. Dr. Hans Sloane concluded in 1688: "Many of the Negroes, being Slaves, and their Posterity after them in Guinea, they are more easily treated by the English here, than by their own Country-People, wherefore they would not often willingly change Masters." [18]

III

Insular officials worried constantly about what one of them called "the discontents of the slaves." The black people studied their white masters with great care and developed capacities for sly tact, resignation, and their celebrated humor to deal with most minor frictions, but mean, heartless, and often cruel overseers or white servant-drivers were another matter. Every plantation had its whipping-post for slaves who would not work, who refused to be overworked, or otherwise offended. More than one black was beaten until his back was bloody, and Taylor reported that sometimes after the whipping, he was rubbed with molasses to attract wasps and other insects to torment him. At first slaves would laugh, then submit silently to the last, and seldom if ever shed tears under duress. At Barbados in the fifties, a number of slaveholders, male and female, were investigated by the Council for whipping Negroes to death.[19]

One recourse for abused and resentful slaves was to run away, and, as mentioned before, many of them did seek freedom. In the first slave statutes to be printed anywhere by English masters, the Barbadians sought in 1654 to restrain the wandering about of servants and slaves, and set a penalty of seven years' additional servitude for any white man who stole blacks "by specious pretence of promising them freedom in another Country." Fugitive slaves often joined with escaped Irish servants in committing robberies, felonies, and, oc-

18. Taylor, Multum in Parvo, II, 547; Jeaffreson, *Young Squire,* I, 224–5; Sloane, *Voyage to the Islands,* I, lviii.

19. R. A. J. van Lier, "The Development and Nature of Society in the West Indies," in Koninklijke Vereeniging Indisch Institut, *Medeling,* No. XCII (Amsterdam, 1950), 8; Taylor, Multum in Parvo, II, 541; Barbados Council Minutes, I, 5, 85, 277; BM: Egerton MSS, 2395, fol. 625.

casionally, murders. Lord Willoughby pleaded with English authorities in 1667 to allow Scots to be brought over to act as a sort of servant-police, "for keeping the slaves in subjection must be provided for." Complaints about runaway slaves leaving Montserrat produced laws in 1670 and 1679 against loitering, meeting together, or "wandering" from their plantations without a ticket from the master or overseer. Despite punishment of captured runaways by severe whippings and forcing them to wear iron yokes called pothooks, the ranks of the fugitives swelled in all of the islands after 1660. Governor Stapleton estimated the 600 Negroes from Barbados and the Leeward Islands had joined the Caribs. The comprehensive code passed in Jamaica in 1675 "for the governing of Negroes," and repeated in Barbados in 1688, contained more provisions about potential or actual runaways than anything else.[20]

Out of fear for their property and the safety of their persons, in peace or war, as the black populations of the British islands increased, the whites worked out in their assemblies an ever stricter discipline, which attained the status of a code for blacks. Lord Willoughby's expressed alarm of 1668 that a Creolian generation might "mancipate" themselves from their masters was no longer fanciful. Petty thievery by individuals was to some extent expected, but at Barbados during the eighties, terrorizing by gangs and robbing of the poor whites had become serious. Some of the blacks went so far as to build up an active secret traffic "with small plantations and people of mean condition" in pots of rum and jugs of molasses stolen from sugarworks. Situations such as these prevailed everywhere.[21]

The complex issue of how properly to rule slaves grew acute in the Caribbean in May 1675 when Fortuna, a woman slave, revealed to her master Giles Hall that the blacks were plotting to rise up in the neighborhood of Speightstown, Barbados, and murder their mistresses, masters, and overseers. Warned in advance,

20. Barbados Council Minutes, I, 90, 108; II, 230; *Acts and Statutes of Barbados* (Jennings), 43, 47, 81, 146; George P. Insh, *Scottish Colonial Schemes, 1620–1686* (Glasgow, 1922), 229–32; *Acts of Assembly . . . of Montserrat,* 20–21, 30, 34; *CSPC, 1675–76,* pp. 236, 499; Taylor, Multum in Parvo, II, 541; PRO: CO 1/36, fols. 148a–9b; *Acts of Barbados* (1721), 137–44; Jamaica Council Minutes, I, 32; III, 11; *Acts of Nevis,* 9.

21. *CSPC, 1661–68,* p. 586; PRO: CO 30/5, fols. 3, 135.

eight days before the appointed time, Governor Atkins called up the militia, who apprehended thirty-five of the conspirators and executed them. "The Lord delivered us," a Barbadian said, but guiltily confessed: "yet we refused to return to him by repentance"; but the Governor blamed the Coromantines, the most numerous tribe involved, for "a damnable design." In gratitude, however, the Assembly recommended the freeing of Fortuna for "her eminent service." [22]

The Jamaicans faced their first serious threat of rebellion in June 1672 when William Growden of St. Elizabeth's Parish was murdered by his slaves, who then fled to the woods and "stood upon their own Defense"; three of them were later captured or killed. As an encouragement for all inhabitants to be on the lookout for future threats to lives and property, the Council awarded £15 to John Vassall, to be shared with the others who had participated in the pursuit. Runaway slaves often fled to the North Side, because it was so sparsely settled, and joined the Maroons, who had maintained themselves there since Spanish times. The latitude allowed slaves in existing ordinances was objected to by Governor Lynch and the Council, who stressed "how much the safety and Interest of all the Planters . . . does consist in restraining by all ways imaginable the Communication of the Negroes one with another," and they ordered that any Negro going off limits must be issued a ticket. In September 1675, when the report of an abortive slave uprising in Barbados reached Jamaica, the Council, as a protective measure, immediately forbade the sale in their island of any slave who had been in that revolt. Planters were asked to employ one white man for every ten blacks. Later, in December, the Governor issued a proclamation in which he attributed insurrections to the "remissness" of the planters and declared that the black code was adequate and that it must and would be enforced.[23]

One slave revolt after another broke out in Jamaica during the eighties. In spite of efforts to control the situation, the "Insolence of Runaway negroes on the Northside" continued. At Madam

22. *Great Newes from Barbados: Intended Rebellion of the Negroes,* 19–20; *CSPC, 1675–76,* pp. 294, 303; *1677–80,* p. 501.

23. Jamaica Council Minutes, I, 188–9, 339–40; III, 11, 16–17, 100–101, 111–13; PRO: CO 1/36, fols. 148a–9b.

Gregg's plantation, 105 blacks rebelled in March 1682; and in June, a year later, 18, mostly Coromantines, rose against Colonel Lucy. A well-armed body of Negroes attacked Mr. Price's house in 1685 and gave way only when the militia arrived; 30 of them were captured and 7 killed, while the remainder fled to the security of the mountains on the North Side, pursued by the militia led by Indian trackers. In 1686 a bounty of £20 was offered to any freeman who killed one of these fugitive slaves, or freedom to a servant. At this time there existed two gangs of Maroons skulking in the fastness of the northeastern parishes of St. Mary, St. George, and St. Thomas; they were known as the Windward and the Cave Negroes, and they lived by snaring wild hogs along a twenty-mile trail and raiding plantations for other food. The last slave revolt of this period occurred at the great Salter estate. More than 500 blacks took the mansion house, killed the overseer, seized fifty fusees and ammunition before marching on the adjoining plantation. There they killed the overseer, fired the great house, and freed the slaves, who refused to join with them. They returned to fortify themselves in Salter's great house, but a body of militia sent in forced them to take refuge in the canes after twelve of their number were killed.[24]

Good or at least indifferent treatment kept the majority of the slaves loyal, such as those who refused to join the insurgents from the Salter estate. Much depended upon the overseers and, again drawing on the Salter estate as an example, the owner and the community paid a high price for absenteeism. Now and again a grateful or kind master freed a slave or two, but most planters frowned on the practice of liberating individuals whom they still looked upon and feared as savage brutes.[25]

24. The Maroons were composed of runaway Negroes and a few Indian women with whom they intermarried. Taylor, Multum in Parvo, II, 548–54; *CSPC, 1681–85,* p. 272; *1685–88,* pp. 82–3, 147, 272; *1689–92,* p. 315; Jamaica Council Minutes, IV, 318–21, 328.

25. For freedoms granted: Barbados Council Minutes, I, 68; II, 319; Davis Coll., VII, Envelope 22; Barbados Council Minutes (1667–82), II, 3, 42. A tantalizing notation: "A Negroes Plantation," appears on a plat of 1665 for land in St. Catherine's, Jamaica. Dawkins Family Papers [plantation survey plats] (Institute of Jamaica), Lib. 2, fol. 33.

IV

So wide was the gulf that separated the mass of the servants and freemen of each island from the rich owners of great estates that the different kinds of lives they led must be clearly distinguished. Nothing would mislead the modern reader more than to gather all of them into one master class merely because they were white. They divided into the many and the few, the low-born and the quality, the poor and the rich, the governed and the governors; and also individually, socially, and culturally into very different categories of human beings. National origins and religious beliefs set them farther apart. Two experiences they did share in common however: a substantial majority had come out to the Caribbean as indentured servants; and everywhere in 1690 all of the white men sensed that the blacks were holding them at bay.

When white servitude was at its peak, 1650–66, the great planters and small, disturbed by the declining quality of the bondsmen, increasingly assumed irrational and callous attitudes toward them. There is no denying that a growing minority of the white servants exhibited turbulent conduct, which ranged all the way from malicious firing of cane fields, robbing masters, trading with slaves for stolen goods, promiscuous sexual relations with one another, or with Negroes, to running away. To curb the "Unruliness, Obstinacy, and Refractoriness" of such people, the Barbadian Assembly codified existing laws with further regulations in 1661. Directed chiefly against Irish servants and transported convicts, these two harsh codes, with very little change, ultimately served as the models for the notorious black codes mentioned earlier in this chapter. Even before these last enactments, Jamaica had adopted the Barbadian regulations.[26]

Almost every aspect of a servant's life and labor was regulated by these laws, which so confined him that during his bondage he became virtually a slave. He could not leave the plantation without

26. The "Tolzey Book" at Bristol lists by name and destination 11,643 individuals, of whom the following are known to have emigrated to the West Indies from 1654 to 1686: to Barbados, 2656; to Nevis, *ca.* 2560; to other islands, 555, or a total of 5771. Ireland, in *JBMHS,* XIV, 48ff. Smith's figures differ somewhat—he assigns 468 of those headed for "other islands" to Jamaica. *Colonists in Bondage,* 309; *CSPC, 1681–85,* p. 318.

a ticket from his overseer or master, and for each two hours of absence he had to serve an additional day. White servants could not marry without the master's consent. Moreover, to lessen sexual laxity, the law required any father of a bastard to serve the mother's master three extra years, and the mother to serve two years more. Suggestive of the lot of the helpless men and women in bondage was the provision to prevent hardened masters from turning off sick servants in order to save expenses, but in nearly every other respect, the codes favored the planters.[27]

The sheer rigor of these codes was, in some ways, self-defeating, for they actually encouraged what they were designed to prevent. Much of the restlessness and viciousness of many indentured servants would never have developed had they been permitted any normal kind of social life. Their whole existence was one of never-ending monotony: exhausting and unvarying daily toil, no recreation at all after sunset, and rarely any religious or social outlets on Sundays. Their bad diet and flimsy cabins were both inferior to what they saw the blacks enjoying. Nor could most of them marry, given the disparity between the sexes, and participate in family life or join in the simple and enjoyable village activities of singing, dancing, and making music as the slaves did. Their acute psychological difficulties stemmed, perhaps, from the ill-concealed contempt in which the Negroes held all "po buckras." When a servant fell ill, he got little help from the plantation physician, and when he died his body was thrown into an unmarked hole as if he were a dog. Père Labat shrewdly pointed out that in the English colonies not many servants, especially among the Irish, gained freedom at

27. *Acts of Barbados* (1721), 22–9; Jamaica Council Minutes, I, 7, 16–17, 32, 46–7. No accounts of the experiences of well-behaved voluntary servants exist, but there are several colorful narratives by transported political prisoners and convicts: Marcellus Rivers and Oxenbridge Foyle, *England's Slavery or Barbados Merchandize* (London, 1659, copy in BM); [Francis Kirkman] *The English Rogue* (London, 1680), IV; [Mary Carleton] *News from Jamaica in a Letter From Port Royal, &c. Written by the German Princess to her Fellow Collegiates and Friends in New-Gate* (London, 1671), [copy at Inst. Jamaica]; *The German Princess Revived, or the London Jilt, Being a True Account of the Life and Death of Jenney Voss* (London, 1684). Two highly respectable victims of the judicial cruelty of Judge Jeffreys wrote vivid reports of servant life: John Coad, *A Memorandum of the Wonderful Providences of God to a poor Unworthy Creature . . . 1688* (London, 1849); and Henry Pitman, *A Relation.*

the end of five to seven years, because their masters usually had ready some legal pretext to keep them longer.[28]

When white men and women ended their terms of service, the new freedom brought them little more than the chance to move about and familiarize themselves with their island for the first time. Now forced to face life alone and ill-equipped, they must have wondered what to do next. Artisans in the country could usually eke out a living, and some of the abler freedmen, principally Scots, rose to be overseers, but the bulk of them had no choice but to resume work on plantations for meager wages, sleep in the same old cabins, and eat the same unappetizing food. Scarcely any opportunities to improve the quality of their lives ever opened up. Their betters dismissed them as "void almost of common civility." Richard Leader, who arrived in Barbados from New England in 1660, wrote back to John Winthrop, Jr., that the prospects for making a good living were excellent, but he was "not in love with this clyme, nor with the people in generall." If conditions were bad for the freedmen, the freedwomen, unless they were married, were even worse off. In Jamaica "the common sort of people seldom marie, according to the Ceremony of the Church of England," Taylor discovered, "but are so full of faith as to take one anothers word, and so live together, and begett children, and if they fall out or disagree, they part friendly by consent." Creole children, he added, seldom lived to be more than thirty-five years old, and they began to decline at thirty. Dr. Hans Sloane commented that "a yellowish sickly look" was the badge of the rank and file of the inhabitants of the Lesser Antilles.[29]

If a newly freed craftsman made his way to Bridgetown, Port Royal, or some other place of trade, and was both industrious and skilled, he was bound to make money. Port Royal is "the most proud and prodigal place I ever beheld," Francis Crow exclaimed in 1685, "for a cooper's wife shall go forth in the best flowered

28. Labat, *Nouveau Voyage,* VI, 196; for kind masters: Davis Coll., VII, Envelope 22; Jeaffreson, *Young Squire,* II, 299.
29. *CSPC, 1661–68,* p. 556; *1669–74,* p. 116; *1693–96,* pp. 446–7; Schomburgk, *History of Barbados,* 273–7; *MHS Colls.,* 2d ser., III, 195–6; Cary to William Helyar, May 22, 1671, Helyar MSS; Jeaffreson, *Young Squire,* I, 186, 255; Taylor, Multum in Parvo, II, 504; Sloane, *Voyage to the Islands,* I, lxxix, 42. For statistics of marriages in Barbados, 1648–90, see BM: Add. MSS, 38,825, pp. 107–295.

silks, and richest silver and gold lace that England can afford, with a couple of Negroes at her tail, there being five Blacks to one White." Town life attracted many other former servants who took such work as was offered and spent their wages in taverns drinking rum and cheap wine with new-found companions and the "crew of wild strumpets" or the common whores on the street (many of both former servants). That Port Royal deserved the epithet Sodom of the West Indies most contemporaries agreed, but Bridgetown always had a large transient population of merchants and mariners to whom its innkeepers and loose women catered. The strange sights of Caribbean seaports caused more than one visitor to marvel: "The common people here goe generally arrayed in good linen, butt many of them bare footed, without either Shoes or Stockins, soe that you shall see a common Woman, only in her Smocke ore linnen peticote, bare footed . . . with a Straw hatt, and tobacco pipe in their mouths and thus they Trampouse about their Streets . . . and thus arrayed will booger [cadge] a cupp of punch calmly with anyone." [30]

V

A very small coterie of the richest planters with extensive holdings of land and hundreds of slaves controlled the agricultural economy of their respective islands; they also presided over their social life and governed the people. Out of the 760 "considerable proprietors" of Barbados, 1660–73, only 74 possessed over 300 acres and 100 slaves; and 175 individuals (6.5 per cent of all planters) owned more than one-half of the white servants, slaves, and land in 1680. It is likely that in Jamaica the proportion of great planters was even less and their holdings more extensive.[31]

The Caribbean sugar and staple barons were almost to a man newly risen, and they exhibited conspicuously the characteristics and behavior of their kind in any age. "We are here generally fiery

30. Crow, in *Jamaica Historical Review,* III, 53; Taylor, Multum in Parvo, II, 502, 504, 509.

31. PRO: CO 1/21, fol. 170; Davis Coll., XV, G, Envelope 42 (list of 74 Barbadian planters and their holdings); Dunn, in *WMQ,* 3d ser., XXVI, 17 (Table IV, 1680).

spirited, and a mean planter thinks himself better than a good gentleman fellow in England," a Barbadian conceded in 1668. Associated with them in the emerging gentry were rich physicians, merchants, and lawyers, nearly every one of whom also had his plantation and slaves. Acute awareness of place and the insecurity of the *arriviste,* when taken with the habit of command, inevitably rendered the average planter hard, arrogant, domineering, condescending to planters and freemen of the lesser sort, and callous and often cruel in his relations with servants and slaves. Although they lacked the leavening gentility of the early leaders, the members of the new planting group could also be kindly, generous, and fabulously hospitable at times, but not one planter of these years rose to the heights attained by James Drax before 1650. The success in satisfying "the sacred hunger of Gold," which spurred them on and was the outstanding trait of them all, is epitomized in the career of Peter Beckford.[32]

With Samuel Pepys's friend "the great Tom Fuller" as his patron, Peter Beckford, first of the name, had "a mind to go to Jamaica" in 1661 in one of the king's ships, and the diarist arranged it. Peter's father Richard was said to have been a tailor of Maidenhead, and he had every reason to be proud of his two sons whose conspicuous careers illustrate the possibility of rising in Restoration society. Thomas, a clothworker and "slopseller" of London, was knighted in 1677. Bred to a mercantile life, well connected through his alderman brother, and, above all, as a nephew of Sir Thomas Lynch, Peter Beckford's destiny in Jamaica was almost predictable. In fifteen years, at the age of thirty-three, he possessed 2238 acres of land upon which he grew sugar and kept cattle pens. In the militia he moved up rapidly from captain to colonel and in 1683 was made commander of the fort at Port Royal, where John Taylor sought his favor and influence. Apparently in 1675 Peter Beckford first went from St. Catherine's to the Assembly, where, at different times, he sat for several parishes until his elevation to the Council in 1691. By marrying Bridget, daughter of Colonel William Bees-

32. Oldmixon's oft-quoted statement that Charles II made knights of 13 Barbadians in 1661 is easily disproved. *British Empire in America,* II, 110–11; *JBMHS,* II, 89–92; *CSPC, 1661–68,* pp. 623–4; *1681–85,* pp. 313, 438; *1689–92,* p. 172; Davies, *Caribby-Isles,* 9; Taylor, Multum in Parvo, II, 252.

ton, one of the foremost planters and officials, he advanced further in the ruling class of Jamaica. None of these activities prevented him from accumulating the 20 estates, 1200 slaves, and £1,500,000 in bank stock which he was said to have owned when he died in 1710. This dazzlingly successful man, who not merely served as president of the council after 1691 and as lieutenant governor in 1702, was described by his contemporaries as "singularly fit" for a soldier and "very active, honest, and sober" as a citizen and planter, and was the founder of what Noel Deerr has called "perhaps the greatest fortune ever made in planting." [33]

Having worked hard to acquire their estates, the newly rich had a compelling urge to emulate those first eminent leaders: Sir Thomas Modyford of Barbados and Jamaica, the Quakers Lewis Morris of Barbados and Samuel Winthrop of St. Christopher and later of Antigua, the Christopher Codringtons, the elder of Barbados, the younger of Antigua and governor of the Leeward Islands. The socially approved setting in this age for a rural plutocracy to indulge its propensity for ostentation was the great plantation house. There it was that the members went to costly extremes that eventually plunged the majority of them deeply into debt.[34]

Sometime after 1650 Sir James Drax built Drax Hall, an impressive edifice of plaster-covered cut-stone in the Jacobean mode, no longer used in England, with a superb staircase and casement windows. Also during the fifties, the Walronds put up Fontabelle in St. Michael's Parish, a large and elegant structure which they ultimately rented to the Assembly for £500 a year for the governor's residence. The only great house to survive, though greatly altered, for hurricanes, fires, rapid decay, and replacement have

33. Several Beckfords seem to have been in Jamaica around 1660, and the family genealogy is difficult to disentangle. There was but one Peter Beckford before 1690, not two as is usually said. *Diary of Samuel Pepys*, ed. Wheatley, I, 295–6; *Caribbeana,* III, 6; Boyd Alexander, *England's Wealthiest Son: A Study of William Beckford* (London, 1962), 29–30; Jamaica Council Minutes, IV, 31–2, 66, 267; *CSPC, 1681–85,* p. 590; Deerr, *History of Sugar,* I, 175–6; Frank Cundall fixed Beckford's estate at £478,000 and his real estate "to as much more." *Governors of Jamaica,* 12–25.

34. *Acts of Barbados* (1721), 147–8; *A Discourse of the Duties on Merchandize, More particularly that on Sugar . . . in Answer to The Groans of the Plantations* (London, 1695), 10–11.

taken away the seventeenth-century buildings erected by the English, is Nicholas Abbey, which was probably of a little later date. Its three curvilinear gables and four chimneys bear witness to the pervasive architectural influence of the Dutch, which is so evident in Samuel Copen's view of Bridgetown in 1695. Actually the so-called "great house" of Barbados and the other islands was very small by current European standards. It was more nearly of the order of the three-story glebe house measuring 40′ by 20′ "from Out to Out" that the vestry of St. John's ordered built in 1679. It was to be roofed with "plaine tyles pinned and laid in Mortar," and to have a ground floor laid with imported paving brick. The knowledgeable vestrymen went to the length of specifying in their minutes the number and exact dimensions of every stick of lumber to be used in the construction—the most informative architectural document surviving from the period.[35] (Plate 15)

Design always depends upon the environment and the materials available. This meant in the West Indies that wooden houses would predominate on every island, and when the local supply of timbers and boards ran out, they had to be brought from New England. Knocked-down "houses ready framed" had been introduced in Barbados before 1650 and soon reached markets all over the Caribbean. New England shingles were used in many instances, but they were expensive and often scarce; thatched roofs remained widely used because the thatch-tree, a kind of palm, grew everywhere. The old church edifice of St. Michael's, Barbados, was repaired in 1664 with "thatching and boarding." Fearful of destructive fires, the authorities forbade construction of "thatch houses" on Nevis. Some planters of Antigua, Montserrat, and Nevis erected stone houses, which, however, collapsed in the earthquakes in 1672. The experience taught the planters "to build low" thereafter. A surprising reversion to medieval construction can be traced to Montserrat in 1668: the specifications called for a new court

35. See the plates in Angus W. Ackworth, *Treasure in the Caribbean* (London, 1949); and *Buildings of Architectural or Historical Interest in the British West Indies* (London, 1951); also Thomas T. Waterman, "Some Early Buildings of Barbados," in *JBMHS*, XIII, pp. 140–43. Barbados Council Minutes, II, 347, 349, 358; Parish Vestry Minutes of St. John's, Barbados, 29, 29a, 39a (House for parish clerk), and Appendix IV of this work; Oldmixon, *British Empire in America,* II, 351.

house to be built with "good and substantial Cratches" or crotchets. Jamaicans, who had ample supplies of lime and stone, found to their amazement that the crotched and timber-framed houses withstood the tremors in 1692, while the stone and brick buildings crumbled.[36]

The abundance of handsome dwelling houses built of brick and stone in Bridgetown and "the many fine ones about the country" elicited praise from John Barbot. There had been a general rebuilding of planters' mansions; in some instances a second rebuilding occurred during the boom years of high sugar prices, for the truth seems to be that the first structures that the sugar planters raised were roomy and comfortable but neither large nor elegant. Most planters preferred to put their money into sugarworks and more slaves. The second and third rounds of mansion-building produced marked improvements and changes in design and construction aimed at increasing the resistance to high winds and for greater comfort. The fact that very good brick and tile were being burned in Jamaica by 1666 encouraged their use in the larger and more elaborate structures. St. Paul's Church in Port Royal, described by Governor Lynch as "the handsomest in America," was the design and achievement of Colonel William Beeston, who was also credited with influencing the planning of several plantation houses, but the most impressive developments in mansion architecture in Jamaica came after 1700.[37]

In a book of the Dawkins family that contains title deeds and plats from 1660 to 1670, one can trace each step in the evolution of the standard story-and-a-half house in St. John's and Clarendon parishes, Jamaica; also the design and size, the pantile roof and projecting eaves of the two-story structure; and finally the tiled

36. Davis Coll., VII, Envelope 14; *CSM Pubs.*, XXIX, 49–50; PRO: CO 1/38, No. 65, fols. 21–2; CO 157/1, fols. 152b, 153a; *Acts of Assembly . . . of Montserrat,* 7–8; *The Late Dreadful Earthquake in Jamaica,* 2; *JBMHS,* XV, 94; Sloane, *Voyage to the Islands,* II, 121–2; BM: Add. MSS, 11,410, fol. 20b; *CSPC, 1675–76,* pp. 237, 466, 499, 500; Labat, *Nouveau Voyage,* VII, 30.

37. Thomas Walduck, a Barbadian planter, wrote many years later of Barbados that the great houses were "nobley built, few . . . in England (except quallaty) comes up to them." T. Walduck, Letter II (1710), BM: Sloane MSS, 2302. Barbot, in Churchill, *Voyages,* V, 644; *CSPC, 1681–85,* p. 313; BM: Egerton MSS, 2395, fol. 609.

hip roof and other types of roofing. Most fascinating of all is a sketch to accompany a re-survey of Salt River Pen, owned by Henry Dawkins in 1667, in which are clearly shown a Dutch story-and-a-half house set on a high foundation and having stepped gables, tiny Holland dormers in the roof, and an end-chimney with two flues. Close by is another building with a curvilinear gable, a circular window in the gable end, and small dormers. The third structure, which is probably the sugar mill, has two tall stories and a hip roof surmounted by a tower as high as the building itself. The Dutch obviously brought design to the English colonists as well as brick and stone, for nothing in Curaçao, St. Eustatius, or Surinam, after 1667, bore a closer resemblance to Old Holland than this plantation group.[38]

When Père Du Tertre visited Barbados sometime before 1657, the vanity of the islanders had not yet extended to furniture: a chest or two, a table, beds, and some benches were about all one ever saw. The inventory of William Clarke, made in 1655, bears out the priest. Woodenware, most of it imported from New England, and pewter served even the rich. In the eighties, however, urged on by their wives and their own desire to display new wealth, the planters began to improve the interiors of their houses with wainscoting, imported hangings, and furniture, a mode developing at this very time among the lesser gentry and mercantile classes in England. In this respect, the Barbadians led the other islanders, but it is significant that the sugar gentry of little Nevis purchased in 1684–85 a "parcel of upholster ware" consisting of chairs with seats and backs of Russian leather and six parcels of "turnery ware" from London: two close-stools from Ireland, and "two dozen chairs from Bristol." The *Port Royal* from London landed in 1687 at Charles Town, Nevis, fourteen bundles of chairs, a table, two desks, a case of drawers—probably all for one planter. Interior elegance had become the vogue by 1690, and an English document of ten years later tells the story:

38. In 1637–38 the English imitated Dutch buildings on Tobago. F. Morales, *Planos y Dibujos Sobre Venezuela Existente En El Archivo General de Indias* (Seville, 1958), Pl. 91. Dawkins Family Papers, Lib. I, fols. 121, 136, 189; Lib. II, 13, 118, 121; Plans I, II, in folio.

	Cabinet Ware	Upholstery
TO JAMAICA		
From London	£1208 5*s.* 3*d.*	£ 740 8*s.* 6*d.*
From Outports	———	332 17*s.* 8*d.*
TO BARBADOS		
From London	£2196 3*s.* 4*d.*	£1570 7*s.* 8*d.*
From Outports	12 0*s.* 0*d.*	140 16*s.* 0*d.*
TO ANTIGUA		
From London	£ 305 4*s.* 6*d.*	
From Outports	———	

Totals	
From London	£6642 9*s.* 2*d.*
From Outports	490 10*s.* 8*d.*
	£7132 19*s.* 10*d.*

By the close of this period in the majority of the better plantation houses, high ceilings, fully glazed casement windows, and "fans in some Parlours, such as are us'd about Montpellier," provided a measure of relief during the dog days. The wives of the wealthiest planters now spent more time indoors and gave increasing attention to procuring fine imported furniture, such as bedsteads with valances, rich brocaded hangings, fine table and bed linens, and silver plate. An estimate of the plate, jewels, household furnishings, etc., in Barbados for 1667 amounted to £500,000.[39]

Like their husbands, the planters' wives were a mixed lot. There was gentle Madam Frances Russell, daughter of the governor of Nevis, who had a fortune of £1500 sterling at the age of fifteen; and then there was "the Irish woman, fit only to be a servant of servants," who presided as mistress of the Jeaffreson household when the overseer was left in charge; and of course there were all

39. Du Tertre, *Histoire générale,* II, 450–52; Davis Coll., II, Envelope 5; Edwin T. Joy, "Furniture for the West Indies," in *Connoisseur Year Book* (1953), 82, 83; (1954), 82, 83, 86; Pares, *West-India Fortune,* 31; Connell, in *JBMHS,* XXIV, 110, 116–21; PRO: CO 1/38, fol. 65; *CSPC, 1661–68,* p. 529; Sloane, *Voyage to the Islands,* I, x; Blome, *Present State of His Majesty's Isles . . . ,* 34.

kinds in between these extremes. Wives, as a rule, outlived their spouses by a ratio of five to one, for unlike their husbands, they abstained from overindulgence in food, wines, brandy, and rum, and had no sexual relations with Negroes. Thomas Tryon commented on their lack of concern for black women; in fact where they "have sole command, as when they are left Widdows, or the like, many of them are more fierce, dogged, pinching, pressing, and severe than the men themselves." Creole women generally overdressed in their efforts to imitate the gentlewomen of England according to travelers; and George Fox berated the Anglican clergy of the West Indies in 1672 for allowing their wives to appear in public "with broidered Hair or Gold or Pearls, or Costly Array," which only encouraged parishioners to think that gain was godliness.[40]

"The Masters, for the most part, live at the height of Pleasure," one observer reported, and another found them living "in all Affluence of Pleasure and Delight. . . ." "What they owe in London does not appear here," said a third. Nevertheless, as John Taylor pointed out as late as 1688, the plantation gentry really enjoyed very few opportunities for recreation of the kind Englishmen loved. They garbed themselves richly in costly imported clothes, as did their wives, wined and dined their friends at home, or appeared in town on gala occasions, such as the reception of a new Royal governor, or the Cockney Feast given annually on October 29 by all of the Barbadian planters and merchants born within the sound of Bow Bells. Marriages and christenings always took place in the great houses rather than the distant church, and burials in the family plot on the plantation, not in the churchyard, and such occasions called for "their best feasts" for the guests who had ridden or driven from far off.[41]

No substantial planter ever went abroad unless on horseback, and as the roads improved on each island, carriages and coaches

40. Trapham, *State of Health in Jamaica,* 55, 68; *Caribbeana,* III, 208; Tryon, *Friendly Advice to the Planters,* 106; *CSPC, 1689–92,* p. 489; Jeaffreson, *Young Squire,* I, 233–6, 263, 270; II, 89; Fox, *To the Ministers,* 19.

41. Blome, *Present State of His Majesty's Isles . . . ,* 39; Blome, *Description of the Island of Jamaica,* 84, 89; *CSPC, 1669–74,* p. 223; Walduck Letter, 1710, BM: Sloane MSS, 2302; Taylor, Multum in Parvo, II, 578, 585, 587; Jeaffreson, *Young Squire,* I, 247, 248; Oldmixon, *British Empire in America,* II, 126.

ranked among the principal badges of status and wealth as well as means of transport for ladies and gentlemen alike. When George Fox landed at Bridgetown in 1671, the Quaker merchant John Rous met him at the waterside with Colonel Chamberlain's coach. Jamaicans tamed their own wild horses for saddle or carriage use, but the Barbadians and other islanders sent to Connecticut or Rhode Island for matched coach horses. The market place at Bridgetown was moved west of St. Michael's Church in 1682 because, among other nuisances, it blocked the passage of horsemen and carriages, including the coach-and-six that a rich planter had put at the disposal of Governor Dutton. But the finest parade of equipages could be seen at St. Iago de la Vega, the Havana of Jamaica, where "the richer sort recreate themselves every Morning in their Coaches or on Horseback, as . . . in Hide Park"; elsewhere the planters and their wives had to be content with driving about the countryside.[42]

The last decade of the period produced a marked increase in social activities that centered in the two large towns. There resident merchants, lawyers, and physicians were joined by members of the rising plantation gentry in an exciting, almost frenetic, search for pleasure. Mr. Francis Hanson pictured a gay Jamaica in 1682: "all Gentlemens Coaches (which are there very numerous) go with six Horses apiece; we have also several Hackney Coaches. The manner of living there for Gallantry, good Housekeeping and Recreations (as Horse Races, Bowls, Dancing, Musick, Plays at a public Theatre, &c.) sufficiently demonstrate the flourishing condition of the Island." He is here referring to Port Royal and Spanish Town together, for the latter was more of a social center because it was the seat of the governor, Sir Thomas Lynch. The Governor's lady gave an entertainment and ball on the king's birthday with a "suitable number of Masqueraders, very curiously habited, and a variety of music." A company of strolling puppet-players performed one season at Bridgetown before they went on to the Leeward Islands. The Barbadians proclaimed King James II with a

42. *HMC, 14th Report,* Pt. 2, III, 272; Taylor, Multum in Parvo, II, 334–5; Fox, *Journal,* 591; *MHS Colls.,* 5th ser., VIII, 427; Dutton to Blathwayt, March 15, 1680/1, Blathwayt Papers (Colonial Williamsburg), XXX; Barbados Council Minutes, II, 364–5; Morden, *Geography,* 569.

procession from Fontabelle to Bridgetown, headed by two regiments of foot followed by all of the judges, the Council, trumpeters, and the Governor; but Port Royal outdid this spectacle when it received the Duke of Albemarle in December 1687 by having a similar military parade from the landing place to the King's House along a street "covered with green cloath," and a "great concourse of Gentry," who later attended a dinner accompanied by bonfires and music.[43]

"Pent up on this Hott sandy point" in Port Royal, resident merchants, privateers temporarily ashore, and the populace found few healthy outlets for their gregarious instincts, unless one counts a bull-and-bear fight at the Bear Garden, cockfights, billiards, shooting at targets for prizes, card games, and every kind of liquor at a tavern. "Young Sparks of the Common Sort" resorted at night to "the Music houses to divert themselves, for the port is very loose in itself, and by reason of Privateers and debauched wild blades which come hither," according to John Taylor, who also mentions that the older, more sedate and proper sort of men contented themselves after sundown with a short "Ambulation." Cards, dice, and gaming tables were patronized daily at Bridgetown taverns, where large sums were wagered. In short, the two seaports offered most of the temptations and tawdry excitement then known to the members of a decidedly male society.[44]

43. Hanson's "Account," *Laws of Jamaica* (Wood), 456; Jamaica Council Minutes, V, 94; *CSPC, 1685–88,* p. 279; Oldmixon, *British Empire in America,* II, 44, 126–7.

44. Taylor, Multum in Parvo, II, 502–4; Oldmixon, *British Empire in America,* II, 126.

XII

Material Success and Social Failure

IN NO RESPECT did the emigrants to the West Indies represent a fair cross section of the society they left behind in the British Isles. Males assembled for the most part from the lesser sort and joined by men of similar backgrounds from other European nations, together with a few gentlemen leaders, made up conglomerates of white men on each of the islands. Noticeably absent from their ranks was any substantial number of those middling Englishmen who figured so prominently at that same time in the building of the New England and Chesapeake societies. Not many of those West Indian colonists, until the Creoles grew numerous, intended to make the islands their permanent home. As a consequence the family became an almost exclusively upper-class institution that, failing to spread, never attained the profound influence it had in the continental colonies. Therefore it is vain to look for a solid base upon which a society resembling that of England could have been formed in any of these islands. The outlook of the colonists was material and secular, and the nature of their failure to construct a valid society becomes evident when their inadequate institutions and way of life are examined.[1]

II

If the inhabitants of the Caribbean settlements were ever to achieve the degree of civilized existence enjoyed by their compatriots in the

1. Taylor, Multum in Parvo, II, 252.

Mother Country, they would have to seek it in Christianity as it was organized and propagated by the Church of England and supported by government, both in England and in the islands. Political and religious upheaval in Britain prevented any planned action from 1650 to 1660. After the Restoration, ecclesiastical indifference or preoccupation at Lambeth and Canterbury proved fatal, for clerical officials never extended episcopal supervision to the West Indies and left the destinies of the Church to local authorities. The familiar union of church and state had to be worked out, if at all, in the colonial assemblies.

The establishment of the Church of England in Barbados provided by the law of 1650 was relaxed within two years by the guarantee, in the articles of submission to Sir George Ayscue and Parliament, of liberty of conscience to all persons, unless their beliefs were inconsistent with civil government. Furthermore, no minister could be deprived of his office without due process of law. When the Penn-Venables Expedition arrived in 1654, the Barbadians asked for and received permission to continue the liberty "which wee soe long have in England fought for." Shortly after the Restoration, however, the Anglican Walronds persuaded the Assembly to pass an act providing that obedience to the Church of England was to be enforced by all constables and justices of the peace; masters and overseers of families (servants included) living within two miles of a church had to attend worship on Sunday mornings; and ministers were directed to use the Book of Common Prayer, to preach, and to catechize children weekly. A second law, of 1661, ordered the churchwardens in all parishes to assess and collect a levy of one pound of sugar per acre for the support of the clergy, the keeping of parish registers, and the reporting of all burials in private plots of persons who lived more than two miles from a churchyard. These two statutes constituted the legal framework for the establishment of the Church of England in Barbados and continued in force long after 1690.[2]

Ecclesiastical establishment took place at different times in each of the other colonies. In the Leeward Islands the Second Dutch

2. *Articles of Agreement, Made and Concluded the 11th day of January, 1651* [1652]; Venables, in RHS, *Camden,* LX, 146; *Laws of Barbados* (Rawlin), 13–15; *Acts of Barbados* (1721), 21–2; Barbados Council Minutes, I, 83.

War disrupted religious life as completely as it did economic activity and civil affairs, but in 1670 Governor Stapleton could report that the Protestant faith was officially proclaimed in all of them and that the proportion of Anglicans to others was eight to one, except on Montserrat where the Roman Catholic Irish outnumbered the English by six to one. On Antigua in 1680, an official found "Ecclesiastical affaires in good order and agreement with the Church of England." The Anglican establishment in Jamaica grew very slowly after 1664 during Governor Modyford's term; not until after 1676 did the Assembly authorize taxes for ministerial support, and ten years elapsed before it completed the organization of civil and ecclesiastical government in the island's fifteen parishes.[3]

Most of the insular vestries attended to the construction of parish churches. At Barbados after 1660, old timber structures with roofs of thatch were replaced by larger and more suitable edifices of stone, and in 1677 ten out of eleven parishes in the island had churches despite the severe hurricane of the year before. Everywhere, in fact, after hurricanes and fires, better churches took the places of those destroyed. The Leeward Islands contained but ten churches in 1676: four in Nevis, two in Antigua, two at St. Christopher, and two in Montserrat. In predominantly Catholic Montserrat, the Anglicans put up a handsome edifice—the pulpit, pews, and all joiners' work made from "the most precious and sweet-scented wood in the country." The Jamaicans lagged behind in building churches, having only six in 1677, but when St. Paul's opened for services in Port Royal on New Year's Day in 1681, it was proclaimed the finest church in the New World.[4]

Ecclesiastical institutions could not be any better than the men who administered them, and the great problem facing those concerned with the moral and ethical standards and behavior of the inhabitants was the lack of able priests to fill the livings that existed. Though most of the time Barbados seems to have been well

3. *Acts of Assembly . . . of Montserrat,* 6; BM: Egerton MSS, 2395, fol. 528b; PRO: CO 1/45, fol. 14; CO 1/36, fol. 146; CO 1/37, fol. 72a; *CSPC, 1681–85,* pp. 6–7; Frank Cundall, *Historic Jamaica* (London, 1915), 22; George W. Bridges, *The Annals of Jamaica* (London, 1827), I, 539.

4. *CSPC, 1675–76,* p. 502; *1677–80,* p. 63; *1681–85,* pp. 147, 314; Vere L. Oliver, *History of the Island of Antigua* (London, 1899), III, 393.

supplied, the want of ministers in the other islands shocked the Royal governors. Jamaica had but three priests in 1666, and only four in 1671: a Scot, two Swiss, and Master John Lemon of Cambridge, reported to be "a very good Preacher and a sober man." In that year Henry Houser of St. Catherine's Parish, preaching before the Assembly and Governor Lynch about "the Torrent of Wickedness and Vice rushing through" Jamaica, called for civil support of an able ministry to "confute the sins of the mighty." The pressing need for clergymen after the re-settlement of the Leeward Islands impelled Governor Sir Charles Wheler to ask Lord Arlington to send over from Cambridge Dr. Francis Turner, Master of St. John's, as Bishop of Nevis to settle the government of the Church and ordain priests in the islands. Sir Charles urged that he bring eight fellows with him but such counsel brought no results, and a flock of about 10,000 Christians in the forty parishes of the Leeward Islands continued to have only four clergymen to shepherd them. "The great Scarcity of Ministers" and the problem of incontinency at Montserrat produced an act in 1678 that made marriages by justices of the peace legal and the offspring legitimate.[5]

In sharp contrast to the Jesuits and other Roman Catholic orders, which sent able and pious men to the French islands, many of the priests of the Church of England proved incompetent or worldly or immoral. Acting as ordinary in 1668, William, Lord Willoughby, governor of Barbados, suspended John Page, minister of St. James's, for scandalous and profane talk, and restored him only upon condition that he preach a sermon the next Sunday testifying to his sorrow and detestation of his unclerical behavior. Sir Charles Wheler notified King Charles II in 1671 that on his arrival in the Leeward Islands three of the four ministers there consisted of "one drunken orthodox priest, one drunken sectary priest, and one drunken person that had no orders." Presumably the fourth was acceptable. With surprising naïveté, the Council of St. Christopher

5. PRO: CO 1/37, fols. 72a–73b; CO 1/27, fol. 11 (I); *CSPC, 1675–76,* p. 424; BM: Add. MSS, 11,410, fol. 199b; Modyford to Clarendon, March 5, 1665/6 (Bodleian: Clarendon MSS, 84, fol. 80), Davis Coll., V; Henry Houser, *An Exact Model or Platform of Good Magistracy* (London, 1693), 6, 18; *Acts of Assembly . . . of Montserrat,* 33–4; *CSPC, 1669–74,* p. 242.

asked for more and better clergymen from England, men of "riper years and better read in divinity than those young graduates that come hither," because the Roman priests in the French part of the island "are questionless men of great learning and parts." If the sermons Richard Scamler preached at Barbados are at all typical, Anglican ministers never spoke directly to their puritan listeners in the plain style or related their sermons to everyday needs but delivered nothing more than an abstract homily.[6]

Following his instructions perhaps too literally, Governor Dutton set about zealously to improve everything about the Church of England in Barbados. As soon as he landed in 1681, he discovered things "in disorder enough": churches ruined or destroyed by recent hurricanes needed rebuilding and vacancies in the clergy required replacements. He found that a clergyman named Grey, who was not in orders, had been tolerated for twenty-four years by previous governors and was in possession of two livings. During this time he had administered the sacraments and married all who applied to him. "Vicious in the whole Course of his life," Mr. Grey confessed to never having been ordained, yet, Dutton wrote to Sir Leoline Jenkins, Jonathan Atkins was highly offended at the suspension of "so famous a person." Because the legitimacy of many Barbadian offspring might be suspect, the distraught official was solicited to pass a bill confirming Grey's marriages of "such vermin" as their parents. Governor Dutton, in explaining his instructions and authority to the members of the Assembly, displayed great dignity but little human understanding, and he reminded them that "you have never made one step for the reducing of the people to their strict observation of their religious duties." When he sought authorization from the Lords of Trade and Plantations for an ecclesiastical court in Barbados, he maintained that "this famous Island" is no longer in its infancy, and its people "can now digest strong meats." Nothing ever came of this effort, and their Lordships should not have been surprised when

6. Barbados Council Minutes, II, 30, 36–7; *CSPC, 1669–74,* pp. 243, 289; *1677–80,* p. 572; Richard Scamler, *Several Sermons: Some Preached in England and Some in Barbados* . . . (London, 1685; copy in Boston Pub. Library), 1–17, 41–80.

word reached London that "above one half of the people, especially of the poorer sorts, never go to Divine Service at all."[7]

Some credence must be given to the clerics' complaints about the oppressions they were subjected to by their vestries, which, they charged in turn, were made up for the most part of "sordid plebeians, the very dregs of the English Nation." To those bodies belonged the power of "placing and displacing" the ministers, which made the latter mere "annual stipendiaries." On the other hand, the surviving minutes of the vestries of St. Michael's and St. John's parishes, Barbados, show that not only did a number of prominent planters serve as churchwardens, but that they had the welfare of their priests very much in mind. Busy governors, though serving as ordinaries, had little time to support the priests except when they sat with their councils to punish flagrant moral offenses, impose public penance in church, or cause offenders to be whipped. When some much-needed Bibles and Prayer Books, shipped out for distribution to the clergy in Barbados, were "embezzled" in 1689, it was Governor Dutton whom the Privy Council ordered to find an explanation without fail.[8]

The presence in the islands from early times of large numbers of settlers of other persuasions than the Anglican posed a variety of problems for Churchmen. Thousands of Irishmen lived in the Caribbean bereft of any spiritual comforts. In 1654 Père Biët determined to learn English in order to serve "more than two thousand Catholics" on Barbados. After he departed, three Irish priests landed at Speightstown, and within two more years, four more arrived. At this point, however, the Secretary notified them that

7. Governor Modyford described frankly the religious state of Jamaica: "alas, My Lord, these five [ministers] do not preach to one third of the Island, the Plantations are at such distance each from the other that it is impossible to make up convenient Congregations or find fitting places for the rest to meete alternatively at each others Houses, as the Primitive Christians did, and there to Pray, Read a Chapter, Sing a Psalm and home againe." He thought that if the settlers had not been instructed in the Christian religion and Thirty-Nine Articles before coming out to the island, they "would have quite forgott or at least little minded among them." PRO: CO 138/1, fol. 104. *CSPC, 1681–85,* pp. 60–61, 148–50, 197–8; Barbados Council Minutes, II, 362, 372; *Caribbeana,* III, 268.

8. *Barbados Diocesan History,* 14, 17; St. Michael's Vestry Minutes, *JBMHS,* XIV and succeeding volumes; St. John's Vestry Minutes, 1640–60, *passim; APC Col.,* II, 131.

they must leave the island within fifteen days. The number of papists declined toward the end of the period, but the Council of Barbados became aware of the activities of two gentlemen planters, Willoughby Chamberlayne and Sir Thomas Montgomerie, who, "perverted" by a Jesuit of Martinique, were endeavoring to convert others to their new faith. Avowing that "This is a Protestant Island, and the parishes are supplied with true, able, and Protestant divines," the Council turned both of the men out of the Council and later declared that thenceforth Roman Catholics were ineligible for any "public employment." [9]

In other islands the Irish Romanists fared somewhat better. Jean Destriche, known as Father Strich, went to St. Christopher in 1650 and set up a chapel at Point des Sables near the English line. Overjoyed, the Irish servants flocked there to receive the sacrament, and soon the priest claimed to have 3000 persons in his congregation. After three months, he crossed to Montserrat, where the English had expelled all Roman Catholic priests, and celebrated the mass daily in the woods until a Carib attack forced him to return to St. Christopher. Aroused by the number of Irish Catholics who attended these covert services, the English feared that they would join the French in case of war and consequently rounded up about 900 of the most fervent of them and shipped them off to the Isle of Crabs more than 500 miles away. Nevertheless, some of those who remained behind secretly crossed to the French part of St. Christopher along hidden paths at night to attend the mass until sometime in 1653 when Father Strich moved along to Guadeloupe.[10]

Because Jamaicans and some of the authorities of the smaller islands of the Leeward group valued settlers more than orthodoxy, and profitable staples above faith, they solicited all comers of any religion whatever. After the separation of the Leeward Islands from Barbados, Sir Charles Wheler's instructions (January 3, 1670/71) directed him to give all possible encouragement to "persons of different judgement and opinion" to come out there to live,

9. Biët, *Voyage,* 276; Gwynn, in *Analecta Hibernica,* No. 4, pp. 233, 235; Oldmixon, *British Empire in America,* II, 39; *CSPC, 1689–92,* pp. 10, 12.

10. Gwynn, in *Analecta Hibernica,* No. 4, pp. 207–12; Pelleprat, *Relation,* Pt. I, 37–50.

and in no instance to molest anyone in the exercise of his religion. In Jamaica, as early as 1664, Governor Modyford was ordered to allow liberty of conscience and permit Christians and Jews to worship according to their lights provided they were otherwise law-abiding. And there was no abatement of this policy, for Lord Vaughan proclaimed the Declaration of Indulgence by beat of drum at Port Royal on March 19, 1674/5, and since at Port Royal in 1688, one might worship at the Church of England, a Presbyterian meetinghouse, a Romish chapel, a "Quackers Meeting House" or a synagogue, "all which Sects live quietly together," it is obvious that toleration still prevailed. About this time, the Council actually gave the Dominican Father Thomas Offler £20 for a chapel "for his Flocke to meet in." [11]

Influential men in the islands looked upon "a powerfull ministry" as "the cheif good." When the vestry of Middle Island Parish on St. Christopher put the minister out of office in 1660 for scandalous living, Samuel Winthrop wrote to his half-brother in Connecticut: "The benefice is the best in the Island, and the people are very desirous, if possible to be supplyed from New England. You will much farther the worke of the Lord if you doe incourage any godly grave minister to accept thereof, for it must not be a young man that must deal with this people, nor one that will seem to winke at their madnesse, but a very seveer reproover of their vices, and one that will teach them by his example to walke soberly as in the daye." The dissenters in Barbados had the opportunity of hearing a New Englander preach when Solomon Stoddard, for reasons of health, went there in 1667, but he returned after a year or so and settled in Northampton. From Jamaica in 1671, the mariner John Blackleach reported to John Winthrop, Jr., that "our New England ministers may not preach with allowance heare, without the bishops licence from England." At Roxbury in Massachusetts-Bay in 1674, John Eliot recorded in the church records: "mr [William] Woodrob, a scotchman, a scholar, had bene at Jamerca, and was too good for them; he came hither, he is well accepted." In succeeding years Jamaica was known at Boston as a place of

11. *CSPC, 1669–74,* pp. 158–9; *1675–76,* p. 186; Jamaica Council Minutes, I, 225–6; II, 65–6; V, 183, 253; Gardner, *History of Jamaica,* 88; Taylor, Multum in Parvo, II, 504.

sin and godlessness. In 1691 Samuel Sewall warned Joseph Sergeant, sailing for Port Royal as his agent: "Keep your N. E. Principles. Hear Gods Word publicly preached every Lord's Day, if it may be without wronging your Conscience. Be a Law to your self." [12]

Buttressed by several ejected English clerics who sought livings in the islands, the spirit of the early conforming puritans persisted throughout this period. John Oxenbridge, unable to preach in England, sailed for Surinam in a "desire and hope of serving Christ there," but when the Dutch took over that colony, he left the Main for Barbados. Thomas Parris, formerly of Boston, made a match between the minister and a sugar heiress, whom he advised to purchase property in New England. "After some fruitlesse essays" in Little England, Oxenbridge accepted a call to the First Church of Boston in 1669. Thomas Bridge, who had had a rigorous training under dissenting ministers in England, crossed to Port Royal in 1686. He lived "in very good esteem with his congregation" until after he was married to the daughter of William Paterson (later a founder of the Bank of England); he was then reported to have "lost his interest with the sisterhood who were his main supporters." Following an adventure in the Bahamas, he sailed northward and eventually he too was called to the First Church of Boston. Another nonconformist, Francis Crow, arrived in Jamaica in 1686 to "find sin very high and religion very low." Only "the better sort of merchants and mechanics adhere to us," he wrote to Giles Firman of Essex. He tried in vain to persuade Mr. Bridge, the "conventicle preacher," to stay at Port Royal and work with him. He too would have gone to New England had he been called, for he was bothered by the intense heat and lack of congenial associates: "I am here deprived of conversation both with scholars and Christians, few here of the better sort caring to see a minister *qua talis* out of the pulpit, having no time nor spirit to entertain

12. Samuel Sewall consigned his goods to Eliakim Mather, then at Port Royal, along with some advice: "Stay where you are, if you can enjoy God's word on the Sabbath from some good minister." *MHS Colls.*, 6th ser., I, 116, 117; 4th ser., VII, 153; 5th ser., VIII, 247, 248; *CSPD, 1683,* p. 94; Sibley, *Harvard Graduates,* II, 112; Oldmixon, *British Empire in America,* II, 134; *CSPC, 1681–85,* pp. 210–11; Boston Record Commissioners, *Sixth Report* (Boston, 1881), 122.

any matured edification in more private Christian communion." [13]

Conforming puritans, dissatisfied with what they considered the lifeless religion and irreligious life of both the priesthood and laity of the Church of England, suddenly discovered an outlet in the new and uplifting faith of the Society of Friends. Only eight years after George Fox began his teaching in England, Mary Fisher and Ann Austin crossed to Barbados to preach "the Truth" and spread Friendly writings amongst a spiritually starved people. Nor were their listeners and readers all humble folk, for John Rous, one of those "convinced" in 1655, published at London the next year *A Warning to the Inhabitants of Barbados, Who Live in Pride, Drunkennesse, Covetousnesse, Oppression, and deceitful dealings;* 600 copies were distributed in his native island. From Northampton gaol in January 1656/7 William Dewsbury announced to the people "scattered into Barbados, Virginia, New England, and other islands" and countries "that the mighty day of the Lord" was coming, and thereafter a steady procession of public Friends from England made Barbados, as George Rofe said, "the nursery of truth." [14]

The secret of the Quakers' success lay in their winning men of piety, probity, and principles to their new sect. John Rous and his rich father Lieutenant Colonel Thomas Rous, Ralph Fretwell, judge of the Court of Common Pleas, Thomas Clarke, owner of a big estate and several hundred slaves, Dr. John Redman, Edward Wright, and several other prominent and wealthy surgeons all adopted the new faith. Though convinced at Portsmouth on Rhode Island, Joseph Borden moved to Bridgetown in 1669 and, in addition to being active in the monthly and quarterly meetings, he

13. After the English regained their part of St. Christopher, some French Huguenots purchased properties there, and in 1671 they applied for a pastor of their own faith, which Sir Charles Wheler granted provided he read the Church of England liturgy. PRO: CO 1/27, fols. 10–11; Waters, *Genealogical Gleanings,* I, 420–1; Shipton, *Harvard Graduates,* V, 18, 20; *CSPC, 1685–88,* pp. 274–5; Crow, in *Jamaica Historical Review,* III, 53, 55–6.

14. John Rous, *A Warning to the Inhabitants of Barbados* (London, 1656; copy in Friends House Library, Tracts, 201/50); William C. Braithwaite, *The Beginnings of Quakerism,* ed. Henry J. Cadbury (Cambridge, Eng., 1955), 224, 270, 401, 402. For a partial list of more than 30 public Friends (men and women) who visited Barbados and Jamaica, see Levy, in Amer. Antiq. Soc., *Proceedings,* LXX, 303–5.

served as a principal link to the other American Quaker center at Newport. "Of good interest and conduct, and an honest man though a Quaker," mariner, fighter, Commonwealth man and member of the Council, Lewis Morris was still being recommended for the Barbados Council in 1666. Such men as these gave the lie to the insistence of the Anglican clergy that the Friends were all tailors and people of the inferior sort. But even many of them who were successful craftsmen stood out as superior in morals and industry when compared with the ordinary white inhabitants.[15]

Although some Friends had to flee to Jamaica in 1658 for refusing to pay rates and to serve in the militia, several meetings had been formed by the next year, and eventually there were five of them in the island. Josiah Coale reported laconically to Fox in 1661: "many convinced daily, and Friends fresh and living, meetings large and precious"; and financial aid from a collection taken in London came the following year. After the visit of George Fox, William Edmundson, and other public Friends in 1671, membership spurted conspicuously; Fox inaugurated women's meetings for the 186 Barbadian Quakeresses. In July 1673 the Grand Jury, exercised over the daily increase in the number of Quakers who, it charged, under the pretense of piety, seduced many ignorant persons from obedience to authority, called upon all families to send their children to be catechized and instructed in Anglican fundamentals. The members added that the ministers had complained that very few parents did this and that only the aged observed the Lord's Day—"a crying sin." [16]

From the advent of George Fox in Barbados in 1671, the Government and Church found the Friends increasingly troublesome and by 1676 had come to fear them. The Friends' efforts to Christianize the Negroes frightened many a planter, and the refusal of the Quakers to serve in the militia against their peaceful tenets aroused bitter resentment. Furthermore the truth of the Quakers'

15. E. M. Shilstone, in *Barbados Advocate Tercentenary* (Christmas No., 1927), 21–3; Besse, *Sufferings of the Quakers,* II, 331–2; *CSPC, 1661–68,* pp. 413, 556, 562; John O. Austin, *Genealogical Dictionary of Rhode Island* (Albany, 1887), 24.
16. Braithwaite, *Beginnings of Quakerism,* 618; Coale to Fox, *Journal of the Friends' Historical Society,* XXXIII, 57; Cadbury, in *JBMHS,* IX, 195–7; *CSPC, 1669–74,* p. 506.

charges against drunken and immoral Anglican priests cut deeply. Tact was never a Friendly trait, and the insistence of the Quakers upon rising in the audience at church and pointing an accusing finger at the parson, and the frankness of their published tracts, which spread the unsavory story of the religious and moral lapses of the colonists to the Mother Country, as well as to the other English colonies, provoked retaliation, repression, and persecution of one Christian by another.

Between 1658 and 1690, in one fashion or another, 260 Friends suffered at the hands of Barbadian authorities, who distrained the Quakers by the seizure of more than a million pounds of their sugar, valued at £10,607 1*s.* 8*d.*, for refusing to bear arms or to supply servants, slaves, and horses to support the militia, as well as for their unwillingness to swear oaths or pay parish levies ("Wages") to support priests of whom they disapproved. Former Justice Fretwell had to pay 7135 pounds of sugar; Colonel Thomas Rous, 25,880; and Lewis Morris, once 6000 for "Church dues" or tithes "so-called," and another time 10,193 pounds. Many of them went to prison for their offenses. Joseph Borden, the rich merchant from Rhode Island, had goods taken from his warehouse shop in 1669 "to the value of 1,440 pounds of sugar," and in 1674 an additional 880 pounds for not riding on patrol. After the passage of an act prohibiting the bringing of slaves to meetings, Ralph Fretwell had to pay £10 apiece for holding a meeting of 80 of his blacks in his own house. Moreover the constables often handled their victims, even women and humble Friends, roughly, sometimes brutally. In 1687 some Friends told Governor Stede pointedly that "we cannot manage well our Estates, when the best of our Negroes and Draft Cattle are taken from us, and not for our Debts, or wronging of any Man, but only for conscience-sake as to God."[17]

17. Joseph Besse gives names and detailed figures in his *Sufferings of the Quakers*, II, 278–343; see also, Roger Longworth to London Friends, Feb. 6, 1686/7, West India MSS (Bos. Pub. Lib.), I, Letter 4. The following tracts dealt with the situation at Barbados: [William Fortescue] *A Short Relation Concerning . . . William Simpson . . .* (London, 1671; copy in Bos. Pub. Lib.); Josiah Coale, *Books and Divers Epistles* (London, 1671); [Lydia Fell] *A Testimony and Warning Given Forth in the Love of Truth . . .* (London, 1676); *A Relation of the Labour, Travel, and Suffering of . . . Alice Curwen* (London, 1688); John Burnyeat, *The Truth Exalted* (London, 1691); also the tracts of Fox, Edmundson, and Vokins previously cited. *Acts of Barbados* (1721), 106.

Quakerism had its roots in the family, and the Friends of Barbados proved no exception. Far more than with any other religious body their meetings were composed of tightly knit families, whether of merchants or planters or craftsmen. Their firm convictions and the absence of sectarian competition caused them to flourish despite persecution (possibly because of it) and to encourage through the meetings any worthy undertaking. It was the sense of the meeting held by Quaker midwives on January 11, 1677/8, that each of them would take gifts for her services only from the parents, and not anything from those who were poor, and that they would sit with the mother in labor in silent meeting "to bear testimony against the World and their ways, who as soon as the Woman is delivered, do run into eating and drinking . . . to the grieving of God's spirit." The midwives also agreed not to use "laced linen" but to "call for plain," and in cases of difficult labor if they needed help "not to go to the World" but advise only with one another "and wait for God's assistance." Apparently the accoucheuses gathered in meetings periodically, for on February 24, 1678/9, the law of 1670 notwithstanding, they decided that it would be proper to accept money from the masters for assisting Negro women in childbirth but nothing from "the poor creatures" themselves. We have no evidence that the women of any other sect ever helped at the lying-in of a slave.[18]

Under guidance from English Friends those of Barbados had organized thoroughly by 1680. They were also corresponding with Quakers in Holland. John Rous was able to assure George Fox that in six "Divisions" (in lieu of parishes) they had weekly meetings, and general monthly, quarterly, and yearly meetings. At Bridgetown in 1686, the Friends also found "Meetings of Business" useful "to see into things; so that All may be keept Sweet and Clean; and that which is contrary may be keept down and judged." Likewise, Children's Meetings where the young repeated the catechism from George Fox's Primer were being held before 1681, when Joan Vokins praised the frequent and comforting Family Meetings of Barbados Friends. Gatherings such as these were the very first of their kind held by the Quakers anywhere, and they filled a felt void in insular

18. Cadbury, in *Journal of the Friends' Historical Society,* XXXVII, 22–4.

life. Quakerism in Barbados embraced and suffused the entire lives of the members.[19]

Public Friends, almost as many women as men, permitted the lay and clerical officials of Barbados no surcease from admonition and censure. Lydia Fell, daughter of the famous Margaret and later the wife of John Rous, gave testimony and warning to the islanders to stop taking away the Friends' goods and saying "that they love God and yet not keep his commands . . . Such are Lyers." "So now consider what is of the World, Evil Thoughts, Envy, Malice, the Lust of the Flesh, the Lust of the Eye, and Pride of Life. . . ." The Quaker indictment had more foundation in fact in Barbados than in England, and it first irritated, then infuriated, all the more because it was true. Governor Atkins closed the Friends' meetinghouse at Bridgetown in 1680 and ordered its seats removed; but public pressure soon forced a reopening. His instructions directed him not to require oaths of the Quakers, who at this time were reckoned as being one-third of all the Barbadians. Late in 1687 King James II notified Governor Stede that the Friends were no longer to be molested in their worship nor fined for neglect of military service exceeding the price of hiring a substitute. From then on they could also hold office without taking an oath. In acknowledging this royal order, Stede said that he had admitted some Quakers to office and had discontinued militia fines. The interest that the Quakers have here, he added significantly, is so great that they ought to make up one whole regiment. The Friends had pretty much won their case in Barbados by this time, though with the founding of Pennsylvania in 1682, many of them began to migrate there.[20]

John Rous of Barbados, accompanied by Mary Fisher and Peter Head, sailed in 1658 to Nevis, where they were welcomed by

19. Rous to Fox concerning organization, 1681, *Journal of the Friends' Historical Society,* XXXIII, 61–3; Roger Longworth to Friends in Amsterdam, 1687, West India MSS (Bos. Pub. Lib.), I, Letter 5; John Beeke (or Becke) to Roger Longworth, Feb. 2, 1685/6, Friends' Historical Association, *Bulletin,* XXIX, 101–2; Vokins, *God's Mighty Power,* 74.

20. Fell, *Testimony and Warning,* 1–4; Shilstone, *Barbados Advocate Tercentenary,* 21–2; *CSPC, 1685–88,* pp. 477, 516–17; Samuel Carpenter to Ralph Smith, Feb. 24, July 10, 1682; Andrew Dury to James Harrison, Sept. 1, 1687, West India MSS (Bos. Pub. Lib.), I, Letters 2, 3, 10.

Humphry Highwood. Although he was not yet a convinced Quaker, Highwood refused to perform his militia duty and consequently was imprisoned for a month. Within two years, the Assembly passed an act to prohibit Friends from landing on Nevis and set a fine of 500 pounds of sugar for any man who wore his hat in court. Despite imprisonments and fines the sect persevered, and finally in 1675 Governor Stapleton agreed to allow the Quakers to watch in their own way without arms; and by this time they had their own meetinghouse in Charles Town. Though they never were a numerous group, the Friends succeeded very early in convincing one of the leading and influential planters, the Puritan Samuel Winthrop.[21]

Friend Jonas Langford landed at Antigua on July 14, 1660, and applied for permission to purchase a large tract of land. Governor Christopher Keynell granted it readily, but a successor Robert Carden sent Langford to prison for speaking up in church after the sermon. He was jailed again, along with Anne Coleman, who came to Antigua in 1664, and Justinian Holliman for holding meetings in planters' houses. Anne Coleman was later banished from the island together with some other Quakers. Prompt intercession by Lewis Morris, who had toured the Leeward Islands recently with Samuel Winthrop, led Lord Willoughby to reverse his deputy's decision, and the Friends returned to Antigua. At this time, Winthrop, who had removed from Nevis to Antigua, Hill, Holliman, and Langford, along with their families, made up all of the Quakers on the island. Imprisonment and fines for refusing to train with the militia elicited a harsh indictment of Captain Paul Lea by Jonas Langford. During the resettlement of the island after the Peace of Breda, 1668–69, Samuel Winthrop served as deputy governor and relaxed the pressure on the Friends; from 1669–71 he served as register, and in 1670 became president of the Council. Groton Hall, Winthrop's plantation, was the center for Antiguan Friends until his death in 1674. Joan Vokins found at Antigua "a handful of plain hearted Friends, and our Hearts were tendered." [22]

21. Besse, *Sufferings of the Quakers,* II, 352–65; BM: Egerton MSS, 2395, fol. 528; Braithwaite, *Beginnings of Quakerism,* 620.
22. Jonas Langford, *A Brief Account of the Sufferings of the Servants of the Lord Called Quakers . . .* (London, 1706), 5–9; Besse, *Sufferings of the Quakers,* II, 370–7; Fox, *Journal,* ed. Nickalls, 626; Mayo, *Winthrop Family in America,*

A few Quakers from Barbados settled in Jamaica in 1658. In an Epistle of 1661 Josiah Coale told the people of the island that they should be meek now that the everlasting God was being preached to them. Jamaica badly needed colonists, and when the Quakers agreed to be quiet in civil affairs, Lord Windsor and his Council declared in 1662 that all inhabitants who would pay their taxes might gather in meetings for "Freedom in matters of Conscience," and also that they would be relieved of bearing arms if they contributed financially to repelling invasions. But in spite of these concessions there was to be no peace, for "the Rude roughness of the sect's temper" bothered the authorities. A theologically wayward Friend, John Perrott, stirred up trouble for the Meeting in 1664 because "the Country Cryed out against him very much." Further difficulties developed during the Second Dutch War when the Quakers declined to serve in the militia, and their refusal to act as sworn jurors brought official action against them. After 1670 a Friend who had paid for three men to watch in his stead at Port Royal could be excused, and in 1675, when Lord Vaughan proclaimed the Act of Indulgence in Jamaica, the Quakers breathed more freely. During his visit to the island, George Fox traveled 300 miles and succeeded in setting up seven meetings, besides one specifically for men and another for women. Governor Lynch said the Quakers and Independents were the chief sects at Port Royal in 1682, and, enjoying toleration, they were more submissive to government and complacent than their brethren in England. He wanted some good ministers to win them back to the Church of England, but Francis Crow reported in 1688 that spiritually dissatisfied Jamaicans "have turned Anabaptists and Quakers. So that the things of God and salvation are at a miserable pass with us." [23]

77–9; BM: Egerton MSS, 2395, fol. 528; Vokins, *God's Mighty Power,* 39, 127, 129.

23. "The Lord hath a very great controversy with this island," Joseph Norris wrote to his brother Isaac at Philadelphia in 1692 after mentioning the earthquake and succeeding illness. Their father, Thomas Norris, was lost in the debacle at Port Royal, and Joseph himself died on September 8, 1692. West India MSS (Bos. Pub. Lib.), I, Letter 14. Coale, *Books and Epistles,* 47; Jamaica Council Minutes, I, 44–6, 104, 166–7, 225–6; II, 65–6; *CSPC, 1661–68,* p. 207; *1681–85,* p. 314; John Taylor, *A Loving & Friendly Invitation to all Sinners to Repent* (London, 1683), 6–8; Burnyeat, *Truth Exalted,* 32; Crow, in *Jamaica Historical Review,* III, 53.

Throughout the initial phase of its remarkable history, the Society of Friends undertook the first and only concerted missionary effort in the American colonies. Commencing in the West Indies, it laid bare a shocking deficiency in the moral and religious condition of the inhabitants, which, with characteristic directness, it condemned out of hand. The Quakers' refusal to bear arms and swear oaths posed very real problems for officials in a region where there was no peace; and the Friendly determination to save the souls of the blacks generated genuine fear. Their great success had been made possible by the failure of the Church of England in the Caribbean, together with the gnawing desire of many former conforming puritans to live more spiritual lives.

III

The weak condition of the Church of England deprived the islanders of the usual moral restraints. The Assembly of Barbados in 1652 moved to reduce offenses and disorders on the Sabbath, such as rioting, drunkenness, swearing, whoreing, shooting at marks, gaming, quarreling, "and many other vitious and ungodly courses." Five years later, a proclamation by the Governor blamed "the continual abounding of cursing and drunkenness, as the root and foundacion of many other crimes and offenses and the disabling and overthrow of divers manual tradesmen, labourers or workmen and the impoverishing (if not ruine) of many families," together with public disorder. Conditions had not improved by 1673 when the Grand Jury presented the lack of proper observance of the Lord's Day, "the profanation of which is a crying sin in the island." Moreover, the enumerated abominations increased daily. Nor were these declarations mere legal hyperbole. From South Carolina, Governor Joseph West reported: "we find that one of our Servants wee brought out of England is worth 2 of the Barbadians, for they are so addicted to Rum, that they will doe little but whilst the bottle is at their nose." [24]

The same kinds of moral lapses were rife throughout the English colonies in the Caribbean. "A Story" Captain Thomas Wal-

24. *Acts and Statutes of Barbados* (Jennings), 79–80; Barbados Council Minutes, II, 174; *CSPC, 1669–74*, p. 506; *1685–88*, p. 569; South Carolina Historical Society, *Collections*, V, 299.

duck of Barbados liked to tell was that "upon all the new Settlements, the Spaniards make, the first thing they do is to build a Church, the first thing the Dutch do upon a new Coloney is to build them a fort, but the first thing the English doe, be it in the most remote parts of the World or amongst the most Barbarous Indians, is to set up a Tavern or *drinking* house." Overindulgence in rum gave rise to a variety of evil consequences, and the efforts of the governors of Jamaica to curb them may have had some good results in the plantation country, but Port Royal was, in the modern phrase, wide open. The Jamaica Council indicated in 1671 that "an awful gaming" was debauching young gentlemen, craftsmen, and other settlers to the extent that the island had a very bad name, trade was affected, and many gamblers had to go to prison or even submit to the final humiliation of "being made Servants." The law forbade gaming in public houses and allowed the diversion only to masters of families having estates of £200. But such class legislation seems not to have stopped the privateers and other sea-faring gentry from playing away all they had.[25]

In these boisterous, contentious, bibulous, and often inebriated social scenes, there was no comfortable place for men and women of gentle birth. Good manners and sound morals simply did not exist for the generality of the colonists. What Madam Margaret Heathcote wrote to her cousin John Winthrop, the younger, from Antigua in 1665 could have been said of all of the islands: "And truely, Sir, I am not so much in love with any as to goe much abroad," for "they be all a company of sodomists that live here." This Puritan gentlewoman, who used Biblical terms precisely, had in mind planters, such as Cary Helyar of Jamaica who, until he married his Priscilla in 1672, lived openly with a mulatto mistress who bore him two sons. When he gave her up he promised her an annuity of £32, provided she would not trouble him and keep herself and the boys off the parish rates. The coarse and abusive language one heard in the islands every day apparently outdid Billingsgate and, inflamed by liquor, both men and women were frequently guilty of defamation of character. The "opprobrious language" used

25. BM: Sloane MSS, 2302, Letter 3; PRO: CO 1/36, fol. 157a; *Abridgement of Laws of Plantations,* 93–4; *Terrible Earthquake at Port Royal* (Broadside, 1692); Jamaica Council Minutes, I, 200–203.

by the Irish of Montserrat in disputes with Scotsmen and Englishmen, "as well in Drink as sober," produced an act in 1668 making it a misdemeanor to use such "Party-words of Distinction" as "*English* Dog, *Scot's* Dog, Tory, Irish-dog, Cavalier, Roundhead" or similar epithets.[26]

Among servants, slaves, and freemen everywhere there was much brawling, and in 1652 the wearing of arms privately by gentlemen had to be prohibited in Barbados, but, astonishingly, no island suffered from many murders or high crimes. It is altogether possible that the prime social function of the privateers and buccaneers was to draw off the criminal elements. No hangman served in Barbados until 1678 when Governor Atkins appointed to the office a fellow who had been convicted upon slim evidence of poisoning his master. Great excitement arose on St. Christopher in 1692 when the news spread of "one Gray, a Notorious Coyner" who came down from the Windward Islands with one Richard Banks, and that the said Gray had brought Tools for Coyning along with him." While the hue and cry for Gray went on, the prospect of an increase in the circulating medium of the Leeward Islands must have titillated the populace.[27]

IV

The arrested institutional growth of both the transplanted English family and the Church in the Caribbean colonies inevitably limited educational advantages. Taken as a group, the settlers never rivaled the capacity of their New England brethren for organizing the family or churches, nor did they possess the widespread literacy of the Puritans. In these respects they seem to have also lagged behind the tobacco planters of the Chesapeake. Material gain motivated the actions of nearly all West Indians, and only a few of them, who were of the puritan temper, perceived the necessity, let alone took any action, "to keep up Learning and all Helps of Education lest degeneracy, Barbarism, Ignorance, and irreligion doe by degrees

26. *MHS Procs.*, 2d ser., V, 105; Cary to William Helyar, Jan. 12, 1672; Bybrook Accounts, 1669–72; Whaley to William Helyar, Dec. 9, 1675, Helyar MSS; Taylor, Multum in Parvo, III, 676, 717–18; *Acts of Assembly . . . of Montserrat,* 10–13.
27. *Acts and Statutes of Barbados* (Jennings), 14–15, 130–31; *CSPC, 1677–80,* p. 202; Jamaica Council Minutes, V, 330.

breake in upon us," as Jonathan Mitchell of Harvard College put it in 1663. To these people, the transmission of English civilization to the Caribbean and the careful preservation of this precious heritage were not, as in New England, of the first importance.[28]

The vestry minutes disclose that intermittently after 1662 masters kept school in the parish church of St. Michael at Bridgetown. What these men taught is not known, but it is doubtful if they went as far as Latin grammar. In 1672 there is a record that the churchwardens bound a poor boy, Joseph Harding, apprentice to John Goodbrand and ordered "two years schooling" for him at the parish charge. Mistress Anne Vaughan was granted permission in 1682 to use the gallery for her pupils and to make necessary alterations at her own charge. Here and there must have existed a petty or a dame school to teach the ABC's to small children. In the country parishes occasionally a schoolmistress, such as Jane Barfoot, conducted a petty school which, according to provisions in their indentures, some apprentices and freemen's children attended. On the larger plantations the master's children sometimes received instruction from an indentured servant or a hired tutor; the Scot John Menzies taught Latin for £25 a year in 1676 on an estate where "I am in Truth nothing a servant but in name." Two generous planters gave land and £1000 for a building for a charity school for the poor white children of St. George's Parish in 1686; and the year before at Speightstown some kind of a "Free-school" opened in a house donated by a Mr. Hancock.[29]

Gradually it dawned upon some Barbadians that their children very much needed regular schooling under official supervision. A Grand Jury of 1668, in calling for the erection of an inland town for security, desired a free school there "to prevent youth seeking education in foreign parts." Again, in 1684, the Grand Jury pointed out "the benefit to our youth if means were taken for education." Very little clerical or official interest in schooling was ever forthcoming, and there was no religious urge to read the Bible and the Catechism. The indifference of the great planters about educating

28. "Harvard College Records," III, *CSM Pubs.*, XXXI, 311.

29. Vestry Minutes, in *JBMHS*, III, 107; XV, 201, 212; XVI, 56, 58, 60, 195; Barbados Council Minutes, II, 399; *Register of the Privy Council of Scotland* (London, 1877–), IV, 651, 671.

ordinary white children naturally extended to the blacks. One of their main objections to converting the slaves to Christianity was that they would have to teach them all English, so they contented themselves, somewhat speciously, with explaining that "the Negroes are a sort of people so averse to learning that they will rather hang themselves or run away than submit to it." Thomas Tryon's scheme for erecting two "Boarding Schools" in each parish, one for English and one for Negro children, where they would be taught to dress, spin, and weave cotton so that in a short time the island could produce "fine Calicoes and muslins" in "publick works" evoked no response at all.[30]

Although an act of 1676 restrained anyone from teaching school who had not taken the oaths of supremacy and allegiance and had received a special license from the governor, Governor Dutton discovered in 1681 that many of the schoolmasters were Quakers and Baptists; he ejected some of them. The Friends did not favor higher education, but they did consider reading, writing, and casting accounts essential for worship and affairs. Writing to the Rhode Island Monthly Meeting, Joan Vokins told about weekly meetings held in Barbados for children who had learned Fox's Catechism at home and remarked that "it do produce a good Effect." Five years later, John Beeke, "a Teacher of Children" at Bridgetown, solicited encouragement from George Fox about "Children's and Schoolmasters' meetings in Barbados," which were the first held anywhere. "At our Children's Meetings . . . we hear the Children," and he has a little boy living with him who knows the primer by heart and "can readily construe the Latin Child's Lessen" and turn the Catechism and proverbs "out of Latin into English." He can also read in the Hebrew Bible. Beeke also sold many books to inland families. At the Bridgetown Friends' School there was a Jewish usher who heard scholars read from the New Testament and taught Christian doctrine from Fox's Primer to several Hebrew children. The members of the Schoolmasters' Meeting agreed to instruct poor children gratis, "and to turn no Children away upon the account of money." Some of "the People of the World's Children" came to meetings, and their parents "seem to be very well satisfied in our Teaching or

30. *CSPC, 1661–68,* p. 620; *1677–80,* p. 611; *1681–85,* p. 750; Tryon, *Merchant's . . . Instructor,* Letter XXXIII, 195–6.

Government." It is far from fanciful to conclude that the schoolbooks and teaching that the Quakers provided for the children of all faiths in Barbados (and on Antigua at the same time) acted as potent proselyting devices for the Society. The innovation of children's meetings filled a tremendous void in the islands.[31]

Substantial planters entertaining social and cultural aspirations began to send their children back to England to be educated soon after the Restoration. "The fathers went out poor and the children come home rich," Sir Charles Davenant observed. "They that are able, breed up their Children in England," was one of Edward Lyttleton's laments. In 1666, for instance, Thomas Easton, a Bristol merchant, agreed to bring to England and educate Willoughby, daughter of Sir James Browne of Barbados, and when she grew up he gave her in marriage to William Yeamans of Barbados. According to John Oldmixon, Thomas Tryon said some of the West Indians sent from £200 to £500 a year to their sons in England, "most of them proving Beaus of the first Rate, and distinguishing themselves by the Gaity of their Dress and Equipage." He warned one planter: "The loose and extravagant Education of your Youth . . . is a sure Indication of Calamity and Misery to your Country, for in a few Years they come to govern the publick Affairs." Schooling for Caribbean youths and girls made up a considerable fraction of the £50,000 spent annually in England.[32]

When Colonel Henry Drax, son of Sir James, died in Middlesex in 1682, he left £2000 to erect and endow "a Free School or College at Bridgetown" because, his will stated, the sons of the richest planters were sent off at the age of twelve to be educated in England

31. When John Beeke went before Governor Dutton in 1680, he denied that the Friends ever taught rebellion, whereupon the official replied: "Well, I must not suffer it." His decision was a hard one for the Quaker, "since I have lost a Very Considerable Estate for my Religion." After Dutton's departure, Friends were not much troubled, and Beeke had his livelihood restored. Beeke to Longworth, Friends' Historical Association, *Bulletin,* XXIX, 101–5; Vokins, *God's Mighty Power,* 62, 74; *Abridgement of Laws of Plantations,* 249; Harlow, *Barbados,* 249–50.

32. Patrick McGrath, ed., *Merchants and Merchandise in Seventeenth-Century Bristol* (Bristol, 1955), xvii; Charles Davenant, *Discourse on the Public Revenue and Trade of England* (London, 1698), II, 96; Lyttleton, *Groans of the Plantations,* 34; Oldmixon, *British Empire in America,* II, 135; *Some Considerations Humbly Offered . . . Concerning the Sugar Colonies . . .* (London, 1701), 4.

and, being so far away from family tutelage, scarcely one ever returned who was "not utterly debauched both in Principalls and Moralls." As late as 1700 the vestry had not acted upon this bequest. Meanwhile, thoroughly disenchanted with English schooling, the Quakers, "especially from Barbados," were sending their youth to Philadelphia by 1685 to study in what is now the William Penn Charter School where Enoch Flower, using "good methods for the best instruction, according to the methods of Commenius," charged only £10 a year for board and instruction.[33]

Unsatisfactory as opportunities for education were in Barbados, they were far worse in the other islands. While living in St. Christopher in 1657, and not yet a Quaker, Samuel Winthrop sent his sons John and Samuel to Boston to be educated for admission to Harvard College, for he deemed "that place more fit for it then this." The next year he informed his half-brother that Mrs. Winthrop and two daughters would soon be coming northward: "I doe not find this country good for children, and, being Gods blessings, desire to provide the best I can for them." Under the tutelage of Deacon Child and Mr. Rowland Evans the boys did well and in ten years were about ready for college, but their father's losses in the Second Dutch War were so great that he had them forgo their Latin and Greek and "learn to write and cypher and gaine some knowledge of accompts" as apprentices to the merchant Richard Wharton. Governor Stapleton found several clerical schoolmasters teaching in Nevis in 1672, but elsewhere none at all—"a shameful neglect." Henry Blake went out from Ireland to Montserrat in 1673 to recoup great losses. He hoped to bring all of his children together on his plantation under an English mistress, but upon the advice of his brother he left his eldest son at school in Ireland.[34]

Thomas Povey made an effort in 1662 to get a yearly stipend of £100 for an Anglican schoolmaster in Jamaica, but he did not succeed. Such schooling as boys and girls received before 1675 was in their homes where older members of the family taught them out

33. Col. Henry Drax's Will, from Fulham MSS, Davis Coll., XIII, Envelope 16; *JBMHS,* XVII, 48, 55; Translation of Robert Webb's Dutch pamphlet, in *Pennsylvania Magazine of History and Biography,* XLIX, 121.
34. *MHS Colls.,* 5th ser., VIII, 244, 245, 246, 251, 254, 259; *Caribbeana,* I, 51, 53, 55.

of hornbooks, primers, psalters, and testaments, which they purchased from John Belfield of Port Royal. The vestry of St. John's Parish and Colonel John Coape each gave £100 to the Reverend Mr. Lemon, a young scholar and preacher, for keeping "a free school he has erected" at Guinaboa. This clerical, pedagogical enterprise continued for about seven years until the schoolmaster married the widow of a poor gentleman. For some reason "Mr. Alene Latrue, Schoolmaster," went on board H.M.S. *Falcon* rather abruptly in 1683, but where he taught is not reported. A few bequests of 100 or 200 pounds were made for schools that never opened and, in 1690, so far as the records show, Jamaica had no schools at all. Most of the planters must have followed the course of Madam Sarah Lyssons of St. Thomas's who employed John Lookmore, "a master of the noble science of defence," to teach her sons. Peter Beckford, who matriculated at Oxford in 1688, was one of the first Jamaicans to go home for his education.[35]

V

Among Caribbean people of all ranks in this age, life was culturally and intellectually barren. No man of the stature of Richard Ligon emerged, and those few planting families that had cultural yearnings could satisfy them only by retiring to England, and not a few of them did. Beyond an occasional Irish piper, one encounters nothing about white men's music, though Dr. Hans Sloane got M. Baptiste, "the best Musician" of Jamaica, to take down the words of songs sung by slaves at a festival and set them to Negro music. The absence of books from insular inventories contrasts oddly with the numbers of books in contemporary New England. It does explain, however, the proposal of two absentee planters in England in 1674 that Lord Vaughan have "a good collection of books in the English tongue" assembled at public expense and distribute them throughout Jamaica "in the most conspicuous places where such of the gentry as are studious may always resort, since there is nothing more

35. Frank Cundall, "Some Notes on the History of Secondary Education in Jamaica," *Handbook of Jamaica for 1911* (reprint: Kingston, 1911), 1–2; Jamaica Historical Society, *Bulletin,* III, 244; *CSPC, 1675–76,* p. 237; *1681–85,* p. 314; Jamaica Council Minutes, IV, 85–6; Cundall, *Historic Jamaica,* 31.

ridiculous than ignorance in a person of quality." In mining language, the Caribbean islands were extractive colonies where the Negroes preserved their rhythms, but little of the English cultural heritage survived. Edward Lyttleton understood this well: "Nothing but England can we relish or fancy: our Hearts are here, where ever our Bodies be. If we get a little Money, we remit it to England . . . When we are a little easy, we desire to live and spend what we have in England." [36]

One exception may be made to the general prevalence of barbarism in the English West Indies, though it involved only a handful of people. In 1666 a committee of the Royal Society of London drew up a list of "inquiries for the Antiles"—based upon Rochefort's *Histoire naturelle et morale* and Ligon's widely read work on Barbados; the lists were given to learned and ingenious persons, usually medical men, who crossed the Atlantic. While serving as a physician on Henry Hasting's plantation in St. George's Parish in 1674, Dr. Thomas Townes worked from a list given to him by Martin Lister, F.R.S. The two struck up a correspondence, and on March 26, 1675, Dr. Townes expressed his deep gratitude for the association: "now I am so remote from the learned world, and I hope and heartily beg you would continue your kindness this way, if for nothing else out of pity to an American . . . most men here being wholly intent upon riches. . . ." Some of the astronomical observations and notes about flora and fauna made by Dr. Townes won publication in the *Philosophical Transactions*. Using a barometer lent by Sir Robert Southwell, a Mr. Crisp observed the weather on St. Christopher in 1680; some unidentified person sent home a catalogue of leaves and seeds, together with samples of sand, in 1683–85. The Royal Society also received a discourse from Nevis about a recent earthquake in the Leeward Islands.[37]

At London in 1672, Dr. William Hughes published *The American Physician; or a Treatise of the Roots, Shrubs, Plants, Trees . . . growing in the English Plantations in America*. Written "in

36. *Analecta Hibernica*, No. 4, pp. 234–5; Sloane, *Voyage to the Islands*, Introduction, I, l–lii; *CSPC, 1669–74*, p. 635; Lyttleton, *Groans of the Plantations*, 34.

37. *CSPC, 1661–68*, p. 379; *Philosophical Transactions, Abridged*, III, 560–1. The fine volume by the late Raymond P. Stearns, *Science in the British Colonies of America* (Urbana, Ill., 1970) contains nearly all that is known about early field work in the West Indies before 1690.

plain and easie Terms" and based upon his personal observations when he was a surgeon on a naval vessel, this was the first English book devoted exclusively to the subject. Hughes blamed the widespread scurvy in Jamaica on the excessive consumption of sugar. While serving as physician to Lord Vaughan, Dr. Thomas Trapham acquired a good understanding of health conditions in Jamaica and the dietary needs of the people, which he published on his return in 1679 as *A Discourse of the State of Health in the Island of Jamaica* —a pioneer English work on the subject. When Dr. Hans Sloane accompanied the Duke of Albemarle to the island in 1687, he began to observe and collect specimens of the flora of Jamaica for the several works that brought him great fame as an innovator in the writing of the natural history of the New World. These medical transients in Jamaica led all of the colonies in both the amount and quality of American contributions to science before 1690.[38]

VI

Two aspects of government and politics profoundly affected the lives of the islanders after 1650. As both white and black populations increased and planters cleared more land for fields of sugar cane, local government had to be extended and strengthened to deal with matters of state and church that could no longer be satisfactorily administered by governors, councils, and assemblies. In the second place, after enjoying what amounted to independence after 1640, the Caribbee Isles submitted in 1651 to Parliament. Thereafter, though they never liked it, the West Indians discovered greater control from home was being exercised and that henceforth Royal officials would more and more determine the course of their lives.

38. John Taylor, the mathematician (fl. 1683–1701) spent the years 1683–88 in Jamaica. During this time he wrote three volumes (still in manuscript) consisting of the journal of his voyage, a vivid detailed description of life in Jamaica, and a diurnal of his experiences as ship's clerk of the frigate *Falcon*. It includes many sketches, maps, and charts, and the most complete account of the discovery and raising of the sunken Spanish treasure by Sir William Phips. See Taylor's Hydrographical Chart of the late discovered Flatts, Bancks, and Rocks . . . called the Ambrogias . . . (1689) in Multum in Parvo, III, facing p. 618. On Dr. Sloane and science in Jamaica, see Stearns, *Science in the British Colonies* (226–46), who somehow does not mention Dr. Trapham's important contribution. *London Gazette,* March 24, 1678–9.

The agency of government with which the colonists had the most frequent and intimate contact was the parish. Before 1652 in Barbados, the law allowed vestries, without any checking whatever or consulting with the parishioners, to assess rates. In answer to numerous complaints, a new act provided for the annual electing of sixteen vestrymen by the "free votes" of the parish, the publishing of the rates for three consecutive Sundays at church, and sending the list to the governor and council, which heard and judged any exceptions before confirming the rates. A justice of the peace could summon the vestry to meet and fine any member 500 pounds of sugar if he failed to attend. By these measures the vestrymen became "Trustees of their Parish" to manage its ecclesiastical, financial, and prudential affairs for one year at a time, and not a closed corporation. The chronic shortage of "able Men to officiate in the highest Places of trust" and the burden on the poorer sort of serving in inferior offices arising in part by the removal of some of the "most Eminent Planters to England" produced a new law in 1669 authorizing the overseers of the poor to serve plurally in parish offices, such as constable and surveyor of the highways, and fixing a fine of 2000 pounds of sugar for refusal. Both Jamaica (1664) and Antigua followed Barbadian precedents closely, and parish government in the Caribbean turned out to be an almost exact copy of English local institutions.[39]

In many of the insular parishes, the churchwardens and vestrymen built church edifices and kept them in repair and housed and paid the minister, when they had one. Their most nagging problem, because it involved the parish levy, was the care of the poor. In a petition to Parliament in 1659, the Barbadian planters pointed out that "the generality of people here are poore." The vestry of each parish and four elected overseers of the poor assisted their unfortunates by out-relief. Because Bridgetown was a seaport and attracted many people from rural parishes, its poverty problem was not typical, but its records have survived. By 1666, the overseers

39. *Acts and Statutes of Barbados* (Jennings), 35–6; *Acts of Barbados* (Hall), 24–5; *Acts of Barbados* (1721), 4, 32–7, 77; C. A. Lindley, Jamaica, 1660–1677 . . . (Ph.D. Thesis, University of Pennsylvania, 1932), 51–2; PRO: CO 1/36, fol. 156a; Jamaica Council Minutes, I, 40–43. For the parish in Britain, see *Vexed and Troubled Englishmen,* 243–7.

and vestry of St. Michael's had 22 indigent persons to each of whom they paid out 100 pounds of sugar a month, and they had also found it necessary to build an almshouse. The vestry also paid the sexton for burying the poor. The next year it began to hire one or more doctors to treat the sick poor at an annual cost to the parish of 5000 pounds of sugar. When by 1683 the Bridgetown Almshouse needed repairs, Dr. Sparke recommended boarding out the inmates who were helpless. On three occasions the authorities paid the passages of people to return to the abodes from which they came: a man and his wife to St. Christopher, Daniel Meers and his family to Antigua, and a woman called only "Urslay" to faraway Boston.[40]

These programs by no means eliminated the relief burden, and parish officers again resorted to English practices. In 1655 they apprenticed a five-year-old boy, Thomas Allington, to Mistress Joan Allen for eleven years. In 1663 "one Bragge, a ropemaker," indicated his willingness to employ several poor or vagrant people in picking oakum, and the vestry requested the judges of the Quarter Sessions to send him some individuals. Because idle beggars had so alarmingly increased, the Grand Jury recommended in 1673 that every parish in Barbados erect a workhouse and procure a stock to employ them; it assumed that if the public initiated the projects, charitable planters would then contribute. Actually, a number of bequests lay unused at the time, or had disappeared, and in 1682 the Council ordered all vestries to make "a diligent and strict inquiry" about such gifts and to report back promptly. "Misapplications of charitable donations" were uncovered in St. Michael's and several other parishes from which Governor Dutton hoped to recover between £4000 and £5000 in money. In general, parish care of the Barbados poor had been effective, for in 1672 Governor Atkins claimed that no persons were any longer to be seen begging for alms.[41]

The litigiousness so characteristic of the English people in this century seemed to intensify in the islands, where it centered round

40. BM: Egerton MSS, 2395, fol. 182; St. Michael's Vestry Minutes, in *JBMHS,* XIV, 125, 126; XV, 20, 119, 121, 122, 125, 126, 127, 203, 206, 207, 209, 211; XVI, 136, 141.

41. *JBMHS,* XIV, 126; XV, 90; *CSPC, 1669–74,* p. 507; *1677–80,* p. 63; *1681–85,* p. 281; Barbados Council Minutes, II, 351, 363, 367–8, 370.

titles to land and boundaries, as well as the unwillingness of men to be "kept under proper Degrees and Distances." There were never enough trained individuals to act as lawyers, justices of the peace, and judges, and as a result, Samuel Barwicke charged that the Barbadians "disfigure the face of Justice amongst us, Every planters babe there undertaking to Comment upon Magna Charta and the Petition of Right, as if the misteries of the Law of Our Nation (which is the onely Established here) were as plaine to them as potatoes." When "some little English Lawyers crept over" to the island bringing "writs of pleas to the increasing of their own estates but to the ruin of many particulars," clerks quickly followed their lead. That tireless reformer, Sir Richard Dutton, "reduced" all the judges and "pretenders to the law" to wearing gowns in 1681 that they might be distinguished from ordinary men, "for till now the lawyers came to bar with swords by their sides, as if they went thither not to beg but to defy justice. Their pleadings, which were nothing but confusion, are now as orderly as Westminster Hall." At this juncture, five Courts of Common Pleas, each with a chief judge and four assistants, and the Court of King's Bench dispensed justice in Barbados; and below them were the familiar justices of the peace who dealt with small causes, either in a quorum for Quarter Sessions or individually.[42]

In the Leeward Islands and Jamaica, the same scarcity of good lawyers and judges limited all judicial affairs. In the seventies Christopher Jeaffreson sent home for law books so that he could handle his own cases at St. Christopher. Sir Nathaniel Johnson found in 1688 that in the courts of Nevis "some matters they will determine by English laws, in others, without any rational disparity, they reject English law; and in another island, the reverse of those decisions will be the judgment given." Much depended upon "the fancy

42. Governor Dutton, according to John Oldmixon, "was a zealous Friend to the African Company [and] used always to sit in Court to judge of the Forfeitures; the Company's Agents were the Informers, and as soon as Sentence was given, they divided the Spoil." *British Empire in America,* II, 46. John Jennings, the Clerk of the Assembly, published at London in 1654 the first collection of *The Acts and Statutes of the Island of Barbados* (copies in LCP and Bos. Pub. Lib.); BM: Egerton MSS, 2395, fol. 184; Bodleian: Clarendon MSS, 84, fol. 357, in Davis Coll., V; *CSPC, 1681–85,* pp. 62, 70; *1699, Addenda,* p. 592; PRO: CO 1/37, fol. 23.

of the judge." In Jamaica in 1665, John Style, a recent arrival from Britain, described the judges of both the courts of Quarter Sessions and Common Pleas as "beasts, drowning the reason that God gave them with strong liquors." Judge Coape "knows not one letter in the book, yet of late he hath learnt to write his name." Long imprisonment in Dublin had not made him a judicious person. Captain Oldfield, condemned in England to hang, was transported to the island as a servant, and three other judges had been "all trained up from boys in rebellion and murder." Such men winked at abuses in the election of churchwardens, and it was Style's crime that he inquired into the disposition of the taxes they had raised. When allowance is made for hyperbole, this account is substantially correct. Governor Sir Thomas Modyford deplored the rude and unseasonable interruptions of court sessions, as well as "impertinent disputes of Lawyers, and Pleaders, not seldom coming drunk into the Courts," which "seem more like a Horse-Fair or a Billingsgate." Severe penalties were to be imposed on drunken lawyers or those violating good order, which, added to an ordinance of 1671 that prevented the increase of lawyers, attorneys, and solicitors, brought about some measure of improvement. Two years later the Assembly passed a law "For the Suppression of Lawyers"—with what result we do not know—but not long after, Lord Vaughan could praise the people of Jamaica for being "very Respectful and Obedient to Authority." Dignity and decorum were accompanying insular maturity.[43]

The preoccupation of Englishmen with their internal difficulties from 1640 to 1660 permitted the men of the Caribbean to improve the opportunity to follow their own paths, as did the Virginians and New Englanders. Trade with the Dutch became so profitable to each side that, confident of support from Holland and Zeeland should it be needed, the insular governments acted as virtually independent republics. The Royalists in Barbados went so far on February 18, 1650/1, as to reject totally the authority of Parliament, in which they were not represented.[44]

43. Pares, *West-India Fortune,* 25–8; *CSPC, 1669–74,* pp. 4, 11; *1685–88,* pp. 158, 510, 525; *Journal of the Assembly of Jamaica,* I, 2, 7, 9; BM: Egerton MSS, 2395, fol. 523; Jamaica Council Minutes, I, 145–7; PRO: CO 1/45, X-2.

44. The political and constitutional history of the several colonies has been treated in detail by Harlow, Williamson, Higham, and Whitson, to whom we have fre-

The tide soon turned, however, for within a year Parliament passed the Navigation Act and sent off the Ayscue Expedition to bring the islands to heel. Then in his Commonwealth phase, Colonel Thomas Modyford wrote to John Bradshaw that the Barbadians wanted the same form of government as the English, and he hoped, though "it may seem immodest," that two representatives could soon be chosen in the island to sit and vote in Parliament. The conquest of Jamaica in 1655 was wholly a Commonwealth undertaking, which the islanders trusted would result in favorable treatment, while at the same time the planters of Barbados reminded Thomas Povey that they had founded their settlement without royal aid and were "now a Colonie, the most envyed in the World," and they expected special favors from the Mother Country.[45]

Prodded and abetted by London merchants after the Restoration, Royal officials determined to tighten bonds with the colonies, especially in regard to trade and fiscal matters. This intent became evident at once with the passage of the Navigation Acts of 1660 and 1663. Proprietary government in the Caribbees gave way to Royal administration and the dictated "grants" of the 4½ per cent duties to the Crown. Sporadically, the vessels of the king's navy helped with the enforcement of the Navigation Laws. When war broke out with the Dutch and the French, the pressure of outside control was felt directly. Over the protests of the Barbadians in 1672, the Leeward Islands received their own governor, and the Caribbees ceased to exist as a political unit. A further feature of influence from overseas was the monopoly of the slave trade, especially that given to the Royal African Company.

The independent spirit of the planters' parliaments always irritated Royal officials. Lord Willoughby, commenting to Lord Clarendon in 1664 about earlier days in the Caribbees, remarked: "It is a new thing to the people here to have the King's authority among

quently referred. The beginnings of the English policy of control are set forth ably by Beer, Andrews, and recently by Thornton. Because the people and their outlook are the concern in this work, the emphasis falls naturally upon the insular rather than the imperial point of view, a somewhat neglected aspect of colonial history. For the decade 1650–60, Watts, *Histoire des colonies anglaises aux Antilles,* is very helpful, especially pp. 18, 37, 55; see also Beer, *Origins of the British Colonial System,* 348–53; *CSPC, 1574–1660,* p. 384.

45. See *Articles of Agreement* (1652), 3–4; *CSPC, 1574–1660,* pp. 373, 374; BM: Add. MSS, 11,411, fol. 9.

them, for in the Earl of Carlisle's time it was Governor and people that did all, but little of my Lord Carlisle's name, being very rarely and seldom used among them." Many years later, in 1672, Governor Dutton protested to the Council for Plantations about the conduct of the Assembly and "the mutinous, ambitious temper of these people who generally aspire to popularity." Speaking for all the islands, a Barbadian candidly conceded that they hoped to have insular representatives in Parliament. Very seldom did either party grasp the fundamental distinction between union and particularism, and realize that a reasonable, workable compromise is always necessary for a successful empire.[46]

Upon one occasion at least, the conjunction of a Royal governor of great ability and understanding and, apparently, some very gifted and reasonable insular councilors and assemblymen yielded excellent results. Sir William Stapleton, an Irishman and a soldier, had served as lieutenant colonel in Sir Thomas Bridge's regiment during the Second Dutch War and had been a prisoner on St. Christopher. William, Lord Willoughby made him deputy-governor for Montserrat because he understood how to govern his countrymen. Stapleton's marriage to Ann, daughter of Sir James Russell, deputy-governor of Nevis, further improved his relations with the planters of the Leeward Islands. As a result, when he was appointed governor, he worked out, quietly and slowly from 1674 to 1682, a federation of the four islands of Nevis, St. Christopher, Antigua, and Montserrat. Each one had its deputy-governor, council, and assembly. Only the governor of the federation could call a general assembly to meet at Nevis (after 1688 at Antigua) to make laws with him and his council for the Leeward Islands. Never popular with the planters, who, nevertheless, did not question its legality, the general assembly was necessary for common action. This particularistic spirit lingered on; in 1689 Lieutenant-Governor Christopher Codrington wrote home from the new seat on Antigua: "I am sorry to have to represent the Island of Nevis to you as a most turbulent and ungovernable people, who are never content with a Governor for longer than he falls in with their desires, however unjust to

46. *CSPC, 1661–68,* pp. 229, 619; *1681–85,* p. 179; on the King-in-Council's support of the rights of Jews against Bridgetown merchants, Barbados Council Minutes, II, 177, 319–21, 324–6; Lyttleton, *Groans of the Plantations,* 23–4.

the other Islands." But this native West Indian proposed as an effective, though unacceptable, remedy the reducing of all of the islands to the English kingdom and "allowing representatives in the English Parliament." [47]

As the newest of the West Indian possessions and one acquired by conquest, the precise constitutional status of Jamaica long remained in question. The Jamaicans were fortunate in having several first-rate governors, among them Sir Thomas Modyford and Sir Thomas Lynch, and a number of highly capable though factious planter-legislators. Under such leadership Jamaica had responsible government for eighteen years after 1660, and after 1664, an assembly that moved steadily toward effective local autonomy. The former Barbadian, Sir Thomas Modyford, who had argued for seats in Parliament, described the Council and Assembly of Jamaica in 1670 as "an humble Modell of our high Court of Parliament," and on other occasions used similar phraseology.[48]

Behind assertions such as these lay a history of determined and adroit action by the legislature. Settlers from Barbados warned their fellow Jamaicans in 1661 against the 4½ per cent duty, which they considered to be the chief cause for the depopulation of Little England. No such grant was ever made to the king, and at the first Jamaica Assembly in 1664, the members voted that no tax should ever be levied without the consent of the governor, council, and lower house, and they inaugurated the long-time habit of omitting any mention of the king or exchequer in all fiscal acts. It also arrogated to insular use all of the advantages of the laws of England. Moreover, before about 1683, Jamaican laws were never sent home for approval by the King-in-Council. When the English government failed to defend the island, Governor Modyford had no other course than to send out the privateers, which was an act of undeclared war. In other ways, too, he countered the "irresponsibility" of the home authorities by becoming a "champion of local autonomy." Sir Thomas Lynch and the Assembly continued on this particularistic path and, when Whitehall hesitated over the logwood issue, the Governor encouraged both cutters and traders. Lord Vaughan came

47. *CSPC, 1661–68,* p. 587; *1689–92,* 175–8; Philip S. Haffenden, "The Crown and the Colonial Charters, 1675–1688," in *WMQ,* 3d ser., XV, 297–9, 464.
48. PRO: CO 1/43, fol. 175; CO 138/1, fol. 97.

out as governor in 1675 to find the Assembly more than ever alert to maintain the rights of Jamaicans, as it saw them. It went so far as to call the Royal African Company to account on the grounds that its charter created a monopoly.

Both by conviction and in action, the government of Jamaica had become so entrenched that predictable failure could only follow Lord Vaughan's attempt to carry out the declaration by the Lords of Trade and Plantations that Jamaica is "in no sort entitled to the Laws of England or to be governed thereby but by the mere grace and grant" of the sovereign. To this assertion, the Assembly opposed government by the consent of the governed; and because of his inability to uphold the Royal prerogative, Lord Vaughan was recalled. The Earl of Carlisle arrived in 1678 with instructions to apply Poyning's Law, which would have deprived Jamaicans of all power to initiate legislation. In an address to his Lordship, the members of the Assembly eloquently stated their resentment that the Lords of Trade and Plantations had countenanced reports that we "are a people full of animosity, unreasonably irregular, violent, undutifull, and transgressing both the bounds of duty and loyalty." Setting factional differences aside, the assemblymen and councilors unanimously opposed remote control, and Whitehall could not impose its will on Jamaica. This dramatic test of strength, 1677–80, resulted in a compromise by which Jamaica came off much better than Massachusetts did in these years. After the struggle had ended, Lord Vaughan recognized the position of the planters: "They being English they think they have the right to be governed as such, and to have their Liberties and properties secured by the Laws of England or others of their own making." At issue had been government by royal grace and favor versus government by the consent of the governed, one which would not be fully resolved until July 2, 1776, in another part of the Empire.[49]

49. Taking as his subtitle "The Rise of an Autonomous Society," C. A. Lindley gives a penetrating account which counterbalances the imperial point of view emphasized by Agnes Whitson in her *Constitutional Development of Jamaica.* See Lindley, Jamaica . . . , pp. 7, 35, 49, 57, 87, 130, 156–7, 187, 200–280, 284, 304, 305–9. Haffenden, in *WMQ,* 3d ser., XV, 298, 464–5; *Journal of the Assembly of Jamaica,* I, 50–51; PRO: CO 1/43, fols. 172, 175.

VII

An overweening greed for profit and a persisting overemphasis on things material prevented any successful rooting and growth of English civilization in the islands of the West Indies. Solely intent upon gain, English merchants and local planters established the first settlements and developed them with male labor, and when white bondage failed to meet their needs, they procured from West Africa hordes of black slaves. The inevitable consequence of such actions was that the family, the church, and a sustaining sense of English community never grew to form a healthy, rounded, friendly society of white people. The presence of the blacks in what seemed to the planters dangerously large numbers blighted insular societies, particularly the spiritual and educational activities of the Church of England. Further adding to the social difficulties of the islands was the unsalutary neglect by the home government of all but the mercantile aspects of colonial life. Only a small fraction of the planters ever really enjoyed the fabulous material prosperity attributed to the Sugar Colonies, and when many of the ablest of them went back home to live in affluence, those whites who remained in each island could never overcome, before 1690, the barbarism that some men of puritan temperament so greatly feared. As one of these thoughtful men read about the state of nature in Thomas Hobbes's great book, it must have reminded him of a Caribbean island: "no commodious Building . . . no Arts, No Letters, no Society, and, which is worst of all, continual feare and danger of violent death; And the life of man solitary, poore, nasty, brutish, and short." [50]

50. Thomas Hobbes, *Leviathan, or the Matter, Forme, & Power of a Commonwealth Ecclesiasticall and Civill* (London, 1651), Pt. I, 62.

No Peace Beyond the Line

THE HISTORY of the Englishmen who settled on the islands of the Caribbean during the seventeenth century is a chronicle of an impressive material accomplishment that was overborne by social failure and human tragedy. After almost two decades of discouraging experimentation with tropical crops, resourceful and determined men, with scant aid from London or Bristol and none from Whitehall, hit upon profitable staples: cotton, indigo, ginger, and, above all, sugar. This they achieved at the suggestion and with the vital aid of their early friends, the Dutch, who also convinced them that to produce merchantable cotton or Muscovado sugar they would have to import not just seeds, plants, and agricultural processes from Brazil but whole industries, entire systems. So successful were the English planters that by the seventies they had won the European market for Muscovado from the Portuguese, and London had become an important sugar-refining center. And the islands supplied most of the cotton for the spinners and weavers of Lancashire.

In the course of forming large estates on which to cultivate ever more sugar to satisfy the demands of the Europeans, the planters blindly perpetrated an unparalleled destruction of natural resources. They first denuded Barbados and the Leeward Islands of timber and vegetation in order to clear land for crops, and in the process they exterminated the wildlife. They then gave over raising provisions and purchased their food at high cost from Ireland and New

England. From the latter they also procured cargo after cargo of wood for buildings and containers. To label the sugar culture a monoculture would be inaccurate, but nowhere in the world of that day was there such concentrated cultivation of sugar and cotton. In executing all this, the West Indians effected an ecological revolution of a thoroughly wasteful kind.

Waste of every sort characterized these colonies throughout the century, but the greatest depletion was in human beings. The inability of the great mass of white settlers to adapt themselves to the strange new environment—to the climate, the diet, deficient housing, overwork—physically and psychologically brought about the death of more than half of them within a few years. When the planters found white servants inadequate, they turned, at the instance of the Dutch, to African slaves for a labor force. In almost every respect, the black man showed himself superior to the white man in adjusting to the new life of the islands, and, because his labor was both cheaper and more efficient, his permanence in the islands was guaranteed. In three brief decades before 1690, any hopes of establishing white men's societies of small farmers vanished as great plantations, populated by African slaves, began to dominate insular agriculture.

Other kinds of waste eroded human life, notably pestilence, war, and violent Nature. These affected Europeans and Africans alike by disrupting their lives, destroying buildings and whatever else they owned, and arousing great fears. From his family, the slave derived some comfort and satisfaction, which were largely denied the white servants and wage laborers, who were overwhelmingly young single males—homeless folk, who had truly nowhere to turn.

The family, the church, and the community were the prime institutions that had made English civilization what it was; they provided the safeguards against barbarism. Human events and conditions in the predominantly rural West Indies stunted them all with the consequence that true societies never developed. As we look back upon these undertakings with the inestimable benefit of hindsight, it is clear that as early as 1690 the sun of the white men was setting and that ultimately time was with the black men. But for them all, there had been no peace.

Appendices

APPENDIX I

CARIBBEAN CHRONOLOGY

First Period: 1623–1650

1623	English at St. Christopher
1624	St. Christopher settled; Dutch attack Bahia in Brazil
1625	English discover Barbados; Dutch and English at St. Croix
1627	Powell settles Barbados; Carlisle Proprietary Patent for Caribbees
1628	Nevis settled from St. Christopher
1629	Spanish attack St. Christopher and Nevis; Providence Island Company
1630	(to 1640) Dutch seize Curaçao, Saba, St. Martin, and St. Eustatius
1631	English settle (Old) Providence Island
*ca.*1632	Montserrat settled by English
*ca.*1633	Antigua settled (both recognized as English by 1636)
1635	Dutch conquered all of Northern Brazil
	French settled Guadeloupe and Martinique from St. Christopher
1637	Prince Johan Maurits [Maurice] builds up Pernambuco
1638	(to 1641) Caribs destroy settlements on Saint Lucia
	(to mid-forties) Dutch monopolize slave trade in Caribbees
1639	Caribs wipe out English on Trinidad
1640	(to 1647) Introduction of sugar culture to Caribbee Isles
1641	Spanish take Providence Island; rebellion at St. Christopher
	Second revolt at St. Christopher, February
1645	Brazilians rise against Dutch; War of Liberation
1647	Plague in Caribbean; Richard Ligon arrives in Barbados
1648	Spanish recognize Dutch in West Indies by Treaty of Munster
	Plague takes off thousands of West Indians
1650	Anguilla settled; Lord Willoughby founds Surinam
	Parliamentary Act forbidding trade with Dutch

Second Period: 1651–1690

1651	Barbados submits to Ayscue and Parliament
	Navigation Law directed against the Dutch, October 9

1652	(to 1654) First Dutch War
1654	Fall of Pernambuco: Dutch and Jews expelled from Brazil
1655	English conquest and settlement of Jamaica First Quakers arrive at Barbados
1659	Fire guts Bridgetown, February 9
1660	Restoration of King Charles II; Navigation Act
1661	D'Oyley erects civil government in Jamaica
1662	Barbuda settled from Antigua; first logwood cut at Campeachy; First Jamaica Assembly convened
1663	Sir Thomas Modyford to Jamaica as governor; Barbadians migrate there; Barbados grants 4½ per cent duty to king; Navigation Act
1664	Nevis grants 4½ per cent duty; English take New Netherland
1665	De Ruyter driven off Barbados; Second Dutch War; English capture Tobago, July 23
1666	Bahamas settled; French declare war January 23; capture St. Christopher and plunder Antigua
1667	English lose Surinam to Dutch, recapture it; Dutch get Surinam by Treaty of Breda; French capture Montserrat
1668	Montserrat grants 4½ per cent duty; Bridgetown fire, April 8
1671	Leeward Islands win separation from Barbados (effected 1672); Sir Thomas Lynch opens new phase of Jamaican development
1672	Suppression of Jamaica privateers begins Sir Thomas Stapleton becomes governor of Leeward Islands (to 1674) Third Dutch War; Royal African Company chartered; Tortola and Virgin Islands captured from Dutch
1673	Fire at Bridgetown, January 24; Third Navigation Law
1674	Christopher Codrington I develops sugar culture in Antigua
1675	Hurricane devastates Barbados, August
1680	Hurricanes destroy buildings and crops in Jamaica and Leeward Islands
1681	Virgin Islands colonized from Antigua; hurricane strikes Jamaica
1689	War with France; French expelled from St. Christopher Epidemic at Nevis takes off 50 per cent of male population
1692	June 7: Port Royal, Jamaica, destroyed by earthquake

APPENDIX II

EUROPEAN WARS TO 1700

1618	↑	Thirty Years' War
1642	│ ↑	English Civil Wars
1648	↓ ↓	Peace of Westphalia
1652	↑	First Dutch War, July 8
1654	↓	Treaty of London, April 5
1665	↑	Second Dutch War, March 4
1666	│	France enters, January
1667	↓	Peace of Breda, July 31 (England, France, and Holland)
1672	↑	Third Dutch War, March 17
1674	↓	Treaty of Westminster, February 9
1689	↑	War of England and Holland vs. France
1697	↓	Treaty of Ryswick

APPENDIX III

A BARBADIAN FEAST

"Give me leave to shew you what feasts they can (when they will) make for their friends, upon their Plantations," Richard Ligon wrote in 1650.[1] THE TABLE OF COLONEL JAMES DRAX AT INLAND PLANTATION: "for the first Course there hath been two messes of meat and both equally good, and this feast is alwayes when he kills a beef, which he feeds extreamly fat, giving him a dozen acres of Bonavist to go loose in, and due times of watering. First then (because beef being the greatest rarity in the Island, especially such as this is) I will begin with it, and of that sort there are these dishes at either mess, a Rump boyl'd, a Chine roasted, a large piece of the breast roasted, the Cheeks bak'd, of which is a dish to either mess, the tongue and part of the tripes minc'd for Pyes, season'd with sweet Herbs finely minc'd, Suet, Spice and Currans; the Legs, Pallets and other ingredients for an *Olio Podrito* to either mess, a dish of Marrow-bones, so here are 14 dishes at the Table and all of Beef; and this he intends as the great *Regalio,* to which he invites his fellow Planters; who having well eaten of it, the dishes are taken away, and another Course brought in, which is a Potato pudding, a dish of Scots Collops of a leg of Pork, as good as any in the world, a fricacy of the same, a dish of boyl'd Chickens, a shoulder of a young Goat dress'd with his Blood and Time, a Kid with a pudding in his belly, a sucking Pig, which is there the fattest, whitest, and sweetest in the world, with the poynant-sauce of the Brains, Salt, Sage, and Nutmeg done with Claret-wine, a Shoulder of Mutton, which is there a rare dish, a Pasty of the side of a young Goat, and a side of a fat young Sho[a]t upon it, well season'd with Pepper and Salt, and with some Nutmeg, a Loyn of Veal, to which there wants no sauce being so well furnish'd with Oranges, Lemons, and Lymes, three young Turkies in a dish, two Capons, of which sort I have seen some extream large and very fat, two Hens with eggs in a dish, four Ducklings, eight Turtle doves, and three Rabbets; and for cold bak'd meats, two Muscovia Ducks larded, and season'd well with Pepper and Salt: and these being taken off the Table, another course is set on, and that is of Westphalia or Spanish bacon, dryed Neats

1. Colonel Walrond's table lacked the beef, but did have fresh fish. Ligon, *Barbados,* 38–9.

Tongues, Botargo [a relish of fish roe], pickled Oysters, Caviare, Anchovies, Olives, and (intermixt with these) Custards, Creams, some alone, some with preserves of Plantines, Bonano, Guavers, put in, and those preserv'd alone by themselves, Cheese-cakes, Puffs, which are to be made with English flower, and bread; for the Cassavie will not serve for this kind of cookery; sometimes Tansies [cooking herbs], sometimes Froizes [pancakes or omelets], or Amulets [medicinal foods], and for fruit, Plantines, Bonanoes, Guavers, Milions [melons], prickled Pear, Anchove Pear, prickled Apple, Custard Apple, water Milions, and Pines worth all that went before. To this meat you seldom fail of this drink, Mobbie, Beveridge, Brandy, Kill-Devil, Drink of the Plantine, Claret-wine, White-wine, and Rhenish-wine, Sherry, Canary, Red sack, wine of Fiall [Madeira], with all Spirits that come from England, and with all this, you shall find as chearful a look, and as hearty a welcome, as any man can give to his best friends." [2]

2. Père Biët mentions a French ship of 200 tons that arrived at Bridgetown in 1654 with a cargo of nothing but brandy to exchange for sugar. "The Encrease of our Westerne Plantations has occasioned the thriving condition of the Maderas by taking of their Wines, and chiefly Barbados," a traveler of the eighties reported. Biët, *Voyage,* 281; BM: Sloane MSS, 2395, fol. 651.

APPENDIX IV

THE GLEBE HOUSE, ST. JOHN'S PARISH, BARBADOS, 1679

THE HOUSE to be built for the Minister is to be Forty Foote long and Twenty one Foote wide from Out to Out and to have a porch building Twelve and Fourteen foote square, A staire building Sixteen and Fourteen foote square Two Shades each of them Fourteen and Twelve foot square, all those dimensions from Out to out./
The body of the House porch & staire must be of stone walls Two foote thick and Eighteen foot high and the shades of the same thicknesse—Tenn Foote high with shadeing and Gable ends./
The Roomes contained in the dwelling house will be as followeth. Viz^{t}:/

In the 1st story

A porch tenn foote sq^{r}:
A Hall Twenty and seventeen foote sq^{r}:
A parlo^{r} sixteen & seventeen foote sq^{r}:
A staire Case Twelve foote sq^{r}:
A shade Twelve & Tenn foot sq^{r}:
A shade Tenn and Twelve foote sq^{r}:

In the 2^{d} story

A porch Chamber Tenn foote square
A Hall Chamber Twenty and seventeen foot square
A parlo^{r} Chamber sixteen and seventeen foote square
A staire Case Twelve foote square
A shade Chamber ten and Twelve foot square
A Shade Chamber Tenn & Twelve foote square

In the 3^{d} story

A Garrit 10 foot square
Hall and parlo^{r} Garritt Thirty six and Seventeen foote square
A staire case in the Garrit Twelve foote square

All the Ground Flooores to be paved belonging to the House with paveing bricks laid in Mortar, all the roofe to be covered with plaine tyles pinned and laid in Mortar./

The Walls to be all plaistered within, pointed without and the Corners Freestone./

The partitions to be on both sides lathed and plaistered./

The second Floore to be laid with boards plained and Joynted./

The Third or Garrett story to be laid with boards plained and Joynted./

In one of the Shades is to be a Chimney and Oven./

Doore Cases this house will need in the 1st story 8 & 7 of which are to be in Stone Walls./ In the 2d Story 5 & 4 of which are to be in Stone Walls./

Windowes in the First story will be needed 9 }
In the Second - - - - - - - - - - - - - - - 8 } These 17 all in Stone walls

The preceeding Doore Cases and windowes being Twenty Eight in Stone Walls must have Lintells of Timber. The Windowes must be all Glassed. The doore cases fitted with Doores, and the three outmost with Locks and Keyes./ Timber for the body of the house &c./ All of Masticke as followeth./

Six beames 3 19½ foote long./ 3 21 foote long all tenn Inches square./

One Hundred Twenty & five foote of Wall plate ten Inches broad Five thick./

Ninty Six Joyce 9 foote 9 Inches long, or Forty Eight Joyce Nine and a half foote long, Forty Eight Joyce Tenn foote long all five and three Inches square./

Five paire of principalls Two pair Eighteen foote long, Three pair fifteen foote Long all seven and Five at bottome, Five square at Topp./

Five Coller beames Each Twelve Foote long Six and Five Inches square Tenn purlins six of them Tenn Foote long. Four Five foote long all six and Five Inches square, Twenty Five pair of small rafters seventeen & a half foote long, or Fifty pair half 10½ foote long, half 7 foote long all Three Inches square./

Timber for the porch building as followeth

Seven Joyce Twelve foote long Six Inches and Three square./ One beame fourteen foote long Tenn Inches and Eight square./ Fourteen Joyce Six foote long five Inches and Two and a half square, Forty-Foote of Wall plate Eight Inches and Foure square./ Two pair of principalls, 1 pair Tenn and a half foote long, 1 pair Thirteen long Six Inches and Five square-Twelve pair of Rafters thirteen foot long or Twenty four pair half five foote long, half Eight foote long all three Inches square./ Seaventy Foure foote of purlin Coller beame and brace Six inches and three and a half./

Timber for the staire Case followeth, viz[t]:

The Standards, Railes braces and Joyce for the staires will require some Twenty five foote Timber./

Fourty Six foote of Wall plate Eight Inches and Foure./

Eighty Eight Foote of Coller beame purlin and brace Six Inches and Three and a half square: Two paire of principalls one paire Twelve foote long, one pair fifteen foote all six Inches and five square, Fourteen paire of small rafters fourteen and a half long and Twenty Eight paire ditto, half six foote long, half Eight foote and a half long all three Inches square./

Timber for the shades followeth

Two Wall plates Tenn Inches and five Thirteen foote long:/ Fourteen Joyce four of which sixteen foote long Six Inches and seaven square. Tenn Joyce fifteen foote long seaven Inches and foure and Two paire of principalls Twenty foot long Nine Inches and Six Square at bottome Six square at Topp, Two pair of purlins Tenn foote long each seaven and Five Inches square./ Twelve pair of small rafters Twenty Two Foote and a half long or Twenty four half tenn foote long and half Twelve and a half foote long all three Inches square./ Four braces Six foote long, Six and foure Inches square. A Mantle Tree for the Chimney and Timbers to lay in the house Wall to fasten the four great shade Joyce thereunto may take some fifteen foote of Timber./ [1]

1. Parish Vestry Minutes of St. John's, Barbados (MS., Barbados Museum and Historical Society), pp. 29–29a.

Index

B

D

E

F

I

Q

R

S

Y

Z

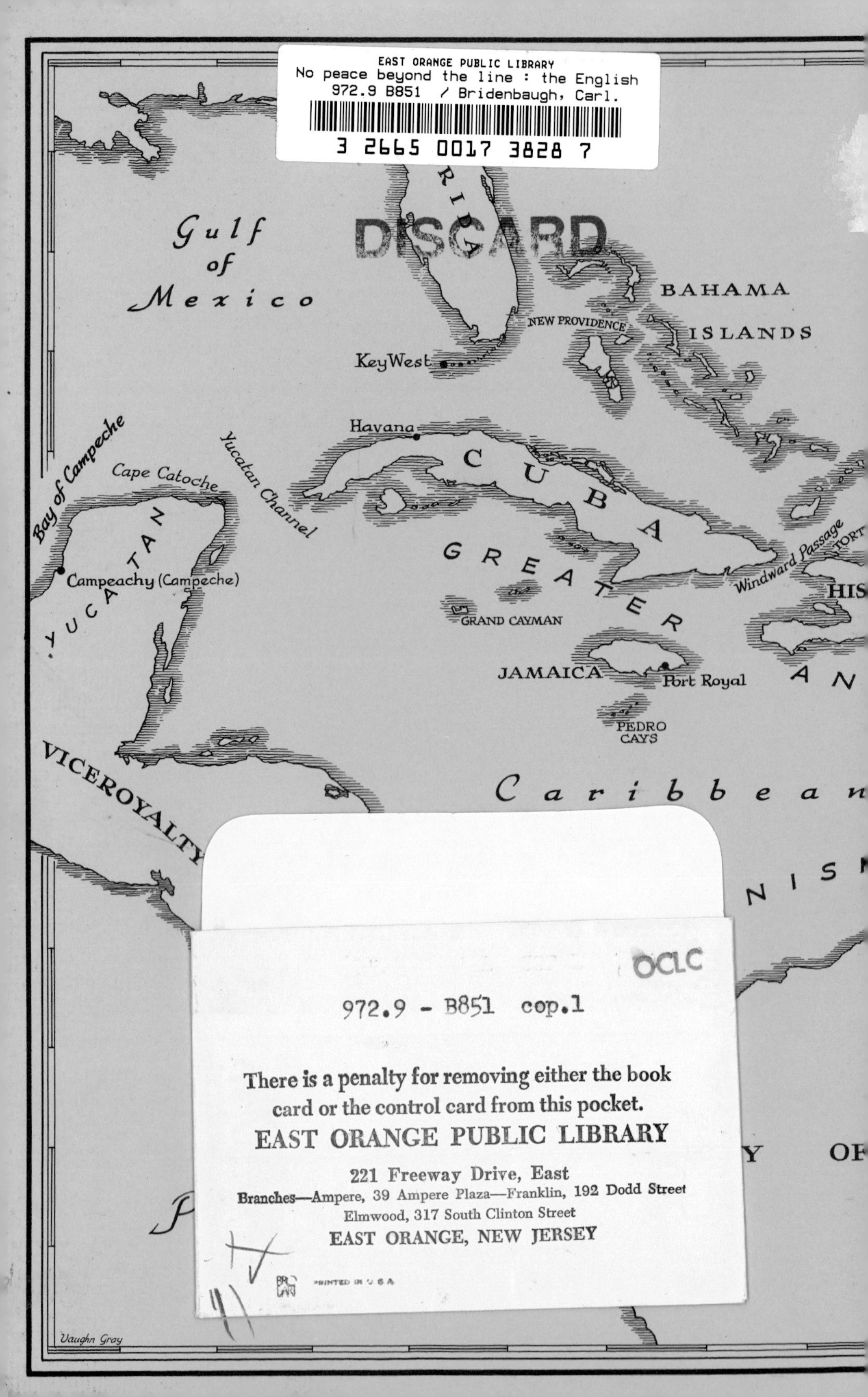
Gulf of Mexico
FLORIDA
BAHAMA ISLANDS
NEW PROVIDENCE
Key West
Havana
CUBA
GREATER
Bay of Campeche
Cape Catoche
Yucatan Channel
YUCATAN
Campeachy (Campeche)
Windward Passage
GRAND CAYMAN
JAMAICA
Port Royal
PEDRO CAYS
VICEROYALTY
Caribbean
Vaughn Gray